Bible Student's Commentary

Joshua, Judges, Ruth

Translated by Ray Togtman

C. J. Goslinga

Regency
Reference Library
Zondervan Publishing House
Grand Rapids, Michigan

THE BIBLE STUDENT'S COMMENTARY—JOSHUA, JUDGES, RUTH

Joshua was orginally published in 1927 in Dutch under the title *Korte Verklaring der Heilige Schrift—JOZUA,* by J. H. Kok, B. V. Kampen, The Netherlands. This translation is based on the third edition (revised), 1955.

Judges and Ruth were orginally published in 1933-38 in Dutch under the title *Korte Verklaring der Heilige Schrift—RICHTEREN–RUTH,* by J. H. Kok, B. V. Kampen, The Netherlands. This translation is based on the third edition (revised), 1966.

Copyright © 1986 by The Zondervan Corporation
Grand Rapids, Michigan

REGENCY REFERENCE LIBRARY
is an imprint of
Zondervan Publishing House
1415 Lake Drive SE
Grand Rapids, Michigan 49506

Library of Congress Cataloging in Publication Data
Goslinga, C. J.
    Joshua, Judges, Ruth.
    (Bible student's commentary)
    Translation of: Het boek Jozua and of Het boek der
Richteren.
    1. Bible.   O.T.   Joshua—Commentaries.   2. Bible.
O.T.   Judges—Commentaries.   3. Bible.   O.T.   Ruth—
Commentaries.   I. Goslinga, C. J.   Boek der Richteren.
English.   1986.   II. Title.   III. Series: Korte
verklaring der Heilige Schrift, met nieuwe vertaling.
English.
BS1295.3.G6713   1986   222'.2077   86–15723
ISBN   0–310–45280–5

The Scripture text used is that of the *Holy Bible:
New International Version* (North American Edition),
copyright © 1973, 1978, 1984 by the International Bible Society,
used by permission of Zondervan Bible Publishers.

Edited by Dick Polcyn
Designed by Edward Viening

Printed in the United States of America

86 87 88 89 90 91 92 93 94 95 / ZO / 10 9 8 7 6 5 4 3 2 1

Contents

Joshua
Introduction

I. *The Content and Significance of the Book*

The Book of Joshua directly continues the history of the Book of Deuteronomy. While the latter ends by reporting the death of Moses, the former begins by recalling this same event. The Book of Joshua then relates God's commandment to Joshua, Moses' successor, to cross the Jordan with the Israelites and to possess Canaan; and it recounts how Joshua fulfilled this mandate. In this account a distinction can be made between the actual conquest of the land and its partition among the various tribes. The Book of Joshua can accordingly be divided into two main sections. The first section (chs. 1–12) describes Israel's crossing the Jordan and, led by Joshua and aided by the Lord's miraculous support, crushing the resistance of the Canaanites, thereby controlling the greatest part of the land west of the Jordan. The second section (chs. 13–24) mainly details the division of the Promised Land, where a particular territory was assigned by lot to each tribe (also to a few individuals, viz., Caleb [14:13–14] and Joshua [19:49–50]). This section then concludes by reporting Joshua's farewell speeches, the renewal of the covenant, and the death of Joshua and Eleazar.

The Book of Joshua, because of its content, has a unique significance that sets it apart from other books of the Bible. This significance is clearly evident in the position the book received in the Canon, namely, directly after the Pentateuch or "five books of Moses." In a certain sense Joshua forms the transition between the Pentateuch and the other books of the Old Covenant. On the one hand, it shows how the entire conquest of Canaan and all that it involved corresponded with the arrangements Moses had already set forth at God's command (e.g., 8:31; 11:15; 13:8, 15, 32–33; 20:2; see Deut. 31:3–8), where Joshua was, so to speak, the executor of Moses' will (11:15, 20, 23). What shines through most of all here is the Lord's covenant faithfulness in fulfilling the promises He had made to the forefathers (21:43–45).

On the other hand, the Book of Joshua also looks toward the future. It contains the assignment to the various tribal territories of precise boundaries that would remain in force during later times. It already depicts the beginning of Israel's residence in the Promised Land. God had given His covenant to Israel, and that covenant now had to take effect throughout the whole life of the nation as it dwelt in freedom and security within the inheritance that had been promised to its forefathers.

The Book of Joshua portrays the nation of Israel at a high point but simultaneously at a crossroads in its life. It contains the glad report that Israel continued to serve the Lord faithfully, even when some time had passed after Joshua's death (24:31); but it also does not hide the fact that the people's hearts basically remained the same (7:1–26; 18:3). It makes a veiled prediction that a remnant of the Canaanites would become a snare to Israel (23:13) and that Israel would be unable to maintain herself on the pinnacle where the Lord had placed her (23:15–16; 24:19–20).

The Book of Judges vividly reveals how lamentably true this prophecy proved to be. The sermon contained in the Book of Joshua— viz., that God's people, though having been blessed by His beneficent deeds, were nevertheless obligated to keep His covenant, to hold on to what they had (Rev. 3:11), and to guard against falling backward in grace—preserves its power at all times.

The predominant note that is sounded in Joshua, however, is not so much one of warning as one of joy and encouragement. Israel is depicted as the chosen army of the living God, led by the Lord Himself as her invisible General, ascending to the summit of victory after victory. Every page resounds with the joyful optimism of faith, for which "mountains are made low and seas dry." Here we encounter the people of the covenant at one of those relatively rare moments when they are allowed to enjoy the favor and fellowship of their God almost without interruption, when strong in faith they are able to perform bold deeds—one of those rare moments in sacred history when the ideal seems to be achieved for a time.

Darkness, however, is not absent in the Book of Joshua—one need only recall the story of Achan—but light nevertheless predominates. The book proclaims the triumph of the Israelite congregation over all its enemies by the mighty hand of God. In this respect it has a striking New Testament counterpart in the Acts of the Apostles. There too the youthful congregation is pictured as standing at a spiritual high point that enables it to accomplish great and startling things. It is true that this congregation as well retained its old nature and thus had a vulnerable spot (cf. Ananias and Sapphira, Acts 5:1–11). But what is central to Acts is that the indwelling power of the Spirit makes the church invincible. By the Spirit's power and the mighty assistance of Christ, the invisible Head of the church who fights for it from heaven, the church marched triumphantly through the world and was able to enter the capital city of Rome in the first century.

Although this parallel cannot be developed further here, it sheds a clear light on the lasting significance of the Book of Joshua for the congregation of the Lord. The central message of this Old Testament book can be summed up in Paul's words: "If God is for us, who can be against us?" (Rom. 8:31).

II. *Joshua, the Servant of the Lord*

Unquestionably the central figure in the book is Joshua, the son of Nun. The book takes its name from him, not because it contains the story of his life, but because he was Israel's leader, under whose direction the events of this book took place.

According to Numbers 13:8, Joshua was born of the tribe of Ephraim. Although his name is given here as Hoshea, verse 16 states that "Moses gave Hoshea son of Nun the name Joshua." Thus these were one and the same person. Joshua's renaming did not necessarily take place on the occasion of the sending of the spies (Num. 13). Most likely it happened earlier, for that event provided no motive to change his name. Moreover it is noteworthy that before Numbers 13 he had always been called Joshua (see Exod. 17:9–14; 24:13; 32:17; 33:11; Num. 11:28; the name Hoshea appears elsewhere only in Deut. 32:44[1]). Moses probably renamed Joshua following the victory God gave him over the Amalekites (Exod. 17:8–16). Whatever the case may have been, the change in Joshua's name has deep significance. Whereas "Hoshea" can be translated simply as "deliverance" or "help," "Joshua" (Heb. *yᵉhôšu[a]'*) means "the Lord is salvation." The name

---

[1] See KJV and RSV margin. NIV has "Joshua" but "Hoshea" in the margin—TRANS.

"Joshua" emphasizes the fact that Israel's salvation and deliverance lay solely in the LORD, the God of the covenant. Joshua bore this name as a promise that he would be the Lord's instrument for saving His people.

The name "Joshua" means more than this, however. No doubt Moses was instructed by God to grant Joshua this splendid name; and surely God's intent in giving this name was that Joshua, who by his deeds would be a type of the great Savior, would also point to Him by his name. The name "Joshua" is in fact the same name as Jesus. *Yᵉšûaʻ*, the shorter, alternate form of Joshua, is found already in the Old Testament (Neh. 8:17); and "Jesus" is merely the Greek form of this. The meaning of the name Joshua first came to full reality in the Son of God. In the fullness of time, when God the Son took on Himself human flesh and blood within the Virgin Mary, God commanded that He be given the name Jesus; for *He* would save His people from their sins (Matt. 1:21).

Joshua had been prominent several times during the wilderness journey. He had commanded the battle against Amalek (Exod. 17:9–13). He alone had been allowed to climb Mount Sinai with Moses (Exod. 24:13; 32:17). He had been Moses' special assistant to keep watch in the sanctuary (Exod. 33:11). He also had been one of the twelve spies (Num. 13:8), the only one besides Caleb who brought a good report of the land and spoke the language of faith (Num. 14:6–9). Through his close association with Moses, Joshua thus gradually had received special preparation for his task. That he had had something to learn is clearly evident from the story in Numbers 11:25–29, for there Moses had to scold his servant for seeking to stop Eldad and Medad from prophesying. At the end of the desert journey, however, the Lord Himself designated Joshua as leader. The moment had then arrived when he was permitted to begin his lifework proper. Moses was commanded to place him before Eleazar the priest; and, in the presence of Eleazar and the entire assembly, Moses imparted to him some of his own glory and dignity by laying his hand on him, thus publicly installing Joshua as his successor (Num. 27:18–23). After Moses died, Joshua was "filled with the spirit of wisdom" (Deut. 34:9), ready to carry on the work of his great predecessor.

The relationship between Joshua and Moses is tellingly illustrated at the very beginning of the Book of Joshua (1:1): Moses is called the "servant of the LORD," but Joshua is called "Moses' aide." Although he succeeded Moses as the leader of the people, Joshua did not have the same status as Israel's great prophet and lawgiver, the mediator of the Old Covenant. This is especially evident in his relationship to Eleazar the priest (Josh. 14:1; 19:51; cf. Num. 27:21–23), which is consistent with the fact that Joshua's association with God was less intimate than Moses' had been. Even after Moses had died, Joshua in a sense remained his servant. He carried out Moses' commands (Deut. 31:7), strictly obeyed Moses' commission (Josh. 11:15), and in all things acted as Moses had instructed (Josh. 8:30–35; 14:2, 5). Joshua's exemplary faithfulness and honesty are illustrated here more than anywhere else. He knew his place and clearly perceived his own special task, namely, to bring Moses' lifework to completion. Since above all Joshua wanted to serve God, he did everything God had commanded him through His servant Moses.

This does not mean, however, that Joshua lacked independence, that he only could follow but could not take the lead. On the contrary, both his person and his life witness to the fact that one who has learned to obey also understands the art of ruling. When Israel's nomadic existence came to an end and it was time to take weapons in hand and conquer Canaan, Joshua, who was a born general, had outstanding qualifications as "the right man in the right place." He won no laurels as a statesman or diplomat (see ch. 9). As a military commander, however, his vast ability is plainly evident in the tactful and decisive manner he carried out his shrewd plans (see, e.g., ch. 8; 10:9; 11:16–17). Joshua's charisma moved the people to accept his leadership and acknowledge him as their superior in wisdom and resolve.

Joshua was able to preserve the unity and solidarity of the tribes. Remaining completely independent and unbiased, he acted with strict fairness in dividing the land to the people (17:14–18). Joshua did not fear men and dared to stand alone (24:15; cf. Num. 14:5–9). The secret of his strength lay in his deep piety (Josh. 7:6–9; 24:15), genuine humility (23:3), selflessness (19:49–50), and "mountain-moving" faith. This faith, which caused the sun and moon to stand still and so enabled the people of God to win a total victory (10:12–14), left an indelible impression on Israel.

Although Joshua stood lower than Moses, he was still rightly called a prophet. He acted in this capacity when he conveyed God's words to the people (3:9; 20:1–6) and when he pronounced admonitions (4:21–24) or curses (6:26). His prophetic role was especially prominent at the conclusion of his life, when with great solemnity he warned the people against unfaithfulness, pointed out their great responsibility, and aroused them to scrupulous observance of the law and motivated them to heartfelt piety (chs. 23–24). Joshua's outstanding life made a powerful impression on the people of Israel (24:31). Significantly, then, Scripture confers the honorary title "servant of the LORD" on Joshua (24:29; Judg. 2:8), a title also ascribed to Moses and granted to the future Redeemer by the prophet Isaiah (Isa. 42:1; 53:11). God treated Joshua according to the rule "those who honor me I will honor" (1 Sam. 2:30).

The Bible—particularly the Book of Joshua—thus casts a glorious light on this God-chosen hero. Apart from his indiscretion in making a treaty with the Gibeonites, there is not a single bad report concerning his professional life. Joshua's work nevertheless remained unfinished at the end of his life. He had been unable to completely expel the Canaanites from the land, and he was far less able to root out Israel's spiritual enemies. Thus Joshua's work and name pointed beyond himself to one greater than he. Joshua was merely a shadow of Him who was to come. But even as a shadow he was permitted to bear the image of the perfect Joshua, our Lord Jesus Christ, who as the "author of their salvation" (Heb. 2:10) triumphed over all the enemies of His people so that He might lead them into the land of eternal rest, the heavenly Canaan.[2]

III. *Author and Date*

Since neither the Book of Joshua nor the rest of the Bible directly speaks to the question of authorship, the composition of the book cannot be ascribed with any degree of certainty to anyone whose name is known to us. A highly questionable Talmud tradition (*Baba Bathra* 14*b*) says that "Joshua wrote his own book and eight verses in the Torah" (these last words refer to Deut. 34:5–12). Although this report cannot be considered decisive on its own merits, this does not mean that Joshua could not have written the book. There is good reason to see whether the data preclude or support his authorship.

The two previous Dutch editions of this commentary argued for the latter position, and various arguments were there advanced to demonstrate its plausibility. Several times I asserted far too dogmatically that the book was almost certainly written by Joshua's own hand. In so doing, however, I largely overlooked the fact that there is but scant mention of any literary activity by Joshua. On the one hand, several

---

[2]See note 16 on page 30.

small sections or verses in the book certainly could not have been written by him. But on the other hand, Joshua's close involvement in nearly everything recounted is a strong reason for ascribing its factual content largely to his own verbal or written reports. Although this cannot be proved, there is nothing that excludes its possibility, and the supporting arguments are cogent. The case that has been made against Joshuan authorship—even by those writers who share my view of Scripture—is far from convincing.[3]

To correctly evaluate the arguments for each position, we must first come to some conclusion as to when the book was written. Happily, there are some important clues for this.

1. Joshua 16:10 states that the Canaanites were still living in Gezer. First Kings 9:16, however, states that the Pharaoh of Egypt had captured this city and destroyed its inhabitants early in Solomon's reign. Joshua 16:10 therefore must have been written previous to this event.[4] Joshua 15:63 similarly reports that since the tribe of Judah did not succeed in completely dislodging the Jebusites, they still inhabited Jerusalem. Because David first conquered this city—or at least the very strong fortress that it had (2 Sam. 5:6–7)—and made it into an Israelite city, 15:63 has to refer to a time before David became king over the Twelve Tribes.[5] Joshua 9:27, which prescribes the duties of the Gibeonites as servants of the sanctuary, allows us to move the date of composition a little earlier; for this verse must have been written before King Saul violated the treaty with them (2 Sam. 21:1–2). As a provisional conclusion, therefore, we can safely say that the Book of Joshua was written and completed *no later than* the beginning of the monarchical period.

2. There is, however, other evidence that points to a much earlier date of composition. Several passages, for instance, give the clear impression of being eyewitness accounts. According to the consonantal Hebrew text, 5:1 should read "until *we* had crossed over" (i.e., over the Jordan).[6] The writer thus here includes himself in the generation

---

[3] Joshua's authorship was still defended by A. Schulz (*Das Buch Josua* [Bonn, 1924], p. 4), but most commentators now reject it with little ado. G. Ch. Aalders (*Oud-Testamentische Canoniek* [Kampen: Kok, 1952], pp. 163–71) rejects it as well, and his arguments will be examined in the text. See also the article by W. H. Gispen in *Bijbelse Encyclopedie*, p. 274.

[4] See also the comments at this verse (p. 131).

[5] The conquest reported in Judges 1:8 apparently remained incomplete and had no lasting result. See Judges 1:21.

[6] The NIV adopts this reading, while the author has "they" in 5:1—TRANS.

that entered Canaan. This evidence is less compelling than it seems, however, for there are good reasons to doubt the accuracy of the text at this point. The vocalized text (the *Qere*) and several Hebrew manuscripts have the third person plural here, and both the Greek and other ancient translations support this reading. These documents thus argue for the translation "until *they* had crossed over"; and this unquestionably fits the context better, which twice speaks of the Israelites in the third person. Possibly a copyist was still thinking of the identical expression in 4:23 and mistakenly inserted the first person in 5:1.

It is difficult to determine which reading is correct and original. Aalders argues that the word *us* in 5:6 ("promised . . . to give us") supports the *Kethib* (the consonantal text) in verse 1, but the text-critical objections to this reading cannot easily be evaded. Verse 6 taken by itself could in fact have been said by an Israelite of a much later period. Because of the above reasons, then, 5:1 cannot decide the question of whether the author was present at the crossing of the Jordan.

Joshua 6:25, however, which states that Rahab "lives among the Israelites to this day," must have been written by a contemporary while she was still alive. Aalders (*Oud-Testamentische Canoniek,* p. 168) disputes the apparent strength of this evidence by arguing that the phrase could mean that she lived on in her progeny. He points out that Rahab's family and all who belonged to her are spoken of in the same context. But this is irrelevant because all the writer says about Rahab's relatives is that they were spared by Joshua. Then the writer again turns to Rahab herself, remarking that after *she* hid the men Joshua had sent as spies "she lives among the Israelites to this day." This can only refer to Rahab as an individual; and the strength of this unambiguous testimony cannot be lessened by applying it to her descendants. The text says nothing about the latter, either here or in 6:23 (cf. 2:13). If the author had wished to speak of Rahab's children or grandchildren, he would have made this clear. On this point we therefore conclude that the author presents himself as someone who has lived through the events he describes.

The unambiguous report in 6:25 is crucial to determining the *time* of composition for the Book of Joshua. Whether this verse can be reconciled with other information and how this then should be done are secondary. Here we have a fixed starting point[7] that is invaluable for

---

[7]I have emphasized this because Aalders attaches too much importance to items of evidence that seem to indicate a later date—evidence that remains rather vague and

those holding to the unity of the Book of Joshua (see next section). If 6:25 was written by a contemporary (who could, however, have been much younger than Joshua), this would be crucial to our view and assessment of the evidence that seems to argue against such an early date.

3. The conclusion reached under point 2 lends greater significance to other passages that vividly and graphically depict various events in the Book of Joshua. This is true of virtually all the stories in the first eleven chapters as well as scenes such as 14:6–12 (the request of the elderly Caleb), 15:16–19 (the meeting of Caleb and his daughter Acsah at her wedding), 17:14–18 (the complaint of the tribes of Joseph and Joshua's reaction), and similarly 22:10–34. The author repeatedly notes small details, as in 2:21 (Rahab's scarlet cord), 5:12 (the manna stops falling), 7:21 (Achan's confession), 8:26 (Joshua holds out his javelin), and 24:26–27 (the memorial stone is set up), to mention just a few. The stories are generally told in a gripping manner, though the matters described in many sections (esp. chs. 13–21) are more like a chronicle. All this creates the impression that the author was personally involved in the events recounted, though it is true that he could have recorded the eyewitness reports of others. There is nevertheless every reason to believe that such significant events for Israel as the entrance into Canaan, the conquest of the land, and the partition of it to the Twelve Tribes would have been committed to writing soon after they happened (see 18:9 and 24:26).

4. There are other passages, however, that many critics believe can be reconciled with a contemporary authorship either only with difficulty or not at all.

Frequently the Book of Joshua states that a certain circumstance or monument still exists "to this day." Obviously an author would not use this expression unless he was already removed from what he was writing about by some length of time. It would nevertheless definitely be wrong to reject the possibility of a contemporary author for this reason alone. The expression itself is too vague to prove much; it does not indicate any definite length of time. Furthermore, a closer

---

that does not disprove the author's clear testimony in 6:25. My disagreement with Aalders' argument is heightened by the fact that he denies any crucial significance even to 5:1, where he reads the first person "we." Given Aalder's position, only one conclusion can be drawn: the author himself crossed the Jordan with the Israelites. We have no choice but to accept the author's own words.

examination of some of the relevant passages reveals some noteworthy things.

The phrase "to this day" occurs in sixteen verses, and in most cases the context does not allow a clear determination of the length of time— viz., 4:9; 5:9; 7:26; 8:28, 29; 9:27; 10:27 (here the expression is strengthened somewhat, lit., "to this very day"; cf. KJV, RSV); 13:13; 14:14 (NIV, "ever since"); 15:63; and 16:10. Additionally we have already discussed 6:25 under point 2. The obvious importance of this verse is that "to this day" can only refer to a part of Rahab's life. Although she may have been quite young when the Israelites entered Canaan and may have lived to a great age, clearly the phrase "to this day" could have been used after as few as forty or fifty years. This is confirmed in 22:3 and 23:8–9, where Joshua, approaching the time of his death, spoke of things that happened during and after the entry into Canaan. Since the conquest of Canaan required only seven years (see section VI) and the partition and allotment of the land took place immediately after that, 22:3 could refer to a period of ten years at most, and 23:8–9 to a period not much longer. As a final example, Phinehas used the phrase "to this very day" in 22:17 to refer to an event from his own life that occurred shortly before the arrival in Canaan (Num. 25:1–3), certainly no more than twelve years earlier.

Thus the phrase "to this day" need only refer to a period of a few years. Aalders concedes this point but then says that "a verse like 16:10 obviously refers to a situation that continued to exist for some length of time after the conquest of Canaan" (*Oud-Testamentische Canoniek*, p. 164). This may be so, but how long did the situation continue to exist? An author with a particular liking for the expression could have used it a mere twenty-five or thirty years after the conquest. The phrase "to this day" thus speaks against authorship by Joshua himself (which Aalders disputes in his argument) but does not preclude the possibility that a younger contemporary could have authored the Book of Joshua.

5. The close of the Book of Joshua (24:29–33) merits consideration because it indicates the *terminus post quem* (as Aalders observes, ibid., p. 168), i.e., things that in any case must have occurred before the book was written. These include the deaths of Joshua, Eleazar, and the elders who had taken part in the conquest of Canaan under Joshua's leadership and had witnessed God's mighty acts of deliverance. The reference in 24:29–33 is not to the entire generation that entered Canaan but only to the "old guard," especially to those who outlived

Joshua. These verses—especially verse 31, which states that Israel served the Lord faithfully throughout the lifetime of these men— clearly cannot be from Joshua's own hand; but nothing obliges us to think of a time very long after his death. In fact the Book of Judges clearly indicates that Israel's growing apostasy began very soon after Joshua's death. According to Judges 3:8, Cushan-Rishathaim was the first foreign ruler to oppress Israel; and this happened as God's punishment on His unfaithful people not more than twenty to twenty-five years after Joshua's death . In the commentary on Judges that follows (p. 237), I date Joshua's death about 1387 B.C. and the first foreign subjection from 1367–1360 B.C.

6. Joshua 10:13 refers to a written source called the Book of Jashar. Since this same work is also cited in 2 Samuel 1:18, De Groot[8] and others hold that it dates from David's time or later and that Joshua was therefore written after that. However, the mention of the Book of Jashar in Joshua can easily be explained by regarding it as a compilation of poetic pieces from various periods that was begun before or during the conquest of Canaan. See comments in 10:13.

7. The arguments for a later date based on 8:33 are equally insignificant. De Groot maintains that the whole pericope in 8:30–35 cannot come from the time of Joshua;[9] and one of his main reasons for this is the phrase "aliens and citizens" in verse 33, which allegedly could not yet have been used at that time. But why not? Moses used the same phrase repeatedly in Exodus, Leviticus, and Numbers (e.g., Exod. 12:19, 48–49); and it therefore could also have been used by Joshua and his contemporaries. (Note 3 at the end of this commentary discusses the position of 8:30–35 in the text.)

8. The phrase "on the other side of the Jordan" (Heb. *bᵉ'ēḇer hayyardēn*), which is found seventeen times in Joshua, is also adduced as proof that the book was written after Israel had long resided in Canaan (see De Groot, ibid., p. 11). De Groot reasons that these words usually indicate the land east of the Jordan. It is significant, however, that the same expression can also refer to the land west of the Jordan, i.e., Canaan proper, the Promised Land in its narrower sense. One therefore cannot simply base his conclusions on only a portion of the relevant passages. Taking stock of this in an extensive note at the end of this commentary, I attempt to demonstrate that the changing reference of the phrase favors the view that the author himself took part

---

[8] J. De Groot, *Het Boek Jozua,* Tekst en Uitleg (Groningen, 1931), p. 10.
[9] Ibid., pp. 10, 99.

in Israel's migration from the east to the west side of the Jordan. This again points to an eyewitness account. (See Note 1 following the text.)

9. In point 1 above, in my attempt to determine the date before which the Book of Joshua must have been written (the *terminus ante quem*), I discussed 15:63 and 16:10. These verses, however, are commonly understood to refer to a time considerably later than the conquest of Canaan under Joshua, as are 15:13–19 and 19:47. Under point 4, however, I pointed out that 16:10 could very easily have been written twenty-five or thirty years after Joshua's death. There is no need to move the date forward. This is also true of 15:63, for Judges 1:8 states that Judah (and Simeon) attempted to capture Jerusalem shortly after Joshua's death. At the same time Judges 1:21 blames the tribe of Benjamin for failing to finish the task.

The circumstances described in Judges 1 extend no further than the time before the first foreign subjection (see point 5 above). The march of the Danites against Laish or Leshem mentioned in Joshua 19:47 (Judges 18 gives a detailed description) falls in this same period (see the commentary on Judges 18, pp. 213, 217–20, and 461–74). Finally, 15:13–19 unquestionably refers to a time during Joshua's life. The conquest of Debir by Othniel and his subsequent marriage to Caleb's daughter Acsah took place shortly after Joshua had assigned Caleb his inheritance (14:13–14). That this story is also included in Judges 1:10–15 (see the comments there, pp. 253–54) does not disprove this point.

10. Joshua 13:13 and 17:13, like 15:63 and 16:10, also report the Israelites' failure to fulfill their mandate to drive out or destroy the original inhabitants of the land. The Geshurites and Maacathites, who lived near the headstreams of the Jordan, are spoken of in 13:13 and the Canaanites of western Manasseh in 17:13. Judges 1:28 repeats this latter verse. Thus these two verses add nothing substantially new.

In summary, the evidence that bears on the question of the authorship and date of the book can be divided into two categories. The first includes those verses that reveal the hand of a contemporary and thus point to an Israelite who himself took part in the entry and the conquest of Canaan west of the Jordan. The second category includes facts and circumstances that arose after the death of Joshua, which do indicate a slightly later period. There is not, however, a single statement that compels us to date the authorship of the Book of Joshua any later than the beginning of the time of the judges.[10] Thus there is no

---

[10] A third category could include those verses that contain no definite clues, but for

difficulty in forming a conclusion that does justice to both categories of evidence. We are not faced with events that are separated by a considerable length of time (e.g., a century or more). On the contrary, the events related in Joshua could easily have happened during the life span of one person. If we date the entry into Canaan at 1407 B.C. and begin the first foreign subjection (under Cushan-Rishathaim, Judg. 3:8) at 1367 B.C., then the time span in Joshua is a mere forty years. A man who crossed the Jordan with Israel at the age of about thirty-five and then lived to eighty could easily have known the entire content of the Book of Joshua, either from his own experience or from the reports of others. If such a person had regularly recorded everything and arranged his material, he could have completed the Book of Joshua in its present form by the end of his life. The author therefore was probably a younger contemporary of Joshua.

This conclusion is significant because it allows for the possibility, which borders on probability, that the author of the Book of Joshua had personal contact with Israel's outstanding general and leader. If this was so, then he not only would have been abreast of the generally known facts, but he also would have had access to information that Joshua alone could have provided—e.g., God's revelations to Joshua (1:1–9; 3:7–8; 5:13–6:5; 7:10–15; 8:18 et al.). Undoubtedly Joshua either would have recorded these divine messages himself or would have quickly conveyed them to a confidant who would have recorded them, which may also have happened with the speeches and commands that Joshua gave to specific individuals and groups (e.g., 1:10, 12; 2:1; 9:22; 18:8; 22:1–8) or to the nation as a whole (23:1–16; 24:1–24). Joshua 24:26, which expressly states that Joshua made a record of his final speech and the covenant renewal ceremony that followed it, shows that he felt the need to record important events from Israel's history even when the Lord did not specifically command him to do so, as far as we know. Indeed, could we expect otherwise from a man who had faithfully served Moses for years (Exod. 24:13; Num. 11:28) and then had carried on Moses' work?

There is every reason, therefore, to believe that a man who was close to Joshua would have taken whatever notes were necessary—either on his own initiative or at the command of his master—and later would have compiled the written account of the conquest of Canaan in a book that was named after Joshua. Such a scribe would naturally have had access to documents and reports from headquarters that defined the

---

this very reason we need not consider them.

boundaries and listed by name the cities of the various tribal territories (see chs. 13–21). He no doubt would have received his information primarily, but not exclusively, from Joshua. We would expect, too, that the author would be in the circle of officers or supervisors repeatedly referred to in the book (1:10; 3:2; 8:33; 23:2; 24:1). The Hebrew name for these men (*šōṭēr*) originally meant "scribe," and Schulz says that "it is virtually certain that those who bore this name were proficient in writing" (A. Schulz, *Das Buch Josue*, Bonn, 1924, p. 4). None of these individuals is known to us by name; but the fact that Joshua, the central figure in the book, had the services of a staff of men who were skillful writers gives us every reason to suppose that the author of the Book of Joshua was a member of this circle.

In conclusion, then, it is most probable that a close confidant of Joshua wrote the book bearing Joshua's name. That Joshua himself wrote the book, a view I held too assuredly in the previous Dutch editions of this commentary, could only be maintained if one qualified it in numerous ways and assumed that the sections that could not have come from Joshua himself were added and interpolated into his work by a later hand. Establishing Joshua as the author of the book would meet with no insurmountable objections, if there were a single sentence anywhere in Scripture that came near to compelling us to regard him as the author. But since this is not the case—and we can do no more than speculate in this regard—the integrity of the book makes it better to assume that it was written by a man who knew Joshua intimately but outlived him by some years. Joshua's influence on the composition of the book named after him would then have been great but indirect.[11] Such a younger contemporary could have described what took place during Joshua's life and after his death, and this view does justice to all the evidence.

Finally, the view that the Book of Joshua was produced toward the middle of the period of the judges or later clashes with the optimistic tone that pervades the book as a whole. Joshua 11:16–23; 21:43–45, and Joshua's speeches in chapters 23 and 24 create the strong impression of being written and spoken soon after the conquest of the Promised Land, when the people still stood on a high spiritual plateau. It is true that the author perceived that some tribes were guilty of a lack of perseverance (see the verses mentioned under points 9 and 10), and

---

[11]C. F. Keil (*Biblischer Kommentar über Josua*² [Leipzig, 1874], p. 8) also holds this view, but his notion that the author was one of the elders is unconvincing. Joshua 24:31 indicates that he rather belonged to the second generation.

24:31 hints that a time of spiritual decline and decay would begin after the death of the elders. Nevertheless, even the final chapter of this book breathes a completely different spirit than that which abruptly confronts us in the first two chapters of Judges. It is highly unlikely that the book would have been written in such a spiritual tone had the author lived during the period depicted in Judges—a time of gross unfaithfulness to God, internal discord, and foreign oppression, which in part meant the undoing of Joshua's lifework. The most reasonable position, therefore, is that the Book of Joshua must have been completed approximately forty years after the entry into Canaan (1407 B.C.), i.e., *ca.* 1367 B.C. (see the discussion below).

In the first two (Dutch) editions of this commentary I hypothesized that Phinehas, the son of Eleazar, supplemented Joshua's original writing with the additional material that could have come from Joshua. This is suggested by the account of the altar of witness that was built by the tribes who returned to the land east of the Jordan (22:10–34). Joshua apparently played no role in this episode, for his name is not even mentioned. Phinehas provided the leadership: he headed up the deputation that was sent to demand an explanation. Since he was a priest, Phinehas was concerned that the unity of the divine worship at the central sanctuary be preserved. Thus, there is reason to believe that the account of the building of that altar of witness came either directly or indirectly from him.

Furthermore, it is possible that Phinehas even authored the whole Book of Joshua. He represented a younger generation than Joshua, and it would be fitting that the report of Eleazar's death and burial came from his own hand. Yet, the fact remains that there are no definite clues that Phinehas was active in writing any part of the book or ever passed on any writings to those who survived him. Nothing would be gained by assuming that Phinehas authored the book. The authority of a biblical book does not rest on the greatness of its author (however attractive such an idea might be) but on the fact that it was inspired by the Holy Spirit. And certainly the Book of Joshua too was inspired by this divine Author.

IV. *The Unity and Independence of the Book*

The previous sections of the Introduction have clearly demonstrated that the Book of Joshua should be regarded as a unity. In this section I will develop this thesis further and defend it against a number of objections.

A book that is a unity is characterized throughout by a central theme that the various individual sections unfold and illumine. This implies that such a book is rounded off in some way—that it is given a suitable beginning and conclusion and that it clearly develops that central idea. The Book of Joshua fully satisfies all these conditions. Its central theme is Israel's settlement in the Promised Land under the leadership of Joshua. The concept of "settlement" includes the entry and conquest of the land and its division to the tribes. Joshua 1:2–9 clearly states this theme at the outset of the book, and scholars have observed that these verses preview the content of the book as a whole. Verse 2 looks forward to 1:10–4:24 (the crossing of the Jordan), verse 5 to chapters 5–12 (the conquest of nearly all of Canaan), verse 6 to chapters 13–22 (the allotment of the land to the various individual tribes), and verses 7–8 to chapters 23–24 (the challenge to remain faithful to the law of Moses). Finally verses 3 and 9 prepare the way for the constantly recurring thought that Israel will possess the land only through the Lord's gracious help (e.g., 6:2; 10:42; 21:43–45; 23:3).

The Book of Joshua is clearly based on a well thought-out plan. This is confirmed by the repeated references to what the Lord has spoken, either directly to Joshua or through Moses (e.g., 1:13; 4:10; 8:27, 31; 10:40; 11:12; 23:5, 10, 14), and by the author's adherence to the thread of the narrative. Repeatedly he pauses to summarize what has preceded and to prepare the reader for what follows. An illustration of this with Joshua's own words is in found in 4:23–24, where the first verse looks backward and the second forward. Similarly verses 16 and 23 in chapter 11 form a conclusion to what has gone before while verse 23 simultaneously announces the account of the division of the land. This pattern is repeated in 12:7–8 and 13:1. Furthermore, the interconnection between 1:5–6; 11:23; and 21:43–45 cannot be missed; and the same thought is repeated, almost as if it were a refrain, in 23:1. Chapters 23 and 24 presuppose the previous account of the conquest and division of Canaan. That the book opens with Joshua's assumption of his office and closes with his death is fully in keeping with its unifying theme: what happened in Israel under Joshua's leadership—or rather what God did for Israel through Joshua—occupies a unique position in sacred history and thus merits a book of its own.

The unity of the Book of Joshua means that all internal inconsistency is precluded. Although critical scholars who oppose scriptural authority

20

claim the book contradicts itself at various points, most of these so-called discrepancies are quite far-fetched; and others vanish if one accepts the book on its own terms. For example, it is arbitrary to suppose there is a conflict between 1:4, where the Euphrates is named as the eastern boundary of Israel's promised territory, and 13:8–12, where this boundary is drawn without mention of the Euphrates. Chapter 1 merely gives a brief and summary description, while chapter 13 defines those boundaries in detail. Furthermore, God's promises were not all fulfilled at once.

Similarly, there is no inconsistency in the fact that chapters 1–12 fail to mention Eleazar, while in chapter 14 and elsewhere Joshua acts in concert with Eleazar and the elders. The change did not occur because of a different perspective on the relation between Joshua and Eleazar but because the former chapters deal with the conquest of the land by force of arms, where the high priest did not play a direct role. He was, however, chosen by God as a leader in the division of the land (Num. 34:17), which is the subject of chapters 14 and following. Finally, there is no irreconcilable conflict between Joshua's warning to put away the foreign gods that still remained (24:14, 23) and the frequent portrayal of the people's obedience to the Lord's law and commandments (e.g., 5:2–11; 7:24–26; 8:33).[12]

More serious is the apparent conflict some see between the statements claiming that Joshua subjected the whole land of Canaan and all its inhabitants (11:16–23; 12:7–8; 21:43–45; 23:1, 4) and the statements that show that much land had not yet been conquered and that many Canaanites had not been destroyed (13:2–6; 14:12; 17:12–18; 18:2–3; 23:5, 7, 12–13). It is remarkable, however, that the author himself seems to have been unaware of any discrepancy, for in verses 4 and 5 of chapter 23 the two views are directly juxtaposed. This by itself should warn us to exercise caution in speaking of a conflict, since clearly the author was unaware of one. The two views in fact are not mutually exclusive, if the following points are kept in mind.

1. If the conquest of Canaan is regarded ideally, then it must be seen as fulfilled in Joshua's time. When regarded factually, however, it remained incomplete. On the one hand, the conquest is described as the fulfillment of God's promise, and this promise applied to the whole land (1:3–4; cf. Deut. 11:24). On the other hand, however, this promise was closely tied to the command to possess the land (1:5–6, 9; cf. Deut.

---

[12] Aalders (*Oud-Testamentische Canoniek,* pp. 165f.) mentions a few other "discrepancies," which I will deal with in loc.

11:25; 31:5). So in a certain sense the promise was conditional. Israel had to take up the sword and subdue every inch of territory if the promise was to be fulfilled. Under Joshua's leadership Israel for the most part answered this demand. But to the extent that the people fell short of this ideal, they failed to fully realize the divine promise.

2. Verses such as 21:43, however, still should not be regarded as exaggerated and incorrect. Joshua's work was not partial but affected the entire land. He subdued both the northern and the southern realms and so eliminated its heathen population that those who remained were as nothing compared to the great work that had already been accomplished. Canaan as a whole had indeed become the land of the Israelites, and the task of conquest and elimination merely had to be completed.

3. From the outset God had intended to grant Israel its inheritance in Canaan only little by little (Exod. 23:29–30; Deut. 7:22).[13] The gradual conquest, therefore, did not intrinsically conflict with the Lord's promise but was in accord with everything that He had spoken to Moses (Josh. 11:23). But this obviously did not excuse the Israelites' negligence (18:3).

The different viewpoints in the Book of Joshua, therefore, should not cause us to doubt its unity. The same can be said of the minor points of difference that some have perceived (e.g., between 8:9 and 12), which will be dealt with in the commentary and Notes. Attempts to demonstrate a different origin for different parts of the book on the basis of linguistic or literary considerations have met with no success, though many commentators claim that such differences exist. They hold that the Book of Joshua consists of diverse, independent narratives and documents that have been combined into a unity. However, when it comes to defining these "sources," these scholars admit that this is anything but an easy task. They say that the Book of Joshua cannot be "dissected" because the diverse "fragments" or "sources" have been too "worked over" and fused together. This very confession, however, bears powerful witness to the unity and indivisibility of the Book of Joshua.

This point can briefly be illustrated by citing the views of J. De Groot and Martin Noth. De Groot (*Het Boek Jozua,* p. 11) does indeed reject the notion that one can know "how a chapter or even a verse is to be distributed over the various sources" and then adds that "this endeavor has failed." When commenting on the lack of a reliable

---

[13] See Keil, *Joshua,*[2] p. 169.

method for accurately determining the antiquity of the various chapters, he even says, "It is a fiction to think one will ever discover this." De Groot therefore is convinced that the attempts to achieve a satisfactory "analysis" of the Book of Joshua are hopeless. But how is this compatible with his view that the Book of Joshua is a compilation of diverse and unconnected sections of various size? He summarily characterizes chapter 6, for example, as a chaos that no longer can be put in order (ibid., p. 90); and he supposes that the original book (from the tenth century B.C.) was later rewritten in a "Deuteronomistic" spirit and then supplemented with a variety of inserted material. He thus comes to the conclusion that "writers from many different times, and probably also from the time of Joshua, worked on the book; the material comes from a variety of hands and from many centuries" (ibid., pp. 10–11).

In contrast to the above strong statement, De Groot's subdivision of the book gives the impression that it was composed very systematically and conceived as a unity. We must therefore ask how the process he has described in the passages cited above could ever have produced such a tightly constructed and well-organized whole as the Book of Joshua. If it is not possible to apply source-critical theories to the book, why then did he not base his understanding and investigation on its self-evident unity? On the one hand, it appears that De Groot, despite the fact that he wished to dissent from source-critical theories, was still strongly influenced by their premise, (e.g., that the Book of Deuteronomy originally existed independent from the Pentateuch). He thereby departed from an unbiased view of the origin of the Book of Joshua and came to regard it as a collection of larger and smaller fragments. On the other hand, De Groot was realistic enough to admit that all the systematic attempts that had been made to assign these fragments to specific sources had been fruitless. We hardly can be tempted to follow him on his inconsistent path.

The position of Martin Noth, whose commentary *Das Buch Josua* (part 7 of Eissfeldt's *Handbuch zum Alten Testament*) appeared in its second edition in 1953, is even more inconsistent. Noth devotes most of the introduction of his commentary to what he calls the literary prehistory of Joshua. He admits that attempts to distinguish in Joshua the same "sources" (Noth speaks of "continuous strands of narrative," p. 8) that are present in Genesis have been unsuccessful. Yet his whole approach betrays his belief in the existence of sources or documents in the Pentateuch. One mainstay of his position is the existence of a great "Deuteronomistic" historical work that arose completely apart from the extensive Pentateuch tradition (p. 16). Noth sees the Book of Joshua as one element of that historical work and discerns no connection between it and the Pentateuch sources J, E, and P. With this basic premise he unfolds his literary-critical reflections on the origin and composition of the Book of Joshua. Noth, with great assurance, theorizes that Joshua 13:1–21:42 had its own literary prehistory, wholly unrelated to the rest of the book. He bases this surprising claim on his understanding of the identity of 13:1a and 23:1b. Noth does not see how both statements could have stood in the original writing. Joshua 13:1a therefore must have been borrowed from 23:1b by a later author to join 13:1–21:42 to the preceding material. But Noth gives no text-critical reason to support his claim that 13:1a is spurious. Apparently we are expected to accept Noth's claim simply on his own authority.

Noth envisions the prehistory of the Book of Joshua as follows. He sees 1:1–12:24 as the work of a "compiler" who gathered the "legends" told in chapters 2–9 and the war reports in 10:1–11:9 and revised and supplemented them in the Deuteronomistic style. According to Noth, the result was a systematically planned Deuteronomistic book that also contained 21:43–22:6 and 23:1–16. Noth then argues that a later hand added 13:1–21:42 and 24:1–33, these also being written in the well-known Deuteronomistic style. (Curiously, Noth asserts on p. 12 that the first "compiler" was probably also the one who first introduced Joshua into the "legends" and "stories" where he originally did not belong. Noth believes that the only event Joshua possibly could have taken part in was the establishment of the covenant at Shechem [ch.24]. Such monstrous claims can hardly be taken seriously. Similar reasoning could eliminate Moses as a lawgiver from Israel's history and Julius Caesar as a conqueror from Rome's history!) In addition to all that, Noth speaks of "accretions" from the post-Deuteronomistic period (e.g., 22:9–34) as well as numerous other additions.

This survey reveals Noth's lack of respect for tradition, not to mention Holy Scripture and its Author. If the Book of Joshua is divisible into as many bits and fragments as Noth claims, one wonders how a work of such outstanding quality could have originated in this fashion. Noth's conclusions appear highly unreliable, and one can only lament the fact that so much time and acumen was expended to mutilate such a splendid book. Noth's critical approach lost sight of the limits of its task and its sphere of competence. Fortunately his conclusions in no way erase the book's own testimony to its inner unity and coherence. Thus it is needless to critique in detail Noth's opinions, which is beyond the scope of this volume. If the reader wishes further information about Noth's starting point, see Aalders's discussion of the Pentateuch problem (*Oud-Testamentische Canoniek,* pp. 83–126, 167f.).

The unity of the Book of Joshua raises the question of its independent status, but there is not a single legitimate reason to deny this. Since the book is governed by one central idea that is fully worked out, it is unique among the books of the Old Testament. Because certain sections of the book agree strongly with parts of the Pentateuch, and because Joshua's work was a direct continuation of Moses', some scholars have concluded that the Book of Joshua and the Pentateuch originally formed a single whole. Thus some have conjectured that the first six books of the Old Testament should properly be entitled the Hexateuch. But there is no indication whatever that the Book of Joshua originally belonged to a larger whole that it was later severed from. In fact there is evidence to the contrary. First, the book is a well-formed whole, both in form and content. Second, it independently recounts a number of facts already recorded in the Pentateuch (e.g., the partition of the land east of the Jordan, ch. 13, cf. Num. 32:33–42; the designation of the cities of refuge, ch. 20, cf. Deut. 4:41–43; 19:1–13). Third, the book contains linguistic idiosyncrasies foreign to the Pentateuch.[14] Finally, the Pentateuch finds its natural conclusion in the death of Moses, though I cannot give the reasons for that here. The fact that the Jews never attached Joshua to the Torah (i.e., "the Law," the books of Moses) but placed it first in the group of sacred books they called "the Prophets" is decisive.[15]

I do not, however, wish to underestimate the inner relationship between the Book of Joshua and the Pentateuch. That relationship can be explained by observing that Joshua's task was to continue Moses' work and to carry out his various commands. In places where the same things are spoken of, it is only natural that the same clauses and expressions should be used (compare 1:3–4 to Deut. 11:24; 1:5–9 to

---

[14] See, e.g., Keil, *Joshua,*[2] p. 9.

[15] For the most part, the hypothetical existence of a Hexateuch has been abandoned. Aalders (*Oud-Testamentische Canoniek,* p. 165) also points out that the Samaritans accepted the Pentateuch, but not the Book of Joshua.

Deut. 31:6–8, 23; 8:29 to Deut. 21:23; 8:30–32 to Deut. 27:2–8; 10:8 to Num. 21:34; ch. 20 to Num. 35:9–28 and Deut. 19:1–13 et al.).

The independence of the Book of Joshua does not mean that it is unrelated to other books of the Bible. On the contrary, the Book of Joshua builds on the Pentateuch; and the Book of Judges ties in with it. Although the biblical books may be relatively independent and have their own meanings, they are nevertheless all parts of a single greater whole. They were not, however, simply joined together at some later date by men. Rather, the divine Author ordained from the time of their origin that they would complement one another and together constitute the written Word of God.

V. *The Interpretation of the Book*

On a literal level the Book of Joshua has relatively few difficulties. Its story is coherent and generally clear. As a rule the book can be readily understood without further elucidation, which will become evident throughout this commentary.

Nevertheless, this section will briefly clarify how a historical book like Joshua should be read and understood. Generally speaking, explaining words and sentences in their immediate context is insufficient for interpreting a book of the Bible. The permanent significance of a particular part of Scripture must also be considered, though this does not warrant exchanging the obvious meaning of the words for an obscure one. It is equally wrong to think that the task of exegesis is complete with a simple exposition of the text. The purpose and aim of exegesis is to determine what the divine Author of Scripture is telling us in a particular passage, what He is revealing as a guide for our faith and conduct. Since this revelation comes to us through the written Word, we can know God's thoughts only to the extent that we understand Scripture. That means Scripture must be regarded as a unity and each Bible book must be seen in its relationship to that unity. Thus the interpretation of a given book depends not only on its own statements but also on the light shed on it by Scripture as a whole.

Because Scripture is an organic unity, each section and each book must be viewed in light of their interconnection as members of a single body. This permits the Bible to be its own primary interpreter. Frequently one passage illumines another. This is especially evident when the Old and New Testaments are placed side by side. The Old Testament cannot be understood correctly if the interpreter does not take the New Testament into consideration, because the New Testament completes the story of the Old Testament. This is more evident in some places than others. For example, the Letter to the Hebrews brilliantly illuminates many Old Testament passages, particularly in the Pentateuch. Every Old Testament book needs to be interpreted in the light of New Testament revelation if it is to be properly understood.

Our reading of the historical books should be guided by a clear understanding of the meaning of the history recorded in the Holy Scriptures. This history is sacred in character and is an integral part of God's special revelation; it reveals His thoughts, not in mere words, but in facts, events, and persons. Therefore those facts themselves have to be interpreted. Placing them in their proper historical and psychological contexts is not enough; we must discover the divine thought that they express. God's counsel of redemption was revealed in both the events of history and the words of the prophets. By classing the historical books of the Old Testament (and Joshua as the first of these) together with the books of prophecy and calling them the "first" or "former" Prophets, the Jews were guided by a correct concept.

God did not inspire those books through the Holy Spirit and see to their inclusion in the Canon merely to acquaint us with Israel's history. The books can be properly understood only if we regard Israel as a type of Christ and His church. This typical character belongs to Israel as a whole as well as to prominent individuals such as Moses, Joshua, David, and Solomon. Furthermore, Israel's history, which foreshadows and prefigures a higher reality, is not that of one nation among many but of the people of God under the old dispensation. This history, which actually happened, simultaneously pointed beyond itself to a higher truth. This is most clearly seen in certain events (e.g., the Exodus) but still must be kept in view in every aspect of Israel's history.

All this applies to the interpretation of Joshua, which is history and should be accepted as such. The first goal of interpretation should be to make the historical narrative as intelligible as possible and to do full justice to it. Although various sections can be discerned in the narrative of Joshua, the book is a single whole; so we should not look for a deeper meaning in each separate verse. We must, however, have a clear understanding of the meaning of the book as a whole (see section I) and of certain of its sections, particularly those that record the most important events. Three examples will illustrate this point.

First, the significance of Israel's passage through the Jordan River

27

(chs. 3–4) is evident in the preparatory speeches and actions (3:2–13), in the miracle that enabled the people to cross (3:15–17), and in the other events that accompanied the crossing (see ch. 4). The unique significance of that event for Israel is indicated by the prophet Micah's recollection of what happened "from Shittim to Gilgal" (Mic. 6:5). Crossing the Jordan has significance for Christians, too. If Israel's desert journey foreshadows the path of the church of Christ through this world, then crossing the Jordan typifies the church's passage through death and the grave to eternal life.[16]

The ark of the covenant led Israel in this crossing; and as soon as the priests stepped down into the river with it, the waters that separated the people from the Promised Land parted, thus enabling every Israelite to pass through. This is another clear picture of the work of Christ, who by humbling Himself in death conquered death itself and cleared a path for His people to the heavenly Canaan. This is not just imagery but prophecy as well. The facts themselves are prophetic of what Christ accomplished for and in His church. God ordained beforehand that these events would happen and be recorded to assure us that He will guide us through the river of death just as securely as He led Israel through the Jordan. Just as Israel had to look on the ark as it stood motionless, so we must fix our eyes on the unshakable cross of Christ. What happened with Israel in the dispensation of shadows must be repeated and fulfilled in the new dispensation as a spiritual reality for the church. That fulfillment must occur. Joshua 3, understood properly, promises that death will be the necessary means by which God's people are enabled to possess their heavenly inheritance.

Second, the Book of Joshua describes the extermination of the inhabitants of Canaan as being extremely harsh and severe. This is not only true of Jericho (6:21) but also of the conquest of Ai and the cities in the north and south of the land (see chs. 8, 10, 11). Did Israel really

---

[16] S. G. De Graaf (*Promise and Deliverance,* trans. H. E. and E. W. Runner, 4 vols. [St. Catharines, Ontario: Paideia, 1977]) takes a different view of this event. He does not see the Jordan and Canaan as the waters of death and heaven, respectively. Rather, "passing through the waters is dying with Christ, in order to live with Him eternally" (1:391). This interpretation seems incorrect, because it gives virtually the same meaning to the passage through the Jordan that belongs to the Exodus and the passage through the Red Sea, and that would conflict with the symbolism in Israel's history. In an earlier discussion of the institution of the Passover, De Graaf correctly observes that "Israel was saved from death and raised to a new life" (ibid., p. 277). But that could not happen again at a later time. In the desert Israel was *already* the people of God en route to the Promised Land. Canaan should therefore be seen as a type of the heavenly homeland.

have the right to act as she did? Was she not guilty of needless cruelty (cf. esp. 10:22–27)? The Book of Joshua does not directly answer these questions but regards the destruction of the native population as something that happened as a matter of course (1:5–6). Clearly Joshua and Israel acted at the Lord's command and with His aid (6:2; 8:1–2; 10:8, 10–11, 40, 42). On the surface this ruthless destruction gives the impression of being cold-blooded and arbitrary; therefore we need to consider what is implied elsewhere in the Bible on this matter. Numerous passages (e.g., Gen. 15:16; Lev. 18:24–30; Deut. 9:1–6; 12:29–31; 1 Kings 21:26; and Ezra 9:11–12) make it clear that the Lord had patiently put up with the sins of the Canaanites (i.e., all the tribes living in Canaan) for a long time; but when Israel entered the land, the measure of the Canaanites' sins was full. God, the righteous Judge of the earth (cf. Gen. 18:25), had resolved to all but annihilate these nations and to give their land to Israel, though Israel also was unworthy. God willed to execute that judgment primarily through the sword of the Israelites, not by water, as in the Flood, or by fire, as in the destruction of the cities in the Valley of Salt. The New Testament adds nothing new to this, though significantly it twice says that God expelled or destroyed these nations (Acts 7:45; 13:19).

All this implies that the extermination of the Canaanites should be seen as a divine judgment whose enforcement was a sacred task, because it was nothing less than the execution of the vengeance of God against a sinful people. God entrusted Israel with this task, and she thereby became His instrument of judgment. Israel's troops were the troops of the living God, and her sword was the sword of the Lord. Only by keeping this in mind can the Book of Joshua's account of Israel's conduct be judged properly. Israel did not act high-handedly; neither were the people driven by sheer lust for blood nor bent on seizing the land. On the contrary, the Book of Joshua impresses us with the scrupulous care, the stern self-restraint, and the huge sense of responsibility with which Israel performed her task (11:12, 15). Furthermore, the constant memory of Moses' warning not to bring the same judgment on themselves by following the sins of the Canaanites (Lev. 20:22–23) could only have made Israel's task more grave. If we correctly understand Israel's actions, we will neither condemn them nor use them as a rule against some nation that exists today. Because Israel's position was unique, the extermination of the Canaanites offers no such rule for today (nor does, e.g., Jehu's destruction of the house of Ahab in 2 Kings 9–10). Israel knew that she had been called to a special task by God Himself.

Because Israel was God's people, His "treasured possession" (Deut. 7:6), during the conquest of Canaan she was specially designated as His earthly army, something that can be said of no other nation. That same designation also applies to the church of Christ, the New Testament continuation of ancient Israel. The account of the extermination of the Canaanites has a twofold message for the church. First, Israel's example foreshadows the church's calling to be the "church militant" in the world. As such, she is to resist the powers of darkness with all that is in her, to cut herself off as resolutely as possible from all association with sin and worldly goals, and to steadfastly combat and uproot the remnants of sin in her midst and also in the lives of her individual members, thereby pushing onward toward the goal of complete sanctification (2 Cor. 7:1). Israel's example makes it clear that the church's punishment for betraying her calling would be exclusion from communion with God. Second, Israel's successes in battle are to encourage the people of Christ. The church, too, fights the Lord's battles; and she can rest assured that no matter how mighty her foes might seem, they will become subject to her if she keeps her banner unstained and draws her strength from Christ.

The division of the land is the third example. A sizable portion of the Book of Joshua is devoted to this matter. It was necessary that each tribe receive its own section of the land and that the boundaries of those sections be accurately marked. The division of the land, therefore, was undertaken with particular care. Joshua, Eleazar, and the elders supervised (14:1; 19:51), and all was done in the presence of the Lord and in accordance with His commands (14:2; 18:10). Casting lots placed the operation directly under God's control, showing that Israel regarded the task as sacred. God's special, divine care in the division of the land foreshadowed an event of deeper significance: the distribution of the benefits that Christ has won for us. Christ not only has secured the promised gift of salvation, He also ensures that it comes into the possession of His followers. He portions it out and puts it into effect.

In the division of Canaan, God clearly regarded not only His people as a whole but also particular tribes and individuals (14:6; 19:49–50) for whom He reserved special inheritances. Christ's work in behalf of His church is similar. When His enemies are finally subdued, Christ will take all who belong to Him into His glory; but the richest diversity will be manifested in their enjoyment of their eternal rest. Each Christian will receive the object of his earthy preparation, his portion of "the inheritance of the saints in the kingdom of light" (Col. 1:12). Each will be given the new name that is written on his own "white stone" (Rev. 2:17) and the place that has been prepared for him in the Father's house, where there are "many rooms" (John 14:2–3).

These three examples adequately show that various parts of the Bible can be understood only if we have a correct view of Scripture as a whole. In the commentary itself, wherever appropriate, I will briefly give the meaning of a particular passage for the New Covenant people of God.

VI. *Chronological Questions*

The question of when the events recounted in the Book of Joshua took place can be answered only in connection with the date assigned to the Exodus, for that date also determines the year Israel entered Canaan, which was forty years later. This, however, is not the place to try to determine when the Israelites were led out of Egypt. Scholars who take the biblical data seriously (esp. Gen. 15; Exod. 12:40; Judg. 11:26; 1 Kings 6:1) generally understand the Pharaoh of the Exodus to be Amenhotep II. Evidence indicates that his predecessor died in 1449 B.C.; thus the Exodus occurred in 1447 B.C. (a date also inferred from 1 Kings 6:1), and the entry into Canaan, in 1407 B.C.[17]

More can be said about the chronology of Joshua's own life. One important question is his age at the time he assumed command of Israel. Although a direct statement is lacking, an approximation can be drawn from various evidence. Joshua 24:29 states that Joshua lived to the age of 110. It also is certain that the conquest of the land took seven years to complete. Caleb states (14:7) that he had been 40 years old when Moses sent him to spy out Canaan and that he now had reached the age of 85 (14:10). The spies had been sent out near the end of the second year after the Exodus, and Israel wandered in the desert for another thirty-eight years after that. Thus Caleb was 78 years old when

---

[17]On this date see W. H. Gispen, *Bijbelse Encyclopedie,* "Exodus" (article), 1950; C. van Gelderen, *Bijbelsch Handboek,* 1935, 1:118ff.; A. Noordtzij, *Gods Woord en der eeuwen getuigenis,* 2nd ed. (Kampen, 1931), p. 317. An early date for the Exodus is also advocated by A. H. Edelkoort, *Uittocht en Intocht,* (1924), pp. 206f., and D. J. Baarslag, *Israel in Egypte,* Libellenserie no. 59–61. On the basis of his archaeological work, J. Garstang (*Joshua, Judges,* [London, 1931]) has determined that the destruction of Jericho and Ai could not have occurred later than 1400 B.C.

the Israelites entered Canaan. Since he was 85 when the land began to be divided, the events recorded in chapters 1–12 must have lasted seven years. Joshua 13:1 states that Joshua had at that time already reached a great age. Undoubtedly he was older than Caleb, and the Book of Joshua gives the impression that he died within two decades after the land was divided. Joshua 23:1 does speak of "a long time," but this could be ten or fifteen years. The division of the land of course took time, especially since the conquest did not go smoothly for some of the tribes (17:13–18) and was not pursued vigorously enough (18:3). The whole process recorded in chapters 13–22 could have required three or four years.

The above considerations suggest that Joshua was between 80 and 90 years old when the Israelites arrived in Canaan, and that allowed him to end his work at the venerable age of nearly 100 years. After that, Joshua still could enjoy a number of years of rest in the Promised Land, but it is doubtful whether he spent this time in idleness. Joshua's actions in chapters 23–24 apparently occurred in his last year of life. My calculations indicate that Joshua must have been almost 50 when the desert journey began. This is confirmed by the fact that he was soon called to lead the people in battle against Amalek (Exod. 17:9). That Exodus 33:11 calls Joshua a young man does not mean that he was younger than our figure; the Hebrew term *na'ar* often refers to a person's status more than his age (cf. Num. 22:22; 2 Sam. 9:9, where it is rendered as "servant"). Compared to Moses, Joshua could very well have been called a young man. If Israel entered Canaan in 1407 B.C., then Joshua would have died in 1387 B.C. (see the commentary on Judges in this series, p. 239).

VII. *Outline*

Part One—The Conquest of Canaan (1:1–12:24)

1. The Divine Mandate (1:1–9)
2. Joshua's Charge to the People (1:10–18)
3. The Mission to Jericho (2:1–24)
4. Israel on the Bank of the Jordan (3:1–6)
5. Crossing the Jordan (3:7–17)
6. Further Details: Memorial Stones From the Jordan (4:1–14)
7. The Crossing Completed and the Monument Erected (4:15–24)
8. Circumcision and the Celebration of the Passover (5:1–12)

Joshua Commentary

Part One

The Conquest of Canaan
(1:1–12:24)

1. The Divine Mandate
(1:1–9)

1:1–2 *After the death of Moses the servant of the LORD, the LORD said to Joshua son of Nun, Moses' aide:* ² *"Moses my servant is dead. Now then, you and all these people, get ready to cross the Jordan River into the land I am about to give to them—to the Israelites.*

Verses 1–9, which appropriately introduce the whole Book of Joshua, contain the divine mandate to possess the Promised Land (vv. 1–2). In the Introduction (p. 20) I have shown that the Book of Joshua unfolds the message of verses 1–9. The narrative of Joshua begins where Deuteronomy ended. "After the death of Moses" (v. 1) refers to the end of the thirty-day mourning period for Moses (Deut. 34:8). The time to act had arrived. The relationship between Joshua and Moses has already been discussed in the Introduction (pp. 8–9). The designation "Moses' aide" does not degrade Joshua but is a title of honor, expressing the fact that he served at Moses' right hand.

We are not told how the Lord spoke to Joshua, neither here nor in the rest of the book, where divine revelations to Joshua frequently are mentioned (e.g., 3:7; 4:1, 15; 5:2, 9; 7:10; 8:1). Joshua 5:13–6:5 alone speaks of a direct appearance of the Lord; apparently the divine

35

messages generally came as an inner voice to Joshua, though at times God may have addressed him audibly (e.g., 7:10). In any case Joshua at once knew that God was speaking to him. This does not conflict with Numbers 27:21, which says that the Lord would address Joshua through the intercession of Eleazar. The historical narrative in the Book of Joshua reveals that as a rule Joshua received his revelations directly from God.

Earlier the Lord told Joshua that he would lead Israel into the Promised Land (Deut. 31:7, 23). Now the Lord called him to assume Moses' place as leader of the people and to begin his life's work. God told Joshua to lead the people from their place of encampment and to cross the Jordan and enter the Promised Land with them. Significantly, the Hebrew text uses the demonstrative pronoun *this* both with "Jordan River" in verse 2 and with "Lebanon" in verse 4.[1] This may indicate that Joshua received this divine revelation on an elevated place from which he could sweep his eyes over the land, just as Moses had seen from afar the country that he was not permitted to enter (Deut. 34:1–4). As the Lord had shown the entire land to Moses, He likewise directed Joshua's gaze first to the Jordan and then to Lebanon. The Jordan was close by, for the people were encamped in the plains of Moab, an area where the Jordan Valley widened. The time had arrived for God to make His promise good. He said to Joshua, "I am about to give"; that is, He was on the verge of giving the land to Israel.

1:3–4 *I will give you every place where you set your foot, as I promised Moses.*
⁴ Your territory will extend from the desert to Lebanon, and from the great river, the Euphrates—all the Hittite country—to the Great Sea on the west.

These two verses, in which the Lord recalls His promise to Moses, have much in common with Deuteronomy 11:24–25 and substantially correspond to the Lord's promise in Exodus 23:23, 27, 31. God was to prove Himself faithful to what He had spoken to Moses and, through him, to the people. The use of the plural form of "you" in the Hebrew text of verses 3 and 4 indicates that through Joshua, God was addressing all the Israelites. As the Lord of heaven and earth, and thus the real Owner of the land, He would allow them to possess every place where they would set their feet.

The full sweep of this divine gift is described in verse 4, which is not an exact fixing of boundaries but a rough sketch of the broad contours

---

[1] See KJV and RSV—TRANS.

of their territory. The southern boundary, defined by the "desert," refers to the desert of Zin, or perhaps the desert of Paran lying south of Palestine in so-called stony Arabia (Num. 13:3, 21). The northern boundary, identified with Lebanon, undoubtedly is a broad reference that includes both the Lebanon and the Anti-Lebanon mountain ranges. Mount Hermon is visible from Mount Nebo, at whose base the Israelites were encamped. Joshua may thus have been standing on the very mountain where Moses died.

The Lord next showed Joshua how the territory promised for Israel, bounded to the south by the desert and to the north by Lebanon, would extend eastward to the mighty Euphrates River in the unseen distance and westward to the Mediterranean Sea. The territory enclosed by this broad outline is further defined as "all the Hittite country," which serves notice that the land was still possessed by Israel's enemies and also anticipates the words of verse 5. "Hittites" here has a broad meaning (as, e.g., also in Ezek. 16:3) and includes the Canaanites. The land is named after the Hittites because the so-called neo-Hittite kingdom probably stretched to Syria in Joshua's day.[2]

1:5–6 *No one will be able to stand up against you all the days of your life. As I was with Moses, so I will be with you; I will never leave you nor forsake you.*
⁶"Be strong and courageous, because you will lead these people to inherit the land I swore to their forefathers to give them.

The rest of God's address returns to the singular form and is directed specifically to Joshua. The promise given to the people in Deuteronomy 11:25 is applied here to him as an individual. No one current owner of the land would be able to stand his ground against Joshua. Resistance would not be absent, but it would be to no avail. Joshua's fortunes in battle would not rise and fall, for as long as he lived he would be victorious, not in his own strength, but because the Lord would be with Him. The Lord never leaves His servants.

Moses' task had been extremely difficult, but God helped him to accomplish it; and Joshua had been a witness to this (Deut. 3:21–22). Now he too would be able to count on the Lord's assistance in the same way. God would neither abandon him to fate nor withhold whatever help was necessary. Moses had already told Joshua this (Deut. 31:8), and to hear it repeated from God's own mouth would surely strengthen Joshua's faith. The almost literal repetition in verse 6 of the promise

---

[2] See *Bijbelse Encyclopedie*, pp. 210f.

from Deuteronomy 31:23 has the same effect. The Lord inspired Joshua with courage.

In the original Hebrew the words "be strong" and "be courageous" are virtually identical in meaning (cf. 1 Cor. 16:13, lit., "be manly, be strong"). Joshua was to march forward fearlessly, heartened by the sure knowledge that he would defeat Israel's enemies and divide their land among his people. Joshua had been chosen for this task by God Himself (Num. 34:17; Deut. 1:38; 3:28) to be the instrument that He would use to accomplish what He had solemnly sworn to the fathers (e.g., Gen. 15:18; 24:7; Exod. 32:13). Joshua, however, was only an instrument; although he would have to fight, it was Yahweh, the God of the covenant, who would give the land to Israel as an undeserved inheritance. Precisely because it was the Lord's own work—and He always keeps His word—Joshua's reliance on His help would have to be unqualified.

1:7–8 *Be strong and very courageous. Be careful to obey all the law my servant Moses gave you; do not turn from it to the right or to the left, that you may be successful wherever you go. ⁸Do not let this Book of the Law depart from your mouth; meditate on it day and night, so that you may be careful to do everything written in it. Then you will be prosperous and successful.*

Whereas verse 2 contains the divine mandate proper and verses 3–6 were to encourage Joshua for his task, the following words of the Lord are more admonitory in character. The opening of verse 7 is almost identical to that of verse 6, but the tone is different. In verse 7 Joshua is warned above all to remain steadfast and immovable (cf. 1 Cor. 15:58) in upholding and keeping the law that the Lord had revealed through Moses. To observe God's commandments faithfully requires greater moral strength and courage than to prove one's bravery in battle. The earnestness and urgency of the words of verse 7 confirm this truth, which is illustrated in the treaty with the Gibeonites (9:14–15). Joshua was to be an example by scrupulously adhering to the law. As a leader, he did not stand above Moses' ordinances but rather had to be doubly on guard against breaking them.

Verses 7 and 8 are strongly reminiscent of Deuteronomy 17:19–20, a part of the law for the king. The king's (leader's) unconditional submission to the Lord's law was vitally important for the entire nation. Moses had written down this law in a book (cf. Deut. 31:9–13), whose contents were now to become flesh and blood in the person of Joshua. He was not to depart from it in his words, thoughts, or whole walk of life. His speech, especially in the administration of justice, had to conform to that law completely. Through continual meditation he had to delve deeper into its meaning. Then he would understand its spiritual depth and be able to follow it meticulously, without neglecting its smallest part. Only if Joshua bound himself absolutely to God's written word would he become a good leader, gaining success in battle and bringing Israel to her destination. In the path of obedience, Joshua would experience the surety of God's promises.

1:9 *Have I not commanded you? Be strong and courageous. Do not be terrified; do not be discouraged, for the LORD your God will be with you wherever you go."*

The Lord closed His address to Joshua by once more sounding a note of encouragement. The rhetorical question points back to what was said in verse 6, thus emphasizing that Joshua could fully expect a successful outcome. Joshua must never succumb to fear or anxiety, for that would be unbelief (cf. Balaam's message to Balak in Num. 23:19: "Does He speak and then not act?"). Joshua was never to rely on his own wisdom or on the great size of the Israelite army, for no support could be found there. The sole source of his strength would be the Lord's presence wherever he went. Joshua's salvation lay in God, and his trust in Him had to be unshakable. In this faith he would be victorious (cf. Judg. 6:14: "Go in the strength you have").

2. Joshua's Charge to the People
(1:10–18)

It is clear from verse 2 that God's command was meant, not just for Joshua, but for the whole nation. This section relates how Joshua began to carry out the divine command by conveying it to the people. It also relates his special appeal to a few individual tribes and their answer to him.

1:10–11 *So Joshua ordered the officers of the people:* [11] *"Go through the camp and tell the people, 'Get your supplies ready. Three days from now you will cross the Jordan here to go in and take possession of the land the LORD your God is giving you for your own.'"*

In obedience to the Lord's command, Joshua immediately ordered the appointed officers (lit., "scribes"; their mention in 3:2; 8:33; 23:2;

24:1; Deut. 20:5–9 shows that this was an important function) to proclaim throughout the whole camp the brief but clear command that the people were to ready their supplies[3] for the march that would take place on the third day. The first objective of the journey was to cross the Jordan and conquer the land, which Israel's sovereign God had given to His people as their rightful possession (v. 11). The three days mentioned here are not the same as those in 3:2 (see the comments there).[4] Verse 11 does not say that the people would be across the Jordan after three days. Rather, Joshua's command meant that on the third day[5] the people were to be prepared to cross to the other side of the Jordan. The command, which is not a prophecy, does not state the exact time the people would arrive there.

1:12–15 *But to the Reubenites, the Gadites and the half-tribe of Manasseh, Joshua said,* [13] *"Remember the command that Moses the servant of the LORD gave you: 'The LORD your God is giving you rest and has granted you this land.'* [14] *Your wives, your children and your livestock may stay in the land that Moses gave you east of the Jordan, but all your fighting men, fully armed, must cross over ahead of your brothers. You are to help your brothers* [15] *until the LORD gives them rest, as he has done for you, and until they too have taken possession of the land that the LORD your God is giving them. After that, you may go back and occupy your own land, which Moses the servant of the LORD gave you east of the Jordan toward the sunrise."*

Although Joshua's command applied to all the tribes, he nevertheless realized that it would be well to say a few words personally to Reuben, Gad, and the half-tribe of Manasseh. Since Moses had given these tribes at their own request an inheritance east of the Jordan (Num. 32; 34:14–15),[6] they had already arrived at their destination. Joshua thus displayed prudent leadership by recognizing their special situation. He reminded them that they had solemnly submitted in the presence of Eleazar and Joshua himself to the obligation Moses had placed on them in the Lord's name (Num. 32:16–32).

Joshua's words here mainly repeat Deuteronomy 3:18–20, which he expanded and altered somewhat (e.g., he spoke of Moses in the third

---

[3] This of course does not refer to the manna. Deuteronomy 2:6 shows that Israel also had access to other provisions, and they were now no longer in the desert.

[4] As, e.g., F.B. Meyer (*Joshua and the Land of Promise* [London], pp. 25, 30) maintains.

[5] "Within three days" in KJV and RSV means "on the third day." Compare Genesis 40:13, 19 with 40:20.

[6] See Note 1 at the end of this commentary.

person) to highlight the privilege that these tribes already enjoyed above their fellow Israelites. In so doing, Joshua provoked their sense of honor and solidarity to make them realize that they must not pull back till the other tribes had received their share of the land. Joshua did not forget to state the requirement that they must furnish their own arms (v. 14). Dressed in battle array, they were to cross the Jordan with the rest of Israel. Not all the men of the two and a half tribes were commanded to help their brothers, however, but only those most fit for battle (cf. 4:13). They were to bear in mind that the conquest would not depend on themselves but on the Lord, who would be faithful to His covenant and promises to give the land to Israel.

1:16–18 *Then they answered Joshua, "Whatever you have commanded us we will do, and wherever you send us we will go. ¹⁷ Just as we fully obeyed Moses, so we will obey you. Only may the* LORD *your God be with you as he was with Moses. ¹⁸ Whoever rebels against your word and does not obey your words, whatever you may command them, will be put to death. Only be strong and courageous!"*

Joshua's words were well received; for the tribes in question, probably speaking through their leaders, confirmed their earlier promise (Num. 32:31) by declaring themselves ready to do what Joshua had commanded. They promised to fully submit to his leadership and to obey him in all things, just as they had done under Moses his predecessor. Quite appropriately they added their wish that Joshua would experience the Lord's help. Without this, their most loyal assistance would be to no avail, for without God's blessing nothing is gained. For their own part, however, they pledged such complete obedience that they even agreed that the death penalty should fall on anyone who would oppose Joshua's orders or be remiss in recognizing his authority. This penalty had in fact already been prescribed in the law (Deut. 17:12), and Joshua must have been encouraged when he heard these tribes acknowledge the importance of order, discipline, and submission to divinely ordained authority. He likewise was heartened by hearing the challenge that had come to him first from Moses (Deut. 31:6), then from the Lord Himself (vv. 6, 7, 9), now echoing from the mouths of these men: "Be strong and courageous!" Thus they expected that their leader would have inner fortitude and be inspired by firmness of hope and strength of purpose. At the same time, they urged this on him and sought to fire his enthusiasm. A new spirit had entered the people, which could only have come from God. In peace of soul

Joshua could say, "Praise be to the LORD . . . in whom I take refuge, who subdues my people under me" (Ps. 144:1–2, NIV margin).

3. The Mission to Jericho
(2:1–24)

2:1 *Then Joshua son of Nun secretly sent two spies from Shittim. "Go, look over the land," he said, "especially Jericho." So they went and entered the house of a prostitute named Rahab and stayed there.*

Joshua rightly knew that God's promises (vv. 3–6) did not excuse him from his duty as general to make practical preparations for the conquest. From Shittim, the site northeast of the Dead Sea where Israel was encamped (cf. Num. 33:49), Joshua sent two men to scout the terrain on the west bank of the Jordan (not the whole of Canaan). They were to spy especially on the fortress of Jericho, which was the first city the Israelites would encounter when they entered Canaan. Jericho lay in an oasis that then had an almost tropical climate and, according to Flavius Josephus, stood sixty stadia (two hours) west of the Jordan. The date palms growing there gave it the name "City of Palms" (Deut. 34:3).

Jericho, whose name means "moon city," was not large but had formidable fortifications. This can still be seen in the remains of the two massive circular walls that have been uncovered northwest of the modern village of Arīhā.[7] There were good reasons why Joshua chose to cross the Jordan and invade Canaan at this precise location. A. Noordtzij describes these as follows:[8]

"First of all, the Jordan formed less of a barrier here than elsewhere. . . . The width of the valley here was a five hour's walk, and a caravan route led past Jericho to the pass of Micmash, which gave access to the hill country. Anyone who managed to seize control of Gilgal and Jericho had gained a firm 'bridgehead' from which he could renew his attack even after an initial defeat. Because of this, Eglon of Moab chose this same route and overpowered Jericho when he sought an inroad into the territory west of the Jordan (Judg. 3:13). The

---

[7] See *Bijbels-Kerkelijk Woordenboek*, 1:155; *Bijbelse Encyclopedie*, pp. 246f. Garstang's (*Joshua, Judges*, pp. 130f.) explorations reveal that the bottom layer of Jericho measured only about 210 by 120 meters. He sets the upper estimate for its population at fifteen hundred people.

[8] *Gods Woord en der eeuwen getuigenis*, 2nd ed., p. 354.

Transjordan offered a solid base of support here, too, and even a good line of retreat. In addition, anyone who pushed through Micmash into the hill country reached the plateau where the cities allied with Gibeon stood. By rendering these powerless, he would drive a wedge into the phalanx of the hill dwellers and divide them into a northern and a southern group."

As could be expected from a circumspect general like Joshua, the spies were sent out secretly . Joshua may have been influenced here by his memory that the majority of the twelve earlier spies pronounced an unfavorable report in public (Num. 13:26–33). The two men reached Jericho unhindered and spent the night at the house of Rahab. Although Rahab was a prostitute, that does not mean she could not also have kept an inn.[9] The men no doubt chose to stay the night at her house for good reasons. There they would arouse the least suspicion and find it easy to exit the city. Obviously God led them there, for at Rahab's house they were safe and would hear exactly what they needed to know. This visit also had the greatest significance for Rahab; it was a turning point in her life.

2:2–7 *The king of Jericho was told, "Look! Some of the Israelites have come here tonight to spy out the land." ³So the king of Jericho sent this message to Rahab: "Bring out the men who came to you and entered your house, because they have come to spy out the whole land."*

⁴But the woman had taken the two men and hidden them. She said, "Yes, the men came to me, but I did not know where they had come from. ⁵At dusk, when it was time to close the city gate, the men left. I don't know which way they went. Go after them quickly. You may catch up with them." ⁶(But she had taken them up to the roof and hidden them under the stalks of flax she had laid out on the roof.) ⁷So the men set out in pursuit of the spies on the road that leads to the fords of the Jordan, and as soon as the pursuers had gone out, the gate was shut.

The arrival of the Israelite spies did not pass unnoticed but quickly came to the attention of the king (at that time every city of any importance had a king). The word "tonight" in verse 2 indicates that it was already evening when the men arrived. By the time the king was informed, it was late enough to be called night. A delegation was immediately sent to Rahab, bearing the king's order that she must hand over her foreign guests. Remarkably, Rahab took the side of the

---

[9]This is even highly probable. See, e.g., Schulz, *Das Buch Josua,* p. 9 (cf. NIV margin in v. 1—TRANS.).

foreigners. While the delegation was outside knocking on her door and demanding entrance in the king's name, Rahab swiftly moved the two Israelite spies to a hiding place on the flat roof. Rahab answered the king's delegation by affirming that the Israelite men had come to her but that she did not report them immediately because she did not know where they had come from. Then she informed the messengers that they had arrived too late; for shortly before the closing of the gates, when it was already dark, the men had left the city. Finally, she slyly advised the king's delegation to pursue the foreigners at once, since they might be able to overtake them.

More can be said about Rahab's answer. Verse 6 adds to the brief statement in verse 4 and reveals what she had concealed from the king's messengers in verse 5. Rahab had on her roof a pile of flax stalks (i.e., raw, unprepared flax) lying in the sun to dry. She had hidden the Israelite spies under the flax pile in case the pursuers decided to search her house. Rahab, however, thought it would be safer to try to put the pursuers on the wrong track; and she was more successful in this than she had expected.

Without suspecting Rahab in the least, the king's messengers took the course she had advised. The gatekeeper let them through at once but then cautiously closed the gate behind them. Believing that the Israelites were en route back to their camp, the pursuers hastened in the direction of the Jordan. The river had several fords where it could easily be crossed when the water was low, or even at flood stage (see 3:15). The pursuit of the spies continued all the way to these fords, but it of course was fruitless.

The rest of the chapter explains Rahab's surprising act of turning against her own people. The whole story should be read in the light of Hebrews 11:31 and James 2:25, which clearly reveal that the key to understanding Rahab's behavior was her faith in the God of Israel. By faith she endangered her own life by keeping the Israelites hidden, thus disobeying the king of Jericho. But this did not excuse all of Rahab's actions. Her response to the king's messengers does not fall in the category of permissible acts of cunning in wartime. It rather was a lie. One might call it a "white lie," but it was a blameworthy act that the above New Testament verses do not defend. The lie did not proceed from faith but from an imperfect notion of God's holiness.

Rahab's intention was good, but the end does not justify the means. Nevertheless, the most important thing is that Rahab, who previously had been a heathen woman of ill repute, in principle aligned herself with

Israel. This was a choice of faith; and we therefore may not condemn her, as does De Groot (*Het Boek Jozua*, p. 79) in regarding her only as a traitor and a deceiver. Rahab's conversion to the one true God meant that she had to break with her own people (cf. Ruth 1:16). Her decision to save Joshua's men was therefore an act of faith. In carrying out this decision, however, she committed a regrettable sin that should surprise no one who appreciates the great weakness that attacks the faith of even the strongest believers (Rom. 7:21).

2:8–11 *Before the spies lay down for the night, she went up on the roof* 9 *and said to them, "I know that the LORD has given this land to you and that a great fear of you has fallen on us, so that all who live in this country are melting in fear because of you.* 10 *We have heard how the LORD dried up the water of the Red Sea for you when you came out of Egypt, and what you did to Sihon and Og, the two kings of the Amorites east of the Jordan, whom you completely destroyed.* 11 *When we heard of it, our hearts melted and everyone's courage failed because of you, for the LORD your God is God in heaven above and on the earth below.*

Once Rahab had gotten rid of the king's henchmen, she went directly to the two foreigners concealed on the roof, to tell them that they could not remain there at rest. It was not the time for sleep, and Rahab had much to tell them. No doubt she first informed them of the danger they had escaped (cf. v. 16). Then she made known her firm conviction that her land had been destined for Israel and told them that both the people of Jericho and all Canaan was seized by fear at Israel's coming. Rahab here used LORD (Heb. *Yhwh*) as the proper name for Israel's God, a name that distinguished Him from the gods of other nations (cf. 1 Kings 18:21).

Verse 9 reports the fulfillment of what was promised in Exodus 15:15–16 and Deuteronomy 2:25; 11:25. The cause of this general terror was the reports of Israel's miraculous passage through the Red Sea (an event that had happened forty years earlier but now was revived in memory as Israel stood at the border of Canaan) and their complete annihilation of Sihon and Og, the two kings of the Amorites. Both events had been ascribed by the Canaanites to the power of Israel's God. Because of them the people melted in fear, and their hearts (the seat of courage) sank at the approach of the Israelites with their dreadful God. Rahab thus could say to the Israelite spies that "everyone's courage failed because of you."

The Canaanites' inner resolve and self-confidence were gone; and there was a secret fear that the battle against Israel would inevitably be lost, not because the Israelites themselves were so capable in battle, but because their God was a "God in heaven above and on the earth below," a God who displayed His power in the air (perhaps this refers to the pillars of cloud and fire that led Israel, Exod. 13:21–22; 14:20, 24) and no less on land and in the water. The last part of verse 11 both resembles Deuteronomy 4:39 and differs from it. Rahab did not express herself as strongly and decisively as Moses had done. To her, Yahweh was a god above other gods but not yet the sole God, for her thinking remained pagan in large measure.

We must carefully distinguish what Rahab said on her own account from what she said of her fellow Canaanites. In verse 9 she declared her personal conviction, while in verses 10 and 11 she reported what all had heard and their general reaction. The difference between Rahab and her people was not that she knew more but that God's Spirit sanctified the news of His great deeds in her heart. Whereas the stories only provoked terror and dismay among the Canaanites, in Rahab they led to faith and a willingness to submit to Israel's God. The visit of Joshua's emissaries then caused her to come to a definite decision and to break with her own gods. That the two men had entered her house with honorable intentions may have contributed to this decision, for their conduct too must have filled her with respect for Israel's God.

2:12–13 *Now then, please swear to me by the* Lord *that you will show kindness to my family, because I have shown kindness to you. Give me a sure sign* [13] *that you will spare the lives of my father and mother, my brothers and sisters, and all who belong to them, and that you will save us from death."*

Rahab's firm conviction that the Lord would grant the land to Israel motivated the request she made here. The Israelites were asked to swear by their God, who now was acknowledged by Rahab, too, that they would repay her help by saving her and her family when the city was captured. She asked the Israelite spies to give her a "sure sign," not a guarantee that they could be counted on, but a clear mark of identification so that she and her family would not be killed by mistake. Rahab desired a sign that would ensure her family's safety.

2:14 *"Our lives for your lives!" the men assured her. "If you don't tell what we are doing, we will treat you kindly and faithfully when the* Lord *gives us the land."*

The men showed that they understood Rahab's request by responding with a strong statement of the promise she desired. Their words mean "we will answer with our lives if you (plural) suffer any harm." "Kindness and faithfulness" (or "kindly and faithfully") is the standard expression for an act of favor performed to satisfy a covenantal relationship or a bond of friendship (e.g., Gen. 24:27, 49; 32:10). Joshua's men explicitly stated the condition that Rahab and her family (who soon would be told of the plan) had to remain silent about "what we are doing." The context indicates that this phrase referrred first to the arrangement they had made, which was not to become generally known, but also included their escape itself. Rahab was thus to send no one in pursuit of them.

2:15 *So she let them down by a rope through the window, for the house she lived in was part of the city wall.*

Rahab had the men climb down a rope hung from a window of her house. This placed them outside the city at once, for the house was built into the thick city wall in such a way that their outer sides partly coincided (the Hebrew literally reads "the wall of the city-wall"). Quite probably the house even extended over the wall a bit.

2:16–21 *Now she had said to them, "Go to the hills so the pursuers will not find you. Hide yourselves there three days until they return, and then go on your way."*

17 The men said to her, "This oath you made us swear will not be binding on us 18 unless, when we enter the land, you have tied this scarlet cord in the window through which you let us down, and unless you have brought your father and mother, your brothers and all your family into your house. 19 If anyone goes outside your house into the street, his blood will be on his own head; we will not be responsible. As for anyone who is in the house with you, his blood will be on our head if a hand is laid on him. 20 But if you tell what we are doing, we will be released from the oath you made us swear."

21 "Agreed," she replied. "Let it be as you say." So she sent them away and they departed. And she tied the scarlet cord in the window.

The conversation apparently took place when the men were already standing at the base of the wall. Indeed, they were probably in a hurry to climb down and only exchanged their final words after that. Some think, however, that the wall was too high for this and that verses 16–21a must therefore have been spoken when the men still were in Rahab's house. Verse 18 then would be translated "through which you will [or 'will have'] let us down," which is in fact a possible reading.

Rahab wisely advised the spies to hide themselves in the hills for

three days, since their pursuers would undoubtedly watch the bank of
the Jordan for the next few days and search the surroundings (see
v. 22). She probably was speaking of the Qarantal Hills west of
Jericho, an area with numerous caves and grottos. Before leaving,
Joshua's men precisely stated their obligations to one another and also
granted Rahab's request for a sign (v. 12). The sentence in verse 17
actually is left unfinished, for it implies a continuation like "if you
break the agreement." Instead, we find a statement of the conditions
Rahab had to meet.[10]

First, when the Israelites approached the city, Rahab was to tie to
her window the rope that she had let the men out with[11] and allow it to
hang down the city wall. The Israelites then would be able to identify
her house. The cord spoken of was braided from scarlet thread and thus
was bright red in color. Next, Rahab was to see to it that her whole
family (and no one else) was inside her house and that none of them
ventured outside. Anyone who did so could no longer be identified as a
member of Rahab's family and thus would stand in danger of being
killed by the Israelites. Such a person's death would be his own fault.
But whoever remained indoors would be safe. The two spies themselves took the responsibility for this. If anyone laid a hand on Rahab's
family inside her house, the guilt for the bloodshed will be theirs. They
then would deserve death for having violated their oath. Joshua's men
thus assumed full responsibility for the oath they had sworn to the
woman who already had saved their own lives.

Besides acting "as innocent as doves," however, the Israelite spies
also took care to be "as shrewd as snakes" (Matt. 10:16). Since they
had given their oath in dead earnest, they must leave no room for
misunderstanding. Thus they repeated (v. 20) the primary condition of
their agreement (v. 14). Rahab must not betray them. If she did, they
would be free from their oath. Rahab consented to all that the men had
said and allowed them to depart. Presumably she did not tie the cord to
her window then and there, for that could have aroused suspicion.
Nevertheless, we are told at once that she did, so that we can see that
Rahab was deadly serious in her promise and her expectation of

---

[10] The author's translation of verses 17–18 reads: "We will be free from this oath
you made us swear. . . . Behold, when we enter the land," etc. Compare the KJV
and RSV. The NIV joins the two sentences by interpreting the Hebrew *hinnēh*
("behold") in verse 18 to mean "unless," and the author's comment thus does not
apply here—TRANS.

[11] If this conversation still took place on top the wall, another rope could be meant.

Jericho's fall. This information closes the account of the events that happened at Jericho.

Since ancient times the fact that the sign that identified Rahab and her family was the color of blood has been regarded as symbolic. This color is seen to express the thought that salvation comes only to those who have been sprinkled with the blood of redemption. Though one must exercise caution in typology, it is a fact that some symbolic meaning often can be found, not only in Israel's ceremonial activities, but also in the Old Testament events themselves. This is not unlikely in the present story, which one can compare to the night that death came on all the firstborn in Egypt, except for those whose dwellings were marked by the blood of the Passover lamb. There too it was decreed that no one should leave his house as long as death still threatened (Exod. 12:13, 22–23). The symbolic meaning of the Passover is much more obvious and deliberate, of course. But it still can be said that the sparing of the houses marked with blood during the Exodus from Egypt is dimly reflected, as it were, in the sparing of the house marked with the red cord during the entry into Canaan. See also the comments in 6:22–25.

2:22–24 *When they left, they went into the hills and stayed there three days, until the pursuers had searched all along the road and returned without finding them.* [23] *Then the two men started back. They went down out of the hills, forded the river and came to Joshua son of Nun and told him everything that had happened to them. They said to Joshua, "The LORD has surely given the whole land into our hands; all the people are melting in fear because of us."*

The spies followed Rahab's advice and hid in the hills for three days. Then they ventured back into the plain after their enemies had searched it high and low in vain. They crossed the Jordan, hastened to Joshua, and told him all that had happened to them. The final impression gained from their experiences is summarized in the encouraging declaration that the land would surely fall into Israel's hands, since the hearts of its inhabitants were already melting in fear. Rahab's testimony had revealed this to them (vv. 9, 11). This news indeed had to be more important to Joshua than the knowledge that had been gained of Jericho's strength, fortifications, and military might. The report of his emissaries implied that the enemy was demoralized. It showed that they had lost confidence in themselves and that their fear of Israel's God had already caused them secretly to despair of victory. The things that had happened to these men under God's direction could only have increased Joshua's confidence.

The Canaanites' despondency and Rahab's firm belief that Israel would triumph gave Joshua two good reasons to march forward courageously. His confidence now came from three different sources: God Himself, the Israelite people (ch. 1), and the news of the mood that prevailed in the enemy territory (ch. 2). In view of this, chapters 1 and 2 can be regarded as an introduction that paints the scene for Joshua's work in broad outline. In chapter 3 he begins to act.

4. Israel on the Bank of the Jordan
(3:1–6)

3:1–2 *Early in the morning Joshua and all the Israelites set out from Shittim and went to the Jordan, where they camped before crossing over. ²After three days the officers went throughout the camp,*

The day after the spies returned, Joshua and the people prepared in the early morning to journey from Shittim to the bank of the Jordan. There the army was to wait a few days before it could cross over. These days, of course, could not be the same as those spoken of in 1:11 or 2:22. The events recounted in chapter 3 follow those of chapter 2, and the spies were probably dispatched right after the command in 1:11 had been issued. Their expedition took at least four or five days and delayed the crossing of the Jordan. Joshua awaited their return at Shittim. Israel then departed for the Jordan on the first of the three days spoken of in verse 2.

We are not told why the Israelites did not cross over immediately, but the reason is easy to surmise. How were the people to cross this river? Verse 15 indicates that the water level was very high, and the overflowing of the banks increased its width considerably. The places that normally could be forded, therefore, were practically impassable, especially since it was not just an army but a whole nation with women, children, and cattle that had to enter Canaan. This would not be possible without some extraordinary help. Israel was thus confronted by an insurmountable obstacle on the border of the Promised Land. The Lord, of course, could have dried up the Jordan at once, but He first wanted the people to experience the great difficulties this river presented so that they might realize their own helplessness and look to Him. The delay at the bank of the Jordan therefore served to test the

Israelites. That we do not read of a single complaint about this disappointing delay reflects favorably on the attitude of the people . On the third day (i.e., two days after their arrival at their present location), the people received another order. Although this was given by the officers, they must have been carrying out what the Lord had previously commanded Joshua.

3:3–5 *giving orders to the people: "When you see the ark of the covenant of the* Lord *your God, and the priests, who are Levites, carrying it, you are to move out from your positions and follow it. ⁴Then you will know which way to go, since you have never been this way before. But keep a distance of about a thousand yards between you and the ark; do not go near it."*

⁵Joshua told the people, "Consecrate yourselves, for tomorrow the Lord *will do amazing things among you."*

The Israelites were told first to be ready to set out at the moment they saw the ark emerge from its tent, carried by the designated priests. The Lord thus no longer intended to guide them by the pillar of cloud (Exod. 13:21). Then they were to follow the ark (cf. Num. 10:33), keeping a distance of about two thousand cubits (i.e., approximately one thousand yards). This shows that although the people were within sight of the river, they had set up their camp some distance from its bank. The command to approach no closer to the ark naturally applied only while the ark was moving, not when it came to a halt (v. 17). By keeping this distance, all the Israelites had a clear view of the ark and could observe how it was God's indirect means for performing the miracle that opened a path never traveled before (v. 16). Verse 4 contains a hint of this miracle, and verse 5 announces it clearly.

Joshua commanded the people, undoubtedly through the same officers spoken of in verse 2, to consecrate themselves in preparation for the next day; for the Lord would then perform the wonders He had promised (Exod. 34:10). This command must have been issued on 9 Nisan (cf. 4:19). The consecration the people had to undergo had both an internal and an external aspect. Exodus 19:10, 14–15 speaks of the external side and commands that one's clothes be washed, but the Israelites had no time for this and probably just put on clean garments instead. In any case, inner consecration was more important in the present context. The people had to prepare for the coming display of God's power by lifting their hearts to Him, dispelling all anxiety, and humbling themselves in His holy presence. To behold God's wonders, one must be in the proper frame of mind.

3:6 *Joshua said to the priests, "Take up the ark of the covenant and pass on ahead of the people." So they took it up and went ahead of them.*

Corresponding to his command to the people in verse 3, Joshua here told the priests what their task would be. They were to carry the ark of the covenant ahead of the people. We should not conclude from the second part of verse 6 that the priests responded to this command at once. Several facts speak against this. First, it is unthinkable that the priests did not receive the command till 10 Nisan, while the people were already informed of what the priests would do on the previous day. Second, the Lord's words to Joshua (vv. 7–8) could not have been spoken after the priests had already departed. Third, the march itself apparently did not begin till verse 14. Verse 6 merely anticipates this in some way. The author's account of the events does not always proceed in chronological order (cf., e.g., 2:21). In chapters 3 and 4 it rather takes more of a topical order that can be summarized as follows.[12] Joshua 3:1–6 tells how the people and the priests were prepared for the miraculous passage through the Jordan. The passage itself is then recounted in three stages: the divine miracle, 3:7–17; details of the crossing, 4:1–14; and the erection of the monument, 4:15–24. Each section begins with a command that the Lord gave to Joshua and then tells how this command was conveyed to the people and carried out. By telling the story in this way, the author was able now and again to anticipate what was coming and to look back on what had already happened (compare 3:12 to 4:2, 4:11 to 4:16–18, 3:16–17 to 4:10). The advantage of such an approach is that it allowed the main elements in the story to be highlighted at every turn and stamped on the reader's memory.

5. Crossing the Jordan
(3:7–17)

3:7–8 *And the LORD said to Joshua, "Today I will begin to exalt you in the eyes of all Israel, so they may know that I am with you as I was with Moses. ⁸Tell the priests who carry the ark of the covenant: 'When you reach the edge of the Jordan's waters, go and stand in the river.' "*

On the morning of 10 Nisan, the Lord promised Joshua that on that very day He would begin to exalt him in the sight of all Israel. God

---

[12] See Keil, *Joshua,*[2] p. 24.

would clothe Joshua with glory so that the people would stand in awe of him and entrust themselves to his leadership. The wonders that would happen would form Joshua's credentials.They would prove that the Lord was with him, just as He had been with Moses. After the passage through the Red Sea, Israel "feared the LORD and put their trust in him and in Moses his servant" (Exod. 14:31). Now they had to come to perceive Joshua as the Lord's servant in the same way.

Along with His promise, the Lord added a few commands. Although verse 8 speaks only of the command to the priests, Joshua must also have first heard from the Lord what he told the people in verses 10–13. There was good reason for the priests to receive a special command: they would take the lead. They were to demonstrate their faith as an example to the people by being the first ones to step into the Jordan. An explicit statement that Joshua conveyed this command to the priests is left out to avoid needless repetition, for historical narrative in the Old Testament often takes for granted that the Lord's commands are passed on (cf., e.g., Exod. 14:15; Deut. 31:14, 28).

3:9–13 *Joshua said to the Israelites, "Come here and listen to the words of the LORD your God. ¹⁰This is how you will know that the living God is among you and that he will certainly drive out before you the Canaanites, Hittites, Hivites, Perizzites, Girgashites, Amorites and Jebusites. ¹¹See, the ark of the covenant of the Lord of all the earth will go into the Jordan ahead of you. ¹²Now then, choose twelve men from the tribes of Israel, one from each tribe. ¹³And as soon as the priests who carry the ark of the LORD—the Lord of all the earth—set foot in the Jordan, its waters flowing downstream will be cut off and stand up in a heap."*

With solemn words Joshua called the people to come and hear the words of their God. When they had answered this summons, Joshua told them what the Lord was going to do. The purpose of His action would be to manifest Himself as the Living One, unlike the gods of the heathen. The Israelites would receive powerful proof that God was both omnipotent and close at hand. Then they would no longer be able to doubt that He had the power to drive out the nations of Canaan ahead of them.

Following Deuteronomy 7:1, seven of these nations or tribes of Canaan are listed. There were in fact more than this (cf. Gen. 15:19–21), but these were undoubtedly the most prominent, especially the Canaanites and the Amorites. Verse 11 is the most important part of Joshua's speech. The sign that would confirm the people's faith was that the ark of the covenant would go ahead of them. It would not just go up to the Jordan but would enter it, as if the river were not even there and there were no rushing current to carry everything away.

The designation of Yahweh as the Lord, the Master of all the earth, is deliberate in verse 11. Israel need not worry; for the ark, the symbol of God's presence and His covenant, would not be stopped by any river. The explanation of how this would happen is in verse 13. Verse 12 forms a parenthesis. Twelve men were to be appointed—one from each tribe—to represent the nation as a whole. The opening of the verse indicates that this was to be done before the crossing. What the Lord had in mind for these men is disclosed in 4:2–3.

In verse 13 Joshua picks up where he had left off in verse 11. The ark would descend into the Jordan, but the waters would not overwhelm it. The water would make a way for the priests at the very moment they put forth their feet to step down into the river. The water would not withdraw till the priests demonstrated their faith by entering the Jordan. Neither would it withdraw later, for the majesty of the Lord's ark would cause the water to shrink back and allow the priests and the ark to pass. The water would not seek another route but—and herein lies the miracle—would pile up some distance upstream and stay in place as a solid wall. Thus a path would be opened through the river, for the water downstream would naturally flow off toward the Dead Sea. Israel's problem of course was with the water coming from upstream. The phrase "cut off" here is synonymous with "come to a stop," but one can think of more graphic illustrations such as snipping a thread or, better, tying an artery.

3:14–16 *So when the people broke camp to cross the Jordan, the priests carrying the ark of the covenant went ahead of them.* [15] *Now the Jordan is at flood stage all during harvest. Yet as soon as the priests who carried the ark reached the Jordan and their feet touched the water's edge,* [16] *the water from upstream stopped flowing. It piled up in a heap a great distance away, at a town called Adam in the vicinity of Zarethan, while the water flowing down to the Sea of the Arabah (the Salt Sea) was completely cut off. So the people crossed over opposite Jericho.*

These verses vividly depict the miracle as the Israelites saw it happen. Verses 14–15 portray the mounting tension that came over the people as the crucial moment approached. The people pulled up their camp in order "to cross the Jordan." This was an act of faith, because the crossing seemed impossible. The priests moved out ahead carrying the ark, and all eyes were fixed on it. They drew nearer and nearer and finally reached the water. But the Jordan was full; in fact, it was more than full, for its banks were flooded. Did the priests then remain on dry land? No, they marched right on, and the miracle happened. The waters recoiled and fled. The Jordan turned back (Ps. 114:3), and the priests walked forward on dry ground.

The parenthetical remark that opens verse 15 needs some explanation. Clearly, Israel had reached the Jordan at the very time its crossing presented special difficulties, the time when its water level was highest. This usually occurred in April, following the snow melt at the river's headwaters on Mount Hermon. At such a time the river exceeded its banks, though this does not mean there was an actual inundation of the Jordan Valley. The Jordan has both a broad and a narrow channel, the latter being its usual course, no wider than about a hundred feet. The depth here is ten to twelve feet, but at the fords it is only around three feet. The edges of this channel are covered with reeds, bushes, and trees. These overgrown banks of the Jordan then form the broader channel. Since they are considerably lower (forty or fifty feet) than the rest of the Jordan Valley on both sides, the broad channel fills up either partly or all the way during rainy periods and harvest time.

When Israel stood at the border of Canaan, the overgrown banks of the river were flooded. The water reached the wider banks; that is why the text speaks of "all its banks"[13] (cf. 1 Chron. 12:15). But the great obstacle that the Jordan presented was not confined just to its width and depth. More dangerous still was the swift and violent current, which could mean serious trouble even for expert swimmers.

The rest of the account is generally clear, though the text permits two possible answers to the question of where the water came to a halt. The Jordan River flows southward through the Arabah or steppe and the rift valley el-Ghor to the Dead Sea. The Israelites approached it from the east. One possibility is to suppose that when the priests bearing the ark stepped into the Jordan, a mass of water built up directly to the north that raised the level of the river abnormally high and spread out all the way to Adam, a town eighteen miles north on the east bank (the site now is called ed-Damiyeh, which lies opposite the ridge Qarn Sartabeh, a name reminiscent of Zarethan). The text also can mean, however, that Adam was the place where the water stopped and piled up.[14] The

---

[13] See verse 15 in KJV and RSV.

[14] This view is supported by the fact that Adam is the precise location where on many occasions "slides from the limestone cliffs on the banks, which there rise to 65 feet, fall into the river and completely dam it up for a time" (De Groot, *Het Boek*

Israelites then could not have seen this, since the town stood "a great distance away"; but they would have learned of it later. In this case the riverbed would have been exposed both north and south of the spot where the ark stood, and the people therefore could have crossed on a very broad front. Baarslag's computations indicate that this indeed would have been necessary.[15] The crossing took place where the Jordan passed by Jericho at a distance of approximately two hours' journey, but the great depth of the Jordan Valley hid the city from view. The name "Dead Sea" is not used in the Old Testament. It rather speaks of the Salt Sea or the Sea of the Arabah (Deut. 1:1; 3:17), the latter being the very long and deep rift that runs along the Jordan and the Dead Sea and continues to the Gulf of Aqabah.

3:17 *The priests who carried the ark of the covenant of the LORD stood firm on dry ground in the middle of the Jordan, while all Israel passed by until the whole nation had completed the crossing on dry ground.*

In obedience to the command given in verse 8, the priests carrying the "ark of the covenant of the LORD"[16] remained standing on the bed of the Jordan. They were not allowed to move on till the whole nation had reached the opposite bank. The priests' motionless stance inspired the people with confidence. They knew that as long as the ark stayed there, the water would not harm them. And they further realized that the same God who called to the waters, "This far and no further," would soon grant them the same protection against their enemies. Section 5 of the Introduction has dealt with the symbolic and prophetic meaning of the passage through the Jordan.

Jozua, p. 82). This last happened in 1927, when the lower course of the river stood empty for twenty-one and a half hours (Garstang, *Joshua, Judges,* p. 137). Just as in the crossing of the Red Sea (Exod. 14:21), God here could have used natural means to stop the water. The miracle then would have been that this happened just "at the moment when Israel needed it" (De Groot, *Het Boek Jozua*). See also F. Schmidtke, *Die Einwanderung Israëls in Kanaän, 1933, pp. 74ff.*

[15] D. J. Baarslag, *Baäls en Burchten,* p. 127.

[16] The Hebrew here literally reads "the ark, the covenant of the LORD." But this expression, though not impossible, is so unusual that the above translation is preferable. It is even the only possible translation if we may assume that the article before '*a*rôn was absent in the original text.

56

6. Further Details: Memorial Stones From the Jordan (4:1–14)

4:1–9 *When the whole nation had finished crossing the Jordan, the LORD said to Joshua,* ² *"Choose twelve men from among the people, one from each tribe,* ³ *and tell them to take up twelve stones from the middle of the Jordan from right where the priests stood and to carry them over with you and put them down at the place where you stay tonight."*

⁴ *So Joshua called together the twelve men he had appointed from the Israelites, one from each tribe,* ⁵ *and said to them, "Go over before the ark of the LORD your God into the middle of the Jordan. Each of you is to take up a stone on his shoulder, according to the number of the tribes of the Israelites,* ⁶ *to serve as a sign among you. In the future, when your children ask you, 'What do these stones mean?'* ⁷ *tell them that the flow of the Jordan was cut off before the ark of the covenant of the LORD. When it crossed the Jordan, the waters of the Jordan were cut off.*¹⁷ *These stones are to be a memorial to the people of Israel forever."*

⁸ *So the Israelites did as Joshua commanded them. They took twelve stones from the middle of the Jordan, according to the number of the tribes of the Israelites, as the LORD had told Joshua; and they carried them over with them to their camp, where they put them down.* ⁹ *Joshua set up the twelve stones that had been in the middle of the Jordan at the spot where the priests who carried the ark of the covenant had stood. And they are there to this day.*

This section records a few details of the crossing, the most important being the taking of twelve stones from the bed of the Jordan. Verses 1–3 indicate that Joshua was commanded to do this by the Lord Himself. God had already ordered Joshua to have twelve men chosen (3:12). Then, after the Israelites had crossed, He told him what these men were to do. The divine command is merely summed up briefly here. Only the gist of it is recorded; but once again it is clear that in all that he did as a leader, Joshua followed God's instructions.

Since the men had already been appointed,¹⁸ Joshua soon had them assembled. He conveyed the Lord's command to them in detail. Each of them was to pick up a stone (apparently a large one) from the very

---

¹⁷ The author's translation omits "the waters of the Jordan were cut off" here and joins "when it crossed the Jordan" to the previous sentence. He then adds the following footnote: "The Hebrew text here repeats the words 'the waters of the Jordan were cut off,' which do not appear in the Septuagint. The repetition could well be the mistake of a copyist"—TRANS.

¹⁸ Joshua may have done this himself. Verse 4 can be translated as either "he had appointed" (KJV, RSV, NIV) or "one had appointed," "that had been appointed." But in 3:12 Joshua commanded the people to choose.

place where the priests were then standing with the ark. These stones from the middle of the Jordan were to serve as an eloquent testimony to the next generation, telling how the waters were miraculously held back and the riverbed exposed by the powerful hand of God. The stones were to be twelve in number because all Twelve Tribes had passed through the Jordan. The men carried out Joshua's command precisely. Verse 8 refers to them as "the Israelites" probably because they represented the entire nation. It is likely that these same twelve men helped Joshua build the monument that stood in the river itself.[19] If anything, this heap of stones in the Jordan testified even more strikingly to the Lord's power to arrest or unleash the river's current as He pleased. The monument rose above the surface of the water, and it still existed at the time the Book of Joshua was written.

4:10–11 *Now the priests who carried the ark remained standing in the middle of the Jordan until everything the LORD had commanded Joshua was done by the people, just as Moses had directed Joshua. The people hurried over, [11] and as soon as all of them had crossed, the ark of the LORD and the priests came to the other side while the people watched.*

While the Lord's commands were being carried out, the priests holding the ark remained fixed in their position. Joshua 3:17 has already said this, but it is deliberately brought into view once again to underscore the fact that this alone made the whole crossing possible. This means, however, that the crossing had to be completed with due haste, for otherwise the priests' endurance would have been overtaxed. The statement that Joshua did just as Moses had directed him harks back to Numbers 27:23 and Deuteronomy 31:7–8. In all that he did, Joshua was deeply dependent on God; and this above all showed his faithful obedience to Moses' instructions. In performing his task, Joshua always saw himself as Moses' servant. Verse 11 does not mean to jump ahead of the story to verses 15–18. Rather, like verse 10, its purpose is to accentuate the requirement that the crossing had to be completely finished before the ark could begin moving. Significantly, this verse mentions the ark first and then the priests. The river's flow had been checked, not by the priests, but by the ark, God's throne in Israel and the visible expression of His presence.

---

[19] The Septuagint has "twelve other stones" in verse 9. "Other" accurately gives the meaning here, but it probably was inserted in the text for clarity. (The author's translation of verse 9 reads "Joshua also set up twelve stones in the middle of the Jordan at the spot. . . ." Compare KJV, RSV, and NIV margin—TRANS.)

4:12–14 *The men of Reuben, Gad and the half-tribe of Manasseh crossed over, armed, in front of the Israelites, as Moses had directed them. [13] About forty thousand armed for battle crossed over before the LORD to the plains of Jericho for war.*

[14] That day the LORD exalted Joshua in the sight of all Israel; and they revered him all the days of his life, just as they had revered Moses.

Fulfilling their promise (1:16), Reuben, Gad, and the half-tribe of Manasseh also crossed the river. Like Joshua, they too complied with the orders of their great leader, Moses (Deut. 3:18–20). Numbers 26:7, 18, 34 gives the total number of men in these three tribes (approximately 110,000 if half of Manasseh's number is used). The 40,000 spoken of here were a choice army picked from these men, which Israel and the Lord Himself regarded as a fulfillment of the pledge these tribes had made. Although the miraculous crossing was the work of God alone, it also was the means by which Joshua's prestige among the people was raised beyond comparison. That such a stupendous miracle had happened under his leadership caused the Israelites to ascribe to him the same glory that had rested on Moses. The reverence that they had had for Moses was now transferred to Joshua, and this was exactly what the Lord had intended. For He fulfilled His promise to Joshua in 3:7 so that he would have the people's full confidence and thus be a fit instrument for leading the Israelites and commanding them in battle.

7. The Crossing Completed and the Monument Erected (4:15–24)

4:15–19 *Then the LORD said to Joshua, [16] "Command the priests carrying the ark of the Testimony to come up out of the Jordan."*

[17] So Joshua commanded the priests, "Come up out of the Jordan."

[18] And the priests came up out of the river carrying the ark of the covenant of the LORD. No sooner had they set their feet on the dry ground[20] than the waters of the Jordan returned to their place and ran at flood stage as before.

[19] On the tenth day of the first month the people went up from the Jordan and camped at Gilgal on the eastern border of Jericho.

For the third time, we see that the successful crossing of the Jordan depended on the priests' holding their position till the last Israelite had reached the opposite bank. The priests were not to move till Joshua

---

[20] The Hebrew here literally reads "toward the dry ground [bank]." "No sooner" is added to the sentence for clarity—TRANS.

commanded them in the Lord's name. Then, at the very moment the priests and the ark reached the western bank and left the riverbed, the water that had been dammed up refilled the channel and followed its normal course. The name "ark of the Testimony," which appears especially often in Exodus, is used to indicate that the testimony, i.e., the stone tablets of the law, were kept there (Exod. 25:16, 21–22; Num. 4:5). The ark, symbolizing God's presence, clearly testified to the people that the miraculous crossing was a special act of divine providence. The day that this happened, 10 Nisan, was memorable. On this very day forty years earlier, every Israelite had selected a lamb for the Passover (Exod. 12:3), four days before the Passover ceremony and the Exodus from Egypt took place. God so arranged things that the annual commemoration of the Exodus would from that day on also call to memory the entry into Canaan, which shows that God's work is a unity. In leading the Israelites out of Egypt and bringing them into the Promised Land, He performed a single act of deliverance (cf. Exod. 6:6–8).

The people set up camp at the place where the town of Gilgal was later built, probably the site of modern Khirbet el-Mefjer, one and a quarter miles northeast of Tell es-Sultan (Jericho).[21] The name Gilgal itself is discussed in 5:9.

4:20–24 *And Joshua set up at Gilgal the twelve stones they had taken out of the Jordan. [21] He said to the Israelites, "In the future when your descendants ask their fathers, 'What do these stones mean?' [22] tell them, 'Israel crossed the Jordan on dry ground. [23] For the LORD your God dried up the Jordan before you until you had crossed over. The LORD your God did to the Jordan just what he had done to the Red Sea when he dried it up before us until we had crossed over. [24] He did this so that all the peoples of the earth might know that the hand of the LORD is powerful and so that you might always fear the LORD your God.'"*

In the camp at Gilgal, Joshua piled up the twelve stones that had been brought from the Jordan and they became a monument to the Lord's sovereign power and faithfulness. This undoubtedly was done before nightfall. When he was finished, he made a brief speech to the people–a speech that is largely the same as what he had told the twelve men in verses 6–7. Nevertheless, there are two important differences. First, the answer that the fathers were to give is shorter, being limited

---

[21] This is the view of Noth and Gispen. The *Bijbelse Encyclopedie* gives the modern name as *en-Nitleh,* and Dalman locates Gilgal near *En-el-Garabe.*

to verse 22b. Verses 23–24 contain Joshua's own words to the people.[22] Joshua impressed on them the immense significance of the event that they had just witnessed. He placed this miracle on the same level as the passage through the Red Sea, something he himself, unlike most of the other Israelites, had taken part in (hence his use of "we"). Second, Joshua told the people God's purpose in this miracle with respect to their enemies. He performed it so that all the nations of Canaan might be filled with a lasting fear of Israel's God (cf. Exod. 14:4, 18; 15:14-16).[23] This whole chapter sheds clear light on the meaning of the miracle recorded in chapter 3.

8. Circumcision and the Celebration of the Passover (5:1–12)

5:1 *Now when all the Amorite kings west of the Jordan and all the Canaanite kings along the coast heard how the LORD had dried up the Jordan before the Israelites until we[24] had crossed over, their hearts melted and they no longer had the courage to face the Israelites.*

This verse does not belong with the previous chapter. Rather, it explains why the Israelites were left undisturbed while they performed the rite of circumcision and celebrated the Passover. The news of Israel's miraculous entry into Canaan caused such widespread consternation that Israel's enemies lost all courage and were unable to cause any trouble. This was the case throughout all Canaan. The mention of the Amorites (in the hill country west of the Jordan) and the Canaanites (further west, on the plain along the Mediterranean coast) only served to summarize the whole population. God provoked this general terror and dismay because He did not want the Israelites to take up arms at

---

[22] The quotation marks in the NIV indicate that the whole of verses 22b–24 is regarded as the descendants' answer—TRANS.

[23] The author's translation has "they" instead of "you" after the second "so that" in verse 24 (cf. NEB). He adds the following footnote: "The Hebrew text here has an unusual second person form in the perfect. A slight change is therefore commonly made in the vocalization to yield the infinitive form with third person suffix. This reading also is supported by the fact that the second 'so that' in verse 24 is subordinate to the first"—TRANS.

[24] The author translates "they" here instead of "we" (cf. RSV, NEB). He adds the following footnote: "The traditional vocalization, several manuscripts, and all the ancient translations have the third person plural here. The first person form in the Hebrew consonantal text may have been copied from the identical phrase in 4:23." See section 3 of the Introduction, pp. 14–15—TRANS.

once but rather to reserve the first few days for religious purposes. It was time for His covenant with Israel to be renewed and reconfirmed to some degree. The Passover would be celebrated on 14 Nisan; and before the whole nation could take part, a number of the males still had to undergo the rite of circumcision.

5:2–3 *At that time the LORD said to Joshua, "Make flint knives and circumcise the Israelites again." ³So Joshua made flint knives and circumcised the Israelites at Gibeath Haaraloth.*

In accordance with ancient custom, flint knives, which were thought to be cleaner than metal ones, were used for the rite of circumcision (cf. Exod. 4:25). The word "again" (v. 2)[25] does not mean that those who were already circumcised had to be subjected to the ritual a second time. Rather, it refers to the nation as a whole. Israel had been circumcised at the time of the Exodus from Egypt and now it was time to be circumcised again. For the people of the covenant, the state of uncircumcision was abnormal and intolerable (cf. Exod. 4:24–26). The promptness with which Joshua obeyed the Lord's command is noteworthy. Possibly the work of circumcision was completed on 11 Nisan, since the greater part of those who were already circumcised likely offered their help. The number of male Israelites has been estimated at around one million, and the proportion of the circumcised to the uncircumcised has been estimated at only one to three or three and a half.[26] Gibeath Haaraloth,[27] the name given to the hill where this rite of purification for the people of Israel took place, preserved the memory of this event.

---

[25] The author has "again the second time." Cf. KJV and RSV—TRANS.

[26] Keil, *Joshua,*[2] p. 40.

[27] The author translated this as "Hill of the foreskins." Cf. KJV, NIV margin— TRANS.

5:4–8 *Now this is why he did so: All those who came out of Egypt—all the men of military age—died in the desert on the way after leaving Egypt.* *⁵All the people that came out had been circumcised, but all the people born in the desert during the journey from Egypt had not.* *⁶The Israelites had moved about in the desert forty years until all the men who were of military age when they left Egypt had died, since they had not obeyed the* Lord. *For the* Lord *had sworn to them that they would not see the land that he had solemnly promised their fathers to give us, a land flowing with milk and honey.* *⁷So he raised up their sons in their place, and these were the ones Joshua circumcised. They were still uncircumcised because they had not been circumcised on the way.* *⁸And after the whole nation had been circumcised, they remained where they were in camp until they were healed.*

Circumcision had to be performed because all who had been born in the desert—the vast majority of the people—remained uncircumcised. But the deeper reason for this, according to verses 4, 6, and 7, was that all the adult males who had departed from Egypt died during the forty years of desert wandering because of their disobedience. Now, in their stead, their sons were to take possession of the Promised Land; but they still had to be circumcised. The failure to circumcise the latter during the desert journey was not because of negligence. Rather, circumcision, the sign of the covenant, could not be administered then because the proper covenantal relationship between Israel and the Lord had been disturbed (cf. Num. 14:28–35, a passage that the present verses hark back to).

In Numbers 14:28–35 the Lord pronounced judgment on the Israelites who did not want to march onward to Canaan. They—all the males twenty years and older—would die in the desert; only their children would enter the Promised Land. Even these children, however, would share in the punishment to some extent; for they would be compelled to roam in the desert for years, "suffering for [their] unfaithfulness" (Num. 14:33). The word translated "unfaithfulness" literally means "prostitution," which characterizes Israel's sin as disloyalty, a breaking of the covenant. The people, because they had refused to go on to Canaan, in effect removed themselves from their covenant with Yahweh; for He had led them out of the "land of slavery" precisely in order to bring them to Canaan.

The Lord had not totally annulled His covenant with Israel but had pronounced a curse on the generation born in Egypt and its children. This curse would only be lifted after that older generation had perished. The penalty for the sins of the fathers doubtless included the withholding of circumcision from their children. This of course refers to the sons born after the events of Numbers 14, which happened a year and a half or two years after the Exodus. Until that time the children surely must have been circumcised in the desert just as they had been in Egypt. Now, at Gilgal, the Lord commanded that circumcision be performed on those who lacked this token of the covenant in order to demonstrate that the covenantal relationship had once again been completely restored. Thus the Lord accepted them as His people in place of their disobedient fathers (v. 7). After the bloody operation had been performed, the newly circumcised rested in their tents a few days till they were healed.

5:9 *Then the* LORD *said to Joshua, "Today I have rolled away the reproach of Egypt from you." So the place has been called Gilgal to this day.*

The further significance of the circumcision can be seen in the Lord's words to Joshua after it was finished. By this ritual He had rolled off Israel's shoulders the reproach and scorn of the Egyptians, which till then had been a burden for them. This of course cannot mean that the Egyptians scoffed at the Israelites because they were uncircumcised. Their derision rather was prompted by the related fact that the Lord had allowed the entire older generation that He had rescued from Egypt to die in the desert.

The Egyptians had no knowledge of the breach in the covenantal relationship between Yahweh and His people, but they did see that the Israelites continued to roam in the desert year after year and were dying off without ever having laid their eyes on the land of Canaan. This could not but have called forth the scorn that Moses spoke of hypothetically in Numbers 14:13–16 and Deuteronomy 9:28. The Egyptians thought that Yahweh was putting the nation to death in the desert because He was unable to bring them into the land He had promised them and "because He hated them." But by having Israel circumcised on Canaan's soil, the Lord removed this reproach that His people had brought on themselves by their own sin. Thus He granted a full confirmation of His covenant and His promises to the generation then alive. Gilgal ("place of rolling"), the name given to the site of this event, would be a lasting reminder of Israel's restoration to honor and the rolling away of her reproach.

5:10–12 *On the evening of the fourteenth day of the month, while camped at Gilgal on the plains of Jericho, the Israelites celebrated the Passover.* *11 The day after the Passover, that very day, they ate some of the produce of the land: unleavened bread and roasted grain.* *12 The manna stopped the day after they ate this food from the land; there was no longer any manna for the Israelites, but that year they ate of the produce of Canaan.*

The Passover was probably no longer observed after its celebration in the second year following the Exodus (Num. 9:1–5), but the right to enjoy this sacrament was now returned to Israel. Following the directions given in the law (Exod. 12:6, 14, 18), the people celebrated the Passover in the evening of 14 Nisan, i.e., after sundown on 13 Nisan, for that marked the beginning of the next day. The newly circumcised, who were sufficiently healed by then and in any case were not unclean, could participate in this feast as well.

The statement in verse 11 that the Israelites ate the produce of the land the day after the Passover might seem somewhat surprising, for 15 Nisan was the beginning of the Feast of Unleavened Bread (Lev. 23:6). On the second day of this feast, i.e., 16 Nisan, the priest waved the sheaf of the firstfruits before the Lord; but before that day no one was to eat of the harvest (Lev. 23:11, 14). This rule assuredly was observed at Gilgal. Israel was first allowed to partake of the grain on 16 Nisan, after the offering of firstfruits had been presented (there is no basis for the KJV's view of this grain as "old corn," see vv. 11–12). Therefore, the phrase "the day after the Passover" has to be understood as including the first day of the Feast of Unleavened Bread, i.e., 15 Nisan, within the Passover itself.

The words "that very day" accentuate the importance of that next day, 16 Nisan. For that is when the manna fell for the last time. The next day it stopped and came no more. The manna was no longer needed, because the Israelites ate the fruit of the Promised Land; and in so doing they already took possession of it symbolically.

This important section of chapter 5 clearly shows that Israel would receive the Promised Land from the hand of the Lord. The weapons and fighting spirit of the army were not the main concern; there was not even a military review. The most important thing by far was that the relationship between the people and God be set right (see also ch. 7). The people had indeed been able to sever this relationship, but they were unable to repair that breach. That was God's work alone. He thus gave the command to circumcise the people and thereby renewed His covenant with Israel. After the circumcision rite had been completed,

God assured the nation through the Passover that He would also be its Ally in the coming battle. Israel, in contrast to the disheartened Amorites and Canaanites (v. 1), stood courageous and strong, assured of the Lord's favor. The nature of sacred history here stands out in bold relief.

9. Joshua and the Commander of the Army of the Lord (5:13–6:5)

5:13–15 *Now when Joshua was near Jericho, he looked up and saw a man standing in front of him with a drawn sword in his hand. Joshua went up to him and asked, "Are you for us or for our enemies?"*

14"Neither," he replied, "but as commander of the army of the LORD I have now come." Then Joshua fell facedown to the ground in reverence, and asked him, "What message does my Lord have for his servant?"

15 The commander of the LORD's army replied, "Take off your sandals, for the place where you are standing is holy." And Joshua did so.

The meeting described here probably occurred immediately after the celebration of the Feast of Unleavened Bread. Joshua presumably was struggling with the question of how Jericho could be captured. An apparition from heaven gave him his answer. The meeting strongly recalls Moses' encounter at the burning bush (Exod. 3:2–6). The figure that appeared to Moses was called not only the "angel of the LORD" but also the Lord Himself (Exod. 3:2, 4); and 6:2 indicates that this same person came to Joshua and called himself the "commander of the army of the LORD".

The "army" is not the army of Israel but that of the angelic hosts (cf. Gen. 32:1; Pss. 103:20–21; 148:2; Dan. 10:13; Rev. 12:7). The title nevertheless takes for granted that this figure also had supreme command over the earthly army led by Joshua. Joshua acknowledged him as his superior by casting himself face down to earth. This, however, was not an act of worship, nor does the title "my Lord" indicate that Joshua recognized the figure as the Lord.[28] Only when commanded to remove his sandals, an image of the removal of all impurity and a token of respect for God's holy presence, did Joshua realize to whom he was speaking. The words "I have now come" may be regarded as the answer to Joshua's previous prayer for help or refer to the Lord's promise in 1:5–6 to be with Joshua. The drawn sword

---

[28]Cf. KJV, RSV, and NIV margin, where "Lord" is lower case—TRANS.

expressed the purpose the Lord had come for: He Himself would fight for Israel.

6:1–5 *Now Jericho was tightly shut up because of the Israelites. No one went out and no one came in.*

² Then the LORD said to Joshua, "See, I have delivered Jericho into your hands, along with its king and its fighting men. ³ March around the city once with all the armed men. Do this for six days. ⁴ Have seven priests carry trumpets of rams' horns in front of the ark. On the seventh day, march around the city seven times, with the priests blowing the trumpets. ⁵ When you hear them sound a long blast on the trumpets, have all the people give a loud shout; then the wall of the city will collapse and the people will go up, every man straight in."

Besides telling Israel that He would fight for her, the Lord also had some special instructions concerning the attack on Jericho. The chapters have been divided incorrectly here, creating the impression that the meeting ended in 5:15. This is not the intention, however, no more than Exodus 3:5 marks the end of the similar encounter of Moses. The Lord's conversation with Joshua continues in 6:2. Verse 1, which is a parenthetical statement that interrupts the story, describes the situation confronting the Israelites at Jericho and is essential to the context. The king of Jericho had shut the city up. The Hebrew here literally reads "Jericho was shutting and shut," thus indicating that the city was sealed to both those entering and those leaving.[29] The king neither considered surrender nor made a foray against Israel. Relying on the strong city walls, he chose to face down this desert nation that had had no experience in storming a fortress.

In the light of Jericho's defiant stance, the meeting between the Lord and Joshua in front of the city gate is even more striking. There the Lord simply told Joshua that He, who had all things under His control, was delivering Jericho and its military might into Joshua's hand. The way He would do this once more testified to God's miraculous power. Israel would thereby again come to realize her total dependence on God, and the nations of Canaan would be given a new reason to tremble. The Israelite soldiers would have to do nothing more than march around the city for six successive days, once each day, and then seven times in a row on the seventh day. After that, the priests who accompanied the army and marched ahead of the ark would sound a signal on their trumpets. The people were then to raise a loud shout; and an invisible hand would cause the walls of Jericho to collapse,

---

[29] Cf. RSV: "shut up from within and from without."

allowing Israel to invade the city, not just through the gates and breaches in the wall, but everywhere at once. The rams' horns with their powerful sound were the same instruments that announced the Year of Jubilee (Lev. 25:9); and their long, continuous blast was also used as a signal in Exodus 19:13.

10. The Fall and Ban of Jericho
(6:6–27)

6:6–7 *So Joshua son of Nun called the priests and said to them, "Take up the ark of the covenant of the LORD and have seven priests carry trumpets in front of it." [7] And he[30] ordered the people, "Advance! March around the city, with the armed guard going ahead of the ark of the LORD."*

Joshua at once proceeded to carry out the charge he had been given. Apparently he made no reply to the Lord's orders, which marks him as a man of strict obedience, even discipline. Moses had taken a different attitude at Mount Horeb in Exodus 3 and 4. Joshua simply did as he had been instructed, thus calling to mind the centurion who could both obey and give orders (Matt. 8:8–9). Probably on the same day, he gave both the priests and the people a brief command concerning the march around Jericho and the order that would have to be followed in this. Joshua obviously must have said more than what is recorded in verses 6 and 7 (see v. 10); but, possibly to avoid needless repetition, the writer only related the gist of Joshua's words. Indeed, the divine command itself is doubtless only recorded in summary form (vv. 3–5); for these verses say nothing of the ark's position within the military procession, nor of the order to place Jericho under the ban (cf. v. 9 and vv. 17–19). Most likely, Joshua also was commanded to have the priests blow on the trumpets the first six days. Verse 5 does not rule this out, since it speaks only of the trumpet blast on the seventh day.[31] The advance guard in the march consisted of that portion of the army that was dressed in full military array,[32] while the rear guard was composed of

---

[30] Following a large number of manuscripts and the most important ancient translations, the NIV here reads the third person masculine singular instead of the plural. Compare the beginning of verse 8—TRANS.

[31] There are, to be sure, a few incongruities in the account; but most of these can be explained very easily in the above manner. Chapter 6 contains no definite discrepancies, and there is no reason at all to accept De Groot's conclusion that it is a chaos (*Het Boek Jozua*, p. 90).

[32] Keil (*Joshua*,[2] p. 46) and others would identify this with the forty thousand spoken of in 4:13, but it must also have included men from other tribes.

men who would not take part in the battle directly, or at least were less
heavily armed.

6:8–14 *When Joshua had spoken to the people,*[33] *the seven priests carrying the
seven trumpets before the* Lord *went forward, blowing their trumpets, and the
ark of the* Lord's *covenant followed them.* [9] *The armed guard marched ahead of
the priests who blew the trumpets, and the rear guard followed the ark. All this
time the trumpets were sounding.* [10] *But Joshua had commanded the people,
"Do not give a war cry, do not raise your voices, do not say a word until the
day I tell you to shout. Then shout!"* [11] *So he had the ark of the* Lord *carried
around the city, circling it once. Then the people returned to camp and spent
the night there.*

[12] *Joshua got up early the next morning and the priests took up the ark of the
Lord.* [13] *The seven priests carrying the seven trumpets went forward, marching
before the ark of the* Lord *and blowing the trumpets. The armed men went
ahead of them and the rear guard followed the ark of the* Lord, *while the
trumpets kept sounding.* [14] *So on the second day they marched around the city
once and returned to the camp. They did this for six days.*

In the description of the first circuit around Jericho, verse 8 says that
the priests went "before the Lord," for He was considered to be
invisibly enthroned above the ark. The ark was carried by the priests
and formed the midpoint of the entire procession (see v. 11). Throughout the march all that could be heard from the army was the flourish of
the trumpets. Joshua had commanded the people, before they had
begun to move out, to remain in total silence till he told them to raise a
shout. Notice that Joshua did not inform the people of the trumpet
signal referred to in verse 5. Possibly he thought it best to let them
know the precise moment by means of an unambiguous verbal
command. At the same time he then would have had the opportunity to
give his final orders (vv. 17–19). In this case Joshua must have spoken
separately with the priests about the moment the signal was to be
sounded (see in v. 16). It appears that the first circuit around Jericho
took place towards evening (v. 11). On the following day the march
was made in the morning (v. 12), for Joshua was not one to
procrastinate or delay.

---

[33] In the Septuagint these opening words of verse 8 are missing and the rest of
verses 8–9 are put in the imperative as the continuation of verse 7. This reading is
incorrect for the following reasons: (1) the command in verse 9 would then be for the
priests, not the people; (2) verse 9 would needlessly repeat the command of verse
7b; (3) the opening of verse 10 would be altogether superfluous; (4) the order of
march would not be given for the first day.

6:15–19 *On the seventh day, they got up at daybreak and marched around the city seven times in the same manner, except that on that day they circled the city seven times.* ¹⁶*The seventh time around, when the priests sounded the trumpet blast, Joshua commanded the people, "Shout! For the LORD has given you the city!* ¹⁷*The city and all that is in it are to be devoted to the LORD. Only Rahab the prostitute and all who are with her in her house shall be spared, because she hid the spies we sent.* ¹⁸*But keep away from the devoted things, so that you will not bring about your own destruction by taking any of them. Otherwise you will make the camp of Israel liable to destruction and bring trouble on it.* ¹⁹*All the silver and gold and the articles of bronze and iron are sacred to the LORD and must go into his treasury."*

Early on the morning of the seventh day, Israel began to march around the city again; and, as God had commanded, they did this seven times. The marching order here is the same as on the previous days. It is explicitly stated that all seven circuits were completed on this one day. If we set the duration of a single circuit at no more than one hour (in terms of the dimensions given in footnote 7 on page 42, approximately one-half hour would really have been enough), this would easily have been possible. In fact there may even have been a brief pause during the march. Since God had commanded the Israelites to encircle the city seven times, they undoubtedly went all the way around it the seventh time as well. No doubt the priests were aware of Joshua's plan to issue a verbal command when the march was completed, and the trumpet sound thus must have ceased for a brief time. At that moment Joshua commanded the people to raise a shout of triumph,³⁴ for they would see at once that the city had been delivered into their hands by the Lord. Jericho had been given to Israel, however, so that the Israelites might devote it right back to the Lord Himself. Jericho was placed under the ban. The Hebrew word here (*ḥērem*) denotes something that is irrevocably and absolutely surrendered to the Lord,³⁵ either to be used in His worship or to be destroyed (Lev. 27:28–29). In this case the ban was destruction. All the inhabitants of Jericho (except Rahab and those with her) were to be killed, along with their animals as well (v. 21). Nor was any Israelite to take any of the Jericho's booty

---

³⁴Joshua perhaps already had informed the people earlier of what he told them in verses 17–19. For they could not all have been within hearing at this moment, and it was essential that none of them miss his words. In this case verses 17–19 would be a repeated and final warning.

³⁵The author translated *ḥērem* and the related verb *ḥāram* in verses 17, 18, 21 et al., as "banned, under the ban" (cf. NEB, JB, NAB, NASB). NIV and RSV have "devoted." Cf. 1 Chronicles 2:7—TRANS.

for his own. Everything there belonged to God and was to be devoted to Him. Whatever was made of gold, silver, bronze, or iron was to be added to the treasures kept in the sanctuary (cf. Num. 31:54; a more severe form of the ban of destruction is found in Deut. 13:16), and the rest of the city was to be destroyed by fire (v. 24). Joshua issued a very grave warning that the Israelites, God's agents in the judgment of Jericho, were not to take any of the devoted things for themselves while performing their duty (v. 18). This would impede the effects of the ban, deny God what was rightfully His own, and bring disaster on Israel. The oneness of the nation of Israel would result in the whole nation being subject to the ban if even a part of the *ḥērem* were stored in its camp.

6:20–25 *When the trumpets sounded, the people shouted, and at the sound of the trumpet, when the people gave a loud shout, the wall collapsed; so every man charged straight in, and they took the city.* [21] *They devoted the city to the Lord and destroyed with the sword every living thing in it—men and women, young and old, cattle, sheep and donkeys.*

[22] *Joshua said to the two men who had spied out the land, "Go into the prostitute's house and bring her out and all who belong to her, in accordance with your oath to her."* [23] *So the young men who had done the spying went in and brought out Rahab, her father and mother and brothers and all who belonged to her. They brought out her entire family and put them in a place outside the camp of Israel.*

[24] *Then they burned the whole city and everything in it, but they put the silver and gold and the articles of bronze and iron into the treasury of the Lord's house.* [25] *But Joshua spared Rahab the prostitute, with her family and all who belonged to her, because she hid the men Joshua had sent as spies to Jericho— and she lives among the Israelites to this day.*

As soon as Joshua had finished speaking, the sounding of the trumpets resumed, no doubt with the distinct, sustained note spoken of in verse 5 (cf. Exod. 19:13), though the words used for it here are not entirely the same. The people broke into shouting. Those not within earshot of Joshua's voice could still hear the trumpet signal, and they too joined in with the shout. The column formed by the Israelite army must have been so long that it completely surrounded the city.[36]

---

[36] In his book *Die grosze Täuschung* (Stuttgart, 1931), pp. 24f., Friedrich Delitzsch attempted to show that the account of the march around Jericho was preposterous by arbitrarily assuming that the width of the Israelite column was only five men. On these terms the entire procession would have extended more than fifty-two miles. We need not take this claim seriously, however. The thought that all the Israelite

Otherwise the men could not have charged in over the ruins from all sides at once and prevented every inhabitant of Jericho from escaping when the wall suddenly collapsed . No serious resistance was offered to Israel's conquest of the city, and the Israelites completed their task virtually without difficulty (24:11 is too general to draw any contrary conclusion). Those who were on top of the wall were buried beneath the rubble at once, and everyone else was put to the sword,[37] everyone, that is, except those found in the house of Rahab.

Joshua, bound by the oath of his men (2:14), kept his word. At his command the two spies went to Rahab's dwelling, which had not collapsed with the wall, and escorted her and her entire family (this apparently is taken very broadly) out of the city. Being unclean, they stayed outside the Israelite camp, but their isolation was not permanent (v. 25). Rahab, who had already been inwardly won over to Israel's God, no doubt made a public break with her idols and openly chose to worship the Lord; and her family must have followed her example. Rahab's faith saved her life (Heb. 11:31), and she became the recipient of grace and honor (Matt. 1:5; James 2:25). When the Book of Joshua was written, Rahab was yet alive (see Introduction, pp. 14–15).

6:26–27 *At that time Joshua pronounced this solemn oath: "Cursed before the* Lord *is the man who undertakes to rebuild this city, Jericho:*
> *"At the cost of his firstborn son*
> *will he lay its foundations;*
> *at the cost of his youngest*
> *will he set up its gates."*
[27] *So the* Lord *was with Joshua, and his fame spread throughout the land.*

The judgment on Jericho was still not complete. The ban placed on it demanded that the city—or rather the place where it once had stood—proclaim a lasting testimony of God's avenging justice (cf. Deut. 13:16). Thus Joshua pronounced a curse on whoever would rebuild the city from its ashes. The people were made to join in this imprecation[38] (perhaps by speaking the "Amen," as in Deut. 27:15–26) and so in effect bound themselves by oath never to reconstruct the city. Strictly

---

men (according to Num. 2:32, approximately 600,000) participated in the march is itself highly improbable, for surely most of the people must have remained in the camp. Moreover the width of the column must have been related to the number of men that circled the city.

[37] A comparison of 8:2, 29, and 10:1 reveals that the king of Jericho met his death by being hanged on a tree. See commentary in 8:29.

[38] See KJV, RSV, "Joshua laid an oath upon them. . . ."

speaking, this imprecation was an act of calling on the name of the Lord and asking Him to punish whoever defied the curse by taking all his sons, from the eldest to the youngest, from him. The rebuilding actually meant a refortification of the city (cf. 1 Kings 15:17; 2 Chron. 11:5; 14:6–7), which is confirmed by the parallel expressions "lay its foundations" and "set up its gates." These clearly refer to building fortifying walls to make Jericho a secure city once again. The curse therefore did not apply to those who made their homes there fairly soon after this (cf. 18:21; Judg. 3:13; 2 Sam. 10:5) but first fell on the man who sought to rebuild Jericho as a fortress (1 Kings 16:34). The miraculous fall of Jericho undeniably proved that the Lord was with Joshua (1:5); thus the entire land came to speak of him as the invincible general of Israel.

The conquest of Jericho occurred in such an extraordinary manner and is described in such great detail because it was the first city that confronted the Israelites as they entered the Promised Land. The Lord therefore chose to use this city as an object lesson for impressing two distinct things on His people: (1) they were receiving the land solely as a gift from God's hand; (2) the land properly belonged to the Lord alone, and they had to consecrate it to Him. The first lesson was taught by the fact that Jericho's fall did not result from a lengthy siege, a successful stratagem, or a powerful assault. The walls collapsed because of God's direct intervention, and the Israelites had to do nothing more than obediently (and apparently uselessly) march around the city and silently await the Lord's action.[39] As in the passage through the Jordan, the Lord lent His aid here in such a striking and miraculous manner[40] that the people could not but have been convinced that they would soon inherit the other cities and the entire land as easily as they had captured this first fortress city.

Credit for the conquest belonged to God alone,[41] which relates to the

---

[39] In keeping with this, in verses 6–7 Joshua issued orders to the priests first and the people second. Furthermore, the ark had the most prominent place in the procession. Verse 11 strongly accentuates this fact: the ark circled the city, and the people were allowed to accompany it. See F.B. Meyer, *Joshua and the Land of Promise*, p. 68.

[40] As of yet the investigation of Jericho's ruins has yielded no clear evidence that the city's fall had no natural cause. See especially Garstang's account. He suspects an earthquake, but this remains uncertain.

[41] Nothing I have said diminishes the truth of Hebrews 11:30, which regards the cause of the walls' collapse from the subjective side. Because of the Israelites' unshaking confidence in God's promise that the walls would collapse, they *had to*

second lesson mentioned above. Israel conquered and took possession of the land for the Lord so that they might dedicate it to Him and live within it as a holy nation. To impress this on the people, Jericho was more severely dealt with than the other cities of Canaan. Human inhabitants, cattle, and material plunder all had to be placed under the ban and devoted to the Lord (see the comments on this in the Introduction, pp. 28–29, and later in chapter 12). The city itself had to be annihilated, and the Israelites were expressly forbidden to rebuild it. Jericho, the gateway to Canaan, was surrendered to the Lord in its entirety; and Israel was allowed to keep none of it. All that remained was the sight of the ruins, a lasting proof of God's avenging justice. But we also must not forget the deliverance of Rahab's household, a permanent testimony to God's free grace.

The sudden fall of Jericho and its total annihilation reveal that the Lord wanted to settle the score with this city and be completely done with it. This completeness is emphasized by the frequently recurring number seven: seven priests, seven trumpets, seven days, and seven circuits on the seventh day. The completeness of the Canaanites' iniquity earned a divine judgment of definitive character. God was bringing a chapter of history to its conclusion, and the events at Jericho offered a graphic image and actual prophecy of events at the close of the age, when there will be seven angels with seven trumpets of doom and judgment (Rev. 8:2). At that time the great and powerful city of Babylon will suddenly fall (Rev. 18:2, 8, 10), accompanied by a great shouting in heaven (Rev. 18:20; 19:1–3). This chapter of Joshua also has a prophetic message for the New Covenant church: it must persevere to the end and carry out its charge obediently (and often seemingly fruitlessly). In particular it must trumpet the continuous warning sound of God's Word in its preaching. And it may rest in the serene confidence that in God's time its great Leader, Jesus Christ (Heb. 2:10), will give the signal that will finally collapse even the strongest bulwark of hostile power to God that holds sway in this world.

---

collapse. Such faith, which will never be deceived (Mark 9:23), consists in disavowing one's own strength and entrusting oneself solely to God's omnipotence.

11. The Violation of the Ban
(7:1–26)

7:1 *But the Israelites acted unfaithfully in regard to the devoted things; Achan son of Carmi, the son of Zimri, the son of Zerah, of the tribe of Judah, took some of them. So the LORD's anger burned against Israel.*

Verse 1, which discloses Achan's secret misdeed, contains the key for explaining the calamity that Israel suffered at Ai (see below). Two things in this verse merit attention. First, the transgression spoken of was imputed to the nation as a whole. The opening words state that the Israelites, not merely Achan alone, violated the ban and broke faith in regard to the devoted things. The nation of Israel was viewed by God as an organic unity, and Achan was a member of that body. His transgression defiled the whole nation and placed it under the ban, since some of the devoted things were in its camp (cf. 6:18; 7:11–12). Second, the final sentence of verse 1 reveals the sacred character of the history recorded in the Bible. Scripture regards facts from God's point of view, recounting history as He sees it and as He Himself makes and directs it. This verse, in saying "so the LORD's anger burned against Israel," specifies a causal connection between Achan's offense and Israel's calamity. Sin always ignites God's anger. Since Achan was acting not merely on his own behalf when he sinned, God's anger was directed against Israel as a whole.

7:2–5 *Now Joshua sent men from Jericho to Ai, which is near Beth Aven to the east of Bethel, and told them, "Go up and spy out the region." So the men went up and spied out Ai.*
³ When they returned to Joshua, they said, "Not all the people will have to go up against Ai. Send two or three thousand men to take it and do not weary all the people, for only a few men are there." ⁴ So about three thousand men went up; but they were routed by the men of Ai, ⁵ who killed about thirty-six of them. They chased the Israelites from the city gate as far as the stone quarries and struck them down on the slopes. At this the hearts of the people melted and became like water.

Circumspect general that he was, Joshua again first sent men to spy out the enemy's strength. The name "Ai" (Heb. *hā'ay*) means "the ruin," clearly not the original name of the city. Ai perhaps was the same city as Aija in Nehemiah 11:31 and Aiath in Isaiah 10:28. Like verse 2, Genesis 12:8 locates it east of Bethel, a city about ten and a half miles north of Jerusalem at the site of modern Beitin. Until recently, it was thought that Ai lay in the hill of ruins at et-Tell.[42] Martin Noth still took this position in his 1953 commentary on Joshua (second edition), but various scholars (e.g., J. Simons) have recognized that there are strong arguments against it.[43] One important item is that already in Joshua's day this site had long been an uninhabited ruin. The identification of Ai with et-Tell is therefore now dubious. Beth Aven lay west of Micmash (see 1 Sam. 13:5), and it perhaps stood at the site of Burqa, north of Mizpah.[44]

Since Ai had few residents, Joshua followed the spies' advice and sent only three thousand men to capture the city, a decision that betrays a certain recklessness. In addition Joshua acted on his own to some degree, for he had not asked the Lord, Israel's supreme Commander, for advice. The outcome of the battle was humiliating for Israel. The men of Ai made a sortie and killed thirty-six Israelites. Joshua's troops were pursued to the stone quarries at the slope of the mountain pass, where the battle ended in a decisive defeat of Israel. The Israelites' mood took an about-face, and everyone was unmanned. In such places as verse 3, "all the people" refers specifically to the army or fighting men; but in verse 7 "people" has a broader reference and includes all Israel.

7:6–9 *Then Joshua tore his clothes and fell facedown to the ground before the ark of the LORD, remaining there till evening. The elders of Israel did the same, and sprinkled dust on their heads. 7 And Joshua said, "Ah, Sovereign LORD, why did you ever bring this people across the Jordan to deliver us into the hands of the Amorites to destroy us? If only we had been content to stay on the other side of the Jordan! 8 O Lord, what can I say, now that Israel has been routed by its enemies? 9 The Canaanites and the other people of the country will hear about this and they will surround us and wipe out our name from the earth. What then will you do for your own great name?"*

Joshua was crushed by what had happened and turned to the Lord, as did the elders of Israel. They all sensed that there must have been a deeper cause for this disaster, but it remained hidden from them. In view of God's clear and certain promises, the defeat was incomprehensible. Joshua and the elders took seriously what had befallen Israel and

---

[42] Garstang, who made a detailed investigation of this area, takes this view (*Joshua, Judges*, pp. 149–59, 355). See also Schmidtke, *Die Einwanderung Israëls in Kanaän*, pp. 104ff.

[43] A concise summary of these is found in *Bijbelse Encyclopedie*, p. 38.

[44] On Beth Aven, see *Bijbelse Encyclopedie*, p. 78; on Micmash, A. Noordtzij, *Gods Woord*,[2] p. 354.

did not merely put it behind them and launch a new attack; it would have been impossible to continue in this manner. Joshua's prayer was first a request for light in the present darkness. It was unthinkable that the Lord would have brought Israel over the Jordan only to allow the Amorites to destroy them. Joshua's faith struggled against this conclusion and asked the question "Why?"[45] His words in verse 7—"if only we had been content to stay on the other side of the Jordan"—imply that it would have been better for the Israelites to remain where they had been than to die in Canaan. At the same time, they acknowledged that the people may have been too bold in their plans and desires. Joshua sensed that the guilt was with Israel, but the exact nature of this guilt remained a mystery. Hence, his words in verse 8: "What can I say?"

The Hebrew word translated as "O" (*bî*) means something like "forgive me if I am being too outspoken." Joshua had no intention of finding fault with what God had done; therefore, he concluded his speech by appealing to the honor of God's name. If Israel's enemies heard what had happened, would they not blaspheme His name? How then could the Lord preserve the sanctity of His name? Does not the honor of God's name demand that His people be victorious? Joshua therefore knowledgeably prayed that what was at stake in this new turn of events was not primarily Israel but God Himself. Even in prayer he followed the example of his teacher Moses (Exod. 32:11–13; Num. 14:15–16).

7:10–12 *The LORD said to Joshua, "Stand up! What are you doing down on your face?* [11] *Israel has sinned; they have violated my covenant, which I commanded them to keep. They have taken some of the devoted things; they have stolen, they have lied, they have put them with their own possessions.* [12] *That is why the Israelites cannot stand against their enemies; they turn their backs and run because they have been made liable to destruction. I will not be with you anymore unless you destroy whatever among you is devoted to destruction.*

After Joshua and the elders had given symbolic expression to their great sorrow and had lain before the ark till evening (v. 6), God's answer came to them, possibly from the cloud above the ark. The Lord's wrath was evident not only in His every word but in the tone He

---

[45] Joshua's words here recall those of the Israelites in Numbers 14:2–3. The important difference, however, is that the people complained without praying. Joshua brought his complaint directly to God; and his attitude was one of humility, more so than Moses' attitude in Numbers 11:10–15.

spoke in. An offense had been committed against the God of Israel; so He had the right to demand a humble confession of sin. Instead of this, however, Joshua approached Him with the question "Why?" (v. 7). It would be less than correct to say that the Lord rejected Joshua's entreaty. Nevertheless, the words "Stand up! What are you doing down on your face?" imply that Joshua was wrong in looking for the cause of Israel's misfortune with God. Israel herself was to blame. The Lord was telling Joshua that His faithfulness must never be doubted. Not He, but the people had been unfaithful.

Verse 13 repeats the command to stand up,[46] but this time God was also ordering Joshua as an obedient servant to be ready to carry out the instructions that followed. A series of accusations against Israel are given in verse 11. Israel had sinned. The Hebrew root literally means "swerve to the side," "take a false step." Their sin in fact was nothing less than a violation of the covenant. That covenant was Israel's privilege, but it also placed the Israelites under obligations. The added words "which I commanded them to keep" show that the binding, obligatory side of the covenant was the main concern here. The people's obligation to give to the Lord what belonged to Him was a direct consequence of the command given the Israelites in 6:18 and a necessary part of their covenantal relationship. Israel's sin is defined more precisely as taking some of the devoted things, i.e., sacrilege, theft of what is sacred. The crime that had been committed was therefore aimed directly at the God of the covenant. It was His covenant and His rights of ownership that had been infringed.

The expressions that follow further portray the gravity of the sin and its aggravating circumstances. The Israelites had stolen, lied, and concealed what they had taken among their own possessions, thinking to use it for their own benefit. If a contrite confession had been made soon enough, perhaps the Lord would not have smitten the people. Instead of this, however, their evil had multiplied, for sin always brings forth more sin. The list in verse 11 makes plain that the Lord had abundant cause for anger and that He held the entire nation responsible for the crime. All Israel was placed under the ban, and this led directly to a twofold choice. Either the people had to bear the consequences of the ban and run from their enemies—for in this condition God could no longer remain with them—or the ban had to be expurgated. The Lord Himself enjoined the latter.

---

[46]The Hebrew word is the same here, but the NIV has "go." See KJV, RSV, NEB, "up," "stand up"—TRANS.

7:13-15 *"Go, consecrate the people. Tell them, 'Consecrate yourselves in preparation for tomorrow; for this is what the LORD, the God of Israel, says: That which is devoted is among you, O Israel. You cannot stand against your enemies until you remove it.*

¹⁴" 'In the morning, present yourselves tribe by tribe. The tribe that the LORD takes shall come forward clan by clan; the clan that the LORD takes shall come forward family by family; and the family that the LORD takes shall come forward man by man. ¹⁵ He who is caught with the devoted things shall be destroyed by fire, along with all that belongs to him. He has violated the covenant of the LORD and has done a disgraceful thing in Israel!' "

Joshua was told that he must at once, that very evening, command the people to consecrate themselves (see in 3:5). Then he must disclose to them the cause of their defeat and order them to assemble the following morning. At that time the Lord Himself would point out the guilty person, not directly, but by lot.⁴⁷ The tribe the devoted things were found in would be indicated first, then the clan, then the family, and finally the man himself who had seized the sacred objects. By thus gradually narrowing in on the guilty party, the Lord would give the entire nation a profound impression of both the gravity of this matter and His divine omniscience. In addition, the guilty person then would still have an opportunity to come forward voluntarily. Once he had been caught, the enforcement of the ban would again be an affair that concerned all Israel; and the nation as a whole would have to take part in the punishment. This punishment would be even more severe than that of Jericho, for the guilty Israelite had stood *within* the covenant and had removed himself from it. He had not committed an offense that could be taken lightly, a sin of weakness. Verse 15 rather calls his crime a "disgraceful thing in Israel."⁴⁸ The man who had done this was to be stoned to death along with his sons and daughters (see v. 25), and their

---

⁴⁷In verse 17 the author has "the lot fell upon the Zerahites." The Hebrew is literally "it [or 'he'] took," but he says it is "probable" that the tacit subject here is "the lot"—TRANS.

⁴⁸The Hebrew word used here always indicates a very serious misdeed (see Gen. 34:7; Deut. 22:21; Judg. 19:23–24; 20:6, 10; 2 Sam. 13:12; Jer. 29:23). All these verses speak of sexual crimes. The offense in Joshua 7 was against purity as well, but in a spiritual sense. The word used in the KJV ("folly") is too weak taken by itself, for the sins spoken of were absolutely incompatible with Israel's character as the Lord's holy covenant nation. Such acts brought disgrace on Israel (cf. Judg. 20:6); and in view of Genesis 34:7 (see NIV margin—TRANS.), one could translate verse 15 as "a disgraceful thing against Israel." See Aalders' *Korte Verklaring* [*Bible Student's Commentary*] in Jeremiah 29:23.

bodies were then to be burned (cf. Lev. 20:14). The same sentence was to be imposed on all the man's possessions, even the stolen goods (vv. 24–25). This was the ban of destruction in its severest form (cf. Deut. 13:15–16).

7:16–21 *Early the next morning Joshua had Israel come forward by tribes, and Judah was taken. 17 The clans49 of Judah came forward, and he took the Zerahites. He had the clan of the Zerahites come forward by families,50 and Zimri was taken. 18 Joshua had his family come forward man by man, and Achan son of Carmi, the son of Zimri, the son of Zerah, of the tribe of Judah, was taken.*

19 Then Joshua said to Achan, "My son, give glory to the LORD, the God of Israel, and give him the praise. Tell me what you have done; do not hide it from me."

20 Achan replied, "It is true! I have sinned against the LORD, the God of Israel. This is what I have done: 21 When I saw in the plunder a beautiful robe from Babylonia, two hundred shekels of silver and a wedge of gold weighing fifty shekels, I coveted them and took them. They are hidden in the ground inside my tent, with the silver underneath."

The next morning arrived, and the Lord's command was carried out. The tribes, clans, and families[51] here must have been represented by their heads, also referred to as leaders (Num. 3:24; 7:2). In the drawing of lots, it was customary to use white and black stones,[52] and the method may have been to have each person select a stone from a pouch (cf. Prov. 16:33). In the present case, the single black stone, for example, would have indicated that the person who drew it was the guilty party.

However this may have been, the use of lots was based on the conviction that God Himself controlled their selection, which truth is indeed evident in the present story. God used lots to disclose something

---

[49] A change in vowels gives the plural here, as in the Greek and Latin translations. The KJV follows the singular in the Hebrew text.

[50] The Hebrew text has "man by man" (cf KJV, RSV). Although various ancient manuscripts and translations have "by families" (hence the NIV reading), the author regards this merely as an emendation based on verse 14 and sticks with the Hebrew text—TRANS.

[51] We should understand these clans as the main subdivisions of the tribes that were usually, but not always, named after the grandsons of Jacob. The word "family" has a broader reference than its standard modern meaning. It denotes a group of families as a division of a clan. On these terms Achan was therefore not a family head but like his father a member of the family of Zimri.

[52] *Bijbels-Kerkelijk Woordenboek*, 1:192; *Bijbelse Encyclopedie*, pp. 311f.

that had been concealed, even though He could of course have chosen to do this directly.

The selection process ended by pointing to Achan. Joshua, gravely but also gently and in a fatherly tone, asked him what he had done. In his words "give glory to the LORD . . . and confess to Him,"[53] the second command is a counterpart to the first. For if Achan denied his guilt, he would be calling God a liar; if he confessed, he would honor God as the omniscient One before whom all things lie open and uncovered (Heb. 4:13). Joshua also used these two commands to remind Achan that God was present. It was not merely man but the Lord Himself who was calling Achan to account. Joshua's words struck the proper chord in Achan; and he openly avowed that the crime he had committed was a sin against God, the true owner of the gold and silver of Jericho (6:19). From the plunder, he had taken a robe made in Babylonia, two hundred shekels of silver, and a wedge of gold. The Hebrew literally reads "robe from Shinar," but this is equivalent to Babylonia, a place where sumptuous garments were woven.

The weight of the silver came to approximately six and a half pounds. The gold wedge was probably an artistic product in the shape of a bar or tongue. Achan used the numeral "one" (Heb. *'eḥad*) in speaking of this gold, and he thus seemed to be trying to extenuate his action by implying that he could have taken more. Since the gold shekel weighed sixteen and a half grams and this number has to be multiplied by fifty, clearly the wedge was quite heavy and very costly. All those stolen valuables were so attractive to Achan that he could not resist his desire to take them (cf. Gen. 3:6; James 1:14–15). He then buried them in his tent, apparently wrapping the robe and the gold wedge together and placing the silver beneath them.

7:22–26 *So Joshua sent messengers, and they ran to the tent, and there it was, hidden in his tent, with the silver underneath.* [23] *They took the things from the tent, brought them to Joshua and all the Israelites and spread them out before the* LORD.

[24] *Then Joshua, together with all Israel, took Achan son of Zerah, the silver, the robe, the gold wedge, his sons and daughters, his cattle, donkeys and sheep, his tent and all that he had, to the Valley of Achor.* [25] *Joshua said, "Why have you brought this trouble on us? The* LORD *will bring trouble on you today."*

Then all Israel stoned him, and after they had stoned the rest, they burned them. [26] *Over Achan they heaped up a large pile of rocks, which remains to this*

---

[53] The author's translation follows the KJV and the NIV margin. The NIV and RSV have ". . . and give him the praise"—TRANS.

day. Then the LORD turned from his fierce anger. Therefore that place has been called the Valley of Achor ever since.

The messengers sent by Joshua found everything in Achan's tent, just as he had said. They took the stolen goods back to Joshua and spread them out on the ground "before the LORD," i.e., in front of the ark. The Lord's rightful possessions were thereby returned to Him. Nevertheless, none of this could be placed with the Lord's treasures in the sanctuary. It was rather set apart for destruction, since the stain of Achan's sin still clung to it. Without a moment's delay, Joshua and Israel proceeded with one accord to execute the ban. As God had commanded in verse 15, this was imposed not merely on Achan himself but also on all his possessions, both living and nonliving.

By violating the ban and bringing goods from Jericho into his tent, Achan in essence made his tent, its contents, and whatever went with it one with Jericho; and all this now fell under the same judgment that had struck the city. In addition, Achan's children could be considered accomplices to his crime, for they hid the fact that he had buried the stolen items in the tent. That nothing was said of Achan's wife (cf. Num. 16:27) perhaps indicates that she had already died. The sentence was carried out in the Valley of Achor. The name Achor was in fact taken from this event, being derived from the verb *'āḵar* ("to afflict, bring disaster on"), the very word that Joshua used twice in his final statement to Achan (v. 25).[54]

Achan had brought evil on God's people and so received recompense from the Lord Himself. Joshua's final words to Achan were simultaneously a signal for the entire nation to begin the stoning. Although verse 25 says that Israel "stoned *him,*" this does not mean that Achan alone was stoned. He was the chief object of the punishment, but the conclusion of verse 25 clearly indicates that his children were stoned with him. After this Achan, his children, and all his possession were burned and then covered with stones. The stones were piled into a large heap above them, a mark of infamy that would recall Achan's sin and serve as a warning to posterity (similar stone heaps were made over the corpses of the king of Ai, 8:29, and Absalom, 2 Sam. 18:17).

The Lord's anger had been appeased and His honor avenged. In making this statement in verse 26, the author harks back to the opening of the story in verse 1, where it is said that "the LORD's anger burned

---

[54] In reaction to this Achan's name also was changed and henceforth was remembered as Achar (1 Chron. 2:7).

against Israel." He then concludes by noting that the valley has been called Achor, i.e., "valley of disaster," ever since. It still has this name in Isaiah 65:10 and Hosea 2:15, where the events of this chapter are alluded to. Joshua 15:7 mentions the Valley of Achor as a point along the northern boundary of the territory of Judah, perhaps best identified with modern Wadi el-Qelt west of Jericho.[55]

The main significance of Joshua 7 is the picture it gives of the holiness of God's covenant with Israel, which did not mean that God would at all times and in all circumstances grant victory and prosperity to Israel. His primary concern was not Israel's glory but the honor of His name. If His people sinned against His commandments, they no less than their enemies would have to endure the consuming fire of His justice. The relationship between the Israelites and their God was purely spiritual and moral in character, and this elevated their religion above that of the heathen nations around them.

This chapter sheds important light on the sober, realistic character of sacred history. Without chapter 7 the picture of Israel during Joshua's day would be too idealistic. That generation, too, was sinful and could succumb to temptation. Chapter 7 demonstrates the truth of this and thus indirectly warns us to be watchful, since the tempter never rests (1 Peter 5:8) and evil lurks everywhere. The New Testament story of the deceit and punishment of Ananias and Sapphira (Acts 5:1–11) has much in common with the account of Achan's sin and execution.

12. The Capture and Destruction of Ai (8:1–29)

8:1–2 *Then the LORD said to Joshua, "Do not be afraid; do not be discouraged. Take the whole army with you, and go up and attack Ai. For I have delivered into your hands the king of Ai, his people, his city and his land. ² You shall do to Ai and its king as you did to Jericho and its king, except that you may carry off their plunder and livestock for yourselves. Set an ambush behind the city."*

After the failure of Israel's first attack on Ai and the events surrounding Achan's crime, Joshua needed special encouragement if he was to proceed with his task. He dared not start over without an express command from God. Therefore, the Lord's first words to Joshua urged him to take courage. He was to overcome his dismay and set out with the entire Israelite army to capture Ai. The outcome of the

---

[55]See, however, *Bijbelse Encyclopedie*, p. 16.

battle was decided from the start. The Lord would give the city, its territory, and all its inhabitants including the king to Israel; but all the people needed to fight to accomplish this.

In stating that the whole army was to be used, the Lord indirectly rebuked Joshua for underestimating the enemy's strength in his first attack (7:3-4). At the same time, however, He wanted to revive the thought that the conquest of Canaan was a task for the entire nation. The Lord then gave Joshua a set of three instructions. Like Jericho, Ai was to be completely laid waste, and all its inhabitants (represented here by the king) were to be put to death. To this extent the conquest of the two cities was the same, but the next instruction introduced a difference. The goods of Ai, both living and nonliving, could be taken by the Israelites. This was because the people would play a more active role here than they did in the capture of Jericho, and also because Ai was no longer the first city that they encountered in Canaan. Therefore the ban did not have to be enforced to its fullest extent (see pp. 73-74). The Lord's final words briefly describe how Joshua was to arrange the attack. Although God here revealed His sovereign rule, He was not ruling out tactful human engagement. On the contrary, He demanded this.

8:3-9 *So Joshua and the whole army moved out to attack Ai. He chose thirty thousand*[56] *of his best fighting men and sent them out at night* ⁴*with these orders: "Listen carefully. You are to set an ambush behind the city. Don't go very far from it. All of you be on the alert.* ⁵*I and all those with me will advance on the city, and when the men come out against us, as they did before, we will flee from them.* ⁶*They will pursue us until we have lured them away from the city, for they will say, 'They are running away from us as they did before.' So when we flee from them,* ⁷*you are to rise up from ambush and take the city. The LORD your God will give it into your hand.* ⁸*When you have taken the city, set it on fire. Do what the LORD has commanded. See to it; you have my orders."*

⁹*Then Joshua sent them off, and they went to the place of ambush and lay in wait between Bethel and Ai, to the west of Ai—but Joshua spent that night with the people.*

Joshua proceeded at once to carry out his instructions. That same day he made all the necessary preparations for the advance against Ai. At the fall of darkness he ordered a select division of his troops to march past the city and to set an ambush behind it, i.e., to the west of it. He disclosed his battle plan and gave them the necessary instruc-

---

[56]This probably should be five thousand. See verse 12 and the comments on it.

tions. Undoubtedly, he also ordered them to be on the lookout for the signal that he would give when they were to make their attack (see v. 18). He added that he had been directed by the Lord Himself to give these orders and that if they followed this plan, victory was assured. The men set out and hid themselves between Bethel and Ai, on the western slope of the hill on which Ai stood, an area strewn with boulders and full of deep crevasses. Verses 3–9 should probably be regarded only as a preview of verse 12 (see note 57 below and Note 2 at the end of the commentary).

8:10–13 *Early the next morning Joshua mustered his men, and he and the leaders of Israel marched before them to Ai. [11] The entire force that was with him marched up and approached the city and arrived in front of it. They set up camp north of Ai, with the valley between them and the city. [12] Joshua had taken about five thousand men and set them in ambush between Bethel and Ai, to the west of the city. [13] They had the soldiers take up their positions—all those in the camp to the north of the city and the ambush to the west of it. That night Joshua went into the valley.[57]*

The next morning Joshua set to work early. He mustered his fighting men and marched ahead of them with the leaders to a point a short distance north of Ai, separated from it only by a valley or depression.[58]

---

[57] The author translated this sentence "but Joshua spent that night in the valley" and added the following note: "The end of verse 13 reads in the Hebrew 'but that night Joshua went into the valley' [cf. NIV]. Several Hebrew manuscripts, however, have *wayyālen,* 'and he spent the night,' instead of *wayyēlek,* 'and he went.' I have followed the former reading in my translation. The two words differ only in their final consonant (the original text only contained consonants), and since the Hebrew characters for *n* and *k* are nearly identical, a copyist could very easily have mistaken the original *n* for a *k*. I have chosen to regard *wayyālen* as the original reading because, in my view, verses 9–11 clearly show that Joshua did not go into the valley that night, but rested in the camp with the people until early morning. But how then can it be said that Joshua spent the night in the valley? If one supposes that verse 13 is referring to the night after the one spoken of in verse 9, it would seem strange that Joshua alone would have gone into the valley that night. Indeed, the word 'valley' in verse 13 is difficult to square with the second half of verse 11. It therefore is easily possible that the received text is not entirely correct here and that we should follow the Syriac translation in reading *'am* ('people') instead of *'ēmeq* ('valley'). For there is only a slight difference in the consonants here. Verse 13*b* would then be a literal repetition of 9*b*. This should not be surprising, for verse 13 merely summarizes the steps Joshua has taken and does not carry the story further. See Note 2 at the end of this commentary"—TRANS.

[58] According to Garstang (*Joshua, Judges,* p. 355), this was the valley of the deep Wadi Muheisin north of Ai. The account was written by an eyewitness.

Here he had the army set up camp on the slopes opposite the city. Most likely the sending of the ambush reported in verse 9 did not take place till the night that followed this march to Ai (see the comments on v. 12 in Note 2 at the end of this commentary). Verse 13 then shows how the main army and the ambush were disposed in relation to each other. The battle formation allowed the two divisions to remain in contact with each other, for they were not on opposite sides of the city. Since they were north of Ai, Joshua and his men could give a signal that would be visible to a lookout posted in the ambush to the west of the city.

There is a discrepancy between the size of the ambush troops in verse 3 (thirty thousand men) and verse 12 (five thousand men), and the attempts that Calvin et al. have made to reconcile these two numbers remain inadequate. Five thousand probably is the correct figure, and the thirty thousand then would be due to a copyist's mistake. Such an error could easily have arisen if the original text followed the Hebrew custom of using letters to represent numbers.[59]

8:14–17 *When the king of Ai saw this, he and all the men of the city hurried out early in the morning to meet Israel in battle at a certain place overlooking the Arabah. But he did not know that an ambush had been set against him behind the city. [15] Joshua and all Israel let themselves be driven back before them, and they fled toward the desert. [16] All the men of Ai were called to pursue them, and they pursued Joshua and were lured away from the city. [17] Not a man remained in Ai or Bethel who did not go after Israel. They left the city open and went in pursuit of Israel.*

The citizens of Ai observed the approach of Israel's army and responded by attacking. The king himself marched with his men to defeat Israel, and they proceeded to a place opposite the Arabah.[60] "All the men" at verse 14 refers only to the men who made this attack. The possibility of danger was discounted, since the men of Ai thought they would be able to retreat into the city if necessary. Joshua thus had the opportunity to carry out his plan. When the first blows were struck, the Israelites made an about-face and allowed themselves to be driven back toward the desert. The king of Ai, already overconfident, resolved

---

[59] The western slope of the hill on which Ai stood undoubtedly did not have enough room to conceal thirty thousand men.

[60] Arabah here probably refers to the plains of Jericho (5:10). By going to a place overlooking those plains, the king hoped to cut off the Israelites' retreat. The men of Ai must have assembled in an area that had been chosen beforehand outside the city gate.

to wipe out the Israelites altogether; and he called for the garrison that had been left in the city and all the able-bodied men to take part in the pursuit. The Israelites feigned terror and turned their retreat into a flight, and the men of Ai were joined in the chase by the citizens of Bethel.[61] The latter must have been stationed as auxiliary troops in Ai before the Israelite ambush had taken its position between the cities. With the departure of these men, Ai was left open and unguarded.

8:18–29 *Then the* LORD *said to Joshua, "Hold out toward Ai the javelin that is in your hand, for into your hand I will deliver the city." So Joshua held out his javelin toward Ai.* [19]*As soon as he did this, the men in the ambush rose quickly from their position and rushed forward. They entered the city and captured it and quickly set it on fire.*

[20]*The men of Ai looked back and saw the smoke of the city rising against the sky, but they had no chance to escape in any direction, for the Israelites who had been fleeing toward the desert had turned back against their pursuers.* [21]*For when Joshua and all Israel saw that the ambush had taken the city and that smoke was going up from the city, they turned around and attacked the men of Ai.* [22]*The men of the ambush also came out of the city against them, so that they were caught in the middle, with Israelites on both sides. Israel cut them down, leaving them neither survivors nor fugitives.* [23]*But they took the king of Ai alive and brought him to Joshua.*

[24]*When Israel had finished killing all the men of Ai in the fields and in the desert where they had chased them, and when every one of them had been put to the sword, all the Israelites returned to Ai and killed those who were in it.* [25]*Twelve thousand men and women fell that day—all the people of Ai.* [26]*For Joshua did not draw back the hand that held out his javelin until he had destroyed all who lived in Ai.* [27]*But Israel did carry off for themselves the livestock and plunder of this city, as the* LORD *had instructed Joshua.*

[28]*So Joshua burned Ai and made it a permanent heap of ruins, a desolate place to this day.* [29]*He hung the king of Ai on a tree and left him there until evening. At sunset, Joshua ordered them to take his body from the tree and throw it down at the entrance of the city gate. And they raised a large pile of rocks over it, which remains to this day.*

The Lord commanded Joshua to signal the troops lying in ambush by raising his javelin in a threatening gesture toward Ai. Israel's general apparently was not with the fleeing army but stood on an elevated place off the field of battle. The signal was perceived by a lookout and made known to the rest of the hidden troops. At once the men in ambush

---

[61]The Septuagint does not mention the men of Bethel, and it is odd that they do not appear in verses 25–26.

burst forth and performed their task flawlessly. The rising columns of smoke proclaimed to the pursuers and the pursued alike that Ai had fallen into the hands of Israel. The roles were reversed; the Israelites halted their flight and began to offer serious resistance. The men of Ai were put on the defensive and forced to flee. But the other Israelite troops advanced to meet them from their own city, and the Aiites found themselves completely surrounded.

All avenues of escape were cut off, and the Aiites fell to the last man before the dreadful sword of Israel. Only the king was kept alive and brought to Joshua. The Israelites then returned to Ai and killed the citizens who had stayed behind, and the city was put to flames and plundered. The fire spoken of in verse 19 had left most of the city untouched, for it was intended only as a signal to the fleeing Israelites. As long as the destruction of Israel's enemies remained unfinished, Joshua continued to hold out his javelin as a symbol of Yahweh's curse on Ai. Finally, however, the task was done, and he drew it back. The city was reduced for all time to a heap of ruins, and the king met his doom after he had been compelled to see his city laid waste. He was hanged on a tree till evening (see Deut. 21:23), probably after he had already been put to death (cf. 10:26). Noordtzij (*Gods Woord*,[2] p. 355), says the execution was to rest the person's abdomen on a pointed stake so that the body was pierced through by its own weight. The king's corpse was finally buried under a heap of rocks.

13. The Public Reading of the Law at Mount Ebal and Mount Gerizim (8:30–35)

8:30–32 *Then Joshua built on Mount Ebal an altar to the* Lord, *the God of Israel,* [31] *as Moses the servant of the* Lord *had commanded the Israelites. He built it according to what is written in the Book of the Law of Moses—an altar of uncut stones, on which no iron tool had been used. On it they offered to the* Lord *burnt offerings and sacrificed fellowship offerings.* [32] *There, in the presence of the Israelites, Joshua copied on stones the law of Moses, which he had written.*[62]

The record of Joshua's military accomplishments is interrupted by a description of the ceremony after the conquest of Ai that was held near

---

[62] The author notes here that "he had written" can refer either to Joshua or to Moses (compare KJV to NIV). He thinks the context indicates that Joshua was the probable subject and thus follows the KJV reading—Trans.

Shechem, on the mountains of Ebal and Gerizim.[63] The text does not explicitly state that the whole nation of Israel accompanied Joshua to this site, but verses 33 and 35 remove all doubt on this score. Because Israel's enemies were overcome with fear, Joshua had the opportunity to march right to the center of Canaan. The Canaanites' resistance had not yet been broken; but it seems that none of their rulers dared confront the Israelite intruders alone, and no alliance had yet been formed (see 9:1). Joshua therefore had the chance to fulfill the mandate that Moses had given the people in Deuteronomy 11:29–30 and 27:2–8. On Mount Ebal he built an altar from the uncut stones found on its slopes (Deut. 27:5–6). A sacrificial feast was then held there containing a meal symbolic of the fellowship between God and His people (Deut. 27:6–7). After this meal, or perhaps while it was being eaten, Joshua had the precepts of the Mosaic law inscribed on stones (not those of the altar) coated with plaster or gypsum, so that the mound of stones would proclaim the Lord's will to the entire land of Canaan. From Ebal, a peak higher than Gerizim, one could survey much of the land. By setting up those tablets of the law, the Israelites signified that God was the Owner of Canaan and that they were seizing it from its pagan inhabitants for Him. The burnt offerings symbolized the people's thankful dedication of their lives, and the fellowship offerings showed that Israel and the Lord were on good terms with each other.

8:33–35 *All Israel, aliens and citizens alike, with their elders, officials and judges, were standing on both sides of the ark of the covenant of the* LORD, *facing those who carried it—the priests, who were Levites. Half of the people stood in front of Mount Gerizim and half of them in front of Mount Ebal, as Moses the servant of the* LORD *had formerly commanded when he gave instructions to bless*[64] *the people of Israel.*

[34]*Afterward, Joshua read all the words of the law—the blessings and the curses—just as it is written in the Book of the Law.* [35]*There was not a word of all that Moses had commanded that Joshua did not read to the whole assembly of Israel, including the women and children, and the aliens who lived among them.*

The ceremony included more than this, however. Israel also had to acknowledge God publicly as her king by formally accepting His law. Joshua, therefore, again following Moses' instructions (Deut. 27:11ff.),

---

[63] See the discussion of 8:30–35 in Note 3 at the end of this commentary.

[64] The NEB has "the blessing should be pronounced first." This translation is possible, but its meaning is unclear.

had the whole law of the Lord recited loudly, probably by priests who had been specially appointed for this task.[65] Part of the Israelites stood on the slope of Mount Ebal and the rest on the slope of Mount Gerizim. The priests and the ark stood between the two groups in the pass or valley where the city of Shechem lay. Deuteronomy 27:11–13 describes in greater detail how the tribes were arranged for this.[66]

The end of verse 33 again evidences that everything was done in accordance with the instructions that Moses had given for blessing the people. In speaking only of blessing, this verse indirectly shows that the Lord's actual intention was to bless His people (cf. Deut. 27:12). The curse was something that would only go into effect if they broke the covenant. Clearly, more than words of blessing were pronounced, however; for verse 34 speaks of both "the blessings and the curses." To avoid all possibility of misunderstanding, verse 35 adds that not a single word was omitted in this public reading. The Hebrew term used indicates that this "reading" was actually a preaching, a public proclamation in the name of the Lord. Everyone had to hear it, for all—aliens and citizens alike—owed obedience to Israel's God.

The covenant that had been made at Mount Sinai was legally ratified in this ceremony. If Israel kept Moses' laws, she was sure to enjoy the Lord's favor in her new homeland. Her foremost duty was to show her thankfulness by faithfully observing God's commandments.

14. The Gibeonites' Deception and Israel's Treaty With Them (9:1–27)

9:1–2 *Now when all the kings west of the Jordan*[67] *heard about these things— those in the hill country, in the western foothills, and along the entire coast of the Great Sea as far as Lebanon (the kings of the Hittites, Amorites, Canaanites, Perizzites, Hivites and Jebusites)— ² they came together to make war against Joshua and Israel.*

Chapter 9 opens with the kings west of the Jordan taking action to form an alliance against Israel, a step prompted by the news that Ai had fallen to Israel and had met the same fate as Jericho (cf. v. 3 and 10:1).

---

[65] The author's translation of verse 34 reads "Joshua had all the words of the law read," while the NIV has "Joshua read. . ."—TRANS.

[66] See J. Ridderbos, *Bible Student's Commentary: Deuteronomy*, p. 251.

[67] Literally, "on the other side of the Jordan." See Note 1 at the end of this commentary.

Joshua 5:1 reveals that these kings at first were overwhelmed with fear. Nevertheless, they did not wish to see themselves crushed without making a serious effort to expel the detested intruders from Canaan. Each king was too weak by himself, for each ruled only over one or a small group of cities. Thus they saw that it was in their interest to cooperate. Verse 2 should not be taken to mean that the armies of these rulers actually combined and marched as one against Israel. Such cooperation could not have been achieved so quickly, for the kings spoken of include those of all Canaan, both north and south. The "western foothills"[68] referred to in verse 1 are equivalent to the Shephelah, a region that includes the coastal plain along the Mediterranean Sea and the lower foothills descending from the highlands. The Lebanon mountain range forms the northern boundary of Canaan. The course that events—or, rather, God's providential control—had taken prevented all Canaan from acting in concert; and Joshua therefore was able to deal separately with the kings of the south (ch. 10) and those of the north (ch. 11).

9:3–8 *However, when the people of Gibeon heard what Joshua had done to Jericho and Ai, ⁴they resorted to a ruse: They went as a delegation whose donkeys were loaded[69] with worn-out sacks and old wineskins, cracked and mended. ⁵The men put worn and patched sandals on their feet and wore old clothes. All the bread of their food supply was dry and moldy. ⁶Then they went to Joshua in the camp at Gilgal and said to him and the men of Israel, "We have come from a distant country; make a treaty with us."*

⁷The men of Israel said to the Hivites, "But perhaps you live near us. How then can we make a treaty with you?"

⁸"We are your servants," they said to Joshua.

But Joshua asked, "Who are you and where do you come from?"

When they learned the fate that had befallen Jericho and Ai, the citizens of Gibeon and its associate cities (see v. 17) did not await the formation of the alliance. Being seized by terror to the core, they considered that their turn could easily be next; for after the ceremony at Ebal and Gerizim, the Israelites had encamped at Gilgal. This was

---

[68]The author translates this as "lowlands" (cf. RSV and JB)—TRANS.

[69]The author's translation here is like that in the NIV margin. He adds the following footnote: "Following several manuscripts and ancient translations, I here read the same word that appears in verse 12 [translated 'provision' in KJV, 'packed' in NIV]. The two words differ only in a single consonant. The form used in the text as we have it does not appear elsewhere and its meaning therefore can only be guessed at"—TRANS.

not the Gilgal near Jericho but another place southwest of Shiloh at the site of modern Jiljulieh.[70] If Joshua were to march south from there, he would soon cover the distance to Gibeon (probably modern el-Jib), a city approximately six miles northwest of Jerusalem. Thus it was natural that the Gibeonites should have sought safety by resorting to a ruse, especially since they knew Israel had been commanded to wipe out all the inhabitants of Canaan (v. 24). The statement in verse 4 that they "on their part"[71] adopted a ruse harks back to Joshua's own trickery at Ai (8:3–8).

A delegation was sent that pretended to have traveled from a distant country, thus giving the Israelites the impression that it was permissible to make a treaty with them. The delegation's dress and the sorry condition of their provisions for their journey were intended to confirm the truth of their words. The tears in their wineskins were not resewn but merely awkwardly mended, as if they had cracked open during the journey. Their clothing and sandals were torn and their bread crumbled and dry as dust. The envoys played their part to perfection. Apparently they were received in a public assembly in the Israelite camp (v. 15), though "men of Israel" (vv. 6, 7, 14) undoubtedly refers primarily to the leaders and tribal heads. The words "we are your servants" (v. 8) were a formal expression of courtesy in the Near East, not a declaration that the Gibeonites had come to submit to Joshua's rule; for their intention was to make a treaty of friendship on an equal footing with Israel. The Israelites' question (v. 7) shows that they had not at all forgotten the Lord's command in Deuteronomy 7:2 and that they were minded to obey it.

---

[70]There was still another Gilgal, but this lay further north in the vicinity of Shechem (cf. Deut. 11:30). The view that there was only one Gilgal is incorrect. Keil has shown that there are sufficient grounds to conclude that Joshua's camp here could no longer have been by the Jordan (*Joshua,*[2] pp. 68ff.; see also Schmidtke, *Die Einwanderung Israëls in Kanaän,* pp. 125f.)

[71]See RSV and NEB, which are close to the author's translation—TRANS.

9:9–15 *They answered: "Your servants have come from a very distant country because of the fame of the LORD your God. For we have heard reports of him: all that he did in Egypt, ¹⁰and all that he did to the two kings of the Amorites east of the Jordan—Sihon king of Heshbon, and Og king of Bashan, who reigned in Ashtaroth. ¹¹And our elders and all those living in our country said to us, 'Take provisions for your journey; go and meet them and say to them, "We are your servants; make a treaty with us."' ¹²This bread of ours was warm when we packed it at home on the day we left to come to you. But now see how dry and moldy it is. ¹³And these wineskins that we filled were new, but see how cracked they are. And our clothes and sandals are worn out by the very long journey."*

¹⁴The men of Israel sampled their provisions but did not inquire of the LORD. ¹⁵Then Joshua made a treaty of peace with them⁷² to let them live, and the leaders of the assembly ratified it by oath.

Joshua sought more information, and the Gibeonites explained why they had come. They were cautious and wily enough to remain silent about the most recent events, since news of these could not yet have reached a distant country. Instead, they spoke only of what had happened in Egypt and the Transjordan.⁷³

Verse 11 gives the impression that Gibeon had no king and was some kind of republic, and verse 17 could imply that it was the leading member in a confederacy of cities. Joshua and the elders actually were already convinced by the time the envoys had finished speaking. Some of them sampled the Gibeonites' bread to confirm what they thought they already knew; and finding the bread indeed dry and stale, they accepted the envoys' whole story as true. In so doing, however, they neglected their one sure means for determining the truth; they failed to seek the Lord's advice. This sin of omission led to a sin of commission as Joshua put away his mistrust, accepted the strangers as friends, and made a formal treaty with them and their city. The treaty, however, contained nothing more than a promise that he would let them live. The elders then ratified the accord by invoking the name of Yahweh.

It is easy to find psychological explanations for Israel's action. The Gibeonites carried out their deception in a masterly way and gave every impression of acting in good faith. Israel also had an understandable

---

⁷²"With them" is literally "for them, in their interest."

⁷³The Gibeonites' cunning can also be seen in that they did not at once call attention to their worn clothing and travel gear but only later in the course of the conversation. To begin by speaking of these things would have aroused suspicion. Such small touches offer internal evidence for the truth of this story, which undoubtedly was related by an eyewitness.

desire to have some friends in the world and not merely enemies. Moreover, there was no absolute prohibition against making treaties (see Deut. 20:10, 15). The Israelites were confronted by an entirely new situation here, however. In their uncertainty about what step to take, they should have remembered that the Lord had promised to enlighten and guide them (cf. Num. 27:21). Here again Israel took a false step that brought trouble because she acted on her own (see in 7:4).

9:16–21 *Three days after they made the treaty with the Gibeonites, the Israelites heard that they were neighbors, living near them.* [17] *So the Israelites set out and on the third day came to their cities: Gibeon, Kephirah, Beeroth and Kiriath Jearim.* [18] *But the Israelites did not attack them, because the leaders of the assembly had sworn an oath to them by the LORD, the God of Israel.*

The whole assembly grumbled against the leaders, [19] *but all the leaders answered, "We have given them our oath by the LORD, the God of Israel, and we cannot touch them now.* [20] *This is what we will do to them: We will let them live, so that wrath will not fall on us for breaking the oath we swore to them."* [21] *They continued, "Let them live, but let them be woodcutters and water carriers for the entire community." So the leaders' promise to them was kept.*

After three days the Gibeonites' deception was unveiled. While the headquarters remained behind in Gilgal (cf. 10:6–7), Joshua at once led a contingent of Israelite soldiers southward in order to demand an account of the Gibeonites.[74] The latter naturally expected the Israelites to come; and they went to meet them at the border of the Gibeonite territory, reminding them of their alliance and that this also applied to the neighboring cities under Gibeon's protection (cf. 10:2). Respecting the oath that had been sworn, Israel's advance troops did not dare to attack and instead turned to the leaders or tribal heads. The people then began to grumble. Nevertheless, the leaders (Joshua seems not to have been present at first and perhaps remained behind in the rear guard) refused to be swayed by this and felt bound by their oath. Once this oath had been sworn and Yahweh's name invoked, the sanctity of that name obliged the Israelites to keep their word. If they did not, the name of the Lord would become an object of contempt among the heathen nations; and His anger would turn against His own people.

---

[74] This interpretation is based on the conclusion that verses 16–17, which both speak of three days, have to be referring to the same interval of time. "On the third day" in verse 17 cannot mean the third day of the march, since the distance from Gilgal to Beeroth, the nearest city, was no more than 9 1/2 miles. This therefore must be the third day after the treaty was made. The meeting with the Gibeonites then must have taken place on the same day that the Israelites marched from Gilgal.

That Scripture does not condemn the leaders shows that they acted rightly, and even stronger proof for this appears when their later disregard for the oath brought judgment on the people (2 Sam. 21). The leaders of Israel thus decided that the Gibeonites might remain alive (v. 20). To punish them, however, and to keep them from mingling with the Israelites and leading them astray, the Gibeonites were compelled to accept the humiliating tasks of woodcutters and water carriers.

9:22-27 *Then Joshua summoned the Gibeonites and said, "Why did you deceive us by saying, 'We live a long way from you,' while actually you live near us? 23 You are now under a curse: You will never cease to serve as woodcutters and water carriers for the house of my God."*

24 They answered Joshua, "Your servants were clearly told how the LORD your God had commanded his servant Moses to give you the whole land and to wipe out all its inhabitants from before you. So we feared for our lives because of you, and that is why we did this. 25 We are now in your hands. Do to us whatever seems good and right to you."

26 So Joshua saved them from the Israelites, and they did not kill them. 27 That day he made the Gibeonites woodcutters and water carriers for the community and for the altar of the LORD at the place the LORD would choose. And that is what they are to this day.

Joshua confirmed the leaders' decision and stated it in greater detail. He summoned the Gibeonites (probably the same men who had come to the camp at Gilgal) to reproach them for their deceit and pronounce a curse on them. Henceforth they would always be the Israelites' slaves and would have to perform the most menial tasks at the house of Israel's God. The ban was thus still imposed on the Gibeonites to a certain extent. The latter gave an explanation for their action and, thankful that they had escaped with their lives, submitted themselves fully to Joshua. Under his protection they would be safe, and the people of Israel doubtless accepted the arrangement that Joshua and the leaders had made. Since it had not yet been decided where the Lord would establish His house, verse 27 does not give the name of the place where the Gibeonites would serve.

Joshua 9 sounds a cautionary note for the people of God. Because its enemies are cunning, the church must always be vigilant. If it does not realize its deep dependence on the Lord at all times and look to Him alone for guidance, it will become trapped unawares in a perilous alliance with the world.

15. Gibeon's Appeal to Joshua for Help
(10:1-6)

Joshua 10:1-6 links chapter 9 to the main event in chapter 10, namely, the triumph at Gibeon. Obviously, this story was put together with care, for it provides an excellent view of the whole course of Israel's march to victory. The passage also sheds light on the events of chapter 9. God allowed Israel to make the alliance with Gibeon because this made it possible for Joshua to destroy the might of all the kings from the south with a single blow. It was inevitable that this treaty would cause the Gibeonites' former friends to turn against them, and it also meant that Joshua would feel obliged to protect them. He thus came to Gibeon, not as an invader, but as one challenged to face the allied kings in battle.

10:1-4 Now Adoni-Zedek king of Jerusalem heard that Joshua had taken Ai and totally destroyed it, doing to Ai and its king as he had done to Jericho and its king,[75] and that the people of Gibeon had made a treaty of peace with Israel and were living near them. ² He and his people were very much alarmed at this, because Gibeon was an important city, like one of the royal cities; it was larger than Ai, and all its men were good fighters. ³ So Adoni-Zedek king of Jerusalem appealed to Hoham king of Hebron, Piram king of Jarmuth, Japhia king of Lachish and Debir king of Eglon. ⁴ "Come up and help me attack Gibeon," he said, "because it has made peace with Joshua and the Israelites."

Ai's utter destruction and the news that the Gibeonites had made a treaty with Israel and in fact had been adopted by that nation caused Adoni-Zedek and his allies to become greatly alarmed. No one had expected this from Gibeon, an important city that could boast greater accomplishments than Ai and had an army of valiant warriors. The Gibeonites' move was regarded as an act of defection that deserved to be punished. The king of Jerusalem, which at that time belonged to the Jebusites, appealed for help to the like-minded kings of Hebron, Jarmuth, Lachish, and Eglon. There probably had been some kind of talks before this (see 9:1-2), but the step taken by the Gibeonites hastened the accord and caused it to be restricted to the southern kings. Action had to be taken at once. If Gibeon were punished, Joshua's ambitions would be thwarted.

---

⁷⁵The author's translation here corresponds to the KJV and NEB. Like the NEB, he puts this sentence in parentheses and says it is not a redundancy but a literal report of the rumor that had spread about Joshua—TRANS.

10:5–6 *Then the five kings of the Amorites—the kings of Jerusalem, Hebron, Jarmuth, Lachish and Eglon—joined forces. They moved up with all their troops and took up positions against Gibeon and attacked it.*

⁶The Gibeonites then sent word to Joshua in the camp at Gilgal: "Do not abandon your servants. Come up to us quickly and save us! Help us, because all the Amorite kings from the hill country have joined forces against us."

The five kings of the south moved against Gibeon. The name Amorites here refers to the native population of Canaan in general. The men of Gibeon rushed a message to Joshua that sounded almost like an SOS. They reminded him of their treaty and urgently asked him to send help at once. The hostile cities lay in the highlands south and southwest of Jerusalem, but except for Gibeon their location is uncertain. Joshua was still encamped at Gilgal (see in 9:6), where he waited for the Lord to make clear what he should do next.

16. The Sun and Moon at the Battle at Gibeon (10:7–27)

10:7–11 *So Joshua marched up from Gilgal with his entire army, including all the best fighting men. ⁸The Lord said to Joshua, "Do not be afraid of them; I have given them into your hand. Not one of them will be able to withstand you."*

⁹After an all-night march from Gilgal, Joshua took them by surprise. ¹⁰The Lord threw them into confusion before Israel, who defeated them in a great victory at Gibeon. Israel pursued them along the road going up to Beth Horon and cut them down all the way to Azekah and Makkedah. ¹¹As they fled before Israel on the road down from Beth Horon to Azekah, the Lord hurled large hailstones down on them from the sky, and more of them died from the hailstones than were killed by the swords of the Israelites.

Joshua responded to Gibeon's plea without delay. Verse 8 shows that he must have turned to the Lord for advice. Joshua received an encouraging answer that in effect applied the promise of 1:5 to his current situation. Although he was thus assured of victory from the outset, Joshua still did not become careless. He called the whole army to battle. The phrase "best fighting men" (v. 7) indicates that there was a distinction between the soldiers who guarded the camp and the attack troops, the fighting men proper used in military campaigns. All the latter set out for Gibeon.

Joshua moved with dispatch and made an all-night march (the distance from Gilgal to Gibeon must have been about twelve and a half miles). Early that morning the enemy, thinking that the Israelites were still some distance away, was taken by surprise. The Lord struck such fear into the enemy army that they could offer no organized resistance and thus suffered heavy losses.[76] They fled toward the northwest, hoping to reach the fortified cities of their alliance (v. 19) by way of the pass at Beth Horon (cf. 1 Sam. 13:18).[77] At Beth Horon the flight turned southward, for Azekah and Makkedah were located southwest of Jerusalem in the lower, western portion of the highlands of Judah (cf. 15:41; 1 Sam. 17:1). Before they reached these cities, however, many of the enemy had fallen to the Israelites; and still more were dashed by the large hailstones that the Lord flung down on His enemies.

10:12–15 *On the day the Lord gave the Amorites over to Israel, Joshua said to the Lord in the presence of Israel:*
>   *"O sun, stand still over Gibeon,*
>   *O moon, over the Valley of Aijalon."*
> [13] *So the sun stood still,*
>   *and the moon stopped,*
>   *till the nation avenged itself on its enemies,*

as it is written in the Book of Jashar.
  The sun stopped in the middle of the sky and delayed going down about a full day. [14] *There has never been a day like it before or since, a day when the Lord listened to a man. Surely the Lord was fighting for Israel!*
   [15] *Then Joshua returned with all Israel to the camp at Gilgal.*[78]

---

[76] Some think that the enemy's confusion was created by a violent thunderstorm (see v. 11). The words "before Israel" in verse 10, however, make it more likely that the sudden arrival of the dreaded Israelites caused them to panic.

[77] This was Upper Beth Horon, five miles northwest of Gibeon, not the Lower Beth Horon (see 16:3, 5) that lay more to the west.

[78] In my view there are good reasons to doubt whether the text as we have it is correct at this point. [Note: the author thus enclosed verse 15 in parentheses—Trans.] Significantly verse 15 does not appear at all in the Septuagint. The Septuagint of course could be in error, but it is possible that it followed a Hebrew text that was missing this verse and that its reading is the original one. No certain conclusion can be reached here, but the latter view is supported by the fact that verse 15 seems out of context in the story. It is unthinkable that Joshua and the Israelites returned to Gilgal at this point in the battle. Some (e.g., Keil) have sought to explain this incongruity by supposing that verse 15 is still part of the quotation from the Book of Jashar; however, this quotation clearly ends in verse 13. Additionally, nothing whatsoever points to such a close connection between verse 15 and the preceding material. The verse, which stands entirely by itself, indicates, perhaps, that the author got ahead of the story here and anticipated the end of the campaign (see v. 43). But this makes little sense, because verse 15 does not even

Verses 10–11 have already shown that the Lord was Israel's partner in battle, but this special divine aid stands out even more strikingly in what happened next. This event formed a high point of unique significance in Israel's campaign against the Canaanites, and it therefore is described in words that have some measure of solemnity. The Israelites' pursuit was in full swing, and Joshua's zeal for battle was ablaze. Fatigue meant nothing to him and his men, for this was a great day for the Lord and Israel. But if their fleeing enemies were to be totally destroyed on this day before nightfall cut short the battle, a miracle would be necessary. And Joshua's faith was indeed great enough to covet such a divine miracle, even to perform one himself by God's power. Although his words were not addressed to God, it is clear from verse 12 that Joshua had a prayer in his heart. He was so certain of being heard, however, that he directly commanded the sun and moon to stand still. This was done "in the presence of Israel," literally, "before the eyes of Israel." One might have expected "in the hearing of Israel," but the author doubtless meant to say that everyone could see Joshua at this remarkable moment.

The people witnessed Joshua's prayer and act of faith with both their eyes and their ears. All Israel saw him standing on the hill at Beth Horon with his hand extended in a commanding gesture toward the celestial bodies. The whole nation also perceived that what Joshua wanted literally came to pass. At this stupendous moment, a trace of the majesty of the heavenly Commander (5:14) rested on Joshua; and Joshua found enough strength in Him to make the host of heaven do his bidding. There is more than one reason to think that Joshua did this at Beth Horon. First, the road began to descend here, and this made it easier for the enemy to flee and increased their chance of escape. Furthermore, Beth Horon was situated between Gibeon and Aijalon and slightly to the north of both. If Joshua faced toward the south from there, he could have beheld the sun to the southeast above Gibeon and the moon to the southwest above the Valley of Aijalon.[79]

---

hint in the outcome of the war (see v. 42). It is therefore better to assume that verse 16 originally came right after verse 14.

It is not hard to explain how the original text could have been altered to its present form. Verses 15 and 43 are identical, and the end of verse 42 repeats that of verse 14 almost verbatim. Possibly when a copyist was checking his work, he thought verse 43 had been omitted and mistakenly inserted it after verse 14. We should remember that in ancient times the verses were neither separated nor numbered.

[79] According to De Groot, Aijalon is equivalent to modern Yalo and lay about a three hours' journey west of Gibeon.

It must have still been morning when Joshua spoke his famous words. For although verse 13 says that "the sun stopped in the middle of the sky," we need not conclude that this was exactly at noon. Joshua was of course mainly interested in the sunlight; but since his aim was in effect to make time stand still, it is easy to imagine why he would have addressed both heavenly orbs visible to him (cf. Ps. 121:6). His exclamation has the form of a Hebrew poetic verse containing two parallel sections. It was written down word for word in the Book of Jashar, and from this book another verse (the first three lines of v. 13) is quoted to show that Joshua's wish was granted.[80] The Book of Jashar, mentioned elsewhere only in 2 Samuel 1:18, apparently was a cumulative collection of songs about the great events in Israel's history. The quotation was included to give the reader a more profound impression of this astounding event, which one of Joshua's contemporaries was moved to celebrate in song. The word "Jashar" is the Hebrew adjective "upright," and the title thus means "Book of the true, faithful Israelite." Or perhaps "upright" refers to the people of God as a whole.

In verses 13a–14 the author says more about the event that inspired this quotation. The sun stood in its place and delayed its setting for approximately one whole day. This does not mean a full solar day but rather a daylight period of around twelve hours. The author describes the event as a miracle that happened objectively, not something that appeared only in the Israelites' imaginations. Therefore, he adds meaningfully in verse 14 that this day, twice as long as a normal day, was absolutely unique in history, especially since the miracle was called forth by a mere man. Nothing can be found to equal either Joshua's display of faith or the response to his prayer. Only in Jesus Himself do we really meet a similar instance of control over the forces of Creation (Mark 4:39), though He says believers are granted the power to do this as well (Matt. 17:20; Luke 17:6). The miracle and the account of it in these verses are dealt with further in Note 4 at the end of this commentary.

Both friend and foe alike knew beyond a shadow of a doubt that the Lord, the God of the heavens, was fighting for Israel. Because of His

---

[80] Hence only part of verse 12 and the first half of verse 13 can be regarded as a quotation. The final sentence of verse 13 does not fit with the quotation at all but gives every impression of being a further description of the miracle related in verse 13a that was added by the author of the Book of Joshua. See Note 4 at the end of this commentary.

miraculous assistance, the Israelites were able to pursue their fleeing enemies many miles farther; and, but for a few insignificant remnants (see v. 20), they succeeded in destroying all the military power of southern Canaan. For verse 15 see footnote 77.

10:16–21 *Now the five kings had fled and hidden in the cave at Makkedah.* [17] *When Joshua was told that the five kings had been found hiding in the cave at Makkedah,* [18] *he said, "Roll large rocks up to the mouth of the cave, and post some men there to guard it.* [19] *But don't stop! Pursue your enemies, attack them from the rear and don't let them reach their cities, for the LORD your God has given them into your hand."*

[20] *So Joshua and the Israelites destroyed them completely—almost to a man—but the few who were left reached their fortified cities.* [21] *The whole army then returned safely to Joshua in the camp at Makkedah, and no one uttered a word against the Israelites.*

In the course of the general stampede, the five kings managed to hide in a cave in the vicinity of Makkedah; but they were discovered and reported to Joshua. Unwilling to delay the pursuit, he had the cave sealed off and guarded and sent his men onward after their enemies, who were scattering into the plain. Not many were left, but those who were had to be slain before they could reach their cities. Since the Lord had handed His enemies over to Israel and deliberately lengthened the daylight hours, it would have been an act of sinful neglect to abandon the pursuit when it was only half finished. Joshua himself stopped at Makkedah, conquered the city (v. 28), and set up camp (v. 21), apparently intending to stay there the night. Makkedah and Azekah presumably were among the fortress cities whose walls the remnants of the enemy army took refuge in. Although the day had been difficult, the Israelites had won a total victory. After marching through the night (v. 9), they had fought through a day that was doubly long; but the Lord had given them extraordinary strength. Now they returned to their camp safe and sound, and no one in the area lay in wait for them or even dared to say a word against them. Evening must have finally been drawing near, for no doubt the sun resumed its normal course as the Israelites were leaving the field of battle.[81]

---

[81] It is clear from the text that the five kings were executed on the same day, but we need not conclude from verse 26 that this happened long before evening.

10:22–27 *Joshua said, "Open the mouth of the cave and bring those five kings out to me." ²³So they brought the five kings out of the cave—the kings of Jerusalem, Hebron, Jarmuth, Lachish and Eglon. ²⁴When they had brought these kings to Joshua, he summoned all the men of Israel and said to the army commanders who had come with him, "Come here and put your feet on the necks of these kings." So they came forward and placed their feet on their necks.*

²⁵Joshua said to them, "Do not be afraid; do not be discouraged. Be strong and courageous. This is what the LORD will do to all the enemies you are going to fight." ²⁶Then Joshua struck and killed the kings and hung them on five trees, and they were left hanging on the trees until evening.

²⁷At sunset Joshua gave the order and they took them down from the trees and threw them into the cave where they had been hiding. At the mouth of the cave they placed large rocks, which are there to this day.

Joshua had the five kings brought out from their hiding place. He then commanded his chief officers to put their feet on the necks of the kings to symbolize their total helplessness and to encourage the whole Israelite army (v. 24) for the battle that awaited them. His words in verse 25 show that this was indeed his intention and that the Israelites were not indulging in a base mockery of their vanquished foes. The five kings then met the same fate as the king of Ai, and their hiding place was turned into their grave.

Joshua's action here can be regarded as a prophetic foreshadowing of Christ's total victory, when all His enemies will be made a footstool for His feet (Ps. 110:1; 1 Cor. 15:25; Heb. 10:13).[82]

17. The Conquest of Southern Canaan (10:28–43)

10:28–33 *That day Joshua took Makkedah. He put the city and its king to the sword and totally destroyed[83] everyone in it. He left no survivors. And he did to the king of Makkedah as he had done to the king of Jericho.*

²⁹Then Joshua and all Israel with him moved on from Makkedah to Libnah and attacked it. ³⁰The LORD also gave that city and its king into Israel's hand. The city and everyone in it Joshua put to the sword. He left no survivors there. And he did to its king as he had done to the king of Jericho.

---

[82] See A. Roorda, *Josua, De Held Gods*, p. 148. See also Note 6 at the end of this commentary.

[83] The author added "the city itself and" here. He included the following note: "The Hebrew text has *'ôtām*, 'them,' here (cf. KJV). Following several manuscripts we should read *'ôtâ(h)*, 'her,' i.e., the city itself"—TRANS.

³¹ Then Joshua and all Israel with him moved on from Libnah to Lachish; he took up positions against it and attacked it. ³² The LORD handed Lachish over to Israel, and Joshua took it on the second day. The city and everyone in it he put to the sword, just as he had done to Libnah. ³³ Meanwhile, Horam king of Gezer had come up to help Lachish, but Joshua defeated him and his army—until no survivors were left.

Joshua took advantage of his defeat of the army of the allied kings and assumed control of the southern part of Canaan, the later territory of the tribe of Judah. The march of Israel's army was a march to victory. On the same day that the five kings were executed, he conquered Makkedah, a city that probably lay close to Azekah, though no evidence of it has yet been unearthed. From there he went to Libnah and then turned south to Lachish, overpowering these two cities as well. All the inhabitants were slain, and the kings of Makkedah and Libnah met the same fate as the king of Jericho (see footnote 37, p. 72; the king of Lachish had already been put to death, vv. 26–27). The Israelites presumably were permitted to plunder the cattle and other possessions, for these cities would not have been subjected to a severer form of the ban than Ai had been (8:2; cf. 11:14).

Verse 32 states that Lachish fell on the second day. The siege thus did not last long but still was longer than with some of the other cities (vv. 28, 35). The reason may have been that King Horam of Gezer arrived with his army during the siege (v. 33) and Joshua had to reckon with him first. Horam, however, also could have come too late, for Gezer lay far north of Lachish, between Ekron and Beth Horon. Because of this we do not read that Joshua captured the city of Gezer. He rather remained in the south. Although the narrative almost has the form of a chronicle, it does not fail to note that credit for the victories belonged to the Lord.

10:34–39 *Then Joshua and all Israel with him moved on from Lachish to Eglon; they took up positions against it and attacked it. ³⁵ They captured it that same day and put it to the sword and totally destroyed everyone in it, just as they had done to Lachish.*

³⁶ Then Joshua and all Israel with him went up from Eglon to Hebron and attacked it. ³⁷ They took the city and put it to the sword, together with its king, its villages and everyone in it. They left no survivors. Just as at Eglon, they totally destroyed it and everyone in it.

³⁸ Then Joshua and all Israel with him turned around and attacked Debir. ³⁹ They took the city, its king and its villages, and put them to the sword.

*Everyone in it they totally destroyed. They left no survivors. They did to Debir
and its king as they had done to Libnah and its king and to Hebron.*

From Lachish, Joshua moved against the neighboring city of Eglon
and took it that same day. Next in line was Hebron, an ancient city in
the center of the hill country that lay far east of Eglon. One city after
another was forced to give way to Joshua and Israel; and when the
villages belonging to Hebron had been subdued, Joshua turned south
again to Debir. One and the same fate befell each of these cities. The
king of Hebron mentioned in verse 37 must have been the successor of
Hoham, the king slain at Makkedah (v. 26). It is obvious that this
whole campaign must have taken several months. With each city, it is
first stated that Israel "put it to the sword" and then that they "totally
destroyed" everyone in it (vv. 28, 35, 37, 39). Possibly the first
expression refers to the slaying of the army and the second to the
extermination of the nonmilitary population.

10:40–43 *So Joshua subdued the whole region, including the hill country, the
Negev, the western foothills and the mountain slopes, together with all their
kings. He left no survivors. He totally destroyed all who breathed, just as the
LORD, the God of Israel, had commanded.* ⁴¹ *Joshua subdued them from Kadesh
Barnea to Gaza and from the whole region of Goshen to Gibeon.* ⁴² *All these
kings and their lands Joshua conquered in one campaign, because the LORD,
the God of Israel, fought for Israel.*

⁴³ *Then Joshua returned with all Israel to the camp at Gilgal.*

These verses summarize the extent and the outcome of Israel's
whole campaign in southern Canaan. The "mountain slopes" (v. 40)
are the hilly region between the highlands or "hill country" to the east
and the lowlands to the west.[84] The Negev is the southern part of
Canaan; and farther south still lay Kadesh Barnea (v. 41), a place
where the Israelites set up camp on two different occasions during their
desert wanderings (Num. 13:26; 20:1). The extreme southern boundary
of the conquered territory is described as running "from Kadesh
Barnea to Gaza" (a city in southwest Canaan). The eastern boundary is
defined by the region of Goshen, a city in the southern hill country
(15:51), and Gibeon, the place where the battle had begun (v. 10).
Aided by God's indispensable help (v. 42), Joshua succeeded in
subjecting this whole territory to Israel, though a few cities (e.g.,

---

[84] The author's translation of verse 40 corresponds to the RSV, where "western
foothills" (NIV) is translated as "lowland" — TRANS.

Jarmuth and Jerusalem) and regions (see 13:2–3) did remain where the conquest later had to be pushed through to completion. Later statements (15:14–15, 63) indicate that not all the inhabitants of the captured cities were put to death. Nevertheless, they were not spared deliberately. The Israelites killed everyone they encountered (v. 40), but many still could have hidden in the hill country or in the desert that later belonged to Judah.

We are explicitly told that the Lord Himself commanded the total destruction of Israel's enemies. Calvin remarked that because it was God's own design that the swords of His people should slay the Amorites, Joshua had no choice but to obey His command. See my remarks in section 5 of the Introduction on the extermination of the Canaanites. After having seized control of all this territory "in one campaign," and thus without a single setback, Joshua and his army returned to their camp at Gilgal in the center of Canaan.

18. The Battle at Merom and the Conquest of Northern Canaan
(11:1–15)

11:1–5 *When Jabin king of Hazor heard of this, he sent word to Jobab king of Madon, to the kings of Shimron and Acshaph, ²and to the northern kings who were in the mountains, in the Arabah south of Kinnereth, in the western foothills and in Naphoth Dor on the west; ³to the Canaanites in the east and west; to the Amorites, Hittites, Perizzites and Jebusites in the hill country; and to the Hivites below Hermon in the region of Mizpah. ⁴They came out with all their troops and a large number of horses and chariots—a huge army, as numerous as the sand on the seashore. ⁵All these kings joined forces and made camp together at the Waters of Merom, to fight against Israel.*

The opening of chapter 11 does not mean that Israel did not have even a moment's respite after her successful campaign in chapter 10, but that the news of Joshua's total victory in the south led to the formation of a strong alliance in the north. The initiative was taken by the king of Hazor, a city that probably lay southwest of Lake Huleh in the later territory of Naphtali (cf. 19:36) and that had hegemony over the northern kingdoms (see v. 10). The location of the cities in verse 1 is not known precisely, but they lay in or near Galilee (cf. 19:25, which mentions Acshaph). The mountains spoken of in verse 2 are the Galilean highlands. Kinnereth is a city or district near Lake Gennesaret, and the Arabah here is equivalent to the Jordan Valley.

The western foothills are the northern extension of those spoken of in 9:1 and 10:40 and embrace the lower coastal region north of Mount Carmel. Naphoth Dor lay to the south of this. Mizpah ("watchtower," "lookout"), which was the name for several elevated points in Canaan (in Gilead, Judg. 10:17; in Benjamin, Judg. 20:1), here refers to one of the northernmost cities lying near Mount Hermon. The Jebusites (v. 3) also dwelt in the north, but it is not known where. A colossal and powerful army, equipped with numerous horses and chariots, thus marched together against Israel somewhere near the Waters of Merom. The latter is usually taken to be Lake Huleh, about seven miles north of the Sea of Galilee. This remains uncertain, but there are no clear alternate possibilities; and verse 8 seems to point to this area as the location of Merom.

11:6–9 *The LORD said to Joshua, "Do not be afraid of them, because by this time tomorrow I will hand all of them over to Israel, slain. You are to hamstring their horses and burn their chariots."*

7 So Joshua and his whole army came against them suddenly at the Waters of Merom and attacked them, 8 and the LORD gave them into the hand of Israel. They defeated them and pursued them all the way to Greater Sidon, to Misrephoth Maim, and to the Valley of Mizpah on the east, until no survivors were left. 9 Joshua did to them as the LORD had directed: He hamstrung their horses and burned their chariots.

Joshua received special encouragement from the Lord and was told that on the next day, by God's help, the whole enemy army would lie slain on the field before Israel.[85] God also commanded him to hamstring their horses (i.e., to cripple them by cutting the tendons of their hind legs) and to burn their chariots. Thus the Israelites would not be tempted to put their faith in the methods of war used by the heathen but would win their battles by God's power, finding their strength in Him alone. Here again, as in 10:9, Joshua took the enemy unawares; and they were soon put to flight. The Israelites set off in hot pursuit, mainly toward the north (Sidon) and the west (Misrephoth Maim, which lay on the Mediterranean Sea north of Acco), but also in part toward the east into the valley at the base of Mount Hermon. The

---

[85] We are not told where Joshua was at this moment. Since, however, he was at most a single day's march from Merom (v. 6), it is likely that Israel had already moved north and stood in the Valley of Jezreel. This is the view of Garstang (*Joshua, Judges,* p. 196), who thinks that Joshua surprised the Canaanites when they were unprepared, so that they could not make use of their chariots.

whole enemy army was decimated; and, as had happened in the south, the might of northern Canaan was thus destroyed in a single battle. Joshua once again carried out God's commands with scrupulous obedience.

11:10–15 *At that time Joshua turned back and captured Hazor and put its king to the sword. (Hazor had been the head of all these kingdoms.) ¹¹Everyone in it they put to the sword. They totally destroyed them, not sparing anything that breathed, and he burned up Hazor itself.*

¹²Joshua took all these royal cities and their kings and put them to the sword. He totally destroyed them, as Moses the servant of the LORD had commanded. ¹³Yet Israel did not burn any of the cities built on their mounds— except Hazor, which Joshua burned. ¹⁴The Israelites carried off for themselves all the plunder and livestock of these cities, but all the people they put to the sword until they completely destroyed them, not sparing anyone that breathed. ¹⁵As the LORD commanded his servant Moses, so Moses commanded Joshua, and Joshua did it; he left nothing undone of all that the LORD commanded Moses.

As in the south, Joshua turned this victory to account by taking concrete control of the land. No sooner had Israel returned from the pursuit than he seized the city of Hazor and put to death its king who had fled there. The heart of the resistance had fallen, and the other cities were taken one by one. Since Joshua's victorious northern campaign no doubt had much in common with that in the south (10:28–42), we are given only a brief description of it. All the enemy's might succumbed to Israel, and everything was placed under the ban. Because Hazor had held the leading position among the northern cities, it received a special exemplary punishment. Verse 13 gives the impression that it was standard for cities in this region to be built on hills. In imposing such a stern judgment on the population of all those cities, Joshua followed as meticulously as possible the orders that he had received from Moses, and that Moses had heard directly from the Lord Himself. His actions in verses 11–12 and 14 were done in obedience to the law concerning the ban (Deut. 20:16–18).[86]

---

[86] See NIV margin in verse 11 and footnote 35, p. 73—TRANS.

19. The End of the Conquest of Canaan
(11:16–23)

11:16–20 *So Joshua took this entire land: the hill country, all the Negev, the whole region of Goshen, the western foothills, the Arabah⁸⁷ and the mountains of Israel with their foothills, ¹⁷from Mount Halak, which rises toward Seir, to Baal Gad in the Valley of Lebanon below Mount Hermon. He captured all their kings and struck them down, putting them to death. ¹⁸Joshua waged war against all these kings for a long time. ¹⁹Except for the Hivites living in Gibeon, not one city made a treaty of peace with the Israelites, who took them all in battle. ²⁰For it was the LORD himself who hardened their hearts to wage war against Israel, so that he might destroy them totally, exterminating them without mercy, as the LORD had commanded Moses.*

These verses are similar to the close of chapter 10, but they are broader in reference. They embrace the conquest of Canaan as a whole and give a summary description of Joshua's work. Verse 16 begins with the regions that he conquered in his southern campaign (see also 10:40–41). Then, in speaking of the mountains of Israel and their foothills, it turns to the central and northern parts of the land (see v. 2). Verse 17 gives the southern and northern boundaries of the territory that Joshua took over. Mount Halak⁸⁸ is a ridge of bare, pale crags south of the Dead Sea stretching eastward toward Seir, the chief mountain range of Edom. Baal Gad probably lay in the valley between the Lebanon range and Mount Hermon. Joshua thus took over all Palestine west of the Jordan, defeating and slaying the kings of that whole region in a war that lasted about seven years (see section 6 of the Introduction). The author was not concerned to provide a complete account of this struggle. In chapters 6–10 he picked out only the most important moments and events. Verse 19 brings out the fact that in this war there was no thought of any kind of rapprochement or truce. Except for Gibeon, all the cities took an implacably hostile attitude toward Israel, which indeed was the Lord's own design.

The hour of doom had struck for Canaan's inhabitants; and in order to bring this about, the Lord saw to it that they made war against Israel and then were crushed by the latter. Ultimately, this therefore was the Lord's work. He Himself handed the Canaanites over to destruction. Their sole thought was not to submit to Israel but to oppose these new invaders to the very end. So the Lord spared His people the temptation

---

⁸⁷Arabah here refers to the western half of the Jordan Valley; see under 3:16.
⁸⁸The author translated this as "the bare mountains" (cf. NEB)—TRANS.

of making peace with the nations that He had doomed to death. Israel was permitted to show them no mercy, and the Lord saw to it that they did not even have the opportunity to do this. Their enemies' hatred thus became Israel's salvation.

11:21-23 *At that time Joshua went and destroyed the Anakites from the hill country: from Hebron, Debir and Anab, from all the hill country of Judah, and from all the hill country of Israel. Joshua totally destroyed them and their towns. *22* No Anakites were left in Israelite territory; only in Gaza, Gath and Ashdod did any survive. *23* So Joshua took the entire land, just as the LORD had directed Moses, and he gave it as an inheritance to Israel according to their tribal divisions.*

Then the land had rest from war.

The destruction and expulsion of the Anakites is no doubt mentioned separately because it was precisely that nation of giants that had frightened ten of the twelve spies Moses had sent into the land (Num. 13:28, 32-33). If Joshua, one of the two who had brought a good report, himself was at least indirectly involved in the writing of this book (see Introduction, section 3), it would be even easier to understand why this nation was singled out. The destruction of the Anakites would show clearly that they were not invincible if only the Israelites trusted in God.

After this there were no Anakites left in the land where Israel settled, though 15:14 seems to indicate that a group of them later came back (see Note 5 after this commentary). They had formerly resided mainly in Hebron and the surrounding area (the hill country of Judah), but some lived also in central and northern Canaan (the mountains of Israel). Anab lay about fourteen and a half miles southwest of Hebron.

Verse 23 states that the conquest of the land had been accomplished and that Joshua thus could turn to its division, the subject of the second part of the book. It has rightly been observed[89] that not all the Canaanites had been destroyed and that the tribes still had very much work to do. This did not alter the fact, however, that control of the land had passed into Israel's hands and that the remnants of the native population thus had the status of fugitives and outlaws. Indeed, God had told Moses beforehand that Israel would take over Canaan gradually (Exod. 23:29-30).

---

[89] Keil, *Joshua,*[2] pp. 95f. See also the Introduction, section 4.

20. Summary of the Defeated Kings
(12:1–24)

12:1–6 *These are the kings of the land whom the Israelites had defeated and whose territory they took over east of the Jordan, from the Arnon Gorge to Mount Hermon, including all the eastern side of the Arabah:*[90]

² *Sihon king of the Amorites,*
who reigned in Heshbon. He ruled from Aroer on the rim of the Arnon Gorge—from the middle of the gorge—to the Jabbok River, which is the border of the Ammonites. This included half of Gilead. ³ He also ruled over the eastern Arabah from the Sea of Kinnereth to the Sea of the Arabah (the Salt Sea),[91] *to Beth Jeshimoth, and then southward below the slopes of Pisgah.*

⁴ *And the territory of Og king of Bashan,*
one of the last of the Rephaites, who reigned in Ashtaroth and Edrei. ⁵ He ruled over Mount Hermon, Salecah, all of Bashan to the border of the people of Geshur and Maacah, and half of Gilead to the border of Sihon king of Heshbon.

⁶ *Moses, the servant of the* LORD, *and the Israelites conquered them. And Moses the servant of the* LORD *gave their land*[92] *to the Reubenites, the Gadites and the half-tribe of Manasseh to be their possession.*

Chapter 12, which forms an appendix to the first eleven chapters of Joshua, does not carry the story further, but merely supplements it by providing a review of Israel's conquests and a complete list of the defeated kings. The first part of the chapter (vv. 1-6) looks back on the conquest of the territory east of the Jordan and the Dead Sea. This of course is not found in chapters 1-11, for the Israelites had already taken possession of the Transjordan under Moses. Nevertheless, it is recalled here because the conquest of the whole land was one single work, begun by the Lord and carried out in His grace. Moses, the Lord's servant, made the first steps; and after Moses' death, Joshua took over the task and finished it.

Verse 1 outlines the territory that was conquered first, the eastern half of Canaan. This was bounded on the south by the Arnon Gorge and on the north by Mount Hermon, and it included the section of the

---

[90] See the footnote in 11:16. Since the Jordan flows southward, the Arabah or Jordan Valley is divided into an eastern and a western half.

[91] The Arabah is the Jordan Valley; the Sea of the Arabah or Salt Sea is the Dead Sea. Cf. 3:16.

[92] The Hebrew text merely has "it" here. What is meant is the territory of Sihon and Og.

110

Arabah or Jordan Valley lying east of the river. King Sihon controlled the southern and western parts of this vast area, while the north and east belonged to Og. The Jabbok River, i.e., its upper course, marked the eastern border of Sihon's kingdom; and in the west it stretched the length of the Jordan from the Dead Sea to the Sea of Gennersaret. In the opening of verse 4 we should have expected to read just "Og" instead of "the territory of Og," but the captured territory was more important to the author than the slain kings. King Og had two royal residences, and his kingdom was adjacent to that of Sihon. Numbers 21:21–35 recounts the defeat of these kings, and the allotment of their land to the tribes mentioned in verse 6 is found in Numbers 32.

12:7–24 *These are the kings of the land that Joshua and the Israelites conquered on the west side of the Jordan, from Baal Gad in the Valley of Lebanon to Mount Halak, which rises toward Seir (their lands Joshua gave as an inheritance to the tribes of Israel according to their tribal divisions— ⁸the hill country, the western foothills, the Arabah, the mountain slopes, the desert and the Negev—the lands of the Hittites, Amorites, Canaanites, Perizzites, Hivites and Jebusites):*

⁹*the king of Jericho*	*one*
the king of Ai (near Bethel)	*one*
¹⁰*the king of Jerusalem*	*one*
the king of Hebron	*one*
¹¹*the king of Jarmuth*	*one*
the king of Lachish	*one*
¹²*the king of Eglon*	*one*
the king of Gezer	*one*
¹³*the king of Debir*	*one*
the king of Geder	*one*
¹⁴*the king of Hormah*	*one*
the king of Arad	*one*
¹⁵*the king of Libnah*	*one*
the king of Adullam	*one*
¹⁶*the king of Makkedah*	*one*
the king of Bethel	*one*
¹⁷*the king of Tappuah*	*one*
the king of Hepher	*one*
¹⁸*the king of Aphek*	*one*
the king of Lasharon	*one*
¹⁹*the king of Madon*	*one*
the king of Hazor	*one*
²⁰*the king of Shimron Meron*	*one*
the king of Acshaph	*one*

[21]	the king of Taanach	one
	the king of Megiddo	one
[22]	the king of Kedesh	one
	the king of Jokneam in Carmel	one
[23]	the king of Dor (in Naphoth Dor)	one
	the king of Goyim in Gilgal	one
[24]	the king of Tirzah	one
thirty-one kings in all.		

Joshua had to finish the work by taking over the western half of Canaan with God's help. Verse 7 draws the boundaries of this territory in the same manner as 11:17. The various sections of the land are then listed in verse 8. The "hill country" probably includes both the southern and the northern highlands, and the "western foothills" similarly, not just the Shephelah, but also the plain of Sharon to the north. As in 11:16, Arabah here refers to the section of the Jordan Valley west of the river.

Verses 9–24 list the kings in their order of defeat, at least to the extent that Jericho and Ai are followed first by the southern and then by the northern kings. The cities in verses 10–13a are all from chapter 10. The names that appear here for the first time refer mostly to places in the far south (v. 14) and the center (vv. 17, 21–22) of Canaan. The location of Lasharon (v. 18) is unknown; but if it lay in the Plain of Sharon, it begins the list of the northern cities. Verses 19–20 and 23a name the most important northern cities, which appeared in 11:1–2. The name "Goyim" (v. 24) could be translated as "nations" or "heathen," but it seems rather to be the proper name of a small tribe in Gilgal ("Galilee," the Septuagint reading, should perhaps be followed here). The cities of some of the kings in this list actually had not been captured by Joshua (cf. 17:11–13; Judg. 1:8, 17).

These verses thus summarize how Joshua completed the first part of his task. If God's people were to dwell in safety in the land that He had chosen for them, they had to begin by not merely subjecting but actually exterminating its pagan inhabitants. The world-historical calling of Israel demanded that she live as a holy nation, isolated from idol worshipers, in a land of her own, there faithfully preserving the Lord's words and His covenant. God therefore ordained that the population of Canaan be destroyed, and Joshua was the man chosen to carry out this divine mandate. In performing this task, Joshua did nothing that tarnished his name. His work revealed him rather as a model of obedience and strict devotion to duty. By faithfully keeping the promises given to Rahab and the Gibeonites, and by punishing Achan with merciless severity, Joshua showed that he was driven by noble and pure motives and did not act arbitrarily.

Joshua's work can only be interpreted properly if we regard him here again as a type of Christ, the Judge of the earth who upholds the justice of God (see Note 6 after this commentary). At the close of the age, Christ too will remove from the earth all who are enemies of the living God and His people. It is necessary that earth's godless inhabitants first be eliminated before it can be a proper habitation for His people. Christ will purge the whole world of all power that exalts itself against God more thoroughly than Joshua purged Canaan. With a refining fire that leaves nothing untouched, the Lord Jesus will purify it from all the stain and pollution of sin. Once this is accomplished, Christ, the Heir of all things (Heb. 1:2), will grant this earth as an inheritance to His coheirs (Rom. 8:17) so that they may possess it in peace for eternity (Ps. 37:9–11).

Part Two

The Division of Canaan Among the Twelve Tribes
(13:1–22:34)

1. The Divine Command to Divide the Land
(13:1–7)

Chapter 13 begins the second part of the Book of Joshua.[1] Joshua had largely fulfilled the first part of the divine mandate that he received in 1:2-9, i.e., the command to conquer the land. Now the Lord directly commands Joshua to begin the second part of his task: the division of Canaan among the tribes of Israel. This was a special favor for Joshua, for he was allowed to crown his work of conquest. Although Joshua may have thought that he would still have to carry on his military operations for some time, the Lord permitted him to lay down his arms and devote his attention to drawing the boundaries of the various tribal territories, a task with far-reaching consequences for Israel's future. It is true that much land remained in enemy hands, but the Lord promised (v. 6) that He would drive them out. God's plan was that the same man who brought Israel into Canaan would supervise the division of the

---

[1]This part of the book contains a host of place names and geographical references, but it would be beyond the scope of this commentary to try to determine their modern equivalents. (The NIV spellings of names have been followed throughout this commentary — TRANS.)

land. Thus Joshua was again a type of Christ: after obtaining salvation for His people, Jesus too grants each believer his allotted share.

13:1 *When Joshua was old and well advanced in years, the LORD said to him, "You are very old, and there are still very large areas of land to be taken over.*

Verse 1 states the reason Joshua was commanded to divide the land: he already had reached a great age. He was presumably more than ninety-seven years old by now (see Introduction, section 6), and the burden of the incessant warfare no doubt had weighed heavily on him. The Lord reminded Joshua of his old age, on the one hand, and of the yet unconquered territory, on the other hand, to make him realize that it would be beyond his powers to take over the remaining land and then still proceed with the division.

13:2–7
"This is the land that remains: all the regions of the Philistines and Geshurites: ³from the Shihor River on the east of Egypt to the territory of Ekron on the north, all of it counted as Canaanite (the territory of the five Philistine rulers in Gaza, Ashdod, Ashkelon, Gath and Ekron—that of the Avvites);² ⁴from the south, all the land of the Canaanites, from Arah³ of the Sidonians as far as Aphek, the region of the Amorites, ⁵the area of the Gebalites; and all Lebanon to the east, from Baal Gad below Mount Hermon to Lebo Hamath.

⁶*"As for all the inhabitants of the mountain regions from Lebanon to Misrephoth Maim, that is, all the Sidonians, I myself will drive them out before the Israelites. Be sure to allocate this land to Israel for an inheritance, as I have instructed you, ⁷and divide it as an inheritance among the nine tribes and half of the tribe of Manasseh."*

The Lord listed for Joshua, region by region, all the territory that still remained under the control of the native population. First, He named the southwestern section of Canaan,[4] the land from the Shihor River (the boundary of Egypt, see 15:4, 47, "Wadi of Egypt") to Ekron (vv.

---

[2] On the Avvites, cf. Deuteronomy 2:23.

[3] The Hebrew text here reads "and Mearah" (cf. KJV, RSV). The NIV follows a few manuscripts of the Septuagint and reads *mēʿarâ(h)* ("from Arah") instead of *ûmeʿ ārâ(h)* ("and Mearah"). Goslinga follows Kittel's proposal of "from Mearah" and notes that "from" is suggested by the subsequent "as far as Aphek." Such a translation, which corresponds to the Septuagint reading, changes the initial waw to a mem—TRANS.

[4] The Geshurites of verse 2 lived in the south (see 1 Sam. 27:8), while the "people of Geshur" in 12:5 and 13:11, 13 lived in the north.

2–3). Verse 4 lists the coastal region inhabited by the Canaanites, an area that extended from Arah or Mearah ("cave") to Aphek, a city northeast of Joppa at the later site of Antipatris (see 12:18; 1 Sam. 4:1). If Mearah is the correct reading (see footnote 3), this probably was a well-known cave in the region of Tyre. "Sidonians" is a general name for the Phoenicians. Verses 5–6 finally mention the northernmost part of the Promised Land, the mountainous country of Lebanon. The Gebalites were the inhabitants of Gebal, a coastal city lying a fair distance north of Sidon.

The Lord willed that the Israelites promptly complete the unfinished remnants of Joshua's task. The outcome was assured from the start, for the Lord Himself would grant them victory. Their previous successes in battle guaranteed this. In dividing the land, Joshua therefore could include the territory that remained unconquered ahead of time. The Lord directly commanded him to begin the division (v. 7), and He added that the land this would embrace was intended only for the nine and a half tribes that had not yet received their territory.

2. The Division of the Land East of the Jordan (13:8–33)

Before sketching the division of the land west of the Jordan River, the author presents an outline of the eastern territory. In 12:1–6 he had summarized the Israelite conquests east of the Jordan, and the same reason that had motivated that review obliged him to state in detail how this territory had been divided among the two and a half tribes. At all times he was concerned to hold in view the unity of the Twelve Tribes; so he could not leave out the allotment of the regions east of the Jordan. To be sure, this land had been allotted under the leadership of Moses, not Joshua; but the author was not interested in Joshua's work as such. On the contrary, he meant to recount the work of God; and this remained a single whole in spite of the fact that various of His servants participated in it.

13:8–14 *The other half of Manasseh, the Reubenites and the Gadites had received the inheritance that Moses had given them east of the Jordan, as he, the servant of the Lord, had assigned it to them.*

⁹It extended from Aroer on the rim of the Arnon Gorge, and from the town in the middle of the gorge, and included the whole plateau of Medeba as far as Dibon, ¹⁰and all the towns of Sihon king of the Amorites, who ruled in Heshbon, out to the border of the Ammonites. ¹¹It also included Gilead, the territory of the people of Geshur and Maacah, all of Mount Hermon and all Bashan as far as Salecah— 12 *that is, the whole kingdom of Og in Bashan, who had reigned in Ashtaroth and Edrei and had survived as one of the last of the Rephaites. Moses had defeated them and taken over their land.* 13 *But the Israelites did not drive out the people of Geshur and Maacah, so they continue to live among the Israelites to this day.*

14 *But to the tribe of Levi he gave no inheritance, since the offerings made by fire to the LORD, the God of Israel, are their inheritance, as he promised them.*

After mentioning Manasseh (v. 7), the author adds (v. 8) that along with the other half of this tribe,[5] the Reubenites and the Gadites had already received their share of the land from Moses, and that this had taken place in full obedience to Moses' orders and the will of God Himself. Verses 9–12 describe their territory in broad outlines, which in fact has already been done in 12:2–5, but in somewhat different terms. Quite appropriately, this description is followed by the historical report that the Israelites had been remiss in driving out the people of Geshur[6] and Maacah, the northernmost inhabitants of the inheritance of these eastern tribes. Verse 14 then states that he, i.e., Moses, assigned no inheritance to the Levites, something that had already been commanded in Deuteronomy 18:1. This statement no doubt was motivated by the fact that the tribe of Levi belonged to the whole nation, including the part residing in the Transjordan. At the same time it prepares the way for the later report that the two and a half eastern tribes also had to cede certain cities to the Levites (21:6–7, 37–40).

13:15–23 *This is what Moses had given to the tribe of Reuben, clan by clan:*

16 *The territory from Aroer on the rim of the Arnon Gorge, and from the town in the middle of the gorge, and the whole plateau past Medeba* 17 *to Heshbon and all its towns on the plateau, including Dibon, Bamoth Baal, Beth Baal Meon,* 18 *Jahaz, Kedemoth, Mephaath,* 19 *Kiriathaim, Sibmah, Zereth Shahar on the hill in the valley,* 20 *Beth Peor, the slopes of Pisgah, and Beth Jeshimoth* 21 *—all the towns on the plateau and the entire realm of Sihon king of the Amorites, who ruled at Heshbon. Moses had defeated him and the Midianite chiefs, Evi, Rekem, Zur, Hur and Reba—princes allied with Sihon—who lived in that country.* 22 *In addition to those slain in battle, the Israelites had put to the sword Balaam son of Beor, who practiced divination.* 23 *The boundary of the Reubenites was the bank of the Jordan.*[7]

---

5 The Hebrew of verse 8 literally reads "with it" [cf. KJV, NIV margin—TRANS.], but the reference is to the other half of the tribe spoken of in verse 7.

6 See footnote 4 above.

7 The Hebrew literally reads "Jordan and territory" (cf. NEB, "adjacent land"), but this "territory" has to be understood as the land along the bank.

These towns and their villages were the inheritance of the Reubenites, clan by clan.

The tribe of Reuben received as its inheritance the land that had been conquered east of the Dead Sea. The words "the entire realm of Sihon" (v. 21) have to be understood as referring only to that part of it in the plateau, for verse 27 shows that another section of Sihon's kingdom was given to the Gadites. Heshbon lay on the border between Reuben and Gad, and it appears from 21:39 that it was also considered a city of the latter tribe. At its northernmost cities (v. 20), the territory of Reuben extended to the east bank of the mouth of the Jordan. The children of Reuben were not allowed to forget that they were living on historic soil, for verses 21–22 remind them of the great things God had done there. They had inherited the land where Sihon had been destroyed and Balaam had received his just deserts. Although these things were well-known, the author nevertheless thought it necessary to call them to memory once again.

13:24–28 *This is what Moses had given to the tribe of Gad, clan by clan:*
²⁵ *The territory of Jazer, all the towns of Gilead and half the Ammonite country as far as Aroer, near Rabbah;* ²⁶ *and from Heshbon to Ramath Mizpah and Betonim, and from Mahanaim to the territory of Debir;* ²⁷ *and in the valley, Beth Haram, Beth Nimrah, Succoth and Zaphon with the rest of the realm of Sihon king of Heshbon (the east side of the Jordan, the territory up to the end of the Sea of Kinnereth).* ²⁸ *These towns and their villages were the inheritance of the Gadites, clan by clan.*

The inheritance of the tribe of Gad is described next. They received the territory north of Reuben, east of the Jordan, and extending northward to the Sea of Kinnereth (v. 27). To the east of the Jordan Valley proper, however, their land did not extend this far north; for it appears from verses 26 and 30 that the city of Mahanaim, north of the River Jabbok, lay on their border. "All the towns of Gilead" (v. 25) means the towns outside Manasseh's share of this region (v. 31). Gad received only the southern part of Gilead but also was given the western half of the Ammonite country up to Aroer (v. 25), a city not to be confused with the Aroer of verse 16.

13:29–33 *This is what Moses had given to the half-tribe of Manasseh, that is, to half the family of the descendants of Manasseh, clan by clan:*
³⁰ *The territory extending from Mahanaim and including all of Bashan, the entire realm of Og king of Bashan—all the settlements of Jair in Bashan,*

sixty towns, 31 half of Gilead, and Ashtaroth and Edrei (the royal cities of Og in Bashan). This was for the descendants of Makir son of Manasseh—for half of the sons of Makir, clan by clan.

32 This is the inheritance Moses had given when he was in the plains of Moab across the Jordan east of Jericho.8 33 But to the tribe of Levi, Moses had given no inheritance; the LORD, the God of Israel, is their inheritance, as he promised them.

These final verses describe the inheritance of the half-tribe of Manasseh, whose land lay north of the Gadites' and stretched up to Mount Hermon. Verse 31 means that the territory named here was given to those descendants of Makir who settled east of the Jordan.9 Since other descendants of Makir came to reside west of the Jordan (cf. 17:3–4), "for half of the sons of Makir" is added for the sake of clarity. Verse 32 closes this account of the distribution of the land east of the Jordan. Because of the great importance of the matter, however, verse 33 repeats the statement in verse 14 that the tribe of Levi received no inheritance from Moses and adds meaningfully that the Lord Himself was their inheritance. God thus fulfilled His promise in Numbers 18:20 by reserving the best share of all for the Levites.

3. The Division of the Western Territory and Caleb's Inheritance (14:1–15)

14:1–5 *Now these are the areas the Israelites received as an inheritance in the land of Canaan, which Eleazar the priest, Joshua son of Nun and the heads of the tribal clans of Israel allotted to them. 2 Their inheritances were assigned by lot to the nine-and-a-half tribes, as the LORD had commanded through Moses. 3 Moses had granted the two-and-a-half tribes their inheritance east of the Jordan but had not granted the Levites an inheritance among the rest, 4 for the sons of Joseph had become two tribes—Manasseh and Ephraim. The Levites received no share of the land but only towns to live in, with pasturelands for their flocks and herds. 5 So the Israelites divided the land, just as the LORD had commanded Moses.*

Chapter 14 begins the account of how the land west of the Jordan was divided among the Israelite tribes, and the narrative recording this

---

8 Literally, "across the Jordan of Jericho eastward."

9 In the author's translation, only the territories mentioned in verse 31 itself are allotted to the descendants of Makir (cf. KJV, NEB). The NIV gives the impression that all the land outlined in verses 30–31 went to the Makirites—TRANS.

whole process runs till the end of chapter 19. Verses 1–5 serve as an introduction. The opening of verse 1 points back to 13:32, thereby bringing out both that something new was undertaken here and that this work tied in with what Moses had done previously. The task was new in four different respects.

1. The division took place under the leadership of Joshua, Eleazar, and the elders or "heads of the tribal clans," all of whom were appointed to this task by God Himself (Num. 34:16–29). The Hebrew for "heads of the tribal clans" is literally "heads of the fathers of the tribes" (cf. KJV), the oldest among the family heads and the successors of the twelve patriarchs.

2. The land was distributed by lot, again in obedience to God's command (Num. 26:52–56; 33:54; 34:13). As these verses had directed, however, the size of the tribes was also taken into consideration in this distribution, the larger tribes being assigned a larger and the smaller ones a smaller inheritance. The lot did not determine the size of the tribal territories directly. It only selected the districts where the various tribes would have to settle. Joshua 19:9 shows that the boundaries that had first been drawn could later be altered somewhat without violating the decisions that had been made by the lot. The precise method that was followed in this allotment is not known with certainty. The rabbis suspect that two containers were used, the names of the tribes being placed in one and the names of the different sections of Canaan on an equal number of slips in the other. The names then could have been drawn from the first container (perhaps by Joshua and Eleazar) in order to determine the sequence in which the individual tribes (represented by the elders) would pick their lots from the second container. There is much to commend this view. In any case the use of lots meant that each tribe could regard its allotment as coming from God's own hand; and it ensured that Joshua and Eleazar could not be suspected of partiality or unjust favoritism. See also the comments in 18:2–4.

3. The division now applied to the land west of the Jordan that had been described and demarcated in Numbers 34:1–12.

4. The present distribution concerned only the nine and a half tribes that had not yet received anything. Verses 3–4a serve to explain this number of nine and a half. There were Twelve Tribes in all. Since Moses had assigned territory to two and a half of these tribes east of the Jordan, nine and a half tribes remained. The tribe of Levi had received no inheritance in Moses' ruling, but this was compensated by the fact that the descendants of Joseph were assigned a double portion.

Manasseh and Ephraim therefore had the same status as the sons of Jacob, and the land still had to be divided among nine and a half tribes. The number twelve was thus preserved. To complete the picture, verse 4b makes clear that the Levites' need for towns and pastureland was not neglected in the distribution, but a detailed statement of what they received does not come till chapter 21. Although the present allotment differed significantly from Moses' division of the Transjordan, everything was again done according to God's instructions to Moses.

14:6–12 *Now the men of Judah approached Joshua at Gilgal, and Caleb son of Jephunneh the Kenizzite said to him, "You know what the LORD said to Moses the man of God at Kadesh Barnea about you and me. ⁷I was forty years old when Moses the servant of the LORD sent me from Kadesh Barnea to explore the land. And I brought him back a report according to my convictions, ⁸but my brothers who went up with me made the hearts of the people melt with fear. I, however, followed the LORD my God wholeheartedly. ⁹So on that day Moses swore to me, 'The land on which your feet have walked will be your inheritance and that of your children forever, because you have followed the LORD my God wholeheartedly.'*

¹⁰"Now then, just as the LORD promised, he has kept me alive for forty-five years since the time he said this to Moses, while Israel moved about in the desert. So here I am today, eighty-five years old! ¹¹I am still as strong today as the day Moses sent me out; I'm just as vigorous to go out to battle now as I was then. ¹²Now give me this hill country that the LORD promised me that day. You yourself heard then that the Anakites were there and their cities were large and fortified, but, the LORD helping me, I will drive them out just as he said."

The rule that the whole distribution had to proceed by lot had one exception. Caleb was the one person who could lay claim to a particular section of Canaan that had been specially promised to him beforehand by God. The way he came forward and spoke—a devout man who remained strong in spite of his years—fits the situation completely and once again forms internal proof for the accuracy and truth of the story.[10] It appears from Numbers 34:19 that Caleb was one of the elders who had supervised the allotment of the land at Gilgal. Because of this he had a good opportunity to come forward with this personal request, but he was also supported in this by some of his fellow members of the tribe of Judah (v. 6). It is unclear why Caleb's father is surnamed "the Kenizzite." According to 1 Chronicles 2:18 Caleb was from the line of Hezron, son of Judah. It is possible that one of the

---

[10] See Note 5 at the end of this commentary concerning the possibility that Caleb made his request right after the Israelites entered Canaan.

members of the line between Hezron and Jephunneh was named Kenaz. (Caleb's brother Othniel is called the son of Kenaz, 15:17, but not Caleb himself; so Kenaz was perhaps Caleb's stepfather.)

Whatever the case may have been, Caleb stepped forward to receive title to a specific part of the hill country of Judah for himself and his household. He emphatically ("you know," v. 6) reminded Joshua of the Lord's promise that they alone among the older generation of Israel would enter Canaan (Num. 14:24, 30). Then he briefly reviewed the facts that formed a basis for his request. He had been sent out to explore the land of Canaan. When he had returned, he brought back an honest report that was inspired, not by fear of men, but by a sincere trust in God. The other ten spies, in contrast, whom he here graciously called "my brothers," terrified the people with their descriptions of the Anakites and their strong fortresses. This was tantamount to apostasy and disloyalty to God, who had promised them the land, while Caleb's conduct displayed a genuine faith in the Lord. Because of Caleb's unwavering faithfulness, Moses swore an oath that Caleb now repeated (v. 9).

Numbers 14 actually does not speak of Moses' swearing such an oath, but it is natural to assume that he conveyed to Caleb the words that the Lord had spoken about him (cf. Num. 14:39). We thus should not really consider this to be an oath of Moses himself but rather an oath of Yahweh (Num. 14:21, 24) that Moses made known to Caleb (see also Deut. 1:34–36). Moses and Caleb understood (no doubt correctly) the Lord's promise to refer particularly to the district of Hebron, the abode of the Anakites, precisely the people that the spies provoked such an outcry about. Quite appropriately the promise therefore meant that this region, which the people had considered impregnable, would be given to faithful Caleb and that he would live long enough to take possession of it (v. 10). This conviction was the basis for Caleb's reasoning in these verses and motivated his request.

Caleb's request itself was also an act of faith, for it required courage to settle where the heaviest fighting could be expected (v. 12). Nevertheless, Caleb's former strength had not left him (he pointed this out to Joshua in v. 11 to help gain his consent). More importantly, Caleb looked to the Lord for help. Verse 12 shows that Joshua too had been a witness to the oath that had previously been sworn (v. 9) and knew that it applied to the hill country where the Anakites lived. Both Joshua's hearing of the oath and the fact that this was the abode of the

Anakites motivated the request Caleb made to Joshua: "Give me this hill country."[11]

14:13–15 *Then Joshua blessed Caleb son of Jephunneh and gave him Hebron as his inheritance. [14]So Hebron has belonged to Caleb son of Jephunneh the Kenizzite ever since, because he followed the LORD, the God of Israel, wholeheartedly. [15](Hebron used to be called Kiriath Arba after Arba, who was the greatest man among the Anakites.)*
Then the land had rest from war.

Joshua obligingly granted Caleb's request and sent him to take possession of Hebron with God's blessing. The author explicitly states that Caleb received this privilege because he served the Lord "whole-heartedly," thus implying that God rewards those who openly honor and confess Him before men.

The final verse contains a brief note on the name Hebron. Formerly this city had been called Kiriath Arba or the "city of Arba" (see RSV margin) after Arba, the forefather of Anak (15:13). This Arba must have been a giant among giants, for the word "greatest" here most likely refers to his height (cf. 12:4 and Deut. 3:11). The chapter ends by repeating the statement in 11:23 that the land now had rest from war, no doubt because Caleb's words in verse 12 could create the impression that the Anakites still presented grave difficulties for Israel. This was in fact not the case, for warfare had generally ceased in Canaan; and the division of the land could thus commence. Note 5 at the end of this commentary deals further with these verses on Caleb and the Anakites.

4. The Inheritance of Judah
(15:1–63)

Chapter 15 begins by accurately drawing the boundaries of Judah's territory (vv. 1–12). In connection with this, it then reports the conquest of Hebron and Debir (vv. 13–20). Finally, a list is given of the cities that were within the inheritance of the tribe of Judah (vv. 21–63).

---

[11]Goslinga's translation of verse 12 differs from the KJV, RSV, and NIV. He regards the two *kî* clauses as parallel and has "Now give me this hill country that the LORD promised me that day, for you yourself heard it that day; for the Anakites are there with great fortified cities"—TRANS.

15:1–4

The allotment for the tribe of Judah, clan by clan, extended down to the territory of Edom, to the Desert of Zin in the extreme south.

² Their southern boundary started from the bay[12] *at the southern end of the Salt Sea, ³ crossed south of Scorpion Pass, continued on to Zin and went over to the south of Kadesh Barnea. Then it ran past Hezron up to Addar and curved around to Karka. ⁴ It then passed along to Azmon and joined the Wadi of Egypt, ending at the sea. This is their southern boundary.*

By God's design Judah, the tribe of royalty, was the first to be chosen by lot to receive a share of the Promised Land. Its territory embraced the whole southern part of the land in its full extent. It stretched south to the kingdom of Edom and extended to the Desert of Zin, the site of Kadesh. Verses 2–4 describe the southern boundary as it started from the southern end of the Dead Sea, ran west through the Desert of Zin, and ended at the point where the Wadi of Egypt flowed into the Mediterranean Sea. The close of verse 4 in the Hebrew literally reads "this will be your southern boundary" (see RSV, NIV margin— TRANS.). The author may have written these words from memory (and thus inaccurately) as a quotation from Numbers 34:3, but they more likely indicate that the boundaries that had been set were read aloud to the tribes under concern. To correctly understand how the territories are demarcated in the chapters that follow, we need to keep in mind that a boundary is said to "go up" or "run up" when it ascends from a lower to a higher elevation and to "go down" in the opposite case. If a boundary continues no farther in a certain direction, it is said to "come out" at a certain point and to "turn" there.

15:5–12

The eastern boundary is the Salt Sea as far as the mouth of the Jordan.

The northern boundary started from the bay of the sea at the mouth of the Jordan, ⁶ went up to Beth Hoglah and continued north of Beth Arabah to the Stone of Bohan son of Reuben. ⁷ The boundary then went up to Debir from the Valley of Achor and turned north to Gilgal, which faces the Pass of Adummim south of the gorge. It continued along to the waters of En Shemesh and came out at En Rogel. ⁸ Then it ran up the Valley of Ben Hinnom along the southern slope of the Jebusite city (that is, Jerusalem). From there it climbed to the top of the hill west of the Hinnom Valley at the northern end of the Valley of Rephaim. ⁹ From the hilltop the boundary headed toward the spring of the waters of Nephtoah, came out at the towns

---

[12] Literally "tongue."

of Mount Ephron and went down toward Baalah (that is, Kiriath Jearim).
¹⁰Then it curved westward from Baalah to Mount Seir, ran along the
northern slope of Mount Jearim (that is, Kesalon), continued down to Beth
Shemesh and crossed to Timnah. ¹¹It went to the northern slope of Ekron,
turned toward Shikkeron, passed along to Mount Baalah and reached
Jabneel. The boundary ended at the sea.
¹²The western boundary is the coastline of the Great Sea.¹³
These are the boundaries around the people of Judah by their clans.

According to verse 5a, the eastern boundary of Judah was formed by
the whole length of the Dead Sea. Verses 5b–11 give the northern
boundary. A comparison with 18:15–19 shows that this largely
coincided with the southern boundary of Benjamin, which is described
there in the opposite direction as here. The mention of the Stone of
Bohan (v. 6) is curious in this context. Bohan was a son of Reuben of
whom nothing further is known, and it is possible that a Reubenite
family settled here rather than in their tribal territory.¹⁴ The land
assigned to Judah extended westward all the way to the Mediterranean
Sea.

15:13–20 *In accordance with the LORD's command to him, Joshua gave to*
Caleb son of Jephunneh a portion in Judah—Kiriath Arba, that is, Hebron.
(Arba was the forefather of Anak.) ¹⁴From Hebron Caleb drove out the three
Anakites—Sheshai, Ahiman and Talmai—descendants of Anak. ¹⁵From there
he marched against the people living in Debir (formerly called Kiriath Sepher).
¹⁶And Caleb said, "I will give my daughter Acsah in marriage to the man who
attacks and captures Kiriath Sepher." ¹⁷Othniel son of Kenaz, Caleb's brother,
took it; so Caleb gave his daughter Acsah to him in marriage.
¹⁸One day when she came to Othniel, she urged him to ask her father for a
field. When she got off her donkey, Caleb asked her, "What can I do for you?"
¹⁹She replied, "Do me a special favor. Since you have given me land in the
Negev, give me also springs of water." So Caleb gave her the upper and lower
springs.
²⁰This is the inheritance of the tribe of Judah, clan by clan:

These verses tell how Caleb took possession of the territory that he
had been granted as his own special allotment. Because the full account

---

¹³The Hebrew text literally reads *hayyāmmâ(h)*, "seaward," and not merely
hayyām, "the sea"; but this is probably a scribal error. The actual reading is "the
Great Sea and territory" (see note 7 in 13:23).

¹⁴We may also note the odd conjecture of O. Proksch that Bohan was the child
born of the incest between Reuben and Bilhah, who according to popular belief was
transformed at once into a stone (see F. M. Th. Böhl, *Genesis* 2:139).

of Judah's military exploits in the first chapter of Judges repeats this same story almost verbatim (Judg. 1:10–15), it is commonly thought that the events reported here happened after the death of Joshua and were inserted into chapter 15 by a later hand. Although the latter point is no doubt true, this forms no evidence for the rest of the above position. Othniel's conquest could hardly have been left out of the comprehensive summary in Judges 1, but it still could have taken place earlier than the events recorded in the first nine verses there. Two things in particular point to this conclusion. First, it is hard to imagine that the old but still vigorous Caleb would have put off the conquest of his inheritance, which he desired so ardently, till after the death of Joshua, a delay that would certainly have come to ten or fifteen years (see section 6 of the Introduction). Second, it is significant that the author inserted this story where one would not expect to find it. He must have done this to show that after the territory described in verses 1–12 had been assigned to Judah, the tribe immediately began with the actual work of conquest. Verses 13–20 thus give one example of this. See also Note 5 at the end of this commentary.

Verse 13 briefly summarizes what happened in 14:6–15 and forms an introduction to the events that follow. Joshua had already driven out the Anakites (10:36–39; 11:21–22); but they apparently returned and settled once more in the neighborhood of Hebron, and Caleb and his men had to destroy them. The names Sheshai, Ahiman, and Talmai refer to families or clans, not to individual persons. After Hebron was conquered, it was Debir's turn. The ancient name of this city, Kiriath Sepher ("city of books"), presumably indicates that it was a center of Canaanite literature and learning.[15] Othniel, Caleb's younger brother (probably his half brother, since Caleb was always called the son of Jephunneh, and Othniel was the son of Kenaz, Judg. 1:13; 3:9, 11), captured Debir and received as a prize Caleb's daughter Acsah. When Acsah came to Othniel and saw the parched ground, she provoked his desire for some more fertile land. Othniel probably thought it more advisable that Acsah bring this request to her father herself. At any rate, it was not Othniel but Acsah who turned to Caleb. Alighting from her donkey was both a token of respect and a sign that she had a request to make, and her wish was generously granted by her father. Verse 20 applies to the whole territory outlined in verses 1–12, Caleb's

---

[15] See A. Noordtzij, *Gods Woord*, 2nd ed., p. 268. According to Noordtzij, the name actually must have been Kiriath Sopher, "city of the scribe."

inheritance forming a small part of this. The highly personal story in the above verses lends sharper relief to the phrase "clan by clan."

15:21–32 *The southernmost towns of the tribe of Judah in the Negev toward the boundary of Edom were:*

Kabzeel, Eder, Jagur, ²²Kinah, Dimonah, Adadah, ²³Kedesh, Hazor, Ithnan, ²⁴Ziph, Telem, Bealoth, ²⁵Hazor Hadattah, Kerioth Hezron (that is, Hazor), ²⁶Amam, Shema, Moladah, ²⁷Hazar Gaddah, Heshmon, Beth Pelet, ²⁸Hazar Shual, Beersheba, Biziothiah,[16] ²⁹Baalah, Iim, Ezem, ³⁰Eltolad, Kesil, Hormah, ³¹Ziklag, Madmannah, Sansannah, ³²Lebaoth, Shilhim, Ain and Rimmon—a total of twenty-nine towns and their villages.

Verses 21–62 list the towns of Judah in four main groups that correspond to the four natural divisions of its terrain: the Negev, the western foothills, the hill country, and the desert.[17] The Negev or south country was the southernmost part of the land of Canaan, an arid plain where the sole means of subsistence was cattle raising. The towns found in this region are again divided into four groups, contained respectively in verses 21–23, 24–25, 26–28, and 29–32.

It seems that an error was made in copying this list, for verse 32 speaks of twenty-nine towns, while thirty-five names appear in the text. The solution to this problem is unclear. One possibility is that the number twenty-nine was a copyist's mistake. Another is that a few names of villages were added that should not be included among the twenty-nine towns. It is also conceivable that after verse 23, which ends the first subgroup of nine towns, a line was omitted that read something like "a total of nine towns and their villages." The number in verse 32 then would refer only to verses 24–32. Although these last verses in fact only contain twenty-six names, a few names could have been left unmentioned. Incomplete lists like this also appear elsewhere and do not present such a serious problem (cf. 19:15, 38).

15:33–47 *In the western foothills:*

Eshtaol, Zorah, Ashnah, ³⁴Zanoah, En Gannim, Tappuah, Enam, ³⁵Jarmuth, Adullam, Socoh, Azekah, ³⁶Shaaraim, Adithaim and Gederah (or Gederothaim)—fourteen towns and their villages.

---

[16]Taking his cue from Nehemiah 11:27, the author followed the Septuagint and read *bᵉnôṭe(y)hā*, "its villages," instead of Biziothiah here. Cf. NEB—TRANS.

[17]See A. van Deursen, *Palestina, het land van de Bijbel* (Baarn, Bosch, Keuning), chs. 7–10.

³⁷Zenan, Hadashah, Migdal Gad, ³⁸Dilean, Mizpah, Joktheel, ³⁹Lachish, Bozkath, Eglon, ⁴⁰Cabbon, Lahmas, Kitlish, ⁴¹Gederoth, Beth Dagon, Naamah and Makkedah—sixteen towns and their villages.

⁴²Libnah, Ether, Ashan, ⁴³Iphtah, Ashnah, Nezib, ⁴⁴Keilah, Aczib and Mareshah—nine towns and their villages.

⁴⁵Ekron, with its surrounding settlements and villages; ⁴⁶west of Ekron, all that were in the vicinity of Ashdod, together with their villages; ⁴⁷Ashdod, its surrounding settlements and villages; and Gaza, its settlements and villages, as far as the Wadi of Egypt and the coastline of the Great Sea.

The western foothills (Heb. *š͎pēlâ[h]*, cf. NEB "Shephelah"[18]) spoken of here lie to the west of the hill country of Judah. This section of Judah actually embraced more than the foothills themselves, for it can be divided into the hilly area descending from the hill country proper (10:40 and 12:8 call this the "mountain slopes") and the plain that extends from there to the Mediterranean Sea. On the whole this was a fertile and heavily populated region. Its towns are divided into four groups. The first of these (vv. 33–36) totals fourteen towns. The text actually includes fifteen names, but it is doubtful whether the last of these was a town; for the Septuagint instead has "dwellings" or, more properly, "(vineyard) walls." In any case, it is reasonable to assume that Gederothaim was counted as one city with Gederah.[19] In the second and third groups the numbers are given correctly (vv. 41, 44). Only the principal towns of the fourth group are named; and the total is not given, probably because Judah had not yet taken actual possession of these towns, and they remained in Philistine hands.

15:48–60 *In the hill country:*

Shamir, Jattir, Socoh, ⁴⁹Dannah, Kiriath Sannah (that is, Debir), ⁵⁰Anab, Eshtemoh, Anim, ⁵¹Goshen, Holon and Giloh—eleven towns and their villages.

⁵²Arab, Dumah, Eshan, ⁵³Janim, Beth Tappuah, Aphekah, ⁵⁴Humtah, Kiriath Arba (that is, Hebron) and Zior—nine towns and their villages.

⁵⁵Maon, Carmel, Ziph, Juttah, ⁵⁶Jezreel, Jokdeam, Zanoah, ⁵⁷Kain, Gibeah and Timnah—ten towns and their villages.

⁵⁸Halhul, Beth Zur, Gedor, ⁵⁹Maarath, Beth Anoth and Eltekon—six towns and their villages.

⁶⁰Kiriath Baal (that is, Kiriath Jearim) and Rabbah—two towns and their villages.

---

[18]The author translated this Hebrew term as "lowland" (cf. RSV)—TRANS.
[19]The author's translation of verse 36 corresponds to the RSV and NIV margin, "Gederah and Gederothaim"—TRANS.

The hill country of Judah is an imposing chain of peaks that traverses Judah from north to south. The terrain is very rocky, but it also contains some fertile valleys and plateaus. The Hebrew text divides the towns of this region into five groups, and here the totals fit exactly and present no problems. Nevertheless, we doubtless still have to assume that the original text contained yet a sixth group of towns. The Septuagint has an additional verse between verse 59 and verse 60 that reads as follows: "Tekoa, Ephrathah (that is, Bethlehem), Peor, Etam, Koulon, Tatam, Sores, Karem, Gallim, Bether, and Manocho; eleven towns and their villages." These towns occupied an important district south of Jerusalem, and some were well-known; so it is inconceivable that they were not present in the original text. In view of this, it is highly probable that our text contains a gap, especially since the eye of a copyist could very easily have skipped from the end of verse 59 to the end of the omitted passage, which read identically ("and their villages"). Verse 60, therefore, gives the sixth rather than the fifth group of towns in the hill country of Judah.

15:61–62 *In the desert:*
Beth Arabah, Middin, Secacah, ⁶²Nibshan, the City of Salt and En Gedi— six towns and their villages.

The last group lists the towns located in the desert, the region that stretched the length of the Dead Sea and extended from there to the hill country. This terrain consists largely of barren, terracelike slopes and contains much limestone and numerous caves. Among its sections were the deserts of En Gedi, Ziph, and Maon, places where David hid during his flights from King Saul. It is not surprising that few cities were found in this inhospitable region where springs were rare.

15:63 *Judah could not dislodge the Jebusites, who were living in Jerusalem; to this day the Jebusites live there with the people of Judah.*

Since the Jebusite fortress lay right on the border of Judah's inheritance (see v. 8), the tribe made an attempt to capture this city. Judges 1:8 states that they were successful (perhaps only in part), but the present verse indicates that the conquest had no lasting result. This verse actually must be a reference to a time after Joshua's death and after the battle reported in Judges 1:8 (see section 3 of the Introduction). The situation described in verse 63 continued to prevail even though the tribe of Benjamin, to whom Jebus or Jerusalem actually had been assigned, also tried to capture the city. Israel's inability to dislodge the Jebusites was no doubt due to her human weakness and indolence; for if the men of Judah had trusted in God and persevered in concert with the Benjaminites, they certainly would have eventually succeeded in expelling them. This was not accomplished till David's time, however (2 Sam. 5:6–9).

It has rightly been noted that the allotment to Judah of such an extensive territory with so many cities can be regarded as the fulfillment of Jacob's prophecy in Genesis 49:8, 11–12.[20] Remarkably, Judah originally did not receive the later royal city of Jerusalem but instead the small and inconspicuous town of Bethlehem (see above), where Judah's greatest king would one day be born.

5. The Inheritance of Ephraim
(16:1–10)

Chapters 16 and 17 describe the inheritance that was given to the descendants of Joseph. Two things should be pointed out here. First, Ephraim and Manasseh each received a separate part of the land, and the boundaries of their territories also are drawn separately. However, only half the tribe of Manasseh is under concern here, for the other half had already received a sizable inheritance in the Transjordan (13:29–31). All this doubtless can be regarded as the fulfillment of Jacob's generous promise to Joseph that these sons would receive a double portion and would be considered equal to his own sons (Gen. 48:5, 22). Second, the unity of these tribes was still preserved in that Ephraim and Manasseh were regarded as one when the lots were drawn.

16:1–4
The allotment for Joseph began at the Jordan of Jericho, east of the waters of Jericho, and went up from there through the desert[21] into the hill country

---

[20] See Roorda, *Josua, De Held Gods*, p. 190.

[21] The author's translation of verse 1 reads as follows: "Then the lot fell to the descendants of Joseph. (The boundary) ran from the Jordan at Jericho, east of the waters of Jericho, and went up from Jericho to the hill country, to the desert of Bethel." He adds the following footnote: "The word *miḏbār* ('desert') is grammatically independent in the Hebrew text. I therefore have followed the Septuagint by transposing it and connecting it with Bethel and by vocalizing '*lh* ('to go up') as a perfect rather than a participle. The sentence reads better this way and fits better with 18:12 (desert of Bethel = desert of Beth Aven)—TRANS.

of Bethel. ²It went on from Bethel (that is, Luz),²² crossed over to the territory of the Arkits in Ataroth, ³descended westward to the territory of the Japhletites as far as the region of Lower Beth Horon and on to Gezer, ending at the sea.
⁴So Manasseh and Ephraim, the descendants of Joseph, received their inheritance.

In saying that the lot "fell" (see note 21 and NEB), the text probably means that this second lot was drawn from the urn (see the comments in 14:1 above). The designated territory then was assigned as a single allotment to the sons of Joseph, no doubt to emphasize their solidarity and to ensure that the territories of the two would not be separated by other tribes. By God's arrangement the most important tribes, Judah and the descendants of Joseph, thus received their share of the land first. The subject of the sentence in verse 1 is missing in the Hebrew, but as in 15:2 it has to be "the boundary" (see note 21). The waters of Jericho were probably a spring east of the city. Verses 1–3 draw only the southern boundary of the territory of the Josephite tribes. Verse 4 makes clear that Manasseh and Ephraim were the only sons of Joseph who received a separate share of the land, for the other sons were included in them (Gen. 48:6).

16:5–9 *This was the territory of Ephraim, clan by clan:*
The boundary of their inheritance went from Ataroth Addar in the east to Upper Beth Horon and ⁶continued to the sea. From Micmethath on the north it curved eastward to Taanath Shiloh, passing by it to Janoah on the east. ⁷Then it went down from Janoah to Ataroth and Naarah, touched Jericho and came out at the Jordan. ⁸From Tappuah the border went west to the Kanah Ravine and ended at the sea. This was the inheritance of the tribe of the Ephraimites, clan by clan. ⁹It also included all the towns and their villages that were set aside for the Ephraimites within the inheritance of the Manassites.

The rest of chapter 16 mainly describes the boundaries of Ephraim's territory. The southern (v. 5) and western (v. 6) boundaries are indicated very briefly, the eastern boundary at greater length (vv. 6–7), while verse 8 gives the northern boundary. Ephraim also received some

---

²²The author translated the Hebrew text literally here and has "from Bethel to Luz" (cf. KJV, RSV, NEB), while the NIV emends it following the Septuagint (see NIV margin). He added the following footnote: "Although Bethel is the same place as Luz (see 18:13), they are distinguished here. See Aalders' comments in the *Bible Student's Commentary* on Genesis 28:19"—TRANS.

towns in the territory of Manasseh (17:8–9), both because it had received the greater blessing of the two Josephite tribes (Gen. 48:19) and was destined to assume a leading role along with Judah, and because presumably its territory was too small.

16:10 *They did not dislodge the Canaanites living in Gezer; to this day the Canaanites live among the people of Ephraim but are required to do forced labor.*

Chapter 16 ends with a remark that resembles 15:63 (see the comments there). Gezer was a city on the border between Ephraim (v. 3) and Dan. It seems that no attempt at all had been made to destroy the Canaanites who lived there. The intent of these and similar remarks is no doubt to make clear that it was only because of Israel herself and her sinful neglect (Deut. 20:16–17) that God's great work of granting her the Promised Land was realized only in part. Verse 10 indirectly admonishes future generations to persevere to the end in their battle with the powers of evil and never to make peace with them. Thus we see that the Book of Joshua contains darkness as well as light.

6. The Inheritance of Manasseh
(17:1–13)

17:1–6 *This was the allotment for the tribe of Manasseh as Joseph's firstborn, that is, for Makir, Manasseh's firstborn. Makir was the ancestor of the Gileadites, who had received Gilead and Bashan because the Makirites were great soldiers. ² So this allotment was for the rest of the people of Manasseh— the clans of Abiezer, Helek, Asriel, Shechem, Hepher and Shemida. These are the other male descendants of Manasseh son of Joseph by their clans.*

³ Now Zelophehad son of Hepher, the son of Gilead, the son of Makir, the son of Manasseh, had no sons but only daughters, whose names were Mahlah, Noah, Hoglah, Milcah and Tirzah. ⁴ They went to Eleazar the priest, Joshua son of Nun, and the leaders and said, "The LORD commanded Moses to give us an inheritance among our brothers." So Joshua gave them an inheritance along with the brothers of their father, according to the LORD's command. ⁵ Manasseh's share consisted of ten tracts of land besides Gilead and Bashan east of the Jordan, ⁶ because the daughters of the tribe of Manasseh received an inheritance among the sons. The land of Gilead belonged to the rest of the descendants of Manasseh.

The allotment spoken of in verse 1 was a part of the allotment in 16:1, for the descendants of Joseph were assigned their land by a single drawing of the lot (see also v. 14). Manasseh is called Joseph's firstborn, not in order to contrast him with Ephraim (who indeed had received the best portion), but with the other sons of Joseph. Although this tribe had already been granted land east of the Jordan, it had another turn following Ephraim in the distribution of the western territory; for Manasseh was the firstborn son who was set apart for a share of God's special blessing (Gen. 48:5). In addition, only half the tribe of Manasseh had received an inheritance on the other side of the Jordan. There the Makirites had settled, or at least part of them, since the clans listed in verse 2 were also descended from Makir.

The name Makir in verse 1 refers first to Manasseh's son himself (Num. 26:29); but since he was no longer alive, it must also be taken as a reference to the Makirites. In the conquest of the Transjordan, these descendants of Manasseh had distinguished themselves by their bravery (Num. 32:39). The "people of Manasseh" spoken of in verse 2 were actually sons of Gilead, the grandson of Manasseh (Num. 26:30–32). Gilead in turn had a grandson named Zelophehad, a man whose daughters laid claim to his inheritance when the land was allotted, since this had been promised to them by God (Num. 27:1–7). They received their due and perhaps even more; for verses 5–6 indicate that they were counted, not as one clan, but as five, so that there were (counting the five male clans of v. 2) ten clans in all. Since it seems unlikely that the daughters of Zelophehad were granted half the entire territory, it is possible that the "ten tracts" spoken of in verse 5 were not all equally large. The names of Manasseh's other sons besides Makir (v. 6) are unknown to us, but it is clear from verse 1 that the descendants spoken of here were in any case Makirites.

17:7–10

> The territory of Manasseh extended from Asher to Micmethath east of Shechem. The boundary ran southward from there to include the people living at En Tappuah. ⁸(Manasseh had the land of Tappuah, but Tappuah itself, on the boundary of Manasseh, belonged to the Ephraimites.) ⁹Then the boundary continued south to the Kanah Ravine. There were towns belonging to Ephraim lying among the towns of Manasseh, but the boundary of Manasseh was the northern side of the ravine and ended at the sea. ¹⁰On the south the land belonged to Ephraim, on the north to Manasseh. The territory of Manasseh reached the sea and bordered Asher on the north and Issachar on the east.

The demarcation of Manasseh's boundaries that follows in these verses is rather vague compared, for example, to the boundaries outlined in 15:2–12 and 18:12–20. Verse 7 apparently draws the southern boundary from east to west (the territory of Manasseh lay north of Ephraim). Verse 9 also is concerned with the southern boundary. The nominal boundary actually ran south of the Kanah Ravine,[23] but since many towns south of this ravine belonged to Ephraim (see 16:9), the boundary in effect coincided with the ravine itself. This apparently is the point of verse 10a (cf. 16:8). The boundary to the west was the Mediterranean Sea; to the north, the territory of Asher; and to the east, the territory of Issachar.

17:11–13

> *Within Issachar and Asher, Manasseh also had Beth Shan, Ibleam and the people of Dor, Endor, Taanach and Megiddo, together with their surrounding settlements (the third in the list is Naphoth).* [12] *Yet the Manassites were not able to occupy these towns, for the Canaanites were determined to live in that region.* [13] *However, when the Israelites grew stronger, they subjected the Canaanites to forced labor but did not drive them out completely.*

The indefiniteness of the above boundaries is at least partly due to the fact that Manasseh's territory overlapped that of Issachar and Asher. Verse 11 names the inhabitants rather than the towns themselves because the people had not yet been able to capture the latter. The statement in verse 12 is graphically illustrated in verses 16–18, while verse 13 clearly refers to the situation that finally was established shortly after Joshua's death (cf. 16:10 and Judg. 1:28).

7. Rejection of the Josephites' Complaint (17:14–18)

17:14 *The people of Joseph said to*[24] *Joshua, "Why have you given us only one allotment and one portion for an inheritance? We are a numerous people and the LORD has blessed us abundantly."*

The following verses show that the two tribes of Joseph were taken together when the land was distributed (cf. 16:1). The complaint of Joseph's descendants is thus concerned with the whole of their

---

[23] The author's translation here corresponds to the KJV and NEB: "south *of* the Kanah Ravine"—TRANS.

[24] Following a number of manuscripts, the NIV here reads *'el* ("to") instead of *'et* ("with")—TRANS.

common territory. It is possible that they already had some knowledge of the territory that was allotted to them and therefore made this complaint at once. More likely, however, this was done some time after the allotment, when their attempts to expel the Canaanites had already proved fruitless (v. 12). The protest of the people of Joseph in verse 16 indeed seems to refer to this. Apparently they had already experienced how much strength the Canaanites still had, particularly in the plain of Beth Shan, and this had caused them to shrink back in fright. This protest was not the first thing they brought up, however. Here, in verse 14, they claimed that they had been treated unfairly in the distribution. Only one lot had been drawn for them; and together they had received only one of the shares or districts that the land initially had been divided into for the purpose of the allotment. This was in spite of the fact that they were such a numerous people and had been specially blessed all along by Israel's God. Ephraim and Manasseh clearly expressed their unity by coming forward as the one house of Joseph and referring to themselves as "we" and "us" (the Hebrew actually has "I" and "me"; cf. KJV and RSV).

17:15 *"If you are so numerous," Joshua answered, "and if the hill country of Ephraim is too small for you, go up into the forest and clear land for yourselves there in the land of the Perizzites and Rephaites."*

Joshua saw through their argument and advised them that, if the hills of Ephraim were too small for them, they should climb the wooded peaks to the north and create room for themselves by chopping down the forest in the land that had belonged to the Perizzites and the Rephaites. This, however, was an enormous task that the people of Joseph were extremely reluctant to undertake. It would have been much easier to go down into the plain, but the iron chariots of its Canaanite inhabitants awaited them there.

17:16 *The people of Joseph replied, "The hill country is not enough for us, and all the Canaanites who live in the plain have iron chariots, both those in Beth Shan and its settlements and those in the Valley of Jezreel."*

Joshua's reply forced the Josephite tribes to confess their fear of the Canaanites. They first remarked that the hill country of Ephraim (i.e., the hills plus the forest that Joshua had spoken of) still would not be large enough for them. Then they pointed out that the remainder of the terrain was controlled by Canaanites equipped with chariots. The plain referred to (the Hebrew literally reads "land of the plain") included both the Valley of Jezreel and the Jordan Valley (i.e., its western bank); the city of Beth Shan stood at the juncture of these two. The territory of these two tribes was actually not too small. All that they lacked was the faith and courage that would enable them to overcome all obstacles.

17:17–18 *But Joshua said to the house of Joseph—to Ephraim and Manasseh—"You are numerous and very powerful. You will have not only one allotment ¹⁸ but the forested hill country as well. Clear it, and its farthest limits will be yours; though the Canaanites have iron chariots and though they are strong, you can drive them out."*

Joshua stuck to the decision he had made. He reminded the Josephites of their great numbers and of how much power they would be able to bring to bear on the battle. The words "you will have not only one allotment" do not mean that they would receive an additional share but are rather a rebuttal of their complaint. Nominally they indeed had only one allotment, but their inheritance was in fact so large that it could serve for both of them. It embraced not only the extensive hill country, where the wooded areas could be brought under cultivation, but also the neighboring valleys that led into this region. Joshua ended by promising Ephraim and Manasseh in the Lord's name that they would triumph over their enemies.

Since Joshua was himself a member of the tribe of Ephraim, his firmness in this situation does him even greater credit. His strict sense of justice prevented him from favoring his fellow tribesmen at the expense of the other tribes.

8. The Division of the Land at Shiloh (18:1–10)

18:1 *The whole assembly of the Israelites gathered at Shiloh and set up the Tent of Meeting there. The country was brought under their control,*

To this point the allotment had taken place at Gilgal (9:6), a place slightly southwest of Shiloh that is probably equivalent to modern Jiljulieh. After the inheritances of Judah and Joseph had been assigned, however, Joshua moved the Israelite camp to Shiloh (modern Seilun), a city located twelve and a half miles south of Shechem (modern Nablus) and twenty miles north of Jerusalem. The reasons for this were not military but religious, for Shiloh was the place where—undoubtedly at God's command (see Jer. 7:12)—the tabernacle was to be set up. From this point on this would be the spiritual center of Israel. In truth, it was no longer necessary to maintain a military camp or headquarters, since the land was under Israel's control. The camp at Gilgal was never intended to be permanent, and it apparently was not an acceptable home for the ark. Shiloh perhaps was preferred because its name means "rest"; for after their long years of wandering, both the tabernacle and the people finally received their promised rest, a shadow of the rest that one day would be brought by the promised Shiloh (Gen. 49:10, see KJV and NIV margin—TRANS.).

Representatives from Judah and the tribes of Joseph were no doubt present when the Tent of Meeting was set up. The sanctuary of Israel's God remained at Shiloh till the ark was removed and then captured by the Philistines (1 Sam. 4:4, 11). After that, the tabernacle was moved to Nob (1 Sam. 21:1) and later to Gibeon (1 Kings 3:4).

18:2–4 *but there were still seven Israelite tribes who had not yet received their inheritance.*
³So Joshua said to the Israelites: "How long will you wait before you begin to take possession of the land that the LORD, the God of your fathers, has given you? ⁴Appoint three men from each tribe. I will send them out to make a survey of the land and to write a description of it, according to the inheritance of each. Then they will return to me.

Although the division of the land should have been finished before the tabernacle was moved, the latter interrupted the process. The allotment therefore did not proceed directly to its conclusion. Instead, it seems that Judah drew its lot first and departed from the camp; and Ephraim and Manasseh then did the same, before the lot was cast for the remaining tribes. The latter remained in limbo at Gilgal and showed little enthusiasm for taking over their share of the land. This was in part a simple matter of inertia. Additionally, the Israelites still had only a rough knowledge of the land and did not know the exact locations of the towns (see v. 9). Furthermore, the Josephites' experience (17:14–18) made them shrink from the thought of renewed warfare. They longed for rest, but it was not the true rest promised by God that they had in mind. Joshua was disturbed at this; and when the tabernacle was moved and set up at Shiloh, he seized this occasion to scold the remaining tribes for their indolence and their ingratitude for the favors God had shown. He would not tolerate any further delay, and he himself took the initiative to push on with the allotment.

For a fair distribution it seemed necessary that a survey first be made of the land and of the numbers of towns in the various tribal territories. Hence Joshua directed that three men be designated from each tribe who would reconnoiter the land that remained undivided, write a description of its main outlines, and make a plan for its distribution.

18:5-7 *You are to divide the land into seven parts. Judah is to remain in its territory on the south and the house of Joseph in its territory on the north. ⁶After you have written descriptions of the seven parts of the land, bring them here to me and I will cast lots for you in the presence of the LORD our God. ⁷The Levites, however, do not get a portion among you, because the priestly service of the LORD is their inheritance. And Gad, Reuben and the half-tribe of Manasseh have already received their inheritance on the east side of the Jordan. Moses the servant of the LORD gave it to them."*

Only seven tribes were taken into account here, since no changes were to be made in the allotments to Judah,[25] the house of Joseph, Gad, Reuben, and the eastern half of Manasseh; and Levi, the tribe that had the best portion, received no inheritance. The word "you" (v. 6) was addressed, not to the scouts who had yet to be chosen, but to the tribes themselves, who were to perform this task in the person of their representatives. It seems that Eleazar and the elders did not themselves urge the Israelites to proceed with their work.

18:8-10 *As the men started on their way to map out the land, Joshua instructed them, "Go and make a survey of the land and write a description of it. Then return to me, and I will cast lots for you here at Shiloh in the presence of the LORD." ⁹So the men left and went through the land. They wrote its description on a scroll, town by town, in seven parts, and returned to Joshua in the camp at Shiloh. ¹⁰Joshua then cast lots for them in Shiloh in the presence of the LORD, and there he distributed the land to the Israelites according to their tribal divisions.*

Everything was done as Joshua had directed. His instructions did not mean that the men had to make actual measurements of the land; they only had to take notes on its extent, its geographical features, and especially the number of towns. Since they were able to complete this task without interference, it is clear that the Canaanites, aware that they were outnumbered, kept quiet as long as they were not attacked. The allotment of the land, as befit its religious character, henceforth took place in the presence of the Lord, i.e., directly in front of His

---

[25] See the comments in 19:9, however.

sanctuary, and under the leadership of Joshua, Eleazar, and the elders (19:51).

9. The Inheritance of Benjamin
(18:11-28)

18:11-20 *The lot came up for the tribe of Benjamin, clan by clan. Their allotted territory lay between the tribes of Judah and Joseph:*

¹²On the north side their boundary began at the Jordan, passed the northern slope of Jericho and headed west into the hill country, coming out at the desert of Beth Aven. ¹³From there it crossed to the south slope of Luz (that is, Bethel) and went down to Ataroth Addar on the hill south of Lower Beth Horon.

¹⁴From the hill facing Beth Horon on the south the boundary turned south along the western side and came out at Kiriath Baal (that is, Kiriath Jearim), a town of the people of Judah. This was the western side.

¹⁵The southern side began at the outskirts of Kiriath Jearim on the west, and the boundary came out at the spring of the waters of Nephtoah.²⁶ ¹⁶The boundary went down to the foot of the hill facing the Valley of Ben Hinnom, north of the Valley of Rephaim. It continued down the Hinnom Valley along the southern slope of the Jebusite city and so to En Rogel. ¹⁷It then curved north, went to En Shemesh, continued to Geliloth, which faces the Pass of Adummim, and ran down to the Stone of Bohan son of Reuben. ¹⁸It continued to the northern slope of Beth Arabah²⁷ and on into the Arabah. ¹⁹It then went to the northern slope of Beth Hoglah and came out at the

---

²⁶The author translated this "and the boundary began in the west and came out at the spring. . . ." He added the following footnote:

There is reason to suspect that a slight error has been introduced into the original text here. The Hebrew literally reads not "in the west," but "westward" (see RSV and NEB margin). The Septuagint replaces the latter with the name of a city, and it apparently therefore read a completely different word here. The context too leads us to expect something different. Verses 12-13 give the northern boundary from east to west, verse 14 the western boundary, and verses 15-19 follow with the southern boundary from west to east. The word "westward" thus seems to clash with the direction in which the boundary is being drawn. I therefore have followed Keil and others in leaving the word more indefinite and translating it as "in the west." Then at least the sentence makes better sense. The most likely solution, however, is that a copyist inadvertently changed the original word (perhaps *miyyām*, "from the west") to "westward" (*yāmmâ[h]*)—TRANS.

The NIV solves the problem by interpreting *yāmmâ(h)* as "on [rather than 'toward'] the west," while the RSV emends the word to "Ephron" in connection with 15:9. Rudolf Kittel simply proposes that *yāmmâ(h)* be deleted—TRANS.

²⁷The Hebrew has "slope facing the Arabah." Beth Arabah (cf. 15:6) is an emendation based on the Septuagint.

northern bay of the Salt Sea, at the mouth of the Jordan in the south. This was the southern boundary.

²⁰ The Jordan formed the boundary on the eastern side.

These were the boundaries that marked out the inheritance of the clans of Benjamin on all sides.

The lot chose Benjamin as the next tribe to receive a share of the land. By God's design the descendants of Jacob's second most-beloved son after Joseph were thus given a position of honor between the tribes of Judah and the Josephites. Because Benjamin was the smallest of all the tribes next to Simeon (cf. Num. 26:14, 41; Ps. 68:27), its territory was not especially large but nevertheless comprised a choice section of the Promised Land. Verses 12–13 give the northern boundary, which coincided with part of the southern boundary of Ephraim (16:1–3). Verse 14 then describes the western boundary, and verses 15–19 the southern boundary that separated Benjamin from Judah (cf. 15:5–9). Geliloth in verse 17 apparently is the same place as Gilgal (15:7). The Arabah at the end of verse 18 is the Jordan Valley, which is quite broad at this point (cf. 3:16; 11:16). Benjamin's territory stretched to the Jordan on the east.

18:21–28 *The tribe of Benjamin, clan by clan, had the following cities:*

Jericho, Beth Hoglah, Emek Keziz, ²²Beth Arabah, Zemaraim, Bethel, ²³Avvim, Parah, Ophrah, ²⁴Kephar Ammoni, Ophni and Geba—twelve towns and their villages.

²⁵Gibeon, Ramah, Beeroth, ²⁶Mizpah, Kephirah, Mozah, ²⁷Rekem, Irpeel, Taralah, ²⁸Zelah, Haeleph, the Jebusite city (that is, Jerusalem), Gibeah and Kiriath—fourteen towns and their villages.

This was the inheritance of Benjamin for its clans.

The remaining verses list the various cities in Benjamin. A few of these, particularly Jericho and Jebus (or Jerusalem; see in 15:63), were very important. The towns were divided into an eastern and a western group. Gibeah (lit., Gibeath, see KJV) was the scene of the events recounted in Judges 19 and 20. The Kiriath ("city") spoken of here is not the same place as Kiriath Jearim (v. 14).

10. The Inheritance of Simeon
(19:1–9)

19:1–8 *The second lot came out for the tribe of Simeon, clan by clan. Their inheritance lay within the territory of Judah.* *²It included:*

Beersheba (or Sheba),²⁸ Moladah, ³Hazar Shual, Balah, Ezem, ⁴Eltolad, Bethul, Hormah, ⁵Ziklag, Beth Marcaboth, Hazar Susah, ⁶Beth Lebaoth and Sharuhen—thirteen towns and their villages;

⁷Ain, Rimmon, Ether and Ashan—four towns and their villages— ⁸and all the villages around these towns as far as Baalath Beer (Ramah in the Negev).

This was the inheritance of the tribe of the Simeonites, clan by clan.

The second drawing of the lot designates the tribe of Simeon as the next in line to receive its inheritance. No boundaries are drawn here, and all we find is a list of the cities that were given to Simeon. The reason is that Simeon received no separate territory but instead had to make its home within Judah. Clearly, Jacob's prophecy about Simeon in Genesis 49:7 came to fulfillment in this manner. The tribe of Simeon was given nothing more than the cities named here, which are listed also in 15:26–32, 42. These and their surrounding villages lay mostly in the Negev, though Ether and Ashan were in the Shephelah or western foothills. Baalath Beer apparently was also named Ramah of the Negev ("height of the south country") to distinguish it from the other places called Ramah (see, e.g., 18:25). Simeon received such a small share of the land because it was the smallest tribe (Num. 26:14; 1 Chron. 4:27),²⁹ and here again we see that God guided the drawing of the lots.

19:9 *The inheritance of the Simeonites was taken from the share of Judah, because Judah's portion was more than they needed. So the Simeonites received their inheritance within the territory of Judah.*

The question of how Simeon's inheritance can be reconciled with the statement in 18:5 is answered by verse 9: the territory of the

---

[28] Whereas the NIV takes Sheba as an alternate name for Beersheba, the author followed the Hebrew literally and regarded these as two distinct places (cf. KJV, RSV, NIV margin). He added the following footnote: "Sheba does not appear in the list of Simeon's cities in 1 Chronicles 4:28, and its location is unknown. Keil supposes that it is the same place as the Shema mentioned next to Moladah in 15:26. It is better to assume, however, that Sheba lay right next to Beersheba ('well of Sheba') and thus could be counted together with it. The total of 13 in verse 6 would then fit with the number of names in these verses. See also Gen. 26:33"—TRANS.

[29] The territory later proved to be too small even for Simeon, however. See 1 Chronicles 4:38–43 and Roorda, *Josua, De Held Gods*, p. 222.

descendants of Judah was too large for them. Apparently the survey made by the twenty-one scouts (18:4, 9) revealed that there was not enough room in the land that remained to be divided, while Judah had more space than it needed. After the men returned, Joshua therefore agreed that one of the seven tribes would receive its inheritance within the boundaries of Judah; and when the lot was drawn, Simeon was designated as this tribe. Thus God's instructions concerning the tribe of Judah were left inviolate (15:1; 18:5; see the comments in 14:1–5), while the other tribes were still treated fairly.

11. The Inheritance of Zebulun
(19:10–16)

19:10–16 *The third lot came up for Zebulun, clan by clan:*
The boundary of their inheritance went as far as Sarid. [11]*Going west it ran to Maralah, touched Dabbesheth, and extended to the ravine near Jokneam.* [12]*It turned east from Sarid toward the sunrise to the territory of Kisloth Tabor and went on to Daberath and up to Japhia.* [13]*Then it continued eastward to Gath Hepher and Eth Kazin; it came out at Rimmon and turned toward Neah.* [14]*There the boundary went around on the north to Hannathon and ended at the Valley of Iphtah El.* [15]*Included were Kattath, Nahalal, Shimron, Idalah and Bethlehem. There were twelve towns and their villages.* [16]*These towns and their villages were the inheritance of Zebulun, clan by clan.*

The sequence God caused the lots to be drawn in did not follow the order of birth of Jacob's sons. This is evident once again in the case of Zebulun, the sixth son of Jacob and Leah; for this tribe was chosen before Issachar, the fifth son (cf. Gen. 49:13–14). Zebulun's territory extended southward to Sarid, and its southern boundary is drawn from that point first to the west (v. 11) and then to the east (v. 12). Verse 13 seems to turn to the eastern boundary, while the line from Hannathon to Iphtah El (v. 14) presumably formed the northern boundary.[30] The western boundary is not described, but it partly coincided with the eastern border of Asher (v. 27). The territory of Zebulun was formed by the fertile region of Lower Galilee, lying between the Valley of Jezreel and the hill country of Naphtali. Oddly, verse 15 gives a total of twelve towns when only five are mentioned. In view of the fact that there is no phrase here like "had the following cities" (18:21) or "the

---

[30]Our conclusions about these boundaries remain tentative, for most of the places in verses 13–14 are of uncertain location.

fortified cities were'' (19:35; the Hebrew of v. 15 literally reads "and Kattah, Nahalal . . ."; cf. KJV, RSV), while some well-known towns of Zebulun are not even mentioned (e.g., Nazareth and the towns mentioned in 1:34–35), it is possible that there once was a list of seven more towns between verse 14 and verse 15. Another possibility, however, is that the author chose to mention only the five most important towns of Zebulun.

12. The Inheritance of Issachar
(19:17–23)

19:17–23 *The fourth lot came out for Issachar, clan by clan.* [18]*Their territory included:*

Jezreel, Kesulloth, Shunem, [19]*Hapharaim, Shion, Anaharath,* [20]*Rabbith, Kishion, Ebez,* [21]*Remeth, En Gannim, En Haddah and Beth Pazzez.* [22]*The boundary touched Tabor, Shahazumah and Beth Shemesh, and ended at the Jordan. There were sixteen towns and their villages.*
[23]*These towns and their villages were the inheritance of the tribe of Issachar, clan by clan.*

The territory of Issachar was surrounded by that of Manasseh (on the south and west), Asher (on the west), Zebulun and Naphtali (on the north), and the Jordan on the east. Only the eastern part of its north boundary is described (v. 22). Its land included the beautiful and fertile Valley of Jezreel.

13. The Inheritance of Asher
(19:24–31)

19:24–31 *The fifth lot came out for the tribe of Asher, clan by clan.* [25]*Their territory included:*

Helkath, Hali, Beten, Acshaph, [26]*Allammelech, Amad and Mishal. On the west the boundary touched Carmel and Shihor Libnath.* [27]*It then turned east toward Beth Dagon, touched Zebulun and the Valley of Iphtah El, and went*[31] *north to Beth Emek and Neiel, passing Cabul on the left.* [28]*It went to Abdon,*[32] *Rehob, Hammon and Kanah, as far as Greater Sidon.* [29]*The boundary then turned back toward Ramah and went to the fortified city of*

---

[31]This word has been added in translation for the sake of clarity—TRANS.

[32]The Hebrew text has Ebron. Since, however, a number of manuscripts have Abdon, the name that appears also in 21:30 and 1 Chronicles 6:74, we can conclude that this was the original reading.

> Tyre, turned toward Hosah and came out at the sea in the region of Aczib,[33]
> [30]*Ummah,*[34] *Aphek and Rehob.*[35] *There were twenty-two towns and their villages.*
> [31]*These towns and their villages were the inheritance of the tribe of Asher, clan by clan.*

The tribe of Asher was given the land along the coast extending northward from Mount Carmel to Sidon. Its southern boundary was Shihor Libnath[36] south of Mount Carmel. Verse 27 gives part of the eastern boundary. The northern part of the eastern boundary is indicated only roughly, for verse 28 gives a list of cities rather than drawing a precise line.[37] Verses 29–30 then describe a line running south from Sidon, but this too ends in a list of cities that seem to define the western boundary. "The region of Aczib" (or "from Hebel to Aczib," see footnote 33) presumably is a section of the coast, which thus did not belong to Asher along its full length. Twenty-four towns are listed in all; so the author perhaps was not including Greater Sidon and Tyre in the total of twenty-two given in verse 30. Where these two Phoenician cities are spoken of, the Hebrew text has '*ad,* "as far as" or "up to." Judges 1:31 ascribes Sidon to Asher's inheritance, however.

---

[33] The Hebrew here is obscure and has been translated in a variety of different ways (cf. KJV, RSV, NEB). The author has "from Hebel to Aczib" and adds the following footnote:
The literal reading of the Hebrew is "from the region to Aczib." This could mean "from the region that stretches to Aczib," but such an expression would be rather unusual and obscure, and one could ask why the text does not simply read "from Aczib." In the Septuagint, the names of two towns appear here and "came out at the sea" forms the end of a sentence. It is very tempting to end our sentence the same way, since this phrase naturally often indicates the termination of a boundary (e.g., 15:4, 11; 16:3; 17:9). Nevertheless, the words that follow the phrase here seem to modify it. The best solution is to take the word *hebel,* which normally means "region," as a place name Hebel, which could be an alternate name for Helbah or Ahlab (Judg. 1:31). The meaning of the sentence then is very clear—TRANS.

[34] Several Greek manuscripts have Acco here (cf. NEB). Perhaps this reading should be preferred, since Acco was a well-known port (Judg. 1:31) and nothing further is known about Ummah.

[35] This is a different Rehob from that spoken of in verse 28.

[36] The author has "the brook of Libnath" (cf. NEB, "swamp of Libnath")—TRANS.

[37] Following the Hebrew literally, the author has merely "and Abdon, Rehob . . ." in verse 28. The NIV has added "it went to" for the sake of clarity—TRANS.

14. The Inheritance of Naphtali
(19:32–39)

19:32–39 *The sixth lot came out for Naphtali, clan by clan:*
*³³Their boundary went from Heleph and the large tree in Zaanannim,
passing Adami Nekeb and Jabneel to Lakkum and ending at the Jordan.
³⁴The boundary ran west through Aznoth Tabor and came out at Hukkok. It
touched Zebulun on the south, Asher on the west and the Jordan³⁸ on the
east. ³⁵The fortified cities were Ziddim, Zer, Hammath, Rakkath, Kinnereth,
³⁶Adamah, Ramah, Hazor, ³⁷Kedesh, Edrei, En Hazor, ³⁸Iron, Migdal El,
Horem, Beth Anath and Beth Shemesh. There were nineteen towns and their
villages.*
*³⁹These towns and their villages were the inheritance of the tribe of Naphtali,
clan by clan.*

Naphtali's territory was formed mainly by the later region of Upper
Galilee, the northeastern section of the land west of the Jordan. This
was a fertile highland area that descended to the lakes of Semechonitis
and Gennesaret. Verse 33 seems to draw part of the northern boundary,
while verse 34a very briefly describes the southern boundary beginning
at the Jordan. The "large tree in Zaanannim" (v. 33) is spoken of once
again at Judges 4:11. Since the total of nineteen in verse 38 is too high,
we have to assume that some of the towns are left unmentioned (e.g.,
Kartan, 21:32).

15. The Inheritance of Dan
(19:40–48)

19:40–48 *The seventh lot came out for the tribe of Dan, clan by clan. ⁴¹The
territory of their inheritance included:*
*Zorah, Eshtaol, Ir Shemesh, ⁴²Shaalabbin, Aijalon, Ithlah, ⁴³Elon,
Timnah, Ekron, ⁴⁴Eltekeh, Gibbethon, Baalath, ⁴⁵Jehud, Bene Berak, Gath
Rimmon, ⁴⁶Me Jarkon and Rakkon, with the area facing Joppa.*
*⁴⁷(But the Danites had difficulty taking possession of their territory, so they
went up and attacked Leshem, took it, put it to the sword and occupied it. They*

---

³⁸The author has "Judah on the Jordan" here (cf. KJV, RSV, and NIV margin). He
adds the following footnote: "The Hebrew text here has the word Judah, which
undoubtedly must be understood as a place name. It is certain, however, that
Naphtali did not border on the territory of the tribe of Judah. A possible solution is
that this was a northern settlement established by the inhabitants of Judah"—
TRANS.

settled in Leshem and named it Dan after their forefather.) ⁴⁸*These towns and their villages were the inheritance of the tribe of Dan, clan by clan.*

Since the territories of the surrounding tribes of Ephraim (on the north), Benjamin (on the east), and Judah (on the south) had already been mapped, it was not necessary that any boundaries be drawn for Dan. The Mediterranean Sea formed its western boundary. Judah and Ephraim probably had to cede a few towns to Dan (cf., e.g., v. 41 and 15:33). The Danites thus were given a section of the foothills and lowland to the west of the highlands of Judah. Nevertheless, because of the Danites' fear and indifference, the greater part of the luxuriant plain was left to the Amorites (Judg. 1:34); and the area that the Danites had actual possession of, therefore, proved to be too small for them. The Hebrew of verse 47 literally says that their territory escaped them, and the RSV and NEB take this to mean that they lost it. This is saying too much, however, as is clear from the story of Samson. Because of the lack of room, some of the Danites marched north and conquered the town of Leshem near the headstreams of the Jordan, an event that is recounted in greater detail in Judges 18.

As a final observation, we can note that the descendants of Jacob's wives, Leah and Rachel, received their inheritances first and then the descendants of Bilhah and Zilpah (i.e., Asher, Naphtali, and Dan), the maidservants of Jacob's wives. There thus was a general order in which the lot distributed the land, though this does not apply to the tribe of Gad, the son of Zilpah, which had already received its inheritance in the Transjordan.

16. The Inheritance of Joshua and the Conclusion of the Allotment (19:49–51)

19:49–51 *When they had finished dividing the land into its allotted portions, the Israelites gave Joshua son of Nun an inheritance among them,* ⁵⁰*as the LORD had commanded. They gave him the town he asked for—Timnath Serah in the hill country of Ephraim. And he built up the town and settled there.*

⁵¹*These are the territories that Eleazar the priest, Joshua son of Nun and the heads of the tribal clans of Israel assigned by lot at Shiloh in the presence of the LORD at the entrance to the Tent of Meeting. And so they finished dividing the land.*

These verses splendidly conclude the account of the division of Canaan. The event that transpires here illustrates the good relationship that prevailed between Joshua and Israel. After each tribe had received its own section of the land, the Israelites gave to Joshua, their faithful leader to whom they owed so much, the city of his choice as his personal possession. That they did this at the Lord's command does not diminish their own willingness. We should not conclude from verse 50 that the Lord had specifically designated Timnath Serah. Rather, He had only directed that Joshua was to be given whatever city he desired. Even this may be saying too much, for it is possible that the Israelites gave Timnath Serah to Joshua merely on the basis of God's express promise to him (and Caleb) in Numbers 14:30. That promise did not mention any details, however; and we do not know whether the Lord made any specific disclosure about this later.

Timnath Serah probably was partially destroyed during the conquest, and Joshua thus would have had to start rebuilding the city. The end of verse 50 also could mean, however, that he enlarged the city or fortified it. Joshua's pure and genuine greatness is shown in that he modestly retired to his home when he could have had himself proclaimed king. A. Roorda fittingly remarks (*Josua, De Held Gods,* p. 252): "Joshua steps down in reverence before his God. Here again, his action calls to mind Him of whom it is said in 1 Corinthians 15:28 that when He has completed His whole work of redemption and all things are subjected to Him, 'then the Son Himself will be made subject to Him who put everything under Him, so that God may be all in all.'"

17. The Designation of the Cities of Refuge
(20:1-9)

20:1-9 *Then the LORD said to Joshua:* [2]*"Tell the Israelites to designate the cities of refuge, as I instructed you through Moses,* [3]*so that anyone who kills a person accidentally and unintentionally may flee there and find protection from the avenger of blood.*

[4]*"When he flees to one of these cities, he is to stand in the entrance of the city gate and state his case before the elders of that city. Then they are to admit him into their city and give him a place to live with them.* [5]*If the avenger of blood pursues him, they must not surrender the one accused, because he killed his neighbor unintentionally and without malice aforethought.* [6]*He is to stay in that city until he has stood trial before the assembly and until the death of the high priest who is serving at that time. Then he may go back to his own home in the town from which he fled."*

> [7] *So they set apart Kedesh in Galilee in the hill country of Naphtali, Shechem in the hill country of Ephraim, and Kiriath Arba (that is, Hebron) in the hill country of Judah.* [8] *On the east side of the Jordan of Jericho*[39] *they designated Bezer in the desert on the plateau in the tribe of Reuben, Ramoth in Gilead in the tribe of Gad, and Golan in Bashan in the tribe of Manasseh.* [9] *Any of the Israelites or any alien living among them who killed someone accidentally could flee to these designated cities and not be killed by the avenger of blood prior to standing trial before the assembly.*

After all the tribes had been assigned their territory, the Lord commanded Joshua that the cities of refuge were to be designated. This was to be done by the Israelites themselves (in the person of their elders), but Joshua was to supervise the procedure. Thus Israel obeyed the instructions that God had already made known in Numbers 35:9–29 and Deuteronomy 19:1–10 and in the brief command given earlier on Mount Horeb (Exod. 21:13), on which these passages are apparently based (cf. also Deut. 4:41–43). Once again Joshua was, so to speak, the executor of Moses' will, though it was God Himself who reminded Joshua of Moses' instructions (vv. 1–2).

There is no need to elaborate here on the regulations concerning the cities of refuge that are briefly summarized in this chapter. See Noordtzij's comments on Numbers 35 and Ridderbos's comments on Deuteronomy 4 and 19 in the two previous volumes of the *Bible Student's Commentary*. The only thing new here is the designation of the three cities west of the Jordan (v. 7; cf. Deut. 19:9). To complete the picture, verse 8 briefly reviews the selection of the cities of refuge in the Transjordan (see Deut. 4:41–43).

One final observation can still be made about the institution of the cities of refuge. The fugitive's stay there was in some sense a period of exile; for though his action may have been unintentional, he still had shed human blood and therefore had to bear the consequences of his carelessness. His exile also would serve as a warning to others. The main purpose of the cities of refuge, however, was to offer divine protection to the offender till the death of the high priest granted him total freedom. This institution of ancient Israel also contains a covert but undeniable reference to Christ, whose death grants a full release from the harsh demands of justice since He has accomplished a real atonement (see Note 6 at the end of this commentary).

---

[39] See footnote 8 in 13:32 and Note 1 at the end of this commentary.

18. The Selection of the Levitical Cities
(21:1–42)

Joshua 21:1–42 recounts the final act in dividing the land: assigning towns to the priests and Levites. This could be done only after each tribe had received its inheritance and the cities of refuge had been designated, for these were also set apart for the Levites (see Num. 35:6).

21:1–3 *Now the family heads of the Levites approached Eleazar the priest, Joshua son of Nun, and the heads of the other tribal families of Israel ²at Shiloh in Canaan and said to them, "The LORD commanded through Moses that you give us towns to live in, with pasturelands for our livestock." ³So, as the LORD had commanded, the Israelites gave the Levites the following towns and pasturelands out of their own inheritance:*

Since their turn had arrived, the heads of the Levitical families stepped boldly before the men who were supervising the division of the land to remind them of the Lord's instructions regarding the towns for the Levites (Num. 35:1–8). Joshua, Eleazar, and the elders responded at once and proceeded to determine which towns the Levites were to reside in. The plan was not that the descendants of Levi would be the sole inhabitants of these towns, but rather that they would be given as much room within them as they needed. While in other cities they could own nothing, here their property would be inalienable. Nevertheless, the selected cities as such would remain the possession of the tribes in which they were located and whose citizens resided in them along with the Levites. This can be inferred, for example, from verse 12 and 14:14 for Hebron (v. 11) and from 15:16–17 for Debir (v. 15).

21:4–8 *The first lot came out for the Kohathites, clan by clan. The Levites who were descendants of Aaron the priest were allotted thirteen towns from the tribes of Judah, Simeon and Benjamin. ⁵The rest of Kohath's descendants were allotted ten towns from the clans of the tribes of Ephraim, Dan and half of Manasseh.*

⁶The descendants of Gershon were allotted thirteen towns from the clans of the tribes of Issachar, Asher, Naphtali and the half-tribe of Manasseh in Bashan.

⁷The descendants of Merari, clan by clan, received twelve towns from the tribes of Reuben, Gad and Zebulun.

⁸So the Israelites allotted to the Levites these towns and their pasturelands, as the LORD had commanded through Moses.

The towns most likely, were designated directly, but the lot then determined the subdivisions of the tribe of Levi that would reside in the respective groups of towns. The Levites were divided into three main clans that were the lines of the three sons of their ancestral father: Kohath, Gershon, and Merari (Num. 3:17). The Kohathites received two allotments, however, since the priests, who were the descendants of Aaron, formed a separate division among them. Verse 4 thus specifically focuses on the Aaronites, and verse 5 distinguishes them from "the rest of Kohath's descendants." Verses 4–8 state how many cities the respective divisions of the Levites received and the tribes in which each allotment lay. The descendants of Aaron were given thirteen towns, the rest of the Kohathites ten, the descendants of Gershon thirteen, and the descendants of Merari twelve. In all, the Levites received forty-eight towns (see Num. 35:7).

21:9–42 *From the tribes of Judah and Simeon they allotted the following towns by name* [10](*these towns were assigned to the descendants of Aaron who were from the Kohathite clans of the Levites, because the first lot fell to them*):
[11]*They gave them Kiriath Arba (that is, Hebron), with its surrounding pastureland, in the hill country of Judah. (Arba was the forefather of Anak.*[40]
[12]*But the fields and villages around the city they had given to Caleb son of Jephunneh as his possession.*
[13]*So to the descendants of Aaron the priest they gave Hebron (a city of refuge for one accused of murder), Libnah,* [14]*Jattir, Eshtemoa,* [15]*Holon, Debir,* [16]*Ain, Juttah and Beth Shemesh, together with their pasturelands— nine towns from these two tribes.*
[17]*And from the tribe of Benjamin they gave them Gibeon, Geba,* [18]*Anathoth and Almon, together with their pasturelands—four towns.*
[19]*All the towns for the priests, the descendants of Aaron, were thirteen, together with their pasturelands.*

[20]*The rest of the Kohathite clans of the Levites were allotted towns from the tribe of Ephraim:*
[21]*In the hill country of Ephraim they were given Shechem (a city of refuge for one accused of murder) and Gezer,* [22]*Kibzaim and Beth Horon, together with their pasturelands—four towns.*
[23]*Also from the tribe of Dan they received Eltekeh, Gibbethon,* [24]*Aijalon and Gath Rimmon, together with their pasturelands—four towns.*
[25]*From half the tribe of Manasseh they received Taanach and Gath Rimmon,*[41] *together with their pasturelands—two towns.*

---

[40]The Hebrew here has Anok, obviously an alternate form of Anak (15:13).
[41]The author substituted Ibleam for Gath Rimmon here and added the following footnote: "The Hebrew text has Gath Rimmon here and not Ibleam. Verse 24,

²⁶*All these ten towns and their pasturelands were given to the rest of the Kohathite clans.*

²⁷*The Levite clans of the Gershonites were given:*
from the half-tribe of Manasseh,
Golan in Bashan (a city of refuge for one accused of murder) and Be Eshtarah, together with their pasturelands—two towns;
²⁸*from the tribe of Issachar,*
Kishion, Daberath, ²⁹*Jarmuth and En Gannim, together with their pasturelands—four towns;*
³⁰*from the tribe of Asher,*
Mishal, Abdon, ³¹*Helkath and Rehob, together with their pasturelands—four towns;*
³²*from the tribe of Naphtali,*
Kedesh in Galilee (a city of refuge for one accused of murder), Hammoth Dor and Kartan, together with their pasturelands—three towns.
³³*All the towns of the Gershonite clans were thirteen, together with their pasturelands.*

³⁴*The Merarite clans (the rest of the Levites) were given:*
from the tribe of Zebulun,
Jokneam, Kartah, ³⁵*Dimnah and Nahalal, together with their pasturelands—four towns;*
³⁶*from the tribe of Reuben,*
Bezer, Jahaz, ³⁷*Kedemoth and Mephaath, together with their pasturelands—four towns;*
³⁸*from the tribe of Gad,*
Ramoth in Gilead (a city of refuge for one accused of murder), Mahanaim, ³⁹*Heshbon and Jazer, together with their pasturelands—four towns in all.*
⁴⁰*All the towns allotted to the Merarite clans, who were the rest of the Levites, were twelve.*

⁴¹*The towns of the Levites in the territory held by the Israelites were forty-eight in all, together with their pasturelands.* ⁴²*Each of these towns had pasturelands surrounding it; this was true for all these towns.*

These verses list the names of the Levitical towns that were ceded by each individual tribe. Judah and Simeon are taken together because Simeon did not inherit a clearly outlined expanse of land (see in 19:1). By drawing the first lot (vv. 4, 10), the Aaronic priesthood received the

---

however, shows that Gath Rimmon lay in the territory of Dan, and it therefore should not be repeated here. The Septuagint has the name of another city here that is probably equivalent to Ibleam, an alternate name for Bileam, which is listed among the Levitical cities in 1 Chron. 6:70. On this basis, it is widely assumed that the text originally had Ibleam or Bileam and that a copyist mistakenly repeated the name Gath Rimmon from verse 24"—TRANS.

group of towns within the territories of Judah and Benjamin. Again, we see that God controlled the allotment, for the Aaronic priesthood thereby came to reside in the towns that lay nearest to Jerusalem (though this city is not named here), the place where the national sanctuary one day would rise. The descendants of Aaron thus dwelt in the southern part of Canaan (vv. 9–19). The rest of the Kohathites received towns in the central part of the land west of the Jordan (vv. 20–26). The descendants of Gershon were assigned towns in the land north of these, but they also received two more towns east of the Jordan in the half-tribe of Manasseh (vv. 27–33). Finally, the Merarites received four towns in Zebulun, but they mainly came to dwell east of the Jordan in towns in the territories of Reuben and Gad (vv. 34–40). Verses 41–42 show that the Israelites strictly obeyed God's instructions and gave the Levites the correct number of towns and also the necessary pasturelands (see Num. 35:2–7).

19. Conclusion and Final Overview (21:43–45)

21:43–45 *So the LORD gave Israel all the land he had sworn to give their forefathers, and they took possession of it and settled there.* *44 The LORD gave them rest on every side, just as he had sworn to their forefathers.* *45 Not one of their enemies withstood them; the LORD handed all their enemies over to them. Not one of all the LORD's good promises to the house of Israel failed; every one was fulfilled.*

These verses do not directly continue the preceding material but rather glance back at the whole of chapters 3–21 and give more or less of a summary and final reflection on them. Although three important chapters still follow in the Book of Joshua, no one would deny that this brief passage actually concludes the historical account of Israel's settlement in Canaan. Looking back on the course of events, the author gratefully acknowledged that the Lord had done all that He had promised before the entry into Canaan (1:2–9). The "good promises" spoken of in verse 45 are the promises that God had given regarding the conquest of Canaan (e.g., Exod. 23:23, 27–30; Deut. 11:31; 31:3–8). To say that not one of these was forgotten or given in vain is no exaggeration. The Lord always fulfills His promises, even in the face of human weakness and unfaithfulness. This was the experience of the ancient Israelites, and it was confirmed once again to believers from the time of the New Testament. One day all God's promises will be fulfilled, and a multitude will then openly acknowledge this with praise and thanksgiving (Rev. 11:17-18; 19:5-7).

Section 4 of the Introduction, which discusses the alleged inconsistencies in the Book of Joshua, deals further with 21:43-45.

20. The Departure of the Transjordanian Tribes (22:1-9)

The account of the conquest and settlement of the Promised Land would be incomplete without the account of Joshua's farewell to the two and a half tribes whose territory was east of the Jordan. This farewell harks back directly to 1:12-18, the passage that records Joshua's orders to those tribes and the promise that they made to him.

22:1-5 *Then Joshua summoned the Reubenites, the Gadites and the half-tribe of Manasseh ² and said to them, "You have done all that Moses the servant of the LORD commanded, and you have obeyed me in everything I commanded. ³ For a long time now—to this very day—you have not deserted your brothers but have carried out the mission the LORD your God gave you. ⁴ Now that the LORD your God has given your brothers rest as he promised, return to your homes in the land that Moses the servant of the LORD gave you on the other side of the Jordan. ⁵ But be very careful to keep the commandment and the law that Moses the servant of the LORD gave you: to love the LORD your God, to walk in all his ways, to obey his commands, to hold fast to him and to serve him with all your heart and all your soul."*

Joshua summoned the tribes of Reuben and Gad and the half-tribe of Manasseh to send them homeward. The exact time this happened is not clear, but it surely must have taken place after the division of the land had been completed. This can be gathered from the words "has given your brothers rest" in verse 4 (1:15 had used even stronger words) and also from the fact that they departed, not from Gilgal, but from Shiloh (v. 9). By that time Joshua had good grounds acknowledging that for a long time they had lent their promised assistance to the other tribes (v. 3; see the comments in 1:12-18). In stating that these tribes had done "all that Moses the servant of the LORD commanded" (v. 2), Joshua was not speaking of the totality of the Mosaic laws but only of the special mandate that had been given to the Transjordanian tribes (Num. 32:20-22). Israel's general also gratefully acknowledged that they had fulfilled their duty and kept the promise that they had made to him (1:17). He discharged them with honor and allowed them to settle permanently in the land that God had given them as their own.

153

The Hebrew term the NIV translates as "homes" in verse 4 literally means "tents" (cf. KJV). The word might seem odd here, but it had become commonplace during the desert journey and thus was used habitually long afterward (e.g., Judg. 20:8 and 1 Kings 12:16 in KJV). Joshua ended by admonishing the Transjordanian tribes to remain faithful to the law of the Lord that Moses had made known to them, for nothing was more important to their common well-being than this. He added a brief but splendid summary of the spiritual content of the whole law: to love the Lord, the God of the covenant, with all one's heart.

22:6-9 *Then Joshua blessed them and sent them away, and they went to their homes. ⁷(To the half-tribe of Manasseh Moses had given land in Bashan, and to the other half of the tribe Joshua gave land on the west side of the Jordan with their brothers.) When Joshua sent them home, he blessed them, ⁸ saying, "Return to your homes with your great wealth—with large herds of livestock, with silver, gold, bronze and iron, and a great quantity of clothing—and divide with your brothers the plunder from your enemies."*

⁹So the Reubenites, the Gadites and the half-tribe of Manasseh left the Israelites at Shiloh in Canaan to return to Gilead, their own land, which they had acquired in accordance with the command of the LORD through Moses.

In blessing the Transjordanian tribes, Joshua simultaneously bid them farewell and wished them the Lord's blessing. The men of Reuben, Gad, and the half-tribe of Manasseh then set out homeward. Verse 7a contains an almost needless reminder of the special position of the tribe of Manasseh, but the purpose of this remark is to certify that in this matter, too, everything was done in accordance with the arrangements ordained by Moses. Curiously, another word from Joshua still follows at verses 7b-8. It might seem that this should have been included in verses 2-5, but this twofold farewell of Joshua has a ready explanation. Verses 2-5 contain Joshua's official address, made primarily in the hearing of the elders, by which he discharged the Transjordanian tribes from their duties. Once they had prepared for their journey and their heavily laden caravan was on the point of leaving the camp, however, he seized the opportunity to remind them that the plundered wealth they were bringing with them rightly belonged to the tribes as a whole, and that a portion of it therefore must be given to those who remained east of the Jordan.

The Lord's instructions to the Israelites after their victory over the Midianites (Num. 31:25-27) had to remain a permanent rule. The Transjordanian tribes had no cause to regret the loyalty they had shown to their brothers by joining battle with them against the Canaanites, for they had been richly rewarded by their share in the plunder taken from the conquered cities. Nevertheless, they had received this reward from God's hand; and they therefore could not selfishly keep it for themselves but had to place it at the disposal of their entire tribes, even those who had tilled the land and kept watch over their homes.

Reuben, Gad, and the half-tribe of Manasseh gratefully returned home with their newly acquired wealth. Gilead refers to the land east of the Jordan. Their departure to their inheritance once again confirms the Lord's promise (21:45) and the words of Moses.

21. The Transjordanian Tribes and the Altar of Witness (22:10-34)

This story bears testimony to the spirit that pervaded the whole nation of Israel and all its tribes at that time. They all desired to maintain the Lord's worship in strict purity, and their obligation to obey His commandments was taken in deadly earnest. Departures from the law would not be tolerated; and, if necessary, they would be forcibly suppressed. The Israelites' experiences in the desert had not been forgotten. It is refreshing to see how fervently they defended God's honor and how zealously they refused to be outdone by their brothers in this.

22:10-14 *When they came to Geliloth near the Jordan in the land of Canaan, the Reubenites, the Gadites and the half-tribe of Manasseh built an imposing altar there by the Jordan.* ¹¹ *And when the Israelites heard that they had built the altar on the border of Canaan at Geliloth near the Jordan on the Israelite side,* ¹² *the whole assembly of Israel gathered at Shiloh to go to war against them.*

¹³ *So the Israelites sent Phinehas son of Eleazar, the priest, to the land of Gilead—to Reuben, Gad and the half-tribe of Manasseh.* ¹⁴ *With him they sent ten of the chief men, one for each of the tribes of Israel, each the head of a family division among the Israelite clans.*

On their return from Shiloh to the Transjordan, the two and a half tribes built an imposingly large altar (the Hebrew literally means "large in appearance") near the Jordan. The word Geliloth in verse 10 could be translated "circles of stones"; but 18:17 shows that it was also the proper name of a place, and the word in fact is equivalent to Gilgal. This site west of the Jordan, therefore, must have been where the altar was erected. The statements in verses 10 and 11 that the site was "in

155

the land of Canaan'' and "on the Israelite side" also show clearly that the altar stood on the western bank of the river. Indeed, we can infer from the whole story that it must have stood there, since only then could it have formed a token of the original unity of the tribes east and west of the Jordan.

As soon as the Israelites heard that this altar had been built, they held a public assembly at Shiloh that included not only the tribal heads but probably also a great number of the fighting men. The step taken by the Transjordanian tribes was generally interpreted as an act of disloyalty, a breach of faith that had to be punished by force of arms and, if possible, purged from the land. It is not surprising that the Israelites regarded it so, since the Lord had explicitly commanded that there must be only one place, chosen by Himself, where they were to present their offerings (Lev. 17:8–9; the command is stated more clearly and at greater length in Deut. 12:4–8, 11, 13, 26–27). This commandment thus forbade anyone to build an altar on his own.

Before proceeding to punish the "guilty" ones, however, the Israelites decided to investigate the matter and to call the Transjordanian tribes to account (see Deut. 13:12–14). The task was delegated to Phinehas and ten heads of families (not tribal heads), but this does not mean that these men were not accompanied by a contingent of soldiers. It seems that Joshua was not present at the assembly, and this would have enabled younger men like Phinehas to take more of a leading role. Phinehas was already famous for his fervent zeal for preserving the holiness of Israel (Num. 25:7–8, 11–13). Section 3 of the Introduction discusses the hypothesis that Phinehas authored verses 10–34.

22:15–20 *When they went to Gilead—to Reuben, Gad and the half-tribe of Manasseh—they said to them:* [16]*"The whole assembly of the LORD says: 'How could you break faith with the God of Israel like this? How could you turn away from the LORD and build yourselves an altar in rebellion against him now?* [17]*Was not the sin of Peor enough for us? Up to this very day we have not cleansed ourselves from that sin, even though a plague fell on the community of the LORD!* [18]*And are you now turning away from the LORD?*

" 'If you rebel against the LORD today, tomorrow he will be angry with the whole community of Israel. [19]*If the land you possess is defiled, come over to the LORD's land, where the LORD's tabernacle stands, and share the land with us. But do not rebel against the LORD or against us by building an altar for yourselves, other than the altar of the LORD our God.* [20]*When Achan son of Zerah acted unfaithfully regarding the devoted things, did not wrath come upon the whole community of Israel? He was not the only one who died for his sin.' "*

Before the men of Reuben, Gad, and Manasseh had had a chance to go their separate ways in the Transjordan, they were accosted by the deputation from Shiloh, which at that time was still the national and religious center of Israel. Phinehas, the deputation's spokesman, immediately launched into an accusation without first taking the time to inquire. The reason for this is completely understandable, however, for the step taken by the Reubenites, Gadites, and Manassites gave the rest of Israel reason to suspect that they were indulging in independent and arbitrary worship. They had not taken care to avoid giving the impression that they took God's commandments lightly. If they had said beforehand that they intended to erect an altar only as a sign and a witness, misunderstanding would have been precluded. Instead of this, however, they acted on their own when they should have consulted with Joshua or Eleazar. To this extent they deserved a reprimand. Since they failed to grasp what was wrong with the course they had taken, Phinehas felt obliged to impress this on them as strongly as possible and to point out the consequences that their action could lead to. He branded their deed as a breach of faith, an act of apostasy, and, more strongly, a rebellion against Yahweh, the God of Israel. These must have been hard words for the Transjordanian tribes to listen to, but at least they caused them to grasp at once why the Israelite assembly had thought it necessary to send out a deputation. Among the western tribes their act had been regarded as a very serious offense.

The seriousness of the eastern tribes' action is further emphasized by Phinehas's proceeding to remind them of the "sin of Peor," when Israel engaged in sexual immorality with the Moabite women and bowed to their gods (Num. 25:1–3). The Israelites had committed a grievous offense at Peor, and the Lord therefore dealt with them severely by sending a plague that killed twenty-four thousand. Although God's anger was thereby put to rest, Phinehas claimed that the aftereffects of this sin had not yet been eradicated. The lust for idolatry and sexual immorality had not been purged from their hearts, and it was above all necessary that this received no new stimulation. All this made it highly irresponsible for the eastern tribes to build this illegitimate altar. As Phinehas saw it, this showed disregard for God's commandments, potentially aroused the people's sinful tendencies, and once again challenged the Lord to unleash His wrath. Phinehas rightly pointed out that, because of the unity and solidarity of Israel, the sin of a part of it would always bring harm on the whole nation, something that had become painfully evident after Achan's crime (7:1–5, 11, 25; see the comments on these verses).

In his words in verse 19—"if the land you possess is defiled"— Phinehas allowed for the possibility that the inner motivation of those who built the altar perhaps was not so wicked. The Transjordanian tribes may have considered their territory more or less unclean, since it was not a part of Canaan proper, the land that had been promised to their forefathers, but instead was separated from it by the Jordan. They were living beyond the soil that was consecrated by the Lord's altar. If this had been their thought, however, they would have built their altar as a kind of adjunct to the altar at Shiloh, partly in order to atone for their residence in an unclean land, and partly to preserve their bond with the hallowed soil (for their altar too stood west of the Jordan).

Phinehas thus supposed that the tribes of Reuben and Gad and the half-tribe of Manasseh may have thought they needed an auxiliary sanctuary because of the impurity of their land (and hence for religious reasons). This indeed approached the truth (as can be seen from vv. 24–27); but by regarding the altar as a place for bringing offerings, Phinehas still misjudged the real intention of these tribes. He told them that if this was why they had built the altar, it would have been far better for them to have come and lived within Canaan. The altar only constituted a partial remedy, for it could not remove the fact that they were living on unhallowed ground. They thus should have made their home alongside the other tribes within the sacred land itself, where the Lord had His abode, for the nine and a half tribes of their brother Israelites would surely have received them with love. Anything would have been better than a rebellion against the Lord that would tear apart the religious and political unity of the twelve tribes of Israel and bring judgment on the entire nation.

22:21–27 *Then Reuben, Gad and the half-tribe of Manasseh replied to the heads of the clans of Israel:* [22] *"The Mighty One, God, the LORD! The Mighty One, God, the LORD! He knows! And let Israel know! If this has been in rebellion or disobedience to the LORD, do not spare us this day.* [23] *If we have built our own altar to turn away from the LORD and to offer burnt offerings and grain offerings, or to sacrifice fellowship offerings on it, may the LORD himself call us to account.*

[24] *"No! We did it for fear that some day your descendants might say to ours, 'What do you have to do with the LORD, the God of Israel?* [25] *The LORD has made the Jordan a boundary between us and you—you Reubenites and Gadites! You have no share in the LORD.' So your descendants might cause ours to stop fearing the LORD.*

> 26 "*That is why we said, 'Let us get ready and built an altar—but not for burnt offerings or sacrifices.'* 27 *On the contrary, it is to be a witness between us and you and the generations that follow, that we will worship the LORD at his sanctuary with our burnt offerings, sacrifices and fellowship offerings. Then in the future your descendants will not be able to say to ours, 'You have no share in the LORD.'*

Since their reasons for building the altar were beyond reproach, it is completely understandable that Reuben, Gad, and the half-tribe of Manasseh at once took exception to Phinehas's accusation with strong and solemn words. In view of the extreme gravity of the matter, they twice invoked God as witness that they were speaking the truth and had not even so much as thought of rebelling against Him. "The Mighty One, God, the LORD" 42 knew their true intention. This profession gave their responses in the character of an oath, an appeal to the one true God whom they also honored as the God of the covenant. How deeply they were disturbed by the accusation is evident, not only from their solemn protestations, but also from their disconnected statements and outcries. So troubling to them was the suspicion of rebellion or apostasy that they called on the Lord not to spare them (i.e., from the hand of the Israelites) if they were indeed guilty of this. The singular form of the verb indicates that the words "do not spare us this day" (v. 22) were addressed to God Himself and were in fact a prayer that interrupted these tribes' response (cf. KJV, where the words are placed in parentheses).

In the Hebrew, verse 23 literally begins "in order to build our own altar," but this has been translated as an independent sentence for clarity. This verse ends by invoking the Lord's vengeance if the Transjordanian tribes had really intended to present their offerings on a separate altar from then on. This was not at all what they had in mind, and they resolutely denied the thought. The Transjordanian tribes rightly felt that the most important question was the purpose for which the altar was built, the function that it was designed to serve. And in verse 24 they proceeded to shed a positive light on this. The possibility

---

42 The author translated this "the God of gods, the LORD" (cf. KJV, NEB). He added the following footnote: "It is possible to read a repetition of three divine names in verse 22, viz., Deity, God, and Lord. The first name is the translation of 'ēl. When used alone, however, this word never denotes the one true God (except in poetic literature), and it is therefore out of place here unless it is connected with 'elōhîm. Hence the translation 'God of gods,' i.e., 'God Most High' (cf. Dan. 11:36)." 'ēl can also mean "strength, might," and the NIV thus regards it as an appellation for God: "the Mighty One"—TRANS.

had entered their minds, probably when they arrived at the Jordan, that in the future the Israelites west of the river might choose to dispute their claim to fellowship with the Lord, His people, and His sanctuary. This possibility was not purely imaginary, for the Jordan not only was the natural boundary of Canaan, but God's promise also had explicitly designated it as the eastern border of the Promised Land (Num. 34:11–12). Canaan had been understood as the land between the Mediterranean Sea and the Jordan River. Thus Reuben and Gad had had to make a special request for permission to settle east of the river (Num. 32:1–5), and they also expressly referred to the western territory as Canaan (Num. 32:32). Now, however, they had become fully alive to the possibility that their settlement in this region could one day induce the rest of Israel to question their claim to a share in the Lord. The western tribes could shut their descendants out; and, most dreadful of all, this would cause their future generations to turn away from the worship of the Lord.

The Transjordanian tribes thus pondered how they could avert this danger. How would they be able later to prove that they were indeed one with the rest of Israel? The construction of an altar provided the solution. This would form a visible witness in later times that the two and a half tribes east of the Jordan had lent their help in conquering the land of Canaan. It would be a sign that they were partners in the seed of Jacob and had a share in the God of Israel. All Israel then would be reminded that the sacrifices offered to the Lord at the altar in the central sanctuary were made on behalf of the Transjordanian tribes as well, and that they, too, had the right to come to the great religious festivals and draw near to God at that altar with their offerings (v. 27).

22:28–29 *"And we said, 'If they ever say this to us, or to our descendants, we will answer: Look at the replica of the LORD's altar, which our fathers built, not for burnt offerings and sacrifices, but as a witness between us and you.'*
[29] *"Far be it from us to rebel against the LORD and turn away from him today by building an altar for burnt offerings, grain offerings and sacrifices, other than the altar of the LORD our God that stands before his tabernacle."*

If they or their descendants were nevertheless told that they had no share in the Lord, the eastern tribes would be able to point to the altar they had built, which had been patterned after the altar at Shiloh. Its vast dimensions made it obvious, however, that it had not been made as a place for bringing offerings but as a sign and a witness to the religious unity between the two groups of tribes. The Transjordanian tribes concluded their defense by emphasizing once more how strongly they abhorred the thought of having any sacrificial altar besides the sole legitimate one. They, too, regarded all self-willed worship as a product of the Evil One, and the Israelites therefore could lay this suspicion to rest.

22:30–31 *When Phinehas the priest and the leaders of the community—the heads of the clans of the Israelites—heard what Reuben, Gad and Manasseh had to say, they were pleased.* [31] *And Phinehas son of Eleazar, the priest, said to Reuben, Gad and Manasseh, "Today we know that the LORD is with us, because you have not acted unfaithfully toward the LORD in this matter. Now you have rescued the Israelites from the LORD's hand."*

Like the defense of the accused tribes, Phinehas's response to them clearly displays the unimpeachable motives that governed both parties in this confrontation. All were concerned with the Lord's interests and truly had the welfare of Israel at heart. The explanation given by the Transjordanian tribes satisfied Phinehas and the Israelite leaders completely, and they had no doubts regarding the sincerity of their brothers. Since no breach of faith had been committed and there was no need for a call to arms, Phinehas gladly proclaimed that the Lord was with Israel. For if their suspicions had proved true, he would have had to conclude that God had departed from the people; and in that case, severe punishment would inevitably have been inflicted on the eastern tribes.

Phinehas and his comrades had prematurely imagined that dark clouds were threatening. The satisfactory explanation of their fellow Israelites, however, had allayed their anxiety and thus, as Phinehas saw it, rescued the whole nation from divine judgment. The previous misunderstanding had been removed; so it was needless to dwell on the question of whether the Transjordanian tribes should have consulted with Joshua and Eleazar before building the altar. Certainly, that would have precluded the misunderstanding; but now that both parties had had their say, the altar could have no ill effects in the future. On the contrary, it could only strengthen the sense of solidarity and brotherhood between the two groups of tribes.

22:32–34 *Then Phinehas son of Eleazar, the priest, and the leaders returned to Canaan from their meeting with the Reubenites and Gadites in Gilead and reported to the Israelites.* [33] *They were glad to hear the report and praised God. And they talked no more about going to war against them to devastate the country where the Reubenites and the Gadites lived.*

[34] *And the Reubenites and the Gadites gave the altar this name: A WITNESS BETWEEN US THAT THE LORD IS GOD.*

The deputation returned to Shiloh, where the Israelites were still assembled. The explanation given by the Transjordanian tribes was accurately reported and found total acceptance. All objections were dispelled, and the altar was regarded in a completely different light. The Israelites were filled with gladness, and they gave praise and thanks to God. No longer did anyone mention the thought of war. The Reubenites and Gadites (the half-tribe of Manasseh is of course included here), on their part, confirmed what they had said by giving the altar a name that simultaneously explained its purpose: "A Witness Between Us that the LORD is God [of all Israel]."

The pericope in verses 10–34 clearly reveals the praiseworthy spirit that prevailed in Israel during Joshua's day, the honesty and truth that governed the people's relations with one another, and the high plateau that they had risen to in their religious life. Misunderstanding obviously was not altogether absent (how could it be otherwise among sinful human beings?); but the manner in which the tribes resolved their dispute, and especially the utterly humble defense of the accused party, should serve as an example both to our "Christianized" society and to the church and its officeholders. The story told here contains a lesson for all times. It shows how brothers engaged in a quarrel cannot fail to be reconciled when both parties are motivated by love for the Lord and the desire to serve Him. That is the first requirement. And second, upholding the Lord's honor will redound to the unity and well-being of His people and confer a lasting blessing on future generations.

Epilogue
(23:1–24:33)

Although these two final chapters cannot be considered a third main section of the Book of Joshua, they still occupy a place of their own; for they record Joshua's parting words to Israel, his "spiritual testament,"[1] and the conclusion of his earthly ministry. They thus form a natural ending to the book. Their great importance lies above all in the way they illustrate how words and deeds go together in God's special revelation. The mighty acts that God performed in His people's behalf remained incomplete without the prophetic word that placed them in their proper light and inspired later generations to remember them and persevere in faithfulness. Chapter 24 is the more important of these two chapters, for it records a meeting that was held between the Lord and His people. Invoking the name of the Lord ("This is what the Lord, the God of Israel, says," v. 2), Joshua first reminded the Israelites of the blessings and privileges they had enjoyed and then proceeded to summon them to continued faithfulness to God, renewed dedication to His service, and the renunciation of all idolatry.

Next comes the high point of chapter 24, an account of the renewal of the covenant between the Lord and Israel. Looking back from here, we see that the assembly and address in chapter 23 were merely preparatory in character, just as in the new dispensation the Lord's Supper, which actually is also a covenant renewal ceremony, is likewise generally preceded by a service of preparation. Chapter 23 is

---

[1] Roorda, *Josua, De Held Gods*, p. 291.

163

also marked by the special warning that it gives against mingling with the heathen peoples who remained in Canaan.

1. Joshua's Farewell Admonition and Warning (23:1–16)

23:1–2a *After a long time had passed and the LORD had given Israel rest from all their enemies around them, Joshua, by then old and well advanced in years, ²summoned all Israel—their elders, leaders, judges and officials—and said to them:*

Chapter 23 begins by calling to mind the successful outcome of Israel's conquest and division of Canaan, which has already been briefly summarized in 21:44 and 22:4. A considerable time had apparently elapsed between chapter 22 and the events that follow. We are not told how long this was, but 23:14 and 24:29 clearly show that Joshua was approaching death. Perhaps he had already reached the age of 110, but in any case the statement of 13:1 that "Joshua was old and well advanced in years" was even more appropriate here. He knew that he did not have long to live, and he still had one important task to perform before his earthly task was fittingly concluded. It was necessary that the people be made fully aware of the immense significance of the events that they had witnessed in his day and of the sacred calling that they would have to live up to in times to come.

In this way Israel would be put in the proper frame of mind for the covenant renewal ceremony that would soon follow at Shechem, where they would repeat and confirm their earlier commitment to obey God's law completely (Exod. 24:7). Joshua thus summoned the representatives of all Israel: the elders, whose age gave them authority over either a tribe or a clan; the leaders (Heb., "heads") of families; the judges, who stood beneath the elders and family heads and had the task of administering justice; and the various classes of officials, who must have had particular duties within the executive arm of government. These groups would enable Joshua's word to reach the whole nation, and their example would have a powerful influence on the people.

Although the site of this assembly is not named, 24:1 clearly distinguishes the assembly at Shechem from this one; and since Shechem is not mentioned in chapter 23, the site must have been Shiloh. Shiloh had been the center of national life ever since the tabernacle had been set up there (18:1), and it was there that the events

164

of 21:2 and 22:1–9 had transpired. If, therefore, the assembly had been held at another location, this surely would have been mentioned.

23:2b–5 *"I am old and well advanced in years. ³ You yourselves have seen everything the LORD your God has done to all these nations for your sake; it was the LORD your God who fought for you. ⁴ Remember how I have allotted as an inheritance for your tribes all the land of the nations that remain—the nations I conquered—between the Jordan and the Great Sea in the west.² ⁵ The LORD your God himself will drive them out of your way. He will push them out before you, and you will take possession of their land, as the LORD your God promised you.*

To explain why he had called Israel together, Joshua began by pointing to his great age. He would not be around much longer to remind them of the things that he wished to impress on them.³ Nevertheless, he proceeded at once to tell the people that they did not really need to hear this from him. They themselves had witnessed what the Lord had done for them, and they needed only to revive their own memories to realize once again that God had been fighting for them. He alone was the reason that they had possession of Canaan. To be sure, the former population of Canaan had not yet been completely eliminated but Joshua reminded the people that he had already allotted to them the territory of the heathen remnants (v. 4); and he assured them that the same God who drove out the other inhabitants before them would certainly continue to fight for them and grant them control of the land that remained unconquered (v. 5).

Joshua's parting words are an exemplary farewell address. He hardly could have had a clearer understanding of his own humble position. He

---

² For the sake of clarity, the word order in this verse has been altered somewhat in the translation. The Hebrew literally reads: "the nations that remain . . . from the Jordan, and all the nations I conquered, and the Great Sea in the west." The sense of this verse requires that the phrase "from the Jordan" be followed by another geographical limit, a *terminus ad quem,* and the word "to" (*'ad*) therefore undoubtedly must have been accidentally omitted from before "the Great Sea" by a copyist. The territory spoken of thus extended "from the Jordan (and) to the Great Sea," or "between the Jordan and the Great Sea." In the Hebrew text these two geographical limits are separated by the phrase "all the nations I conquered" (cf. KJV and see Keil, *Joshua,*² p. 176), but it is not possible to preserve this locution in English. The conquered nations and their suvivors all lived in a single, undivided expanse of territory extending from the Jordan River to the Mediterranean Sea, and the translation therefore clearly reproduces the meaning of the original text.

³ Calvin rightly noted that Peter's words in 2 Peter 1:13–15 accurately express Joshua's frame of mind here.

realized that he had finished his task. Nevertheless, since he really had been nothing more than a participant in God's work, he was content to place its future unfolding in the Lord's hands. At the same time that he prepared Israel for his own departure, therefore, he comforted the people by pointing them to the God who always remains the same and never fails in His promises.

23:6–8 *"Be very strong; be careful to obey all that is written in the Book of the Law of Moses, without turning aside to the right or to the left. ⁷Do not associate with these nations that remain among you;⁴ do not invoke the names of their gods or swear⁵ by them. You must not serve them or bow down to them. ⁸But you are to hold fast to the LORD your God, as you have until now.*

Although the Lord's faithfulness could not be doubted, the people of Israel would never behold the fulfillment of His promises and take full possession of Canaan unless they on their part remained faithful to Him and His commandments. The Israelites owed obedience to all God's commandments without exception, and they especially were to be on guard against associating with the remnants of the former population of Canaan. This constituted the main danger that had to be made unmistakably clear to the people. Because of this the Israelites were not even to mention the names of the pagan gods, for that would imply that they had some reality or significance. Not only the Canaanite nations, but the names of their gods also had to disappear from the face of the earth; and Israel was to have no part in paying homage to these deities.

On the contrary, the Israelites were to persevere in serving the Lord, their covenant God, just as they had done "until now" (v. 8). This does not mean that they had not already gone astray more than once in the past. Still the nation on the whole had come to know the Lord as its God, especially in the Exodus from Egypt and at Mount Sinai; and it had never totally ceased from serving Him. Obedience had rather increasingly taken hold of the nation's life, and it thus could generally be said that the people desired to serve the Lord. This was true above all during the time of Joshua. Verse 8, therefore, is telling the Israelites that they must not deny their past but must continue along the path that

---

⁴The Hebrew in verses 7 and 12 literally reads "these nations, these ones remaining among you."

⁵The Hebrew here literally reads "cause to swear." On the basis of the Aramaic, Syriac, and Latin translations, however, a slight emendation (mainly in the vocalization) has been introduced to give the reading "swear."

they had followed till then, faithful to the ultimate choice that they had made regarding the foundation of their life.

23:9–10 *"The LORD has driven out before you great and powerful nations; to this day no one has been able to withstand you. ¹⁰One of you routs a thousand, because the LORD your God fights for you, just as he promised.*

Joshua reinforced this exhortation by once more reminding the people of what God had done for them. Not only had He promised to drive Israel's enemies out of the land (e.g., Deut. 7:1; 11:23, 25; Josh. 1:5), He already had fulfilled this promise; and He would continue to do the same in the future. The Israelites were, therefore, obliged to devote their whole life to His service, for this was His rightful due.

23:11-13 *So be very careful to love the LORD your God.*
¹²*"But if you turn away and ally yourselves with the survivors of these nations that remain among you and if you intermarry with them and associate with them, ¹³then you may be sure that the LORD your God will no longer drive out these nations before you. Instead, they will become snares and traps for you, whips on your backs and thorns in your eyes, until you perish from this good land, which the LORD your God has given you.*

Israel indeed had to serve the Lord for the sake of her own well-being, and Joshua thus followed his exhortation with a word of warning. This was a matter of life and death for the people, and to turn away from God would mean certain ruin. If the Israelites did associate with the heathen nations around them and became united with them, the Lord would withdraw His help. He would never drive out the Canaanites that remained in the land unless Israel joined battle against them. For the sword of Israel was His chosen instrument for accomplishing that task; and if the people failed to unsheath that sword and instead made friends with the conquered nations, the Lord would spare these nations and turn them into Israel's undoing. They would become "snares and traps" for the Israelites, "whips on [their] backs and thorns in [their] eyes" (v. 13). Although these four expressions all go together, it seems best to regard the first two more as allusions to the spiritual and moral harm that would be done to the Israelites when the heathen Canaanites led them to idolatry, and the latter two as references to the physical harassment they would suffer at the hands of the nations they had spared once these regained their power and resumed the offensive. The inevitable result would be the undermining of Israel's strength and the ruin of the nation.

It is unclear whether the end of verse 13 is speaking of exile or deportation from Canaan. The Hebrew literally reads "until you perish from off this good land . . ."; it is possible, however, to translate this "until you meet your ruin" (or, cf. NEB, "vanish from the good land"). The verse in any case means that Israel would be destroyed and therefore would cease to inhabit the land of Canaan. This could be the result of deportation but also of death coming from wars and other calamities. The phrase in question is taken from Deuteronomy 11:17 and 28:21, where the context makes it extremely unlikely that exile is considered the cause of the destruction (Deut. 28 first mentions exile in v. 36). The context of the present verse is likewise unfavorable for the thought that Joshua had exile in mind, since the enmity of Canaan's former inhabitants could hardly have led directly to Israel's deportation. Joshua probably meant that they would die within the Promised Land itself.

The situation is somewhat different in verses 15b–16, for there the nations of Canaan are no longer being spoken of. The Israelites rather are reminded of "all the evil" (v. 15) that the Lord had threatened them with, one instance being deportation to a foreign land (Deut. 28:36–37, 64). The conclusion of chapter 23 can therefore be regarded as an allusion to a future time of exile [the author has "vanish from the good land" in v. 16; cf. NEB—TRANS.]. This was not the first time that the people heard the warning Joshua gave to them in verses 11–13, for once again he was only following the example of his great teacher Moses (see Exod. 23:33; 34:12; Num. 33:55; Deut. 7:16).

In a sense Joshua laid Israel's future and fate in her own hands and told the people that obedience to the Lord would mean their salvation but disobedience their ruin. God's faithfulness did not relieve them of their duty to be faithful but rather should have been their strongest reason for responding to Him in a similar fashion. Joshua thus aroused the Israelites' sense of their own responsibility. His grave warning simultaneously made clear that turning away from the Lord would not only be an act of disloyalty and ungratefulness but also the greatest folly, for "all who hate me love death" (Prov. 8:36).

23:14–16 *"Now I am about to go the way of all the earth. You know with all your heart and soul that not one of all the good promises the LORD your God gave you has failed. Every promise has been fulfilled; not one has failed.* [15]*But just as every good promise of the LORD your God has come true, so the LORD will bring on you all the evil he has threatened, until he has destroyed you from this good land he has given you.* [16]*If you violate the covenant of the LORD your God, which he commanded you, and go and serve other gods and bow down to them, the LORD's anger will burn against you, and you will quickly perish from the good land he has given you."*[6]

In the final verses of chapter 23, which form the peroration of Joshua's speech, Israel's aged leader brought home the gist of his parting words in a vivid and grave manner. He again declared that his end was near, but he also called on the Israelites to consider what they had witnessed and lived through and to acknowledge with all their heart and soul that God had made good His promises. No one who had eyes to see could deny this. The mere fact that Israel was living in Canaan was irrefutable proof of God's faithfulness. This, however, could only increase the people's certainty that He also would not hesitate to carry out His threats.

What Joshua had in mind in these verses could have been no mystery to Israel, for at the end of the desert journey Moses had on more than one occasion not only foretold God's rich blessings but also provided explicit lists of His dreadful curses (Deut. 8:19–20; 11:26–27; Deut. 28–29). In addition, after the people had entered Canaan, the whole law, both its blessings and its curses, had been read publicly in the ceremony at Mount Ebal and Mount Gerizim (Josh. 8:34). If the Lord's threats were carried out, the Israelites would have no one but themselves to blame; for this would only happen if they violated the covenant that God had "commanded" them (v. 16). This does not mean that the Lord's covenant consisted solely of commandments; it was primarily an act of grace. Nevertheless, it simultaneously imposed obligations on the people and tied them absolutely to God's will. If the Israelites chose to sever this bond and shirk these obligations, especially by succumbing to idolatry, they would ignite God's wrath against themselves and (like the former population) make themselves unworthy to continue as owners of Canaan.[7]

---

[6]The final part of verse 16 ("the LORD's anger will burn against you, and you will . . .") is missing in the Septuagint, and the conditional in 16a instead is attached to verse 15. This, however, does not give us reason to omit verse 16b.

[7]See the comments in verse 13.

Joshua's farewell address—its final verses in particular—was grounded in his awareness of the holiness of God's covenant with His people, a reality that never would lose its importance. This covenant never implied that the people of God could at all times count on His blessing and assistance and that He would always take their side, regardless of how they acted. No one can lightly take shelter under the Lord's covenant faithfulness. Only as they guard against "being polluted by the world" (James 1:27) and make God's honor their first concern can people depend on His favor and help. God's blessing is only experienced in treading the path He has shown. If His people depart from this, they will find that their own God has turned against them (Deut. 6:15). The Lord wants a holy people, not because He needs them, but because they need Him.

2. The Renewal of the Covenant at Shechem (24:1–28)

24:1 *Then Joshua assembled all the tribes of Israel at Shechem. He summoned the elders, leaders, judges and officials of Israel, and they presented themselves before God.*

The national assembly at Shechem undoubtedly was held shortly after the gathering at Shiloh. It was attended by the same persons listed at the beginning of chapter 23, but more members of the nation also may have been present. Verse 1 speaks of "all the tribes of Israel," a phrase that accentuates the representative nature of this meeting more strongly than the brief mention of "all Israel" in 23:2. In no case could any of the tribes be absent or inadequately represented at Shechem.

Shechem was not chosen as the site of the assembly because it was the geographical center of Canaan. Rather, in former times the Lord Himself had consecrated this spot as a "holy place" (see v. 26) and had designated it as a site where He wished to reveal Himself. This was where the Lord had appeared to Abraham soon after he had settled in Canaan and where Abraham had built Him an altar (Gen. 12:6–7). This also was where Jacob had buried the foreign gods that were found in his household (Gen. 35:2–4). At Shechem the voice of history spoke both of God's faithfulness in fulfilling His promise to Abraham and of Israel's solemn calling to make a radical break with all idolatry. These were the two main lessons that Joshua wanted to drive home to the Israelites; so Shechem was admirably suited to the purpose of the assembly. Its own history could only increase the gravity of his words and stamp them indelibly on the people's memory.

According to verse 1b, the assembly formally began when the Israelite representatives "presented themselves before God." This probably involved a solemn invocation by Joshua of the name of the Lord (as Calvin remarked). Thus all would be aware of the religious character of the meeting and would utter their words and make their decisions in the knowledge that the omniscient God was looking on. There is no indication that the ark of the covenant had been moved to Shechem or that an altar was set up. The "presenting before God" therefore was not merely an external act but an actual drawing near to Him in which the people lifted up their hearts to meet Him and hear His word.

24:2–4 *Joshua said to all the people, "This is what the Lord, the God of Israel, says: 'Long ago your forefathers, including Terah the father of Abraham and Nahor, lived beyond the River and worshiped other gods. ³But I took your father Abraham from the land beyond the River and led him throughout Canaan and gave him many descendants. I gave him Isaac, ⁴and to Isaac I gave Jacob and Esau. I assigned the hill country of Seir to Esau, but Jacob and his sons went down to Egypt.*⁸

Joshua pronounced that word in the Lord's own name. The opening of verse 2 clearly shows that he had received an explicit command from God to tell the people the things that follow. He stepped forward as one whose mission as the servant, ambassador, and prophet of Israel's God gave him a just claim to the people's attention. His first aim was to

---

⁸In the Septuagint this verse contains the following additional words: "and there became a great and populous and mighty nation. But when the Egyptians mistreated them. . . ." The second sentence then leads directly into verse 5. Some are of the opinion that the translators of the Septuagint added these words to the Hebrew text on their own on the basis of Deuteronomy 26:5–6. This could be, but it is also possible that the words in question were originally present in the Hebrew text and were later accidentally omitted by a copyist. The Hebrew word for "Egypt" is identical to the word for "Egyptians," the last of the additional Greek words; and the eye of a copyist could have easily jumped from the former to the latter word and caused him to omit what came in between. In my view it cannot be determined whether the additional words were inserted (and therefore are spurious), something that would have been unnecessary, or whether they were later omitted (and therefore are genuine). If the latter is the case, the Septuagint translators must have had access to a better Hebrew text, a possibility that also might be indicated by the respective readings in 15:59. It cannot be denied, at any rate, that the Septuagint's words fit very well in the text.

remind the Israelites of the special favors that the Lord had granted them in the past (vv. 2–13), and on this basis he then confronted them with their calling to serve Him faithfully (vv. 14–15).

Joshua's statements about Israel's origins show that her history was really a history of God's gracious acts. The nation was descended from Terah, who through Abraham was the forefather of Jacob, and through Nahor the forefather of Rebekah, Leah, and Rachel (Haran, Terah's third son, is not mentioned here because he was not a forebear of Israel). These ancestral fathers lived in the land beyond the Euphrates River, first in Ur and then in Haran (Gen. 11:31), places where the worship of the one true God had perhaps not been lost altogether, but had in any case degenerated and become mixed with idolatry. We do not know what idols were worshiped in Terah's house, but at least some light is shed on this by what we are told about Laban's family. They worshiped the teraphim or "household gods" (Gen. 31:19, 30); thus even Jacob's family was not spared the presence of "foreign gods" (Gen. 35:4). These and other idolatrous practices must have already been present in the house of Terah, and Abraham no doubt would have carried on with them if God had not intervened. But God pulled him out of this partly idolatrous environment and brought him to the promised land of Canaan, accompanying and protecting him in his travels; and this act of God's special grace and electing love remained decisive for the rest of Abraham's life.

As far back as Israel could look in her history, the hand of God was visible. It was not natural events that brought the nation into existence but the extraordinary presence and overflowing grace of God. One element in this, of course, was the fulfillment of God's promise to grant offspring to Abraham (Gen. 12:2). The words "I gave" in verse 3 perhaps are an illusion to the fact that Isaac was not the first son of Abraham. Ishmael, however, is not mentioned because he did not belong to the chosen line. Esau, Jacob's twin brother, is indeed mentioned, but only in passing. Joshua was concerned solely with the offspring who had been called of God. Behind this whole story lurks the sovereign, electing grace of God, who declared that "I have loved Jacob, but Esau I have hated" (Mal. 1:2–3). Joshua's history of the origins and growth of Israel next briefly mentions the sojourn of Jacob's offspring in Egypt, a place where they did increase greatly in number but were forced to endure the chains of slavery far from Canaan. Was this the purpose of Abraham's call and removal from his homeland, the outcome of God's promises?

24:5–7 " *'Then I sent Moses and Aaron, and I afflicted the Egyptians by what I did there, and I brought you out. ⁶ When I brought your fathers out of Egypt, you came to the sea, and the Egyptians pursued them with chariots and horsemen as far as the Red Sea. ⁷ But they cried to the LORD for help, and he⁹ put darkness between you and the Egyptians; he brought the sea over them and covered them. You saw with your own eyes what I did to the Egyptians. Then you lived in the desert for a long time.*

The period in Egypt was obviously not the purpose of Abraham's call but merely prepared the way for the next act of God's grace, Israel's deliverance from the "land of slavery," which thenceforth would have such great significance for the nation. In an altogether unique manner, Israel's history was the work of God's own hand. In the persons of Moses and Aaron, He provided the nation with indispensable leadership just when that was needed. By sending the ten plagues, He caused the Egyptians to let His people go. He Himself showed the way during the Exodus; and after preventing the Egyptians from harming His people, He caused them to die in the sea. It was also His doing that the nation was kept safe and miraculously provided for during its long stay in the desert. Clearly, the Lord never did His work halfway. He had a goal in mind for Israel, and His firm hand guided the nation irresistibly toward that goal.

24:8–10 " *'I brought you to the land of the Amorites who lived east of the Jordan. They fought against you, but I gave them into your hands. I destroyed them from before you, and you took possession of their land. ⁹ When Balak son of Zippor, the king of Moab, prepared to fight against Israel, he sent for Balaam son of Beor to put a curse on you. ¹⁰ But I would not listen to Balaam, so he blessed you again and again, and I delivered you out of his hand.*

A particularly obvious example of God's perfect work is what He did with the Amorites and with Balak and Balaam. The Amorites tried to prevent Israel from reaching her destination and future territory by means of the sword, and Balak and Balaam sought to achieve the same end by means of curses. In consequence the Amorites, the peoples of Sihon and Og, were destroyed and their land taken over (Num. 21:21–35), and Balaam's intended curses were changed into blessings (Num. 22–24), thus opening the route to Canaan.

---

⁹The alternation between the first and the third person might be surprising here, but there is no reason to amend this to the first person (cf., e.g., Gen. 19:24).

24:11–12 " *'Then you crossed the Jordan and came to Jericho. The citizens of Jericho fought against you, as did also the Amorites, Perizzites, Canaanites, Hittites, Girgashites, Hivites and Jebusites, but I gave them into your hands.* 12 *I sent the hornet ahead of you, which drove them out before you—also the two Amorite kings.*10 *You did not do it with your own sword and bow.*

Next a series of divine miracles is recounted, each one more marvelous and overwhelming than the last: the crossing of the Jordan, the conquest of Jericho, and, above all, the total victory over every one of the militant and populous nations of Canaan. Israel had not succeeded in battle because of her sword or her bow. The credit belonged to the Lord alone, who fought for the Israelites and "sent the hornet ahead of them." This expression should not be understood literally. The hornet is a large, aggressive wasp that nests by the thousands in the caves and crevasses of Palestine's rocky ground. Its sting is extremely painful and can be felt for days afterward, and a number of stings inflicted simultaneously can even be fatal.11 A band of hornets could therefore form a grave pestilence and create severe problems for an army. Nowhere in the Book of Joshua, however, do we read that Israel's enemies were actually attacked or put to flight by wasps or hornets. The victory over the two Amorite kings in the Transjordan mentioned in verse 12 also was not brought about by a plague of insects; or, at any rate, Numbers 21:21–35 says nothing about this. This silence is significant, for in other cases we are explicitly told when the Lord used elements of nature to intervene in a battle in a special way (e.g., 10:11).

The possibility cannot be denied, of course, that the Lord at one time or another sent a plague of insects against His enemies; but since we have no particular information on this, it is more likely that the phrase "sent the hornet" has to be understood figuratively.12 It then would

---

10The author has "like the two Amorite kings" here and adds the following footnote: "The Masoretic text does not have the word k^e ('like'), and a literal translation therefore would put 'the two Amorite kings' in apposition with 'them.' This could not be what Joshua meant, however, for he has already spoken of the Amorites in verse 8. Nevertheless, in view of 2:10 and 9:10 it is highly likely that the previous words refer to Sihon and Og. If we assume that k^e (a single consonant in Hebrew) was present in the original text, the verse reads very well and corresponds in meaning to Deuteronomy 31:4"—Trans.

11See *Bijbelse Encyclopedia*, pp. 218f.

12Ridderbos also takes this view in his comments in Deuteronomy 7:20 in the *Bible Student's Commentary*.

refer to the fear and terror that seized these enemies when the Israelites approached them and Joshua's troops came into view.[13]

The Book of Joshua in fact speaks often of this fear (2:24; 5:1; 10:2, 10; 11:7-8), and this more than anything else was the result of the Lord's invisible help for Israel. Before the fighting even had begun, He deprived her enemies of all courage, paralyzed their resistance, and caused them to despair of victory (2:9-11; 4:24; 9:24). None of the battles that we read about gives the impression of being a protracted struggle in which the outcome hung long in the balance and each side had a nearly equal chance of victory. On the contrary, it always is clear that the Canaanites' defeat was assured from the outset and that the Israelites had to do nothing more than carry out God's sentence on the inhabitants of the land (see section 5 of the Introduction). This is how we must understand the statement in verse 12, that the Israelites did not overcome their enemies with their own "sword and bow."

If the "hornet" is understood literally, one would have to conclude that the Israelites did not even have to put their weapons to use. In numerous passages, however, it is stated explicitly that the Israelites defeated their enemies by putting them to the sword. The end of verse 12 therefore can only mean that Israel's victory was a direct result of God's powerful assistance and that their sword did nothing more than harvest the fruits of this victory (cf. Ps. 44:3).

24:13 *So I gave you a land on which you did not toil and cities you did not build; and you live in them and eat from vineyards and olive groves that you did not plant.'*

In consequence of the Lord's efforts on their behalf, the Israelites enjoyed the great privilege of making their home in such an excellent land, of living in its cities and eating of the fruits of its soil. They must never forget that all this wealth was a gift to them. But for God's grace, they would have received nothing; and all that they owned was an inheritance from the Lord. What had been promised to their ancestors had been miraculously given into the possession of that current generation.

---

[13] The "hornet" thus does not stand for human beings, as Garstang supposes in his claim that it refers symbolically to the Egyptians. This view is extremely uncommon, and the arguments against it can be found in Gispen's remarks in Exodus 23:28 in the *Bible Student's Commentary*. According to Köhler (cited by both Gispen and Noth), the Hebrew word in question does not even designate an insect but is rather derived from an Arabic term meaning "fright" or "discouragement."

24:14–15 *"Now fear the LORD and serve him with all faithfulness. Throw away the gods your forefathers worshiped beyond the River and in Egypt, and serve the LORD. ¹⁵But if serving the LORD seems undesirable to you, then choose for yourselves this day whom you will serve, whether the gods your forefathers served beyond the River, or the gods of the Amorites, in whose land you are living. But as for me and my household, we will serve the LORD."*

Thus this generation had the solemn obligation to live a life of thankfulness to Him who had granted them all this as an undeserved favor. Israel lived as the people of the Lord in the land of the Lord, and they were to serve Him and Him alone. This service was not to be merely external and formal but sincere, genuine, and steadfast, motivated by heartfelt devotion. The people therefore had to put away all traces of idolatry that might still remain among them.

Although Israel's religious life at that time may have been relatively pure, even exemplary, the people still had not disengaged themselves entirely from idols (Ezek. 20:7–8; 23:3, 8) and the worship of demons that had originated in Egypt (Lev. 17:7; Deut. 32:17). We do not read that they handed over any idols on the present occasion, but their idolatrous tendencies certainly must have been strong enough to justify Joshua's grave warning. Israel's later history confirms this, for idolatry was the temptation the people succumbed to again and again.

Joshua was aware that the whole future of Israel depended on its faithfulness to the Lord. Nevertheless, he did not seek to impose his own sentiment on the people. They had to choose to serve the Lord of their own free will. They must not be given the opportunity to say later on that they were forced into this service or that they did not have the chance to take their own stand. Joshua thus treated the Israelites as a mature people. He was not even content with their tacit agreement, for he commanded them to make a public choice on that very day. If they had any objection to serving Yahweh, their covenant God, they had to state this unequivocally and take full responsibility for their choice. Then they could turn to the gods of Mesopotamia or Canaan. But in any case, they could not remain in indecision. Joshua's words made it unmistakably clear that serving Yahweh was absolutely incompatible with idolatry. A choice had to be made, and he at least had made his own choice. However Israel decided, for Joshua and his family the service of the Lord was the only acceptable course.

24:16–18 *Then the people answered, "Far be it from us to forsake the* LORD *to serve other gods!* [17] *It was the* LORD *our God himself who brought us and our fathers up out of Egypt, from that land of slavery, and performed those great signs before our eyes. He protected us on our entire journey and among all the nations through which we traveled.* [18] *And the* LORD *drove out before us all the nations, including the Amorites, who lived in the land. We too will serve the* LORD, *because he is our God."*

Joshua fell silent. The people were called on to respond, and their answer left nothing in doubt. In the person of their elders, they indignantly rejected Joshua's supposition that they might be unfaithful to the Lord. This would never be, for they acknowledged the Lord and none other as their God. Already they belonged to His covenant, and that covenant had brought nothing but good to them. It was the Lord who delivered them from Egypt (the people here called to mind the opening of the Ten Commandments, Exod. 20:2, where the terms of their covenant with the Lord were explicitly stated), and He had been the source of all the acts of grace that Joshua had just reviewed.

Possibly verse 18 singles out the Amorites merely as an example of "all the nations." More likely, however, the mention of this nation is a response to what Joshua had said in verses 8 and 11–12 and thus refers specifically to Sihon and Og. It thus would form an indirect acknowledgement that the territory east of the Jordan also belonged to the land that the Lord had given to His people. The people's choice was therefore identical to Joshua's: they too would serve the Lord.

24:19–20 *Joshua said to the people, "You are not able to serve the* LORD. *He is a holy God; he is a jealous God. He will not forgive your rebellion and your sins.* [20] *If you forsake the* LORD *and serve foreign gods, he will turn and bring disaster on you and make an end of you, after he has been good to you."*

At first Joshua was not completely satisfied with this answer. The matter was too important to be decided hastily and on impulse, without giving due consideration to all that the decision involved. He thus told the Israelites that they would not be able to serve the Lord. They were not to think that they had the strength to do this on their own, and they should not have made a promise that they could not keep, for their God was holy and demanded that their entire life bear the stamp of holiness. He also was a jealous God (cf. Exod. 20:5) who would not share His honor with any other gods and would leave no breach of faith unpunished.

The end of verse 19 does not mean that the Lord was utterly

unforgiving, but He sought to make the Israelites fully aware of their obligation to obey. The people could expect that if they broke the covenant, they would be punished in accordance with the terms of the covenant; for their relationship to the Lord was as exclusive as a wife's to her husband. If Israel became unfaithful, they would have to suffer the consequences (cf. the threat in the second commandment, Exod. 20:5, and Exod. 23:21). Joshua made it clear that in this case the Lord would "turn" (v. 20), i.e., take a different attitude toward them than He had till then. Whereas He had thus far been their benefactor, He then would become their enemy and destroy them.

24:21–24 *But the people said to Joshua, "No! We will serve the LORD."*
[22] Then Joshua said, "You are witnesses against yourselves that you have chosen to serve the LORD."
"Yes, we are witnesses," they replied.
[23] "Now then," said Joshua, "throw away the foreign gods that are among you and yield your hearts to the LORD, the God of Israel."
[24] And the people said to Joshua, "We will serve the LORD our God and obey him."

The Israelites, notwithstanding Joshua's words in verse 20, made an unequivocal pledge to serve the Lord. Joshua bound them to this pledge by solemnly declaring that the people themselves were witnesses. He thereby sought to bring home to them how critical their decision was and how great their responsibility (cf. Eccl. 5:4; Luke 9:57–62; 14:25–33). The Hebrew phrase translated "you are witnesses against yourselves" (v. 22) is usually taken to mean that the Israelites themselves would have to testify as their own accusers if they ever should later turn away from God. It seems to me, however, that Joshua was speaking of the present, not the future, just like the people themselves at the end of verse 22. At that time, however, the people were not witnesses against themselves, for they had not yet become unfaithful. The word "witnesses" here thus does not refer to one who testifies but to one who sees and hears.

The Israelites would have to answer for the fact that they had made their choice publicly and in the hearing of everyone. All of them were witnesses in regard to one another and in regard to the nation as a whole.[14] No one would thenceforth be able to deny that at Shechem the nation of Israel had chosen to serve the Lord. Joshua's meaning, in

---

[14] The author thus translates verse 22 "you are witnesses in your own regard," not "you are witnesses against yourselves"—TRANS.

other words, was that each member of Israel was thereby proclaimed a witness of what had just transpired. It is unusual, of course, to make someone who has undertaken a pledge into his own witness. In this case, however, there could be no objection to this; for everything had taken place in a public, national assembly that was attended by so many.

The people's brief response—"witnesses" (i.e., "we are witnesses"; the Hebrew merely has the one word "witnesses")—shows that they had no doubt about what Joshua meant. They affirmed that they fully appreciated what had happened on that day. Joshua then once again admonished the Israelites to make a permanent break with all idolatry; and he seemed to be speaking mainly of their inner motivation, not their outward acts. For he added that they must yield their hearts to the God of Israel (and not to idols), the rightful owner of their undivided love. The people repeated their pledge to obey and serve the Lord, who had already shown Himself to be their God; they would remain faithful to Him.

24:25–26 *On that day Joshua made a covenant for the people, and there at Shechem he drew up for them decrees and laws.* ²⁶ *And Joshua recorded these things in the Book of the Law of God. Then he took a large stone and set it up there under the oak near the holy place of the LORD.*

The repeated promises and declarations that the Israelites had made in response to Joshua's example and urgent advice served to renew their commitment to serve the Lord. Verse 25 confirms this by stating that Joshua made a covenant "for the people" or "with the people." The Hebrew allows for both translations here (KJV, RSV, and NEB thus have "with," while NIV and NEB margin have "for"). "For the people" would be a correct translation if this were taken to mean that Joshua induced the Israelites to accept the obligations involved in God's covenant. One even could say that he enjoined the covenant on them; but this would be a little too strong, since formally he left the people free to make their own choice. Because "for the people" also can mean "on behalf of the people," however, "with the people" is the better translation. Joshua here did not act on behalf of the people but on behalf of the Lord. Joshua stepped forward as the representative of Israel's God and pronounced His word to the nation (v. 2). This lent authority to Joshua's own words and allowed him to establish "decrees and laws" for Israel. Verse 25 is not speaking of new "decrees and laws" but rather means that Joshua recalled Yahweh's requirements and claim on Israel and gained the people's spoken assent to these. In view of this the ceremony can be called a *renewal* of the covenant (cf. Deut. 29:1).

According to verse 26, Joshua wrote down "these things" (i.e., the words exchanged between himself and the people and the confirmation of the covenant itself) in a record that was given a place in the "Book of the Law of God." This probably was the same document that Deuteronomy 31:24–26 says was placed beside the ark of the covenant as a potential witness against Israel. It appears that the record was made in the presence of the people and not after the assembly had ended. In this way all would know that what had been spoken and performed at Shechem had also been put in writing.

Joshua perhaps did not do all the writing himself, since he certainly could not have done so while speaking. Instead, the account of his words and of all that happened at the assembly were probably recorded by another person present. We can only guess who this may have been; but there is reason to think that Phinehas acted as a scribe on this occasion, since his priestly office gave him access to the place where the lawbook was deposited. This remains uncertain, of course, but it is only a side issue. In any case we can be sure that the chapter preserves Joshua's own words.

24:27–28 *"See!" he said to all the people. "This stone will be a witness against us. It has heard all the words the Lord has said to us. It will be a witness against you if you are untrue to your God."*
28 Then Joshua sent the people away, each to his own inheritance.

One final step still had to be taken by Joshua. He had to take all possible measures to help preserve Israel's memory of the choice the people had just made. So he set up a large stone under an oak tree near the holy place where he had addressed the nation (see the comments in 24:1) and declared that this stone would be a "witness against you." Stones were set up to commemorate special events on other occasions as well (e.g., Gen. 28:18–22; 1 Sam. 7:12). The specific purpose of Joshua's stone was to serve as a continual reminder to the people of the pledge they had taken at Shechem to remain faithful to God. He spoke of it as if it were a living person, saying that it had heard all the words that had come to Israel from God and that its mere presence testified to the covenant that had been made. But this meant that it would also be a witness against the people if they should ever turn away from the covenant. Joshua's words seem to contain the tacit assumption that someday this would in fact happen (cf. Deut. 31:26–29; "witness against you" actually means "accuser," Num. 5:13; Mic. 6:1–2). At the same time, however, he implied that the setting up of this stone as a silent witness ought to prevent the people from ever being untrue to their God.

After this final warning, Joshua allowed the representatives of Israel to depart. His task was finished, though we do not read that he formally resigned his office.[15] This, however, was because his office was not permanent. His task had been to lead Israel as it took control of Canaan, and in this capacity he could have no successor. In his final years he therefore did not in any sense reign as a king over Israel but rather retired to his home at Timnath Serah (19:50). There he resided as a mere citizen, though he was no doubt a "first among equals." He had addressed the people in the Lord's name for the last time, and the choice of his successor over Israel was left to the Lord.

3. The Death of Joshua and Eleazar (24:29–33)

24:29–31 *After these things, Joshua son of Nun, the servant of the LORD, died at the age of a hundred and ten.* [30] *And they buried him in the land of his inheritance, at Timnath Serah in the hill country of Ephraim, north of Mount Gaash.*

[31] *Israel served the LORD throughout the lifetime of Joshua and of the elders who outlived him and who had experienced everything the LORD had done for Israel.*

Joshua's rich and eventful life lay behind him. He had not been compelled to abandon his task halfway through, for he had lived long enough to bring it to completion and even to see and enjoy the fruits of his labors. But the best still remained for him, his entrance into his eternal rest. God most likely took Joshua to Himself soon after the assembly at Shechem. The hand that recorded his death also honored him with the noblest of epitaphs: "servant of the LORD." Joshua was permitted to share this title with Moses even though he was granted a mere two talents instead of the latter's five (Matt. 25:15).[16] He was buried near his home at Timnath Serah, a place that is very likely identical to modern Khirbet Tibneh. Many tombs are found in the rocks

---

[15] Keil, *Joshua,*[2] p. 184.
[16] Cf. F. B. Meyer, *Joshua and the Land of Promise,* p. 188.

here,[17] and it has traditionally been maintained that one of these is Joshua's own. The Septuagint preserves the tradition that the Israelites placed in Joshua's grave the flint knives that he had circumcised them with at Gilgal (5:2), but there is no evidence for this in Scripture.

Through his person, words, and conduct, Joshua exerted a powerful influence for good that lasted considerably beyond the end of his life. According to verse 31, Israel remained faithful to the Lord as long as the older generation of the conquest was still alive. "Elders" here is probably a specific reference to those Israelites who, like Joshua and Caleb, had marched out of Egypt and had not died in the desert. They thus could remember the Exodus from the time of their youth, especially the miraculous crossing of the Red Sea; and "everything the LORD had done for Israel," therefore, would embrace God's whole work of deliverance, from the Exodus through the entry into Canaan. This older generation that still knew Egypt formed living proof that God had faithfully fulfilled the promises made to the patriarchs.

24:32 *And Joseph's bones, which the Israelites had brought up from Egypt, were buried at Shechem in the tract of land that Jacob bought for a hundred pieces of silver from the sons of Hamor, the father of Shechem. This[18] became the inheritance of Joseph's descendants.*

Brief and prosaic though it is, the account of Joseph's burial in this verse is worth reflecting on. In its own right the Israelites' compliance with Joseph's final instructions (Gen. 50:25), that they take his bones from Egypt (Exod. 13:19) and bury them in the soil of the Promised Land, was a pious act of loyalty. Beyond this, however, the lesson comes through that whoever believes God's promises in absolute earnest will be richly rewarded and never put to shame, even if the fulfillment of these promises is sometimes delayed for centuries (Heb. 11:13, 22). The most important thing in verse 32 is not the Israelites' action but what the Lord Himself did. In the sight of all, He showed that Joseph's hope had a sure foundation and was not in vain.

Fittingly enough, the site chosen for Joseph's grave was the very plot of ground that Jacob had legally purchased in order to erect an altar to the God of Israel there (Gen. 33:19–20). The exact amount that he had

---

[17] Keil, *Joshua,*[2] p. 184. Mount Gaash is also spoken of in 2 Samuel 23:30 and 1 Chronicles 11:32. For the location see De Groot, *Het Boek Jozua,* pp. 150f., and Garstang, *Joshua, Judges,* p. 402.

[18] The Hebrew has "they became," but the Vulgate and Syriac translations have the singular.

paid for this land is impossible to determine. The Hebrew literally states that he bought it for one hundred kesitahs (see NIV margin), a unit of unknown value. The kesitah appears also in Job 42:11; but there too it is unclear how much this was worth in comparison, for example, to the shekel. It indeed seems likely that it was worth more than the silver shekel; but in any case it probably was not a coin but rather a ring or bar of silver whose value depended on its weight.[19] We are not told when exactly the burial of Joseph's bones took place. Perhaps it was done while Joshua was still alive; but possibly he merely gave the instructions, and Phinehas saw to it that they were carried out after his death.[20]

24:33 *And Eleazar son of Aaron died and was buried at Gibeah, which had been allotted to his son Phinehas[21] in the hill country of Ephraim.*

The report of the death of Eleazar suitably concludes the Book of Joshua. Eleazar was as important to Joshua as Aaron had been to Moses, and in some ways even more important (Num. 27:21). He was not as prominent as his father; but among the older generation in Israel, he was second only to Joshua (v. 31). His death together with Joshua's thus closed the era of Joshua's leadership. Although we are told neither the time of Eleazar's passing nor his age, we can assume that his life ended soon after (or perhaps even before) that of Joshua. Like the latter, he was buried in the territory of Ephraim. Gibeah, the site of his grave, is distinguished from the other places of the same name (in Benjamin, 1 Sam. 13:2; 15:34, and in Judah, Josh. 15:57) by the statement that it was allotted to Phinehas. It seems that Phinehas received this place as his own special inheritance, perhaps because of the extraordinary zeal he had shown for maintaining the purity of the Lord's worship (Num. 25:7–13; Josh. 22:13).

The location of this Gibeah is uncertain. One difficulty is that according to Joshua 21:9–19, the descendants of Aaron received towns only in the tribes of Judah, Simeon, and Benjamin, and not in Ephraim. Some have attempted to resolve this by claiming that the hill country of Ephraim extended deep into Benjamin (Judg. 4:5), well beyond the

---

[19] See Bohl, *Bijbels–Kerkelijk Woordenboek,* 1:111, and *Bijbelse Encyclopedie,* p. 173.

[20] To this day there is a tradition that locates the grave of Joseph at the foot of Mount Gerizim, at a spot along the path to Jacob's well.

[21] The Hebrew here literally reads "in Gibeah of Phinehas, his son, which had been allotted to him in. . . ."

boundary of the tribe of Ephraim. Gibeah then could be identical to the Levitical town of Geba in Benjamin (21:17).[22] Others identify it with Jibia, a place in Ephraim near Timnath Serah, which thus would have been assigned to Phinehas as an exception to the general rule for the Aaronites.[23] This is unlikely, however. The site of Eleazar's burial simply can no longer be determined.[24]

According to the tradition preserved in the Septuagint at the end of chapter 24, the Israelites made a circuit with the ark when Eleazar was buried. Phinehas thereupon was installed as priest and later was interred in the same grave. The note in section 3 of the Introduction discusses the question of the probable author of 24:19–33.

---

[22] See Keil, *Joshua*, 2:185.

[23] E.g., Oettli (in Strack und Zöckler, *Kurzgefasster Kommentar*), *Josua*, p. 204.

[24] The Hebrew term Gibeah means "height" or "hill" and is translated this way in the KJV and NEB. It seems more likely, however, that Phinehas (like Joshua) received a special inheritance that was named Gibeah.

Appendix

NOTE 1

The phrase "on the other side of the Jordan" (Heb. $b^{e'}\bar{e}\underline{b}er\ hayyard\bar{e}n$) is used seventeen times in the Book of Joshua. Generally it is qualified further; but sometimes it occurs without a modifier, and it clearly does not always refer to the same area. The data can be summarized as follows: Six times (1:14; 2:10; 9:10; 14:3; 17:5; 22:4) the phrase is left unmodified and indicates the region on the east bank of the Jordan. Seven times (1:15; 12:1; 13:8, 27, 32; 18:7; 20:8) it has a modifying phrase ("toward the sunrise," "eastward," "in the east") and likewise refers to the area east of the river. In 9:1 the phrase is used without a modifier in reference to the region on the west bank of the Jordan. And in three places (5:1; 12:7; 22:7) it has a modifier ("seaward" or "westward") and likewise indicates the area on the western bank.

The variation in geographical reference cannot be explained simply by attributing it to a change in the author's viewpoint. It is not true that before the river was crossed he always used the phrase to indicate the western bank and after the crossing always the eastern bank. In those places where the phrase is left unmodified, there is one instance before the crossing where the author used it in reference to the land east of the Jordan (1:14), and one after the crossing where he used it to refer to the land to the west (9:1). Since the directional modifier is included in ten cases and left out only in seven, the author apparently did not regard a further specification of the meaning of the phrase as redundant. In six out of the seven cases where the phrase is used by itself, it refers to the east bank. Two of these times it is spoken by persons who were themselves situated west of the river (Rahab, 2:10; the Gibeonites, 9:10).

In view of the above facts, we have to be extremely cautious in attempting to draw any conclusions about what "on the other side of the Jordan" means. The places where a modifier is used certainly can have no decisive bearing on this attempt, for there the author himself felt that the phrase by itself was ambiguous. Joshua 12:1 and 7, for example, clearly fall in this category. The

185

strong ambiguity of the phrase in other passages no doubt partly results from the fact that the story unfolds on both sides of the river; the book recounts Joshua's leading Israel from the east to the west side of the Jordan and their settlement in the latter territory.

It is natural that this change of location could cause a participant in the migration to use the phrase with some inconsistency. The shift in meaning thus indirectly confirms that the author was personally involved in the events he wrote about (see Schulz, *Das Buch Josua,* p. 3). This also could explain the unusual usage of the phrase in 9:1. If the author had long been accustomed to speaking of the land west of the river as "on the other side of the Jordan," understandably he still could have used the phrase in the same sense on one occasion after he had crossed to the west side. He was, however, careful to make his meaning clear, for the context in 9:1 leaves no doubt that he had the west side of the river in mind. Indeed, there is no room for misunderstanding in other passages as well where the phrase is left unmodified.

The most difficult passage is 1:14, where Joshua used the phrase for the land east of the Jordan when he was still on that same side of the river. A possible explanation of this is that the Hebrew terms in question here mean "on the *side* of (the Jordan)." This is unquestionably their meaning in 22:11 and, for example, Exodus 28:26 (NIV, "next to"); and since the territory of the tribes that Joshua was addressing in 1:14 stretched alongside the Jordan, he could have had this same sense in mind. This, then, would form an exception to the rule, for the most common meaning is certainly "on the other side of (the Jordan)." And once the Israelites had settled in Canaan, it very soon became standard to use the phrase for the eastern bank (14:3; 17:5), which was the normal meaning for the Canaanites as well (2:10; 9:10); hence the English term "Transjordan."

In summary, the phrase "on the other side of the Jordan" in the Book of Joshua (1) most often has a directional modifier added because of its neutral meaning; (2) in the remaining cases refers to the land east of the river as a rule, unless the context forbids this (9:1); and (3) indirectly argues for an authorship by one of Joshua's contemporaries because of its shifting meaning. Although the phrase appears without a directional modifier seven times, the NIV translates it simply as "on the other side of the Jordan" only in 22:4. In all other cases it is translated "east of the Jordan" or "west of the Jordan."

NOTE 2

Various scholars maintain that 8:3–12 does not form a coherent whole. According to Schmidtke, the general view is that two different sources (J and E) have been "fused together" in this pericope, but in such a manner that it would be "hopeless" to attempt to separate them (*Die Einwanderung Israëls in Kanaän,* p. 105). De Groot offers the hypothesis that an original shorter recension later was expanded and supplemented (the text is much shorter in the Septuagint, see *Het Boek Jozua,* p. 96).

Verses 12–13 are considered especially problematic here, since they seem out of context. Nevertheless, we must make a serious attempt to understand the traditional text as an integral whole. The verses present the following picture. Joshua first broke camp, or at least made all the necessary preparations for the march (v. 3a). As night approached he sent out the troops that would wait in ambush (vv. 3b–9). He himself remained in the camp with the people that night, and the next morning he and the main army advanced to a point north of Ai and encamped there (vv. 10–11). This march could not have gone quickly, for the Israelite camp was still at Jericho (7:2); and since Ai was somewhere near Bethel, the journey had to have taken the whole day. Verses 12–13 then can be conceived as a parenthesis in which the author does not carry the story further but rather summarizes the steps taken by Joshua and reviews the position of his army. In this case, however, the end of verse 13 still would have to refer to the night that followed Joshua's march to Ai; for the battle that begins in verse 14 could not have come till the next day.

In itself the thought that verses 12–13 repeat what has already been said forms no serious objection to this view. More important is its necessary assumption that the ambush troops were able to hide west of Ai for a full day and night without being discovered. Garstang tries to evade this problem by supposing that Joshua and his main army marched on to Ai through a valley (thus he explains the end of v. 13) the same night that he sent out the ambush. Such a solution is attractive, but it is contradicted by the clear statement in verse 10 that Joshua proceeded to Ai during the daytime.

Another way to escape the difficulty is to assume that verses 3b–9 give a preview of how Joshua followed God's instructions to set an ambush. Verses 10–11, then, would report the advance of the entire army, including the ambush, and their encampment north of Ai at evening; and the actual dispatching of the ambush would not come till verse 12. The ambush would only have had to travel a short distance that next night and could have been ready to act early the following morning. On these terms verse 12 does carry the story further, and verse 13 alone reviews the position of the army. The night at the end of verse 13, then, would have to be the same as that of verse 9. It is obvious that, on this view, the appropriate tense in verse 12 would be the simple past, i.e., "Joshua took . . . and set. . . ." We still cannot rule out the earlier view altogether, however, for the flow of the story suggests that verse 12 does hark back to 3b and that the pluperfect therefore is the appropriate tense. Verse 13 remains the same in either case. Although it adds nothing new, we still cannot follow the Septuagint and delete it (as is done in the NEB); for if verse 14 came right after verse 12, we would get the impression that the king of Ai attacked Joshua's troops on the same day that they arrived near the city. Verse 13 therefore excludes this possibility.

Appendix

NOTE 3

Because 8:30–35 interrupts the account of Israel's military activities, many have questioned the position of this pericope in the text. In the Septuagint these verses come after 9:2; and although there is probably no one who would claim that they fit better here, this is thought to be an indication that their position is uncertain. Some think the pericope should follow 5:13–15, and a few place it right after 24:27. De Groot himself makes no choice but claims that the order of the narrative is governed by literary rather than chronological concerns. The author allegedly wished to draw a parallel between the work of Joshua and Moses and, more specifically, between the reading of the law on Mount Ebal and the granting of the law on Mount Sinai in Exodus 20.

1. There are no text-critical reasons for moving 8:30–35. The narrative in the Septuagint is certainly out of order, presumably because 9:1–2 have been misplaced slightly.

2. The events themselves forbid that the pericope be placed either after 5:15, for Israel is still there by the bank of the Jordan, or after 24:27, for we cannot suppose that Joshua waited that long to fulfill the command in Deuteronomy 27.

3. The real objection to the present position of these verses is that we are told nothing about Israel's journey from Ai to Shechem or their conquest of the latter. This is true of course, but we do not read anything about this later, either. Our conclusion, therefore, has to be that the Book of Joshua does not explicitly recount all Israel's conquests. The book apparently did not intend to tell the whole story of Israel's doings. But then, nothing forbids us to assume that after the defeat of Ai, Joshua at once turned north and pushed on all the way to Shechem. The route to there in fact stood open to Israel. We might wish for more information, but we have to be content to read between the lines that Joshua also took over the district between Bethel and Shechem, for this is included in the territory outlined in 11:16–19.

4. It is true that the order in the narrative does not always have to be purely chronological. Nevertheless, an author is forbidden to make any connections that do not exist in reality. If he indeed wished to draw a parallel between events from the lives of Joshua and Moses, that parallel was either historical or it was false; and we cannot accept the latter possibility. On the other hand, it would be difficult to prove—and it in fact never has been proved—that the order here cannot be chronological.

5. Our conclusion, therefore, is that 8:30–35 has not been moved from its original position. Schmidtke, among others, also holds this view. According to him, there is no evident reason why a redactor would have inserted the passage in this precise place unless the tradition had in some way compelled him to do so (*Die Einwanderung Israëls in Kanaän,* pp. 110f.).

NOTE 4

The pericope in 10:9–14, which recounts the battle at Gibeon and the miracle of the sun standing still, has been the subject of many careful and penetrating studies both in the commentaries on Joshua and in numerous articles.[1] The questions that arise here are concerned mainly with the relationship between the solar miracle and the hailstorm. Were these two separate phenomena or were they related, perhaps even two sides of the same event in nature? Did the Lord's help in the battle (v. 14) consist in the stopping of the sun, in the hurling down of the hail, or in both? Or in other words, what is the relation between verses 9–11 and verses 12–14 and, within the latter verses, between verses 12–13a and verses 13b–14? What exactly does the quotation from the Book of Jashar include, and are verses 13c–14 the conclusion of this quotation or the author's resumption of the narrative from 9 to 11? Very divergent views have been expressed on all these questions, and the composition of chapter 10 as a whole has often been drawn into the dispute.

Roman Catholic writers think that an important clue can be found in the words of Jesus son of Sirach in the apocryphal book Ecclesiasticus 46:4–5, where it is said of Joshua: "Was it not through him that the sun stood still and made one day as long as two? He called on the Most High, the Mighty One, when the enemy was pressing him on every side, and the great Lord answered his prayer with a violent storm of hail" (NEB). From this it is inferred that the hailstorm was the Lord's means for bringing about the enemy's ruin. The stopping of the sun, on the other hand, is either regarded as something that did not really happen (e.g., Schulz) or is explained away as a mere concealment of the sun behind the dark cloud banks from which the hail descended (e.g., Van Hoonacker, Van Mierlo). Even apart from the fact that the testimony of Jesus Ben Sirach cannot simply be taken as authoritative for our exegesis of Joshua, however, that writer clearly understood the stopping of the sun as a real event in verse 4 and in fact said that it "made one day as long as two." But we also can note in passing that his picture of Joshua as pressed by the enemy on every side when he called to the Lord cannot be reconciled with the clear words of verses 9–11. In our exegesis of these and the following verses, our sole concern should be the text itself; and we need not consider the testimony of Jesus Ben Sirach.

Both Schulz and De Groot give fairly extensive surveys of the numerous views and "explanations" of the pericope in question; and, in the interest of brevity, I here refer the reader to their commentaries. In the following remarks I will merely supplement the interpretation that I have already given and, by repudiating views that conflict with the text, show that it has sufficient warrant.

---

[1] De Groot gives an extensive list of literature in *Het Boek Jozua,* p. 154, and to this we can add J. Alfrink, "Het stilstaan van zon en maan in Jozua 10:12–15," *Studia Catholica* 24 (1949).

1. The pericope should be regarded as an integral whole, and its entire content has to be accepted as reliable history whose truth is guaranteed by the divine authority of Holy Scripture. Therefore we must reject all "explanations" that claim there is a fundamental discrepancy between the parts of this pericope (e.g., between the quotation from the Book of Jashar and the verses that enclose it). Equally unacceptable is the method that smooths over difficulties by butchering the text and deleting parts of it. Schulz, for example, regards verses 12–14a as a later insertion (*Das Buch Josua*, p. 28); but as De Groot rightly observes of this "surgical method" (*Het Boek Jozua*, p. 107), "the problem vanishes here for lack of material."

2. Verses 9–11 and verses 12–14 have to be considered separately. Taken by themselves, 9–11 obviously present no difficulties. They give a brief but, nevertheless, clear picture of the defeat of the Amorites. We even could call it a complete picture, for it not only shows us how the battle began but also how it unfolded and came to an end. Notice that the Amorites were thrown into confusion at once. They soon took flight and were overtaken and killed all the way to Azekah, above all because of the extraordinary hailstorm. The hail did not begin to fall already at Gibeon, nor did it hold off till the end of the chase. Rather, it hit the Amorites when they were on the road near Beth Horon, that is, halfway through the battle and probably around noon; and it continued till evening, or at least till the final victory described in verses 20–21 had been achieved. The "solar miracle" is not yet spoken of in these verses.

3. In verses 12–14 we must distinguish the quotation from the Book of Jashar from the words that the author himself added to it. The quotation itself clearly ends in the middle of verse 13 after "avenged itself on its enemies," for this is followed by the statement "as it is written in the Book of Jashar" (v. 13b). Then the author describes the effect of the miracle spoken of in verse 13a and adds his own comments on this event (vv. 13c–14). The question, however, is where exactly does the quotation begin? It probably would be impossible to reach a definite conclusion about this. We do know that the two quotations from the Book of Jashar in the Old Testament, namely, this passage and 2 Samuel 1:17–27, contain poetic material. But it is reasonable to assume that these poetic pieces, like many of the Psalms, were introduced by a brief historical statement or a superscription.

I therefore take the view that the opening words in the Hebrew text of verse 12—"then spoke Joshua to the LORD"—have to be ascribed to the author himself, and that the quotation proper begins with "on [or 'in'] the day" (*bᵉyôm*).[2] The Book of Jashar then would have "Joshua said" instead of "and he said" at the end of this opening statement, but the author of the Book of

---

[2] Goslinga's translation of verse 12 exactly parallels the RSV, which reads: "Then spoke Joshua to the LORD in the day when the LORD gave the Amorites over to the men of Israel; and he said in the sight of Israel. . . ." Since the NIV rearranges the word order in this sentence, the RSV (also KJV) reading must be consulted to understand his argument.

Joshua had no need to repeat the proper name here. That is, the quotation from the Book of Jashar would begin: "On the day when the LORD gave the Amorites over to the men of Israel, Joshua said in the presence of Israel. . . ."

In support of this we can note that the author's introduction in verse 12 would then state that Joshua spoke to Yahweh, a fact confirmed in verse 14, while it is not evident from the quotation itself that Joshua prayed to God. Verse 12a (in the KJV and RSV) thus forms a transition from the narrative to the quotation. The advantage of this view is that the author's opening word in verse 12—"then" (*'āz*)—would bring out that Joshua's call to the sun and moon took place, not after, but during the battle, and that in the ensuing pursuit it became clear to all that this call was not in vain but was answered by God in a miraculous way. If we turn to verse 11 to fix more precisely the moment that this "then" refers to, we there find the fleeing enemy caught in the hailstorm on the road near Beth Horon. Joshua's momentous call certainly would not have been made long before this. See the comments in the text at 10:12–14.

4. In verses 13c–14 the author resumed his narrative again. He amplified the words of 13a by reporting that the sun came to a stop in the middle of the sky and delayed its setting for almost a whole day. Then he expressed his reverent amazement at the wholly unique and miraculous manner in which the Lord fulfilled what Joshua's faith had given him the confidence to ask for. In both the positive and the negative statements that the author made, it is unequivocally clear that he regarded this departure from the normal course of nature as an objective phenomenon. For him the extraordinary and unnatural lengthening of the day on which the Lord handed the Amorites over to Israel and answered Joshua's prayer was a historical fact. If one chooses not to believe this, he does so on his own account; for there are no reasonable grounds for denying that the author himself believed it and sought to record it in clear words. The most basic question is whether one believes in miracles, in the power of God the Creator over the forces of nature and the motions of the celestial bodies. Anyone who does not believe in this can only regard these verses as a myth, but he then has no inner point of contact with their content. Whoever does have this belief, on the other hand, is best able to understand the enormous significance of this episode and to grasp the author's purpose in reporting it.

It goes without saying that this standpoint does not eliminate all the problems and questions that arise. One might still ask, for example, at what point in the day Joshua could see the sun above Gibeon and the moon over Aijalon. It is entirely unreasonable for De Groot to assert that "whoever accepts the literal interpretation would better renounce all attempts to explain or illuminate it by means of physical science, for nothing more can be said from that point of view" (*Het Boek Jozua*, p. 107). De Groot would disqualify precisely those persons who take the biblical account at its word. But may we not also ask what star it was that the Magi saw in the East and see whether this might not shed some light on the date of Jesus' birth? Can one seriously claim that a person who wants to explain and interpret Scripture must begin by abandoning any belief in God's miraculous power, a power that, as it were, became flesh and blood precisely in the biblical authors?

5. It would be wrong to think that the author's own words stand in contrast to those of the quotation. According to De Groot, Joshua called on the sun and moon "to look down on the battle that was underway in the very same poetic fashion that Isaiah called upon the heavens and the earth" (ibid., p. 108). In support of this he appeals to Isaiah 1:2. A simple comparison of this verse with Joshua 10:12–13 reveals, however, that the two passages are altogether different. The meaning that De Groot wants to read into the quotation ("to look down on") simply is not there, and he therefore is completely wrong in saying that "we thus cannot credit Joshua with the stopping of the sun and moon. The stopping is rather a literary device of the author of the Book of the Righteous" (ibid., p. 109). The facts are unmistakably clear here. Joshua called for the sun and moon to stand still, and the next verse uses the very same verb to state that the sun did indeed stand still (a synonymous verb is used with the moon). The words literally describe the facts.

Various studies devoted to this pericope attempt to escape the notion that the sun actually stood still by understanding the verb used in the quotation to mean "cease shining." The blazing sun allegedly had to "be still" or "keep silence" by holding back its rays. This then would have happened when the dark thunderclouds concealed the sunlight, sending the hailstones clattering down and at the same time refreshing the weary warriors with cool air. In such an interpretation, however, the words of Scripture are obscured rather than clarified. De Groot and Schulz also reject this as a biased view. But in the final analysis, neither of these commentators—one a Protestant, the other a Roman Catholic—is prepared to accept the miracle of the sun standing still in the sky.

6. In my view many scholars have difficulty with this pericope precisely because of this dogmatic objection. The clear and deliberate meaning of the passage is rejected, and one then either tries to give it another meaning or proceeds to delete parts of it. The text itself presents no insurmountable difficulties at all, however, though it does not answer all our questions. Ultimately these questions can be reduced to one: How can we explain the fact that the sun shone without interruption for an entire day while, at the same time, large hailstones fell for hours on end? The latter, after all, requires that the sky be darkened with clouds. Is this not inconsistent? In other words, how can we reconcile verses 9–11 with verses 12–14? This is the question that I posed at the beginning of this note.

It is my view that we simply have to accept the two groups of verses at face value, even though (as so often happens) this leaves certain problems for which we cannot find a satisfactory solution. In the present context these problems are physical in nature. The text, however, gives us no detailed information about the atmospheric conditions during this event, and for this reason we should not magnify the problems needlessly. Nothing is said about black clouds or a thunderstorm, not to mention total darkness. Elsewhere we see that the Lord could send rain and loud thunderclaps in the middle of the day and entirely without warning; in 1 Samuel 7:10 and 12:18, He did this in answer to the prayer of Samuel. In the same way He here answered Joshua's prayer by commanding the sun to stop in its course till the enemy was destroyed, but this does not necessarily imply that the sky remained bright and unclouded for the rest of the day. Besides this, the sunlight does not vanish entirely during a hailstorm. What was miraculous in this event was not the brightness of the day but the doubling of its length, which was brought about by the Lord's own hand.

As far as His special intervention is concerned, the Lord fought for Israel in two different ways. First, He fulfilled Joshua's bold wish that the (apparent) motion of the sun on its path would temporarily come to a halt. How the Lord accomplished this is beyond our knowledge. The important thing is that it did indeed happen (cf. the miracle of the shadow's backward motion on the sundial of Ahaz, 2 Kings 20:9-11; Isa. 38:8). Second, He bombarded the enemy army with gigantic hailstones. Schulz is therefore in some sense correct to say that the solar miracle and the hailstorm were two independent events. Nevertheless, they were parallel phenomena of nature, both of which were due to an extraordinary divine intervention, and both of which meant the ruin of Israel's foes. Their common purpose was to grant Israel a complete victory and to show that Israel's God had control even over the forces that moved in the heavens (cf. Judg. 5:20).

NOTE 5

The Book of Joshua contains two different reports about the destruction of the Anakites, and it is unclear how these are to be brought into harmony with each other. Joshua 11:21-22 states that Joshua destroyed them totally, and the cities of Hebron and Debir are mentioned in particular. These verses undoubtedly mean to say that this happened in connection with the conquest recounted in 10:36-39, where the same cities are spoken of. In 14:12-13, however, Caleb said there were Anakites still living in the hill country of Judah whom he wished to expel from their fortified cities, and Joshua then gave him Hebron as his inheritance. And in 15:13-20 we read how he drove the Anakites out of Hebron and conquered Debir. Were the cities of Hebron and Debir then conquered on two different occasions? To this we may ask, Why not? After Joshua's great campaign through southern Canaan, the Anakites could have infiltrated the land once again from Gaza, Gath, and Ashdod (11:22) and taken over Hebron and Debir a second time. The fact that 10:36-39 says nothing about Caleb, Othniel, or the events of 14:12-13 and 15:13-20 supports this conclusion.

One might object, however, that we read nothing at all about a retaking of Hebron by the Anakites and that such an event would be difficult to square with the strong words in 11:22. In addition, 13:1-7 does not list the hill country of Judah among the districts that still remained in enemy hands. Baarslag, therefore, supposes that Caleb's words in 14:6–12 had already been spoken when Israel first set foot in the Promised Land (*Israel in Egypt*, p. 24, note). Such a position is not intrinsically impossible; and it is even supported by the observation that the end of 14:15 ("then the land had rest from war") would make better sense than if there were still Anakites to fight.

There are also serious objections to this view, however. First, 14:6–13 would then break the chronological order of the narrative. And second, the Gilgal in verse 6 would have to be the Gilgal near Jericho (4:19). There would be only a single conquest of Hebron and Debir, and 15:13–19 would be speaking of the same events as 10:36–39. This is quite unlikely, though we could grant that the latter passage could have ascribed the conquest to Joshua (cf. 11:21–22) because he was the commander-in-chief under whom Caleb fought. Beyond this, however, Caleb's statement in 14:10 that he received the Lord's promise forty-five years ago presents a serious difficulty, for that was less than forty years before Israel was at the Gilgal by the Jordan. Baarslag actually just dismisses this objection, and he is not sufficiently mindful of the fact that the Book of Joshua does not tell us everything that happened in connection with the conquest of Canaan.

Besides all this, Baarslag's dogmatic assertion that the military campaign reported in Judges 1:1–20 is in fact the same as that of Joshua 10 certainly fails to do full justice to the biblical data concerning the progress of the conquest. According, to him the notion "that the future territory of Judah was conquered *twice* definitely has to be rejected" (ibid., p. 18); but he hereby is taking issue not merely with a certain view but with the picture that is clearly presented in Scripture. The Bible distinguishes between the main military campaign of Joshua throughout the entire land and the work that remained after that for the various individual tribes (cf. 23:4–5 and section 4 of the Introduction). In performing this more minor but no less necessary part of the conquest, the tribes were extremely negligent. Nearly all that they did in this regard is summarized in Judges 1 (the capture of Hebron and Debir in vv. 10–15 forms an exception here, for that happened during Joshua's lifetime). Therefore it is even less comprehensible how the rather trifling ventures of Judges 1 could be placed in the great campaign of Joshua 10.

Remarkably, Baarslag first writes (ibid., p. 17): "Everyone must no doubt be struck—at least on a first, superficial reading—by how the stories of the conquest of southern Canaan in the Book of Joshua and the beginning of the book of Judges are so enormously and totally inconsistent in virtually every respect." Then, a few pages later (pp. 22f.), he nevertheless makes an almost violent attempt to harmonize these two so totally inconsistent pictures. He can only do this at the expense of the traditional text, for his view demands that the words "after the death of Joshua" at the opening of Judges 1 be eliminated. In this fashion one can of course achieve any solution one wishes, but the procedure is purely arbitrary; and Baarslag cannot make amends by emphatically declaring that he here holds "completely to the book of Joshua as historically reliable" (p. 19, note). These words simply cannot be accepted as a statement of principle, for the reliability of a particular portion of Scripture cannot be made dependent on our own insight.

Judges 1 and Joshua 10 merit equal acceptance, and this in fact presents no difficulties whatsoever if one only recognizes that Judges 1—as is clear from its own words—is concerned with a later time and speaks of different events than Joshua 10. The latter chapter deals with the main conquest of Joshua as the commander of all Israel. The former, in contrast, summarizes the military activities of the various individual tribes after Joshua had died. This is so obvious that even Rudolf Kittel, who takes a very critical view of the biblical data and maintains in his classic work (*Geschichte des Volkes Israel* [Gotha, 1923], 1:396) that Judges 1 recounts events that happened during Joshua's lifetime, still is compelled to acknowledge that Israel had to have acted in concert before the tribes began their individual offensives. He holds to the historicity of the division of the land and points to the unity of the tribes at Mount Sinai and their joint wanderings during the lifetime of Moses (p. 408). Judges 1 also presupposes that the tribes previously had acted together under a central leadership. Kittel thus says that this chapter "can in no case be the beginning of an independent story, but rather points back to a preceding narrative in which Joshua must have played the leading role" (pp. 409–10). This line of thought is almost entirely in keeping with the picture presented in the Bible.

NOTE 6

A few friendly critics have issued a mild caveat and asked whether I have not at times taken the matter of typology too far in this commentary. I believe that this is not the case, though I do agree that the exegete has to be more careful in this than the preacher. For this reason I have at some points expressed myself less strongly than I did in the first edition of this commentary. It is still clear, however, that Joshua was called to his sublime task by God Himself. He was the Lord's instrument for destroying the enemies of the theocracy and granting the Promised Land to God's people of that day. God even had his name deliberately changed from Hoshea to Joshua, the Hebrew equivalent of Jesus (see Introduction, pp. 4–5). His life task thus formed a subordinate part of the larger work of Christ Himself. It prepared the way for His coming and for the establishment of the kingdom of God in this world. Therefore the pattern of Joshua's work opens a perspective on the future. His victories foreshadow the final victory of Christ. The statements I have made are therefore fully justified in my view and in no way tend to spiritualize the historical facts of the narrative. See also section 5 of the Introduction.

Judges
Introduction

I. *Name, Content, and Outline of the Book*

The Book of Judges, which is mainly the record of the work of those men whom Scripture calls the judges, is appropriately named. Its clear purpose is to portray the unfolding of Israel's history from the death of Joshua to the advent of the monarchy, an era usually designated as the period of the judges. Even the chapters that do not speak directly of the judges themselves (1, 9, 17–21) are closely related to the actual stories about them, for these parts of the book describe the circumstances that made it necessary for a judge to arise. The title of the book, therefore, fits perfectly with its content,[1] which can be briefly summarized as follows.

Chapter 1 recounts the attempts made by various tribes after the death of Joshua to take full possession of the territory that had been allotted to them and emphasizes the fact that these efforts were abandoned all too soon. Chapter 2 tells how the angel of the Lord severely reprimanded the people for their negligence (vv. 1–5) and follows with a general description of the period of the judges (vv. 6–23). Judges 3:1–4 then adds a list of the nations that the Lord allowed to remain in Canaan. After this, the histories of the various judges and the events that directly called forth their rise as Israel's leaders and military commanders are related in varying detail. The

---

[1] The book does not present the histories of all the judges. Eli and Samuel are missing, even though they too can be considered judges (see 1 Sam. 4:18 [NIV margin]; 7:15; 8:1–2). The end of section 3 below discusses a possible reason for this.

judges appear in the following order: Othniel (3:7–11), Ehud (3:12–30), Shamgar (3:31), Deborah (chs. 4–5; ch. 5 contains the song of Deborah), and Gideon (chs. 6–8). Chapter 9 tells of Abimelech's reign as king at Shechem and his fall. Chapter 10 then resumes the histories of the judges, beginning with Tola and Jair (vv. 1–5). After an introduction in 10:6–16, the history of Jephthah is recounted in 10:17–12:7; and this is followed by the brief mention of Ibzan, Elon, and Abdon (12:8–15). The extensive and dramatic account of Samson's birth, marriage, heroic exploits, and death in chapters 13–16 concludes the histories of the judges.

The last five chapters contain two independent narratives, both of which probably date from the opening phase of the period of the judges. Chapters 17–18 tell how Micah the Ephraimite began to practice idolatry in his house and how a group of Danites carried off the contents of his shrine and his own personal priest and then captured the town of Laish. Chapters 19–20 follow with the story of a scandalous crime committed by the inhabitants of Gibeah and the ensuing civil war in which the tribe of Benjamin was almost completely destroyed. The final chapter then tells how the Israelites, fearing that the Benjamites would die off completely, gave them the virgins from Jabesh Gilead and offered them the opportunity to abduct the girls from Shiloh. The book closes with the characteristic statement: "In those days Israel had no king; everyone did as he saw fit" (21:25).

Corresponding to this survey of its contents, the Book of Judges can be divided into three main sections. The first section (1:1–3:4)[2] is a preface that broadly outlines the conduct of the Israelites during the period of the judges with regard to the Canaanites and their gods, and thus also with regard to the Lord Himself. It simultaneously reveals the Lord's special guidance and His intentions for Israel during this era. The second section (3:5–16:31) recounts the history of the Israelites' repeated subjection to their many enemies, both domestic and foreign, and tells how they were delivered and restored to prosperity by their various judges, from Othniel to Samson. The third section (chs. 17–21) concludes the book. Although this can formally be regarded as an appendix, it poignantly pictures the appalling decline of Israel's

---

[2]Others would close this section in 3:6. Although this difference of two verses is not significant, verses 5–6 cannot be considered the end of the preface. This has in fact already ended in 2:23, while 3:1–4 was merely added as an appendix. Verses 5–6, on the other hand, belong with verse 7, for these three verses together describe the events that motivated the divine judgment in verse 8.

religious and moral life and negatively illustrates why the nation needed the kind of powerful, central authority that first emerged in the monarchical period.

II. *The Unity and Composition of the Book*

The Book of Judges contrasts with Joshua and Ruth, its immediate neighbors in the Old Testament canon. Whereas the latter two books deal with rather narrowly defined topics and are highly uniform in the way they handle their material, Judges at first appears to be, not a unity, but an accumulation (almost a "stringing together") of historical data, diverse narratives, and religious reflections. The book is concerned with numerous persons and events from a period that lasted for more than three hundred years after the death of Joshua, and it presents no complete or tightly coherent history of this era. Consequently its unity does not stand out vividly. A first impression, however, should not be allowed to decide the question, for unity is not at all absent. Closer inspection reveals that the distinct parts of the book are governed by one central thought, something that already came to light in my outline in section I.

The obvious purpose of the Book of Judges is to exhibit the peculiar character of the period of the judges and the significance of this era in the whole history of divine revelation. This purpose clearly emerges in the second part of the book, which is by far the largest. Here a close connection is drawn between the rise of most of the judges and the religious condition of the nation. The actual careers of the judges, at least of the so-called major judges, are placed in a kind of frame[3] that begins each story with the statement that the Israelites sinned against the Lord and gave Him reason to punish them and ends by reporting the number of years that the land had peace or the length of the judge's reign (see 3:5–7 and 3:11; 3:12 and 3:30; 4:1 and 5:31; 6:1 and 8:28; 10:6 and 12:7; 13:1 and 16:31).

The narrative draws its strength from the multitude of episodes unfolded on these pages, and it is only through their combined effect that we receive an adequate picture of the period of the judges. The continual need for a new judge to deliver the nation from oppression makes it abundantly clear that the Israelites were predisposed toward

---

[3]This does not mean that the actual events of history are altered to fit this frame, which itself is a history of a higher order. The frame places the facts in their proper light and unveils the causal relations between them.

unfaithfulness and unable to remain on the right path apart from external compulsion. Again and again they fell back into their old evil ways, departing from Yahweh, the God of the covenant, to serve idols. Then God would surrender His people to oppressors for a time of affliction. But when the measure of their suffering was full, God would answer His people's cry of distress by sending a deliverer to defeat their enemy and bring them back to worshiping Him, the one true God. After the death of each of these judges, however, a new period of decline would set in; and the resurgent apostasy would compel the Lord to punish the nation once again.

Judges 2:11–19 presents a deliberate sketch of the course of Israel's history during this period. More powerful than this cyclic scheme, however, is the voice of history itself in the chapters that follow, where the religious and moral decay of the nation is depicted with mounting intensity. The fixed, recurrent statement that "the Israelites did evil in the eyes of the LORD" is at once monotonous and eloquent.

The multitude of episodes in the second section, which forms the main body of the Book of Judges, therefore does not detract from its unity. On the contrary, it appears to be closely related to the plan and purpose of the author. The other sections of the book also are made subordinate to the unfolding of that plan. The period of the judges was not independent of the epoch that preceded it, and the history recounted in 3:5–16:31 confronts us with the question of why Israel changed so markedly between the time of Joshua and the time of the judges. The answer to this is found in the preface to the book.

This preface consists of two clearly distinct parts. The first (1:1–2:5) presents a survey of the military endeavors of the tribes of Judah (and Simeon), Benjamin, Manasseh, Ephraim, Zebulun, Asher, Naphtali, and Dan; and in each case it is stated that the tribe in question did not persevere to the end in destroying the Canaanites. In punishment for this disobedience to God's express command (see Deut. 7:1–2), the Lord Himself would use the heathen population that remained in Canaan to oppress the Israelites and would turn their gods into a snare for His people. This by itself already largely explains the peculiar course of Israel's history during the time of the judges. God granted the surviving Canaanite population the power to subjugate His people again and again to judge Israel for failing to exterminate these nations. Similarly the Israelites' negligence in breaking down the pagan altars induced God to abandon His people to idolatry for a time, allowing them to suffer its disastrous consequences.

This brief explanation is fleshed out in the second part of the preface (2:6–3:4), where the course of Israel's history after the death of Joshua is regarded more or less internally. Picking up the thread from Joshua 24:28–31, the author states in 2:10–15 that the people's tendency toward unfaithfulness was because a new generation had grown up that had not witnessed the mighty deeds that God had performed during the entry into and conquest of Canaan. This generation began to provoke the Lord by following after the gods of the Canaanites. God therefore punished them grievously by repeatedly abandoning them to the power of the surrounding, hostile nations. In fulfillment of the prediction that the Canaanite gods would become a snare to Israel (2:3), the people proved unable to resist the temptation to idolatry; and they thereby brought God's vengeance on themselves. The profoundly sinful character of idolatry stands out in bold relief here. Clearly there is no contrast at all between these verses and 2:1–3.

Verses 16–19 continue to amplify the first part of the preface by directly announcing the coming of the judges and showing that this office demonstrated God's great goodness and long-suffering. Even more significantly, verses 20–23 state that God's motive for allowing the survivors of the heathen nations to remain in Canaan was to test the Israelites and see whether they would keep His covenant, and 3:1–2 elaborates this thought a little further.[4] From this point of view we thus see that the whole course of Israel's history during this period was ordained and directed by God in a way that would make the people fully alive to the absolute distinction between themselves, as the nation of the one true God, and the heathen nations with whom they had such close contact because of their own negligence. In this manner the Israelites' hidden motives and the degree to which they recognized and respected this distinction were continually brought to light. For as the people themselves had to admit in their better moments, their contact with the heathen was always harmful, both to their freedom and to their religious life, while their deliverance in each case came from the very God whom they had so faithlessly forsaken.

There is no need to belabor these thoughts further. Already it is abundantly clear that 1:1–3:4 forms an extremely important part of the

---

[4] Judges 3:1–2 does not give a second divine motive. It rather describes the Lord's testing and shows that He used the enmity of the surviving Canaanites to compel Israel (for her own good) to choose sides. "The purpose, which at first sight seems twofold (at 2:22 and 3:2), is basically only one" (J. Bachmann, *Das Buch der Richter*, p. 184).

Book of Judges. Although these verses are clearly prefatory, they are also indispensable. Without them the book would be a torso, for they present the historical, psychological, and theocratic foundation for the work of the judges and unveil the perspective from which the whole period of the judges has to be viewed. Thus there can be no argument against the inner unity between the first and the second parts of the book. The common theme of both is the path by which God led His people Israel during the time of the judges, or, better, the battle that the Lord fought with the Israelites in order to make them submit to His service, to accustom them to His discipline, and to preserve them from mingling with the heathen and ruining their religious and moral life. In this battle the Lord continually made use of judges who raised the people from the humiliation they found themselves in for a time and pointed them in the right direction.

It could be expected that this central thought would not come through with equal clarity in every part of the book. In some sections God's guidance and specific intentions are expressly spoken of; in others it seems as though He left the nation to herself for a time, especially in the third main part of the book, chapters 17–21. I have already touched on the peculiar character of these chapters at the end of section I. The events that they relate actually interrupt the unfolding of the historical narrative, which is not taken up again till 1 Samuel 1. These chapters were deliberately placed at the end of the book to characterize the period of the judges as a whole and to show how it served as the necessary preparation for a new era. Just as the first main section ties in with the time of Joshua, the third points forward to the time of the monarchy. Remarkably, however, the material for these chapters is taken almost from the beginning of the period of the judges (see, e.g., 18:1 and 20:28), even though it is treated retrospectively from the point of view of the monarchy. This comes out in the recurrent statement that typifies this whole section: "in those days Israel had no king" (17:6; 18:1; 19:1; 21:25), which the first and last of these verses accentuate by adding: "everyone did as he saw fit."

Chapters 17–21 nevertheless contain evidence that Israel actually had not yet fallen so far. Micah indeed had gone astray, but neither he nor the Danites were bent on idolatry or the worship of Baal. The nation still was profoundly conscious of the unity and solidarity of the Twelve Tribes. There was a general outrage at the atrocity committed by the men of Gibeah. That the Lord's advice was sought before the people began to act, the high priest's authority was recognized, oaths

201

were honored, etc., points to a period early in the time of the judges, when the decline of the nation had not yet become so serious as, for example, during the time of Deborah (see 5:8, 16–17). This makes it all the more remarkable that we read nothing about God's direct intervention or control in these chapters.

In chapters 17–18 various individuals do speak of God and express their belief that He was with them (17:13; 18:10), but nowhere is it said how God acted or how He judged what took place. In chapter 20 the Lord's responses to the people's questions are so brief that they cannot always tell for sure whether they have chosen the right course. And in chapter 21, there is no answer at all to the prayer of the people recorded in verse 3. No prophet stepped forward to admonish them or to clarify God's purpose and plan. It seems as if God has left the people on their own. Although He in fact is Israel's king, He hardly makes His authority felt. This of course was not without reason, for one of the essential features of the period of the judges was God's intention "to test Israel and see whether they will keep the way of the LORD" (2:22). Because this was the Lord's plan and method, it was necessary that He largely withhold His direct guidance of Israel's national life, especially during the early part of this era. Chapters 17–21 present a striking illustration of how things went with the Israelites when they were left more or less to their own devices. The third main section of the Book of Judges, therefore, serves to unfold the same theme that governs the first two sections. The whole book is a unity, clearly having been constructed according to a definite design.

I accept the unity of the Book of Judges mainly on the basis of the book's content, but its form also supports my case. The unity of the book has been challenged in many ways from both points of view. In regard to its content, many alleged inconsistencies have been pointed out, e.g., between 1:8 and 1:21, 1:18 and 3:3, 2:22 (and 3:4) and 3:2, 17:10 and 17:11 et al.[5] The comments on these various verses will examine the question of how real these inconsistencies are. A more general discrepancy is thought to be found in the contrast between the recurrent use of the word "Israelites" (3:7, 12; 4:1, 23–24; 6:1–2; 8:33; 10:6 et al.), which has to refer to the nation as a whole, and the narrative's continual focus on only one or a small group of tribes (4:6; 5:14–18; 7:23; 8:1; 10:18; 13:25).[6]

To be sure, the work of most of the judges undeniably seems to have

---

[5]See, e.g., E. König, *Einleitung in das Alten Testament*, p. 251.
[6]See, e.g., W. Nowack, *Handkommentar zum Alten Testament*, p. vi.

been limited to only a part of the nation of Israel. (This cannot be demonstrated in the cases of Othniel and Ehud, however. The fact that the former came from Judah and the latter from Benjamin in no way proves that they delivered and governed only their own tribes.) Nevertheless, the national and religious unity of Israel had not yet been lost entirely, and the author of the Book of Judges holds to this unity. By using the word "Israelites" or "Israel," he continually brings out that he is speaking of the people of the covenant as a whole, a nation that so faithlessly deserted its faithful God and still was delivered by Him again and again. The history that is recounted in the book is the history of that nation, not of its several individual tribes. And even though the whole nation was not always handed over to the oppressor, it was indeed the whole nation that forsook the demands of the covenant. There is no trace of an absolute inconsistency here. It is true that the battles were local in character and involved only a few of the tribes. Nevertheless the benefits that flowed from the judges' work usually extended, not merely to the tribes they freed, but to others as well. Therefore it could justly be said after each war of liberation that "the land" had peace for some length of time (3:11, 30; 5:31; 8:28), or that the judge in question led "Israel" (8:33–35; 12:7; 15:20; 16:31). It is quite arbitrary to suppose both that the word "Israelites" always refers to all Twelve Tribes, and that the work and authority of the judges were confined within the boundaries of the tribes they belonged to. Proceeding in this fashion does not uncover inconsistencies that lie within the text but rather imposes them on it.

The same thing happens when the formal unity of the book is disputed on the basis of differences in historical method and religious viewpoint, which supposedly are found on nearly every page. Whenever two accounts of some topic do not coincide completely, some commentators immediately assume that the author uncritically drew his material from two distinct sources, and sometimes also that he interpolated one or more verses in order to harmonize mutually discrepant accounts. The fact that 2:6 begins with the death of Joshua, for example, is regarded as sufficient evidence that 1:1–2:5 could not have been written as a preface to the Book of Judges.[7]

It is commonly thought that in nearly all the major stories in Judges (i.e., those about Ehud, Deborah and Barak, Gideon, Jephthah,[8] Micah

---

[7] König, *Einleitung in das Alten Testament*, p. 251.

[8] The story of Samson is not mentioned here because even the critics I am speaking of almost unanimously regard this as a literary unit. See pp. 209–10 below.

and the Danites, and the crime and punishment of the Benjamites), two distinct narratives concerning the events described were combined into one and then incorporated into the religio-historical "schema" that runs as a continuous thread through the whole central part of the book. This thread is supposedly found in those passages that portray the Israelites' periods of oppression as a punishment sent by God Himself in response to the people's unfaithfulness (2:6–3:8; 3:12; 4:1–2; 6:1; 8:33–35; 10:6–16; 13:1). According to this theory, the view of Israel's history found in these passages dates from many centuries later than the events recounted in the original narratives. This religious viewpoint, however, does not come to expression in 1:1–2:5, in chapter 9, and in chapters 17–21.

To explain this it is claimed that the person who outlined the "religious schema" was acquainted with these chapters (or at least chs. 9 and 17–21) but rejected them as unsuited to his purpose, and that a later redactor then reincorporated them. Such a theory ends by reducing the Book of Judges to fragments instead of explaining how it came into being. It assumes that the book in its present form was the work of many different hands and that it in no way can be regarded as a literary unity. Various commentaries thus give the impression that "the author of the book of Judges [was] surrounded by a quantity of manuscripts, out of which he selected larger and smaller fragments which he fit together as well as he could."[9]

---

[9]A. Noordtzij, "The Old Testament Problem," translated by Miner B. Stearns in *Bibliotheca Sacra* 98 (1941), p. 239. The following statement from one of the commentators who adopt the critical viewpoint shows that this judgment is not exaggerated. "It must be borne in mind that any hypothesis we may frame is much simpler than the literary history of which it attempts to give account. J, E, JE, D, R, etc. represent, not individual authors whose share in the work can be exactly assigned by the analysis, but stages of the process, in which more than one—perhaps many—successive hands participated, every transcription being to some extent a recension" (G. F. Moore, *Judges,* International Critical Commentary, vol. 7, 2nd ed. [New York: Charles Scribner's Sons, 1895], p. xxxiii, note 2). This quotation shows that the proponents of the theory discussed above in the text generally take the view that the so-called sources of the Pentateuch also stand behind the Book of Judges. Indeed, several commentaries on this book were written at the time when the source hypothesis of the Wellhausen school was almost universally accepted as correct. These include the commentaries of Nowack and Moore mentioned above, and also K. Budde, *Das Buch der Richter,* 1897 (in Marti's *Kurzer Handkommentar*) and S. Oettli, *Buch der Richter* (in Strack and Zöckler's *Kurzgefasster Kommentar,* 1893). Between 1890 and 1900 much was written about the composition of the book. König and Oettli think that the presence of J and E in Judges cannot be demonstrated, and the same position is taken by A. Schulz, *Das*

It is obvious that such a conception of the origin and composition of Judges completely fails to appreciate its peculiar character as a part of divinely inspired Scripture. At the very outset the contents of the book are branded as unreliable, for it is assumed that the historical data have been altered to fit the "religious schema" of the redactor from the so-called Deuteronomistic school. Additionally, this theory does not accept the book in the form in which it has come down to us but instead dismembers it (or at least attempts to do so)[10] into a host of fragments that have no intrinsic unity. From this standpoint the existence of an actual *Book* of Judges is in fact denied. The desire to reduce the material to fragments has gone to an extreme and by and large annihilated the book as an object of exegesis.

Our starting point in this commentary is and should be the conviction that the book is a unity, even though some of its parts may vary in origin. A mere respect for tradition demands this general outlook. One at least has to begin by regarding the tradition as trustworthy; and if a work presents itself as an independent whole, we therefore should make a serious attempt to grasp it as such. Such an attempt is lacking, however, if one ignores the clear intent of the author, deliberately introduces all kinds of discrepancies, and then supposes that the author or redactor has taken the most disparate data and either thoughtlessly thrown them together or clumsily tried to harmonize them.

Even apart from a believing acceptance of Scripture, one is obliged to accept the unity of the book as long as this is not ruled out by internal or external evidence. If we respect the veracity of Scripture, we have even less warrant for explaining the so-called discrepancies discerned with our limited knowledge and insight by assigning the material to a diversity of "sources" with varying degrees of credibility. And this conclusion is only reinforced by our previous observation that

---

Buch der Richter (Bonn, 1926), pp. 4f., and R. Kittel, *Geschichte des Volkes Israel*, vol. 2, 3rd ed. (1907), pp. 16ff. Kittel strongly opposes views like that of Moore in the above quotation. On the other hand, the presence of J and E is defended by C. H. Cornill, *Einleitung* (1913), pp. 102ff., and others. E. Sellin, *Einleitung* (1929), p. 66, thinks the latter position is probably correct; and J. Garstang, *Joshua, Judges* (London: Constable and Co. Ltd., 1931), pp. 3f., regards it as certain.

[10]The fact that the distribution of the historical material among the various presumed "sources" is practically a hopeless undertaking can be seen from Sellin's remark (*Einleitung*, pp. 67f.) on chapters 17 and 18: "The distribution among J and E here is indeed even more uncertain than in the rest of the book of Judges." A glance at Nowack's *Übersicht über die Quellenscheidungen* (*Handkommentar*, pp. xxiv ff.) also is enough to convince one that the book could not have originated in such a manner.

the Book of Judges is not at all a loose assemblage of episodes but rather a systematic treatment of some select historical material from a definite religious point of view. Although an unmistakable slant pervades the book from beginning to end, this by itself casts no doubt on its reliability. On the contrary it forms further evidence for its unity.

The unity of the Book of Judges in no way precludes the possibility that it may also in some sense be a composite product. If this is understood to mean not a mere stringing together of passages taken from various "sources" but rather an independent and purposeful use of older writings in which the author at times preserved the very words of the latter, such a thought is not at all unacceptable. Indeed, it is highly improbable that a book embracing the history of more than three centuries could have been written without making use of written information concerning the events of that era. The author of Judges, therefore, undoubtedly had access to such information. That he nowhere mentions such a written source by name (as Josh. 10:13 mentions the Book of Jashar) may be because he had no particular reason to do so. If the author was the first person to write a historical account of the period of the judges—and if there was not yet any kind of complete and authoritative collection of stories about the judges— then it would have been impossible for him to appeal to an earlier historical work. He still must have had sources, but these would have consisted of disconnected stories and factual reports that were handed down either orally or in writing. A large part of the author's work, then, would have been to track down, collect, verify, and present an orderly arrangement of these traditions. I am not claiming that this is indeed what happened, but such an idea seems very plausible for the following reasons.

1. As has been noted above, the Book of Judges contains no reference to an existing work on the same period, even though such references are not uncommon elsewhere (see Josh. 10:13; 2 Sam. 1:18; 2 Chron. 12:15; 13:22).

2. The facts about the lives and deeds of the various judges undoubtedly did not at once become common knowledge throughout the whole nation, and personal details must have been known only in small circles. Such things may have been preserved in writing, but this does not mean that the records were circulated. There thus must have been someone who made a collection of these written reports.

3. Most likely, this collection was not made simply to disseminate the facts themselves more broadly but primarily to transmit the voice of

history to future generations of Israelites and to enable them to perceive God's guidance in that history. So the person who combined the stories that had been handed down into a unified narrative would have been none other than the author of the Book of Judges. See the note at the end of this section.

My reconstruction is obviously only a theory and not fact. The possibility must be granted that the Book of Judges contains an earlier collection of writings that was reworked, amplified, and placed in the service of one central idea. Any attempt to determine the origin of the book and the manner it was composed has to exercise caution. We have no direct testimony in this regard; and our argument therefore has to proceed solely on the basis of internal evidence such as style, the nature of the historical reports, etc. It is obvious that no certain and indisputable conclusions can be reached by this route. In particular it is impossible to determine precisely where the author has reproduced a specific written source literally, to what extent he may have altered or amplified such a source, or the number and kinds of sources that he used. Yet it is still valuable to formulate an idea of how he proceeded and perhaps to provide a natural explanation for the various idiosyncrasies (e.g., differences in style) found in the book. So I will present a hypothetical outline of how the Book of Judges could have come into existence.

The author, who undoubtedly was acquainted with the Book of Joshua and lived during the early years of the monarchy (see the next section), proceeded to write a history of the period of the judges to highlight the lessons it had for his own generation. With this in mind, he tracked down and gathered the written records and oral traditions concerning the actions of the various tribes and the work of the judges, and then he arranged his material. He probably first composed the second part (3:5–16:31), the main body of the book, and added 2:6–3:4 as an introduction. These central chapters record what was most important to him, the constant alternation between apostasy and repentance, sin and grace, that coincided with the rise and death of the various judges and marked this period of Israel's history.

The great differences in length among the individual histories, some of which are extensive and some very short, probably corresponds to the varying amounts of material that the author had on the different figures. If he found only a brief note on a certain judge, he probably preserved this unaltered but connected it with the flow of his historical narrative (e.g., 10:1–2). If he had also heard an oral tradition concerning the same person, he could have joined this to the written record with his own words. This seems to be what happened in 10:3–5. Verses 3 and 5 were probably taken from a written chronicle, while verse 4 appears to be the author's own formulation of an oral tradition. Such details concerning the number of children of a great ancestor are long remembered by posterity. A similar case is found in 12:8–15, where once again verses 11–12 differ from the surrounding verses in that they consist solely of names and numbers. Judges 3:31 also gives the impression of being a tradition that was preserved orally and was first committed to writing in its present form by the author.

The histories of the major judges—Othniel, Ehud, Deborah, Gideon, Jepthath, Samson—contains so many details, often of a kind that could have been known only by the judges themselves (e.g., 3:20–23), that they undoubtedly could not have been written without the reports of contemporaries. The author probably wished to record everything that was known to him, and to do this he perhaps had to combine diverse stories about the same events into a single whole. On the whole, however, he must have confined himself to a faithful presentation of what he found in his sources, not only in the case of the song of Deborah (ch. 5), but also in the greatest part of the stories themselves. His task was not to reconstruct history but rather, by looking to the facts themselves, to discern its voice and allow it to speak. He did this especially in those passages that open and close the individual histories, where Israel's oppression by her enemies is always portrayed as Yahweh's punishment for her unfaithfulness, while the long periods of peace and rest are credited to the rule of the judges sent by God. These passages are often called the frame within which the history is set.[11] There can be no objection to this term as long as it does not imply that the historical facts have been twisted and distorted to fit the requirements of a particular schema. Such a view would be tantamount to a denial that the Scriptures are historically reliable. The frame does not mangle or fictionalize the facts but rather places them in their proper light. What was at stake during the time of the judges was the preservation of the covenant between Yahweh and Israel, the upholding of His claim on His people. This is not a theory or perspective that was devised later on. Rather it is something that was felt by the judges

---

[11]The passages are as follows: 3:5–8; 3:12; 4:1–2; 6:1; 8:33–35; 10:6–16; 13:1 (opening), and 3:11; 3:30; 4:23; 5:31b; 8:28 (closing). Judges 9:55–57; 12:7; 15:20; and 16:13b also can be considered closing passages, though they do not speak of a period of peace.

themselves and that even comes through to some degree in the original stories (e.g., in the song of Deborah, 5:8; Gideon's battle against the Midianites, 7:18, 20; Jephthah's declaration and vow, 11:11, 27, 30–31; Samson's cry to the Lord, 15:18).[12]

The story of Abimelech in chapter 9 interrupts the series of histories of the judges, since this figure cannot be included among the latter. Nevertheless, it is very easy to surmise why the author might have chosen to insert this section after the story of Gideon rather than saving it for the final part of the book, where it also would have fit very well. He perhaps drew it from the same source as the account of Gideon's life; but in any case it forms a very suitable illustration of the fact that God controls the course of history and takes vengeance on sin (here the sin of ingratitude, 8:34–35).

Chapters 13–16, which recount the history of Samson, also occupy a rather special place in the book. From a literary point of view, this section forms a self-contained unit. The story is much fuller than that of any of the other judges and provides a remarkably gripping account of Samson's birth, character, conduct, and lifework. Curiously, however, very little is said about his official work as a judge. He won no great victory, at least not like those of Barak, Gideon, and Jephthah; and he did not free Israel from the yoke of the Philistines. Nevertheless, the author tells the story of Samson with a special fondness and presents his material in a very orderly and well-constructed narrative. Nowhere do we get the impression that he had to base his account on earlier documents and traditions that had to be combined into a unified whole. May we perhaps explain these unique features by supposing that chapters 13–16 are entirely the author's own writing, that he did not have to look elsewhere for his material since they deal with a person and a period that were still very close to him? This is an attractive thought.

If the author of Judges was a younger contemporary of Samson, or at least a contemporary who outlived him, he would have had a much better opportunity to display his own talent as a writer in the depiction of Samson's life and personality than in the rest of the book. He still would have confined himself to the actual facts, but he would not have been bound to a tradition that had long been fixed in a definite form and that he had no authority to use in his own way. This would have made it easier for him to write the story of Samson in one piece and to leave his

---

[12]This has been pointed out by Oettli, *Buch der Richter*, p. 216, and König, *Dictionary of the Bible*, "Book of Judges," vol. 2, p. 816.

own mark on this part of the book. Of course, the first reason for this special focus on Samson was the importance of the man himself. Nevertheless, if my hypothesis is correct, the literary unity displayed in chapters 13–16 also has a ready explanation; and the story of Samson then would form a important part of the author's own written contribution to the book he composed (see section 3 below).

Chapters 17–21 only require a few remarks. The two stories presented here do not mention any of the judges; therefore, there was no reason to insert them at any particular point in the book's survey of this part of Israel's history. The author does make clear that these events took place virtually at the beginning of the period of the judges. In addition, his material here was different from the rest of the book, for oppression by a foreign enemy is not even alluded to. He therefore must have set these stories aside till he had finished the most important part of the book and then attached them later to round off his account of the era. Their position at the end of the book shows that these chapters were intended to characterize the whole period from a particular point of view, and this comes out even more clearly in the repeated statement: "in those days Israel had no king" (17:6; 18:1; 19:1; 21:25). These words, which could not have been present in the original stories, were undoubtedly added by the author of Judges himself and show that he knew from his own experience the blessings that a monarchy could bring. Apart from this, he most likely left the stories that had come down to him unchanged.

The above-mentioned statement does not mean, however, that all the Israelites' misery during the time of the judges was due to the absence of a king and that their own sin and idolatry played no role in this. Such a thought is completely foreign to the author. Chapters 17–21 do not stand in contrast to chapters 2–16 and may not be detached from them. Rather they have to be read in the context of the preceding material, for they form an indispensable supplement to it. The author merely wishes to bring out in these chapters that one of the indirect causes of the degeneration and decline that Israel underwent during the time of the judges was the lack of a strong, centralized, and hereditary authority such as he knew in his own day. If the entire nation had been like Gideon (8:23), the monarchy would have been unnecessary. These final chapters reveal, however, how soon after the death of Joshua and the older generation Israel succumbed to the religious and moral decay that caused the period of the judges to contrast so unfavorably with the early years of the monarchy.

After having completed the steps that I have outlined up to now, the author was nearly done with his work. All that was lacking was a clear picture of the change that Israel had undergone between the days of Joshua and the period of the judges. The question of how the nation had dealt with Joshua's final will and testament, and particularly with his command to purge the Canaanites from the land completely and to take over the unconquered regions (see Josh. 17:18; 18:3; 23:5, 10), demanded an answer. It also was necessary to sketch the actual balance of power in Canaan, since this now totally different from what it had been during the lifetime of Joshua. In a word a preface was needed to depict the judges' work in broad outline; thus the author composed 1:1–2:5.

I have already spoken of the content and significance of this part of the book (see pp. 196–97), but it is also extremely appropriate as an introduction to the entire book.[13] First, we should note that the tribe of Judah is treated at relatively great length. Fully a half of the first chapter is devoted to this tribe's campaigns (vv. 3–20), which largely met with success though they were not pursued to the end (v. 19). Judah distinguished herself favorably by making a serious effort (in league with Simeon) to conquer its allotted territory and to eliminate all non-Israelite inhabitants. This explains why this tribe recedes so much into the background in chapters 3–16.[14] It is true that Othniel, the first judge, came from Judah (3:9–11); but after this we hear nothing of this tribe till the Philistines and Ammonites begin to oppress Israel (10:7–9; 15:9–11). In spite of its importance, Judah is not even mentioned in the song of Deborah. In the light of 1:1–20, this can be explained by the fact that the corrupting influences on Judah's religious life were weaker than in the other tribes and did not take effect as soon. The minor role that the tribe of Judah plays in the second and main section of the book would be virtually inexplicable without this preface.

Second, it is significant that chapter 1 contains some valuable items of information mainly on those tribes that occupy center stage in the rest of the book or that produced the major judges. These include in particular the repeated remark that the original, heathen population of

---

[13]This is undeniably true, and it has been pointed out especially by E. Bertheau, *Richter und Rut* (Leipzig, 1845), pp. xvff., Oettli, *Buch der Richter,* p. 216, and C. von Orelli, *Realenzyclopädie für protestantische Theologie und Kirche,* 3rd ed., in article by A. Hauck, p. 769.

[14]The situation is somewhat different in chapters 17–21, where Judah headed the attack against the Benjamites (20:18). Like the events in 1:1–20, however, the story told there happened quite soon after the death of Joshua.

the land was not completely eliminated, leaving seedbeds of idolatry everywhere to spread their contagion to Israel again and again. Apart from this more general item, however, we can also point out some more specific connections between chapter 1 and many later parts of the book. Verses 12–15 thus prepare the way for 3:9–11, and the brief remark on the Kenites in verse 16 sheds light on 4:11. The tribes whose exploits are noted include Benjamin, the native tribe of Ehud (3:15); and Ephraim, which proved to be a powerful force for Israel many times in the book (5:14; 7:24–25; 8:1; 12:1) and probably gave birth to Deborah (4:5); also Manasseh, the tribe of Gideon (6:15); and Zebulun and Naphtali, which distinguished themselves in the battle against Sisera (4:10; 5:18). Barak was from Naphtali (4:6), and this tribe also fought in Gideon's army (7:23).

Asher and Dan appear in the poorest light in chapter 1. Asher not only left the Canaanites in peace, it also failed to exact tribute from them and even settled for a subordinate position within its own territory. A comparison of 1:31–32 with 28–30 and 33 shows that while the other tribes tolerated the presence of the Canaanites, Asher conversely was in effect tolerated by the Canaanites. Judges 5:17 accordingly reproaches this tribe for its indolence, but its prompt response to Gideon's call for help in 7:23 still tells in its favor. Dan also took only weak action against the native population. There undoubtedly is a close connection between verse 34 and the story told in chapter 18 (see esp. 18:1). Rather than manfully fighting against the Amorites, the Danites retreated and caused a massacre in the peaceful city of Laish. This same cowardice can be seen in the story of Samson, the great Danite (13:2) whose comrades left him to stand alone in battle.

All this shows that chapter 1 is indeed introductory in character and as such ties in well with the rest of the book. Chapter 2:1–5 also is introductory, and the author has inserted this old tradition in just the right place, since it connects perfectly with the first chapter and prepares the way for what comes later in the book. The Book of Judges in its present form therefore has a twofold preface or introduction, namely, 1:1–2:5 and 2:6–3:4; and it seems that the explanation for this peculiar feature lies in the manner in which the book came into being. As I have suggested above, 2:6–21:25 was composed first, and 1:1–2:5 was only written later. The author apparently felt that the preface in 2:6–3:4 did not provide enough preliminary information and therefore added 1:1–2:5. In this first preface, however, he only included whatever items seemed necessary in view of the work as it stood at that point. We can only guess where he took his information from here, but the peculiar structure of chapter 1 perhaps gives us a clue.

The chapter is more or less fragmentary in character.[15] The conquests of Judah and Simeon are described briefly, but seemingly in full, while only a single campaign of Ephraim and Manasseh is spoken of (vv. 22–26). In the case of the other tribes, we are given nothing more than a chroniclelike list of what they did or failed to do. We can easily imagine that the author had a written source from which he could quote as much as he wished. Since he merely wanted to summarize the situation after Joshua's death, he abridged this source and limited himself to a brief statement of the outcome of most of the tribes' efforts. He made an exception to this rule only in the case of Judah (for the reason given on pp. 211 above) and to some extent also for the important tribes of Joseph. It is possible that some of his information was generally known and did not have to be taken from a written source. This could include verse 21, for Benjamin's failure to conquer Jerusalem certainly would not have had to be dug out of ancient documents, and perhaps also verse 29. For the most part, however, he would have needed written accounts to confirm his knowledge of circumstances and events that lay a few hundred years in the past.

I therefore offer the following hypothesis in this regard. It is not at all unlikely that the priests kept a record of the successes, failures, and general fortunes of the various tribes in the central sanctuary at Shiloh, a place that continued to have great prestige during the early years of Israel's history. This was where the "Book of the Law of God" was kept (Josh. 24:26), and probably also where the Book of Joshua was completed and stored.[16] There, too, the high priest Phinehas and his subordinates no doubt realized the great importance of making a written record of the main events that took place after Joshua had died. At Shiloh some type of chronicle thus would have been kept for a number of years concerning the history of the Twelve Tribes, or at least of the tribes that had settled west of the Jordan, and this chronicle would have been the source from which the author took his material for 1:1–2:5. It seems very likely therefore that chapters 17–18 and 19–21 would have come from this same source.

In conclusion, I want to emphasize that the above arguments are

---

[15]Oettli calls chapter 1 an "excerpt from a larger context" (*Buch der Richter*, p. 215).

[16]The preceding commentary on Joshua (p. 19) advocates the possibility that Phinehas added the finishing touches to the Book of Joshua.

concerned solely with the human side of the origin, or rather the growth and composition, of the Book of Judges. In no way have I diminished the divine side of that process. Behind the Book of Judges stands the inspiration of the Holy Spirit, but this divine role in its production escapes our perception and study. We can be sure, however, that the work of the Holy Spirit did not render the work of a human author unnecessary but rather demanded and embraced it. For this reason we have to do full justice to the historian's own activity in tracking down, sorting, and preparing his material. The Book of Judges was his work too; but the Spirit of God drove him onward from beginning to end, enlightening his mind and leading him infallibly into all truth. Like the rest of the Bible, the Book of Judges is therefore altogether divine and altogether human.

NOTE

I here will present a brief response to the article by H. Mulder in the *Gereformeerde Theologische Tijdschrift* (1948, no. 2), entitled "De ontstaan-stijd van de beide aanhangsels van het boek Richteren (ch. 17–21)."[17] In regard to Mulder's objection to my view that the book forms a unity and that its distinct sections are governed by one central thought, the reader can consult pages 198–214 above. On page 8, I concluded that chapters 17–21 unfold the same theme found in chapters 1–16, which strongly suggests that a single author put the book together according to a specific plan that he had conceived beforehand (see the beginning of section III below).

Mulder, who agrees with my conclusions in many other respects, attempts to show that the Book of Judges is not an integral whole. He poses the question of whether chapters 17–21 actually form an appendix (p. 103), and his argument tends to an affirmative answer. Granted, from a purely formal point of view, the chapters in question can be called an appendix (see pp. 197–98 above). In terms of their content, however, they unquestionably form an integral part of the book and merely give their own version of its one, central idea (see pp. 9–10). A. Noordtzij expresses this as follows: "Judges 3:5–16:31 presents what we perhaps could call a longitudinal cross section of the period of the judges. . . . Judges 17–21 gives a vertical cross section" (*Bijbelsch Handboek* [Kampen, 1935], vol. 1, pp. 444–45). This image correctly brings out the close connection between chapters 17–21 and the earlier material.

Mulder, in contrast, takes the following view: "When the first part of the book was already in existence, a later writer added chapters 17–21 because he thought that the account of the period of the judges would be incomplete if these internal affairs were left unmentioned. He did not wish to interrupt the train of

---

[17] I.e., "The date of origin of the two appendices to the book of Judges."

thought that was consistently carried through in the first 16 chapters, and for this reason he simply added the latter chapters as an appendix'' (p. 104). Mulder thus views the final part of Judges as having been attached to it later, not part of the book's original design. He gives no date for this; but on page 113, he says that it possibly did not happen till David had conquered Jerusalem. This would therefore be considerably later than the beginning of Saul's reign, the date Mulder assigns to the actual writing of these chapters (p. 106). I can concur with this latter date entirely, but this compels us to inquire why the author of chapters 1–16 could not have also written chapters 17–21 and included them in his plan for the book. Disregarding the fact that the book is largely an abridgment of older documents and might even incorporate much material from them verbatim, we must ask why Mulder objects to the view that the book as a whole was composed by a single person. His article gives no clear and convincing answer to this question.

Mulder calls attention to the perplexing fact that chapters 17–21 "occupy a peculiar position within the framework of the book" (p. 103). "Their natural, chronological place would be at the beginning, and there is reason to think that this even would improve the overall logical design of the book" (p. 104). To support this latter claim, he appeals to G. F. Moore's commentary, which was written from a strongly critical point of view. True, few would maintain that chronological order has been observed here. This, however, gives no commentator the right to tamper with the traditionally accepted unity of the book and to detach an important part from the whole. The author was free to organize the book according to his own design, and he chose to do so in the following manner. First, he gave a chronologically ordered survey of the work of the judges; then he recounted a few events that illustrated and typified Israel's decline during this era. What does it matter that he took these events from the beginning of the period under concern, which as a whole extended from Joshua to Samuel? Here too he was completely free to make his own choice. By using these early events, he took the opportunity to show "how soon after the death of Joshua and the older generation Israel succumbed to the process of religious and moral decay that caused the period of the judges to contrast so unfavorably with the early years of the monarchy" (see p. 210 above).

Mulder refers to this statement and rejects it by arguing that I have sought to find "some kind of contrast between the time of the judges and the monarchy which actually could not have been intended , since these chapters come before the period of the judges proper" (p. 104). But what does this objection amount to? Mulder here takes issue with something that is purely incidental and diverts our attention from the main point, namely, that Israel's decline set in so soon and that the author wished to bring this out by taking his examples from the very beginning of the period he was recounting. Mulder himself in fact calls this whole period, including its opening years, the period of the judges (see the first quotation from p. 104 of his article). His objection therefore hardly refutes my case. The article does not discuss my view of how chapters 17–21 unfold the central theme of the whole book, nor my remarks about why they were placed at the end (p. 201); and my previous statements on these two points can therefore be left as they stand.

We thus see that Mulder's only real reason for rejecting the unity of the Book of Judges is because chapters 17–21 violate the chronological order. Taken by itself, however, this argument is inadequate. His standpoint raises further questions in that it makes these chapters into a mere appendix that is more or less independent of the rest of the book. According to Mulder, the chapters do not belong where they stand. He regards their inclusion as the (rather arbitrary) act of a writer who thought that the account of the period of the judges would be incomplete if these internal affairs were left unmentioned. One might ask whether the Bible's historiography really aims so much at being exhaustive, but our main concern here is the implication that this "writer" (he actually would have been a redactor, since the stories were already written) added the chapters at the wrong place. From Mulder's viewpoint, which regards chronology as the primary criterion, the writer rather should have attached them as an appendix to the Book of Joshua, since the events that they relate happened soon after Joshua's death. But would the chapters really have fit better there?

Mulder actually ends up in the predicament of having a book consisting of two parts that do not form a whole. Although he says that "inspiration does not stand or fall with the acceptance of one or two authors" (p. 104), the work of the Holy Spirit that we call inspiration applies, not merely to the written words alone, but also to the overall design that stands behind Scripture as a whole, and each of its books in particular. He is the primary author of every book; and once He gives us a book, no one can say that a certain part really does not fit because it violates the chronological order.

Mulder of course does not say this or draw this conclusion. He too will acknowledge that the redaction of each book in the Bible bears the stamp of the Holy Spirit's authority. And he no doubt would apply this principle also to the work of his presumed "writer," who in a later century added chapters 17–21 to a previously existing Book of Judges. Even Mulder would have to admit, however, that the writer's alleged motive for doing this (viz., that the account would be incomplete without these "internal affairs") was an inadequate and rather superficial reason for including something in the Canon.

It is much better, therefore, to begin by assuming that chapters 1–16 and chapters 17–21 do form an integral whole. Although these two parts came into being separately, they were joined together by the one person whom we have called the author of the Book of Judges. By no means was this author guided by a mere desire to be exhaustive. Rather, he perceived that the events contained in chapters 17–21 would lend their own accent to the message he wished to bring and give it added depth. Inspired by the working of God's Spirit, he thus welded the diverse data he had gathered into a single book that was no mere compilation and did not need to be expanded. He organized this book in such a manner that the introduction or first section tied in with the time of Joshua, while the third and final section pointed forward to and paved the way for the monarchy. And the fact that the material for this closing section was taken from a time slightly before the appearance of the first judge presented no problems for him. It is my hope that a close perusal of what I have written will be enough to dispel all of Mulder's objections to my view.

III. *Author and Date*

Only if we hold to the unity of the Book of Judges, as I have argued in the previous section, is it possible to speak of its author. For if this part of Scripture is allowed to disintegrate into numerous larger and smaller fragments that were continually enlarged by a variety of redactors and then arbitrarily put together, its "unity" would be a mere semblance or product of chance; and it would make no sense to ask who wrote the "book." If, on the other hand, one perceives that a single mind was at work in the composition of the book—despite the fact that older sources were used liberally and that many facts and stories were doubtless quoted from them verbatim—if one cannot close his eyes to the unmistakable unity that overarches its diverse parts, then one cannot escape the question of who it was that succeeded so well in transmitting the voice of history from centuries earlier in such an arresting manner to his own people.

The answer to this question will never be known, however. Nowhere in the Bible do we receive any definite clue as to the name of the author. Not a single passage speaks of him either directly or indirectly. Only in Jewish tradition do we find a name. A note in the Talmud states that Samuel wrote his book and also Judges and Ruth (*Baba Bathra* 14b). If this information is based solely on an ancient tradition, we cannot attach much value to it. Nevertheless, the thought that Samuel could be the author of Judges (we will not concern ourselves with the other two books) is so inherently attractive that I believe it is important to see whether the evidence speaks for or against authorship by him. We must therefore examine whatever hints can be found within the book itself as to the time when it was written. The following passages merit attention in this regard.

1. Judges 1:21; 1:26; 10:4; and 18:12 all contain the phrase "to this day." The three latter verses do not help us, since the phrase there applies to place names that for an unknown length of time remained in use. Judges 1:21, however, not only speaks of the tribe of Benjamin's failure to dislodge the Jebusites, but also states that the latter continued to live in Jerusalem with the Benjamites "to this day." In connection with the first half of the verse, this last statement can only mean that Jerusalem remained entirely in Jebusite hands. They are said to live

"with the Benjamites" only because the city lay within Benjamin's territory.[18] In my view, we are not to think that the Jebusites and Benjamites lived together within the city walls (though the words themselves do allow this interpretation), for Benjamin neither captured the city nor occupied it at all.[19]

The author rather means to say that Jerusalem remained unconquered. Judges 19:12 clearly shows this as well ("an alien city, whose people are not Israelites"); and indeed the whole context of this verse implies that it would have been dangerous for an Israelite to stay in Jerusalem. This situation still prevailed when 1:21 was written, and the verse therefore must date from before David's conquest of Jerusalem reported in 2 Samuel 5:6–9. Since David's conquest took place shortly after he had been enthroned as king over all the tribes at Hebron following Ish-Bosheth's death (previously he had been king only over Judah, 2 Sam. 5:5), the Book of Judges could not have been written later than the beginning of David's reign.

2. This extremely important conclusion is confirmed to some extent by 1:29, which states that the Canaanites were not expelled from Gezer but continued to live there among the Ephraimites. The meaning of this verse is similar to that of verse 21: Gezer lay in Ephraim's territory, but in reality it remained a Canaanite city.[20] This situation lasted till Solomon's time, when a Pharaoh of Egypt captured Gezer, killed its Canaanite inhabitants, and presented it as a gift to Solomon (1 Kings 9:15–17). Judges 1:29 therefore must have been written no later than the beginning of Solomon's reign, but it is possible that it dates from considerably earlier. As a general conclusion, the two verses we have discussed thus far (vv. 21 and 29) forbid us to date the writing of Judges later than the beginning of the monarchy.

3. The repeated phrase "in those days Israel had no king" (17:6;

---

[18] Judges 1:8 speaks of a conquest of Jerusalem by the tribe of Judah that took place after Joshua's death. After that, however, Judah extended its conquests in another direction (v. 9) and did not prevent the Jebusites from resettling the city. Benjamin seems to have made no attempt at all to take Jerusalem. See the comments in 1:8 and 1:21.

[19] If one wishes to infer from verse 21 that there were Benjamites living within the walls of Jerusalem, he would have to grant that there were people from Judah there too. Joshua 15:63 makes precisely the same statement about Judah that this verse makes about Benjamin. In that case, however, Jerusalem undoubtedly could have been considered an Israelite city, while the Levite in Judges 19:12 says exactly the opposite.

[20] For the relation between Judges 1:29 and Joshua 16:10, see the note at the end of the commentary on chapter 1 (pp. 258–59).

18:1; 19:1; 21:25) points this same way. As I have already observed (pp. 25–26), these words indicate that the author himself lived during the monarchy and regarded it as a welcome improvement over the previous era. In his eyes the benefits of kingly authority contrasted favorably with the disarray in civil and religious life, the internal discord, and the instability in the administration of justice that marked the period of the judges, and especially the interludes between the reigns of the various judges. The author therefore could not have written this phrase before the monarchy had been established. This conclusion takes us an important step further in our investigation, for it means that the Book of Judges must have been written between the beginning of Saul's reign and the eighth year of David's reign.

I believe we can go even further, however. The phrase "in those days Israel had no king" unquestionably draws a contrast between the monarchy and the period that preceded it and casts an unfavorable light on the latter in comparison to the former (this contrast comes out especially in 17:6 and 21:25). This makes it highly likely that it was written near the beginning of Saul's reign, before his rule fell into disfavor. For it is less easy to see how the author could have extolled the monarchy during the time Saul went from bad to worse and disappointed the hopes of Samuel and the people, when he was possessed by an evil spirit and committed arbitrary and cruel deeds (see 1 Sam. 15; 16:14; 18:10–11; 22:16–19). The phrase would in fact fit better with the beginning of David's reign than here. Even an enthusiastic supporter of David, however, could hardly have closed his eyes to the discord and confusion produced by the conflict between David and Ish-Bosheth, a situation that certainly made the monarchy seem something less than an advantage. It is therefore safest to place these words during the time when the verdict on Saul still seemed very good and the prospects even better, when he succeeded in restoring the nation's unity (1 Sam. 11:7–8), armed the people for war and punished their enemies severely (1 Sam. 14:47–48, 52),[21] and was still regarded even by Samuel as the Lord's anointed (1 Sam. 15:1).

4. Judges 18:31 forms an important final item of evidence here. The end of this verse clearly shows that Shiloh had ceased to be the religious center of Israel. This happened when the Philistines carried off the ark, for from that moment the Lord no longer made His abode in

---

[21] See C. F. Keil, *Josua, Richter, und Ruth*, Biblischer Kommentar über das Alte Testament, vol. 3 (Leipzig, 1874), p. 197, who in this connection also cites Saul's elimination of the mediums and spiritists (1 Sam. 28:9; cf. v. 3).

Shiloh (Ps. 78:60–61). It is even possible that the city and sanctuary were destroyed on that occasion (Jer. 7:12; 26:6).[22] Samuel then took up residence in Ramah and also stayed in other places (1 Sam. 7:16–17), and Shiloh is not mentioned again till the time of Solomon. We can therefore conclude from 18:31 that Judges was written after the death of Eli, a result that indirectly confirms and is fully consistent with what we have found thus far.

5. There is only one verse in the book that flatly contradicts this result and would seem to force an entirely different conclusion on us. In 18:30 it is said that the Levite Jonathan and his descendants continued to serve as priests for the tribe of Dan till the Exile, or, literally, "the day of the captivity [i.e., deportation] of the land." This phrase has to refer to the deportation of those who lived in the northern regions of the Ten Tribes to Assyria by Tiglath-Pileser, king of Assyria, in ca. 732 B.C. (2 Kings 15:29). If the author of the Book of Judges knew of this event, he unquestionably must have lived centuries later than Saul and Samuel. The passages discussed under points 1 through 4 above emphatically contradict this, however. These passages do not allow for an alternate interpretation in the light of 18:30 that would fit with this verse. On the contrary, the two sets of evidence are incompatible. The verses we have dealt with above could not have been written by someone who lived later than David and Solomon, while 18:30 could not have been written before the Assyrian deportation that it speaks of. In my view, this conflict cannot be resolved unless we assume that 18:30 was inserted by a later writer. We need not think that the whole verse was added but only its four final words in the Hebrew, i.e., "until the time of the captivity of the land."[23] If these words were originally

---

[22] See A. Noordtzij, *Om de heilige erve,* vol. 1, p. 46.

[23] The following arguments can be made in support of this solution.

1. Judges 18:30's statement of the time that the priestly work of Jonathan and his sons came to an end is altogether superfluous. It is hard to think that these words come from the writer of verse 31b, who there concludes the story contained in chapters 17–18 (which he borrowed from an older source) by stating that Micah's idols were used "all the time the house of God was in Shiloh." The time given here doubtless applies also to verse 30, and the author thus meant that both the priesthood of Jonathan's family and the idol worship in Dan continued for as long as God's house remained in Shiloh. But he says nothing about what happened thereafter. His words do not set a limit and do not mean that these things persisted *only* for that long. On the contrary, he remains silent about the situation in his own day and only reports what he knew for certain concerning the simultaneous existence of the lawful worship at Shiloh and the illegitimate cult at Dan. Since verse 31 must have been written shortly after the fall of Shiloh, it hardly is likely

absent from verse 30, the discrepancy is removed and therewith the problem that this verse seemed to raise for our above result. The testimony to the book's date that we have gathered from the passages cited under the first four points is thus left unimpaired.

We therefore conclude on the basis of internal evidence that the Book of Judges must have been written near the beginning of the period of the monarchy, and probably in the first half of Saul's reign. This result fits extremely well with the hypothesis that Samuel was its author, which does violence to none of the historical facts; and even though this must remain an unproven hypothesis, it is worth noting that the following points speak in its favor.

First, there is no question that, generally speaking, the Book of Judges is written in the spirit of Samuel. This can be seen in the somber tone of its stories, its harsh condemnation of idolatry, its religious view of history, and in the way it persists in regarding the nation of Israel ideally, as a single whole. On all these counts the book accords fully with what we would expect from the prophet Samuel, a man whose vigorous acts of reformation formed a single-minded attempt to root out idolatry altogether, to promote the religious and political unity of the nation, and to accustom the people to an orderly life in accordance with the Lord's commandments (1 Sam. 7:3–6, 12; 12:9–11, 14–15, 20–25). Doubtless Samuel had an earnest desire that the memory of the history of the judges would live on in Israel in the following generations and that the hard lessons and the punishments that God had used to educate the nation in the previous centuries would not sink into oblivion (cf., e.g., 1 Sam. 12:6, 10–11, 15, 21, 24). A written account of the period of the judges would have been an outstanding way to preserve the memory of that history.

---

that the author would have specified another date at the end of verse 30, not to mention one that referred to a later time.

2. Even if the idols vanished (either through theft or in some other way) after the sanctuary at Shiloh had been destroyed, this would not mean that the priestly position and function of Jonathan's descendants automatically had to come to an end. These were two different states of affairs that should not simply be regarded as inseparable, though Mulder wrongly disputes this (*Gereformeerde Theologische Tijdschrift* [1948], p. 109). Van Gelderen thinks differently, stating that "it is natural to think that Jeroboam's golden calf was designed as a replacement for the silver one that had vanished," and "the descendants of the . . . Levite were still at work in Dan in Jeroboam's day, where he apparently maintained their services" (see Korte Verklaring on 1 Kings 12:29, 31).

3. There would be too many objections to other solutions. See the comments in 18:30.

Second, Samuel was just the right man for this task. He stood at the end of the period recounted in the Book of Judges and was thus able to gain a comprehensive view of its unique character and significance. Simultaneously, he formed the link between this period and the time of the monarchy, and this gave him the opportunity to compare the two and to arrive at the judgment of them which, at least to some extent, comes through in the book.[24] Samuel undoubtedly was also well acquainted with the fortunes of the various tribes and judges. Having been raised at Shiloh,[25] he came into contact with persons from all parts of the land who brought their offerings there; and after the fall of the sanctuary in that city, he came to play an increasingly central and commanding role in the nation and stayed regularly in different areas of the country (1 Sam. 7:16). It would therefore not have been much trouble for him to gather the necessary data for making a written account of the histories of the judges and of the whole period following Joshua's death. The plan for this work could have already matured while he was active as a judge, even though he did not actually carry it out till his old age under Saul's rule.

Third, my hypothesis is supported by the likelihood that the story of Samson was written by a person who stood near to him in history (see pp. 209–10). This again makes Samuel a suitable candidate (see p. 235 below). At the same time an authorship by Samuel would shed some light on why the account of Samson's work closes the period of the judges. Another author would most likely have allowed this period to run to the beginning of Saul's reign and would thus have dealt also with Eli and Samuel. If Samuel himself wrote the book, however, the absence of an account of his own life and work, which was closely linked to and in fact formed a single whole with that of Eli, would be easy to understand.

In conclusion, the task of committing God's revelation to writing was

---

[24] I have especially those verses in mind that call attention to the benefits brought by the monarchy (17:6 et al.). Although Samuel did not welcome the monarchy enthusiastically (see 1 Sam. 8:6), he nevertheless dropped his resistance when the Lord commanded him to listen to the people (v. 22); and his growing knowledge of Saul even gladdened him and filled him with hope (1 Sam. 10:24; 11:14–15; 12:2, 13). In the early years of Saul's reign, Samuel regarded him as the man who would realize his ideals and "in whose hands his life's task would be secure" (A. Noordtzij, *Om de heilige erve*, vol. 1, p. 59). And even when Samuel was no longer able to cherish this hope (1 Sam. 13:13–14), he still did not immediately lose all reason to prefer the firm rule of Saul to the time of the judges.

[25] See the hypothesis about Shiloh that is proposed on at p. 213.

so supremely important—so important that the Lord chose and prepared His instruments for it with particular care—that we must find it highly improbable that Samuel, the great man of God, could have played no role in the composition of the Book of Judges at the beginning of the period of the monarchy. Even if he himself did not write the book, we still have every reason to believe that it was undertaken at his initiative and in his spirit and brought to completion under his direction.

IV. *Chronological Questions*

In this section we will deliberately focus on the chronological information found in the Book of Judges. The book contains various numbers giving the lengths of Israel's alternating periods of oppression and freedom. By themselves these numbers present no difficulties; but if they are taken together and compared with other biblical data, a chronological problem emerges that has yet to find a completely satisfactory solution. The lengths of these periods are as follows:

3:8	Subjection under Cushan-Rishathaim	8 years
3:11	Judgeship of Othniel, time of peace	40 years
3:14	Subjection under Eglon	18 years
3:30	Judgeship of Ehud, time of peace	80 years
4:3	Subjection under Jabin	20 years
5:31	Judgeship of Deborah, time of peace	40 years
6:1	Midianite oppression	7 years
8:28	Judgeship of Gideon, time of peace	40 years
9:22	Rule of Abimelech	3 years
10:2	Judgeship of Tola	23 years
10:3	Judgeship of Jair	22 years
10:8	Ammonite oppression	18 years
12:7	Judgeship of Jephthah	6 years
12:9	Judgeship of Ibzan	7 years
12:11	Judgeship of Elon	10 years
12:14	Judgeship of Abdon	8 years
13:1	Philistine oppression	40 years
15:20 (16:31)	Judgeship of Samson	20 years
	Total	410 years

This total, however, does not give us the correct length for the period of the judges as a whole. Strictly speaking, we also have to include the time of Eli and Samuel in this period. The forty years of Eli (1 Sam.

4:18) can be ignored, since they practically coincided with the first period of Philistine control;[26] and nowhere are we told how long Samuel ruled as judge. First Samuel 7:2 does indicate that approximately 20 years had passed between the death of Eli and Samuel's action at Mizpah that led to the defeat of the Philistines there (v. 11). If, for convenience, we make the battle at Mizpah the end of the period of the judges, we therefore will have to increase our total of 410 by 20 years. But since the 20 years of Samson's judgeship fell completely within the "days of the Philistines" (Judg. 15:20; 16:31), we can subtract this 20 again and keep our total of 410 years.

This number still does not cover the entire era, however. For when the Israelites first were subjected to foreign rule (3:8), some years had already passed and, though they preceded the first judge, they still must be included in the period of the judges. This was the time immediately after Joshua's death when the military exploits reported in chapter 1 took place, the time when the older generation died off and was followed by a new one that did not remain faithful to Yahweh (2:10–13). Twenty years would not be too long for this interval, especially since the atrocious crime of the Benjamites and the events that it led to (chs. 19–21) probably happened then as well (see the comments in ch. 19). Thus we arrive at a provisional total of 430 years.[27]

First Kings 6:1 shows that this number is too high, however, since there it is stated that the building of the temple, in the second month of

---

[26] Following C. van Gelderen (*Bijbelsch Handboek* [1935], vol. 1, pp. 129f.), I here assume that the time of Philistine oppression spoken of in 13:1 ended with the death of Samson and that the defeat at Aphek in 1 Samuel 4:1–2 ushered in a second period of Philistine domination. The date of this battle was 1080 B.C. or a few years later (see my *Korte Verklaring* on 1 Samuel, 2nd ed. [Kampen: Kok, 1959], pp. 35, 75).

[27] A direct statement of the length of this period may be found at Acts 13:20 (KJV), where Paul in his speech at Antioch says that it was 450 years from the occupation of Canaan to the appearance of Samuel. There is a question, however, whether this number belongs with verse 20 or verse 19. If it goes with verse 19 (as in the NIV), the number refers to the time between Jacob's journey to Egypt and the division of Canaan (400 years in Egypt, 40 in the desert, and 10 for the conquest). The manuscripts indeed favor this latter reading. I do not think that the number 450 should be regarded as decisive even if it goes with verse 20, however, since we cannot assume that Paul is here substituting his own independent calculation for the one that can be gathered from the Old Testament evidence. He undoubtedly followed the traditional computation according to which the period of the judges lasted for about 450 years (the total of 410 for the numbers in Judges plus the 40 years of Eli spoken of in 1 Sam. 4:18).

Solomon's fourth year, commenced 480 years after the Exodus. For if we figure 430 years for the period of the judges (till the battle at Mizpah), 40 years for the desert journey, 20 years for the time from the entry into Canaan to Joshua's death,[28] 50 years for the combined reigns of Samuel and Saul, and 40 years for David's reign,[29] the first three years of Solomon's reign already give a total of 583 years (430 + 153), a number that far exceeds the 480 of 1 Kings 6:1.

Throughout the ages both Jewish and Christian commentators have attempted in various ways to explain and remove this discrepancy. I will not bother to give a summary of these attempts here, especially since some of them do not do justice to the historical reliability of Scripture. Only if we begin by accepting that the Bible is indeed reliable will we be able to perceive and pose the problem correctly. Now, it might generally be true that "the Bible's chronology confronts us with numerous difficulties" and that it, "not to mention Semitic chronology as a whole, is largely foreign territory to us."[30] This, however, does not excuse us from asking in the case of each individual book of the Bible whether its chronological data are both internally consistent and in agreement with the evidence that can be found elsewhere. And the fact that our first impression seems to deny this in the Book of Judges should not induce us at once to abandon the search for a solution. At the very least we must consider the most obvious approach for showing that the numbers found in Judges do not necessarily conflict with 1 Kings 6:1.

We begin by asking whether it is possible that some of the periods of oppression and some of the judgeships took place simultaneously rather than in succession, as the unsuspecting reader might casually assume. There is at least one passage in the book that quite clearly answers this question in the affirmative. We read in 10:7 that the Lord sold or abandoned the Israelites into the hands of the Philistines and the Ammonites. The rest of chapter 10 and chapter 11 speak solely of the

---

[28] In the preceding commentary on Joshua, pp. 34f., I have figured 20 years for this. This constitutes a minimum that has been chosen to keep the numbers, which are only approximations, from becoming needlessly large. The number certainly could not have been less than 20, however (Keil figures a mere 20 years; *Kommentar,* p. 231), since it is hard to believe that Joshua, who died at the age of 110, could have been older than 90 when the Israelites first arrived in Canaan.

[29] Second Samuel 5:4 gives this as the length of David's reign. For Samuel and Saul, see p. 234 below; for the 40 years of Eli (1 Sam. 4:18), see p. 239.

[30] Noordtzij, *Gods Woord en der eeuwen getuigenis,* 2nd ed. (Kampen, 1931), pp. 238f.

Ammonites, however, while chapter 12 continues with the history of Jephthah and follows with a few minor judges. Since we then hear once again of a Philistine oppression in 13:1, this must be the same thing that was mentioned in 10:7. The latter verse apparently means to say that Israel was attacked and subdued on two different fronts at the same time. It is understandable, however, that the author should have dealt with these concurrent events in two separate stages for the sake of a coherent account.

First, the author tells us the whole story of what the tribes east of the Jordan underwent; and only then does he turn to the Philistines' simultaneous subjection of the western tribes that had already been announced in 10:7. It has rightly been pointed out that the Israelites' turn to evil spoken of in 13:1 does not necessarily refer to the time following Abdon's death.[31] The first part of this verse is, rather, the standard formula for introducing a new manifestation of Yahweh's wrath, and it in fact serves to connect the material that follows with 10:6. If, therefore, we conclude that 13:1ff. is concurrent with and not later than 10:7ff., this has an important consequence for the chronology of the book. The Philistine and the Ammonite oppressions then began at the same time; and since the 18 years of Ammonite rule fell completely within the 40 years of the Philistines, we only have to include the latter in our reckoning. The simultaneity of these chapters also has a second consequence: the judgeships of Jephthah, Ibzan, Elon, and Abdon (12:7–15) largely ran parallel to that of Samson; and their work therefore must have been restricted to only a part of Canaan.[32] For this reason we also do not have to count all the years of their rule in our computation of the length of the period of the judges. These two results allow us to eliminate a considerable number of years

---

[31] Keil (*Kommentar*, p. 224), who is the main advocate of the solution to the chronological problem given in the text, emphasizes that the end of chapter 12 lacks the statement that "the land had peace for so many years." We should not read too much into the absence of these words, however, since the author still implies that Jephthah and the judges who followed him preserved the peace for some number of years. But this peace must only have prevailed in the part of Canaan where they were active (see the next note).

[32] Although Ibzan, Elon, and Abdon come right after Jephthah in chapter 12, it is highly unlikely that they carried on their work east of the Jordan. Ibzan was from Bethlehem, not Bethlehem Ephrathah, but another place in the territory of Zebulun (Josh. 19:15). Elon too was a Zebulunite; but Abdon was from Ephraim and no doubt exercised his office in Pirathon, the site of his burial. The line of reasoning followed in the text implies that Abdon was still a judge when Samuel led Israel. There are problems with this, however, as I will show on pp. 231–2.

from our total figure. Nevertheless, there is more than one objection to the thought that this constitutes a solution to the chronological problem in Judges.[33]

1. The number of years that are eliminated in this manner is far from enough. The sum of the years of the Ammonite oppression and of the judgeships of Jephthah, Ibzan, Elon, and Abdon (18 + 6 + 7 + 10 + 8) is 49. If this number is subtracted from our above total of 583 years (p. 225), the remainder is still 534, considerably more than the 480 years between the Exodus and the building of the temple. Besides this, it is not unlikely that the judgeships of Ibzan, Elon, and Abdon overlapped to some extent (see pp. 235 below). Judges 12:8–15 does not forbid this; and if it is true, the number of years that we are eliminating from the total will have to be reduced slightly. Our problem therefore remains unsolved.

2. The above "solution" has failed to take 11:26 into account, an extremely important verse that we have overlooked up till now. In his negotiations with the Ammonites, Jephthah raised the argument that the territory the Ammonites wished to claim as their own had already been inhabited by Israelites for 300 years. We should not conclude that this is the exact number of years, but there can be no doubt that 300 years was approximately how long it had been since this area had been conquered in the last year of Israel's desert wanderings (Num. 21:21–26; Deut. 1:3–4). If we date Jephthah's rise as judge toward the end of Ammon's ascendancy, the list on page 223 indicates that this would have been 319 years after the invasion of Cushan-Rishathaim. This number still has to be increased by at least 40 years (the 20 years of Joshua's leadership and 20 more years between Joshua's death and Cushan-Rishathaim; see p. 224), giving a total of 359 years. This does not square with 11:26, however; for even if we assume that Jephthah was using a round number, a difference of almost 60 years is too great. We are therefore forced to examine the period before Jephthah in order to see whether it is possible to eliminate another sizable span of time from our total.

One thing has already become clear. On more than one occasion,

---

[33] Keil believes that it does solve the problem. We should note, however, that for the period between the beginning of the conquest of Canaan under Joshua and the beginning of Cushan-Rishathaim's rule, Keil figures only 20 years (compared to our 40), and for the combined reigns of Samuel and Saul only 40 years (compared to our 50). In his view the first of these figures is supported by the evidence concerning Othniel's age (see the comments at 3:9–11).

different judges were simultaneously at work in different parts of the land; and this means that some of the lengths of time stated in the book are included in others, and that they cannot all figure into our total for the period of the judges as a whole. It seems to me that this offers the most natural solution for the apparent discrepancy between the evidence within the book itself and that found elsewhere, particularly in 1 Kings 6:1, and indeed also for the problem in 11:26. Not surprisingly, I have therefore followed the hint found in 10:7 in searching for such a solution to the chronological problem. In my view, however, the result that has been achieved by this route can be supplemented at another point in the historical narrative, where the events again can be regarded as concurrent rather than successive.

I here have in mind the period of peace that prevailed between Ehud's victory over the Moabites and the judgeship of Deborah. Judges 3:30 states that the land had peace for eighty years, and 4:1 says that after the death of Ehud the Israelites gain turned to evil. This then is followed by the story of the Canaanite oppression in the north. It would seem that Jabin began to tyrannize the Israelites at the end of the eighty years, but the text actually does not state this. And although Judges 4:1 speaks of Ehud's death, it does not state that it came at the end of the eighty years mentioned in 3:30. In fact these two verses are separated by the very curious report in 3:31, that Shamgar arose after Ehud to strike down the Philistines and deliver Israel. I call this statement curious, because its position in the text indicates that Shamgar's work fell within the eighty years of 3:30 and still followed Ehud's death. This means that Ehud did not rule as judge for eighty years, something that indeed is highly improbable even on its own terms. But we also can conclude from this that the report that the land had "peace" for eighty years should not be taken too strictly. The Philistine invasion that Shamgar thwarted with his oxgoad may have been more or less of an isolated event, but it still disturbed the peace that the land was enjoying. And in any case we should not think that the entire land of Canaan was peaceful. This is clearly evident in 5:6–8, which depicts the desolate situation caused by the Canaanite oppression during the days before Deborah's rise to power.

Remarkably, these are called the days of both Shamgar and Jael. Shamgar, hence, was a contemporary of Jael, and thus also of Deborah. What is more, Shamgar's work as judge (in the south) and Jabin's rule (in the north) ran parallel to each other. In connection with our above finding on Shamgar, this means that Jabin's tyranny too fell within the eighty years of 3:30 and happened relatively soon after Ehud's death, as 4:1–2 indeed indicates. One could expect that Ehud's influence had its greatest effect in his immediate environment: Benjamin, Judah, and southern Ephraim (3:27). After his death, apostasy first took hold in the remote parts of northern Canaan. The peace in that region was therefore short-lived, and the Israelites soon were subjected to the harsh yoke of Jabin and Sisera for twenty years (4:2–3).

We still can go beyond this result. Since the attacks of Midian and its allies produced havoc throughout almost the whole of Canaan from north to south (6:4, 35), the forty years of peace in 5:31 and the eighty years of 3:30 in all likelihood ended at the same time. After this there is no more talk of "peace." We can therefore conclude that the twenty years of Jabin's rule and the forty years of Deborah fell completely within the eighty year period spoken of in 3:30. This period began with the judgeship of Ehud, to which we can assign twenty years. After this came the twenty years of Canaanite oppression in the north, with Shamgar's work in the south falling in the latter half of this interval. Deborah began to prophesy and to administer justice shortly thereafter (4:4–5), and after the victory over Jabin and Sisera the entire land had peace for forty more years. But this means that sixty years (twenty plus forty) have to be subtracted from our previous total for the period of the judges as a whole.

We can now proceed to a final computation of the total number of years. On page 224 we arrived at a total of 430 years, figuring from Joshua's death till the battle at Mizpah. Subtracting the 60 from this leaves 370 years; and if we assume that 43 more years are eliminated by the parallel between 13:1ff. and 10:7ff. discussed above (pp. 226–28), the remainder is 327 (370 - 43) years. These years then can be dated from 1387 to 1060 B.C.

The period spoken of by Jephthah in 11:26, which we computed at 359 years on page 227, will also have to be decreased by 60 years. Since this leaves 299 or roughly 300 years, the objection discussed under point 2 above is also completely removed by our present reckoning. In a list at the end of this section, I will give the dates of the events from Judges according to our standard system of chronology. My figures here are greatly aided by the fact that we now know almost for certain that the building of the temple commenced in 967 B.C. On this basis the year of the Exodus has to be set at 1447 (967 + 480) B.C[34] Using these

---

[34] For these dates the reader may consult Böhl, *Bijbelsch-Kerkelijk Woordenboek,* vol. 1, pp. 264, 304; Edelkoort, *Uittocht en Intocht* (1924), pp. 206f.; D.J. Baarslag,

two dates as our fixed points of reference, we can determine the boundaries of the period of the judges with fairly great precision. On page 224 above, the battle at Mizpah (1060 B.C.) was chosen as the end of this period. On page 225, the combined reigns of Samuel and Saul were figured at 50 years. In my commentary on 1 Samuel, pages 34f., I argue that 28 of these 50 years belonged to Samuel. If, therefore, we end the period of the judges at Saul's enthronement, it lasted 355 (327 + 28) years in all, running from 1387–1032 B.C.

NOTE

In my above argument I have seriously considered the views of C. Van Gelderen (*Bijbelsch Handboek,* vol. 1, pp. 124–30), who heeds the solution that I offered in the first edition of this commentary for the problems presented by the chronological information in Judges. At some points in the present edition, I have corrected my views in accordance with his. For example, I now set the advent of the Philistine and the Ammonite rule in the same year; and I allow the end of the Philistine oppression spoken of in Judges to coincide with Samson's death. Van Gelderen, however, objects to my proposal that both the twenty years of Jabin's rule (4:3) and the forty years of tranquility spoken of in 5:31 fell within the eighty-year period of peace that 3:30 attributes to the work of Ehud. Van Gelderen instead achieves the "necessary reduction" in the number of years mainly by having the years of the judges Tola and Jair coincide almost completely and by allowing both the Philistine and the Ammonite oppression to begin already in the year of Gideon's death. In addition, he uses the so-called antedating system in figuring the lengths of the various periods. In this system, the final year of each period is also counted as the first year of the next period, and every time interval specified in the book is therefore shortened by a year. This gives a welcome reduction of around fifteen years for the period of the judges as a whole.

It seems to me, however, that this system of reckoning is inadvisable in the present context. Although it might be demanded by the chronology of the kings of Israel and Judah, as Van Gelderen points out on page 125, this has no bearing on the Book of Judges. The hereditary succession of monarchs ensured that the respective periods of rule were continuous, and the overall total, therefore, would be too high if one counted both the year of a given king's death and the first year of his successor's reign. The reigns of the judges, however, were always separated by a time of anarchy; and there was no hereditary succession.

Israël in Egypte, ch. 4, p. 122; A. Noordtzij, *Gods Woord en der eeuwen getuigenis,* 2nd ed., p. 311; C. Van Gelderen, *Bijbelsch Handboek,* vol. 1, p. 119. In the *Bible Student's Commentary,* see Gispen, *Exodus* (Grand Rapids: Zondervan, 1982), pp. 21–24. In the *Korte Verklaring,* see Van Gelderen, *De boeken der Koningen,* 2nd ed., vol. 1, the comments in 6:1, and C.J. Goslinga, *1 Samuel,* 2nd ed., pp. 35f.

It is even very likely that the advent of each instance of foreign rule was separated from the previous judge's death by a brief transition period in which the Israelites clearly departed from serving their God. A comparison of 8:33–35 and 9:2 thus shows that some time had probably elapsed between Gideon's death and the beginning of Abimelech's rule. The latter, in turn, certainly must have lasted somewhat longer than the three years mentioned in 9:22, for its end does not come till 9:54. In my view, we must therefore continue to count each one of the years that the book speaks of.

The following objections can also be made to Van Gelderen's position.

1. It is highly unlikely that the simultaneous invasions of the Ammonites from the east and the Philistines from the south began right after Gideon's death. Chapter 9 does not even contain a hint of these, nor do the brief reports on Tola and Jair in 10:1–5. In itself, the notion that these two judges ruled at the same time (in Ephraim and Gilead, respectively) presents no overwhelming problems. Are we really to believe, however, that the Israelites were seriously attacked and subdued on two fronts in their day even though we find not a single word that alludes to this? And would it not be very strange that such a severe and widespread oppression should have begun and been sustained at the very time when two judges were ruling? Nowhere in the Book of Judges do we encounter such a thing, which indeed would conflict with the rule stated in 2:18. What is more, it cannot be denied that 10:6–18 strikingly illustrates the statement in 2:19 and offers a fitting description of a period when no judge ruled. If Tola and Jair lived and worked at this time, they would not even have deserved to be called "minor" judges unless they took strong action against both the enemies from without and the apostasy within. There is therefore no way that I can follow Van Gelderen at this point.

2. The dates that Van Gelderen assigns to some of the judges also have some improbable consequences. He dates the Ammonite oppression from 1122–1105 B.C. and also has Abimelech's reign begin in 1122. Tola began to rule after Abimelech's death in 1118, and Jair in 1116. He then gives the following list:

1105–1100	Jephthah rules as judge in Gilead
1100–1094	Ibzan rules as judge in Judah[35]
1094–1085	Elon rules as judge in Zebulun
1085–1078	Abdon rules as judge in Ephraim.

On page 130, Van Gelderen dates the Philistine oppression from 1122–1083 and Samson's work from 1102–1083. Now, 10:2 assigns twenty three years to Tola, and 10:3, twenty two years to Jair. According to Van Gelderen's antedating system, this would mean that Tola was judge from 1118–1096 and Jair from 1116–1095. A simple comparison of the dates thus shows that Tola was governing in Ephraim at the same time that Jephthah ruled in Gilead. This would mean, however, that in the story told in 12:1–6, Jephthah was fighting

---

[35] On the question of whether Ibzan was judge in Judah or Zebulun, see p. 235 below.

against Tola when he defeated the Ephraimites at the fords of the Jordan—the one judge against the other! Van Gelderen's starting point is already undermined by this implication alone. It is likewise unthinkable that when Jair was judge in Gilead and the Ammonites set up their camp there, the Israelites should have turned to Jephthah, whom they had previously driven away, to gain the commander they needed (see 10:17–18; 11:6–7, 10). Indeed, the question that the Gileadite leaders asked in 10:18 implies that there was at that time no judge in the area.

The dates that Van Gelderen assigns to Abdon are also improbable. For it seems to me that this judge's rule in Ephraim must have ended at least some time before the battle at Aphek in 1080 B.C., where the Israelites, apparently without a commander appointed by God, suffered a bloody defeat at the hands of the Philistines and lost the ark of the covenant (1 Sam. 4:10–11). This must have happened shortly after Abdon's death, and he could not therefore have been active till 1078. Making him a contemporary of Samson presents no problems. All that I have observed under this point thus shows that Van Gelderen's dates are hard to accept. I have to conclude that the work of both Tola and Jair preceded the advent of the Ammonite and the Philistine oppression, as chapter 10 indeed clearly indicates.

3. Van Gelderen makes no specific objection to my proposal that the sixty years of Jabin, Deborah, and Barak fell within the eighty years of peace that 3:30 attributes to the work of Ehud. He merely observes: "Nowhere do I find that the numbers of years given in chapters 3–9 contain adequate evidence for simultaneity. For the events there are recounted in great detail and they all concern the land west of the Jordan, if not exclusively, then still for the most part" (p. 125). This statement is correct, and it is true that the text only gives us reason to suspect that some of the events were concurrent without forcing this conclusion on us. Nevertheless, if the information at the end of chapter 3 and the beginning of chapter 4 is examined closely, this suspicion cannot be suppressed. There is no need to repeat what I have said on pages 228–29. Van Gelderen does not deal with that at all, and he thus presents not a single argument that could refute my reasoning there. I therefore believe, that the position I have taken can be maintained without qualification.

In my view the case is decided above all by 5:6. There it is clear not only that Shamgar and Jael were contemporaries (which Van Gelderen naturally has to accept on the basis of this verse), but also that Israel was in a very sorry state during their time, apparently because of Jabin's oppression in the north and that of the Philistines in the south (though the latter seems to have been more of a passing phenomenon, 3:31). Since 3:31 indicates that Shamgar arose not too long after Ehud, the statement in 3:30 that the land had "peace" has to be taken with a grain of salt (as I have already observed). Judges 4:4–5 gives the impression that during the years when the north was languishing under Jabin's iron hand, Deborah was able to exercise her authority with relatively little interference throughout much of the land, particularly its central region, and that the people could come to her for judgment. The appearance of Shamgar, then, should be dated slightly before or at the same time as Deborah. If the work of these judges is allowed to fall completely within the eighty years of 3:30, enough time is also left for Tola and Jair. Van Gelderen's chronology, in contrast, squeezes these two into a difficult position (see 1 and 2 above).

The weakness of Van Gelderen's "solution" thus lies in the fact that, however attractive it may appear on first consideration, one encounters new difficulties when he checks it more closely, which show that it has certain loose ends that have not been accounted for. Granted, in dealing with a period where so much of the data is obscure, one can only draw guarded conclusions and must always leave open the possibility that further research (e.g., into Egyptian history) might shed more light and uncover a new and better answer to the difficulties. But I am unable to recommend the solution provided by Noordtzij's notion of a dual chronological system. According to him, "we find, at any rate, two chronological systems in the Old Testament that continually intersect one another, and it is necessary that we do not confuse these. Sometimes, we find small numbers that make clear the temporal sequence of individual facts and events. At other times, we encounter a single number that embraces an entire era. It is these latter numbers that have something artificial about them. The writer does not use the number 40 and its multiples in order to teach us that Israel's history consisted of successive periods of twenty, forty, eighty, or more years. Rather, such numbers are the result of his attempt to organize the historical facts in accordance with generational intervals" (*God's Word*, p. 240). Noordtzij seems to have had especially the Book of Judges in mind when he wrote these words. For this is precisely where one constantly encounters the juxtaposition of numbers like 20, 40, and 80; others like 8, 7, 3, and 6; and even large, unrounded numbers like 22 and 23. Noordtzij, in fact, declares that his theory has a concrete application to Judges (ibid., p. 310). But if he means by this that the round numbers are actually of no use to us, it seems to me that he does not do justice to the biblical data.

The following general remarks should be made in this regard.

1. Many of the lengths of time given in the historical books undoubtedly should not be taken as a precise statement of the number of full years. Large round numbers like 40 and 80, especially, can be regarded as only approximately accurate. One proof of this is that David's reign is said to have lasted 40 years (2 Sam. 5:4), even though 5:5 states that he reigned 7½ years in Hebron and 33 years in Jerusalem, and thus strictly speaking 40½ years in all.

2. The above example also shows, however, that one should not rashly underestimate the chronological value of the numbers in Scripture, for the number 40 here is still approximately correct. Forty years is also definitely the correct length for the journey through the desert (Deut. 1:3; 2:14). It might be true that the writer "organized the historical facts in accordance with generational intervals," but this interval still was not arbitrarily determined. On the contrary, the figure of forty years for the period in which a new generation arose is in full accord with reality.

3. One of the numbers that has met with the most doubt is that found in 1 Kings 6:1, where the building of the temple is said to have commenced in the "four hundred and eightieth year" after the Israelites' exodus from Egypt. Since this total is equivalent to 12 times 40, many regard it as far too artificial to be historically correct. Some have also concluded that the number is without value because they think the Exodus has to be placed during the reign of the Egyptian pharaoh Merneptah (1234–1214 B.C.). The biblical evidence definitely contradicts this date, however, and shows that the Exodus must be placed near the middle of the fifteenth century B.C.—more precisely in 1447, and thus exactly 480 years before the temple began to be built in 967.

John Garstang has forcefully defended the historical reliability of 1 Kings 6:1 in his book *Joshua, Judges* (London, 1931). On the basis of his archaeological work in Palestine, and especially in Jericho, Ai, and Hazor, he has established that most of the towns mentioned in Joshua and in Judges 1–5 flourished during the years 2000–1600 and entered their decline or even were destroyed between 1600 and 1200, most often before 1400. He consequently dates the Exodus in 1447, the year that Pharaoh Thutmose III died, and the entry into Canaan in 1407. Since Joshua's conquest of Canaan took seven years in all, this means it was finished exactly in 1400 B.C. Garstang too has the construction of the temple begin in 967, and he also accepts the 300 years spoken of by Jephthah in 11:26 as completely accurate. The fact that he does not start out with the intention of vindicating the biblical data makes his conclusions all the more remarkable. Indeed, he is even very arbitrary with these data at times and does away entirely with the "minor" judges Tola, Jair, Ibzan, Elon, and Abdon. But his skepticism does nothing to diminish the powerful testimony that his archaeological work has brought to light.

Following is my chronological overview of the main events from the Exodus to the building of the temple.

Exodus from Egypt	1447 B.C.
Entry and conquest of Canaan	1407–1400
Death of Joshua	ca. 1387
Local conquests, punishment of the Benjamites, etc.	1387–1367
Subjection under Cushan-Rishathaim	1367–1359
Judgeship of Othniel, time of peace	1359–1319
Moabite oppression	1319–1301
Judgeship of Ehud, time of peace	1301–1281
Subjection under Jabin	1281–1261
Shamgar	ca. 1265
Deborah, time of peace	1261–1221
Midianite oppression	1221–1214
Judgeship of Gideon, time of peace	1214–1174
Civil war under Abimelech	1174–1171
Judgeship of Tola	1171–1148
Judgeship of Jair	1148–1126

A few of these items require a brief comment.

1. Although Eli lived within the period that Judges deals with, I have not listed him separately because the book does not mention him; and he seems to have had no direct influence on Israel's government. In addition his lifetime coincided with other persons who played a more dominant role, particularly Jephthah, Samson, and Abdon.

2. I also have left out Samuel's sons (1 Sam. 8:1), since they were not judges in the true sense (see footnote 36 on p. 246); and they performed their duties along with and under their father rather than after him (see 1 Sam. 7:15).

3. I have figured around 40 years for the Philistine oppression because Samson must have been born after it started, was active as judge for 20 years, and could hardly have come forward as Israel's champion before he was 20 years old. Van Gelderen places Samson's death in 1083 because he has the Philistine oppression begin in 1122. It obviously would be impossible to determine the exact year, but a few years at least must have passed between Samson's death and the battle at Aphek (see footnote 26 on p. 224).

4. I have assumed that the judgeships of Jephthah through Abdon partly overlapped one another. It is true that 12:8–15 has "after him . . . led Israel" in each case, but the text does not rule out that this be interpreted "after him . . . came to the fore as leader." Van Gelderen also accepts this as a possible meaning (p. 128), even though he does not think that it necessarily has to be followed. In my view it is indeed necessary, since Abdon has to have died before the battle at Aphek (see pp. 231–32 above). The judgeships of Ibzan and Elon, on the other hand, did not overlap, since both belonged to the tribe of Zebulun. Van Gelderen places Ibzan in Judah, but it is unlikely that Judah had a judge in Samson's time (see 15:10–15 and the comments in 12:8).

V. *The Period of the Judges*

Although I have already discussed the peculiar character of the period of the judges in passing (see the beginning of section 2 above), there still is a need for a separate section that sketches this character more fully and inquires into the unique significance of this era (and thus of the Book of Judges itself) within divine revelation as a whole.

The office of judge was held by the following persons:(1) Othniel, (2) Ehud, (3) Shamgar, (4) Deborah, (5) Gideon, (6) Tola, (7) Jair, (8) Jephthah, (9) Ibzan, (10) Elon, (11) Abdon, (12) Samson, (13) Eli, (14) Samuel.[36] Only the first twelve of these appear in the Book of Judges, and a distinction is usually made among these between the six "major" and the six "minor" judges. These adjectives are somewhat arbitrary, but they bring out the fact that very little is known of the latter group, while the vocation and lifework of the former are sometimes recounted in great detail.

The NIV translates the single Hebrew verb *šāpaṭ* as both "judged" and "led," "judge" and "leader" (cf. the text and marginal notes in 2:16–19; 3:10; 4:4; 10:2; 12:7; 2 Sam. 7:11; 2 Kings 23:22; 1 Chron. 17:6, 10 et al.). The roles of judge and leader in Israel therefore had much in common. A judge in the broad sense (see, e.g., Deut. 1:16; 16:18; Josh. 8:33) was a person who spoke, upheld, and administered justice. Justice was clothed with divine authority in Israel, and the task of such a judge was to apply the law of God to the Israelites' daily life and to make its authority felt (see Deut. 17:18–20; 19:17–18; 25:1). This actually was part of the general task of Israel's government; and Moses, for example, thus performed the duties of a judge. In this broad sense judgeship was a common and permanent office in Israel.

The judge in the sense of leader was somewhat different. He too had the Lord's justice at heart and was called to uphold it, to restore it, and to establish and maintain its control over Israel's life. He did this, however, not so much through his words, by holding court, but through his deeds, by actively liberating and ruling the nation. Whenever the people fell under foreign subjection because of their own sinfulness, a judge or leader would arise after some time had passed, who first would take up the sword against the enemy to defend Yahweh's just claim on Israel. After he had broken the foreign yoke and delivered the people, however, he also would lead them back to a life of obedience to the divine law that they had so wickedly violated; and he would continue to

---

[36] Abimelech cannot be counted among the judges, as I will explain in the comments on chapter 9. This title also cannot be given to the sons of Samuel, for though they were appointed by their father, God did not call them; and the people in fact did not recognize them (see 1 Sam. 8:1–5). Samuel's sons did exercise judgment, but he himself remained Israel's leader (see, e.g., 1 Sam. 10, 12). Bedan in 1 Samuel 12:11 (see KJV, NIV margin) is no doubt an alternate name for one of the judges, or perhaps Barak (see the commentary on 1 Samuel, in loc.).

exercise some form of ruling authority till the time of his death. God Himself would give him a special mandate to do all this, and his victory over Israel's enemies would confirm this divine calling in the eyes of the people.

The judgeship in this sense was thus a unique and extraordinary office. It was not needed for the administration of justice, since there was no lack of ordinary judges in Israel. Indeed, although the majority of the judges did no doubt act in a judicial capacity, we cannot be certain that all of them did (e.g., Shamgar and Samson). Their "judging" was rather equivalent to ruling (cf. 1 Sam. 8:5–6, NIV margin), which they did in wartime by liberating the people from foreign tyranny and in peacetime by restoring and establishing the Lord's authority over the nation's life. Most of the "minor" judges seem to have done only the latter. Although their careers, therefore, did not begin with a military feat, their stories make clear that their divine appointment was beyond question. For if they had been nothing more than ordinary judges, they would not have been given a place in the Book of Judges. Nevertheless, the stories of the "major" judges, who are also referred to as Israel's deliverers (2:16; 3:9, 15; cf. Neh. 9:27), give us a more characteristic picture of what the judges did. In every case these individuals are marked by a special and inescapable divine commission giving them the authority to lead the nation in battle and to preserve it from again becoming unfaithful to God's covenant.

The work of the judges therefore has much in common with what Moses and Joshua did earlier and what the kings did later. What is distinctive is the unusual manner in which they arose to prominence, and this is related to the special significance of the period in which they lived. Through Moses, the Lord had freed His people from Egypt and brought them to the border of Canaan, and Joshua had been the instrument by which He had enabled them to take possession of the Promised Land. What had been foretold to the patriarchs had then been fulfilled for the time being, and Abraham's offspring lived in freedom and prosperity in the land that God had promised to give him. The Israelites now had to conduct themselves and unfold their common life there in a manner that was fitting for a nation chosen by God. Now "began a new era in which the privileged nation that was the second party in the covenant was called to display its thankfulness and in which its faith and obedience were consequently put to the test."[37]

---

[37] Ph. J. Hoedemaker, *Zonde en Genade, De Tijd der Richteren* (Amsterdam), p. 22.

One could say that God left the Israelites more or less to themselves at this time. The nation had outgrown its childhood, and it now had to manifest its spiritual maturity by consciously and steadfastly living up to its covenant with the Lord. It had all that it needed to do this. Through Moses, God had provided Israel with all the necessary laws and ordinances, and she also had received the promise of God's almighty aid and protection. She knew her calling over against the other nations, and shortly before his death Joshua had once again admonished her to fulfill this calling faithfully. Israel also had national independence, and her elders gave her an organized government that was sufficiently stable. In Shiloh the Israelites had a national sanctuary where the high priest could draw near to the Lord on behalf of the whole nation, and where they could experience and strengthen their inner unity by celebrating the great religious festivals at regular intervals. All that was lacking was a visible head, a human ruler; but this was exactly what God had planned. For He Himself was Israel's King, and the ark of the covenant was the visible symbol of His presence. Israel had a unique privilege here. It was governed directly by God Himself, and there was no need for a human individual like Moses or Joshua to act as mediator. The years that followed Joshua's death were intended to be an era of theocracy in its purest form.

The Lord Himself made this clear when He answered Samuel's complaint with the words: "It is not you they have rejected, but they have rejected me as their king" (1 Sam. 8:7). The Israelites already could perceive that this was God's purpose, however, from the fact that no successor was appointed to follow Joshua.[38] Even when the people had turned away from Him a few times, the Lord took no steps at all toward establishing a monarchy but instead was content to send a judge whose mandate and powers were limited. The Israelites were well aware and in fact took for granted that the judges were not kings and did not hold a hereditary office. The nonhereditary character of their office formed a salient difference between judgeship and kingship; and when it became evident that the people would rather have done away with this difference, Gideon opposed their arbitrary wish with the words "the LORD will rule over you" (8:23). If they had understood this and acted accordingly, it would have been pointless for God to send any more judges; for Israel's manner of life should have made them unnecessary. The whole institution of the judgeship thus had only

---

[38] The Lord also explicitly declared that the period of the judges was intended as a time of testing for Israel (2:22; cf. 3:1–4).

secondary importance and was a mere product of circumstance. Speaking from a human point of view, we could say that God sent each judge in the hope that he would be the last. Only after the people had repeatedly made it obvious that they were too spiritually immature for a pure theocracy did He allow a hereditary monarchy in Israel.[39]

When the period of the judges began, the Israelites stood at a turning point. Would they use their privileges rightly, or would they instead fall from the high plateau on which God had placed them? The latter, of course, is what happened. Their decline set in quite soon and gradually worsened, even though the Lord arrested this process time and again and repeatedly gave the nation a chance to return to the right course. On three different occasions He explicitly reprimanded them for their idolatry in order to bring them to repentance (2:1–3; 6:8–10; 10:11–14). Again and again He restored them to a right relationship with Himself, drove out their enemies, and taught them to live according to His law once more; but each time they returned to their old evil ways. The period of the judges is thus also characterized by Israel's inconstancy. The religious and moral quality of the nation's life continually rose and fell as it vacillated between faithfulness and unfaithfulness to its covenant God. Never was there a constant and uninterrupted decline. There were indeed forces that pulled the people downward, but others worked for their good and sometimes even triumphed temporarily. What is more, the latter forces finally were able to maintain the upper hand. At the end of the era of the judges, we do not find a total collapse into spiritual bankruptcy but rather the figure of Samuel, the great reformer.

No one could deny that reformation was necessary at that time. The situation may not have been hopeless, but Israel's decay had assumed very alarming proportions. The following summary should give the reader an accurate picture of Israel's development during the period of the judges.[40]

---

[39] This of course does not mean that the Israelites were able to frustrate God's hidden purposes. Hoedemaker remarks: "According as it became clear that man's unbelief rendered him unable to take possession of God's gift and to fulfill His calling, but instead caused him to sink deeper and deeper, to the very same degree God was changed—not in His plan and purpose, but in the way He revealed Himself. God as it were allowed His action to be determined by man's, stooping ever lower and ever again holding and drawing back, but always in such a manner that this stooping down and drawing back paved the way for a new and glorious revelation of His grace" (*Zonde en Genade*, p. 19).

[40] Noordtzij (*Gods Woord*, pp. 357–60) gives a detailed account of the period of the judges from which my synopsis in the text is partly drawn. C. von Orelli's

1. The Israelites failed to get rid of the remaining Canaanites. They did not carry out Joshua's last will and testament (Josh. 23). This negligence was the basic error that had harmful repercussions throughout all of Israel's life. The nation forgot that it had a divine calling to fulfill. It spared its bitterest enemies, partly out of misplaced generosity and partly out of fear and laziness.

2. Because the Israelites did not eliminate the Canaanites, a large number of them continued to live in Israel; and this led to a certain amount of fraternization that ended in actual intermingling. In many places the Canaanites were merely tolerated, but in others they held the upper hand and were the predominant influence. Life in Canaan became a compromise between the old and the new population, for Israel was not immune to the effects of Canaanite religion and culture. Israel adopted many of the practices of the original inhabitants, and thus also the paganism that was inherent in those practices. The people intermarried with their former enemies and worshiped their gods (2:11–13; 3:5–7). The Canaanites' friendship proved to be a greater danger to Israel than their hostility.

3. Intermingling with the Canaanites caused the Israelites' religious thought to become seriously corrupted. They largely lost their awareness that the Lord is the one, true God and that He can be served only in holy and spiritual worship. Even judges like Gideon and Jephthah no longer had an unspoiled notion of this (8:27; 11:31). The pagan gods all stood on the same level, and their power and influence were restricted to certain places. Many Israelites now placed Yahweh alongside these gods. He was regarded as mightier and more exalted and not strictly equal to them (6:31–32; 11:27), but the pagan gods too were accepted as real and had to be reckoned with and honored (8:33–35). Yahweh therefore was no longer acknowledged as the one God, as Moses had taught the people (Deut. 6:4). But this meant that the religious unity and independence of Israel had also been lost. Once paganism had been given a legitimate place, the unifying power of the one true religion in its antithesis to all forms of paganism no longer had any effect. This is why the central sanctuary at Shiloh declined in prestige, why no high priests are mentioned (e.g., as spiritual advisers to the judges) between Phinehas and Eli, why private shrines like those of Gideon and Micah (8:27; 17:5) offended no one at all, and why the servants of the

---

description in *Realenzyclopädie für protestantische Theologie und Kirche,* "Richter in Israël" (article), is also worth reading. In *Israël en de Baäls,* 2nd ed. (1929), pp. 50–54, J. Ridderbos deals in particular with the process of decay in Israel.

legitimate sanctuary were so poorly provided for that they sometimes wandered about destitute (17:7–8).

4. These same factors also had a harmful effect on the Israelites' sense of national unity. The story in chapters 19–21 shows that this at first remained very strong. It gradually grew weaker, however, as can be seen from such things as the song of Deborah, the opposition that Gideon and Jephthah experienced, especially from Ephraim, and the people's desertion of Samson and willingness to surrender him to the Philistines. All concern for Israel as a whole and the national interest was gone. Each tribe had regard only for its immediate private interests, and jealousy divided the nation's powers. The inspiration that had come from faith in the God of the covenant had waned, and with it the love and sense of solidarity between the sons of the one house of Jacob. Had it continued along this path, Israel would finally have been assimilated by the pagan world and ceased to exist as both a religious and a national entity.

God, however, averted this disaster, and He did so by using forces that were already present—stored up, as it were—in the nation itself. Along with all the darkness, we therefore can also point to some bright spots.

5. As I have already observed on page 238–39, God forcefully stemmed the tide of decay in Israel by periodically calling forth judges. The work of these leaders not only strengthened the people's bond with the Lord, but also heightened their national awareness. Dutch writers have with good reason compared them to the House of Orange. God did not drop these leaders from above but rather raised them up from out of the nation itself. They and their devout lives, therefore, were not isolated phenomena. On the contrary, they arose from circles of followers where the sincere fear of the Lord had been preserved and where the decline and decay that had become manifest in Israel was a cause of grief.

6. The spiritual pinnacle Israel stood on when she entered Canaan was perhaps unequaled in either her earlier or her later history. She was unable to maintain herself at this level, but it is clear that a faithful nucleus remained, and even that this nucleus was rather large. Without this, Samuel's reforming work could not have found such widespread acceptance. The Book of Judges itself contains scant evidence of this devout core, but we can point to the decisive stand of Gideon's father and the piety of Samson's parents, not to mention some of the utterances of the judges themselves. Much more importantly, however,

the stories of Ruth and of Samuel's birth also both fall within the period of the judges. The Book of Ruth brings us into a circle of pure Israelite piety and elevated moral conduct. Elkanah's family represents the part of the nation that was still keenly aware of its bond to the sanctuary at Shiloh, and Hannah's song of praise could only have proceeded from a life that was rich in faith and prayer. The brief story of Ichabod's mother also is significant in this regard (1 Sam. 4:19–22).

7. The period of the judges was a time of great contrasts in which the most contradictory motives came to expression in Israel. Here we find tender piety alongside merciless savagery, dauntless faith alongside craven fear, virtuous chastity alongside gross immorality, peaceful village life alongside unrestrained warfare. Clearly Israel had not yet achieved equilibrium during this period. It was like a gifted youth, seething with vitality, but lacking in self-control and constantly going to extremes. The typical Israelite of this day has therefore often been found in Samson,[41] a man who could be both indomitably strong and weakly compliant, who had a humble life of prayer but also was easily swayed by the temptations of the flesh, who fell deeply but displayed genuine repentance. In the Lord's law and covenant, Israel had a rich spiritual inheritance; but she still had to learn to order her life in certain ways, and she constantly went astray in this. At the same time, however, the Lord's guidance enabled Israel to grow to maturity in preparation for a new era. The nation still had a future, and the storms and stress of the period of the judges were powerless to sweep away the good seed that would produce such an outstanding harvest in David's day.

The period of the judges as it is portrayed in Scripture had its own place in God's guiding plan for Israel and in the history of His revelation.[42] Picking up from my previous remarks on this on pages 198–99, I here can add the following points.

1. The period of the judges was necessary in order to convince the Israelites of their own inner weakness. Israel had to learn that she was unable to fulfill her divine calling without the external support of the

---

[41] See, e.g., von Orelli, *Realenzyclopädie,* p. 766.

[42] Noordtzij (*Gods Woord,* p. 362) is guilty of an overstatement when he calls this "the darkest period in the life of Israel." This view is too pessimistic and one-sided and cannot explain how a figure like Samuel could have arisen. The period of the judges is comparable to the Middle Ages. The widespread darkness in both eras was offset by many bright spots that alone made the later reformations possible. Israel's darkest period was rather the one that preceded and continued to exist during the Exile.

monarchy,[43] and the nation had to be prepared for that monarchy. David had to be preceded by the period of the judges just as Christ had to be preceded by David.

2. The nation had to learn from harsh experience that the friendship of the pagan inhabitants of the land and any concessions that were granted to them could only be harmful to it and threatened the survival of both its religious and ethical and its national life. In this process the people's minds became open for the words of Samuel, the great judge and prophet who finally called them back to obedience to the God of their forefathers, the God who had delivered them from Egypt and brought them to Canaan.

3. The period of the judges cast an especially strong light on the unshakable faithfulness of Israel's God. No matter how often the people reverted to their old sins, no matter how stubbornly they chose to follow forbidden paths, the Lord continually gave ear to their entreaties for help. He made clear to them that they did not deserve such help (6:7–10; 10:11–14) and that His acts of deliverance were a gift of pure grace. The Lord had His own reasons for doing this. The Book of Judges does not expressly state what these reasons were, and other books of the Bible speak more clearly in this regard.[44] God spared Israel for the sake of the covenant that He had established with Abraham. It was because He was the God of the covenant that He did not abandon Israel. He had marked out this nation for an exalted destiny, and He steadfastly refused to give up on His plan. Properly regarded, the Lord's faithfulness to Israel was first of all faithfulness to Himself. And this faithfulness was His people's salvation.

The period of the judges was also significant in one final respect. God saw to it that the necessary records were made of this part of Israel's history and included in a book of the Bible because He also had something to say to the Israel of the New Covenant. The message that is proclaimed to us in the Book of Judges can be briefly summarized as follows. The Book of Judges forms an eloquent protest against any

---

[43]This does not mean that the Israelites were able to serve God better under the kings. The monarchy too fell short of its expectations, just as the old dispensation as a whole brought out its inherent insufficiency more and more clearly. Within the terms of this dispensation, however, the period of the judges necessarily led to the institution of the monarchy.

[44]E.g., 1 Sam. 12:22; 1 Chron. 16:7–36; 2 Chron. 20:6–12; Neh. 9:27–31; Pss. 105:8–11; 106:45. Verses like Judges 2:18 and 10:16, which speak of God in human terms, do not bring out the fact that the way God dealt with Israel was connected to His whole plan of salvation.

marriage between the church and the world. The church of Christ must never forget that it finds itself in a world that is hostile to its King and its service to Him. Never should it overestimate its own strength or underestimate that of the enemy. Never may it allow itself to be drawn into a compromise with this enemy or to indulge the hope that it can defeat him by meeting him halfway. Any alliance that it makes with the world is tantamount to a denial of its very nature and can only bring harm to God's kingdom. Church history contains countless illustrations of what happens to the church when it ignores this warning and fails to be on guard against the insidious march of corruption. Indeed, every individual Christian as well must constantly be at war with both the enemy who would ensnare him from without and the sin that seeks to cripple his strength from within.

Whoever gives ear to this warning in Judges, however, will also perceive the second part of its message. The book bears powerful testimony to the fact that the Lord has infinite patience with His people and is unchangingly faithful, that He is not grudging in His forgiveness of sin and gladly answers prayers. Never will He become weary in helping His own. His church can rest assured that the world will never overcome it because it is built on the firm rock of Jesus Christ, who is the same "yesterday and today and forever" (Heb. 13:8).

VI. *Outline*

Part One—Preface: Israel's Relations With the Remaining Canaanites (1:1–3:4)

    A. Israel's Failure to Destroy the Canaanites (1:1–2:5)
        1. The Military Exploits of Judah and Simeon After Joshua's Death (1:1–21)
        2. Successes and Failures of the Other Tribes (1:22–36)
        3. The Lord's Rebuke of Israel at Bokim (2:1–5)
    B. Israel's Submission to the Canaanite Gods; God's Leading of His People During the Period of the Judges (2:6–3:4)

Part Two—Israel Under the Judges From Othniel to Samson: The Cycle of Punishment and Deliverance (3:5–16:31)

    A. Othniel's Deliverance of Israel From Cushan-Rishathaim (3:5–11)
    B. Ehud's Deliverance of Israel From the Moabites; Shamgar's Heroism (3:12–31)

Judges
Commentary

Part One

Preface: Israel's Relations With the Remaining Canaanites
(1:1–3:4)

A. Israel's Failure to Destroy the Canaanites
(1:1–2:5)

1. THE MILITARY EXPLOITS OF JUDAH AND SIMEON AFTER
   JOSHUA'S DEATH (1:1–21)

1:1 *After the death of Joshua, the Israelites asked the* LORD, *"Who will be the first to go up and fight for us against the Canaanites?"*

The opening of the Book of Judges implies that two things had gone before. First, the last years of Joshua's life had been a time of peace in which the Israelites began to enjoy the fruits of his victory (Josh. 11:23; 21:44; 23:1). Second, the death of Joshua had, in effect, been taken as a sign that Israel's weapons had lain at rest long enough and that the time had now arrived for the people to carry out Joshua's will and to fulfill their pledge of obedience (Josh. 24:22, 24) by rooting out the remaining Canaanites. No doubt the elders of the tribes west of the Jordan held a meeting shortly after Joshua's death to discuss what should be done. They resolved to resume the battle; but being unwilling to take action without the Lord's guidance, they first went to Him with the question of which tribe should be the first to march against the Canaanites. As far as we know, this is the first time that the Israelites asked the Lord for advice in this way. Their altered circumstances demanded this step, for the nation no longer had a leader like Moses or Joshua who received instructions directly from God. They may in fact have done this already under Joshua, because when he was commissioned, Moses stated that Eleazar the priest would inquire of the Lord for him (Num. 27:21). Moreover, Joshua 9:14 tells that the people failed to seek God's will on one occasion. The Book of Judges, nevertheless, speaks of such turning to the Lord repeatedly (20:18, 23, 27, 28). In the last of these verses, clearly the high priest (i.e., Phinehas) inquired on the people's behalf, and he (i.e., Eleazar) undoubtedly also did so in 1:1, using the divinely ordained Urim and Thummim (Exod. 28:30; Num. 27:21).[1] The question that the Israelites brought to the Lord sounds rather surprising at first. Indeed there was no need for one tribe to act first and for the others to await their turn. Each could have begun at once in its own territory. The question is quite understandable and shows great wisdom, however. For it was desirable that a single tribe begin the battle as a signal to all the others and also to the Canaanites that the cease-fire had come to an end. And if this tribe did not launch out on its own but was rather selected by God, the entire nation would be sure to understand its calling and to follow suit.

1:2 *The LORD answered, "Judah is to go; I have given the land into their hands."*

The Lord's answer shows that the Israelites were right to begin by asking this question. Judah was chosen to go first. God apparently had a special preference for this tribe, for Judah had also received the richest blessings from Jacob (Gen. 49:8–12). The Lord's answer also contains a promise of victory that corresponds with what He had foretold to Joshua (Josh. 1:3). This promise actually applied not merely to Judah but to all the tribes if only they would set their hands to the task.

1:3–7 *Then the men of Judah said to the Simeonites their brothers, "Come up with us into the territory allotted to us, to fight against the Canaanites. We in turn will go with you into yours." So the Simeonites went with them.*

⁴When Judah attacked, the LORD gave the Canaanites and Perizzites into their hands and they struck down ten thousand men at Bezek. ⁵It was there that

---

[1] This does not imply that the people were assembled at Shiloh. They also could have been at Shechem (Josh. 24:1).

they found Adoni-Bezek and fought against him, putting to rout the Canaanites and Perizzites. ⁶Adoni-Bezek fled, but they chased him and caught him, and cut off his thumbs and big toes.

⁷Then Adoni-Bezek said, "Seventy kings with their thumbs and big toes cut off have picked up scraps under my table. Now God has paid me back for what I did to them." They brought him to Jerusalem, and he died there.

The men of Judah's proposal that the Simeonites fight with them is completely understandable. While the time for combined action was past and each tribe was now responsible to purge the pagan population from its own territory, there was nothing inherently wrong with the tribes' helping one another out. In the present case there was good reason to do so, not only because Judah and Simeon, who were both sons of Leah, were very closely related, but above all because the inheritance of Simeon lay entirely within the borders of Judah (Josh. 19:9). "Come up" (v. 3), like "go up" (v. 1), actually means "climb up" in this context; for the battle first had to be waged in the Judean highlands.

The men of Simeon acceded to Judah's proposal and prepared for war, and the Canaanites and Perizzites mobilized their troops at the same time. Adoni-Bezek (i.e., "lord of Bezek," a title) led out an army of ten thousand men that was defeated by Judah and Simeon in a clash at Bezek. Verse 4 and verse 5 are speaking of one and the same battle, the former verse stating the main outcome and the latter turning to some of the details. The name Bezek appears elsewhere only in 1 Samuel 11:8, where it refers to the place where Saul marshaled his troops before marching to battle at Jabesh Gilead. It is unlikely that this was the site of the battle in verse 4, however; for it lay quite a ways north, near to Beth Shan and the crossing of the Jordan, while the campaign of Judah and Simeon took place in the south. Presumably there was another Bezek that lay in Judah.

Adoni-Bezek, the commander, was overtaken in flight and cruelly maimed to humiliate him and incapacitate him for battle. No doubt this was an objectionable procedure, for the Israelites' task was to slay their enemies, not to maltreat them. The Lord's will was nevertheless at work even here, as Adoni-Bezek himself acknowledged. He had performed the same brutal act on some seventy kings (the number should not be taken literally), whom he then condemned to scrounge on the ground like dogs for the scraps of food that fell or were thrown to them from the royal table. Now, stung by his conscience, he acknowledged that divine vengeance had caught up with him. The men of Judah and Simeon took him to Jerusalem; and since the author adds that he died there (v. 7), we can infer that his death came shortly after his arrival.

1:8–9 *The men of Judah attacked Jerusalem also and took it. They put the city to the sword and set it on fire.*
⁹*After that, the men of Judah went down to fight against the Canaanites living in the hill country, the Negev and the western foothills.*

The allied tribes next attacked Jerusalem, the city of the Jebusites.[2] Strictly speaking, this was not part of their task, since Jerusalem lay just inside the boundary of Benjamin (Josh. 18:16, 28). But as long as this powerful city remained in enemy hands, it would pose a constant threat to the men of Judah and Simeon; so it had to be captured without delay. Faithful to His promise, God gave Jerusalem into the hands of the Israelites; and they put its inhabitants to death and burned the city (cf. the fate of Ai, Josh. 8:24, 28). It is unclear whether or not the stronghold of Zion was captured as well (see 2 Sam. 5:6–9).

Judah and Simeon then marched onward, and the task of keeping the city of Jerusalem under Israel's control was left to the tribe of Benjamin (see in v. 21). Verse 9 fails to mention Simeon only because Judah played the leading role in the campaign. The two tribes conducted warfare throughout almost the whole territory that had been allotted them: the Judean hill country, the Negev or southern district, and the western foothills lying between the highlands and the Mediterranean Sea.[3] Verse 9 uses the verb "went down" because their march gradually descended to lower elevations, beginning in the hill country and ending in the coastal plain.

In reading this account, we must keep in mind that Judah and Simeon were not taking over terrain that was altogether new to them. The entire region described in these verses had already been conquered by Joshua (Josh. 10:40); and after Canaan had been divided, the tribe of Judah (which received the first lot, Josh. 15) and later that of Simeon (Josh. 19:1–9) undoubtedly settled there. The various individual tribes must have gone to live in their inheritances while Joshua was still alive, for this is presupposed especially by Joshua 22–24. The present campaign of Judah and Simeon, therefore, only aimed to purge their

---

[2] Joshua had previously killed the king of Jerusalem (Josh. 10:23, 26), but he did not attack the city.
[3] Only the desert of Judah (Josh. 15:61) is left unmentioned.

allotted territories of the Canaanites who had survived the earlier warfare or had returned later.

1:10–15 *They advanced against the Canaanites living in Hebron (formerly called Kiriath Arba) and defeated Sheshai, Ahiman and Talmai.*

11 From there they advanced against the people living in Debir (formerly called Kiriath Sepher). 12 And Caleb said, "I will give my daughter Acsah in marriage to the man who attacks and captures Kiriath Sepher." 13 Othniel son of Kenaz, Caleb's younger brother, took it; so Caleb gave his daughter Acsah to him in marriage.

14 One day when she came to Othniel, she urged him to ask her father for a field.4 When she got off her donkey, Caleb asked her, "What can I do for you?"

15 She replied, "Do me a special favor. Since you have given me land in the Negev, give me also springs of water." Then Caleb gave her the upper and lower springs.

The outcome of this campaign does not come till verses 17–19, for the author first inserts an account of the conquests of Hebron and Debir. This does not mean, however, that these cities were taken during the present campaign of Judah and Simeon. Clearly, Hebron and Debir were conquered on two different occasions. The Israelites first subjected them on Joshua's great campaign through southern Canaan (Josh. 10:36–39); but since the Anakites later resettled them (see Josh. 14:12), they had to be captured a second time by Caleb and (in the case of Debir) Othniel. Since Caleb had already been given Hebron as his portion when the division of Canaan had just commenced (see Josh. 14:6–15), seven years after Israel had arrived there, it is likely that he captured the city shortly thereafter and that the conquest of Debir and the marriage of Othniel and Acsah followed without delay. Caleb undoubtedly settled in Hebron at once and did not first take up residence in another place.5 This means, however, that the events recorded in verses 10–15 happened already during Joshua's lifetime. (Below I give reasons why this story was nevertheless included in Judges 1.) The author is not wrong to credit Judah with the victory over the Anakites (v. 10), for Caleb did not defeat them single-handedly but in league with his fellow tribesmen. Judah is named as the victor only because the author is here recounting the military exploits of this tribe.

---

4 The Hebrew text literally reads "the field" here. The Septuagint does not have the definite article, and it probably was not present in the original text. Its insertion here can easily be explained by dittography.

5 See the preceding commentary on Joshua, pp. 120–21.

And if this has caused him to downplay Caleb's role, he makes amends in verse 20 by stating that it was Caleb who drove out the descendants of Anak; for it cannot be denied that verses 10 and 20 are speaking of the same event. Aside from a few minor differences, the entire pericope in verses 10–15 can also be found in Joshua 15:14–19.[6]

One of these differences is the statement in verse 13 that Othniel was younger than Caleb. There thus would have been no great difference in age between Othniel and Caleb's niece that stood in the way of their marriage. Acsah probably had been staying in Hebron, but she came to Debir. When she arrived (v. 14), she at once told her groom that it would be to their advantage to get some fertile land from Caleb as well. Not one to procrastinate, she seized the first opportunity; and they approached her father together. Acsah then made her request, and Caleb immediately granted it.[7]

The inclusion of this story in its present context can be explained as follows. When Judges 1 was written, by far the largest part of the book had already been completed (see section II of the Introduction, p.215); and the person who composed this preface was thus able to incorporate material that would shed a proper light on the rest of the book. Since Judges 3 contains the story of Othniel, the first judge, there was good reason to include an account of Othniel's military feat at Debir. In this way the reader is alerted to the fact that this first judge had already made a name for himself in Israel.

1:16 *The descendants of Moses' father-in-law, the Kenite,[8] went up from the City of Palms with the men of Judah to live among the people of the Desert of Judah in the Negev near Arad.[9]*

In view of the fragmentary character of Judges 1, it is not surprising that the author has inserted a brief report on the Kenites. Jethro or

---

[6] The relationship between the two stories is discussed in the note at the end of the comments on Judges 1. See also the comments in Joshua 15:14–19 in the preceding commentary.

[7] Garstang, *Joshua, Judges,* pp. 210–14, makes some interesting observations about the location and history of Debir and tells of an upper and a lower pond by the city. See also Noordtzij, *Gods Woord,* pp. 51, 268, et al.

[8] The definite article is missing in the Hebrew text. The Septuagint does have the article, which there is preceded by the name Jethro or Hobab. This apparently indicates that the Hebrew text originally contained no name but most likely did have the definite article.

[9] It is doubtful that the original text has been accurately preserved here. The Septuagint reads differently and in some manuscripts does not have the name Judah.

Reuel, the father-in-law of Moses, has previously been represented as a Midianite (see Exod. 2:16; 3:1; 18:1; Num. 10:29); but here he is called a Kenite (cf. Judg. 4:11). There probably had been a branch of the Kenites who left their home in Canaan (Gen. 15:19) and intermingled with the inhabitants of Midian already before the time of Moses. Some of these Kenites migrated back to Canaan with the Israelites (see Num. 10:29–32; 24:21); and after crossing the Jordan, they stayed in the area of the City of Palms (i.e., Jericho). They now marched along with the men of Judah and Simeon and settled down in the vicinity of Arad. Verse 16 indicates that the Kenites were on good terms with the Israelites. Although a separate nation, they were Israel's ally, both here and elsewhere in Canaan (cf. 4:11; 5:24).

1:17 *Then the men of Judah went with the Simeonites their brothers and attacked the Canaanites living in Zephath, and they totally destroyed the city. Therefore it was called Hormah.*

Verse 17 follows with a report on the conquest of Zephath, a city that, like Arad,[10] lay in the deep south of Canaan. This region had been allotted to the tribe of Simeon (Josh. 19:4). The two tribes now marched together against Zephath and utterly destroyed it, thereby devoting it to the Lord (see NIV margin). The Hebrew text contains a play on words here. Hormah, thenceforth the name of the city, is related to the previous verb translated as "destroyed" and thus literally means "destruction" (see NIV margin). The reason why this conquest receives special mention is probably found in Numbers 21:1–3, where the Israelites vowed to destroy the cities of the king of Arad utterly. The people perhaps had failed to fulfill their promise in the case of Zephath, which lay within the border of the Promised Land. But the men of Judah and Simeon finally carried out the vow; and the name Hormah, which Moses had given to the entire district, was applied to the city of Zephath in particular. The Book of Joshua has in fact already used this name for the city in advance (12:14; 15:30; 19:4).

The problem with the present translation is that "Desert of Judah" usually refers to the region between the hill country and the Dead Sea, while Arad lay far to the south of this (ca. nineteen miles south of Hebron). Apparently the name Judah originally did not follow "desert" but was later accidentally repeated by a copyist. The sentence then should read "people of the desert in the Negev near Arad." The translation "south of Arad" (KJV, NASB) is unacceptable both grammatically and geographically.

[10] Garstang, *Joshua, Judges*, p. 357, has identified this city with Tell Arad.

1:18 *The men of Judah also took Gaza, Ashkelon and Ekron—each city with its territory.*

From here the march turned back to the north and followed the Mediterranean coast. The men of Israel conquered Gaza, Ashkelon, and Ekron, three Philistine cities, together with their surrounding territories. Gaza was the southernmost and Ekron the northernmost of the three. The campaign had to pass by the cities of Ashdod and Gath without capturing them, and even the three conquered cities did not remain in Israel's hands permanently. Notice that verses 17–18 only mention a few details; more must have happened than is recorded here.

1:19 *The* LORD *was with the men of Judah. They took possession of the hill country, but they were unable to drive the people from the plains, because they had iron chariots.*

This verse describes the final outcome of the men of Judah's campaign. They succeeded in conquering and maintaining control of the hill country, but they were unable to hold their position in the land of the Philistines, the lowland plains that lay west of the hill country along the Mediterranean coast. Their success in the highlands and foothill regions is ascribed to God Himself, for without His help the Israelites would have met with failure even there. But was the Lord then unable to grant them victory in the lowlands as well? Most certainly He was not, and verse 18 shows that He at first did so. Verse 19 does not contradict this, but it does form a rather unexpected sequel to the previous verse.[11] Each verse suggests an entirely different situation. Verse 18 recounts the final act in the allied tribes' campaign, while verse 19 describes how things stood for Judah in the period that followed.

Judah was the undisputed master of the hill country, but the coastal plain escaped its grasp. How can this contrast be explained? The author gives us a hint by stating that the inhabitants of the plains had iron (i.e., iron-plated) chariots. The Israelites felt that they were no match for

---

[11]Some have claimed that verses 18 and 19 are in total conflict (e.g., Moore, *Judges,* p. 37), but I have shown in the text that they can be reconciled. The author would never have written verse 18 if he had not known from ancient documents that Judah had initially conquered Gaza and the other two cities. Whereas verse 18 was undoubtedly drawn from a very early source, it seems to me that verse 19 contains the author's own report on the situation that prevailed throughout the greater part of the period of the judges.

these and did not dare to attack. Their trust in the Lord's help was not strong enough. Since He had enabled them to capture even the seemingly impregnable fortress of Jerusalem, they surely should have had faith that He was strong enough to neutralize the enemy's chariots (see Josh. 17:18). Here they fell short, however—not at first, but in the course of time.

It seems that Judah and Simeon halted their campaign after the conquest of Ekron (v. 18). They had accomplished a great deal, but they were guilty of two serious omissions: (1) they failed to pursue their enemies to the last nook and cranny (see in v. 18); (2) they did not immediately establish Israelite settlements in all the conquered cities and territories, nor did they prevent them from being reconquered by the enemy. As a result, once the men of Judah and Simeon had returned to their homes, the surviving Philistines (3:3) reappeared on the scene, resettled the land that had been taken from them, and consolidated their position there as much as they were able. The men of Judah, in contrast, did not dare to venture into the plains again. Their courage and pluck had grown slack, and they began to lose faith before the difficulties that confronted them. Besides this, they were enjoying their rest. They felt secure in the highlands and were content to leave the coastal plain to the Philistines, heedless of the threat that this could pose in the future.

1:20–21 *As Moses had promised, Hebron was given to Caleb, who drove from it the three sons of Anak.* 21 *The Benjamites, however, failed to dislodge the Jebusites, who were living in Jerusalem; to this day the Jebusites live there with the Benjamites.*

For verse 20, see the comments in verse 10. As I observed there, Caleb's victory at Hebron preceded the present campaign of Judah.[12] At verse 21 the author notes that the men of Benjamin were remiss in expelling the Jebusites from Jerusalem. Their neglect was all the more serious because they really had to do nothing more than reap the harvest that had been prepared by Judah and Simeon (see v. 8). They merely had to find and destroy the Jebusite hideouts and then settle down in Jerusalem themselves, but they probably never even made a serious attempt to do this. As a result the Jebusites soon had the city rebuilt and refortified. They thus continued to make their home within

---

[12] Goslinga's translation brings this out by putting verse 20 in the past perfect tense—Trans.

the territory of Benjamin, and Jerusalem remained a non-Israelite city (see 19:11–12) till the time of David (2 Sam. 5:6–7). As a foreign settlement in the heart of Israel's territory, Jerusalem had a highly unusual position (see pp. 217–18 above).

2. SUCCESSES AND FAILURES OF THE OTHER TRIBES (1:22–36)

On the whole the contents of verses 22–36 are more negative than positive. This, however, was because the author is seeking to bring out how remiss the Israelites were in completing the conquest of the land; and we therefore should not conclude that their successes were limited to what is explicitly mentioned here. Indeed, these go no further than the conquest of Bethel (which is cited as an example of how things went when the Israelites had faith that God would help them fulfill their mandate) and the subjection of some of the Canaanites to forced labor. On the other hand, we also should not infer that whatever places are left unmentioned were taken over by Israel. These verses do not give us a complete list, as is obvious from the absence of Issachar. The absence of this tribe cannot mean that it succeeded in conquering its entire inheritance, for this consisted mainly of the Valley of Jezreel, a region whose heavily armed inhabitants caused the Ephraimites and Manassites to recoil in fright already during the time of Joshua (Josh. 17:16). We are told nothing about later attempts at conquest.

In general, the Israelites had better results in the hill country than in the valleys and plains (see in v. 27). The tribe of Issachar probably joined forces with Zebulun and Naphtali (it is mentioned next to them in the song of Deborah, 5:15, 18) and made up for lost time by taking advantage of the defeat of Sisera. Verses 22–36 also say nothing about the tribes that settled east of the Jordan: Reuben, Gad, and the half-tribe of Manasseh. Presumably, the documents used by the author contained nothing of significance about the tribes that are left unmentioned.

1:22–26 *Now the house of Joseph attacked Bethel, and the LORD was with them.* ²³ *When they sent men to spy out Bethel (formerly called Luz),* ²⁴ *the spies saw a man coming out of the city and they said to him, "Show us how to get into the city and we will see that you are treated well."* ²⁵ *So he showed them, and they put the city to the sword but spared the man and his whole family.* ²⁶ *He then went to the land of the Hittites, where he built a city and called it Luz, which is its name to this day.*

Following the example of Judah and Simeon, Ephraim and the half-tribe of Manasseh, which together formed the house of Joseph (Josh.

16:1, 4), joined forces to take over the remainder of their allotted territory. Although their march began later, it still must have taken place at about the same time as that of the southern tribes. The land assigned to Ephraim and Manasseh lay roughly in the center of Canaan. They began by laying siege to Bethel, a city that actually belonged to Benjamin's inheritance (Josh. 18:22) but was situated right on the border of Ephraim (Josh. 16:1–2). Bethel (formerly called Luz, Gen. 28:19) had previously been conquered by Joshua (Josh. 12:16), probably after the destruction of Ai; and its citizens had been killed in battle (Josh. 8:17, 22). The present verses show, however, that it had once again passed into Canaanite hands. Now the city was made a permanent possession of Israel.

The Israelite spies accosted a man from Bethel outside the city gate and, by promising to spare his life, persuaded him to show them a route by which they could easily take the city by surprise. With the Lord's help, their plan was successful. Judgment was executed on the inhabitants of Bethel, but the man and his family were allowed to escape unharmed. Unlike Rahab, who became a member of Israel after the fall of Jericho (Josh. 6:25), he departed for the land of the Hittites and preserved the memory of his native city by building a new city called Luz there. The location of this city is unknown, for "land of the Hittites" is too general an expression (cf. Josh. 1:4). The most likely possibility would be somewhere near the mountains of Lebanon.

1:27–29 *But Manasseh did not drive out the people of Beth Shan or Taanach or Dor or Ibleam or Megiddo and their surrounding settlements, for the Canaanites were determined to live in that land.* 28 *When Israel became strong, they pressed the Canaanites into forced labor but never drove them out completely.* 29 *Nor did Ephraim drive out the Canaanites living in Gezer, but the Canaanites continued to live there among them.*

In contrast to the fate of Bethel, a number of cities in the territory of Ephraim and Manasseh were spared. Manasseh dealt leniently with the cities that had been assigned to it within the inheritances of Asher and Issachar (Josh. 17:11). Since these cities—except for Dor on the seacoast—lay mainly in the Valley of Jezreel, it is clear that this region remained unconquered. The end of verse 27 states that the Canaanites were determined to hold their ground here, and their weapons and chariots left no doubt about their intentions. The Israelites therefore did not dare to engage these valley dwellers in battle; and when they later felt strong enough, they were content to subject them to forced labor. We are not told the precise form that this servitude took, but it most likely consisted in the payment of tribute in money or goods and the performance of certain tasks (cf. the duties of the Gibeonites, Josh. 9:23, 27). In any case, Manasseh's policy disobeyed God's command to destroy the Canaanites utterly (Deut. 7:2; 20:16–17). Ephraim similarly left Gezer, the most important city on the coastal plain, in enemy hands (see Josh. 16:10).

1:30–33 *Neither did Zebulun drive out the Canaanites living in Kitron or Nahalol, who remained among them; but they did subject them to forced labor.* *[31] Nor did Asher drive out those living in Acco or Sidon or Ahlab or Aczib or Helbah or Aphek or Rehob, [32] and because of this the people of Asher lived among the Canaanite inhabitants of the land. [33] Neither did Naphtali drive out those living in Beth Shemesh or Beth Anath; but the Naphtalites too lived among the Canaanite inhabitants of the land, and those living in Beth Shemesh and Beth Anath became forced laborers for them.*

Since the powerful tribes of Joseph were so delinquent, it is not surprising that we read similar reports about the smaller tribes of Zebulun, Asher, and Naphtali. These tribes had inherited the northernmost part of Canaan, lying between the Mediterranean Sea on the west and Lake Gennesaret and the upper reaches of the Jordan on the east. They too fared best in the highland regions (of Galilee), while a large number of towns, including the important coastal cities of Acco and Sidon, remained in Canaanite hands. The Asherites especially, who had been assigned the land along the sea, had to accommodate themselves to the multitude of Canaanites who could not be expelled; and they in fact lived as foreigners within their own territory.

1:34–36 *The Amorites confined the Danites to the hill country, not allowing them[13] to come down into the plain. [35] And the Amorites were determined also to hold out in Mount Heres, Aijalon and Shaalbim, but when the power of the house of Joseph increased, they too were pressed into forced labor. [36] The boundary of the Amorites was from Scorpion Pass to Sela and beyond.*

The tribe of Dan, finally, was compelled by the Amorites to retreat into the hill country of Ephraim. Since their inheritance lay mainly in the plain, the Danites were left almost no room to settle in. Because of this, part of the tribe searched for a home elsewhere (see ch. 18).

---

[13] The Hebrew literally reads "not allowing him." The Septuagint, which is followed by the NIV here, has "not allowing them" and thus seems to have read the plural—Trans.

Mount Heres ("mountain of the sun") might be the same place as Ir Shemesh ("city of the sun"), a city that was allotted to the tribe of Dan in Joshua 19:41. The comment in verse 36 on the boundary of the Amorites' territory is only remotely related to the preceding verses. The Scorpion Pass (Heb. "pass of Akrabbim") was located on the southern boundary of Judah (Josh. 15:3), while the Danites' territory lay to the northwest of this tribe. The location of Sela ("rock") is uncertain, but it is also sought in the southern part of Canaan.[14] The following Hebrew term, which the NIV translates as "and beyond," literally means "and upward" (see KJV, RSV, NEB). "Upward" would indicate that the boundary ran toward the hill country of Judah. Verse 36 therefore might be taken to indicate that the Amorites originally lived largely in the southern part of Canaan, as indeed is clear from Deuteronomy 1:7, 44. But the verse would then be speaking of the situation that prevailed when the Israelites entered Canaan, before this region had been conquered by Judah.

NOTE

There are in general three possible explanations for the almost literal correspondence between some of the verses in Judges 1 (vv. 10–15 [and 20], 21, 27–28, and 29) and certain passages in the Book of Joshua (15:13–19; 15:63; 17:11–13; and 16:10, respectively).[15] First, we could suppose that the author of Judges 1 borrowed these passages from Joshua. Against this it is usually argued that the verses in Joshua are obviously later interpolations, while those in Judges 1 are completely at home in their context.[16] This objection loses its force, however, if we assume that the author of Judges 1 was able to consult the Book of Joshua in its final form. Nothing forbids us to think that the interpolation of a few additional passages into the original Book of Joshua happened relatively soon after Joshua's death.[17] The first chapter of Judges was not composed till a few centuries later than this (see pp. 217–21 above), and its author therefore could have made use of Joshua. This, however, does not yet

---

[14] Keil suggests that it was a rock in the Desert of Zin (see Num. 20:8–11; *Kommentar*, p. 209), while Moore proposes a high, bare rock southwest of the Dead Sea (*Judges*, pp. 55f.). The latter possibility is preferable to the former, for Sela then would lie northeast of the Scorpion Pass; and this would point the boundary toward the north (the same cannot be said of Keil's proposed location). Like the NIV, Moore translates "to Sela" rather than "from Sela." This emendation of the text, however, might conflict with the following words, which literally mean "and upward" (Moore and NIV, "and beyond.")

[15] See my discussion of this issue in the commentary on Joshua, p. 160.

[16] See, e.g., Moore, *Judges*, p. 5.

[17] See the commentary on Joshua for this.

explain the differences (e.g., between Judg. 1:27 and Josh. 17:11) that show that the verses in question were not simply quoted directly. These differences also form an objection to the second possibility, namely, that the Book of Joshua drew some material from Judges 1. This position indeed has little to recommend it. No reason at all can be found why information from Judges 1 should have been inserted into the much older book of Joshua. In addition, the accounts in Joshua are sometimes more precise, while the author of Judges 1 makes it evident that he is speaking of events from the distant past.[18] Most commentators therefore follow a third route and assume that the authors of the passages in question both took their material from the same source but did not reproduce it in exactly the same way. This, of course, was because they wrote at different times and had different purposes in mind. I personally favor a combination of the first and third positions. The author of Judges 1 would then not only have consulted his ancient chronicle (see pp. 213 above) but would also have examined the material in Joshua that had been drawn from this same source. And because he was writing so much later, his reports took a somewhat broader view even when he was speaking of the same things (cf., for example, the meanings of "to this day" in Judg. 1:21 and Josh. 15:63). He thus was not merely repeating known facts.

3. THE LORD'S REBUKE OF ISRAEL AT BOKIM (2:1–5)

2:1–5 *The angel of the LORD went up from Gilgal to Bokim and said, "I brought you up[19] out of Egypt and led you into the land that I swore to give to your forefathers. I said, 'I will never break my covenant with you, 2 and you shall not make a covenant with the people of this land, but you shall break down their altars.' Yet you have disobeyed me. Why have you done this? 3 Now therefore I tell you that I will not drive them out before you; they will be [thorns] in your sides and their gods will be a snare to you."*

4 When the angel of the LORD had spoken these things to all the Israelites, the people wept aloud, 5 and they called that place Bokim. There they offered sacrifices to the LORD.

---

[18] For example, a contemporary would have placed the comment in verse 20 on Caleb right after verse 10, instead of ten verses later. The remark in verse 13 that Othniel was younger than Caleb would have been needless for contemporaries, and Joshua thus omits it. The author of Judges 1, in contrast, had good reason to include it.

[19] The Hebrew verb form here would usually be translated "I will bring you up," but such a reading is impossible in this context. Some commentators have therefore supposed that this verb originally was preceded by a word meaning "I have said." There is no need to take recourse to such a conjecture, however. The given translation can be supported by a number of analogous cases (see *Gesenius' Hebrew Grammar*, tr. A. E. Cowley [Oxford, 1910], section 107b).

This brief but extremely important pericope raises a variety of questions that unfortunately cannot all be given an adequate answer. To understand this passage correctly, we have to assume that it is closely related to the previous material. Judges 1 speaks of human actions and circumstances that developed in history. In 2:1–5 we are told how God regarded these, and we perceive at once that we again are dealing with sacred history. These verses, which form an essential part of the story of how God led Israel, offer a unique perspective that allows us to view the events and developments of the period of the Judges in their proper light. My comments on this pericope can be organized in terms of the following questions and observations.

1. Who is it that speaks to the Israelites in verses 1–3? Verse 1 calls him the "angel of the Lord." This name is never used for a human messenger or prophet but always for someone God Himself is manifested in and who therefore shares His being (cf. Exod. 3:2–6; 23:20–23; 33:2), though His person is still distinct. We need not concern ourselves here with this distinction between the divine persons as long as it is clear that it is God Himself who appears and addresses the people. The angel of the Lord often comes forward like this in the Book of Judges (see 5:23; 6:11; 13:3), and the words in verses 1–3 could only have been spoken by God Himself.

2. When did this theophany (divine manifestation) take place? It must have happened after it became clear that the Israelites were not living up to their mandate to destroy the Canaanites but before the oppression of Cushan-Rishathaim (3:8) had begun. If approximately fifteen years had elapsed between the death of Joshua and the beginning of this time of oppression, the theophany will have to be placed in the second half of this interval (see my chronological overview on p. 234–35), when the warfare of chapter 1 already lay in the past. The end of verse 2 presupposes that God had given the Israelites enough time to fulfill their mandate before He came to rebuke them. See the next point.

3. Where and on what occasion did the angel of the Lord appear? The text contains a few items of information that at least point us toward a conclusion. According to verse 1, the angel of the Lord set out from Gilgal and "went up" to Bokim. Bokim therefore must have been located in the hill country. This implies, however, that the Gilgal spoken of was not the place where Joshua had set up camp (Josh. 9:6; 10:6 et al., which also lay in the hill country) but rather the place of the same name near Jericho (see Josh. 5:9). I will say more about this under

point 4. The location of Bokim is unknown, but apparently it was an important and well-known place. Verse 5 indicates that the name Bokim ("weeping") was first given to the site after this event, in memory of the widespread weeping that verse 4 speaks of. In verse 1 the author deliberately used the name in anticipation of this, but the place of course must also have had another name. This becomes even more obvious when we note that some type of national assembly was apparently being held there. According to verse 4 the angel of the Lord spoke to "all the Israelites," and the people therefore must have been gathered together. The meeting would not have been attended by each individual Israelite, of course, but a great number of the elders from the various tribes would have been present.

Joshua convened similar assemblies (Josh. 23 and 24), and they also were held in the early church. There must have been a specific reason for the meeting, however—the assembly at Mizpah (20:1), for example, had such a reason (and was attended by more than just the Israelite leaders)—and we are told nothing about what this may have been. Therefore it seems likely to me that the angel of the Lord appeared at one of the great religious festivals that the Israelites were obligated to attend. The entire nation was present in a sense in the persons of its representatives. Since the national sanctuary stood at Shiloh, there is good reason to look for Bokim there or in the immediate vicinity and perhaps to connect the angel's appearance with the festival spoken of in 21:19. It appears from 20:26–27, however, that the ark of the covenant was kept at Bethel for a time (see 20:23, 26; 21:1–4, which also speak of weeping); and the Septuagint's identification of Bokim with Bethel therefore cannot be ruled out. The events in 2:1–5 probably took place shortly after those in chapters 19–21. See pages 141–52.

4. Why does verse 1 mention Gilgal? To answer this question it is important to realize that the names Gilgal and Bokim form a contrast. Some commentators have rightly called attention to the relationship between this theophany and the previous one at Gilgal (Josh. 5:13–15).[20] Gilgal's favorable light in Joshua 5 suggests that the nation's covenantal relationship to the Lord reached a high point there. The anathema that in a sense still rested on the people was removed; their normal covenantal relation to God was restored; the rite of circumcision was performed; the Passover was celebrated; and they ate of the produce of the Promised Land for the first time. The Lord then

---

[20] See Keil, *Kommentar*, p. 211; D. Hoek, *Het boek der Richteren voor de gemeente verklaard* (1907), pp. 33f.

appeared to Joshua just before the battle at Jericho to assure him of His almighty aid. At Gilgal the Israelites received their mandate in the power of faith. Now, at Bokim, the warfare lay behind them, and their weapons had been put to rest. But the angel of the Lord came from Gilgal to Bokim to remind them of their past and make them aware of how far they had fallen since then.

We should not imagine that the angel literally followed a road from the one place to the other.[21] The author only meant to say that the same divine Person who had commanded the Israelites to conquer Canaan now came to call them to account for their failure to fulfill this mandate to the end. The words "from Gilgal to Bokim" thus express the decline that Israel had undergone during this interval. This explains why the author chose to use the name Bokim, which was more telling than the standard geographical name, already in verse 1.[22]

5. The divine message itself has four main thoughts.

a. The Israelites were reminded that they owed their whole existence as a nation, their deliverance from Egypt, and their possession of the Promised Land to no one but the Lord.

b. They were told that they had an entirely unique relationship to Yahweh. He had adopted Israel as His own special possession and promised never to break His covenant; but He also had commanded them to shun the inhabitants of Canaan and to destroy both them and their altars (see Exod. 19:5–6; 23:32–33; 34:12–15; Deut. 7:2–6; Josh. 23:12–13; their covenantal obligations actually included much more than this, but the angel was focusing on the things Israel had fallen short in). The Israelites were to regard Canaan as God's property; they therefore were to purge it of all the remnants of idolatry, especially since the altars would form a temptation toward new acts of idolatry.

c. The divine messenger confronted the people with their sins. He accused them of ignoring His voice; and in His divine displeasure at such ungratefulness, He asked why they had done this and how they could have acted so. Israel thus was censured for disobeying the terms of the covenant stated at the beginning of verse 2. This divine reproach, of course, was made in view of the half-hearted and unfinished efforts of the tribes recorded in chapter 1.

---

[21] It is possible, however, that this apparition of the angel of the Lord was seen leaving Gilgal on the same day.

[22] According to H. Rossier, "Bokim sets the character for the whole book of Judges, just as Gilgal does for the book of Joshua" (*Opwekkingen, beschouwingen over het boek der Richteren* (The Hague, 1928), p. 28.

d. The Lord announced how Israel would be punished for her transgression. He did this by recalling some words that He had previously pronounced in warning (see Num. 33:55; Josh. 23:13). The Hebrew at the beginning of verse 3 literally means "I also said" (cf. KJV, NEB, NASB). Following verse 2, however, the repetition of this threat meant that it now would be carried out; and the present tense is therefore appropriate. Israel had become guilty of the sin of Achan. They spared what had been devoted to destruction (see Josh. 7:1, 11–12) and associated with things that had been anathematized; therefore they made themselves liable to divine judgment. This judgment would consist of God's refusal to expel the Canaanites or to eliminate them in some other way.[23] Instead, they would remain alive so that they could oppress the Israelites.

With divine irony the Lord ensnared the people in their own folly. Their sin came back to haunt them. Since they had taken the easy way out and spared the Canaanites, their new neighbors would prove to be a troublesome burden to them. The Hebrew text of verse 3 literally reads "they will be as sides to you," but this apparently is an abbreviation for "they will be thorns in your sides" (cf. Josh. 23:13; Num. 33:55), i.e., "they will oppress you." What was worse, the Israelites would be infected by the Canaanites' idolatry and would suffer incalculable spiritual harm. The people would come to realize that every departure from God's commandments results in punishment, and that whoever makes peace with sin becomes its slave.

6. Verses 4–5 tell the effects of the Lord's rebuke. The Israelites broke out into loud weeping. Apparently they had not yet become hardened in their sin and insensitive to the angel's earnest voice. Everyone was overcome with dismay, and to express their sincere sorrow they decided to offer sacrifices (which no doubt included sin offerings) at this site that had been sanctified by the angel of the Lord's presence. In spite of this, however, there was no turn for the better. During the period of the judges, the Israelites would have to be rebuked and struck down many times over before they forsook their idolatry

---

[23] This judgment is something completely different from God's promise in Exodus 23:29–30, that He would not drive out the Canaanites all at once but gradually. That was in the nation's own interest but did not relieve them of their duty to root out the pagan population to the last person. Now that they had proved to be remiss in this, however, God's refusal to drive out the Canaanites was turned into a judgment. See the comments in 2:22.

and came to understand that "to obey is better than sacrifice" (1 Sam. 15:22).

B. Israel's Submission to the Canaanite Gods; God's Leading of His People During the Period of the Judges (2:6–3:4)

Chapters 2:6–3:4 constitute the second half of the preface to the Book of Judges. In content this section is not a continuation of 2:5 but rather runs somewhat parallel to the first part of the preface (1:1–2:5). Both sections begin with the time of Joshua and end by reporting that God decided no longer to drive the Canaanites out of the land. In the first part of the preface, this decision was motivated by the Israelites' half-hearted attempts to root out the inhabitants; in the second, by their participation in the Canaanites' idolatry, their ungrateful betrayal of God, who had shown them such rich favors.[24]

2:6–9 *After Joshua had dismissed the Israelites, they went to take possession of the land, each to his own inheritance.* [7] *The people served the LORD throughout the lifetime of Joshua and of the elders who outlived him and who had seen all the great things the LORD had done for Israel.*

[8] *Joshua son of Nun, the servant of the LORD, died at the age of a hundred and ten.* [9] *And they buried him in the land of his inheritance, at Timnath Heres in the hill country of Ephraim, north of Mount Gaash.*

The almost verbatim repetition of a few verses from the final chapter of the Book of Joshua (24:28–31) shows that the author of Judges intended to pick up his story where Joshua left off. The great similarity between these two sets of verses should not cause us to overlook the few noteworthy differences, however. Their contexts alone are enough to lend them a distinct color, for in Joshua 24 they are used to end a story, while in Judges 2 they serve as the introduction to the account of a new epoch. This explains the difference in sequence: verse 7 corresponds to Joshua 24:31, and verses 8–9 to Joshua 24:29–30. Additionally, verse 6 clearly cannot mean (like Josh. 24:28) that Joshua dismissed the people from the national assembly at Shechem, for the previous verses have not spoken of this. The verse must rather have a broader meaning, as indeed can be seen from the added statement that

---

[24] For a discussion of the preface as a whole, see the Introduction, pp. 199–201, 211–14.

"they went to take possession of the land."[25] Joshua's dismissal of the Israelites does not merely refer to their departure from Shechem. It also means that when the division of the land had been completed, he sent off the various tribes to settle in their allotted territories and to complete the work of conquest (see, e.g., Josh. 22:6; cf. 19:51; 21:43; 23:1).

The Israelites remained faithful to the Lord throughout the lifetime of Joshua and the elders who outlived him. The word elders here refers to those who functioned as local authorities and clan leaders during the lifetime of Joshua (see Josh. 23:2; 24:1) and who also were among the oldest members of the nation. Most of them outlived Joshua because they all were considerably younger than he. Joshua's (and Caleb's) real contemporaries had all died in the desert (Num. 14:29–30). These elders of Israel had witnessed with their own eyes and ears all the great deeds that the Lord had performed for Israel from the Exodus to the conquest of Canaan. Under their leadership the Israelites continued to observe God's covenant faithfully.[26]

2:10 *After that whole generation had been gathered to their fathers, another generation grew up, who knew neither the Lord nor what he had done for Israel.*

Change did not come till Joshua had departed this earth and "that whole generation [of the elders] had been gathered to their fathers," i.e., had passed from the community of the living into that of the dead. A new generation arose that could not speak from their own experience of the great miracles that God had performed to deliver His people. They did not know the Lord as He had made Himself known in the passage through the Red Sea, at Mount Horeb, and at Jericho. And they did not appreciate their freedom and rest in the Promised Land. To them the presence of the Canaanite survivors was not something abnormal that could only be endured temporarily. Obviously this younger generation would not have arisen all at once but rather replaced their elders gradually. Verse 10 does not rule out the

---

[25] See J. Bachmann, *Das Buch der Richter* (Berlin, 1868), p. 163.

[26] Further comments relating to verses 6–9 can be found in the commentary on Joshua, pp. 184–85. Timnath Heres is the same place as Timnath Serah, and both names were presumably in use at that time. In the fourth century it was claimed that Joshua's grave still existed near Tibneh in the former territory of Ephraim, at a site that probably was rediscovered by Guerin in 1863. See Moore, *Judges*, p. 68; Garstang, *Joshua, Judges*, p. 402.

possibility that part of the older generation also began to fall away, as chapter 1 indeed makes clear; nor does it deny that part of the new generation might still have had a sincere reverence for the God of their fathers.

2:11–13 *Then the Israelites did evil in the eyes of the LORD and served the Baals. [12] They forsook the LORD, the God of their fathers, who had brought them out of Egypt. They followed and worshiped various gods of the peoples around them. They provoked the LORD to anger [13] because they forsook him and served Baal and the Ashtoreths.*

The decline in Israel's religious life also did not set in at one particular point in time. It began almost imperceptibly and in more than one place, and it probably was already underway when the angel of the Lord appeared at Bokim. Verse 11 first makes the general statement that Israel "did evil in the eyes of the LORD" and then explicitly says that they "served the Baals." The next verse describes their sin as forsaking the Lord; for though the people continued to honor Him as God, they no longer conceived of Him as the only God. By serving other gods besides Yahweh, they forsook His true worship and violated the first commandment. The Israelites thus became guilty of ingratitude toward their Redeemer and degraded themselves by bowing to the gods of the heathen, the very gods whose impotence before Yahweh had been so clearly demonstrated. Their actions provoked the Lord and, as it were, challenged Him to respond.

Verse 13 describes Israel's sin further as serving Baal and the Ashtoreths. Although the name Baal appears first in the plural (v. 11) and then in the singular, no contrast is intended. Baal is the name of the male deity who was worshiped everywhere in Canaan. He could also be spoken of in the plural, however, since the form of his cult often differed among the various cities and tribes, each of which regarded him as its own tutelary deity. The name Baal literally means "lord" or "master." In Shechem he was worshiped as Baal-Berith (8:33; 9:4, 46) and in Ekron as Baal-Zebub (2 Kings 1:2–3, 6, 16). Molech too was a kind of Baal (Jer. 32:35), and Psalm 106:37–38 shows that the Israelites even participated in the cult of this abominable deity. Ashtoreth, the female deity worshiped throughout Canaan alongside Baal, is similarly referred to in both the singular and the plural. She represented the female power of nature and was the goddess of fertility. Baal seems to have been conceived more as a god of the heavens, the god of lightning (see 1 Kings 18). Closely related to Ashtoreth is the goddess Asherah, whose name was also used to denote the sacred pole or tree trunk that symbolized her (see in 3:7).

The author does not explain how the Israelites came to forsake their God so faithlessly.[27] He merely states that this happened and describes it in no uncertain terms as an apostate betrayal of the Lord.

2:14–15 *In his anger against Israel the LORD handed them over to raiders who plundered them. He sold them to their enemies all around, whom they were no longer able to resist. ¹⁵Whenever Israel went out to fight, the hand of the LORD was against them to defeat them, just as he had sworn to them. They were in great distress.*

The Lord showed His profound displeasure with His people's unfaithfulness by withdrawing from them the help and protection that they so desperately needed. He sold (i.e., handed over and abandoned) them to their surrounding enemies, who were thus allowed to plunder them. They became unable to hold their own in battle, and their military efforts all met with failure. Rather than defeating their enemies, they were smitten by the Lord's powerful hand, which had turned against them. In this way the Lord enabled Israel to see that He made good on His threats as well as His promises and strictly abided by what He had spoken and sworn (Exod. 23:33; Lev. 26:17, 25, 36–37; Deut. 28:25, 29; Josh. 23:12–13, 15–16).[28] At the same time, however, it is also clear from this that God had not yet abandoned the Israelites entirely. His punishments were motivated by the covenantal relationship that He continued to maintain, and their purpose was to lead His people to repentance.

---

[27] See section V of the Introduction for a discussion of this (pp.236–42). In *Israël en de Baäls*, pp. 50–52, J. Ridderbos presents a list of factors that could possibly explain why Israel succumbed to the Canaanite influence. This same work also discusses the Baals and other Canaanite deities (see esp. pp. 20, 72). Further material on these can be found in G. Ch. Aalders, "Baäl" and "Astarte," *Christelijke Encyclopedie* (2nd ed.); Obbink-Brouwer, *Inleiding tot de Bijbel* (1928), pp. 4, 29f.; M. J. Mulder, *Baäl in het Oude Testament* (The Hague, 1962); K. Dronkert, *De Molochdienst in het Oude Testament* (Leiden, 1953).

[28] The word "sworn" in verse 15 does not mean that God pronounced an oath to reinforce a specific threat. It rather brings out the fact that by virtue of the Lord's covenant with Israel, the threats that had been given actually had the force of an oath (cf. Exod. 24:1–8; Deut. 29:12, 21 ["all the curses of the covenant"]; Josh. 24:19–24; Hos. 2).

2:16–17 *Then the LORD raised up judges, who saved them out of the hands of these raiders.* *17 Yet they would not listen to their judges but prostituted themselves to other gods and worshiped them. Unlike their fathers, they quickly turned from the way in which their fathers had walked, the way of obedience to the LORD's commands.*

These verses likewise reveal that God did not promptly reject His chosen nation once and for all. Whenever the Israelites were in great distress, He sent leaders to deliver them. Verse 16 says that the Lord "raised up" these judges, meaning that He called them, entrusted them with their task, and gave them the ability to perform it. The judges did not act on their own. Rather, they were the instruments through whom the Lord Himself brought deliverance, so that the Israelites might perceive His goodness and be moved to obedience. This goal was never achieved, however. The people proved unwilling to listen to their judges, and their guilt therefore became all the greater. Not only did these divinely sent judges bring freedom to Israel—a great gift in itself—but as visible leaders they also made it easier for the people to remain faithful to the Lord. By being as heedless of these judges as they had been of God Himself, the Israelites only increased their guilt.

Verse 17 clearly indicates that Israel's disobedience happened already during the lifetimes of the respective judges, for it says that the people "quickly" abandoned the path of their fathers. This cannot refer to the original departure from the Lord that verse 11 speaks of but rather must mean that the nation turned away again and again during the reigns of the judges themselves. So although the judges did succeed for a short time in turning the Israelites back to the covenant paths that their pious ancestors had walked during the time of Joshua (v. 7), it became evident soon enough that the people's hearts remained unchanged; for each time they once again fell back into their old sin of "prostituting" themselves to other gods. As a violation of their "marital" bond to the Lord, idolatry was tantamount to spiritual prostitution and adultery for Israel (Exod. 34:15–16; Deut. 31:16).[29]

---

[29]Goslinga's translation of the end of verse 17 resembles the NEB—"they did not obey the LORD"—and he interprets these words as a summary condemnation of Israel's conduct. The NIV, in contrast, interprets the Hebrew clause in question to mean "unlike their fathers" (cf. the RSV—"and they did not do so") and transposes these words to the beginning of the sentence —TRANS.

2:18–19 *Whenever the* LORD *raised up a judge for them, he was with the judge and saved them out of the hands of their enemies as long as the judge lived; for the* LORD *had compassion on them as they groaned under those who oppressed and afflicted them.* ¹⁹*But when the judge died, the people returned to ways even more corrupt than those of their fathers, following other gods and serving and worshiping them. They refused to give up their evil practices and stubborn ways.*

My understanding of verse 17 is confirmed by these next two verses, which shed further light on verses 16–17. First, we are told that each time the Lord granted Israel a judge, He protected the nation against foreign tyranny for as long as the judge lived. The reign of a judge was therefore always a time of blessing and prosperity. Credit for this did not belong to the judge himself but to the Lord, who was moved to compassion at hearing the groans of His people under the oppression of their enemies. Only by His aid were the judges able to gain and to preserve the freedom of the nation. The Israelites did not take God's fatherly exertions on their behalf to heart, however; for as soon as the judge died, they returned to their old ways and outdid their fathers in wickedness. The word "fathers" does not refer to the contemporaries of Joshua (as in v. 17) but rather to the immediately preceding generations who had turned from the path of obedience under the previous judges.

Each generation went further astray than its predecessors. Since this unmistakable decline always resumed with the death of a judge, it is clear that the judges could only restrain the outward manifestations of the people's corruption and did not succeed in eradicating it from their hearts. Verses 18–19 do not deny this, for they only state that the nation remained free from foreign oppression throughout the lifetimes of the judges, not that its spiritual condition was sound. Once a judge died, the Israelites' outward behavior became doubly corrupt, which shows that the corruption then so brazenly exposed must have already been present beforehand. The sin of idolatry, never completely done away with, continued to rear its head again and again. The final part of verse 19 incisively states that the people simply refused to part with "their evil practices and stubborn ways" (lit., "hard" or "stiff-necked ways"; cf. Exod. 32:9; 33:3).

2:20–22 *Therefore the LORD was very angry with Israel and said, "Because this nation has violated the covenant that I laid down for their forefathers and has not listened to me, ²¹I will no longer drive out before them any of the nations Joshua left when he died. ²²I will use them to test Israel and see whether they will keep the way of the LORD and walk in it³⁰ as their forefathers did."*

Verses 16–19 have summarized the entire period of the judges which will later be recounted at length in the ensuing chapters of the book. Therefore it would be wrong to think that verses 20–22 are speaking of something that happened after verse 19. The Lord's anger was not first ignited against Israel at the end of the process described in verses 16–19. Rather, this happened already before it began, as verse 14 indeed makes clear. Verses 14 and 20 are speaking of one and the same thing: the outbreaking of the Lord's anger. The latter verse, however, also informs us of a decision He made that explains the course of events sketched in verses 14–19. The report of this decision in verses 20–22 takes the form of a divine soliloquy.

The author—who here speaks of God in human terms—was not implying that the Lord revealed these words at that particular point in time. Rather, he means that from a certain moment (namely, when Israel's idolatry provoked His anger) the Lord refrained from helping Israel against her enemies and decided not to destroy the pagan peoples that remained in the land. Since 2:1–3 likewise shows that the Lord withdrew His (conditional) promise to root out the Canaanites at a specific moment, it is interesting to try to determine the temporal relation between verses 20–22 and verses 1–3. Both passages speak of the same thing, and there undoubtedly is a close connection between them. It therefore seems very plausible to me that the purpose of the angel of the Lord's appearance at Bokim was to inform the Israelites of the divine decision in verses 20–22 (insofar as that was necessary). The time that verses 14 and 20 allude to would then have been shortly before the theophany at Bokim.

In verse 20, where the Lord pondered His decision, the nation's guilt is given as the reason He chose to follow a different course of action. The Israelites had violated the covenant. The further statement that this had been "laid down for their forefathers" (the same Hebrew verb is used in Josh. 7:11) shows that the Lord actually meant "covenantal

---

³⁰The Hebrew text has *bām* ("in them") here, but there is no plural antecedent for this pronoun. The NIV, therefore, follows the Greek, Latin, and Syriac translations and several Hebrew manuscripts in reading *bāh* ("in it" [viz., way]).

obligations'' here. God's covenant gave rights, or rather privileges, to Israel; but it also imposed obligations on them. By ignoring their obligation to refrain from serving foreign gods (Exod. 34:14–16), the people had alienated themselves from God; therefore the Lord called them "this nation" rather than "my nation" (cf. Isa. 6:9–10). The Israelites also stopped listening to God's voice as it had come to them, for example, through Joshua (e.g., Josh. 23:16).

Verse 21 follows with the actual content of God's decision. Because the Israelites had acted so faithlessly, the Lord concluded that He too was released from His covenantal obligations; thus He resolved to spare the nations that Joshua had left behind in Canaan when he died. That a portion of these nations—tribes or remnants would be more accurate—had been destroyed after Joshua's death (1:1–25) is not mentioned, since the conquest of Canaan had mainly been Joshua's work.

If God had said no more, we would have to regard this sparing of the Canaanites as nothing more than a punishment for Israel's sin (cf. 2:3). In verse 22, however, the Lord explicitly stated that His decision also had another purpose.[31] He intended to use the surviving pagan peoples to test Israel and to see whether or not they would walk in His ways. Previously God had had another plan for these nations: annihilation. His leniency toward them had only been provisional, since He did not wish to root them out all at once (as v. 23 states). This had actually been in Israel's own interest (see Exod. 23:29–30; Deut. 7:22); but it meant that the judgment of the Canaanite nations would only be postponed, not revoked. Thenceforth, those nations would have an entirely different standing. God would spare them to give Israel the opportunity to make a definite choice to show whether or not she intended to serve the Lord as her forefathers had done (vv. 7, 17).

Since the Israelites had already displayed their weakness and succumbed to the Canaanite gods (vv. 11–13), the new course that God was taking contained a grave danger. Israel possibly would go even further astray and become liable to divine condemnation. On the other

---

[31]Commentators disagree on the question of whether verse 22 is still reporting the Lord's words or whether the author of the book is once again speaking. (This possibility is more plausible if one consults the NASB translation, which is closer to Goslinga's than is the NIV—TRANS.) The first possibility is the most natural reading of the text and creates no difficulties whatsoever. The second possibility leaves the opening of verse 22 hanging and gives rise to the serious problem that the author then would twice (v. 22 and 3:1) speak of a hidden divine motive that is revealed by God Himself neither in verse 3 nor in verse 21.

hand, however, the people might also prove that they had taken the Lord's chastisement to heart and were capable of repentance. In putting Israel on trial, God therefore was motivated not only by avenging justice but also by fatherly love and pedagogical wisdom. His pedagogical aims, however, were not disclosed to the people themselves. The Lord had subjected the Israelites to similar tests in the past (Exod. 16:4; Deut. 8:2, 16; see also the comments in 3:1–4).

2:23 *The LORD had allowed those nations to remain; he did not drive them out at once by giving them into the hands of Joshua.*

In verse 23 the author appends a brief comment to verses 21–22 to explain why these pagan nations were still left in Canaan when Joshua died. This was not because of Joshua's negligence, but because God had intended to destroy the Canaanites gradually (see the comments in v. 22 and footnote 23 at page 263).

3:1–2 *These are the nations the LORD left to test all those Israelites*[32] *who had not experienced any of the wars in Canaan* 2 *(he did this only to teach warfare to the descendants of the Israelites*[33] *who had not had previous battle experience):*

Chapter 3:1–4 concludes the preface to the histories of the judges proper. Picking up from 2:20–23, the author lists the nations that God had decided to spare and also somewhat clarifies His purpose for these nations. By repeating the same words He had used in His soliloquy, the Lord left no doubt that these were the same nations spoken of in verses 21–22. The purpose of the Lord's decision is then stated more precisely. First, the writer observes that the decision pertained to "those Israelites who had not experienced any of the wars in Canaan." A fair number of Israelites were still alive (e.g., Othniel) who had taken

---

[32] The Hebrew text literally reads "Israel" here.

[33] The Hebrew text in verse 2 literally reads: "[he did this] only for the sake of the knowledge of the descendants of the Israelites, to teach them warfare" (cf. KJV). Goslinga argues that the word "knowledge" has to have an object, and the only possibilities for this are "wars" in verse 1 or "warfare" in verse 2. Since either choice is awkward, he opts for the Septuagint reading, which omits "knowledge" altogether and reads "only for the sake of the descendants of the Israelites, to teach them warfare." According to him the word "knowledge" (Heb. *da'at*) could have been accidentally inserted into the original text by a copyist, since the words *da'at* (which also can mean "to know," "to see") and "test" occur together in similar contexts elsewhere (see v. 4 and Deut. 8:2; 13:3). The NIV translation essentially follows the Septuagint here—TRANS.

part in the conquest, and many of these were distressed at the nation's spiritual decline. The Lord's "test" applied not to them but to the new generation that 2:10 says had no firsthand knowledge of all that He had done when Joshua led Israel against the Canaanites. This generation had less of an advantage than its predecessors because it had not witnessed the awesome and inspiring spectacle of how the Lord had led His people from victory to victory; thus it had not been blessed by the glorious experience of a war waged in the strength of faith. But this generation would receive some measure of compensation for its lack, since the Lord was going to give them the opportunity to learn warfare by sparing the surrounding nations.

The Lord put the descendants[34] of Israel to the test only because this was in their own true interest. To spare them this test would have been harmful, since the worshipers of Baal then could have pursued their sinful ways undisturbed; and the whole nation would have sunk much deeper. The Lord thus provided something that would continually restrain them; for His "test" not only would allow the Canaanites to survive, but it also would allow them to oppress the Israelites (2:3, 14–15). Those nations were Israel's enemies, and their continued presence in the land meant that the people would have a life of constant warfare. Instead of the promised rest, there would be fear, unrest, oppression, and resistance. But all this would contain a hidden blessing for the Israelites. They would be compelled to prove themselves in battle, and they thus would have the chance to share in the experience of their ancestors from Joshua's day.

The final words of verse 2 present some difficulty. The Hebrew text here contains a limiting clause that restricts the meaning of the previous words, "to teach warfare to the descendants of the Israelites." A literal translation would be: "at least those [i.e., descendants] who had not experienced them before" (cf. KJV, RSV). The pronoun "them" has to refer to the wars spoken of in verse 1. The Lord therefore was not concerned to teach warfare to all the Israelites but only to those who had not experienced the previous battles. They would come to learn of the earlier warfare that they had not had the benefit of sharing in. Obviously these later generations could no longer take part in the previous battles that verse 1 speaks of; but if we understand this

---

[34]The Hebrew word here is the same term that appears in 2:10, and it thus could also be translated "generations" (cf. KJV, RSV). According to Goslinga, the use of the plural indicates that the author was speaking not merely of the new generation referred to in 2:10 but also of later generations—TRANS.

warfare more generally as the Lord's holy war against His enemies—with all its miraculous rescues and inspiring victories—then they still would be able to share in the experience of their predecessors.[35] The Lord would rekindle this ancient warfare by allowing the Israelites' pagan neighbors to oppress them, and then He would deliver them through the judges. The war that would be waged by the later generations (under Barak, Gideon et al.) would in essence be the same one that their pious forefathers had fought in and had told them about (see 6:13); thus they too would gain firsthand knowledge of that ancient struggle.[36] Although the pagan nations had survived solely because of Israel's neglect, God in His goodness still intended to use this evil to eventually benefit His people. Only through direct experience of battle against their foes would the new generation of Israelites learn to be vigilant and to trust in God alone.

Many commentators claim that since the purpose the author of Judges ascribes to God in verse 2 is not expressed by God Himself in 2:22, he was placing a variant interpretation on God's motives. The above comments, however, show that this was not the case. Proper exegesis of verse 2 reveals that its purpose is to explicate the nature of the Lord's "testing" of His people. He would test the Israelites by giving them the direct experience of actual warfare, and constant combat would reveal whether or not they would keep the Lord's covenant. If they remained faithful in battle and placed their confidence in God (as the judges and the better part of the nation did), they would show that they had chosen for the Lord. If they instead shrank from conflict out of fear and indolence (see, e.g., 5:15–17; 15:10–13), they would have to bear their guilt.[37]

---

[35] Verse 2, therefore, is not speaking of the civil wars of chapters 9, 12, 20.

[36] Goslinga's translation, which differs from the NIV and other English versions, brings this out even more clearly. He thinks that the antecedent of the relative pronoun that begins the restrictive clause at the end of verse 2 (see text above) is not "descendants" but "wars" (in v. 1). He thus translates verse 2: "to teach them warfare, at least those [i.e., wars] that they had not previously experienced" — TRANS.

[37] In my judgment the above comments do full justice both to the words of verse 2 and to its context. Exegesis of the verse is made more difficult by the peculiar syntax, which might be due to a minor corruption of the original text (see footnote 33). I have mainly followed the exegesis of Bachmann, whose excellent commentary (*Das Buch der Richter*) is marred only by the fact that it does not go beyond the fifth chapter of the book. See also pp. 199–200 and footnote 4.

3:3–4 *the five rulers of the Philistines, all the Canaanites, the Sidonians, and the Hivites living in the Lebanon mountains from Mount Baal Hermon to Lebo Hamath. ⁴They were left to test the Israelites to see whether they would obey the LORD's commands, which he had given their forefathers through Moses.*

The list of nations given here has much in common with that of Joshua 13:2–6; and since Joshua 13:1 marks the end of Joshua's acts of conquest, this is hardly surprising. It is striking that all the nations mentioned lived either in the south (more precisely, the southwest; viz., the Philistines) or the north of Canaan. For although "all the Canaanites" could possibly also embrace the coastal inhabitants living between the land of the Philistines and the land of the Sidonians (or Phoenicians), both the latter nation and the Hivites, who inhabited the Lebanon mountains, were to be found solely in the north. Baal Hermon was the peak at whose foot stood the town of Baal Gad (Josh. 13:5), and Lebo Hamath (or "the entrance to Hamath") was the northernmost point of the Promised Land. The Canaanites spoken of here must therefore also have lived primarily in the north (see Josh. 13:4). Various regions are thus left unmentioned that, according to Judges 1:27–36, continued to be populated by their native inhabitants throughout the period of the judges. From this we can see that the author was only concerned to list the nations that lived beyond the reach of Joshua's conquests, not those that had largely been destroyed and survived only as scattered remnants within the conquered territory. The Lord spared these nations only for Israel's benefit. They became instruments in His hand for testing the Israelites to see whether they would heed His commands. The need for such a test does not detract from God's omniscience. He merely wanted to enjoy the sight of His people's obedience, and it therefore pleased Him to control events in a way that would bring their hidden motives to the surface. Faith, after all, has to be proved in action. See also the comments in 2:22.

Part Two

Israel Under the Judges From
Othniel to Samson:
The Cycle of Punishment and Deliverance
(3:5–16:31)

A. Othniel's Deliverance of Israel From
Cushan-Rishathaim
(3:5–11)

The connection between this section (particularly vv. 5–6) and the preface to the book deserves a few comments. Chapter 3:5–11 contains the story of the first judge and includes both the background for and the outcome of his work. This therefore begins the actual history of the period of the judges. Strictly speaking, the interval between Joshua's death and the first advent of foreign oppression cannot be considered part of this period, and 3:5 thus picks up the story somewhat later than 1:1 and 2:6. Here we are given a description of the situation that unfolded after the angel of the Lord appeared at Bokim (2:1–5). This theophany served as a warning, and after this warning the Lord undoubtedly gave the Israelites some time to repent before He subjected them to foreign rule. Verses 5–7 tell how Israel behaved during this interlude. Because of this, there is no abrupt break between verse 5 and the end of the preface in verse 4, but clearly verses 5–6 cannot belong to the preface itself (see footnote 2, p. 197).

3:5-7 *The Israelites lived among the Canaanites, Hittites, Amorites, Perizzites, Hivites and Jebusites.* *⁶They took their daughters in marriage and gave their own daughters to their sons, and served their gods.*
⁷The Israelites did evil in the eyes of the LORD; *they forgot the* LORD *their God and served the Baals and the Asherahs.*

The author opens the main body of the Book of Judges by outlining the situation that gradually unfolded in the years following Joshua's death. The Israelites were living in peace among a people who should have been their enemies: the remnants of the native population of Canaan. Verse 5 mentions not only the nations of verse 3, which were barely touched by Joshua's conquests, but also those within the conquered territory that had great numbers of survivors. Israel began to intermingle with her new neighbors, taking their daughters as wives and giving her own daughters in marriage to pagans whom God had anathematized. This was a much more serious offense than the formal treaty that Joshua made with the Gibeonites in Joshua 9. Here Israel's distinct identity was compromised, and the contrast between her and the pagan nations began to fade even on a religious level. The descendants of Jacob, the Lord's own allies, committed the very sin that was most displeasing to their partner in the covenant. Forsaking Him, their Liberator and King, they gave honor to the Baals and the Asherahs, the gods and goddesses of the heathen.

The name "Asherah" might have meant "bringer of good fortune." It is sometimes used for the sacred pole or tree trunk (which perhaps had a crudely carved bust of the deity) that was dedicated to this goddess (see, e.g., Exod. 34:13); but its juxtaposition with "Baals" indicates that here it refers to the goddess herself (see the comments in 2:11-13).

3:8 *The anger of the* LORD *burned against Israel so that he sold them into the hands of Cushan-Rishathaim king of Aram Naharaim, to whom the Israelites were subject for eight years.*

Enraged at Israel's violation of the covenant, the Lord permitted Cushan-Rishathaim, a foreign king, to overpower them. For eight years the Israelites were compelled to serve him, probably by paying a heavy tribute. Nothing further is known about this foreign tyrant from Aram Naharaim. Although many English versions render the Hebrew name for his land as Mesopotamia, his domain did not lie in the region between the Tigris and Euphrates rivers that the Greeks called by this name. Rather, it was located along the Upper Euphrates, particularly in the region of Haran.[1] Aram Naharaim literally means "Aram of the two rivers." Verse 10 simply has "Aram," a word that often is translated as "Syria" but which here and elsewhere (e.g., 1 Kings 10:29) has a broader reference.

Cushan-Rishathaim[2] may have been ruler of the kingdom of Mitanni, an important Near Eastern power between 1700 and 1500 B.C. that controlled the region of Aram Naharaim. In that case he probably was the vassal of a Hittite king and was attempting to extend his power southward. There can be no certainty about this, however.[3] Whatever his own plans may have been, the Lord was using him to chastise Israel.

3:9 *But when they cried out to the* LORD, *he raised up for them a deliverer, Othniel son of Kenaz, Caleb's younger brother, who saved them.*

The Lord's chastisement achieved its purpose, for the Israelites turned to Him for help. Their cry to God expressed not only the pain of their affliction but also their awareness that its cause lay in their abandonment of Him. Faithful to His promise, the Lord sent a deliverer in the person of Othniel, Caleb's younger brother (1:13), who was then the preeminent representative of the older generation that had witnessed God's mighty deeds in the conquest of Canaan.[4]

3:10 *The Spirit of the* LORD *came upon him, so that he became Israel's judge and went to war. The* LORD *gave Cushan-Rishathaim king of Aram into the hands of Othniel, who overpowered him.*

It was the working of the Spirit of the Lord on Othniel that made him into a judge. By calling this the Spirit of the Lord rather than the Spirit of God, the author makes clear that the Israelites owed their deliver-

---

[1] See Böhl, "Mesopotamië," *Bijbels-Kerkelijk Woordenboek*, vol. 1; Gispen's article in *Bijbelse Encyclopedie* (1950).

[2] The name Cushan, which occurs elsewhere only in Habakkuk 3:7 as the name of an Arabic tribe, in this context is probably the Hebrew form of a foreign title. Rishathaim, which literally means "double wickedness," might be a similar Hebraic deformation that reduced this ruler's title to a contemptuous epithet: "Cushan the archvillain." See Noordtzij, *Gods Woord*, p. 362; Garstang, *Joshua, Judges*, p. 263f.

[3] See Van Gelderen's remarks in *Bijbels Handboek*, vol. 1, p. 126.

[4] About forty years had passed since the conquest of Canaan; so Othniel must have been seventy-five or eighty years old. See the chronological table at the end of section IV of the Introduction and Joshua 14:10.

ance to the God of the covenant, who stood in a special relationship to them. The Spirit of Yahweh was seeking to revive their memory of this relationship and to reassert His claim of ownership on them. To accomplish this He called Othniel, set his faith ablaze, and endowed him with the gifts and abilities that he would need to deliver Israel. Verse 10 states that Othniel "became Israel's judge," or, literally, "judged Israel." This does not mean that he was active for a long time but simply that he stepped forward to avenge Cushan-Rishathaim's trampling of Israel's rights and to secure justice.

The word "judge" is almost equivalent to "deliverer" (see 2:16). Othniel thus set out with an army of Israelites and, with the Lord's help, won a decisive victory over the foreign tyrant that put an end to his supremacy in Canaan. This does not mean that Cushan-Rishathaim himself was taken prisoner and his territory subjected to Israel. Othniel was not bent on conquest, and we are in fact given no hint as to where the battle was fought. Tradition has preserved only a very few details from this whole episode. The overt cause for the clash may have been a campaign that the king of Aram was conducting to extend or consolidate his power. Although Othniel himself represented the southern tribe of Judah, presumably this first oppression affected virtually the entire nation, especially since it was not the work of a small neighboring tribe but of a great kingdom lying far to the north.

3:11 *So the land had peace for forty years, until Othniel son of Kenaz died.*

The land enjoyed a time of peace for forty years. The report of Othniel's death does not necessarily mean that this came at the end of this forty-year period.[5] It rather serves to close this episode and simultaneously to prepare the way for the announcement of Israel's renewed apostasy in verse 12.

---

[5] Although the NIV has "until," the Hebrew literally just means "and Othniel . . . died" (cf. KJV, NASB—TRANS.).

B. Ehud's Deliverance of Israel From the Moabites; Shamgar's Heroism
(3:12–31)

3:12–14 *Once again the Israelites did evil in the eyes of the LORD, and because they did this evil the LORD gave Eglon king of Moab power over Israel.* [13] *Getting the Ammonites and Amalekites to join him, Eglon came and attacked Israel, and they took possession of the City of Palms.* [14] *The Israelites were subject to Eglon king of Moab for eighteen years.*

The abrupt announcement of a new turn to evil in verse 12 implies that the Israelites' inner corruption came to the surface soon after Othniel's death. Once again they openly committed deeds that were hateful to the Lord, particularly idolatry and the sins related to it (see vv. 6–7). A new generation had grown up after the oppression of Cushan-Rishathaim that ignored the lessons of the recent past and turned down a path that would inevitably lead to divine punishment. Since the Israelites abandoned their God, the Lord also abandoned them and gave Eglon, the king of Moab, power to overcome at least a part of the nation. He joined forces with the Ammonites and the Amalekites and invaded Canaan; and although the Israelites attempted to resist, their efforts were in vain because the Lord refused to help (2:14–15). After defeating them, Israel's enemies took possession of the unfortified City of Palms (i.e., Jericho), the gateway to the land west of the Jordan. The battle probably took place west of the river, somewhere in the vicinity of this city. Seemingly, Eglon did not extend his conquests much farther than Jericho, but his victory there enabled him to exact tribute from the Israelites. For eighteen long years they had to submit to the Moabite yoke and cringe beneath their power.

3:15 *Again the Israelites cried out to the LORD, and he gave them a deliverer—Ehud, a left-handed man, the son of Gera the Benjamite. The Israelites sent him with tribute to Eglon king of Moab.*

This punishment worked for Israel's good, however; for the people again were reminded that the Lord was their God and turned to Him for help. The Lord responded by calling Ehud the son of Gera, a man from the tribe of Benjamin, to cast off the foreign yoke. If verse 15 is taken alone, we might think that Ehud was acting on his own, without a special divine mandate, when he made his surprise attack on Eglon and called the Israelites to war. Only after his success would it then have become clear that his work had found God's approval. Since verses 20 and 28 show that Ehud was consciously acting in the name of the Lord, however, such an interpretation is unacceptable. Ehud was not a self-appointed liberator. He was called and ordained by God, for God "gave"[6] Israel a deliverer. Had it been otherwise, Ehud would not have belonged among the judges who acted by divine right; and the Book of Judges unquestionably grants him such a position.

The absence of a statement that "the Spirit of the LORD came upon him," as verse 10 says of Othniel, is not crucial. Verse 30 also does not state that Ehud "judged" Israel (perhaps because it was not known how long he did so); we can, however, infer from 4:1 that he, like the other judges, moved Israel to observe the Lord's covenant for a time. For it was only after he died that they again became apostate.

Ehud came from the tribe that had to suffer the longest and the hardest under the Moabite oppression. He was from the clan of Gera, a grandson of Benjamin (1 Chron. 8:3; cf. 2 Sam. 16:5; Gen 46:21 lists Gera among Benjamin's sons). His left-handedness does not necessarily mean that his right hand was impaired. For 20:16 states that in the conflict between Benjamin and the other tribes, the Benjamite army had seven-hundred left-handed slingshot artists. These men as well as Ehud must therefore have been unpracticed with their right hand. The esteem and confidence that Ehud enjoyed among his people is shown by that fact that he was delegated to bring the annual tribute to Eglon. If, as seems likely, he had already done this more than once, he would have had some inside knowledge of the situation at Eglon's residence.

3:16–19 *Now Ehud had made a double-edged sword about a foot and a half long, which he strapped to his right thigh under his clothing. 17 He presented the tribute to Eglon king of Moab, who was a very fat man. 18 After Ehud had presented the tribute, he sent on their way the men who had carried it. 19 At the idols near Gilgal he himself turned back and said, "I have a secret message for you, O king."*

The king said, "Quiet!" And all his attendants left him.

Before setting out this time, Ehud made a short double-edged sword. According to the rabbis, the unit of length in the Hebrew here was equal to a short cubit.[7] The deadly weapon was thus more of a dagger

---

[6] "Gave" here translates the same Hebrew verb as "raised up" in 2:16. See the comments in loc.—TRANS.

[7] The NIV gives the approximate English equivalent as "about a foot and a half" — TRANS.

than a sword. Ehud concealed this by strapping it to his right thigh under his clothing. Seemingly unarmed, he arrived at the Moabite king's palace at the head of a procession of Israelites who carried the tribute.[8] Eglon, we are told, was an obese man. Ever on the lookout, Ehud quickly formulated his plan; but to carry it out, he would have to be left alone. Having managed to avoid all suspicion, he left the king's court with his men and accompanied them to the idols at Gilgal, where he himself turned back. Eglon must have resided at Jericho. The Gilgal spoken of here was not the place by the Jordan, east of Jericho, where Joshua had had the Israelites circumcised (Josh. 5:9–10), nor was it the Gilgal in central Canaan that long served as Joshua's camp (Josh. 10:7; 14:6). Rather, it was the Gilgal of Joshua 15:7, which stood opposite the Pass of Adummim, southwest of Jericho on the road to Jerusalem.[9] Eglon had had idols erected there as a sign of his power, and there may have also been a Moabite outpost at this site. Anyone coming or going from the territory of Benjamin would have had to pass these idols. Verse 26 gives the impression that Eglon's power did not extend farther westward; and by bringing his men to Gilgal, Ehud therefore ensured their safety. When he was readmitted to the king's presence, he pretended to have a secret message; and at Eglon's command to keep silent, all the royal attendants left. This, of course, was exactly what Ehud wanted.

3:20–23 *Ehud then approached him while he was sitting alone in the upper room of his summer palace and said, "I have a message from God for you." As the king rose from his seat, [21] Ehud reached with his left hand, drew the sword from his right thigh and plunged it into the king's belly. [22] Even the handle sank in after the blade, which came out his back.*[10] *Ehud did not pull the sword out, and the fat closed in over it. [23] Then Ehud went out to the porch;*[11] *he shut the doors of the upper room behind him and locked them.*

The king was sitting alone in a private room that was probably situated on the roof of his summer palace.[12] Such roof chambers,

---

[8] An illustration of this method of bringing tribute can be found in Noordtzij, *Gods Woord*, p. 408: "Jehu before Shalmaneser III, followed by the bearers of 'gifts.'"

[9] According to Keil, *Kommentar*, p. 237.

[10] The Hebrew term rendered as "back" (*paršᵉḏōn*) does not occur elsewhere, and its translation is therefore far from certain. Goslinga's translation resembles the KJV and RSV: "and the dirt [i.e., contents of the bowels] came out." He adds the following note:

We can only guess what the term *paršᵉḏōn* means. One problem is that it is impossible to determine the subject of the verb "came out" at the end of v. 22

which were often surrounded by slats that would break the sunlight but allow for the circulation of air, can still be found today in the Near East. The opening of verse 20 seems to imply that this particular room had both an inner and an outer section (see also v. 24). Ehud, who was already in Eglon's presence (v. 19), stepped up to him in the inner chamber[13] after the attendants had left and said in a solemn voice: "I have a divine word for you." The Hebrew term he used is very general and can mean both "word" and "thing, matter, affair." We could therefore also translate this as "I have some divine business for you," but perhaps the closest approximation in English is the NIV's "I have a message from God for you." In any case Ehud cannot be accused of deceit. He merely used a somewhat vague and ambiguous expression that clearly announced his divine mission. For though he did not use the personal name of Israel's God—the name "Yahweh"—the king could not have doubted that he as an Israelite was bringing a message from his own God.

Eglon stood up, partly out of curiosity but partly also out of respect, since to the pagan mind the God of Israel was still an actually existing and even fearsome deity. What could this God have to tell him? Completely unsuspecting Eglon stood directly in front of Ehud, and the latter seized his opportunity. Grasping his razor-sharp dagger in his left hand, Ehud plunged it with such force into Eglon's bloated belly that the dagger vanished, handle and all. The stroke was lethal, and Ehud thus did not need to withdraw his weapon. Seeing the king collapse to the ground with his entrails falling out, his sole concern was to get to safety. Keeping his wits about him, he went out to the porch, locked the door to the king's room from the outside, and calmly left the palace.

[the NIV has transposed this final clause]. Some think that Ehud is the subject, but this conflicts with the fact that he does not leave the room until v. 23. Others [e.g., the NIV and NEB] think that the subject is "sword" and that *parš*ᵉ*ḏōn* indicates the point of exit. The traditional Jewish interpretation sees a connection between *parš*ᵉ*ḏōn* and *pereš*, a word for the contents of the bowels, and regards *parš*ᵉ*ḏōn* as the subject of the clause. I have chosen to follow this view but will not guess as to how the form *parš*ᵉ*ḏōn* could have originated—TRANS.

[11] The Hebrew *misd*ᵉ*rôn* , translated as "porch," also is obscure. Although this is its only occurrence in the Old Testament, it seems to be related to a stem meaning "row" or "series" and thus might indicate a colonnade or portico.

[12] The author's translation of this difficult Hebrew phrase corresponds to the RSV rather than the NIV—TRANS.

[13] The apparent inconsistency that some have thought to find between verse 19 and verse 20 is easily explained in this manner.

A few brief remarks about the ethical implication's of Ehud's deed are in order here.

1. In terms of principle, Ehud's act was no different than Israel's destruction of the Canaanites under Joshua, Samuel's killing of Agag (1 Sam. 15:33), and other cases where divine judgment was carried out by men at God's own command. Ehud came forward to uphold the rights of God and to take vengeance on His behalf against the Moabites and their king, and it is in this light that his actions have to be judged. Even though the Moabites were the Lord's instrument for punishing Israel, they still remained His enemies and had no right to occupy His sacred land and oppress His people. And although God had not given Ehud a special command to kill Eglon, his duty and right to do so were a direct consequence of his calling as judge.

2. Ehud cannot simply be accused of a treacherous act of assassination. He was attempting to overthrow his nation's enemy, and Moab could have expected that the Israelites would attempt to regain their freedom. Eglon and his attendants acted very foolishly, and Ehud cannot be condemned for playing on their credulity and carelessness. Nor can he be blamed for the way he cleverly managed to avoid suspicion or took advantage of his left-handedness.

3. It cannot be demonstrated that Ehud acted out of base motives such as personal hatred or vindictiveness. If there was anything reprehensible in the manner he performed his task—his more or less ambiguous words, for example, or his almost pitiless cruelty—this of course cannot be excused. We must bear in mind, however, that human beings are always imperfect instruments in God's hand and that the main thing here is the essence of Ehud's deed, not the incidental factors.

4. The Bible does not condemn Ehud's action either directly or indirectly. Rather, it presents it as God's way of delivering Israel at that time and place. Nevertheless, his special position as judge obviously forbids us to use his deed to justify other acts of tyrannicide.[14]

---

[14] See J. Bachmann, *Das Buch der Richter,* pp. 231ff.; D. Hoek, *Het boek der Richteren,* pp. 65f.

3:24–25 *After he had gone, the servants came and found the doors of the upper room locked. They said, "He must be relieving himself in the inner room of the house."* ²⁵*They waited to the point of embarrassment, but when he did not open the doors of the room, they took a key and unlocked them. There they saw their lord fallen to the floor, dead.*

After Ehud departed, the king's servants returned but were surprised to find the doors of the upper room locked. The lock must have been on the inside, since Ehud would otherwise have immediately fallen under suspicion for fastening it. Instead, the servants' first thought was that the king must be "relieving himself." The Hebrew text actually contains a euphemism here that literally reads "covering his feet" (see KJV).[15] The king's upper room thus must have been equipped for this. The servants waited a considerable length of time, expecting that the king, who seemingly did not wish to be disturbed, would signal them to come in by opening the door himself. Finally, being at a loss what to do and fearful that they had neglected their duties, they brought the key, opened the door,[16] and found Eglon lying dead on the floor.

3:26–30 *While they waited, Ehud got away. He passed by the idols and escaped to Seirah.* ²⁷*When he arrived there, he blew a trumpet in the hill country of Ephraim, and the Israelites went down with him from the hills, with him leading them.*
²⁸*"Follow me," he ordered, "for the LORD has given Moab, your enemy, into your hands." So they followed him down and, taking possession of the fords of the Jordan that led to Moab, they allowed no one to cross over.* ²⁹*At the time they struck down about ten thousand Moabites, all vigorous and strong; not a man escaped.* ³⁰*That day Moab was made subject to Israel, and the land had peace for eighty years.*

Ehud had escaped in the meantime and managed to avoid being overtaken. He reached Seirah, a place of unknown location that must have lain somewhere in the hill country of Ephraim. There he signaled to his countrymen with a trumpet. When a host had assembled, he told how the Moabite king had fallen; and he promised victory in the Lord's

---

[15] The expression is based on the fact that the ample garments of an ancient Near Eastern person would completely cover his feet when he squatted to the floor. See Bachmann, *Das Buch der Richter*, p. 226.
[16] Doors in the ancient world were locked by means of a bolt that could be fastened not only from the inside but also from the outside by means of a strap or even by hand. Such a bolt, which probably was also used here, could then be opened only by a key.

name if they followed him. His appeal found a ready response, and the Israelites' return to the Lord revived their fighting spirit. Emerging from the forests and caves of Ephraim's hills, great numbers of them marched down with their courageous commander and took possession of the fords of the Jordan, cutting off the Moabites' retreat to their homeland. They did not rest till they had destroyed the entire army of "vigorous [lit., 'fat, well-fed'] and strong" Moabites. The nation of Moab was thus humiliated, and for eighty years no hostile power dared to cross the Jordan (but see pp. 228–30).

3:31 *After Ehud came Shamgar son of Anath, who struck down six hundred Philistines with an oxgoad. He too saved Israel.*

On pages 228–29 and 234 in the Introduction, I have discussed the date that should be assigned to Shamgar's work. His judgeship could not have lasted long, but we need not confine it to the heroic feat mentioned in this verse. The words "in the days of Shamgar" in 5:6 strongly suggest that Shamgar was a man of influence and authority for at least some length of time. The end of verse 31 ("he too") clearly means to place Shamgar along with Othniel and Ehud among the judges or deliverers that the Lord "raised up" (2:16). Nevertheless, it seems likely that Shamgar's activity and influence did not extend very far. He must have come from one of the tribes whose territory bordered on the coastal plain where the Philistines resided. When Jabin was oppressing the northern tribes, a band of Philistines invaded Israelite soil. Shamgar perceived them (perhaps while he was plowing the field behind a yoke of oxen); and, armed only with an oxgoad, a stick about eight feet long with an iron point at one end and a flat, chisel-shaped iron at the other, he attacked and killed six hundred men. The survivors fled in panic, and the Philistines did not dare to cross their border again for some time. Shamgar's deed has much in common with that of Samson in 15:15 (cf. also 2 Sam. 23:8, 18). He undoubtedly was an extraordinarily strong man, but the deliverance that he brought to Israel came ultimately from the Lord.

C. Deborah and Barak
(4:1–5:31)

1. DEBORAH AND BARAK'S DEFEAT OF JABIN AND SISERA (4:1–24)

Although the relationship between chapters 4 and 5 will be discussed at greater length at the beginning of chapter 5 (see pp. 294–95 below) and in the comments on the biblical text itself, I wish also to make some brief remarks at the outset. A few minor differences have been pointed out between these chapters. Chapter 4, for example, mentions only Naphtali and Zebulun, while chapter 5 also names other tribes. The latter chapter does not name Jabin or Mount Tabor, the place from which the attack was launched. In spite of these differences, however, the two chapters have so much in common that one cannot doubt that they are describing the same historical event. Indeed, if the author of chapter 4 had been unsure about a certain point, he doubtless would have been careful to avoid writing anything that conflicted with the authoritative song of Deborah.

There also is no reason to suppose that chapter 4 itself is an amalgamation of two entirely distinct stories, namely, the battle against King Jabin of Hazor and a completely different battle against Sisera of Harosheth. Such a view is taken, for example, by Moore (*Judges*, pp. 108f.) and Edelkoort (*Uittocht en Intocht*, pp. 176ff.), the latter holding that this is the same Jabin that is spoken of in Joshua 11. Accepting the traditional text as historically reliable does leave some difficulties, but this does not compel us to tear the story asunder. The most serious problem is that verses 9–10 have Barak's army assemble in Kedesh of Naphtali, while verse 11 puts the same place near to Zaanannim and verse 17 implies that it lay close to the battlefield. Possibly verse 11 is speaking not of Kedesh in Naphtali but of Kedesh in Issachar (1 Chron. 6:72). Garstang (*Joshua, Judges*, p. 301) identifies the latter town with *Tell Abū Qedeis*, which would put it between Taanach and Megiddo and thus right by the battlefield (see 5:19). The Zaanannim spoken of likewise could be a place other than the Zaanannim in Naphtali (Josh. 19:33; the Hebrew text spells the name differently in the two verses; cf. KJV). And the problem in verses 9–10 also is not insurmountable. Indeed, nothing forbids leaving such perplexities unresolved till we succeed in finding further light (e.g., through archaeological work in Palestine). The comments that follow will also touch on some of these points.

4:1–3 *After Ehud died, the Israelites once again did evil in the eyes of the LORD.* *²So the LORD sold them into the hands of Jabin, a king of Canaan, who reigned in Hazor. The commander of his army was Sisera, who lived in Harosheth Haggoyim. ³Because he had nine hundred iron chariots and had cruelly oppressed the Israelites for twenty years, they cried to the LORD for help.*

For the probable date of Ehud's death, see the Introduction, pp. 228–30, and the chronological table on p. 234. The turn away from the

Lord most likely began in the northern tribes, where the influence of Ehud's work had been felt the least. These tribes were the first to be punished; for the enemy that invaded Israel was Jabin king of Hazor, a city of northern Canaan that lay southwest of Lake Huleh in the territory allotted to Naphtali. Joshua had captured and burned this important city (Josh. 11:10–13), but the Canaanites managed to rebuild it because of the Naphtalites' indifference (Judg. 1:33). Here they took the offensive, and the threat of 2:3 (cf. Josh. 23:13) was carried out to such an extent that this Canaanite king was free to tyrannize the Israelites at his pleasure. Israel was powerless against Jabin in the face of his strong army, his nine hundred iron chariots, and his formidable general Sisera. The latter resided in Harosheth Haggoyim ("Harosheth of the Gentiles"), a military center (v. 13) whose exact location is unknown.[17] The people of Israel groaned under this heavy foreign yoke for twenty years before they once again learned to call on the Lord for deliverance.

4:4–5 *Deborah, a prophetess, the wife of Lappidoth, was leading Israel at that time. ⁵ She held court under the Palm of Deborah between Ramah and Bethel in the hill country of Ephraim, and the Israelites came to her to have their disputes decided.*

God heard the Israelites' prayer, and to answer it He turned to two individuals whom He had already given some advance preparation for the task of delivering Israel. The first was Deborah, a woman who had the divine gift of prophecy. She was thus an instrument through whom the Lord revealed Himself, and as God's mouthpiece she was able to settle difficult legal disputes. According to verse 5, she held court under the palm tree that bore her name, between Ramah and Bethel. There, in the heart of Israelite territory, life could still go on in relative tranquility. That God allowed the highest legal matters to be decided by a woman rather than a man was a departure from the usual order in the social and spiritual life of Israel. Deborah was first of all a prophetess, secondly an administrator of justice, and she then also became a judge

---

[17] Harosheth Haggoyim is usually identified with Harithiyeh, located on the Kishon River at the foot of Mount Carmel. Garstang, however, has sought it in the nearby Tell el-Harbaj (*Joshua, Judges,* p. 297). If either view is correct, this would mean that Jabin controlled all northern Canaan from his home in Hazor and that his power extended even to the Valley of Jezreel. See Van Deursen's article in the *Bijbelse Encyclopedie.*

in the sense of deliverer. She was in no way a lesser judge because she was a woman.

4:6–7 *She sent for Barak son of Abinoam from Kedesh in Naphtali and said to him, "The LORD, the God of Israel, commands you: 'Go, take with you ten thousand men of Naphtali and Zebulun and lead the way to Mount Tabor. ⁷I will lure Sisera, the commander of Jabin's army, with his chariots and his troops to the Kishon River and give him into your hands.'"*

Deborah summoned Barak, God's second instrument for putting a stop to Jabin's oppression. Barak came from Kedesh in Naphtali, a town that lay even farther north than Hazor.[18] Undoubtedly Deborah was following God's instructions here. The deliverer had to come from the tribe that had suffered the most under Jabin's tyranny. Possibly Barak himself had felt the weight of Jabin's yoke and had exiled himself in the hill country of Ephraim. Regardless, the Lord commanded him through Deborah to marshal an army of ten thousand men from Naphtali and Zebulun on Mount Tabor and promised that he would win a total victory over Sisera. God Himself would lure (the Hebrew verb used here literally means "pull, drag") Jabin's commander to a place where Barak could easily make a surprise attack from the hill.

4:8–10 *Barak said to her, "If you go with me, I will go; but if you don't go with me, I won't go."*

⁹"Very well," Deborah said, "I will go with you. But because of the way you are going about this, the honor will not be yours, for the LORD will hand Sisera over to a woman." So Deborah went with Barak to Kedesh, ¹⁰where he summoned Zebulun and Naphtali. Ten thousand men followed him, and Deborah also went with him.

With success assured from the outset, Barak still wavered, saying that he would only march if Deborah went with him. The Lord's promise should have been enough for him, but Barak's faith was too weak. He also lacked obedience. It would not have been wrong for him merely to express a wish that Deborah accompany him; but by making this a condition of his going, he sinned against the Lord. Deborah's response rebuked him for his lack of faith. She said that she would

---

[18] But perhaps there was another place of the same name, otherwise unknown to us, that was located more to the south. The Kedesh by Hazor seems problematic in that it lay a good twenty-five miles north of the battlefield. Moreover, it would have been difficult for Barak to recruit an army so close to Hazor. See the comments in verses 10–11.

indeed go with Barak, but the credit for the victory would belong to a woman and not to him. Deborah and Barak went to Kedesh together, where Barak assembled an army of men from Zebulun and Naphtali who answered his summons. The fact that a full ten thousand responded, just as Deborah had said (v. 6), was already a fulfillment of God's promise. With the Lord's powerful support, there was no shortage of men willing to risk their lives for Israel's freedom. Barak's troops no doubt were divided into groups for the march from Kedesh to Tabor, for it was essential that this take place in secrecy. It seems problematic that Barak mustered his army at Kedesh, since from there they would have had to march past Hazor, Jabin's capital city, to reach Mount Tabor lying far to the south.[19]

4:11 *Now Heber the Kenite had left the other Kenites,[20] the descendants of Hobab, Moses' brother-in-law,[21] and pitched his tent by the great tree in Zaanannim[22] near Kedesh.*

The same problem returns in another form in verse 11, where we read that Heber pitched his tent near Kedesh. Verses 17 and 22 indicate that Heber's tent stood near enough to the battlefield for Sisera and Barak to reach it on foot. One therefore might assume that here, at least, another Kedesh is intended than the one north of Hazor, but then it would be strange that this place is not distinguished from the Kedesh in Naphtali in verse 6. Moreover, the proximity of this Kedesh to Zaanannim also argues against such an assumption (but see the remarks on p. 287). Verse 11 obviously has been included because of its relevance to the account of Jabin's flight and death in verses 17–22. Apparently Heber was on friendly terms with Barak (see v. 22). The Hebrew text literally reads "Cain" at the beginning of verse 11 (see

---

[19] Another problem is that the ten thousand men from Zebulun and Naphtali constituted Barak's entire army in chapter 4 (see v. 14), while 5:14–15 also has other tribes offering their help. These latter troops from the south did not assemble at Kedesh before the march, however, but probably first joined forces with Barak at the Kishon River. See note 58 on p. 312.

[20] The Hebrew text literally reads "Cain" here.

[21] The Hebrew text has "father-in-law," but an alternate vocalization of the consonants gives the word for "brother-in-law." The latter translation is preferable, since in Numbers 10:29 Hobab is clearly Moses' brother-in-law. The Septuagint reading can be interpreted either way.

[22] The Hebrew text spells Zaanannim differently here than in Joshua 19:33 (cf. the KJV of both verses). These may be variant forms of the same name, but see the remarks at p. 287.

note 20), but the reference clearly is to the group of Kenites that migrated to Canaan with the Israelites (cf. Num. 24:21–22 in NASB).

4:12–13 *When they told Sisera that Barak son of Abinoam had gone up to Mount Tabor, ¹³ Sisera gathered together his nine hundred iron chariots and all the men with him, from Harosheth Haggoyim to the Kishon River.*

Sisera learned that Barak had marched with his army to Mount Tabor. Mount Tabor stood northeast of the Valley of Jezreel, a lowland region that was crossed toward the northwest by the Kishon River and its multitude of tiny tributaries. Harosheth Haggoyim presumably lay northwest of this valley. Sisera concentrated all his power in the valley of the Kishon. The Israelites' position on Mount Tabor may have been favorable, but they could not stay there forever. As soon as they dared to come down into the valley, Sisera intended to shatter them with his iron chariots. We have to imagine Sisera waiting to meet Barak at the foot of the isolated peak of Tabor.[23]

4:14–16 *Then Deborah said to Barak, "Go! This is the day the LORD has given Sisera into your hands. Has not the LORD gone ahead of you?" So Barak went down Mount Tabor, followed by ten thousand men. ¹⁵ At Barak's advance, the LORD routed Sisera and all his chariots and army by the sword,[24] and Sisera abandoned his chariot and fled on foot. ¹⁶ But Barak pursued the chariots and army as far as Harosheth Haggoyim. All the troops of Sisera fell by the sword; not a man was left.*

Although Sisera was sure of victory, he had not reckoned with Israel's mighty Ally. He thought that the Israelites would not dare to

---

[23] A fine description of Mount Tabor can be found in A. Kuyper, *Palestina*, pp. 45–46.

[24] Goslinga's translation, which adheres very literally to the Hebrew, reads: "the LORD threw Sisera and . . . into confusion before the edge of the sword before Barak" (cf. the KJV). He adds the following footnote:

It is hard to find an appropriate meaning for the phrase "before the edge of the sword." The best course is to imagine Barak and his men storming down the slope with drawn swords and Sisera and his army being seized by panic at the sight. But it is odd that the verse does not simply read "before the sword of Barak." It also seems much more likely that the panic of Sisera's seasoned warriors would have been caused by a phenomenon of nature than by the sight of the Israelites' swords (see the comments under 5:20). Moreover, the Hebrew phrase in question appears in a very unusual context here. It nearly always occurs in connection with "put" (1:8, 25; Josh. 10:28, 30, 32; etc.) or "fall" (v. 16), where it means "by the edge of the sword." This cannot be the meaning here, however, since verse 15 seems to describe an act of God that preceded the actual meeting of the armies. The sense attack, but Deborah commanded Barak in the name of the Lord to pounce on the enemy. The Lord Himself would lead the way; and with Him as their invisible General, Israel would be victorious. This time Barak obeyed without a word of protest. He marched down the slope with his men, a seemingly foolhardy move, but the Lord was fighting for Israel. The Lord threw Sisera's army into confusion (the NIV translates the verb as "routed"—TRANS.), just as He had done before to the Egyptians and the Amorites (cf. Exod. 14:24–25 and Josh. 10:10, where the same Hebrew verb is used). We are not explicitly told how God did this, but 5:20 seems to point to a violent natural phenomenon or a sign in the heavens that provoked such a panic (cf. Exod. 23:27) that men and horses rushed about in disarray and finally fled. There never was an organized battle; and although the enemy may have offered patches of resistance (cf. 5:19), Barak and his troops mainly just had to chase and cut down Sisera's soldiers. The pursuit lasted all the way to Harosheth Haggoyim, and at the end not a single enemy soldier remained alive. It was just as if the days of Joshua had returned.

4:17–20 *Sisera, however, fled on foot to the tent of Jael, the wife of Heber the Kenite, because there were friendly relations between Jabin king of Hazor and the clan of Heber the Kenite.*

[18] Jael went out to meet Sisera and said to him, "Come, my lord, come right in. Don't be afraid." So he entered her tent, and she put a covering over him.

[19] "I'm thirsty," he said. "Please give me some water." She opened a skin of milk, gave him a drink, and covered him up.

[20] "Stand in the doorway of the tent," he told her. "If someone comes by and asks you, 'Is anyone here?' say 'No.'"

Sisera was seized by panic and fright. In the mad scramble it was impossible for him to escape on his chariot; so he took to foot. He ran, not toward Harosheth Haggoyim, however, but to the Kenite settlement. Jabin, king of Hazor, was on peaceful terms with the clan of Heber, who apparently had taken a neutral position.[25] Sisera went to the tent of Jael. (Even today among the Arabs the tent of a woman is an inviolable place and therefore completely safe.) She saw him approach-

---

would be clearer if the phrase were absent. Did a copyist insert it accidentally because his eyes wandered to verse 16? The possibility cannot be ruled out, but there is no way to prove it—TRANS.

[25] If Heber indeed lived near Kedesh in Naphtali, Sisera could just as easily have fled to Hazor. It makes sense that he would not have wanted to enter the city of Jabin as a fugitive, but not that he covered such a great distance without seeking a hideout nearer by and without falling into Israelite hands.

ing and, since she apparently knew him, invited him inside. The Hebrew word that she used literally means "turn aside," and its effect in this context was thus "turn off the road and come in." Sisera naturally was glad to hear these friendly and soothing words.

On entering Jael's tent, Sisera at once lay down on the floor to rest. Jael placed a covering over him, not only for his comfort, but also to conceal his presence. Having gained his complete trust, she showed him the greatest courtesy and hospitality. He asked for some water, and she gave him milk that had been preserved and kept cool in a leather pouch. Another authentic touch in the story is the precautionary measure that Sisera took to avoid discovery. He asked Jael to stand in the tent doorway to avert possible pursuers. Then he sank, dead-tired, into a deep sleep.

4:21–22 *But Jael, Heber's wife, picked up a tent peg and a hammer and went quietly to him while he lay fast asleep, exhausted. She drove the peg through his temple into the ground, and he died.*

²²Barak came by in pursuit of Sisera, and Jael went out to meet him. "Come," she said, "I will show you the man you're looking for." So he went in with her, and there lay Sisera with the tent peg through his temple—dead.

Now was the time for Jael to act. As she stepped forward to kill Israel's oppressor, the author deliberately called her by her full name, "Jael, Heber's wife," thus emphasizing that this was done by a woman. She took the wooden tent peg, her chosen instrument for the task, and gripped the hammer securely in her hand. According to G. F. Moore, "among the Bedouins pitching the tent is women's business, and so no doubt it was in ancient times; the mallet and pin were accustomed implements, and ready at hand."[26] Silently Jael approached the place where Sisera lay, and with firm hand and unerring strokes she drove the peg into his temple and through his head into the tent floor. Sisera writhed in pain and died almost instantly. Jael then went out of the tent, and just at that moment Barak arrived in pursuit of the enemy leader. When Barak had discovered that Sisera was no longer with his troops, he apparently left the pursuit to others so that he could search for and apprehend him. It was to Barak's credit that Deborah's prediction that "the honor will not be yours" (v. 9) did not cause his zeal to slacken. His zeal in fact carried him right to Jael's

---

[26]*Judges*, p. 124.

tent, but there he beheld the fulfillment of the prophetic words: "the
LORD will hand Sisera over to a woman" (v. 9).

4:23–24 *On that day God subdued Jabin, the Canaanite king, before the
Israelites.* [24] *And the hand of the Israelites grew stronger and stronger against
Jabin, the Canaanite king, until they destroyed him.*

Jabin's hour of doom had finally struck. His army and his general had
been annihilated. The Lord had humiliated him and turned the
Israelites' tyrant into their lackey.[27] He resisted for as long as he could,
but Israel increasingly gained the upper hand. Finally, nothing was left
of Jabin and his might, and the land again could enjoy a period of peace
(5:31).

2. DEBORAH'S SONG OF TRIUMPH (5:1–31)

Following the historical account of Israel's victory over the Canaanites in chapter 4, chapter 5 celebrates this same victory in the song of
Deborah. The two chapters are relatively independent of each other.
Chapter 5 is more ancient, for Deborah's song was composed when the
impact of the victory was still fresh in her mind (see v. 1). The author
of chapter 4 no doubt knew the song; but numerous details show that he
also consulted other sources, and he in fact did not even include all the
material from chapter 5 in his account. The chapters are therefore
complementary; and, as my commentary will demonstrate, there is no
inconsistency between them.

In examining the relation between these two chapters, we must keep
in mind that the former is written in prose and the latter in poetry. In
chapter 4 we have the words of an historian, while in chapter 5
Deborah, driven by the Spirit, presents her poetic and prophetic vision
of the marvelous things that had just happened in Israel. Although
verse 1 says that Barak sang this song along with Deborah, we should
not infer that he composed part of it. That would detract from the unity
of the song, which was a spontaneous outpouring of the heart. Verse 7
explicitly identifies Deborah as the author; and both the feminine
singular form of the Hebrew verb for "sang" in verse 1 and the use of

---

[27] It probably is not accidental that Jabin was given the title "king of Canaan" (or
"Canaanite king") three times in this chapter. The name "Canaan" comes from the
same stem as the verb that is translated "subdue, lay low." The Hebrew text thus
contains a play on words that could be translated "God laid Jabin low, the king of
Lowland."

the first person singular pronoun in verses 3, 9, 13, and 21 also indicate a single author. Verses 12 and 15 give us no reason to doubt an authorship by Deborah.

The song of triumph by this Israelite prophetess belongs among the masterpieces of world literature. It has been a source of perpetual fascination because of its pure simplicity, its extremely vivid imagery, its powerful yet subtle expression, and its high emotion and blazing enthusiasm. The whole of this poem is life and movement, and Deborah poured her entire soul into writing it. In B. Wielenga's words, "It is the effusion of a heart that glows with amazement and leaps with enthusiasm, deeply moved with gratitude to God. It is the product of a lucid mind that perceives God's work in history, but also of an artistic soul with a mastery of bold and novel images, original and musical vocabulary, and a personal sense of rhythm."[28] But its very authenticity, vibrancy, and simplicity make it the common property of the ages. It was not Deborah alone who was singing this song; the liberated people of God were speaking through her mouth. The spiritual background and significance of the sober facts recorded in chapter 4 only become clear through this song. For Deborah shows us that even in the relatively insignificant and often barbarous minor wars of Judges, what was really at stake were spiritual values and realities: the preservation of God's people, the triumph of His cause, and the coming of His kingdom. Deborah, therefore, just like Moses on the bank of the Red Sea (Exod. 15), was already singing her song of triumph for the church of the New Testament (see Rev. 15:2–4).

The song of Deborah cannot be divided according to a definite scheme into distinct strophes of similar length. Its overall rhythm is determined not by some artistic device but by its thought content. Three main sections can be distinguished within it. The first (vv. 2–11) is a hymn in honor of the Lord, who remembered His covenant and brought about a splendid reversal of Israel's fortunes. The second (vv. 12–22) depicts the mighty struggle of the faithful in Israel, who with God's help are enabled to win a total victory over the enemy. The third section (vv. 23–31), which forms an epilogue, celebrates the ignominious end of the enemy commander as a cause of bitter disenchantment in his home but a source of glad hope for all who love God.

---

[28] *De Bijbel als boek van schoonheid,* 2nd ed., p. 245.

NOTE

The numerous obscurities in the Hebrew text of Judges 5 have given rise to many small differences among the various translations of the song of Deborah. At some points Goslinga's translation diverges from the NIV and corresponds more closely to the RSV and the NASB. Similar differences can in fact be found among all the English versions. To do justice to Goslinga's commentary on Judges 5, it therefore seemed advisable to depart from our normal procedure in the *Bible Student's Commentary* of using the NIV text. Instead, a close English translation of the author's Dutch translation of the song of Deborah has been substituted in the verse-by-verse commentary. For the reader's convenience, however, the NIV text has been added in its entirety at the outset, using Goslinga's division into three strophes—TRANS.

5:1–31 *On that day Deborah and Barak son of Abinoam sang this song:*

> ² *"When the princes in Israel take the lead,*
> *when the people willingly offer themselves—*
> *praise the LORD!*

> ³ *"Hear this, you kings! Listen, you rulers!*
> *I will sing to the LORD, I will sing;*
> *I will make music to the LORD, the God of Israel.*

> ⁴ *"O LORD, when you went out from Seir,*
> *when you marched from the land of Edom,*
> *the earth shook, the heavens poured,*
> *the clouds poured down water.*
> ⁵ *The mountains quaked before the LORD, the One of Sinai,*
> *before the LORD, the God of Israel.*

> ⁶ *"In the days of Shamgar son of Anath,*
> *in the days of Jael, the roads were abandoned;*
> *travelers took to winding paths.*
> ⁷ *Village life in Israel ceased,*
> *ceased until I, Deborah, arose,*
> *arose a mother in Israel.*
> ⁸ *When they chose new gods,*
> *war came to the city gates,*
> *and not a shield or spear was seen*
> *among forty thousand in Israel.*
> ⁹ *My heart is with Israel's princes,*
> *with the willing volunteers among the people.*
> *Praise the LORD!*

> ¹⁰ *"You who ride on white donkeys,*
> *sitting on your saddle blankets,*
> *and you who walk along the road,*

consider ¹¹*the voice of the singers at the watering places.*
They recite the righteous acts of the LORD,
the righteous acts of his warriors in Israel.

Then the people of the LORD
went down to the city gates.
¹²*'Wake up, wake up, Deborah!*
Wake up, wake up, break out in song!
Arise, O Barak!
Take captive your captives, O son of Abinoam.'

¹³*"Then the men who were left*
came down to the nobles;
the people of the LORD
came to me with the mighty.
¹⁴*Some came from Ephraim, whose roots were in Amalek;*
Benjamin was with the people who followed you.
From Makir captains came down,
from Zebulun those who bear a commander's staff.
¹⁵*The princes of Issachar were with Deborah;*
yes, Issachar was with Barak,
rushing after him into the valley.
In the districts of Reuben
there was much searching of heart.
¹⁶*Why did you stay among the campfires*
to hear the whistling for the flocks?
In the districts of Reuben
there was much searching of heart.
¹⁷*Gilead stayed beyond the Jordan.*
And Dan, why did he linger by the ships?
Asher remained on the coast
and stayed in his coves.
¹⁸*The people of Zebulun risked their very lives;*
so did Naphtali on the heights of the field.

¹⁹*"Kings came, they fought;*
the kings of Canaan fought
at Taanach by the waters of Megiddo,
but they carried off no silver, no plunder.
²⁰*From the heavens the stars fought,*
from their courses they fought against Sisera.
²¹*The river Kishon swept them away,*
the age-old river, the river Kishon.
March on, my soul; be strong!
²²*Then thundered the horses' hoofs—*
galloping, galloping go his mighty steeds.

²³*'Curse Meroz,' said the angel of the* LORD.
  'Curse its people bitterly,
  because they did not come to help the LORD,
    to help the LORD *against the mighty.'*
²⁴*"Most blessed of women be Jael,*
  the wife of Heber the Kenite,
  most blessed of tent-dwelling women.
²⁵*He asked for water, and she gave him milk;*
  in a bowl fit for nobles she brought him curdled milk.
²⁶*Her hand reached for the tent peg,*
  her right hand for the workman's hammer.
 She struck Sisera, she crushed his head,
  she shattered and pierced his temple.
²⁷*At her feet he sank,*
  he fell; there he lay.
 At her feet he sank, he fell;
  where he sank, there he fell—dead.

²⁸*"Through the window peered Sisera's mother;*
  behind the lattice she cried out,
 'Why is his chariot so long in coming?
  Why is the clatter of his chariots delayed?'
²⁹*The wisest of her ladies answer her;*
  indeed, she keeps saying to herself,
³⁰*'Are they not finding and dividing the spoils:*
  a girl or two for each man,
  colorful garments as plunder for Sisera,
  colorful garments embroidered,
  highly embroidered garments for my neck—
 all this as plunder?'

³¹*"So may all your enemies perish, O* LORD!
  But may they who love you be like the sun
  when it rises in its strength."

Then the land had peace forty years.

5:1 *On that day Deborah sang this song with Barak the son of Abinoam:*

The "day" spoken of here is not that of Jabin's destruction (4:24) but rather the day of Sisera's downfall referred to in verse 22. It is possible that Deborah sang this song, not on that very day, but at a public festival of thanksgiving held shortly thereafter. First, what was left of the enemy had to be destroyed, and Israel's army had to reassemble. Barak took part in this song, perhaps by chiming in with Deborah and repeating her words at certain points: e.g., at the end of verses 9 and 11 and in verses 22 and 31.

5:2–3

> *"That the leaders*[29] *took the lead in Israel,*
> *that the people willingly offered themselves,*
> *praise the LORD!*
> ³*Hear, you kings! Listen, you rulers!*
> *I, I will sing to the LORD,*
> *sing praises to the LORD, the God of Israel!*

These first two verses are introductory in character and form the overture to Deborah's song. Verse 2 is a general call to praise the Lord. It was because of Him that the local leaders or princes (this applies even to Barak) did not shirk their duty to attack the enemy but instead marched ahead of their men in full awareness of their responsibility (v. 9). This action of Israel's leaders was decisive, since good leadership produces good followers. The common people also proved that they were willing and ready. They spontaneously answered the call to battle and, with weapons in hand, rallied behind their leaders (see 4:10). This was no reckless adventure undertaken in a spirit of mad frenzy. On its deepest level it was rather an act of faith that came from the Lord. Because of this Deborah's song of praise to the God of Israel was also meant for the kings and rulers of the heathen. When it was fully alive to its prophetic mission, the nation of Israel had a message for the entire world (see Ps. 2:10).

After directing her call to others in verse 2, Deborah herself set the example in verse 3. She who had been an eyewitness to God's great deeds had no choice but to tell of them. Indeed, she must sing of them to His glory.

5:4–5

> *"LORD, when you went out from Seir,*
> *when you marched forth from the field of Edom,*
> *the earth shook, the heavens poured,*
> *the clouds poured down water.*
> ⁵*The mountains quaked before the LORD,*

---

[29] At Numbers 6:5 and Ezekiel 44:20, the singular form of this Hebrew noun refers to an untrimmed head of hair. Here and in Deuteronomy 32:42, the plural must be a reference to persons distinguished by such uncut hair, i.e., leaders or princes (see König, *Hebraisches und Aramaisches Wörterbuch*). The related verb is therefore translated "took the lead."

> *even Sinai before the* LORD, *the God of Israel.*

Deborah begins to tell of God's glory by depicting His majestic approach as He came to deliver His people. Here she used words and names that recalled Yahweh's coming to His people in the desert by Mount Sinai. At that time Israel proceeded toward Sinai from Egypt, i.e., from the west; and God, as it were, came to meet them from the east, from Edom. The meeting itself took place at Mount Sinai. Israelite singers later would constantly call to memory the stupendous revelation described in Exodus 19 and 20, where the Lord entered into a covenant with His people (e.g., Deut. 33:2; Ps. 68:7–8; Hab. 3:3). For them this was not merely an event from the past but rather the firm historical foundation for the special bond between Yahweh and Israel that had continued into the present and held the promise that they would be delivered many times in the future. This also was why Deborah turned her mind back to Sinai.

Deborah did not exactly give a description of the Lord's coming to Sinai.[30] Instead, she named this mountain, as well as Seir and Edom, to evoke the thought that He had come from there to His people's aid. In this way she drew a connection between the Lord's revelation in the desert of Sinai and the nation's recent deliverance from the hand of Sisera. What she meant to say was that the God who had just come to liberate her people was the very same God who came to the Israelites at Sinai and took them under His protection. His most recent coming was merely an extension of His coming back then. The way Deborah described this new coming—especially her mention of heavy storms—is probably related to the special, miraculous means that the Lord used to help Israel (see in vv. 20–21).[31]

In describing how God came to Israel, the prophetess turned in reverence to the Lord Himself. He "went out" as a warrior and "marched forth" as a king (cf. Hab. 3:12–13). This not only made the

---

[30] Exodus 19 and 20, for example, say nothing about the heavy rains that Deborah spoke of in verse 4. This may be a minor difference, but it is significant.

[31] This seems more plausible than to think that verses 4–5 give a description of the Lord's coming to Israel in the desert. The topic of Deborah's hymn is the victory over Sisera, and we have to assume that in these verses she was carrying out her resolution in verse 3 to sing praise to the Lord. Verses 4–5 otherwise would not fit with the whole. Deborah indeed had in view the latest manifestation of God's power to deliver. She depicted this as emanating from the Sinai peninsula because its source lay in the fundamental revelation that God gave of Himself when He delivered Israel from Egypt and established a covenant with them at Sinai.

earth shake; it also, as it were, melted the heavens away and caused the clouds to burst. Seir is the name of the chief mountain range of Edom; but here, like "field of Edom," it refers simply to the land of Edom itself, whence the Lord had formerly come to meet His people (as Deborah poetically imagined this; see above). His approach caused even the immovably solid mountains to tremble; and Sinai, the mighty peak where the law was given, drew the poetess's special attention. Deborah's meaning in verses 4 and 5 can be summarized as follows: "Lord, when You went out to battle, even Your greatest creatures were so powerfully agitated that Your victory was assured in advance."

5:6

> *"In the days of Shamgar son of Anath,*
> *in the days of Jael, the roads were deserted,*
> *and those who had traveled by the high roads*
> *took to winding paths.*

In verses 6–8 the songstress depicts the sad condition that the Israelites had brought on themselves and their land during the time of oppression before she arose as judge. Curiously, she named this time after Shamgar and Jael.[32] She of course did not mean that these two were responsible for the situation that prevailed. On the contrary, she wished to honor them as persons who still left their mark during those dark days. This was clearly the case with Shamgar, since he was active as judge between the time of Ehud and Deborah (3:31).[33]

All we know of Jael from before the time of the battle at the Kishon River, however, is that she, as a Kenite, was not oppressed like the Israelites. The fact that Sisera imagined he would be safe with her (4:17) shows, rather, that she lived in peace with the Canaanites (although she may have secretly been well-disposed toward Israel).[34] In any case the present verse leads us to suppose not only that Jael sided with Israel in her heart but also that the disaffection from Jabin's rule in

---

[32] The Hebrew text clearly implies that the "days of Shamgar" and the "days of Jael" were the same. The meaning therefore cannot be "the time from Shamgar to Jael."

[33] For the date of Shamgar's work, see the Introduction, pp. 229ff. This verse strongly supports the view that the influence of a judge did not always affect the entire land (see pp. 206–7).

[34] Because of this some think that the Jael of verse 6 was either another person or an alternate name for Shamgar. The author certainly would not have left this unmentioned, however.

her immediate surroundings made her sympathies known. The meaning of this verse is clear. The roads were abandoned and lay in disuse. No one ventured on the main highways for fear of being robbed or killed. Those who had to travel and were accustomed to taking the high roads, e.g., merchants, chose to use winding detours and hidden, unbeaten paths where they could better escape detection. Trade and commerce all but came to a halt.

5:7

> Leaders were absent in Israel,
>   absent until I, Deborah, arose,
>   arose a mother in Israel.

Public life in Israel was governed by fear. There was a general lack of leaders, and a man like Shamgar in the south was a rare exception. Those who had the ability to lead did not have enough faith and courage to stand up against Jabin. This situation remained unchanged till Deborah's intervention brought about a turn for the better. In repeating the word "arose," the prophetess shows how moved she was at recalling her public assumption of leadership. Because of the position of women in that culture, this may have been an extremely trying experience. Nevertheless, the Lord had called her, and in obedience to His voice she became a "mother in Israel." This pregnant phrase means that she became a mother in regard to all the Israelites, a woman who gave her all to save her people, who took their needs to heart and identified with them, and who by her motherly devotion and vigorous leadership aroused her compatriots and infused them with a new spirit.

5:8

> When new gods were chosen,
>   then war came to the gates.
> Truly, not a shield or spear was seen
>   among forty thousand in Israel.

Deborah discloses the deeper reason why the Israelites had fallen to such a depth of humiliation and misery. Their own apostasy had given their enemy the power to oppress them. Since the people chose new gods (Deut. 32:16–17) and forsook Yahweh to bow before the idols of the pagan survivors, the Lord carried out His threat (2:3) and deprived them of their peaceful life. Their enemy devastated the land and appeared at their city gates, provoking such fright that no one had the courage to raise a shield or spear against them. These and other weapons were not entirely lacking (as in 1 Sam. 13:19–22), but no one dared to use them either for defense (shield) or for attack (spear). All courage was gone. The oppressed tribes easily could have sent forty thousand armed men against Sisera; but their betrayal of the Lord, the rightful God of Israel, had deprived them of their independence and crippled their moral strength.

5:9

> *My heart goes out to[35] the commanders of Israel,*
> *who willingly offered themselves among the people:*
> *praise the LORD!*

This remained Israel's situation till God Himself saw fit to bring about a favorable turn in their fortunes. Deborah makes a surprising transition to this turnabout in verses 9–11, which stand in splendid contrast to verses 6–8. There we beheld a nation, alienated from its God, that groaned under the enemy's yoke and hid impotently behind the walls of its cities. Here we hear the rejoicing of a people reconciled to God and, with the enemy expelled from the land, able to enjoy peace and prosperity.

Deborah's call to praise the Lord in verse 2, which could well be called the theme of her song, returns in somewhat altered form in verse 9. Almost poignantly she proclaimed that her heart went out to Israel's commanders. Words like these show us how much the poetess lived in her song and how personally involved she was in the events that it celebrates. As a mother in Israel, she lovingly remembered the men who gave themselves willingly to save the nation. As a prophetess she rejoiced that men could still be found who were ready to rise up for the honor of Israel's God and lead the people in battle against their enemies.

The commanders spoken of here are the same individuals that Deborah called "leaders" in verse 2. What there was said of the people in general, here is said of the commanders in particular, namely, that they willingly came forward and offered themselves. These individuals indeed deserved special mention; for they ran the greatest risks and had the hardest task, especially in the confused and abnormal circumstances that then prevailed (cf. Isa. 3:6–7). With commendable modesty, Deborah did not even speak of herself, even though she had

---

[35] The Hebrew literally reads "my heart to the commanders," i.e., "my heart is inclined to, belongs to," etc.

303

been God's instrument for creating the remarkable turnabout that lies between verse 8 and verse 9. Her call to praise the Lord is addressed not merely to the commanders but to the people in general.

5:10–11

"You who ride on white[36] donkeys,
*   you who sit on carpets,*
*   you who travel on the road—*
*   take note!*
[11] Far from the noise of the archers,[37]
*   at the watering places,*
there let them recite the righteous acts of the LORD,
*   the righteous acts of his leaders in Israel.*
Then the people of the LORD went down to the gates.

In verse 10 the prophetess addresses specific groups of persons with her call to consider carefully what the Lord had done. The words she used bring out the fact that peace, prosperity, and public security had basically returned to Israel after the victory over Sisera. The white donkeys spoken of were rare and formed a symbol of affluence. Thus Deborah was speaking to distinguished persons and members of the ruling class (see 10:4; 12:14). The next phrase is aimed at those who sit restfully at home on a blanket or carpet. They are not necessarily the rich, for Deborah's emphasis here falls on the privilege to sit or lie down undisturbed. Finally, she addressed those who traveled the roads, i.e., merchants, who could move about unmolested and no longer had to take side paths. All these, who now could enjoy the fruits of victory and the benefits of peace, were not to accept those gifts thoughtlessly. Rather, they were to consider them carefully, take them to heart, and speak of them (the Hebrew verb literally means "consider, ponder," but it does not exclude the meaning "tell of"; cf. RSV).

The same was to be done by the fourth group that Deborah spoke of.

---

[36] This Hebrew term, which is used here only in the Old Testament, denotes the light color of the Arabian ass: according to some, silvery gray, but more likely white.

[37] This translation gives a plausible solution to the problems in verse 11a. The rabbis' translation "archers" (the Hebrew term is extremely rare) is preferable to the other possibilities and fits best with the preposition *min* at the beginning of the verse. In Genesis 27:39, Numbers 15:24, and Proverbs 20:3, this preposition means "far from." On this interpretation the verse begins by describing the location of the watering places negatively: they are "far from the noise of the archers." D. Hoek takes a similar view in *Het boek der Richteren*, pp. 102, 105.

Although they are not addressed directly in verse 11, she made an oblique reference to the shepherds encamped with their flocks by the watering places in Israel's meadows. When Sisera's plundering bands threatened the entire land, these shepherds had to leave their villages (v. 7). Now, however, they were able to carry on their tranquil labor far from (i.e., without being disturbed or terrorized by) the "noise of the archers," a general reference to all the tumult of war. This clamor had been silenced, and the herdsmen also could enjoy the blessings of the deliverance God had granted. But this meant that they also would have to sing of the righteous acts of the Lord, acts by which He upheld His rights, confirmed His covenant, and executed judgment on His enemies. Because the Lord used men to do this and destroyed the Canaanites by means of Israel's sword, these righteous acts could also be ascribed to those who served Him by leading Barak's army. These men gave themselves for His cause and fought the "wars of the LORD" (Num. 21:14). The Lord's deeds had been performed in the sight of Israel, and they therefore gave the whole nation reason to praise God.

In the end of verse 11 Deborah tells how she saw the delivered people, who could again can be called "people of the LORD," return to their city gates. They entered the cities, not to take shelter behind the walls, but to resume normal life. Presumably, she said that they "went down" because so many of them had been hiding in the hills and once again could make their homes in the cities of the plain. This had not yet happened when Deborah sang her song, but she presented it as the direct result of the Lord's righteous acts. The description of the total change in Israel's life concludes with this vivid stroke.

5:12

> "Awake, awake, Deborah!
>   Awake, awake, sing a song!
>   Arise, Barak! Lead away your captives,
>   son of Abinoam!

Next, Deborah begins to describe the great battle from which the Israelites emerged victorious . One thing she focused on was the people's morale, or lack of it, in this war for their national freedom. The different responses of the various tribes gave her the opportunity to praise and to find fault. And she brought out with particular clarity how the Lord's special assistance enabled the Israelites to inflict a crushing defeat on their foes (vv. 12–22).

To pay just tribute to this glowing episode from Israel's history and bring the battle back to life in her poem—in Herder's words, "to fight the mighty battle over again"[38] —Deborah aroused herself to song four times over. Her subject seems too overwhelming and her language too weak. It would take a supreme effort of mind and spirit to compose her song and give voice to the great things God had done. The prophetess's call "awake, awake" is on its deepest level "a cry for help from the Spirit of the Lord" (cf. Pss. 57:8; 108:1–2).[39]

In verse 12b Deborah was casting her thoughts back to the time *before* the decisive battle, not after it.[40] This therefore begins the song of triumph in a narrow sense, where Deborah herself sang of the "righteous acts of the LORD" (v. 11). Her words "Arise, Barak" refer not to the moment of attack in 4:14 but to 4:6, for she was bringing out the fact that the call to battle went from her to Barak. "Lead away your captives" is actually a promise. If Barak was obedient, he would soon be in a position to take captive his foes (see 4:7). This does not mean, however, that he was not permitted to kill them.

5:13–15a

  "Then came down[41] the remnant[42] of the nobles,
    the people[43] of the LORD came down[41] with me as heroes:
  [14]from Ephraim, those whose root was in Amalek,
    following you, O Benjamin, with your hosts;
  from Makir commanders came down,
    from Zebulun, those who marched off under the recruiter's staff;[44]

---

[38]Quoted in Strack and Zöckler's *Kommentar,* p. 241.

[39]H. Hoekstra, *Het lied van Debora* (Utrecht), p. 66.

[40]This must be the case, since the following description of the advancing Israelite soldiers likewise refers to the time before the battle. The words "lead away your captives" thus do not mean "carry off those whom you have already captured" but, more generally, "take captive your enemies."

[41]A small change in the traditional vocalization, accepted by most commentators, gives the perfect form *yārad* ("came down") twice in verse 13.

[42]The Hebrew term *śārîd* denotes the survivors of a battle, but in Isaiah 1:9 it seems to have the more general meaning "remnant, remainder." This is perhaps also the meaning here, assuming that the text is reliable. It then would refer to those who escaped Jabin's oppression. According to Keil, verse 13a indicates that the number of nobles, relatively speaking, had become very small.

[43]The Hebrew accents place the word "people" with verse 13a (cf. KJV). I have followed most commentators in joining it to 13b, however (the NIV does the same— TRANS.), since it does not fit with the syntax of 13a and 13b would otherwise lack an appropriate subject. Making "the LORD" into the subject would completely break the train of thought.

[44]These words are usually translated "those who bear the commander's staff" (cf. NIV). This ignores the preposition *be* before "staff," however, and gives the Hebrew verb a meaning that it has nowhere else.

> ¹⁵*also princes*⁴⁵ *in Issachar, together with Deborah.*
> *And like lightning*⁴⁶ *was Barak;*
> *into the valley they rushed*⁴⁷ *at his heels.*

Deborah's trumpet signal to Barak set all Israel in motion. The thrill of joy that this sent through the prophetess can be seen not only in verses 2 and 9 but, above all, in her broad description of the advance of the Israelite troops and their commanders. Her frequent use of the verb "came down" (elsewhere the word is often "advanced [to battle]") must mean that the people had largely retreated into the hill country and now had to descend to the battlefield in the valley of the Kishon. One might think that it refers to the descent from Mount Tabor at the moment of attack (4:14), but Tabor is not mentioned here. Furthermore, since the tribes spoken of here are contrasted with those who did not join the fighting, it is unlikely that a particular moment of the battle was being spoken of.⁴⁸ Verses 13–15a are nothing more than a detailed account of how the people and their leaders willingly offered themselves for Israel's freedom (cf. vv. 2, 9).

Regrettably, the text of these verses is obscure at certain points, and changes in the traditional vocalization do not always provide a solution. The terse, poetic style only increases the difficulties. In verse 13a Deborah says that at the time she summoned Barak (v. 12), the nobles came down; and in 13b she says the same of the people (i.e., the

⁴⁵The Hebrew text is problematic here. It literally has "my princes"; but since Deborah was not from the tribe of Issachar, I have followed the ancient versions and almost all modern commentators in reading simply "princes" (cf. NIV).

⁴⁶After the name "Deborah" the Hebrew text literally reads "and Issachar thus Barak." It is impossible to make sense of these words, even if, as is often done, one interprets them to mean "and as was Issachar, so was Barak" (cf. NASB). Some have therefore proposed that the name Barak really refers to his tribe Naphtali, but this is rather far-fetched. In that case the name "Naphtali" would have been added. We are forced to address the text-critical question of whether the name "Issachar" originally stood in the second line of verse 15. The Septuagint reads "and Barak thus Barak." On this basis we can assume that the Hebrew term *bārāq* occurred twice in the original text. Since this term means "lightning," its first occurrence can be understood as the common noun and its second as the proper name of Israel's general. Barak, then, would be compared to a flash of lightning. On this conjecture the Hebrew text originally read *ûḇārāq kēn bārāq*. The first "Barak" later could have been replaced in some manuscripts by the "Issachar" from the previous line because of a copyist's slip.

⁴⁷The Hebrew verb literally means "were forcibly sent, driven," which fits very well with the image of lightning.

⁴⁸In verse 15, in contrast, the text compels us to think of the descent from Mount Tabor. See the comments on that verse.

soldiers or army) of the Lord, whom she described as an army of "heroes." She added that they came "with me" (lit., "for me") to show that they did this in obedience to her word and went to battle in her company (for Deborah went with the army, cf. v. 15; 4:9–10).

In verse 14 Deborah applied her words of praise for the nobles and the people in general to the various tribes in particular. The sequence in which these tribes are listed has no special significance. From Ephraim came those who were rooted, i.e., who had settled, in the hill country of the Amalekites southwest of Shechem (cf. 12:15). They and the troops from the neighboring tribe of Benjamin formed a single division, with the Benjamites (who had many slingshot artists, 20:16) in the vanguard. Makir, the half-tribe of Manasseh living west of the Jordan and north of Ephraim,[49] was noted for its able captains. Zebulun is said to have marched off under (lit., "by") the recruiter's staff, probably because it, like Naphtali, had to field a specific number of soldiers (4:6).[50] These would have been enlisted and organized by a particular officer (cf. 2 Kings 25:19; Jer. 52:25) who then led them off under his staff (i.e., command).

Issachar, a tribe that had suffered especially hard under Jabin's tyranny, is mentioned last among the tribes that flocked to the battle. This tribe, too, had no lack of leaders or princes, but the words in verse 15a, of course, apply also to the common soldiers. The assumed verb in the first line of this verse is "came down" from the previous verse. The words "together with Deborah" apply also to the tribes mentioned in verse 14 and correspond to "with me" in verse 13. If the Septuagint reading in the second line of verse 15 is correct, Deborah then turned her attention to Israel's general, who made a worthy showing of himself in the battle. To describe Barak in his triumphant onslaught she used the image of lightning, a symbol that is appropriate both because of its swift and inescapable stroke and because of its deadly power. It would have been most natural to compare Barak to a flashing thunderbolt (his very name in fact means "lightning") if the victory was indeed caused by a severe storm that God sent to frighten the enemy (see under v. 20). Inflamed by his example, Barak's men swiftly descended on Sisera's army from the heights of Mount Tabor (4:14–15).

---

[49] The Manassites east of the Jordan were also descended from Makir (Josh. 13:31), but this half of the tribe is designated by the name "Gilead" in verse 17.

[50] See Bachmann, *Das Buch der Richter,* p. 390.

5:15b-16

> *In the divisions of Reuben*
> *there were great resolves*[51] *of heart.*
> [16]*Why did you stay sitting among the cattle stalls,*
> *listening to the shepherds' piping?*[52]
> *Among the divisions of Reuben*
> *there were great searchings*[51] *of heart!*

The poetess next turns her mind to the tribes that shrank from the battle, repudiating the unity of the nation and violating its solidarity. She first upbraided the Transjordan tribes, which subsisted largely by cattle-breeding (Num. 32). Her word to Reuben was one of biting sarcasm. The divisions or clans of Reuben across the Jordan had spoken much about Deborah and Barak's call to arms, but they never got around to acting. Sitting among the cattle stalls,[53] they had mused and deliberated for so long that the time for them to help passed them by. Their great "resolves" turned into great "searchings"; but the only result was that they continued to be diverted by the shepherd's flute, a sound they preferred to the war trumpet.

5:17

> *Gilead stayed beyond the Jordan;*
> *and Dan, why did he linger by the ships?*
> *Asher sat on the coast of the great sea*
> *and stayed by his landings.*

Gilead also remained beyond the Jordan and was not to be seen at the battlefield. The name Gilead, who was the grandson of Manasseh, refers first of all to the eastern half of this tribe. It undoubtedly also includes the Gadites, however; for they had settled between Reuben and eastern Manasseh and possessed part of the region named Gilead (see Josh. 13:25, 31). Sisera had not posed a direct threat to this area, but this gave the Gileadites no excuse for leaving their brothers in the

---

[51]"Resolves" and "searchings" translate two different Hebrew words that are almost homonymic. This wordplay, which berates the Reubenites for their failure to turn intentions into deeds, is lost in translation.

[52]The Hebrew literally means "whistling of the flocks." The verb cannot denote the lowing or bleating of animals, however; so the reference must be to the sound of shepherds' flutes.

[53]The dual form of the Hebrew noun may be significant. Some have proposed that these were stalls arranged in two parallel rows, or stalls that had two separate sections; cf. NIV margin, "saddlebags."

lurch. Dan and Asher also neglected their sacred fraternal duties, either out of laziness or because they were too preoccupied with their selfish material interests. The Danites were reproached for lingering by the ships. This does not mean that they themselves were seafarers but probably that they traded with Phoenician navigators at Joppa (see Josh. 19:46), where their territory touched the coast.[54]

The Asherites remained fishing by the seacoast (the Hebrew literally reads "coast of the seas," i.e., the Great or Mediterranean Sea), unwilling to leave their homes by the landings (not port towns, but coves or bights on the coast). Their apathy was all the more reprehensible because their territory lay in the north and bordered on the tribes that had been oppressed the most: Naphtali, Zebulun, and Issachar (Josh. 19:24–31). The tribes that Deborah denounced had weakly succumbed to a spirit of indolence and leisure, expedience and self-interest, that partly alienated them from their fellow Israelites. Remarkably, Jacob's words to Issachar in his parting address are here applied to Reuben (v. 16), while what there was said of Zebulun here is said of Dan and Asher (see Gen. 49:13–15).[55]

5:18

> *Zebulun is a people who risked their lives unto death,*
> *Naphtali too, on the heights of the field.*

Zebulun, Naphtali, and Issachar as well showed considerably more concern for their nation's plight than could have been expected from Jacob's predictions (see Gen. 49:13, 14–15, 21). "Concern" is actually too weak a word, particularly for the first two tribes, who were especially worthy of Deborah's praise. The people of both Zebulun and Naphtali risked (the basic meaning of the Hebrew verb is "despise, disdain") their lives unto death, placing them in jeopardy for the sake of Israel's freedom. In this, regard the two tribes were equally deserving.

The phrase "on the heights of the field" actually applies to both

---

[54]This seems to indicate that the Danites had not been completely driven from their territory along the coast (1:34), though the Hebrew verb translated "linger" in verse 17, which literally means "stay as an alien," would show that they had a subordinate position. But since the Danites are here mentioned in the context of the northern tribes (Asher, Zebulun, Naphtali), it is also possible that Deborah was speaking of their settlement in the north (ch. 18).

[55]This is clearer in the other English versions than in the NIV. See the NIV marginal note in Genesis 49:14—TRANS.

tribes as well and can be understood in two different ways. It cannot refer to the battlefield itself, since this lay in a valley. We could, however, take it as a reference to the hill country where Zebulun and Naphtali lived, so that verse 18 would be speaking of the willing self-abandon with which they left their territories for the battle. More likely the phrase indicates the slopes of Mount Tabor from which they pounced on the enemy, heedless of their own lives. This latter interpretation nicely complements and in a sense returns to the thought of verse 15a. What there was said of Barak's troops in general here is applied in particular to the two tribes that played the main role in the assault. After her digression in verses 15b–17, Deborah thus would be returning to the very moment of the fierce and glorious onslaught.

The special tribute paid to Zebulun and Naphtali in this verse may imply that their forces constituted the main body of Barak's army. The other tribes probably only contributed relatively small contingents of troops. This might have a bearing on the fact that chapter 4 speaks solely of Zebulun and Naphtali (see footnote 19, p. 290). Chapters 4 and 5 cannot be called totally inconsistent, for the former chapter does not expressly deny the presence of troops from the other tribes. It is remarkable that Judah and Simeon (which lived within Judah's territory, Josh. 19:1, 9) are not even mentioned. If they did not offer their help, we should have expected that Deborah would rebuke them along with the others. The best explanation is that these two tribes were themselves threatened at that moment (perhaps by the Philistines, see pp. 228, 234–35) and were not in a position to help. Thus they could not have been accused of laziness or cowardice. There is no certainty about this; but we at least can assume that Deborah never summoned Judah and Simeon to the battle, since she otherwise would surely have censured them for their absence.

5:19

> "The kings came, they fought;
>   then fought the kings of Canaan
> at Taanach, by the waters of Megiddo;
>   they took no spoils[56] of silver.

Deborah now proceeds to a broad description of the battle itself and its outcome. These next few verses quiver with all the suspense of the

---

[56] The Hebrew term usually refers to unjust gain, but it also can simply mean "piece." Thus another possible translation is "they took not a piece of silver."

battle, in which men and horses, stars and rivers, heaven and earth took part. The poetess's style and vocabulary become so personal (especially in v. 21) that we cannot always be certain about her meaning. The scene of the battle is the Valley of Jezreel. This is traversed from east to west by the Kishon River, which in the northwest runs along the foot of Mount Carmel into the plain of Acco and empties into the Mediterranean Sea. Near to where the Kishon reaches Mount Carmel lay Harosheth Haggoyim, Sisera's base and the place from where the kings marched out to battle (4:13).

The kings that verse 19 speaks of were allies of Jabin (there was a similar coalition during the time of Joshua; see Josh. 11:1–5). Chapter 4 does not explicitly mention them, but it also says nothing that contradicts the existence of such an alliance. Sisera himself may have ruled a city-state, since verse 28 seems to be speaking of a royal residence (see also the comments in 10:11–12). We should not infer from this verse (nor from Ps. 83:9–10) that Jabin took part in the battle; chapter 4 clearly indicates that he was absent (e.g., vv. 7, 13, 24). The towns of Taanach and Megiddo both lay south of the Kishon River, and "waters of Megiddo" must be a reference to the Kishon itself along with its tributaries.

Since Mount Tabor lay northeast of the Valley of Jezreel, the battle probably unfolded as follows. Sisera and his army marched past Taanach and Megiddo and proceeded northward over the Kishon in the direction of Mount Tabor, leaving behind a contingent of men to occupy the crossing of the river. At the foot of Mount Tabor the advance troops were thrown into confusion and forced to retreat before Barak's onslaught.[57] Sisera's army tried to withdraw to their camp by recrossing the Kishon, but most of them were swept away by the turbulence of the swollen waters (v. 21). This took place across from Taanach and Megiddo.[58] Those who were left then fled, perhaps along both banks of the river, in the direction of Harosheth Haggoyim (4:16). Verse 19 does not mention these later events, but the fact that the Canaanite kings were defeated is already clear from the mocking words "they carried off no silver, no plunder"; i.e., instead of taking spoils,

---

[57] This must have happened near Endor, south of Mount Tabor (Ps. 83:10).

[58] It is well possible that the fleeing army was attacked near Taanach by the troops arriving from Benjamin, Ephraim, and Manasseh (and thus from the south), since it seems that these were not present on Mount Tabor (cf. 4:10, 14). See E. Meier's comments in Bachmann, *Das Buch der Richter,* p. 423. A detailed description of the battlefield including photographs and maps can be found in Garstang, *Joshua, Judges,* pp. 92–95, 296–302.

they lost the battle. The Israelite soldiers, of course, did not take treasures to the battle, but a Canaanite victory doubtless would have been followed by a raid for plunder (see v. 30).

5:20

> From the heavens the stars fought,
>   from their courses they fought against Sisera.

The kings' defeat was not the work of Barak and his men, however. Deborah in fact says nothing about Israel's army here. The Canaanites' undoing was rather a power that came from above. Verse 20 can be interpreted in two different ways. First, the "fighting of the stars" can be regarded as a poetic embellishment of the thought that it was the Lord Himself who fought against Sisera. It is also possible, however, that some natural phenomenon in the air up above frightened the enemy. The latter choice seems preferable to me. The first remains a possibility, since the Lord certainly did come down to help Israel. But verse 20 seems to imply that He did so by means of elements and forces in the atmosphere above. This was not necessarily an actual miracle. More likely an exceptionally severe thunderstorm, perhaps accompanied by hailstones (see Josh. 10:11), threw the enemy into a panic and also caused the Kishon to overflow its banks. Such a picture does not conflict with the poetic character of verse 20, for I am certainly not taking the verse literally (as if the stars themselves could have fought against Sisera like animate beings). The poetry of the verse lies in the fact that Deborah imagined the forces from above as a direct participation of the stars in the battle on Israel's side. Both the help from below (v. 21) and the help from above took on concrete form in her mind.

5:21

> The river Kishon swept them away,
>   the militant river, the river Kishon.
> March on, O my soul, with strength!

The Kishon is no mighty river. According to Garstang, only in the area of Harosheth Haggoyim was it wide and deep enough to be considered dangerous.[59] Nevertheless, in the rainy season the water could rise high enough to make it unfordable. Because of the special circumstances that accompanied the battle, the water level rose so

---

[59] *Joshua, Judges,* pp. 296f.

abnormally high and the current became so swift and torrential that the Canaanites who fled into the valley were swept away by its force. The verse does not mean that the Kishon merely carried off the corpses of the soldiers who had already been slain. On the contrary, the river itself destroyed them and pulled them to a watery grave.

The Hebrew term *q°dûmîm* in the second line of this verse is very likely an epithet for the Kishon that describes the fatal consequences it had for Israel's enemy. Unfortunately, we cannot be sure about its meaning. The term occurs nowhere else but seems to be related to a stem meaning "be before" or "meet." On this basis it is usually interpreted to mean either "antiquity" (as in the NIV, "age-old"—TRANS.) or "(hostile) meeting, attack" (hence Goslinga's "the militant river"—TRANS.). The latter choice makes better sense in this context (see, e.g., E. König, *Hebraisches und Aramaisches Wörterbuch*), since the Kishon is poetically imagined as the assailant or adversary of the Canaanites (cf. NEB—TRANS.). Possibly, this was a previous nickname for the river that Deborah merely took over because it was so appropriate to the occasion. Since the word is in the plural, a literal translation would be "river of attacks."

The third line of verse 21 presents a new problem. The translation I have given (which corresponds to the NIV —TRANS.) makes good sense in itself and does not do violence to the Hebrew text, but Deborah's emotional outburst seems out of place here. The description of the battle has not yet ended, and a new section of the poem has not begun (as, e.g., in v. 12). Other translations have therefore been offered, but these usually are either quite far-fetched,[60] or they are based on groundless emendations of the text. However one chooses to render the Hebrew, clearly Deborah was here addressing herself ("my soul"). We are therefore confronted, whether we like it or not, by a lyrical interruption of the portrayal of the battle in verses 19–22. Thus it is best to accept the obvious meaning of the Hebrew words. Deborah's challenge to herself to proceed with strength may seem superfluous to us, but it forms further proof of how the poetess's entire soul *lived* in her song and of how the stirring power of her subject matter almost overwhelmed her. The strong emotion she felt is already evident from her repetition of the name "Kishon"; so it was not without reason that she called to her soul, "Faint not!"

---

[60] This applies to the King James translation (also suggested by Bachmann): "O my soul, thou hast trodden down strength." The sense is unnatural, and the translation is not completely accurate.

5:22

> *Then were the horses' hoofs shattered*[61]
> *from the driving, the driving of his valiant ones.*

The poetess immediately turned her gaze back to the battlefield. Her last vision of the enemy was one of an army in frenzied flight. Those who had not been swallowed up by the Kishon mounted their chariots in an attempt to escape this valley of ruin. Even this did not avail, however; for the drivers pushed their steeds so relentlessly that their hoofs were shattered, either from pounding against the hard ground or because their feet collided with one another. The repetition of the word "driving" (or "galloping," NIV —TRANS.) nicely evokes the frenzy of the flight (the Hebrew term might even be considered onomatopoeic). The possessive pronoun "his" refers either to Sisera (v. 20) or to the enemy in general.

5:23

> *'Curse Meroz,' says the angel of the* LORD,
> *'curse utterly its inhabitants!*
> *For they did not come to help the* LORD,
> *to help the* LORD *as heroes.'*

Although we would not notice this from the formal structure, verse 23 begins the third and final part of Deborah's song (compare v. 12, the beginning of the second part). The connection between this and the previous section is very intimate, and there is not the slightest break in the unity of the poem. Nevertheless, this unity is transformed as the poetess's thought progresses. Here there is a particular change in tone. Deborah begins to settle the accounts by doling out curses and blessings according to how the people acted in regard to their defeated enemy. Whereas verse 22 was still speaking of how the battle ended, the prophetess here proceeds without pause to an account of what happened after the battle.

The form that this takes is first of all a cursing of the city of Meroz and its inhabitants. Their sin was that they did not hasten to join in the pursuit of the fleeing enemy. This pursuit did not come to an abrupt end but was continued in several directions for as long as possible (see

---

[61] A slight change in the vocalization gives the *pual* form, *hullᵉmû*, "were struck [to pieces]," i.e., "shattered." The Hebrew has the active form "struck" without an object, which is rather obscure. I have therefore followed the ancient versions, all of which have a passive or intransitive form (cf. KJV —TRANS.).

4:16–17). The citizens of the Israelite cities nearby obviously should not have passively looked on; they were obliged to rally behind Barak's warriors. The people of Meroz did not do this, however. Those who surely should have joined the chase and had every opportunity to do so "did not come to help the LORD," i.e., to help the Lord's cause and His people. Their neglect was an even greater sin than that of the tribes that stayed away before the battle (vv. 16–17). Because of their Laodicean attitude, the Merozites were struck by God's curse. The angel of the Lord himself, who shared God's nature and was responsible for Israel's success (see 2:1), placed this curse in Deborah's mouth.[62] Understood literally verse 23 is a command from Deborah to her listeners to pronounce a curse, but the meaning is obviously "cursed be Meroz." The curse must have gone into effect, for the city is never mentioned again; and we have no idea where it was located.

5:24–27

> "Blessed[63] above women be Jael,
>   the wife of Heber the Kenite,
>   blessed above tent-dwelling women!
> [25] To him who asked for water[64] she gave milk;
>   in a bowl fit for nobles she brought cream.
> [26] Then she reaches her hand for the peg,
>   her right hand for the workmen's hammer;[65]
> she strikes Sisera, nails his head through,
>   shatters and pierces his temple.
> [27] Between her feet he writhed, he fell, he lay still;
>   between her feet he writhed and fell;
>   where he writhed, there he fell—dead."

The blessing of Jael stands in sharp contrast to the cursing of Meroz. By her bold deed she who was not even an Israelite and had no need to choose sides gained the honor of victory (see 4:9); and Deborah thus pronounced a blessing on her in the name of the Lord. Jael was thereby

---

[62] Deborah meant to bring out that her curse of this city that had traitorously let the enemy pass by was pronounced not on her own authority but in obedience to God's express command. This, however, does not diminish the fact that her entire poem was inspired by the Spirit of God.

[63] The Hebrew term could also be translated "praised," but the contrast with "curse" in verse 23 makes "blessed" a better choice.

[64] Literally, "he asked for water" (cf. NIV —TRANS.). These words have the effect of a subordinate clause; however, the coordination is purely formal, for Deborah was focusing on Jael's action.

[65] Notice the contrast between "workmen's hammer" and "bowl fit for nobles."

exalted above all other women,[66] in particular, all those who lived in tents, viz., the wives of the nomads or wandering herdsmen like Heber (cf. 8:11). The description of her slaying of Sisera is so incomparably vivid that we almost see the entire scene unfold in detail before our very eyes.

Wielenga says that the poem here is "masterfully graphic, frighteningly realistic."[67] We see Jael, with exaggerated courtesy, offer Sisera her finest drinking vessel and then reach with the same hand for the lethal weapon. We hear the hammer strike home and witness the convulsive twisting of Sisera in his death throes. Remarkably, Deborah praised not only the slaying of Sisera but also the preceding hospitality by which Jael was able to ensnare him (see the comments below on the ethic of her action). The name of the enemy general is omitted in verse 25 only because Jael's deed was already widely known.

"Cream" at the end of this verse is the same as the "milk" of the previous line (to distinguish the two would conflict with 4:19); the poetic parallelism merely repeats the same thought in different words.[68] The "bowl fit for nobles" was a drinking vessel used by the upper class that others would keep on hand in case such a person visited.

Verse 26 harks back to the beginning of 4:21: Jael grasped the hammer and tent peg and approached Sisera. Keil's view that the first line is speaking of her left hand is rather contrived;[69] the poetic parallelism forbids such an interpretation. The following words graphically depict the quick, deadly strokes of Jael's hammer and their effect on Sisera, who writhed (literally, "bent his knees"), half-awakened, under the intolerable pain, collapsed in an agony of convulsions, and finally lay motionless, violently dispatched from life. "Between her feet," the literal meaning of the Hebrew, is virtually equivalent to "at her feet." At the very spot where he writhed and collapsed, he died, nailed fast to the floor of Jael's tent.

Verses 24–27 have a decisive bearing on the question of whether Jael should be praised or blamed for her deed. Since Deborah openly praised her in God's name, it seems clear to me that her motivation was pure and her object divine. If she had not basically been driven to this

---

[66] Cf. Judith 13:18.

[67] *De Bijbel als boek van schoonheid,* p. 248.

[68] The Hebrew term denotes the thick or fatty part of the milk and has thus been taken as a reference to curds or butter. As in Deuteromony 32:14, however, it is merely a synonym for "milk."

[69] *Kommentar,* p. 260.

deed by the Spirit of God, such a blessing would never have been spoken. It is possible that she sinned in carrying out her appointed task—e.g., in the way she performed it, her choice of weapons, and perhaps also in her private thoughts, but this should not be our main concern. Deborah neither directly nor indirectly condemned her for these things. We cannot even find fault with the cunning that she used to accomplish her goal, since verse 25 shows that she received divine approval for the hospitality by which she managed to trap Sisera. Certainly she would have been at fault had she refused to take him in and thus given him the opportunity to escape. Cunning was the obvious course for Jael, and as such it was not forbidden.

Nevertheless, we get the impression that Jael went too far and crossed the boundary between cunning and (subjective) deceit. Her kindness was too exaggerated in the way she went out to meet Sisera, invited him inside, and assured him of his safety (4:18). The contrast between her initial civility and the gruesome attack on Sisera that followed is so great that we have to question her integrity. Indeed, Deborah's blessing does not make Jael into a saint. And we cannot save her with the excuse that she did not conceive her plan for killing Sisera until he lay sleeping in her tent. There is no ground for this notion; and it is in fact ruled out by verse 25, which also belongs to the blessing. When Jael saw the fleeing general approaching, she immediately recognized him (4:18) and conceived her plan to kill him in some way.

But we also have no reason to suppose that it would have been better for Jael to surrender the sleeping Sisera to Barak. First, possibly Jael knew of the prophecy that the honor of victory would belong to a woman (4:9). When the Lord delivered Sisera into her hand, she therefore could well have concluded that she was the one chosen to execute his sentence. Second, any hesitation to act would have been blameworthy. Proof for this, again, is that Jael is honored with God's blessing for her deed (see, in contrast, the curse pronounced on those who spare the Lord's enemies, Jer. 48:10). Jael's act has much in common with what Ehud did to Eglon and Jehu to the family of Ahab (2 Kings 9–10; see the comments on Ehud's deed, pp. 285 above).[70]

5:28–30

*"Out of the window peered Sisera's mother,
  loudly she cried through the lattice:*

---

[70] Cf. also Bachmann, *Das Buch der Richter*, pp. 288–97; A. Kuyper, *Vrouwen uit de Heilige Schrift*, pp. 55–57.

> 'Why is his chariot so long in coming?
>   Why is the clatter[71] of his chariots delayed?'
> [29] The wisest of her ladies answered her
>   (but she repeated her words to herself):
> [30] 'Are they not finding and dividing the spoil?—
>   a girl or two for every man,[72]
>   spoil of colorful garments for Sisera,
>   spoil of colorful garments embroidered,
>   a set of colorful embroidery[73] for my neck[74] as spoil!'

After cursing Meroz and blessing Jael, Deborah unexpectedly turns her eyes to a third group: Sisera's mother and her ladies, who anxiously and futilely awaited the general's return. The remarkable beauty of this part of the poem, and particularly its depth of psychological insight, leaves an unforgettable impression on the reader. The poetess unfolds a fantasy that is perfectly true to the realities of life. Bringing Sisera's mother, so proud of her son, to center stage at this point is a masterly stroke that confronts the reader with an eloquent series of contrasts. First, there is the contrast between Jael, the victor crowned with honor, and Sisera's mother, the bereaved victim. Second, the mother's anxious premonitions are contrasted with the frivolous assurances of her attendants. And, finally, there is the contrast between the almost desperately cheerful expectations of these women and the cruel reality of which the reader is already aware. This small piece of literature is unsurpassed in its magnificent and biting irony.[75] Its irony is not one of

[71] Since the Hebrew term literally means "steps," some have thought that it denotes the hoofbeats of the horses joined to the chariots (cf. RSV, NASB). This is possible; but since the chariots rather than the horses are spoken of, it seems better to conceive the term more generally as a reference to the monotonous clatter of the vehicles themselves.

[72] Literally, "for a head a man," i.e., "per man." Compare the expression "per capita."

[73] The Hebrew has the dual form here. Other possible translations are "colorfully embroidered double garment" or "two pieces of colorful embroidered work."

[74] This translation (which corresponds to the NIV—TRANS.) follows the consonants of the Hebrew text but changes the vocalization from the construct plural to the first person singular suffix. The Hebrew literally reads "the necks." Some translators connect this to the following word and have "for the necks of the spoil," which could be interpreted as a reference to the necks of the abducted women (the KJV has "for the necks of them that take the spoil"; cf. also NASB, NEB). But this is an extremely unnatural expression that seems out of place in the context. The plural construct form could easily have arisen through a minor change in the vocalization.

[75] This is the opinion of Lowith, cited in Moore, *Judges*, p. 167. Moore's own comments in this work may also be compared to what I have said above.

hate but the sacred irony of divine wisdom, power, and justice, an irony that laughs at men's vain attacks against God and His kingdom and exposes their futile hopes to scorn (Ps. 2:4–6).[76] Deborah's words are a product, not of vindictiveness or malicious delight in the misfortunes of others, but of a sacred love and zeal for God, His people, and His justice.

Sisera's mother awaited her son in his palace at Harosheth Haggoyim (4:2). With great impatience she leaned out one of the upper windows and watched ("peered"; the Hebrew term literally means "looked down from above"; cf. Gen. 26:8; Ps. 85:11) for his return. Unable to relax, she kept a constant lookout by the lattice; but after seeing and hearing nothing, she loudly bewailed her failure to comprehend why Sisera had not yet appeared and there were no hoofbeats to announce the approach of the other chariots. She suppressed the thought of defeat, for it was too dark to mention aloud. But where then could they be? The answer, given by the wisest ladies of her court, shows just how blind and uncomprehending these women were (see 1 Cor. 3:19–20).

The second line of verse 29 can be understood in two different ways. First, it could mean that Sisera's mother gave the same answer to her question in verse 28 that her companions did.[77] Second, as Keil has observed, it could mean that she kept repeating her own words and anxious questions to herself while she was listening to her ladies' answer. In the first case she accepted her companions' reassuring words; in the second, her misgivings were too great. Both possibilities make sense psychologically. The Hebrew term that begins the clause literally means "also, even," but it can also have the adversative force of "but." In my view the fact that the verb in verse 29b (which is different from that in 29a) nowhere has the meaning "reply" is decisive.[78] A literal translation would be "she caused her words to

---

[76] Bachmann, *Das Buch der Richter*, pp. 477ff., also discusses the beauties of these verses and their double-edged irony. Wielenga overlooks the latter in his words "only a woman's heart . . . can laugh with such poignant sorrow" (*De Bijbel als boek van schoonheid*, p. 248). This is one-sided at the least, and it is unfair to Deborah. The poetess was a prophetess as well.

[77] This is the NIV's interpretation—TRANS.

[78] It *can* mean "answer" or, with the accusative of the person or the preposition *lᵉ*, "give someone an answer." It also is found in the expression "bring words back," in the sense of "bring an answer, make report" (cf. Prov. 22:21 NEB). In that case, however, the "words" are the answer itself, not the question that is answered. Since "her words" in the Hebrew of verse 29b (cf. NASB) refers to the questions of verse 28, the meaning here differs from Proverbs 22:21. If the pronoun "her" were not in

return to herself," and only the second of the above possibilities does justice to this. The meaning is thus that the dark forebodings of the mother's heart could not be dispelled by the cheerful fancies of her "wise" but ultimately superficial ladies, who said that Sisera and his men had failed to appear simply because they were "finding" and "dividing" the spoils of battle (v. 30). The forms of these Hebrew verbs would indicate that they were still engaged in this and hence were unable to return.

Deborah further describes the ladies' picture of the supposed plunder. Quite plausibly the string of loosely connected phrases that follows in verse 30 indicates that these were brief exclamations of the ladies in which each tried to outdo the comforting fantasies of the others. The Hebrew term translated "girl" originally meant "womb"; in this context it is a rather coarse expression equivalent to "bedmate" (cf. NEB). Besides his share of the abducted women, Sisera also has supposedly received a wealth of fine clothing, which the court ladies described partly as simply colored and partly as embroidered in a variety of colors. Each of them imagined that the general had already come home to adorn her neck with some of this colorful attire.

5:31

"So will perish all your enemies, O LORD!
But those who love Him are like the sun, rising in its strength."

Then the land had peace forty years.

Deborah abruptly broke off her picture of Sisera's home. She did not wish to amuse herself with this image of the distress of her nation's enemy, for her only concern was with God and His purposes. With great solemnity she ends her song by turning to the Lord and voicing her certainty that all His foes would perish like Sisera, who thus is portrayed as an enemy of Yahweh Himself. In contrast, all who love God are like the sun, which at its rising dispels the powers of darkness and destroys them with invincible strength. Deborah was not speaking of the sun in its midday strength, for it is already like a champion at the moment it crosses the horizon (Ps. 19:5). This is the image of those who stand on the Lord's side in this world. Israel was thus here given a promise that would surely be fulfilled if it remained faithful to Yahweh—and not Israel alone, for the promise in these closing lines

---

the Hebrew, we would not have to understand the verse this way. See Bachmann, *Das Buch der Richter,* pp. 489ff.

never grows old and is spoken to all ages (cf. Matt. 13:43; Rev. 1:16). The author closes this portion of his book by reporting that the victory of Deborah and Barak kept the land free from foreign oppression for forty years.

D. Gideon
(6:1–9:57)

1. GIDEON'S CALL (6:1–32)

6:1–6 *Again the Israelites did evil in the eyes of the LORD, and for seven years he gave them into the hands of the Midianites. ²Because the power of Midian was so oppressive, the Israelites prepared shelters for themselves in mountain clefts, caves and strongholds. ³Whenever the Israelites planted their crops, the Midianites, Amalekites and other eastern peoples invaded the country. ⁴They camped on the land and ruined the crops all the way to Gaza and did not spare a living thing for Israel, neither sheep nor cattle nor donkeys. ⁵They came up with their livestock and their tents like swarms of locusts. It was impossible to count the men and their camels; they invaded the land to ravage it. ⁶Midian so impoverished the Israelites that they cried out to the LORD for help.*

The opening of chapter 6 has to be read in connection with the closing line of 5:31. The peace broke down after forty years because the Israelites once again became unfaithful to the Lord and brought punishment on themselves. The spirit of Deborah was foreign to the generation that had grown up in the intervening years; and they fell back into the sins of their ancestors, particularly that of idolatry (v. 10). Faithful to His threats (Lev. 26:14–17; Deut. 28:15, 33, 43–44), the Lord therefore subjected His people to renewed oppression. His instrument this time was the Midianites, a nation that was related to Israel through Abraham's marriage to Keturah (Gen. 25:2).

Verse 2 shows how harsh this oppression was. Out of fear for the Midianites, the people hid themselves and their belongings in the hills, making use of the clefts, caves, and elevated strongholds that were still known during the author's day. Although the Hebrew verb in this verse literally means "made" (cf. RSV), the meaning is clearly that they prepared these places and fitted them for human habitation. They were forced to take such action because of the methods used by the Midianites, who were not bent on combat and bloodshed. Their aim was not to destroy the Israelites but to despoil them. After the Israelites had planted their crops and the harvest was approaching, the Midianites would cross the Jordan each year with the Amalekites and "other eastern peoples" (i.e., the Bedouins or Arabic desert nomads) to raid the countryside, pitching their tents there and plundering the fields and storehouses. Whatever they did not steal, they would ravage or burn, ruining whatever was left of the harvest. Then they would march onward, first crossing Canaan from east to west and then turning south along the coast to Gaza. Behind them they left a path of desolation, void of grain and living animals. Finally they would go back to the limitless deserts east of Palestine, only to return again at harvest time the following year.

According to verse 5, the eastern peoples came with their herds— literally, their livestock, but these were camels rather than cattle or sheep—and their tents and settled in the land for a time as if they were its legitimate owners. So numerous were they that, like swarms of locusts, they literally left nothing that could be eaten behind them. Apparently not a single battle was fought between them and the Israelites. Fearful of their awesome numbers, the people's only concern was to find shelter for themselves and their possessions. Every year their situation grew more precarious. Finally, after this had gone on for seven years, they began to cry to the Lord for help.

6:7-10 *When the Israelites cried to the LORD because of Midian, ⁸he sent them a prophet, who said, "This is what the LORD, the God of Israel, says: I brought you up out of Egypt, out of the land of slavery. ⁹I snatched you from the power of Egypt and from the hand of all your oppressors. I drove them from before you and gave you their land. ¹⁰I said to you, 'I am the LORD your God; do not worship the gods of the Amorites, in whose land you live.' But you have not listened to me."*

The Israelites' cries of distress did not go unanswered. The Lord sent a prophet to tell them that their misery was caused by their failure to obey God's commandments. Verses 8-10 briefly summarize the message of this unknown prophet. He spoke in the name of Him who, as the legitimate God of Israel, had a claim to the people's obedience and worship. Then he reminded them of two great mercies the Lord had shown them: their deliverance from slavery in Egypt and the expulsion of the Canaanites from the Promised Land. The words "all your oppressors" refer particularly to the rulers who forcibly tried to obstruct Israel's entrance into Canaan (Sihon and Og, for example); but they also could include Jabin and Sisera (chs. 4-5), who actually did oppress the people.

Verse 10 recalls the great and fundamental act of mercy in which the

Lord made a covenant with the Israelites to be their God (Exod. 20:2) and also His explicit commandment against worshiping the gods of the Amorites. The nation indeed had been warned, but it had not listened (cf. 2:1–2). Although the message of this prophet contained no promise of deliverance, it did serve to prepare the people for deliverance. They had to learn to turn to God, not merely out of need, but with full consciousness of their guilt.

6:11–13 *The angel of the* LORD *came and sat down under the oak in Ophrah that belonged to Joash the Abiezrite, where his son Gideon was threshing wheat in a winepress to keep it from the Midianites.* *12 When the angel of the* LORD *appeared to Gideon, he said, "The* LORD *is with you, mighty warrior."*

13 "But sir," Gideon replied, "if the LORD *is with us, why has all this happened to us? Where are all his wonders that our fathers told us about when they said, 'Did not the* LORD *bring us up out of Egypt?' But now the* LORD *has abandoned us and put us into the hand of Midian."*

We are not told directly what effect this sermon had. That it did bear fruit, however, is clear from the story of Gideon. After the prophet had gone through the land preaching penance, the angel of the Lord himself, who had previously come to Israel at Bokim (2:1–5), made an appearance. Taking on the form of a man, he sat under the oak in Ophrah (apparently this was a well-known tree), a town inhabited by the clan of the Abiezrites (see v. 24).[79] The town leader was Joash, whose son Gideon ("hewer, [one who] cuts down") was busy threshing wheat. The Hebrew verb in verse 11 literally means that he beat out the ears with a stick, the method used by the poor (Ruth 2:17, see KJV).

Although wheat was usually threshed on an open threshing floor, Gideon had chosen to do this in the winepress, where no one would expect to find wheat. This not only illustrates the hardship that the nation had to endure; it also shows how dejected and disheartened they had become. Fear of the Midianites had crippled the Israelites. This, however, did not stop the angel of the Lord from addressing Gideon as a "mighty warrior" and promising that the Lord was and would be with him. He was not looking at what Gideon was in himself but at what God would make of him and accomplish through him (cf. John 1:42).

Gideon displayed his modesty by ignoring the angel's compliment and applying his promise, not to himself, but to his entire nation. In

---

[79] Ophrah must have been located north of Shechem. Böhl (*Bijbels-Kerkelijk Woordenboek*, vol. I) identifies it with Far'ah, Garstang (*Joshua, Judges*, p. 319) with Sileh. See also the article in the *Bijbelse Encyclopedie*.

Gideon's view the Lord must *not* have been with Israel, for then "all this" would not have come over them. He doubtless was thinking here, among other things, of the slaughter at Tabor in which the Midianites had killed his brothers (8:18–19). The Lord certainly *could* have brought deliverance. Fathers were in fact still telling their children about the great wonders He had performed in the past. But God had abandoned and rejected the Israelites. Gideon nevertheless did not deny that He had reason to do so.

6:14–16 *The LORD turned to him and said, "Go in the strength you have and save Israel out of Midian's hand. Am I not sending you?"*

15 "But Lord," Gideon asked, "how can I save Israel? My clan is the weakest in Manasseh, and I am the least in my family."

16 The LORD answered, "I will be with you, and you will strike down all the Midianites together."

The unknown visitor countered Gideon's objections by revealing more clearly who He was, thus showing that the God of Israel was indeed with Gideon. It was only the Lord who could say, "Go in the strength you have [i.e., the strength that I now give you through my word] and save Israel out of Midian's hand. Am I not sending you?" The Lord's word should have been enough for Gideon, and all his doubts should have been put to rest. Gideon thus understood that the person whom he had taken for a mere traveler was speaking with divine authority, and so he addressed him as "Adonai" or "Lord." Gideon still objected, however. Another person would be a better choice, and he was not in a position to deliver Israel. His clan, the Abiezrites, was the weakest in Manasseh; therefore he had very little power and influence. Moreover he was the youngest of his father's sons. No one would follow him and his efforts surely would meet with failure. But the angel's answer defeated all Gideon's protests and forced him to ignore himself completely: "I will be with you, and you will strike down the Midianites as if they were but one man."

6:17–18 *Gideon replied, "If now I have found favor in your eyes, give me a sign that it is really you talking to me. 18 Please do not go away until I come back and bring my offering and set it before you."*

And the LORD said, "I will wait until you return."

It increasingly dawned on Gideon who his visitor really was. Nevertheless, he still was not completely certain. He therefore respectfully asked the unknown man for a sign. Gideon's request was completely understandable. The call to be Israel's deliverer was incredible to him. Was he deceiving himself? Had all this actually happened? Was it really the Lord Himself who had appeared to him? Why should he have been granted such a special favor? In need of greater assurance, he asked for a sign that would convince him his eyes were not lying and would remove all reason for doubt. Such a desire was acceptable under the Old Covenant because of the way God revealed Himself then (see Gen. 15:8; 24:12–14; Exod. 4:1–9; Num. 17). It certainly does not form evidence of unbelief, though the need for a sign does show that man had fallen short in his relations with God. Gideon wished to know whether he was really speaking to the Lord, as his visitor's words seemed to imply. His additional request in verse 18 did not intend to dictate what the sign should be, for he had no idea what the Lord would do with the food he presented (v. 21). He merely was asking the Lord not to end His visit, desiring the opportunity to honor Him by offering a gift. Possibly, Gideon remembered how Abraham offered a meal to the Lord (Gen. 18:5–8). In any case his desire to honor his lofty guest in this manner was not in the least surprising. The Lord graciously acceded to Gideon's request, thereby letting him know that He would also satisfy his wish for a sign.

6:19–24 *Gideon went in, prepared a young goat, and from an ephah of flour he made bread without yeast. Putting the meat in a basket and its broth in a pot, he brought them out and offered them to him under the oak.*

20 The angel of God said to him, "Take the meat and the unleavened bread, place them on this rock, and pour out the broth." And Gideon did so. 21 With the tip of the staff that was in his hand, the angel of the LORD touched the meat and the unleavened bread. Fire flared from the rock, consuming the meat and the bread. And the angel of the LORD disappeared. 22 When Gideon realized that it was the angel of the LORD, he exclaimed, "Ah, Sovereign LORD! I have seen the angel of the LORD face to face!"

23 But the LORD said to him, "Peace! Do not be afraid. You are not going to die."

24 So Gideon built an altar to the LORD there and called it The LORD is Peace. To this day it stands in Ophrah of the Abiezrites.

The meal that Gideon served was far from meager. He slaughtered and prepared a young goat and made unleavened bread from an ephah (21 or 22 liters) of flour. There thus must have been no lack of food in Joash's house. Then Gideon brought all this out to the oak tree, where the angel was still seated, and the latter commanded him to set down the meat and bread on a rock that lay there and to pour the broth over it. The rock thereby became an altar, Gideon's gift an offering, and the visitor revealed himself as God (v. 20 therefore calls him "the angel of God"), the true owner of everything who thus had the right to accept offerings.

The sign itself then follows. Touching the food with His staff, the Lord caused fire to leap from the rock and consume the offering. Then He vanished at once from Gideon's sight. At one and the same moment, He proved His deity to Gideon and gave him a token of His grace by accepting the offering. Gideon, meanwhile, had been frightened to death by the miraculous sign, and perhaps even more by the angel's sudden disappearance. Finally, he realized beyond a shadow of a doubt that the human apparition he had been speaking with was none other than the angel of the Lord, a person both distinct from and one with God Himself. But this meant that Gideon must die; for God had said, "No one may see me and live" (Exod. 33:20). Gideon's words— "Ah, Sovereign Lord! I have seen the angel of the Lord face to face"[80]—express his great fear that the Lord had come to him because He was angry and intended to kill him. Although this fear was unwarranted in view of God's promises (see also 13:22–23), it nevertheless was a natural expression of Gideon's sense of his own nothingness in the face of God's glory and might.

The Lord dispelled Gideon's fear at once by calling to him (undoubtedly in an audible voice; cf. Gen. 22:11, 15): "Peace! Do not be afraid. You are not going to die." This served as a new sign to Gideon that the Lord was with him. Thankful for the revelation he had been favored with, he spontaneously built an altar at this site that God had sanctified by His presence. In memory of the comforting words he had received, Gideon named the altar "The Lord is Peace." By building this altar, Gideon expressed his confidence that the Lord would uphold His covenant and deliver Israel. At the time this story was written, the altar was still standing in Ophrah of the Abiezrites (a different town than the Ophrah in Benjamin, Josh. 18:23).

---

[80] Goslinga's translation of this literally reads: "Alas, O Lord God! For this reason have I seen the angel of the Lord" (viz., because He is angry with me and wants to kill me)—Trans.

6:25–26 *That same night the LORD said to him, "Take the second bull from your father's herd, the one seven years old. Tear down your father's altar to Baal and cut down the Asherah pole beside it. ²⁶ Then build a proper kind of altar to the LORD your God on the top of this height. Using the wood of the Asherah pole that you cut down, offer the second bull as a burnt offering."*

The angel of the Lord's appearance was necessary to convince Gideon that he indeed had been called by God. Once he knew of this calling and had a heightened sensibility for divine revelations, however, we do not read of such an appearance again. On the night after the above events, the Lord commanded Gideon to destroy the cult of Baal and to restore the true worship of Israel's God. In the words of Keil, "the Lord allies Himself with Gideon in the first revelation; in the second, He demands that Gideon ally himself with Him and confess Him as his God."[81] Before stepping forward as his people's liberator, Gideon needed to perform a deed that showed that he recognized Yahweh as the sole God of Israel and her rightful sovereign. His liberating work had to be defined by his divine calling to uphold the trampled rights of the Lord. Gideon therefore had to begin with an act of religious reform.[82] Figuratively speaking, he had to "start from Jerusalem," i.e., from his father's house.

Gideon's father, Joash, had been too weak to take action against the public spirit that tolerated the worship of Baal. He had even agreed that an altar be built in Ophrah to Baal as Canaan's guardian deity and that a sacred pole crowned by the bust of Asherah be placed next to it (see in 3:7). Gideon was commanded to go to that altar with a bull from his father's herd, specifically, "the second bull . . . the one seven years old." Bulls apparently were distinguished as first, second, third, etc., according to their position, size, or age. The deliberate mention of this bull's age could perhaps be an allusion to the seven years of Midianite oppression, the bull itself then symbolizing Israel as it rededicated itself to the Lord after this length of time. This, in any case, is what burnt offerings signified, though they also included the thought of atonement (see Lev. 1:3–4).

Before offering the bull, Gideon had to build an altar to the Lord on top of the bluff or stronghold of Ophrah and thus in a clearly visible place. The Hebrew expression *bammaʿarākā(h)* in verse 26 is rather

---

[81] *Biblische Kommentar*, 2nd ed., p. 266.
[82] See the lecture of G. H. J. W. J. Geesink, "Gideons Hervormingsdaad" (1887).

obscure,[83] but it most likely has to do with the construction or equipping of the altar. A literal translation would be "in an orderly pattern" (cf. NASB, NEB) or "with equipment." The Lord explicitly required that the Asherah pole be used as the firewood. The cult of Baal and Asherah could not coexist with the worship of the Lord but had to be destroyed. That God here ignored the Mosaic laws and commanded that an offering be brought by a man who was not descended from Aaron and did not even belong to the tribe of Levi shows how abnormal things had become in Gideon's day. One could almost think that the Israelites were living back in the patriarchal times.[84]

6:27–32 *So Gideon took ten of his servants and did as the LORD told him. But because he was afraid of his family and the men of the town, he did it at night rather than in the daytime.*

[28] In the morning when the men of the town got up, there was Baal's altar, demolished, with the Asherah pole beside it cut down and the second bull sacrificed on the newly built altar!

[29] They asked each other, "Who did this?"

When they carefully investigated, they were told, "Gideon son of Joash did it."

[30] The men of the town demanded of Joash, "Bring out your son. He must die, because he has broken down Baal's altar and cut down the Asherah pole beside it."

[31] But Joash replied to the hostile crowd around him, "Are you going to plead Baal's cause? Are you trying to save him? Whoever fights for him shall be put to death by morning![85] If Baal really is a god, he can defend himself when someone breaks down his altar." [32] So that day they called Gideon "Jerub-Baal," saying, "Let Baal contend with him," because he broke down Baal's altar.

Gideon performed his task discreetly but thoroughly. His fear of his family was really more a matter of caution than timidity, for he felt that he would be hampered in the fulfillment of his mandate if he acted during the daytime. He therefore chose to do his work in the dark, but this does not mean he acted that very night. Time was needed to form his plans and to find collaborators. He secured the help of ten servants who apparently were secretly opposed to the cult of Baal and finished his work without disturbance by daybreak. Gideon thus managed to confront his fellow townsmen with an accomplished fact. Not only the

---

[83] The NIV translates this as "proper kind of," but see the marginal note—TRANS.

[84] Cf. H. Hoekstra, *De Heere is vrede* (1917), p. 63.

[85] Or "during the morning," i.e., "this morning" (cf. KJV).

fact, but also its perpetrator become known soon enough; and since the altar to Baal apparently did not belong to Joash alone (v. 25) but to all the citizens, the men demanded that Joash hand over his son to be punished for desecrating the city shrine.

Gideon's deed had the opposite effect on Joash, however. He acknowledged that his son did the right thing and decisively took sides against Baal and his devotees. Not only did he reproach his fellow townsmen for pleading Baal's cause and defending his rights; he even jeopardized his authority as clan leader by upholding the worship of the Lord as the sole legitimate God in Israel. He imposed the death penalty on whoever took Baal's side; and he sported with the deity by calmly observing that if Baal were God, he could defend himself. This statement gave rise to Gideon's nickname Jerub-Baal, which literally means "let Baal contend [with him]." The person of Gideon was a living challenge to Baal to show that he was God. But since Baal obviously did not have the power to avenge himself, the name gradually turned into a title of honor for Gideon with the meaning "contender with Baal."

Gideon's deed thus had a surprising result. In his own circle the power of Baal had been broken in principle. The forces of evil held sway among the people, not because there was no one who worshiped Yahweh, but because those who did so kept silent and lacked the courage to oppose either the followers of Baal or the invading foreigners. But now there had been a turn for the better. The initial impact of Gideon's destruction of the Baal cult had raised his prestige so high that he could boldly take the lead in the battle for Israel's independence. With Gideon it is clearer than with any of the other judges that the struggle against foreign gods and the struggle against foreign oppression were one and the same. Israel belonged entirely to the Lord. No one else had any claim either to the nation or to the land of Canaan. No idol belonged among God's sacred people, and no foreign foot belonged on His sacred soil. The task of the true judge was to rid the land of both.

2. THE EQUIPPING, ENCOURAGING, AND TESTING OF GIDEON
(6:33–7:8)

6:33–35 *Now all the Midianites, Amalekites and other eastern peoples joined forces and crossed over the Jordan and camped in the Valley of Jezreel.* [34] *Then the Spirit of the LORD came upon Gideon, and he blew a trumpet, summoning the Abiezrites to follow him.* [35] *He sent messengers throughout Manasseh, calling them to arms, and also into Asher, Zebulun and Naphtali, so that they too went up to meet them.*

The account of how God prepared and, as it were, educated Gideon for his task is remarkable for its length and detail. Chapter 6:11–32 has recounted how he was called and molded into a judge and a servant of Israel's God. The next section focuses on the training that he received to be a general in the Lord's service. To introduce this, the author turned back to the invasion of the land of Israel by the hordes of the Midianites and their allies, something that actually preceded the events of verses 11–32. Verses 13–16 clearly show that Israel's enemies were already in Canaan at that time (cf. also v. 11: Gideon was called at harvest time). They had joined forces across the Jordan, crossed the river undoubtedly at Beth Shan, and camped in countless numbers in the fertile Valley of Jezreel.

The Lord equipped Gideon for battle by granting him His Spirit, providing him with an army, and strengthening his faith (by the signs in vv. 36–40). The first of these is the most important. The Hebrew literally means that the Spirit of the Lord "put Gideon on," i.e., like a garment. This is usually taken to mean that he clothed Gideon like armor. In the Hebrew phrase, however, the man is conceived as the garment in which the Spirit envelopes Himself, the instrument that He makes use of. The meaning is therefore that the Spirit of the Lord entered into Gideon, filling him and making him capable of great deeds.

In consequence of the Spirit's action, Gideon stepped forward as a leader. He sounded the trumpet in Ophrah and the surrounding area; and the Abiezrite clan both heard his signal and, as the text clearly means, rallied behind him. The other clans in Manasseh responded in similar fashion. Verse 34 is speaking only of the western half of Manasseh, which included the descendants of Abiezer (Josh. 17:1–13). The other half of the tribe that had settled east of the Jordan (Josh. 13:29–32) did not take part in the battle. The Manassites spoken of here, therefore, lived west and southwest of the Valley of Jezreel, a region that had been assigned primarily to the tribe of Issachar. Gideon's messengers also found a ready response in Asher, Zebulun, and Naphtali. Since these tribes lay north of the Valley of Jezreel, their men could join forces with the army in Manasseh only by taking a western detour around the valley. This required some time, of course, but in the end Gideon had mustered an army of thirty-two thousand men (see 7:3).

6:36–40 *Gideon said to God, "If you will save Israel by my hand as you have promised—look, I will place a wool fleece on the threshing floor. If there is dew only on the fleece and all the ground is dry, then I will know that you will save Israel by my hand, as you said." ³⁸And that is what happened. Gideon rose early the next day; he squeezed the fleece and wrung out the dew—a bowlful of water.*

³⁹Then Gideon said to God, "Do not be angry with me. Let me make just one more request. Allow me one more test with the fleece. This time make the fleece dry and the ground covered with dew." ⁴⁰That night God did so. Only the fleece was dry; all the ground was covered with dew.

Gideon found no cause for pride in the fact that his army was sizable but evidenced his humility and awareness of how dependent he was by asking God for a sign to confirm his faith. Remarkably, these verses use only the name "God"; "Lord," which was used consistently in the previous section (except in v. 20), does not appear here at all. This could express the thought that the "LORD" who had called Gideon (vv. 14, 16, 23–24) was not only the God of Israel but also the God of heaven and earth who performs wonders and signs with the elements of nature.

Gideon's request began by respectfully reminding God of His promise (v. 16) and then described the sign that he wished to receive. The Hebrew word translated "will save" in verse 36 is actually a participle that literally means "are saving," i.e., "active and ready to save." "Wool fleece" in the Hebrew has the definite article and thus indicates a piece of sheepskin that Gideon already had at hand. Both Gideon's entreaty and the kind of sign he requested were acceptable to the Lord. He did exactly what Gideon desired, and so conspicuously that it could not possibly have happened by chance. The ground was dry and the fleece soaking wet.

Emboldened by this answer to his prayer, Gideon went a step further (cf. Abraham's plea for Sodom, Gen. 18:32). With even deeper reverence than before, he asked for the opposite of the first sign. This would be even more striking and marvelous, since it is in the nature of wool to absorb moisture. The second sign would therefore go against nature and demonstrate God's power to do what seems impossible to men even more clearly. Since Gideon's request was not a demand made in unbelief or an arbitrary test of God's faithfulness and power, the Lord readily answered it. These signs served to strengthen Gideon's faith, which would soon have to undergo a double test itself. They also fully assured him that the same God who can do as He wills with the dew of the heavens would also shower His grace on Israel and fill the weary nation with new strength.

7:1–3 *Early in the morning, Jerub-Baal (that is, Gideon) and all his men camped at the spring of Harod. The camp of Midian was north of them in the valley near the hill of Moreh. ² The LORD said to Gideon, "You have too many men for me to deliver Midian into their hands. In order that Israel may not boast against me that her own strength has saved her, ³ announce now to the people, 'Anyone who trembles with fear may turn back and leave Mount Gilead.' "*[86] *So twenty-two thousand men left, while ten thousand remained.*

Shortly after the second sign had been given, Gideon and his men marched out to meet the enemy. This must have happened after the men from the northern tribes and the Manassites had assembled at one place (see 6:35). We have no idea where this might have been, but it probably was not Ophrah. Clearly, the enemy hordes were encamped in the Valley of Jezreel. Gideon must have approached them from the south (probably the southwest); for when he reached the spring of Harod, the Midianite camp lay to the north, spreading outward from the hill of Moreh into the valley. The enemy therefore was situated between Gideon's army and this hill. The battlefield itself undoubtedly was located in the eastern part of the Valley of Jezreel. There in the southeast stood the northernmost spur of Mount Gilboa, at the foot of which the spring Ain Jalud[87] forms the source of the brook Nahr Jalud. The terrain here corresponds perfectly with what verses 1 and 4–5

---

[86] The Hebrew is rather obscure here. The verb translated "leave" appears nowhere else. Its stem, which is also the root of the word translated "wreath" in Isaiah 28:5, seems to be related to an Arabic word meaning "weave" or "wind." A possible translation is therefore "make a detour, turn off the normal route." The name "Gilead" is also odd, since we know nothing of a mountain by this name west of the Jordan. One cannot help wondering whether the name is not a mistake for Gilboa.

[87] This modern name does not correspond to the biblical name, but the Old Testament uses no other name for the spring (1 Sam. 29:1 undoubtedly is speaking of the same spring). See Garstang, *Joshua, Judges,* p. 94. In *Dein Reich Komme* (April, 1932), W. Marzinkowsky tells of a settlement called "Ain Harod in Galilee." If this refers to the same fountain, the ancient name would appear to have been revived.

reveal about the position of the Israelite encampment. The camp apparently lay on a height or slope at the foot of which the spring of Harod had formed a brook or pool. North of this point and separated from it by a valley stands the Jebel Dahi or Little Hermon, commonly identified with the hill of Moreh.[88]

Before Gideon even had time to devise a plan of attack, the Lord, the Israelite army's real Commander, instructed him to give those whose courage had left them a chance to turn back. The Israelites had called on the Lord for help (6:7), and He therefore wanted to make it abundantly clear that their deliverance came from no one but Him. They then would have no cause for boasting. To Gideon's disappointment, more than two-thirds of his army took advantage of the opportunity to depart.[89] Apparently the sight of the enemy army dampened the enthusiasm of most of them and replaced it with despondency and fear. So there were only ten thousand men left from Gideon's once sizable army.

7:4-7 *But the* LORD *said to Gideon, "There are still too many men. Take them down to the water, and I will sift them for you there. If I say, 'This one shall go with you,' he shall go; but if I say, 'This one shall not go with you,' he shall not go."*

5So Gideon took the men down to the water. There the LORD *told him, "Separate those who lap the water with their tongues like a dog from those who kneel down to drink." 6Three hundred men lapped with their hands to their mouths. All the rest got down on their knees to drink.*[90]

---

[88] We have every reason to accept this proposal of Bertheau (*Buch der Richter und Rut*, pp. 119f.; see also Ebers and Guthe, *Palestina*, vol. 1, p. 286 et al.). The only objection to it is that we know of no other places where the name Moreh is applied to the Little Hermon. Bertheau points out, however, that the Little Hermon does not appear elsewhere in the Old Testament. The Moreh near Shechem (Gen. 12:6; Deut. 11:30) is entirely out of the question.

[89] The men probably took the same route they had come by. They then would not have traveled directly to their tribes and homes but would first have gone to a specific place behind the front (Mount Gilead?), turning home only from there. For most of them (especially for the northern tribes), this was a detour (see footnote 86 and the comments in 6:35). Such a route would have had two advantages: (1) the departing soldiers would not hinder the movements of Gideon's select troops and provoke a premature clash with the enemy; and (2) if necessary, they could quickly be called back (as in fact happened in v. 23).

[90] Goslinga's translation of this verse corresponds to the NEB rather than the NIV: "The number of those who lapped was three hundred, and all the rest went down on their knees to drink, putting their hands to their mouths." He adds the following note:

> [7]*The LORD said to Gideon, "With the three hundred men that lapped I will save you and give the Midianites into your hands. Let all the other men go, each to his own place."*

Even this number was much too large; so the Lord commanded Gideon to take his troops down to the spring of Harod (see v. 1), where He would sift them yet again. Only after Gideon had obeyed this command did the Lord tell him the sign he must look for. All the men were to drink (probably in small, easily observable groups), and Gideon was to separate those who drank as a dog drinks from those who got on their knees to drink. The latter formed the overwhelming majority, for only 300 men drank the water like a dog (see below). Amazingly, the Lord instructed Gideon to send the 9,700 home and promised to deliver Israel with the tiny group of 300 men. Gideon had to be content with this promise. His trust was to not lie in his own military might but solely in God's word.

It almost seems as if the Lord were sporting with Gideon, for He gave him an army only to take almost all of it away. But Gideon held fast to God's promise and passed His test with flying colors. We do not read of a single word of protest from him in these verses, and his quiet obedience forms clear proof of his faith (see Heb. 11:32). One cannot help asking whether the sign that the Lord used (v. 5) was purely arbitrary and external or whether it pointed to a difference in the spirits of the two groups. The latter is undoubtedly the case. The 300 threw themselves flat on the bank, hastily gulped down a little water, and had already returned to their ranks when the others had just kneeled down. The 9,700 did not show the same alacrity; they took their time and remained on their knees long enough to draw up several handfuls of water. The first group was nimbler and quicker and thus better prepared for battle. Some think that these men drank while standing, stooping down to scoop up some water with their hands. This way of

---

The final six words follow "lapped" in the Hebrew text, but in this position they make the whole sentence unintelligible. For those who lapped the water like dogs (v. 5) did *not* bring their hands to their mouths, but lay flat on their breasts and put their mouths to the water. In contrast, those who got on their knees could not drink the water unless they brought it to their mouths with cupped hands. I therefore suspect that the words in question originally stood at the end of verse 6. A copyist may have accidentally skipped them and later added them in the margin, and they then could have been reinserted into the text a line too high in a later copy. Some important manuscripts of the Septuagint omit the words entirely and instead have "with their tongue," an apparent emendation of the unintelligible text—TRANS.

drinking could never be compared to that of a dog, however (see footnote 90), nor can one think that they then could have acted more quickly than if they had drunk in the manner described above. We have to assume that God used this simple method to sift out the most spirited and dedicated of the 10,000 soldiers.[91]

7:8 *So Gideon sent the rest of the Israelites to their tents but kept the three hundred, who took over the provisions*[92] *and trumpets of the others. Now the camp of Midian lay below him in the valley.*

At the end of verse 7, the soldiers who were to depart are called "the people" in the Hebrew text (the NIV has "all the other men"—TRANS.). The text literally reads "all the people" (cf. KJV), which is not surprising, since the 300 who stayed with Gideon formed a tiny minority of only 3 percent. At the beginning of verse 8 the Hebrew again has "the people";[93] so this cannot refer to the 300 (as in the KJV). The meaning is rather that the 300 men took over the provisions (or at least as much as they needed) and the trumpets of the departing soldiers. The latter would be able to find food on their journey, and they no longer had need of the trumpets.

It seems that Gideon had already conceived the plan of frightening the Midianites with a powerful blast of trumpets, since he otherwise would have allowed those leaving to keep their trumpets. If there was an average of one trumpet per 100 men, the 300 trumpets would have included those of the 22,000 soldiers who had departed earlier. The 9,700 undoubtedly marched off by the same route as the latter (see footnote 89). Verse 8 ends by describing Gideon's position as he stood on the verge of the decisive battle. The verse as a whole thus summarizes the final result of his preparations (6:33–7:7): the army he started with had virtually disbanded, only a small troop remained with him, and the enemy was situated below him in the valley.

---

[91] I make a further assumption about the 300 men in footnote 101.

[92] Following the Septuagint and most commentators, the construct form *ṣēdat* should be read here instead of *ṣēdâ(h)*, which otherwise would need the definite article.

[93] The NIV transposes the first clause to the end of the verse and renders *hāʿ ām* ("the people") as "the others." Compare the RSV and NASB —TRANS.

3. GIDEON'S SURPRISE ATTACK ON THE MIDIANITES (7:9-22)

7:9–12 *During that night the LORD said to Gideon, "Get up, go down against the camp, because I am going to give it into your hands.* ¹⁰*If you are afraid to attack, go down to the camp with your servant Purah* ¹¹*and listen to what they are saying. Afterward, you will be encouraged to attack the camp." So he and Purah his servant went down to the outposts of the camp.* ¹²*The Midianites, the Amalekites and all the other eastern peoples had settled in the valley, thick as locusts. Their camels could no more be counted than the sand on the seashore.*

Evening was doubtless already near by the time Gideon's army had finally been picked (vv. 2–7) and the unneeded soldiers had been sent off (v. 8). The author therefore went on to speak of "that night" (or "that same night," KJV, RSV) when he really meant "the night that followed." The Lord wanted Gideon to act without delay. He commanded him to attack the Midianite army that very night and promised that he would be victorious. To dispel the slightest trace of doubt or apprehension from Gideon's mind, however, the Lord first gave him the opportunity to sneak down to the edge of the camp with his servant Purah (who perhaps accompanied him from his home), where he would be able to eavesdrop on a conversation that would reveal the mood in the camp. Then his heart would no longer tremble, and he would have the courage to lead his men to victory.

Gideon grabbed this opportunity. Together with Purah, he carefully penetrated right up to the outposts of the camp. The Hebrew in verse 11 literally means "edge of the armed men in the camp." This phrase is readily understandable if we assume that the camp also contained a great number of women and children, who were encamped farther back in the valley along with the herdsmen and cattle. The army itself was positioned directly opposite Gideon. Verse 12 reminds us how incredibly numerous the invading hosts were. Was it not foolhardy to launch out against such a superior force? The events that follow proved the contrary.

7:13–14 *Gideon arrived just as a man was telling a friend his dream. "I had a dream," he was saying. "A round loaf of barley bread came tumbling into the Midianite camp. It struck the tent with such force that the tent overturned and collapsed."*

¹⁴*His friend responded, "This can be nothing other than the sword of Gideon son of Joash, the Israelite. God has given the Midianites and the whole camp into his hands."*

The Lord saw to it that Gideon and Purah could listen in unnoticed as a sentry told his comrade of a disturbing dream he had had. The Hebrew term *ṣᵉlûl* (NIV, "round loaf") in verse 13 does not occur elsewhere, and its meaning is uncertain. The older versions simply have "cake," a translation that makes good sense in the context. Possibly, however, the word refers to the shape of the barley bread (hence the NIV translation). The loaf obviously was round, for it rolled into the Midianite camp, reached "the tent" (i.e., a certain tent seen in the dream that represented the whole camp), and overturned it. Both speakers agreed that such a dream had to have a deeper meaning, and the listener's interpretation was unequivocal: the rolling loaf was the sword of Gideon and the dream was an omen of the Midianite army's downfall.

This interpretation was certainly correct. The Midianite soldier had received a nocturnal revelation from God (he used this general name, not the personal name "Lord") of what would befall his army. The barley loaf was a perfect symbol for Gideon, since he was leading the agrarian Israelite nation against the nomadic invaders.

The important thing for Gideon and Purah, however, was not whether the interpretation was correct but the fact that both the dream and the interpretation unveiled the secret fears that Gideon's coming had aroused in the Midianites' hearts. They sensed that a new spirit had come over Israel. The Midianites were starting to feel threatened, and the Lord saw to it that they expressed their feelings while Gideon was listening. Gideon hardly could have found stronger proof that God was with him. The Midianites themselves confessed their despondency, and he therefore could have had no doubt that the Lord had absolute control even over the hearts and the most secret thoughts of His enemies.

7:15–18 *When Gideon heard the dream and its interpretation, he worshiped God. He returned to the camp of Israel and called out, "Get up! The LORD has given the Midianite camp into your hands." ¹⁶Dividing the three hundred men into three companies, he placed trumpets and empty jars in the hands of all of them, with torches inside.*

¹⁷"Watch me," he told them "Follow my lead. When I get to the edge of the camp, do exactly as I do. ¹⁸When I and all who are with me blow our trumpets, then from all around the camp blow yours and shout, 'For the LORD and for Gideon.' "

No wonder Gideon knelt to the ground in grateful worship. With such a God on his side, he could not fail to be victorious. He returned at once to his own camp and marshalled his men for the night attack. Because of his trust in God, however, he did not strike out before taking careful thought. On the contrary, he took advantage of what the Lord had allowed him to hear; for the plan that Gideon devised aimed more to frighten the enemy hosts and provoke a panic in their camp than to defeat them by force of arms. The steps that he took were calculated to increase the Midianites' fear to the point of desperation. He divided his soldiers into three equal companies and instructed them to approach the enemy camp from three different sides (see v. 18), holding their trumpets in one hand and the jars with torches inside in the other. Then they were to watch him and follow his example. Because this could, at best, only be done by the men who were with him and not by the two other companies, Gideon went on to explain his plan in greater detail. We have to assume that verse 17 abbreviates his words and that he also instructed the men to break their jars and ignite their torches. The most important thing, however, was that they all acted at the right moment.

As the commander, Gideon would give the signal; and when he and those with him sounded their trumpets, the other companies were to blow theirs also and shout out the battle cry "For the LORD and for Gideon." Gideon did not even mention the use of swords, for the Lord Himself would be fighting for Israel. His plan assumed that the military part of the Midianite camp was relatively small, while those who accompanied the army were spread out over a large part of the Valley of Jezreel.

7:19–21 *Gideon and the hundred men with him reached the edge of the camp at the beginning of the middle watch, just after they had changed the guard. They blew their trumpets and broke the jars that were in their hands.* ²⁰ *The three companies blew the trumpets and smashed the jars. Grasping the torches in their left hands and holding in their right hands the trumpets they were to blow, they shouted, "A sword for the LORD and for Gideon!"* ²¹ *While each man held his position around the camp, all the Midianites ran, crying out as they fled.*

Gideon probably first sent off the divisions that had to cover the greatest distance and then approached the camp with his own one hundred men. They arrived at a favorable moment. The night was divided into three watches, and the first of these had just ended. The guard had been changed, and all was quiet in the camp once more. The author's account shows that Gideon's plan was followed to the letter.

Only the battle cry—"a sword for the LORD and for Gideon"—
departed from his instructions (v. 18), but this was not important.

Gideon's unusual tactics were a complete success. Rudely awakened
from their sleep by the deafening blast of trumpets, the Midianites
imagined they were being stormed by a huge army. The torches
flickering on all sides told them they were surrounded. The pandemoni-
um of shattering jars deluded them into thinking that the Israelites had
already entered the camp and were creating havoc there. And the battle
cry with the dreaded names of Yahweh and Gideon did the rest. The
enemy was thrown into a panic. While Gideon and his 300 men merely
held their positions, waving their torches and blowing their trumpets,
the camp rushed about in wild confusion.

7:22 *When the three hundred trumpets sounded, the LORD caused the men
throughout the camp to turn on each other with their swords. The army fled to
Beth Shittah toward Zererah as far as the border of Abel Meholah near
Tabbath.*

The Midianites did not even think of putting up a fight. They shrieked
in terror and hoped only to escape. But the Lord, amazingly, came to
Israel's aid by causing the enemy army to destroy itself. In their terror
the fleeing soldiers were unable to recognize one another in the dark,
one turning his sword against the other and violently trying to force his
way out of the camp. The attempted escape turned into a senseless
slaughter in which the very size of the army contributed to its ruin. To
restore order was out of the question. Finally, a remnant managed to
escape in the direction of the Jordan.

The location of Beth Shittah is unknown, but some think the name is
preserved in modern Shutta, on the road that leads from the Valley of
Jezreel to Beth Shan (modern Beisan). This was an obvious path of
escape that would have taken the Midianites to the crossing of the
Jordan east of Beth Shan. They must have turned from this route,
however, for Abel Meholah lay ten miles south of Beth Shan, probably
right on the bank of the Jordan.[94] Zererah is generally identified with
Zarethan, but this cannot be the Zarethan of Joshua 3:16 and 1 Kings
7:46, which lay much too far south. There must have been another
place of the same name near Beth Shan (see 1 Kings 4:12).[95] Since the

---

[94] Goslinga therefore has "bank of Abel Meholah" in verse 22—TRANS.

[95] Van Gelderen identifies this Zarethan with modern Tell es-Sarem (*De Boeken
der Koningen,* vol. 1, p. 91).

Hebrew text literally states that Abel Meholan was "above" Tabbath, the latter place must have been farther downstream.

4. THE PURSUIT AND DESTRUCTION OF THE MIDIANITES
(7:23–8:21)

7:23 *Israelites from Naphtali, Asher and all Manasseh were called out, and they pursued the Midianites.*

As we have seen in verse 22, the Lord's astonishing assistance broke the overwhelming might of Midian almost with a single blow. Before the Israelites had even drawn their swords, He had granted them a victory that Isaiah 9:4 compares to the greatest act of deliverance of all. But they had to complete this victory by pursuing the fleeing Midianites, a name that of course refers to the entire enemy army. Gideon therefore sent for more Israelite soldiers. Since these came from Naphtali (which here includes Zebulun), Asher, and Manasseh, they must have been the same men that he had sent home in verses 3 and 8 (see 6:35 and footnote 89). Calling them back did not conflict with God's previous command to allow them to depart; for now that the Lord had lent His marvelous aid, the people had to demonstrate their own willingness to fight for their freedom. They could not remain passive but had to actively pluck the fruits of God's work.

7:24–25 *Gideon sent messengers throughout the hill country of Ephraim, saying, "Come down against the Midianites and seize the waters of the Jordan ahead of them as far as Beth Barah."*
So all the men of Ephraim were called out and they took the waters of the Jordan as far as Beth Barah. [25] *They also captured two of the Midianite leaders, Oreb and Zeeb. They killed Oreb at the rock of Oreb, and Zeeb at the winepress of Zeeb. They pursued the* [96] *Midianites and brought the heads of Oreb and Zeeb to Gideon, who was by the Jordan.*

Gideon sent out a special call to the Ephraimites, since this tribe, which bordered on the Jordan, was in the best position to thwart the Midianites' attempt to flee. He ordered them to come down from their mountain hideouts and strongholds (see 6:2) and to cut off the enemy's escape by seizing the river crossings. To do this they of course had to get there before the Midianites. The exact location of Beth Barah is not

---

[96] Following the ancient versions (Greek, Latin, and Syriac), the object marker *'ēt* should be read here instead of *'ēl*.

known, but it probably lay south of Abel Meholah and Tabbath (v. 22). The Ephraimites discharged their task successfully and even managed to capture and kill two Midianite leaders. Oreb ("raven") was killed at the rock of Oreb and Zeeb ("wolf") at the winepress of Zeeb, two places that obviously received their names from this event.[97]

Although the number of Ephraimites was too small to block the escape of the entire Midianite army, they did manage to harass the soldiers who got past them and to pursue them up to the Jordan. It seems that the pursuit was not carried beyond this point, however. The heads of Oreb and Zeeb were brought to Gideon on the other side of the Jordan.[98] Gideon and his men naturally would have led the pursuit, and they thus were the first to reach and cross the river (see 8:4). The Ephraimites overtook them on the opposite bank,[99] probably when Gideon stopped in order to give his men a brief rest. His reply to the Ephraimites in 8:2–3 seems to imply that they caught up with him before he had captured the other two Midianite leaders.

8:1–3 *Now the Ephraimites asked Gideon, "Why have you treated us like this? Why didn't you call us when you went to fight Midian?" And they criticized him sharply.*

²But he answered them, "What have I accomplished compared to you? Aren't the gleanings of Ephraim's grapes better than the full grape harvest of Abiezer?

³God gave Oreb and Zeeb, the Midianite leaders, into your hands. What was I able to do compared to you?" At this, their resentment against him[100] subsided.

The men of Ephraim unjustly criticized Gideon because he had not called them to fight against the Midianites earlier. They did not add that they certainly would have come, however. Their words in fact show that this was quite unlikely, for they resented the fact that the honor of victory belonged to Gideon, a Manassite. It is true that Gideon had sent no messengers to them before the battle (6:35), but this doubtless was because he knew that they would have been unwilling to help. Indeed they could have come on their own but instead remained in the security

---

[97] Isaiah 10:26 shows the significance that was attached to the Ephraimites' exploit (cf. also Ps. 83:11).

[98] Goslinga has "to Gideon on the other side of the Jordan" in verse 25 (cf. KJV and RSV)—TRANS.

[99] Or they may have crossed the Jordan more to the south and came to meet Gideon from there.

[100] Literally, "from against him"; i.e., their anger turned away from him.

of their mountain hideouts. So now they gave vent to their wounded ambition, thinking that Gideon also only wanted to win glory for his own tribe.

Gideon's answer totally disarmed them, however. With great wisdom, piety, and self-control, he modestly stated that his accomplishment was very small compared to theirs. In the first place he did not represent all Manasseh but only the clan of Abiezer.[101] Moreover, although he had been granted the grape harvest—i.e., he had been permitted to strike the first blow and put the enemy to flight—in this case the gleanings were more important. Ephraim could boast the heads of Oreb and Zeeb, while Gideon had not yet been able to capture a single Midianite leader. Gideon also pointed out that their success was due to God alone; credit did not belong to any man but to the Lord Almighty. His words put the Ephraimites' anger to rest, and a dangerous fraternal quarrel was thus averted before it started.

8:4–9 *Gideon and his three hundred men, exhausted yet keeping up the pursuit, came to the Jordan and crossed it. ⁵He said to the men of Succoth, "Give my troops some bread; they are worn out, and I am still pursuing Zebah and Zalmunna, the kings of Midian."*

⁶But the officials of Succoth said,[102] "Do you already have the hands of Zebah and Zalmunna in your possession? Why should we give bread to your troops?"

⁷Then Gideon replied, "Just for that,[103] when the LORD has given Zebah and Zalmunna into my hand, I will tear your flesh with desert thorns and briers."[104]

⁸From there he went up to Peniel and made the same request of them, but they answered as the men of Succoth had. ⁹So he said to the men of Peniel, "When I return in triumph, I will tear down this tower."

Since the fleeing soldiers numbered over ten thousand and the Israelite army was not sufficiently united, the pursuit inevitably became somewhat scattered. Significantly, only the three hundred choice

---

[101] Gideon's words in verse 2 strongly imply that his three hundred choice warriors came mainly from his own clan of Abiezer. Those who were the first to follow Gideon (6:34) turned out to be the ones who passed God's test at the spring of Harod (7:7).

[102] The Hebrew verb here is singular ("he said"). It may be permissible to follow a few of the ancient versions in reading the plural, but this is not strictly necessary.

[103] Another possible translation is "Very well, but when the LORD has given. . . ." See footnote 168 in 11:8.

[104] Although the Hebrew verb translated "tear" generally is not used with a double accusative, verse 16 shows that it is possible to read this clause this way. The 'et̲ is therefore an object marker.

soldiers under Gideon's direct command continued the pursuit deep into the Transjordan. Israel's leader was well aware that if the Midianites were to be permanently discouraged from reinvading Canaan (see v. 28), his task had to be carried out to the end. Verses 18–21 show that he was also motivated by the desire to punish those who had murdered his brothers.

We are not told where Gideon crossed the Jordan. Although he was on the enemy's track, the latter had gained considerable ground because of their swift camels. But his men managed to overcome their exhaustion and keep up the pursuit. When they finally reached Succoth, Gideon naturally expected that the citizens of this Israelite city would provide his troops with bread (the Hebrew literally means "round, flat loaves of bread"). Since he was pursuing Israel's common enemy, this was the least they could do. The men of Succoth's refusal to help was therefore nothing less than a short-sighted and cowardly act of treason against the nation, and the mockery in their words only increased their guilt. Their distrust of Gideon was rooted in unbelief toward God. Their question to Gideon in verse 6 literally seems to be asking him to show them the cut-off hands of Zebah and Zalmunna. Although the Hebrew term *kap* generally means "palm" or "hollow hand," it sometimes is used particularly for hands that have been cut or broken off (see Deut. 25:12; 1 Sam. 5:4; 2 Kings 9:35).

Gideon did not allow himself to become discouraged. Certain that the Lord would help him, he threatened the men of Succoth with a harsh but well-deserved punishment. Because they had spurned his request, he would thrash their naked flesh with "desert thorns and briers," the hardest and sharpest of all spiny plants. Without further delay Gideon proceeded onward to Peniel, but there his appeal for food found a similar response. Once again he announced a just punishment: the city's tower, which formed the strength and the pride of its citizens, would be leveled to the ground. Peniel and Succoth both lay on the Jabbok River. Succoth (perhaps identical to modern Tell Deir 'alla)[105] stood near the point where the Jabbok emptied into the Jordan, and both places apparently were located south of the river (see Gen. 32:31–32; 33:17). Succoth lay west of Peniel, for whereas Jacob had traveled westward toward the Jordan, Gideon was moving away from the river toward the east (see v. 11). He and his men undoubtedly managed to find food elsewhere; without it they could never have traveled the miles that lay ahead.

---

[105] See the *Bijbelse Encyclopedie.*

8:10–12 *Now Zebah and Zalmunna were in Karkor with a force of about fifteen thousand men, all that were left of the armies of the eastern peoples; a hundred and twenty thousand swordsmen had fallen. ¹¹Gideon went up by the route of the nomads east of Nobah and Jogbehah and fell upon the unsuspecting army. ¹²Zebah and Zalmunna, the two kings of Midian, fled, but he pursued them and captured them, routing their entire army.*

Zebah and Zalmunna had marched with their army to Karkor. Although the exact location of this is unknown,[106] verse 11's mention of Jogbehah indicates that it lay somewhere near Rabbah, the capital city of the Ammonites, and therefore far to the southeast of Peniel. The army of the "eastern peoples" had shrunk considerably; 120,000 had already fallen, either by the swords of their own comrades (7:22) or by the Israelites' swords. The survivors still constituted a sizable force of 15,000 men, however; and this caused them to become careless. They also felt secure in their current location, confident that the Israelite farmers would not have followed them this far east of the Jordan. They therefore rested from their hasty flight, leaving the camp completely unguarded; and Gideon was given another chance to surprise the enemy.

Gideon probably marched eastward from Peniel through the valley of the Jabbok and then turned south on the "route of the nomads [tent-dwellers]," a caravan route east of Jogbehah leading down to the Bedouins' country, which still has the same name today. Jogbehah is undoubtedly identical to modern Ajbeihat northwest of Amman (ancient Rabbah). Nobah must have stood slightly north of this. It cannot be the same place that Numbers 32:42 speaks of, for this lay far to the north in the territory of eastern Manasseh, while Jogbehah lay in the territory of Gad (Num. 32:35). Gideon took the enemy army by surprise, and they fled in confusion and fright. Zebah and Zalmunna, the two kings of Midian, attempted to escape as well; but he overtook and captured them. The army apparently did not even put up a fight, and Gideon abandoned the pursuit once they had been scattered and deprived of their commanders.

---

[106] It may be identical to the ruins of Karkagheisch, near Jogbehah, that Burkhardt speaks of (see Keil, *Kommentar*, p. 285). Garstang proposes the oasis of Karkar (*Joshua, Judges*, pp. 322f.), but this lay 150 miles southeast of Succoth; and we do not get the impression that Gideon traveled this far.

8:13-17 *Gideon son of Joash then returned from the battle by*[107] *the Pass of Heres.* [14]*He caught a young man of Succoth and questioned him, and the young man wrote down for him the names of the seventy-seven officials of Succoth, the elders of the town.* [15]*Then Gideon came and said to the men of Succoth, "Here are Zebah and Zalmunna, about whom you taunted me by saying, 'Do you already have the hands of Zebah and Zalmunna in your possession? Why should we give bread to your exhausted men?'"* [16]*He took the elders of the town and taught the men of Succoth a lesson by punishing them with desert thorns and briers.* [17]*He also pulled down the tower of Peniel and killed the men of the town.*

Rather than killing Zebah and Zalmunna at once, Gideon brought them along to show them to the cities that had scornfully refused food to his men. The statement that he returned "by the Pass of Heres" indicates that he went back by a different route, which would explain why he reached Succoth first. Aiming to enter the city by surprise, he approached it from an unexpected direction, namely, by the mountain road of Heres, which presumably lay south of Succoth and perhaps is identical to modern El-Herat. As the divinely appointed judge of Israel, Gideon certainly had the right to punish this city. He was not seeking personal revenge but simple justice (compare the cursing of Meroz in the song of Deborah, 5:23). He in fact exercised great restraint in this, for his punishment was limited to persons in positions of responsibility: the officials and the elders.

Gideon accosted a young man—the word can also mean "servant," but that is unlikely here—outside the city walls and interrogated him. This youth was apparently quite knowledgeable, for he was able to write down for Gideon the names of seventy-seven distinguished citizens. Armed with this list, Gideon entered the city without warning and displayed before its citizens the two captured Midianite kings about whom they had taunted him. He repeated their mocking words almost verbatim, only adding "exhausted men" to accentuate how vile their action had been. Then he also carried out his threat in verse 7 to the letter. Taking the elders—all the persons whose names had been written down for him (v. 14)—he used the "desert thorns and briers"

---

[107]The Hebrew text perhaps should be emended slightly here by omitting the second preposition (*l*[e]) before *ma'[a]lēh*. Presumably this *lamed* was accidentally inserted on the analogy of the preceding word *milḥāmâ(h)*. As it stands, the Hebrew means "from above," which does not fit with "Heres." The ancient versions offer no help here.

he had spoken of to teach them a bitter and painful lesson, i.e., he thrashed them with these but did not kill them.

The Hebrew text here literally reads simply "he taught the men of Succoth with these" (cf. KJV, RSV). We have no ground for assuming that the text originally read "he thrashed [or 'tore,' NIV] them." The ancient versions seem to support this, but they might be giving interpretative translations that bring out the correspondence of verse 16 to verse 7. It was not necessary that the author describe the execution of Gideon's punishment with the same graphic terms that Israel's leader had used in the former verse. The meaning of the text is obvious here. Peniel was punished also and apparently even more harshly than Succoth. But Gideon no doubt only killed the men of this city because they offered resistance. Perhaps they made a stand within the tower itself so that he could not carry out his threat without bringing them down as well.

8:18–19 *Then he asked Zebah and Zalmunna, "What kind of[108] men did you kill at Tabor?"*

"Men like you," they answered, "each one with the bearing of a prince."

[19]Gideon replied, "Those were my brothers, the sons of my own mother. As surely as the LORD lives, if you had spared their lives, I would not kill you."

Gideon still had a third sentence to carry out. Zebah and Zalmunna also had to receive their just punishment. Although verse 18 proceeds to this immediately, we are not to think that the execution of these kings took place right after the punishment of Peniel. The presence of Gideon's son Jether (v. 20), a young man who surely did not belong to the three hundred, implies that the Israelite army was back in the vicinity of their commander's home, probably at Ophrah.[109] Unlike Oreb and Zeeb, therefore, the two Midianite kings did not receive a summary execution. This was not because Gideon wanted to put his victims on display in Israel, but because they had shed blood within Gideon's own clan and had to be put to death as criminals. Their execution probably took place in the presence of the entire family of Joash, Gideon's father.

The event that Gideon was speaking of in his question to Zebah and Zalmunna has not even been alluded to in the previous verses. We can infer from his words, however, that his brothers had not been killed in fair combat but had rather been treacherously murdered by a group of

---

[108]The Hebrew interrogative means "where" in all other cases (cf. RSV), but here it has to mean "what manner of" or "in what condition."

[109]See D. Hoek, *Het boek der Richteren*, p. 212.

Midianites led by Zebah and Zalmunna. Tabor is probably the mountain of that name, though it could possibly be another place. The Midianites may have been staying there in order to find pasture for their animals. Since Zebah and Zalmunna immediately understood what Gideon was talking about, the murder must have taken place quite recently, perhaps shortly before Gideon received his call, and under very special circumstances. His question does not mean to ascertain whether or not they were guilty but to let them know exactly whom they had assaulted and what they were being sentenced for. They realized at once that their victims belonged to Gideon's family; and without attempting to excuse themselves or hide anything, they answered, "Men like you, each one with the bearing of a prince." Gideon then exclaimed, "Those were my brothers, the sons of my own mother," thus making clear that they were his full brothers, born of both his father and his mother. It therefore was no wonder that they resembled him and embodied the nobility of his lineage.

Gideon forgot that he was first of all a judge, not an avenger of his family's blood, when he declared under oath that he would not kill the captive kings if they had spared his brothers. As a judge and a servant of the Lord, he could under no condition spare the lives of these enemies of the Lord's people. Blood vengeance was not forbidden to him, but it was secondary; and he was wrong to put his family interests before those of the Lord.

8:20–21 *Turning to Jether, his oldest son, he said, "Kill them!" But Jether did not draw his sword, because he was only a boy and was afraid.*

²¹Zebah and Zalmunna said, "Come, do it yourself. 'As is the man, so is his strength.'" So Gideon stepped forward and killed them, and took the ornaments off their camels' necks.

Gideon's confused priorities led him to entrust the task of killing Zebah and Zalmunna to his son Jether rather than to his own soldiers. This would humiliate the Midianite kings and simultaneously give his son the opportunity to prove his manhood.[110] Jether, however, was unequal to such a test and did not dare to go at these stalwart sons of the desert. The latter, in turn, begged to be spared such an indignity: Gideon himself might attack them, but the task was more than child's play. Accepting their invitation, Gideon cut down the two kings and

---

[110]In later times the Saracens also had their captives slaughtered by boys, "who thereby proved their manhood." See Kittel, *Gestalten und Gedanken in Isräel,* p. 78.

claimed as his own the gold or silver ornaments that hung on long cords from the necks of their camels.[111]

5. GIDEON'S REJECTION OF THE KINGSHIP, HIS LATER LIFE, AND HIS DEATH (8:22–35)

8:22–23 *The Israelites said to Gideon, "Rule over us—you, your son and your grandson—because you have saved us out of the hand of Midian."*
23 But Gideon told them, "I will not rule over you, nor will my son rule over you. The LORD will rule over you."

The successful pursuit of the Midianites and the execution of their two kings had ended Israel's struggle for its national freedom. Before turning home, however, the Israelites with Gideon asked that he and his descendants rule over their part of Israel. He was not offered the kingship over all Israel. Most likely only the tribes mentioned in 6:35 were speaking here, and probably Issachar as well. The selfish and ambitious nature of the Ephraimites (8:1–3; cf. also 12:1) makes it extremely doubtful that members of this tribe were present. After their meeting with Gideon by the Jordan, they had probably returned to their homes. But the army of the other tribes was more or less united, and it would therefore have been natural for them to reassemble somewhere after they had abandoned the pursuit of the Midianites.

The Israelites' request was motivated by gratefulness toward Gideon, by their sense of solidarity (v. 22 thus calls them "Israelites," or, literally, "men of Israel"), and perhaps also by the need for a central authority that would give expression to the tribes' unity. Nevertheless it seems that they failed to appreciate the fact that the Lord was already their king. Thus Gideon declined their flattering offer (though the word is not used, they were actually offering his family dynastic control). This does not mean that he rejected the very idea of a monarchy.[112] He simply did not feel called to the office of king, and he could hardly regard a request that did not come from an official national assembly as a divine appointment. Moreover, as long as the Israelites recognized the Lord's rule, no human king would be necessary.

---

[111] These probably were shaped like a crescent or half moon (cf. RSV). The term used for them is not pure Hebrew and appears elsewhere only in Isaiah 3:18. The death of Zebah and Zalmunna is alluded to in Psalm 83:11.

[112] This is the view of various modern critics who date the text to the time of Hosea (or later). See Moore, *Judges*, p. 230.

8:24–27 *And he said, "I do have one request, that each of you give me an earring from your share of the plunder."*[113] *(It was the custom of the Ishmaelites to wear gold earrings.)*

25 They answered, "We'll be glad to give them." So they spread out a garment, and each man threw a ring from his plunder onto it. 26 The weight of the gold rings he asked for came to seventeen hundred shekels, not counting the ornaments, the pendants and the purple garments worn by the kings of Midian or the chains that were on their camels' necks. 27 Gideon made the gold into an ephod, which he placed in Ophrah, his town. All Israel prostituted themselves by worshiping it there, and it became a snare to Gideon and his family.

After unequivocally declining the kingship, Gideon made his own request. But although his intent may have been to strengthen the unity of the nation under the Lord's rule, he in fact committed an offense against His kingship by making an unauthorized change in Israel's ritual. The fact that Gideon did not realize this and thought he could bring honor to his nation's God in this way shows how strongly even he had been influenced by the Canaanites.[114] He asked his men for the earrings they had plundered from the enemy. Almost every one of them had seized such an earring, since the invaders, who were Ishmaelites, usually wore many rings.

In this context "Ishmaelites" seems to be a general name, almost equivalent to "Bedouins" or "desert people,"[115] that refers more to their mode of life than to their lineage. Thus here it can include the Midianites, who were not descended from Ishmael (Gen. 25:1–2, 13–15; see also Gen. 37:25–28). These nomads, who often conducted trade by means of caravans, were fond of jewelry (as they still are today) and would use it to adorn both themselves and their animals.

Gideon's men eagerly accepted his request (cf. Exod. 32:2–3), and each of them threw his earring onto a garment that had been spread out on the ground. The total amount of gold he collected came to 1,700 shekels, i.e., about 62 pounds if a shekel was equal to approximately ⅗ of an ounce[116] (but see the NIV marginal note on v. 26—TRANS.). The ornaments and other valuables that verse 26 excludes from this total

---

[113] Literally, "earring of his plunder." The translation "earrings" (RSV) or "an earring" (NIV) is possible; but the verse gives the impression that when the plunder was divided, each person received a single ring. (Goslinga's translation thus reads "his plundered earring"—TRANS.)

[114] See Noordtzij, *Gods Woord*, pp. 366f.

[115] See Moore, *Judges*, p. 231; Kautzsch, *Die Heilige Schrift des Alten Testaments*, note in verse 24.

[116] See *Bijbels-Kerkelijk Woordenboek*, vol. 1, p. 280; cf. p. 88.

could not have been items that the people kept for themselves. These things had belonged to the Midianite kings; furthermore, the verse is speaking of the weight of gold that Gideon did in fact collect. Since Gideon asked only for the earrings, the people undoubtedly kept most of their plunder. But the pendants and other items that are not included in the 1,700 shekel total must have formed his own personal contribution to his project; for he had taken the ornaments of the kings and their camels (v. 21), and he certainly would also have received a sizable share of the rest of the spoils.

Gideon made an ephod from the treasures he had gathered. Although commentators formerly regarded this ephod as some kind of idol, the Hebrew term can never have this meaning. It rather was simply the upper garment worn by the high priest, which had a breastpiece attached to the front of it and two shoulder pieces for holding it in place. The descriptions in Exodus 28 and 39 show that the materials for such an ephod were extremely costly—it was woven with gold thread and contained numerous jewels—and it therefore was not surprising that Gideon needed a large amount of gold to produce it.[117] We need not assume that this ephod was an exact copy of the one described in Exodus 28.

The new sacred garment was placed and kept at Ophrah, Gideon's hometown. Although the Hebrew verb used in verse 27 usually means "place" or "set up," this does not necessarily have to indicate that the ephod was an idol. The verb can also mean "lay down," as with the fleece in 6:37; and in the present context we could use the more neutral translation "give a place to." The ephod must have been kept in a room from which it could be taken whenever a divine oracle was wanted. Ephods were worn by priests, even in pagan nations,[118] as a means for communicating with the deity.

Gideon must have thought that he could separate the ephod from its legitimate high priestly function in the tabernacle at Shiloh and use it to receive divine oracles independently. He thus introduced an unlawful change in Israel's ritual, perhaps thinking that the tribe of Ephraim (where Shiloh was located) had no right to possess the national

---

[117]See Noordtzij, *Gods Woord*, p. 367, who points out that much gold was also used to pay the workers. Also see G. Aalders, "Gideon," *Christelijke Encyclopedie*, 1st ed. (Kampen: Kok, 1925).

[118]See Böhl, "Efod," *Bijbels-Kerkelijk Woordenboek*, vol. 1, and Obbink-Brouwer, *Inleiding tot den Bijbel* (1928), pp. 32f. Both these scholars reject the conception of the ephod as an idol image.

sanctuary. Gideon's illicit act had dire consequences. He seduced the nation ("all Israel" seems to refer to more than just the above-mentioned northern tribes) into abandoning the legitimate sanctuary and prostituting itself to the ephod; and he brought on himself and his family the judgment that had been imposed on violators of the second commandment (Exod. 20:5). We cannot tell whether Gideon himself functioned as a priest; but if not, he certainly must have installed others in the office (cf. 17:5).

8:28–32 *Thus Midian was subdued before the Israelites and did not raise its head again. During Gideon's lifetime, the land enjoyed peace forty years.*
    ²⁹Jerub-Baal son of Joash went back home to live. ³⁰He had seventy sons of his own, for he had many wives. ³¹His concubine, who lived in Shechem, also bore him a son, whom he named Abimelech. ³²Gideon son of Joash died at a good old age and was buried in the tomb of his father Joash in Ophrah of the Abiezrites.

These verses tell how Gideon's life ended. His work as judge consisted mainly in breaking the yoke of the Midianites, whom he defeated so totally (without conquering their territory, however) that they never again thought of making another raid on Israel. For the rest of Gideon's lifetime, approximately forty years, the land was therefore able to live in peace. This was the fruit, not only of his military efforts, but also of his religious reform that undermined the Baal cult and restored his people's relation to the Lord, at least in principle. Recalling this earlier reform, the author once again called him "Jerub-Baal," a name that he had kept in spite of his later errors.

Gideon returned to his private home, but we can infer from verse 33 that he remained a dominant figure. Nevertheless, he had some personal flaws that compromised his influence on society. That he had numerous wives and seventy sons does not do him credit. Even though devout Israelites might not have been greatly offended by such polygamy at that time,[119] it indicates a sensual propensity that reflects unfavorably on the judge Gideon. Scripture in fact condemns his polygamy indirectly by showing how the very size of his family led to a conflict among his sons that resulted in Abimelech's atrocious crime (9:5). The birth of this son is specially mentioned because of the role he would play in chapter 9. His mother was not a wife within Gideon's own house but a concubine who lived in Shechem (she was not a slave,

---

[119]See G. Aalders, "Gideon," *Christelijke Encyclopedie.*

however; see 9:18 and the comments in 9:3). The Hebrew verb used in verse 31 indicates that Abimelech was given to him as a secondary name, probably because this son very soon stood out among all his brothers.[120] Gideon died at a "good old age." Assuming that he was no older than thirty-five or forty when the Lord called him, he lived to the age of seventy-five or eighty.

8:33–35 *No sooner had Gideon died than the Israelites again prostituted themselves to the Baals. They set up Baal-Berith as their god and* [34] *did not remember the LORD their God, who had rescued them from the hands of all their enemies on every side.* [35] *They also failed to show kindness to the family of Jerub-Baal (that is, Gideon) for all the good things he had done for them.*

After Gideon's death the Israelites fell back into the worship of Baal. The generation that had been his co-witnesses to Midian's unexpected downfall departed too; and the newcomers, who had had no firsthand experience of this amazing deliverance, were all the more prone to the Baal cults because their predecessors, Gideon included, had failed to preserve the purity of the Lord's worship. They even went so far as to worship Baal under the name Baal-Berith, i.e., "Baal of the covenant." By thus regarding Baal as a god who had a covenant with Israel, the people actually substituted him for the Lord, who had formerly revealed Himself to them as the God of the covenant (Exod. 24:8; Josh. 24:25). Israel thus fell prey to syncretism.[121]

The center, or perhaps the fountainhead, of this form of Baal worship seems to have been Shechem (see 9:4, 46). By their apostasy the Israelites showed that they had forgotten what had been done for them by both the Lord and Jerub-Baal, whose family had an enduring right to

---

[120]The verb does not mean simply "name" but rather "confer a name on [as a by-name or new name]" (see 2 Kings 17:34; Neh. 9:7; Dan. 1:7; 5:12). For this reason Abimelech could not have meant "my father is king," since Gideon certainly would never have given such a name. The name probably instead meant "Father is king," with "Father" being a reference to God Himself. See Oosterhoff, *Israëlietische persoonsnamen* (1953), pp. 67f.; Keil, *Kommentar*, p. 291; Moore, *Judges*, pp. 235f. Also see Obbink-Brouwer, *Inleiding tot den Bijbel*, p. 35, who translates the name "my father is king" and assumes that the monarchy was already established under Gideon.

[121]This is the view of Keil, *Kommentar*, p. 291; Hoekstra, *De Heere is vrede*, p. 176. Another explanation of the name Baal-Berith is "Protector of covenants among men"; see Oettli, *Buch der Richter*, p. 258, Hoek, *Het boek der Richteren*, p. 227.

their gratitude. In regard to these later developments, see sections II and V of the Introduction and the comments in 2:11–13.

6. ABIMELECH'S MURDER OF HIS BROTHERS AND INSTALLATION AS KING AT SHECHEM (9:1–21)

The story of Abimelech and his rule at Shechem has to be regarded as an appendix to the story of Gideon. It cannot be placed on the same level as the histories of the judges themselves, for Abimelech was in no sense a judge and is never called one. He was not a man of God whom the Lord called to deliver the nation and to lead it back to a life of obedience to His commandments. On the contrary, he was a person who took advantage of the lack of a central authority and violently seized the kingship with the support of a group of Baal worshipers. His story is included in the Book of Judges only because it typifies this period to some degree. It provides a striking illustration of the decline that set in after Gideon's death and clearly displays the disastrous turn of events that was brought on by the latter's weaknesses.

One peculiarity is that, in this case, the Israelites were not punished for their sin through a new advent of foreign (or at least, non-Israelite) oppression. Instead, their judgment took the form of internal discord and bloody civil strife, the inevitable outcome of the previous decline in their religious and moral life (see 8:33–35). Although most critical scholars claim to perceive a different spirit in chapter 9 than in chapters 3–8, it clearly preaches the very same message of divine justice and recompense (see especially vv. 23–24, 56–57).

9:1–5 *Abimelech son of Jerub-Baal went to his mother's brothers in Shechem and said to them and to all his mother's clan,* ²*"Ask all the citizens of Shechem, 'Which is better for you: to have all seventy of Jerub-Baal's sons rule over you, or just one man?' Remember, I am your flesh and blood."*

³*When the brothers repeated all this to the citizens of Shechem, they were inclined to follow Abimelech, for they said, "He is our brother."* ⁴*They gave him seventy shekels of silver from the temple of Baal-Berith, and Abimelech used them to hire reckless adventurers, who became his followers.* ⁵*He went to his father's home in Ophrah and on one stone murdered his seventy brothers, the sons of Jerub-Baal. But Jotham, the youngest son of Jerub-Baal, escaped by hiding.*

Some time after his father's death, Abimelech, driven by a lust for power (see the comments in 8:31), traveled to Shechem to gain the support of his mother's brothers and, through them, the entire population of the city. Not satisfied to occupy a prominent position at Ophrah alongside Gideon's other sons, he wanted to be the undisputed and sole ruler. But to achieve this he needed his mother's family to stir up open opposition in Shechem against his brothers' supposed plan to rule Israel as an oligarchy. We cannot infer from his words in verse 2 that Gideon's other sons indeed had such a plan. Abimelech was only trying to frighten his family into making a quick choice between a government by many and a monarchy. And he added that, if they preferred the latter (as is tacitly assumed) and all the citizens (literally, "lords," "owners") of Shechem agreed, they should remember that he was their own flesh and blood and therefore had a right to their support.

Abimelech's uncles reported his words to the Shechemites and easily won them over, for they regarded Abimelech as their own kinsman. Realizing that Shechem would share in his glory if he succeeded, the inhabitants of the city even went so far as to offer him material help in the form of seventy shekels of silver (i.e., about 2½ pounds; see in 8:26)[122] taken from the treasury in the temple of Baal-Berith. All this indicates that Abimelech's uncles were very prominent citizens who had a large following in Shechem, and they must therefore have found it insulting when Jotham called their sister a "slave girl" (v. 18). There is no evidence, however, that Shechem was still in Canaanite hands and that the present chapter is describing a revolt of the native population against their Israelite masters.[123] Abimelech said nothing about a difference in nationality, and verses 22 and 55 clearly show that he was an Israelite ruler. The city had in fact been captured early in Joshua's campaigns, and it became a center of Israelite life (Josh. 8:30–35; 24:1), even though some Canaanite elements might have remained there.

Abimelech used the silver he had been given to hire a group of "reckless adventurers."[124] The first of the two Hebrew terms used here literally means "empty"; in the present context it is equivalent to "worthless," "unprincipled," "immoral." The meaning of the second term is less certain. Some think it denotes faithlessness, but its cognate forms in other languages seem to point more to recklessness or unscrupulousness.

---

[122] But see the NIV marginal note in verse 4—TRANS.

[123] This is the view of Moore, *Judges*, pp. 238, 243, and E. Sellin, *Wie wurde Sichem eine israelitische Stadt?* (1922). Noordtzij, *Gods Woord*, p. 368, rejects such a position.

[124] D. Hoek's notion that the task of these mercenaries was to stir up the citizens of Shechem against Gideon's sons is entirely groundless (*Het boek der Richteren*, p. 230). Abimelech's kinsmen had already done this quite successfully (vv. 3–4).

Accompanied by this band of criminals, Abimelech marched to Ophrah and made a surprise attack on his brothers, probably during the night. All of them were brutally murdered with the exception of Jotham, who managed to hide himself. The gruesome detail that they were all killed—slaughtered, as it were—on a single stone implies that Abimelech performed the whole massacre himself, probably to ensure that not one of his brothers escaped. He then would have missed Jotham, his youngest brother; but the survival of a single member from Gideon's family would not have stopped Abimelech from having himself proclaimed king.

9:6 *Then all the citizens of Shechem and Beth Millo gathered beside the great tree at the pillar in Shechem to crown Abimelech king.*

Abimelech returned to Shechem, where the citizens rewarded his act of "tyrannicide" by crowning him king. It is not clear why this verse (also v. 20) mentions Beth Millo along with Shechem, especially since verses 2–3, 7, and 18 speak only of the citizens of Shechem when the citizens of Beth Millo must have been intended as well. What could have been the relationship between these two places? Beth Millo must have been an independent part of the city of Shechem. It then would have been included under the name Shechem; but for the sake of completeness, it could also be named separately. Shechem thus may have been the "lower city" and Beth Millo the "upper city," that was built on a hill and contained the tower of Shechem.[125] This tower is spoken of in verses 46–49, where, remarkably, the "citizens of the tower of Shechem" are distinguished from the people of Shechem itself; for the city had been demolished and its inhabitants put to death already in verses 42–45. It is natural to assume that this distinction parallels the distinction between Shechem and Beth Millo and that the latter was nothing other than the tower of Shechem along with the section of the city where it stood. This position is strongly supported by the fact that the word Millo (perhaps a Canaanite term; its derivation is uncertain) has to denote a fortress or stronghold, since the Millo in

---

[125]This is the view of C. Spielmann, *Jotham* (Halle, 1901), p. 71. For the location and history of Shechem, see, e.g., Noordtzij, *Gods Woord*, pp. 46f.; Böhl, *Bijbels-Kerkelijk Woordenboek*, vol. 1, pp. 279f., and *Palestina in het licht der jongste opgravingen* (1931). According to Böhl, the tower of Shechem stood at Tell Balatah, in the eastern part of the valley between Mount Ebal and Mount Gerizim, while Shechem itself lay farther west in the valley, probably at Tell Sufar (pp. 61–67). The designations "upper" and "lower" city therefore might not be appropriate.

Jerusalem was an important fortification in that city (see 2 Sam. 5:9; 1 Kings 9:15, 24: 11:27; 2 Chron. 32:5, NIV marginal notes).[126] In my view the tower of Shechem itself would then have been called the Millo, while Beth Millo referred to the whole "upper city" including its stronghold.[127]

Abimelech was crowned by the citizens of Shechem and Beth Millo at a place that had great historical importance: the oak of the monument at Shechem.[128] This was undoubtedly the stone of witness that Joshua had set up in order to keep alive the memory of the covenant renewal ceremony at Shechem (Josh. 24:26–27). Abimelech and his followers could no longer comprehend its silent testimony. Although Keil, Oettli, and others have claimed that the temple of Baal-Berith stood at this same site, this is mere conjecture. I will say more about the location of this shrine in verse 46.

9:7–15 *When Jotham was told about this, he climbed up on the top of Mount Gerizim and shouted*[129] *to them, "Listen to me, citizens of Shechem, so that God may listen to you. 8 One day the trees went out to anoint a king for themselves. They said to the olive tree, 'Be our king.'*

9 "But the olive tree answered, 'Should I give up[130] *my oil, by which both gods and men are honored, to hold sway over the trees?'*

10 "Next, the trees said to the fig tree, 'Come and be our king.'

11 "But the fig tree replied, 'Should I give up[130] *my fruit, so good and sweet, to hold sway over the trees?'*

12 "Then the trees said to the vine, 'Come and be our king.'

13 "But the vine answered, 'Should I give up[130] *my wine, which cheers both gods and men, to hold sway over the trees?'*

14 "Finally all the trees said to the thornbush, 'Come and be our king.'

---

[126] See Van Gelderen's remarks in the *Korte Verklaring* in 1 Kings 11:27.

[127] I therefore reject the notion that Beth Millo means "house of Millo" in the sense of "people of Millo" (see vv. 6 and 20 in the KJV). It may be tempting to understand the name this way since it then would parallel "citizens of Shechem" and since it clearly refers to the population and not merely to the place itself. Applying a place name to its inhabitants is normal linguistic usage, however, while the above understanding of Beth Millo is not. Such a view would be acceptable only if Millo were a personal name or if the one thousand or so inhabitants (v.49) belonged to a single clan. Place names prefixed by "Beth" are common.

[128] The NIV translates this "great tree at the pillar in Shechem." The Hebrew term translated as "pillar" or "monument" is obscure, and both Goslinga and the NIV emend it—TRANS.

[129] Literally, "and raised his voice and shouted and said. . . ."

[130] According to *Gesenius' Hebrew Grammar* (§ 63 k), Bertheau, and Keil, these peculiar verbal forms are the Qal perfect.

15 "The thornbush said to the trees, 'If you really want to anoint me king over you, come and take refuge in my shade; but if not, then let fire come out of the thornbush and consume the cedars of Lebanon!'

When he heard what had happened in Shechem, Jotham decided to rebuke the city's inhabitants for their ingratitude and to warn them of the dire consequences their action would have. This was a bold step, but he was cautious enough to remain outside the city and proclaim his message from Mount Gerizim. He probably did not stand at the summit (2,850 ft.) but on an outcropping that formed a natural platform above the city, low enough so that he could be understood by the citizens.[131] Their attention was drawn by the hearing. Jotham then proceeded to tell a fable that would sting their consciences once they grasped its moral. The use of the fable to convey a specific truth in poetic form is extremely rare in the Old Testament (2 Kings 14:9 is the only other example); parables were used more commonly for this purpose. Jotham's fable has trees as its actors. Wishing to anoint a king over themselves, they offer this dignity first to the olive tree, then to the fig tree, and then to the vine; but in each case they are firmly turned down. Surprised and almost horrified by the offer, all three ask whether one could expect them to give up[132] their useful and beneficial mode of life to rule over the trees. They could not perform both tasks at once; so they would have to renounce their role of bringing gladness to "gods and men" and exchange their true worth and glory for a mere semblance of glory, namely, the exalted but precarious position of "waving over the trees."

Jotham's fable was not condemning the kingly office itself but alluding to the dangers that accompany this office and make it an undesirable task. The threefold rejection accentuates this, for none of the initial candidates for the office wanted it. At their wits' end, all the trees (this is the first time the word "all" is used) finally make their offer to the thornbush. He is willing to accept it, but because the trees

---

[131]The place is still called "Jotham's pulpit" today; see Böhl, *Palestina,* p. 103, and the comments in verse 7 in Moore, *Judges,* and Oettli, *Buch der Richter.* A. Van Deursen gives a clear drawing of the site in *Palestine het land van den Bijbel,* p. 163.

[132]"Give up" in verses 9, 11, and 13 translates a Qal perfect verb form. D. Hoek (*Het boek der Richteren,* p. 234) puts the first of these in the past tense and has "have I then lost" in verse 9. But since he translates the second perfect form as "should I depart," the first one could also be put in the present. The three perfect forms are equivalent and according to *Gesenius' Hebrew* Grammar (§ 106 n) are to be regarded as *perfectum confidentiae.*

have only turned to him as a last resort, he first sets a condition that takes advantage of his thorniness. Grinning sardonically, as it were, he says that if they are serious about their offer and really want him as king, they are welcome to come and take refuge in his shadow. According to Moore, "the irony of the fable has its climax in the seriousness of this pledge of protection."[133] The trees will soon discover that they have gotten a king who cannot help but prick and wound them, even when he attempts to show kindness. A more fitting satire of kings like Abimelech could hardly be found than this thornbush offering its shade. The king-to-be has yet more to say, however. If the trees are not serious about recognizing him as king (i.e., "but if not"),[134] he will unleash on them a raging fire that will consume even the cedars of Lebanon, the greatest and fairest of trees. This threat was no empty boast; thornbushes are easily set aflame and can often quickly spread a fire through an entire forest or field (see Exod. 22:6; Isa. 9:18).

9:16–20 *"Now if you have acted honorably and in good faith when you made Abimelech king, and if you have been fair to Jerub-Baal and his family, and if you have treated him as he deserves— 17 and to think that my father fought for you, risked his life to rescue you from the hand of Midian 18 (but today you have revolted against my father's family, murdered his seventy sons on a single stone, and made Abimelech, the son of his slave girl, king over the citizens of Shechem because he is your brother)— 19 if then you have acted honorably and in good faith toward Jerub-Baal and his family today, may Abimelech be your joy, and may you be his, too! 20 But if you have not, let fire come out from Abimelech and consume you, citizens of Shechem and Beth Millo, and let fire come out from you, citizens of Shechem and Beth Millo, and consume Abimelech!"*

Jotham gave the application of his fable by making a sharp accusation against the citizens of Shechem. His lesson for them closely parallels the words of the fable, particularly the answer of the thornbush in verse 15, but the thought changes somewhat. For although "really" in that verse and "honorably" in verse 16 translate the same Hebrew words (*be'emet*),[135] the meaning is different in each case.

Verse 15 is asking whether the trees (i.e., the Shechemites) were

---

[133] *Judges*, p. 248.

[134] Keil's interpretation of these words as "if you do not find the expected protection by me" (*Kommentar*, p. 295) is rather odd and does not fit the context.

[135] Goslinga thus has "honestly" in both verses. Cf. the RSV, which has "in good faith" (NASB, "in truth") both times—TRANS.

acting honorably or truthfully toward the thornbush (i.e., Abimelech), while in verse 16 Jotham is asking whether the Shechemites acted "honorably and in good faith" toward Jerub-Baal and his family when they made Abimelech king. One cannot call this a serious discrepancy between the fable and its application,[136] however, since the similarity between Abimelech and the thornbush that is brought out in verses 19–20 is the main point of the fable. Another difference lies in the fact that the trees did not really want the thornbush as king, while the citizens of Shechem did in fact sincerely want Abimelech. This, however, formed a deliberate satire of the Shechemites' folly: they had what even that creatures devoid of reason never would have done.

We also should remember in this context that Abimelech too was a son of Gideon and therefore belonged to the "family of Jerub-Baal." If the Shechemites wished to defend their action by saying that they were showing honor to Jerub-Baal and being loyal to his family by crowning Abimelech, Jotham could rightly object that they were not speaking "honorably and truthfully" (in the same sense as v. 15; see footnote 135). They never could really have meant to pay homage to the family of Gideon, for they had had Gideon's legitimate sons killed and had made the murderer, the son of Gideon's slave girl (see in v. 18), into their king.

My above demonstration that the fable (vv. 8–15) and its moral (vv. 16–20) indeed fit together (although it is true that no analogy is perfect) has already basically explained the latter verses. As the translation shows, the sentence that begins in verse 16 is not completed till verse 19. Verse 16 contains a conditional clause that is resumed in verse 19 and then followed by the main clause. Verses 17–18 form a parenthesis that, as it were, offers internal proof that these are indeed Jotham's very own words. The mention of Gideon at the end of verse 16 moved him to describe in powerful and glowing terms what his father had done for the people. He fought for them and placed his own life in peril to free them from the Midianites' oppression. The tribe of Ephraim, to which Shechem belonged, too had shared in the fruits of his victory. With a fine sense of drama, Jotham chose this moment to disclose his true identity. Instead of repeating the name "Jerub-Baal" from verse 16, he called him "my father"; and the storyteller thus suddenly revealed himself as the son who had arisen to defend his father's honor. The son, in turn, turned into a preacher who confronted his audience

---

[136]This is the view of Moore, *Judges,* p. 245. Others go even further and hold that the fable has been transposed from a completely different context.

with a picture of the man who had risked his life for their sake and to whom they owed so much.

In verse 18 the preacher became an accuser who hurled down his indictment from Mount Gerizim by describing the hideous ingratitude with which the men of Shechem rewarded Gideon's selfless action. They had rebelled against his family, killed his sons by consenting to Abimelech's murderous plan and offering him monetary support (vv. 3–4), and enthroned Abimelech as their king. Jotham called the latter "the son of his slave girl" because his mother was only a concubine of Gideon, so that Abimelech actually was not equal to his father's legitimate sons. He was indeed the Shechemites' kinsman, but since he was the least worthy of Gideon's sons, they had dishonored themselves by choosing him as their king. The free citizens of Shechem (the Hebrew here satirically calls them "lords") had actually displayed a slavish mentality by consenting to be ruled by the son of a slave woman. In the end they would get what they had asked for.

The accuser finally turned into a prophet of doom. His words in verse 19 are pure irony. The possibility that was entertained in verse 16— namely, that the Shechemites had acted "honorably and in good faith"—has already been revealed as a blatant falsehood by the parenthesis. Jotham nonetheless continued to entertain it so that he could mockingly play the role of a well-wisher. If they have acted honorably, he said, then they should congratulate one another; i.e., he joined them in wishing one another well. If they have not, however, he had a double threat for them in verse 20: fire would come from Abimelech to consume them, and fire would come from them to consume Abimelech. A friendship based on ambition, ingratitude, disloyalty, and bloodshed could only have disastrous consequences for both sides. The application here goes beyond the fable, since the latter had spoken only of a fire coming from the thornbush (v. 15).[137] But since in this case both sides were guilty (see vv. 24, 56–57), the king and the citizens would have to execute judgment on each other.

9:21 *Then Jotham fled, escaping to Beer, and he lived there because he was afraid of his brother Abimelech.*

Once he had finished speaking, Jotham realized he was no longer safe there. Abimelech would want to kill him just as he had killed his brothers. Jotham therefore fled in haste, probably toward the south

---

[137]See Keil, *Kommentar*, p. 295.

(Mount Gerizim stood south of Shechem). Beer ("well"), the place where he settled, is usually identified with El-Bireh south of Bethel; but this remains uncertain.

7. GOD'S REQUITING OF ABIMELECH AND SHECHEM (9:22–57)

9:22–24 *After Abimelech had governed Israel three years, ²³God sent an evil spirit between Abimelech and the citizens of Shechem, who acted treacherously against Abimelech. ²⁴God did this in order that the crime against Jerub-Baal's seventy sons, the shedding of their blood, might be avenged on their brother Abimelech[138] and on the citizens of Shechem, who had helped him murder his brothers.*

Three years had passed since the citizens of Shechem crowned Abimelech as their king (v. 6). His power must have extended beyond Shechem itself, for verse 22 says that he governed "Israel." He could not have been king of all Twelve Tribes, however; at most, his domain covered the tribes of Ephraim and Manasseh, which had assumed a leading position during Gideon's battle against the Midianites. The fact that his kingship was illegitimate may be expressed by the particular Hebrew verb (*śûr*) used in verse 22.[139] But the basis of his rule, the friendship between Abimelech and Shechem, proved to be unstable when after three years the Shechemites began to rebel against him. We are not told the direct cause of their disaffection, but sacred historiography here displays its true character by revealing the primary and deepest cause: God sent an evil spirit between Abimelech and the citizens of Shechem. The Lord had even the demonic powers under His complete control. He used this spirit to disrupt the good relations between Abimelech and the Shechemites and to sow a seed of dissension that would produce an uprising.

The fact that God adopted such a course shows to what depths Israel

---

[138]This sentence presents a problem in that it conjoins an intransitive and a transitive verb. A literal translation would be "in order that the crime against the seventy sons of Jerub-Baal, their blood, might come and be brought on Abimelech their brother. . . ." The word "on" here is to be construed with both "come" and "be brought."

[139]Abimelech can in a sense be considered a forerunner of Saul, even though the latter did assume the throne lawfully. For Abimelech exalted himself by capitalizing on the longing for a king that prevailed in some circles (see 8:22), and in this he "represented in his own time the same spirit that later became manifest in the rejection of Samuel and Jehovah and the installation of Saul" (Ph. J. Hoedemaker, *Zonde en Genade*, p. 159).

had sunk and how far the people had become estranged from Him. By permitting an evil spirit to influence them, He was acknowledging that His people had fallen from their high rank and had become basically the same as the pagans whose gods they worshiped. This is why verse 23 (also vv. 56–57) does not call Him "the LORD," a name that pointed to the special relationship between the Israelites and their covenant Partner, but instead uses the more general term "God." God here was acting as the righteous Ruler of the world. Because He is holy, He punished both Abimelech and the Shechemites for their criminal alliance by alienating them from each other. In so doing He avenged their crime and brought the blood of Jerub-Baal's sons (the Hebrew term for blood often connotes blood that has been shed violently; see Deut. 19:10, 13; Ps. 106:38) not only on the murderer himself but also on those who aided him in his evil plot (v. 4).

9:25 *In opposition to him these citizens of Shechem set men on the hilltops to ambush and rob everyone who passed by, and this was reported to Abimelech.*

Verse 25 gives only a brief and incomplete account of how the Shechemites displayed their disloyalty to Abimelech. They set an ambush in the hilltops (probably Mount Ebal to the north and Mount Gerizim to the south of Shechem) to harm his interests. Abimelech apparently was no longer in the city, probably because he had moved his residence.[140] This could have been either a cause or an effect of his estrangement from the citizens of Shechem, but in both cases it would have harmed their relationship.

Because he had moved, those chosen to bring tribute to Abimelech had to travel to his new residence. Verse 25 perhaps means that the Shechemites sought to harm their king by plundering those bringers of tribute. But because they also robbed others ("everyone who passed by"), Abimelech's regime fell into ill favor with all the travelers and merchants who had to use the highway that ran past Shechem.[141] The steps taken by the men of Shechem did not yet constitute open revolt,

---

[140]The text does not say where, but the most likely choice is Arumah (v. 41), since no other place is named. The source that the author used for this story may have contained some information on this before verse 25 that he chose to leave out because of his later mention of Arumah. Spielmann (*Jotham*, p. 145) thinks that Abimelech was away on a campaign against the Philistines.

[141]See Keil, *Kommentar*, p. 296. His view that the ambushers were also lying in wait for Abimelech himself is unlikely, since the king would never have traveled to Shechem without his army.

but they were serious enough to report to Abimelech and called for a strong response.

9:26–29 *Now Gaal son of Ebed*[142] *moved with his brothers into Shechem, and its citizens put their confidence in him.* [27] *After they had gone out into the fields and gathered the grapes and trodden them, they held a festival in the temple of their god. While they were eating and drinking, they cursed Abimelech.* [28] *Then Gaal son of Ebed said, "Who is Abimelech, and who is Shechem, that we should be subject to him? Isn't he Jerub-Baal's son, and isn't Zebul his deputy? Serve the men of Hamor, Shechem's father! Why should we serve Abimelech?*[143] [29] *If only this people were under my command! Then I would get rid of him. I would say*[144] *to Abimelech, 'Call out your whole army!' "*

Before Abimelech could respond, however, the situation at Shechem became critical. Gaal the son of Ebed entered the city with a band of his

---

[142] Several Hebrew manuscripts and also the Syriac translation have the name Eber here. The Septuagint has Jobel or Obed, and the Vulgate also has Obed. It is therefore well possible that the name Ebed was not original, but to decide between the other names on text-critical grounds would be extremely difficult. The possibility that Ebed is authentic cannot be discounted, and I have therefore retained the spelling of the Masoretic text (in vv. 26, 28, and 30). The name is also found elsewhere (Ezra 8:6).

[143] Goslinga emends the Hebrew text here and translates this verse as follows: "Who is Abimelech, and who is Jerub-Baal's son, that we should be subject to him? Is he not a Shechemite, and Zebul his deputy? *You* be servants, you men of Hamor, Shechem's father! But why should *we* serve him?" He adds the following footnote:
Since the Hebrew text of verse 28 is difficult to make sense of in its context and is regarded by many as more or less corrupt, my translation departs from it in two different places. The ancient versions offer text-critical grounds for emendation, for the Septuagint has "son of Shechem" instead of "Shechem" [see the NIV translation above], and instead of the verb "serve" [see NIV] it has "his servant," a difference that is based on a minor change in the vocalization. In connection with this the following object marker is read as the preposition "with": "his servant with the men of Hamor." The Vulgate reads the verse similarly. Although this reading makes better sense than the Masoretic text, it is entirely inadequate in its context and has a very unnatural syntax.
Verse 28 has two main problems, the first lying in the words "who is Shechem?" This parallels the question "who is Abimelech?" and must have the same meaning, especially since it is followed by the words "that we should be subject to him [viz., Abimelech]." But since Shechem could not have been another name for Abimelech, the second question must have originally contained another name. The Septuagint has "son of Shechem" (or "Shechemite") here, but this could not have been the original reading for two different reasons. First, it would be odd to call Abimelech the "son of Shechem"; second, this should be the answer rather than part of the question. The only logical solution is that "who is Abimelech?" was originally paralleled by the question "who is the son of Jerub-

kinsmen under his command. We do not read of this Gaal elsewhere, but he and his brothers apparently were adventurers and freebooters who hoped to find refuge in Shechem. Presumably they had crossed

---

Baal?'' Nabal similarly asks "who is David, and who is the son of Jesse?'' in 1 Samuel 25:10. And the answer to this twofold question must then have followed in the rhetorical question "is he not a son of Shechem, and is not Zebul [likewise a Shechemite] his deputy?'' Gaal thus declares that Abimelech (and Zebul) is a Shechemite so that he can draw the conclusion that he and his brothers, who were not Shechemites, did not have to obey him. The Hebrew names *ben-yᵉrubba'al* and *ben-sᵉkem* could have changed places due to the error of an early copyist.

The second problem lies in the words "serve the men of Hamor, Shechem's father" [see the NIV translation above]. In the first place, it is not clear to whom Gaal could have been addressing these words (the first part of v. 28 offers no clue), nor is it clear who the "men of Hamor" could have been or why Gaal uses this name. In the second place, it is difficult to see why Gaal would have urged the Shechemites (if that is whom he was addressing) to serve the men of Hamor, since verse 29 shows that he himself wanted to take command. In addition, it makes no sense for him to ask "why should *we* serve him?'' In view of his own ambitions, this should rather have been "why should *you* serve him?'' The solution to this puzzle is found at the end of verse 28, where the emphasis should fall on "we" rather than "him" [in the NIV, "Abimelech" at the end of v. 28 translates the Hebrew pronoun "him"—TRANS.]. The deliberate addition of the independent pronoun for "we," especially since it is in pause, places this beyond doubt. This "we" has to refer to Gaal and his own men, who stand in contrast to the men he is addressing. But to clarify this second part of the verse I still have to make the following hypothesis. The object marker *'et* before "men of Hamor" may have originally been *'attem,* the pronoun for "you," which in its unvocalized form differed by only a single consonant. An inattentive copyist could have omitted the *mem,* so that the remaining two consonants were understood as the object marker. This would have distorted the syntactical function of the words "men of Hamor," which were originally vocative, and obscured the connection between Gaal's command and his following question. If my conjecture is correct, the imperative form, "Be servants!'', is fittingly addressed to the "men of Hamor," and there is a clear contrast between the command and the question. Gaal's meaning is thus "if you want to be servants of Abimelech, that's up to you, but we who are not Shechemites have no intention of serving him.'' See also the comments on verse 28.

This translation of verse 28 has the great advantage of understanding the whole verse as a clear expression of one thought. The diverse parts of the verse then follow each other naturally and fit together coherently. Moore presents a clear summary of most of the positions that have been taken in *Judges*, p. 259. In *Oud Testamentische Studien* (1950), pp. 146ff., G. J. Thierry offers an alternate solution that likewise departs from the Hebrew text. My translation finds support in Kittel, *Geschichte des Volkes Israel*, vol. 2, 3rd ed., p. 46, and to some extent also in C. Spielmann, IT Jotham, p. 149.

[144]The Hebrew is problematic here, so *wayyō'mer* has been changed to *wᵉ'ōmar* following the Septuagint (see NIV margin).

over (the literal meaning of the Hebrew verb) to the Shechemites' side and traveled to the city from their former hideout. The prevailing discontent with Abimelech's rule certainly would not have been unknown to Gaal. In all likelihood he was a Canaanite and not an Israelite (see v. 28), though his name could be either Canaanite or Hebrew in origin (the derivation of the name Ebed is uncertain, see footnote 142).

The citizens of Shechem extended a glad welcome to Gaal. They needed no longer to fear Abimelech's displeasure; for if he tried to attack, Gaal and his men would protect their city. But this caused them to become overconfident. It was the time of the grape harvest, and all the people went out to the fields to gather the fruits. The winepress was trodden; and they held a festival of thanksgiving where, drunk with wine, they openly cursed Abimelech. The Hebrew term translated "festival" in verse 27 literally means "offerings of praise" (it appears elsewhere only in Lev. 19:24). Here it refers to a harvest feast at which offerings were presented to the god Baal-Berith and meals were held.

Gaal seized this opportunity to arouse the inhabitants of Shechem against Abimelech. To understand his words in verse 28 properly, we must keep in mind that he and his brothers, though they took part in the festival, were aliens in Shechem and that the Shechemites had not yet openly defected from Abimelech or allied themselves with Gaal against their king. Verse 29 shows that the authority of Zebul, Abimelech's deputy, was still recognized; and in verse 39 the citizens of Shechem let Gaal and his men stand alone against Abimelech (see under v. 39). Most explanations of verse 28 wrongly assume that Gaal was regarding himself and his brothers as one with the men of Shechem. The actual situation was somewhat different.[145] When he used the word "we," he was speaking of himself and his followers, who were not Shechemites and had no intention of submitting to Abimelech or his deputy Zebul. His words were designed to make the Shechemites, in whose presence he was speaking, envious of the freedom that he and his followers enjoyed. He thus said to his own men, "Who is Abimelech, and who is Jerub-Baal's son, that we should be subject to him? Is he not a Shechemite and Zebul his deputy?" In other words, "Why should we, free men, stay here, where we must obey Abimelech and Zebul?" Then he turned to the Shechemites and said scornfully, "*You* be servants, you men of Hamor, Shechem's father! But why should *we* serve him?"

---

[145]To understand the comments that follow, the reader must consult Goslinga's translation of verse 28 in footnote 143 — TRANS.

Once again Gaal made clear that he and his followers had no desire to serve Abimelech, but he was also slyly implying that he intended to leave the city. He knew well that the Shechemites would rather keep him; and he in fact was willing to stay, but only if they submitted to his command (v. 29). Gaal did not overtly call for a revolt. Instead, he cunningly provoked the Shechemites' desire for independence. This is why he also addressed them as "men of Hamor, Shechem's father" (Gen. 33:19; 34:2) and called Abimelech "Jerub-Baal's son." Those names made his hearers feel that it was beneath their dignity to be subject to Abimelech, since they belonged to the city's aboriginal population and Abimelech was only half a Shechemite. Moreover, his father Jerub-Baal was none other than the infamous opponent of the Baal cult, the god held in such high esteem at Shechem. The name "men of Hamor" may have fit only the non-Israelite citizens, but this genuinely pagan element must have played the leading role at the festival in Baal-Berith's temple.

Gaal's true motives emerged when he offered to be the Shechemites' commander. He took care to express this as a wish, saying that if they submitted to him, he would chase Abimelech from his throne and challenge him to "call out [his] whole army." This boast was another trick on Gaal's part, for it aimed to make the Shechemites think that Abimelech's army was small and could provoke little fear even when it attacked in full numbers.

9:30–33 *When Zebul the governor of the city heard what Gaal son of Ebed said, he was very angry. [31] Under cover he sent messengers to Abimelech, saying, "Gaal son of Ebed and his brothers have come to Shechem and are stirring up the city against you. [32] Now then, during the night you and your men should come and lie in wait in the fields. [33] In the morning at sunrise, advance against the city. When Gaal and his men come out against you, do whatever your hand finds to do."*

Oddly, we are not told how the Shechemites reacted to Gaal's words. He undoubtedly found a favorable response (see v. 31), but the people perhaps were not yet ready to risk an open revolt. Apparently there was no need for this, however, since Zebul, Abimelech's deputy, did not stand up for the king and apparently ignored Gaal's seditious talk. Zebul seems to have played a double role.[146] Although he was officially Abimelech's representative, he actually sided with the Shechemites

---

[146] See Noordtzij, *Gods Woord*, p. 368.

and did not want the king to return (see v. 41). He also did not want to see the city fall into Gaal's hands, however; and since he was too weak to expel him and his gang by himself, he pretended to be his friend (or at least not to be his enemy; see vv. 36–37) while he covertly sent warning to Abimelech.[147] His messengers first had to impress the king with the gravity of the situation.

The translation "stirring up" in verse 31 is undoubtedly correct, even though the verb in question has this meaning nowhere else and always means "besieging" when used of a city. The given translation takes its cue from this, however. For Gaal and his brothers were indeed making an assault against the city and forcing it to turn against Abimelech, not by a siege from without, but by the power of persuasion.

The messengers presented a plan of attack by which the king would be able to lay hold of Gaal and his band. That same night the king and his army were to march to the outskirts of Shechem and hide themselves for an attack at daybreak. When Gaal and his men marched out of the city—his boasting in verse 29 betrayed his plan to do so— they would fall into Abimelech's trap, and he would have his chance to defeat them. Remarkably, Zebul's plan did not ask Abimelech to enter the city and take control. Everything was to take place outside the city walls. Within the city itself the king would not be welcome, and he perhaps also would not be safe there. Abimelech no doubt knew this, and he wisely accepted Zebul's plan so that he could first deal with Gaal separately. How he did this is told in verses 34–41.

9:34–37 *So Abimelech and all his troops set out by night and took up concealed positions near Shechem in four companies. [35]Now Gaal son of Ebed had gone out and was standing at the entrance to the city gate just as Abimelech and his soldiers came out from their hiding place.*

[36]When Gaal saw them, he said to Zebul, "Look, people are coming down from the tops of the mountains!"

---

[147]The Hebrew term that the NIV translates as "under cover" in verse 31 could also be the proper noun "Tormah" (see the marginal notes in the RSV and NASB). Goslinga chooses to regard it as such and makes the following comments:

Whether or not the Hebrew term *tormâ(h)* designates a place, and where this may have been located, is uncertain. Since a place-name would be quite appropriate here, however, there is good reason to regard it as such. The name Tormah is so much like Arumah in verse 41 that it could be a variant form of this. The ancient versions almost all have "in secret," but this seems to be a mere guess, since the word *tormâ(h)* is found nowhere else. A derivation from the stem *rmh* ("deceive, betray") would be unusual and is very much in doubt—TRANS.

Zebul replied, "You mistake the shadows of the mountains for men."
³⁷But Gaal spoke up again: "Look, people are coming down from the center of the land, and a company is coming from the direction of the soothsayers' tree."

Abimelech set out that very night with all his troops (the Hebrew word "people" here means "soldiers") and marched toward Shechem. To escape detection and ensure the success of his attack, he divided his men into four companies. They held their positions till morning, when Gaal and his men marched out through the city gate (the entire context, especially vv. 39–40, shows that he was not alone). We are not told why he left the city. The usual explanation is that he wanted to protect the people working in the fields against a possible attack, or that he was going out on a raid and intended to return to the city at nightfall. It is equally possible, however, that Gaal planned (or was pretending; see the comments in v. 28) to leave the city for good because he would not submit to Zebul and could not gain the full allegiance of the Shechemites. Whatever was his reason, Zebul, knowing that Gaal would march out that morning, escorted him from the city (v. 36).

As soon as Gaal was outside the gate, he stopped to survey the terrain; and Abimelech and his men arose from their hiding places. They actually launched their attack too soon, since Gaal was not yet in the open field and could have retreated into the city. Zebul cleverly prevented him from doing this, however, first by feigning ignorance and then by piquing Gaal's vanity. When Gaal perceived the "people" (here, as in numerous other places, the Hebrew word actually means "soldiers") descending from the hilltops, Zebul first told him that what he saw was only the shadows of the mountains, mockingly pretending that Gaal had been frightened by mere phantoms. But when the troops came closer and their presence was unmistakable, Gaal again asserted that he saw soldiers coming at him from the "center of the land," and another company approaching from the "soothsayers' tree."

The Hebrew term translated "center" here means "navel," and it perhaps should be taken literally. The "Navel of the Land" could have been a mountain in the vicinity of Shechem (see v. 36). It is most commonly identified with Gerizim, since, as the highest peak in the area, this mountain would have deserved such an unusual name. The fact that Abimelech probably arrived from the south (where Arumah and Thebez lay; see vv. 41 and 50) also supports this identification. We can only guess why Mount Gerizim would have been called the "Navel of the Land," however. Perhaps the people living near Shechem regarded it as the center or heart of Canaan (just as the navel marks the center of the belly), but we have no evidence to confirm this (the Hebrew term appears in only one other place, Ezek. 38:12).[148] "Soothsayers' tree" is probably a Canaanite name for the "great tree of Moreh" in Genesis 12:6 ("Moreh" means "teacher" or "soothsayer"); but it probably should not be identified with the oak of the monument where Abimelech was crowned in verse 6 (see the comments there).[149] Apparently Gaal at first could not see the other two companies of soldiers from where he was standing.

9:38–41 *Then Zebul said to him, "Where is your big talk now, you who said, 'Who is Abimelech that we should be subject to him?' Aren't these the men you ridiculed? Go out and fight them!"*
³⁹So Gaal led out the citizens of Shechem and fought Abimelech. ⁴⁰Abimelech chased him, and many fell wounded in the flight—all the way to the entrance to the gate. ⁴¹Abimelech stayed in Arumah, and Zebul drove Gaal and his brothers out of Shechem.

Zebul finally stopped his chicanery. He reminded Gaal of his boasting and dared him to show his mettle and attack the men of whom he had previously spoken so contemptuously (vv. 28–29) but now seemed to fear. Gaal, knowing that he would be finished in Shechem if he shrank from the battle, marched with his men against Abimelech in full view of the city's citizens, who had suddenly become neutral.[150] After suffering a disastrous defeat in which many of his men were wounded, Gaal sought to take refuge within Shechem's walls. But Zebul let him in one gate only to chase him out the other. Gaal and his gang were no longer welcome in Shechem, for Zebul had achieved his goal: with Abimelech's help he had gotten rid of his dangerous rival without having to send Shechemites to war. He also had managed to keep up his pretense of loyalty to Abimelech. The king, apparently content with his victory, returned to Arumah, a place that some scholars identify with modern El 'Ormeh, about nine miles southeast of Shechem. But he did not forget what the Shechemites had done to him (vv. 25–27) and made plans to take violent revenge.

---

[148] According to Böhl, Shechem stood "almost at the exact center of the territory west of the Jordan" (*De geschiedenis der stad Sichem en de opgravingen aldaar* [Amsterdam, 1926], p. 4).

[149] Noordtzij, *Gods Woord*, p. 352.

[150] Goslinga's translation of verse 39 corresponds to the NIV marginal note: "Gaal went out in the sight of the citizens of Shechem"—TRANS.

9:42–45 *The next day the people of Shechem went out to the fields, and this was reported to Abimelech. ⁴³So he took his men,¹⁵¹ divided them into three companies and set an ambush in the fields. When he saw the people coming out of the city, he rose to attack them. ⁴⁴Abimelech and the companies¹⁵² with him rushed forward to a position at the entrance to the city gate. Then two companies rushed upon those in the fields and struck them down. ⁴⁵All that day Abimelech pressed his attack against the city until he had captured it and killed its people. Then he destroyed the city and scattered salt over it.*

Abimelech probably kept his troops ready to return to Shechem at a moment's notice while he awaited a favorable report from his spies. He did not have to wait long. The very next morning the people of Shechem went out to work in the fields, thinking that they no longer had anything to fear from Abimelech. As soon as he heard of this, he called out his troops, divided them into three companies, and had them set an ambush in the fields near Shechem. When most of the citizens had gone out the gate and the city was nearly empty, his army made a surprise attack. He himself and the company with him took a position in front of the city gate; and while the other two companies attacked and killed the people in the fields, he and his own men captured and finished off the fugitives. Abimelech then entered Shechem itself, where he killed everyone he found and reduced the city to ruins. The walls and gates were torn down, and the ground was strewn with salt. No similar act of destruction can be found anywhere in the Old Testament, but in numerous passages salty ground indicates a barren and uninhabited wasteland (Deut. 29:23; Ps. 107:34; Jer. 17:6; Ezek. 47:11; Zeph. 2:9). Abimelech's unusual and dramatic action thus symbolized that Shechem would from that time on remain desolate and abandoned. First Kings 12:1 shows, however, that the city was later rebuilt. This can be explained by the fact that verses 42–45 are speaking only of the city of Shechem proper, which did not include Beth Millo (see the comments under v. 6).

---

¹⁵¹The Hebrew literally reads "the people," but since verses 42–43 use the same word for the citizens of Shechem, "men" is a better translation.

¹⁵²Following the Vulgate and some manuscripts of the Septuagint, Goslinga changes this to "company" (cf. KJV, RSV)—TRANS.

9:46–49 *On hearing this, the citizens in the tower of Shechem went into the stronghold[153] of the temple of El-Berith.* *47 When Abimelech heard that they had assembled there,* *48 he and all his men went up Mount Zalmon. He took an ax[154] and cut off some branches,[155] which he lifted to his shoulders. He ordered the men with him, "Quick! Do what you have seen me do!"* *49 So all the men cut branches and followed Abimelech. They piled them against the stronghold and set it on fire over the people inside. So all the people in the tower of Shechem, about a thousand men and women, also died.*

Abimelech's thirst for revenge was not yet satisfied. The citizens of the part of the city that is here called the "tower of Shechem" had also been disloyal to him and deserved to be punished. Verse 46 indicates that the temple of El-Berith (or "the god Berith," identical to Baal-Berith in v. 4) stood in this section of the city. Although it may have been separate from the tower, the two buildings probably stood so close together that they formed a single fortified structure.[156] The temple thus would have been a component of the tower of Shechem (or Beth Millo; see in v. 6). The people of Shechem's tower, who shortly before had spoken so contemptuously of Abimelech in the temple (v. 27), were afraid to fight and sought the protection of their civic deity. They took refuge in the stronghold of the temple, which probably was a spacious underground vault (see v. 49: "set it on fire over the people inside") where food may have been stored against a possible siege. Even here they were not safe, however, for Abimelech took drastic measures.

---

[153] The Hebrew term here, which comes from an unknown root, appears elsewhere only in 1 Samuel 13:6. Since in that verse it almost certainly refers to a pit or underground hiding place, here it must mean a grotto or vault under the temple. Verse 49 supports this view.

[154] The Hebrew oddly has the plural here (cf. NEB). Since Abimelech obviously could not have taken up all the axes, some conjecture that the text originally had "his axe," the reading of the Vulgate and some manuscripts of the Septuagint. But if this was the original reading, it would be virtually impossible to explain how the definite article and the plural suffix later came to be added. Possibly the Hebrew text is authentic, and the name Abimelech [the NIV changes this to "he"—TRANS.] here denotes his entire army, as also happens with Gaal in verses 35 and 39. His men then would not be mentioned explicitly only because the following words applied to Abimelech alone.

[155] The Hebrew has "branch of trees," though the word translated "branch" (which is found nowhere else) is of uncertain meaning. The RSV and NEB have "brushwood"—TRANS.

[156] The archeological findings support this view. See Noordtzij, *Gods Woord*, p. 46; Böhl, *Palestina*, p. 62; A. Van Deursen, *Palestina het land van den Bijbel*, pp. 163ff.

When Abimelech heard where the citizens had hidden, he and his men climbed Mount Zalmon, a densely wooded hill in the vicinity of Shechem (see Ps. 68:14; some think Zalmon was an alternate name for Mount Ebal, while others identify it with modern Selman, a peak connected to Mount Gerizim). There he cut down some branches (see footnote 155), heaved them to his shoulder, and commanded his men to do the same. They all marched back to the temple, where they placed their wood on top of the stronghold and ignited it. The fire spread to the roof of the underground vault, and all the people of Shechem's tower— approximately one thousand men and women—perished from the intense heat and the suffocating smoke. Their trust in Baal-Berith was revealed as futile, and Jotham's prophecy that fire from Abimelech would consume the citizens of Shechem and Beth Millo (v. 20) found its fulfillment.

9:50–55 *Next Abimelech went to Thebez and besieged it and captured it.* *[51] Inside the city, however, was a strong tower, to which all the men and women—all the people of the city—fled. They locked themselves in and climbed up on the tower roof. [52] Abimelech went to the tower and stormed it. But as he approached the entrance to the tower to set it on fire, [53] a woman dropped an upper millstone on his head and cracked his skull.*

[54] Hurriedly he called to his armor-bearer, "Draw your sword and kill me, so that they can't say, 'A woman killed him.'" So his servant ran him through, and he died. [55] When the Israelites saw that Abimelech was dead, they went home.

These verses recount how Abimelech met his death at Thebez, a town about six miles north of Shechem on the road to Beth Shan, probably identical to modern Tubas. Thebez must have been a vassal city of Abimelech where the Shechemites had instigated a revolt like their own, since it otherwise could not be said that Shechem was responsible for Abimelech's downfall (see vv. 20, 56–57). Abimelech marched from Shechem to Thebez and besieged and captured the city, while all the citizens took refuge in the strong tower. Although the given translation places "all the people of the city" in apposition to "all the men and women," it is possible that the words refer to a separate group (for the phrase could be translated "and all the lords of the city"). They barricaded the entrance to keep Abimelech out and then climbed onto the flat roof to watch and harass him from there.

Abimelech, a man whose cruelty knew no limits, once again used fire as his weapon and marched directly up to the tower gate to set it aflame. He was thwarted by an unknown woman, however, who was able to drop an "upper millstone" on his head from her position directly above him on the roof. Hand mills were made from two circular stones (see Deut. 24:6; Job 41:24), between one and two feet in diameter and two to four inches thick, that were particularly hard and heavy. The stone shattered Abimelech's skull, and he quickly commanded his armor-bearer to stab him so that it could not be said that he had met his death at the hands of a woman. He obviously could not escape this disgrace, however (see 2 Sam. 11:21). The Israelites returned home after their king's death, and his illicit monarchy came to an end. He had no successor, and the people remained too divided to establish a united kingdom.

9:56–57 *Thus God repaid the wickedness that Abimelech had done to his father by murdering his seventy brothers. ⁵⁷God also made the men of Shechem pay for all their wickedness. The curse of Jotham son of Jerub-Baal came on them.*

These final two verses assert that the downfall of Abimelech and the Shechemites was an act of divine retribution for their sins. The Hebrew in both verses literally reads "God caused the wickedness to return," which not only means that He punished them, but also draws an inner connection between the crime and the punishment and shows that the partnership in evil was disastrous for both sides. The Shechemites' disloyalty to Gideon's family reduced them to servitude under Abimelech's tyranny, and the cruel king met his own cruel death in his subjects' revolt. God thus caused Jotham's curse (v. 20) to be fulfilled on both sides.

E. Jephthah
(10:1–12:15)

1. THE JUDGES TOLA AND JAIR: ISRAEL'S RENEWED APOSTASY AND REPENTANCE (10:1–16)

10:1–2 *After the time of Abimelech a man of Issachar, Tola son of Puah, the son of Dodo, rose to save Israel. He lived in Shamir, in the hill country of Ephraim. ²He led Israel twenty-three years; then he died, and was buried in Shamir.*

The words "after the time of Abimelech" of course do not mean to grant this degenerate son of Gideon a place among Israel's judges. On the contrary, the statement that Tola "rose to save Israel" implies that things had gone wrong during Abimelech's time. Tola thus stepped

374

forward to restrain the corruption in Israel's religious and social life that had been fostered by the upstart king. Although he was from the tribe of Issachar (the names Tola and Puah had already appeared earlier in this tribe, Gen. 46:13; Num. 26:23), he lived in the village of Shamir in the hill country of Ephraim. Perhaps his family had taken refuge there during the time of the Midianite invasions. In any case his residence in Shamir implies that the Ephraimites also recognized his authority. Although Abimelech came between them, Tola must have been the divinely ordained successor of Gideon. The exact location of Shamir, where he lived till the end of his life and was buried, is unknown.

10:3–5 *He was followed by Jair of Gilead, who led Israel twenty-two years. ⁴He had thirty sons, who rode thirty donkeys. They controlled thirty towns in Gilead, which to this day are called Havvoth Jair. ⁵When Jair died, he was buried in Kamon.*

Tola's judgeship in western Canaan was followed by that of the Gileadite Jair east of the Jordan. We are not exactly told that Gilead was his home, but since Havvoth Jair, the towns controlled by his sons, lay in this region, he must have lived there as well. The name Havvoth Jair (or settlements of Jair, see NIV margin) had already been given to these towns in Bashan by an earlier Jair from Manasseh who had captured them during Moses' time (see Num. 32:41; Deut. 3:12–14). Perhaps the name had later fallen into disuse, for the author of verse 4 implies that up to his own day the name "settlements of Jair" referred to the judge Jair (and not to his earlier namesake),[157] whose thirty sons had each taken over one of these towns. The donkeys they rode on were a sign of their wealth and prominence (cf. 1:14; 5:10; 1 Sam. 25:20). After having judged Israel for about as long as Tola, Jair died and was buried in Kamon, a place of unknown location.[158]

The dearth of information on Tola and Jair does not mean that their leadership was unimportant or did little good for Israel. It probably does imply, however, that their achievements were not as remarkable as those of someone like Gideon. Almost nothing is said about how

---

[157]The son of Segub mentioned in 1 Chronicles 2:22 was undoubtedly the earlier Jair.

[158]The ancient historian Polybius lists a Kamoun after Pella, which would put it east of the Jordan; and Eusebius mentions a Kammona in the Valley of Jezreel. But this evidence is too vague to allow us to identify the ancient town. See Keil, *Kommentar*, p. 302; Moore, *Judges*, p. 275.

they managed Israel's internal affairs, but this is related to the author's purposes (see sections II and V of the Introduction). Further information on Tola and Jair can be found in the lengthy note beginning on page 230; their dates are listed on page 234.

10:6–10 *Again the Israelites did evil in the eyes of the L*ORD*. They served the Baals and the Ashtoreths, and the gods of Aram, the gods of Sidon, the gods of Moab, the gods of the Ammonites and the gods of the Philistines. And because the Israelites forsook the L*ORD *and no longer served him,* ⁷*he became angry with them. He sold them into the hands of the Philistines and the Ammonites,* ⁸*who that year shattered and crushed them. For eighteen years they oppressed all the Israelites on the east side of the Jordan in Gilead, the land of the Amorites.* ⁹*The Ammonites also crossed the Jordan to fight against Judah, Benjamin and the house of Ephraim; and Israel was in great distress.* ¹⁰*Then the Israelites cried out to the L*ORD*, "We have sinned against you, forsaking our God and serving the Baals."*

Verses 6–9 are very similar to 2:11–15, both in their vocabulary and their content. What was said there of the period of the judges in general is said here of the period that directly preceded the judgeship of Jephthah. Verse 6, naturally, does not imply that the sin of idolatry was altogether absent during the days of Tola and Jair and then suddenly reappeared. These judges had merely suppressed it as much as they could, but it became more and more prevalent after their deaths. The resurgent apostasy affected the entire nation, not merely a few tribes. The gods that were served were not only those of the Canaanites (the Baals and Ashtoreths, see 2:11–13) but also those of Aram or Syria, of Sidon, of Moab, of the Ammonites, and of the Philistines (see 16:23; the Sidonian, Moabite, and Ammonite deities are named in 1 Kings 11:5, 33). The Israelites therefore succumbed to the idolatry of nations that lived both east and west of the Jordan, and both north (Sidon) and south (Philistia) of Canaan. The people's sin was twofold: they worshiped foreign gods, and they forsook the Lord (see Jer. 2:13).

Verse 7 too is speaking of all the Israelites. In punishment for their sins, the Lord handed them over to the Philistines and the Ammonites. The Philistine and the Ammonite oppressions are announced together because they began simultaneously, and their first eighteen years coincided (see section IV of the Introduction, pp.225–26,, 230–32, 235). This thus could be considered Israel's nadir during the period of the judges. The Ammonites are named second because the author will focus exclusively on them in the next part of the book. The first part of verse 8 could be referring to the Philistines as well, but the second half of the verse speaks of the Israelites east of the Jordan and thus has only the Ammonites in mind.

The words "that year" might seem somewhat redundant, especially since the second half of verse 8 contains no additional verb in the Hebrew (see the KJV).[159] One would think that the mention of the eighteen years of oppression would be enough (cf. 4:3; 6:1). The words make good sense in connection with the expressive verbs "shattered" and "crushed," however. What the author means is that Israel's enemies shattered their resistance at once and the people were severely oppressed in the very same year that the Lord "sold" them. The name "land of the Amorites" anticipates Jephthah's words in 11:19–22 by recalling that the region the Ammonites were invading had formerly been taken from the Amorites (Num. 21:21–25). Gilead here is a general name for the whole Transjordan (see Josh. 22:9).

The Ammonites, who lived east of the Transjordan, were not content to limit their invasions to Israel's border regions. Verse 9 states that they also crossed the Jordan to attack the tribes of Judah, Benjamin, and Ephraim; and the end of the verse shows that they had great success.[160] They no doubt were aided by the fact that these same tribes were also being hard pressed on their western borders by the Philistines. The Ammonites' penetration beyond the Jordan apparently did not come at the beginning of the eighteen years spoken of in verse 8 but later, when the oppression reached its extreme. Then the eastern tribes could not look to their brothers west of the river for help. In their great need, they finally turned to the Lord and acknowledged that their misery had been caused by their twofold sin (see under v. 6).

10:11–14 *The LORD replied, "When the Egyptians, the Amorites, the Ammonites, the Philistines,* [12]*the Sidonians, the Amalekites and the Maonites oppressed you and you cried to me for help, did I not save you from their hands?* [13]*But you have forsaken me and served other gods, so I will no longer save you.* [14]*Go and cry out to the gods you have chosen. Let them save you when you are in trouble!"*

The people's consciences had thus been awakened; but as in the time of the Midianite invasions (see 6:7–10), the Lord did not grant

---

[159]The words are omitted in the Vulgate and a few manuscripts of the Septuagint, but there is no reason to regard them as spurious. The Septuagint tries to evade the problem by translating "at that time"; the Syriac has "from that year." (One must consult the KJV to understand the problem here; the NIV takes care of it by dividing v. 8 into two sentences and adding the verb "oppressed" in the second—TRANS.)

[160]This is the first time that we have heard of Judah since 1:19. For the reasons for this, see the Introduction, p. 211.

deliverance at once. First, He severely reprimanded the Israelites. We are not told how He did this, but He most likely spoke through the high priest (as in 1:1–2). He could not have revealed Himself directly to the people's consciences,[161] for His words are very explicit; and verse 15 shows that they formed part of a dialogue with the Israelites. The Lord therefore must have given this revelation on some specific occasion and through a particular person. He asked a rhetorical question that confronted the people with what they already knew full well: He alone had been their deliverer in former years. First, He reminded them of the great deliverance from Egypt; then He listed other nations from whom He rescued them. The Amorites had attempted to obstruct Israel's entrance into Canaan under Sihon and Og (Num. 21:21–35). The Ammonites and the Amalekites had attacked the Israelites in league with the Moabites (3:13), and the Amalekites later also joined forces with the Midianites (6:3). The Philistines made a raid against Israel during the time of Shamgar (3:31). We are not explicitly told of an invasion by the Sidonians, but they are listed among Israel's enemies in 3:3; and it is not unlikely that they were among Jabin's allies (4:2; 5:19).

The Maonites present the biggest problem. The Hebrew text literally reads "Maon," which could be either the Maon of 1 Samuel 23:24 in eastern Judah or the town of the Meunites in 2 Chronicles 26:7, located south of the Dead Sea and east of Petra. Nowhere do we read of a Maonite attack, and it has rightly been observed that the inclusion of this tribe in the list is as strange as the omission of the Midianites.[162] But it would be even stranger to think that the name Maon is spurious; so we have to assume that the Maonites had indeed oppressed Israel.[163] The Hebrew sentence structure is irregular here. Verse 11 begins a question; but instead of completing this, verse 12 changes to a declarative statement. For the sake of clarity, this has been translated as one continuous question.

The Lord's previous acts of mercy made the Israelites' sins all the more reprehensible. Forsaking His worship, they went and served other gods. The Lord therefore no longer intended to save them. He instead sent them back to the gods they had chosen, saying that if they

---

[161] Keil considers this a possibility (*Kommentar,* p. 304).

[162] See Moore, *Judges,* p. 280.

[163] The text probably was corrupted here very early, but it is impossible to determine what the original reading was. The Septuagint has Midian or Canaan, the Vulgate has Canaan, and the Syriac version has Ammon. Only the Targum has Maon. The diversity of translations might indicate that the ancient versions found the name Maon strange and guessed at the original reading.

were really gods, they could save the Israelites from their distress (cf. Deut. 32:37–38).

10:15–16 *But the Israelites said to the LORD, "We have sinned. Do with us whatever you think best, but please rescue us now." ¹⁶Then they got rid of the foreign gods among them and served the LORD. And he could bear Israel's misery no longer.*

The Israelites responded to the Lord's rebuke with a renewed and even more abject confession of their guilt. They acknowledged His right to punish them, but this did not restrain them from imploring Him to deliver them from their imminent doom at the hands of the Ammonites. To show how serious they were, they destroyed their pagan idols and altars and began to serve the Lord once again. Although each individual might not have felt sincerely sorry for his idolatry, there was a public break with this hideous sin that signified a national act of repentance; and this certainly was preceded by an inner change of heart on the part of many.

Speaking in human terms, verse 16 states that the people's changed attitude caused the Lord to change. No longer was He able to endure the sight of His people's misery. The Hebrew literally says that His soul became short, i.e., impatient, because of the misery of Israel. Once Israel had repented, the Lord no longer looked on their sins. These were hid from His eyes, as it were, and in His deep love He could not permit their suffering to continue. The close of verse 16 implies that the Lord would begin to help Israel and that the deliverance that followed was ordained by Him.

2. JEPHTHAH'S DEFEAT OF THE AMMONITES, HIS VOW, AND ITS FULFILLMENT (10:17–11:40)

10:17–18 *When the Ammonites were called to arms and camped in Gilead, the Israelites assembled and camped at Mizpah. ¹⁸The leaders of the people of Gilead said to each other, "Whoever will launch the attack against the Ammonites will be the head of all those living in Gilead."*

Once Israel had basically been restored to a right relationship with the Lord, the author began to describe how the Lord used the judge Jephthah to deliver His people. Corresponding to their inner change of heart, the Israelites had an outward change in their behavior; for they at once made an armed stand against their oppressors. The Ammonites made plans for a new attack and marched into Gilead (they apparently

379

had not left a permanent garrison in Israel); but this time the Israelites (i.e., the Transjordan tribes) immediately countered them with an army of their own. This perhaps caused the enemy to move more cautiously, for the following verses show that they delayed their attack.[164]

The exact location of Mizpah (perhaps identical with Ramath Mizpah, Josh. 13:26), the site of the Israelite camp, is unknown; but it must have lain in the vicinity of modern es-Salt.[165] The Israelite army lacked a strong commander who enjoyed general respect. Verse 18 literally reads "and the people, the leaders of Gilead, said to each other." In other words, the leaders gave expression to the general view: there was no obvious choice for Israel's general. This is the first time that the Israelites found themselves in the remarkable predicament (the situation was different in 1:1) of being without a divinely appointed judge. The need for such a commander was felt so strongly that the men of Gilead offered control of their entire territory to whoever would launch the attack.

11:1–3 *Jephthah the Gileadite was a mighty warrior. His father was Gilead; his mother was a prostitute. ²Gilead's wife also bore him sons, and when they were grown up, they drove Jephthah away. "You are not going to get any inheritance in our family," they said, "because you are the son of another woman." ³So Jephthah fled from his brothers and settled in the land of Tob, where a group of adventurers gathered around him and followed him.*

The result of the Gileadite leaders' deliberation is found in 11:5. Before coming to this, the author turned back a few years to recount the history of the man who would shortly be unveiled as Israel's new commander. Since the events of 11:1–3 preceded those of 10:10–18, it would be appropriate to put these three verses in the pluperfect tense.[166] The clan of Gilead (grandson of Manasseh, Num. 26:29) or land of Gilead ("Gileadite" could mean either of these) did in fact have an able warrior, but he was living in exile. This was Jephthah, the son of a prostitute, who had been fathered by a man named Gilead.[167] His half-brothers, the legitimate sons of Gilead, had expelled him to keep

---

[164]But see what 11:13 and the comments there say about the Ammonites' intentions.

[165]This is the view of Keil, Oettli, Böhl, and others. Böhl thinks especially of the hill Osha' in the hill country of Gilead (*Bijbels-Kerkelijk Woordenboek,* vol. 1, p. 211). Genesis 31:23–25, 49 shows that Mizpah indeed lay in this hill country.

[166]Goslinga's translation in fact does so—TRANS.

[167]Nothing else is known about this Gilead.

him from getting a share in the family inheritance. This no doubt happened after their father's death. Jephthah was forced to take refuge in the land of Tob, a place somewhere in Syria (2 Sam. 10:6, 8), where he lived a freewheeling life at the head of a band of "adventurers." These were not necessarily miscreants but failures and outcasts like Jephthah himself, who wished to live outside normal society. Their periodic raids for food spread Jephthah's fame as a bold and shrewd commander.

11:4–11 *Some time later, when the Ammonites made war on Israel, ⁵the elders of Gilead went to get Jephthah from the land of Tob. ⁶"Come," they said, "be our commander, so we can fight the Ammonites."*

⁷Jephthah said to them, "Didn't you hate me and drive me from my father's house? Why do you come to me now, when you're in trouble?"

⁸The elders of Gilead said to him, "Nevertheless,¹⁶⁸ we are turning to you now; come with us to fight the Ammonites, and you will be our head over all who live in Gilead."

⁹Jephthah answered, "Suppose you take me back to fight the Ammonites and the LORD gives them to me—will I really be your head?"

¹⁰The elders of Gilead replied, "The LORD is our witness; we will certainly do as you say." ¹¹So Jephthah went with the elders of Gilead, and the people made him head and commander over them. And he repeated all his words before the LORD in Mizpah.

The words "some time later" (literally, "after days") naturally do not refer to the beginning of the Ammonite oppression in 10:7–8 but to the attack on Gilead that came near the end of the eighteen years. In verse 4 the author thus returned to the moment he had arrived at in 10:17–18. That the elders of Gilead called Jephthah back from the land of Tob so that he could lead Israel against the Ammonites shows that he must have been an extremely capable commander. This undoubtedly was a very difficult decision, and it is to their credit that they were able to swallow their pride. As clan leaders the elders of Gilead must have sanctioned the act of Jephthah's half-brothers. They therefore were co-responsible for Jephthah's banishment and his condemnation to a

---

¹⁶⁸Although the Hebrew term usually means "therefore" (cf. KJV), such a translation seems inappropriate here. It is not clear what "therefore" could refer to, and it would not make sense with either of Jephthah's two questions. The term is used absolutely more than once in response to an objection or rebuke, where it has the force of "very well," "that may be, but," or "nevertheless" (see Gen. 4:15; 30:15; footnote 103 in Judg. 8:7).

vagabond existence, a fate that he could only have regarded as a bitter injustice.

It is not surprising that Jephthah began by rebuking the elders of Gilead for their past conduct toward him, even though he did not reject their offer. The deputation that sent for him may even have contained members of his own family. In any case they satisfied his displeasure by acknowledging that his complaint was just and by offering to bestow on him the highest honors. Their mere coming to him shows that they were serious about reconciliation. In addition, they were willing to grant him, not only supreme command over the army, but also supreme authority over "all who live in Gilead," i.e., over the entire Transjordan, once the war had ended. They did not have a hereditary monarchy in mind, however.

Jephthah acceded to the elders' proposal; but to avert all possible misunderstanding, he first repeated their words, both the condition and the reward. He had to have no doubt about their sincerity. Verse 9 literally reads "if you are taking me back to fight," but this can be rendered "suppose you take me back to fight." He did not forget to mention that the outcome of the battle lay in the Lord's hands. Although Jephthah's words do not literally have the form of a question, they are interrogative in tone. He was not making his own demand here but merely asking for a confirmation of the elders' promise in verse 8. The latter satisfied his wish by taking a solemn oath. They appealed to God as their witness (the Hebrew literally means "Yahweh is hearing") and used the standard formula for oaths ("if we do not do," which is equivalent to "we will certainly do") to declare that they were willing to do as Jephthah said. Jephthah then accompanied the elders of Gilead to the army, where he was installed as head and commander.

At this point there was a remarkable harmony between the people and their leaders. Jephthah accepted his high office by solemnly pronouncing before the Lord and the people the commitment that he had made to the elders to fight against the Midianites with God's help. As the Lord had been called as witness between Jephthah and the elders (v. 10), so now the bond between Jephthah and the people was likewise solemnized in His presence. There is no need to assume that there was a sanctuary at Mizpah or that sacrifices were offered on this occasion. Nevertheless, it is not unlikely that the ceremony took place in the presence of one or more priests. Significantly, this was the first time that a judge was chosen by the people, almost in a constitutional manner. Judges had previously always been sent by the Lord and were then instinctively recognized as such by the people. Here, however, the people acted first; and God subsequently approved their choice (vv. 29, 32) and accepted the elders' procedure.

11:12–13 *Then Jephthah sent messengers to the Ammonite king with the question: "What do you have against us that you have attacked our country?" ¹³The king of the Ammonites answered Jephthah's messengers, "When Israel came up out of Egypt, they took away my land from the Arnon to the Jabbok, all the way to the Jordan. Now give it*¹⁶⁹ *back peaceably."*

The following verses reveal Jephthah's outstanding gifts, his firm self-restraint, and his love of peace. That he began by negotiating, and the way he proceeded in this, show that he was much more than a common brigand. Instead of making a precipitate attack, he sent messengers to the Ammonite king with the questions "What do you have against us? Why have you invaded our country?" The king's answer was that the Israelites unlawfully seized territory from Ammon when they came out of Egypt. To Jephthah's talk about "our country," he replied that it was "my land." He therefore wanted Israel to give back the land extending southward to the river Arnon (modern Wadi Mojib) that flowed into the east coast of the Dead Sea, westward to the Dead Sea and the Jordan River, and northward to the Jabbok (modern Nahr ez-Zerga), the chief eastern tributary of the Jordan.

The eastern boundary of this region was the Syrian desert, the farthest extent of the Ammonite kingdom east of Gilead. It is extremely doubtful that this disputed area had ever belonged entirely to Ammon; they probably had only controlled part of it (see Josh. 13:25, "half the Ammonite country"). In any case Israel had taken this territory, not from the Ammonites, but from Sihon of the Amorites, as Jephthah shortly would argue. We can infer from the king's answer that his goal in this attack was not to penetrate beyond the Jordan but to occupy Gilead itself and claim it permanently for the Ammonites.

11:14–22 *Jephthah sent back messengers to the Ammonite king,* ¹⁵*saying:*

"This is what Jephthah says: Israel did not take the land of Moab or the land of the Ammonites. ¹⁶*But when they came up out of Egypt, Israel went through the desert to the Red Sea*¹⁷⁰ *and on to Kadesh.* ¹⁷*Then Israel sent messengers to the king of Edom, saying, 'Give us permission to go through*

---

¹⁶⁹The Hebrew pronoun is in the plural. It therefore does not strictly refer to "my land" but rather to the cities in the conquered territory.

¹⁷⁰The Hebrew has "Sea of Reeds"; see Deuteronomy 2:1.

*your country,' but the king of Edom would not listen. They sent also to the
king of Moab, and he refused. So Israel stayed at Kadesh.*

¹⁸*"Next they traveled through the desert, skirted the lands of Edom and
Moab, passed along the eastern side of the country of Moab, and camped on
the other side of the Arnon. They did not enter the territory of Moab, for the
Arnon was its border.*

¹⁹*"Then Israel sent messengers to Sihon king of the Amorites, who ruled
in Heshbon, and said to him, 'Let us pass through your country to our own
place.'* ²⁰*Sihon, however, did not trust Israel to pass through his territory.
He mustered all his men and encamped at Jahaz and fought with Israel.*

²¹*"Then the LORD, the God of Israel, gave Sihon and all his men into
Israel's hands, and they defeated them. Israel took over all the land of the
Amorites who lived in that country,* ²²*capturing all of it from the Arnon to the
Jabbok and from the desert to the Jordan.*

Jephthah sent a new deputation to the Ammonite king, this time with
a lengthy, well-argued defense of all that Israel had done in the past. He
mentioned Moab along with Ammon because much of the territory the
Ammonites claimed had belonged to Moab, even though the king had
concealed this fact. During the desert journey, the Lord had forbidden
Israel to take territory from Moab or Ammon (Deut. 2:9, 19, 37); and
Jephthah was certain they had obeyed this command. He therefore
directed his messengers to let history speak for itself.

The Israelites had scrupulously avoided provoking trouble with these
nations and likewise with Edom, which they were similarly forbidden
to attack (Deut. 2:5). When they arrived at Kadesh on their journey
from Egypt (this was their second stay at Kadesh, in the fortieth year of
their desert wanderings; Num. 20:1, 14; cf. Deut. 1:46; 2:1, 14), they
asked the king of Edom (Num. 20:14–21) and probably also the king of
Moab (Numbers does not mention this, but Jephthah could easily have
known it from oral tradition) for permission to pass through their
territories. When both kings refused, the Israelites circumvented Edom
and Moab. They would have reached Moab from the south if they had
traversed Edom; but they instead skirted the eastern border of Moab by
marching northward along the upper reaches of the Arnon, which in
that time formed the eastern and (from its turn to the west at Aroer,
Josh. 13:9) northern boundaries of Moabite territory. The kingdom of
Moab had formerly extended north of the Arnon, but Sihon king of the
Amorites had taken this upper region from the previous Moabite king
(Num. 21:26). When the Israelites arrived at the lower reaches of the
Arnon, they therefore stood on Moabite territory, but in the land of
Sihon.

Once again the Israelites tried to preserve the peace by sending the Amorite king a request for permission to pass through his land (Num. 21:21–22). Sihon distrusted Israel's motives. When he sent his army against them, they attacked at once; and the Lord granted them a total victory. They naturally took over his territory, not only the area around the capital city of Heshbon, but all the land from the Arnon to the Jabbok. Jephthah pointedly added that this region was at that time inhabited by Amorites, not Ammonites. The precise location of Jahaz is unknown, but it must have been north of the Arnon, somewhere between Medeba and Dibon.[171]

11:23–24

"Now since the LORD, the God of Israel, had driven the Amorites out before his people Israel, what right have you to take it over? 24 Will you not take what your god Chemosh gives you? Likewise, whatever the LORD our God has given us, we will possess.

On the basis of this historical review, Jephthah asserted that the Ammonites had no right to this part of Israel's land. The Lord, Israel's own special God, drove the Amorites out before His people; so it was preposterous for the Ammonites to claim that they had the right to expel the Israelites. Jephthah then presented an argument that the Ammonites must have found incontrovertible. He first asked whether they did not have the right to take possession of whatever (literally, "him, who") their god Chemosh gave them; then he stated that the Israelites too could take over land from which the inhabitants had been rooted out by their God. It would be wrong to conclude from this that Jephthah actually believed in the existence and power of the god Chemosh. He never would have denied that the God of Israel was the sole God. A prophet might have spoken differently,[172] but Jephthah was here speaking as a political negotiator, not a prophet.

It certainly was permissible for Jephthah to use such reasoning to make the Ammonites realize that their occupation of Gilead was unjust, even by the standards of their own, pagan thinking. Chemosh was actually a Moabite god; and it is exceedingly strange that Jephthah referred to this deity in his argument rather than to the Ammonite god

---

[171] See, e.g., Böhl, *Bijbels-Kerkelijk Woordenboek*, vol. 1, p. 149; Garstang, *Joshua, Judges*, p. 385.

[172] See Noordtzij, *Gods Woord*, p. 364, who concedes that Jephthah left open the question of whether Chemosh really existed. This means, however, that he did not really acknowledge the existence of Chemosh but was merely being tactful.

Molech or Milcom (see 1 Kings 11:7, 33; 2 Kings 23:13). Even if one supposes that the Moabite god was worshiped in the kindred tribe of Ammon, he still would not have become the special deity of the Ammonites and their land. Jephthah's words give the distinct impression that he was speaking to Moabites rather than Ammonites. Various scholars have therefore proposed that the Ammonites conquered the land of the Moabites south of the Arnon before they marched against Israel.[173] In that case they would have adopted the cult of the god of that land, and they thus would have invaded Israel's territory north of the Arnon from the land of Chemosh and as his devotees. This still is the best explanation for Jephthah's reference to Chemosh. It also is possible, however, that the special bond between the Ammonites and the god Milcom did not come into being till the time of the monarchy.

11:25–26

Are you better[174] than Balak son of Zippor, king of Moab? Did he ever quarrel with Israel or fight with them? *26For three hundred years Israel occupied Heshbon, Aroer, the surrounding settlements and all the towns along the Arnon.[175] Why didn't you retake them during that time?*

Jephthah had no doubt that the Ammonite king would find his argument in verses 23–24 irrefutable. He therefore went on to assert that if the king did not drop his arrogant claim, he would be doing something that even Balak, king of Moab, had never considered. Jephthah's question—"Are you better than Balak?"—is really asking whether the Ammonite king had greater rights than the king of Moab (not whether he was stronger or morally better). This is clear from his entire line of argument and also from his next question: "Did he ever quarrel with Israel?," i.e., make legal claims against Israel. Balak had not done this even though a large part of the land that Israel conquered had belonged originally to Moab (see pp. 388–89). Since Balak had recognized Israel's rights and refrained from molesting the people, how could the Ammonite king now call these rights into question? He had even less reason to do so now that the Israelites had lived in the disputed territory for three hundred years (on this number, see pp.

---

[173]E. König, *Geschichte der alttestamentliche Religion*, 2nd ed. (1915), p. 120; Böhl, *Bijbels-Kerkelijk Woordenboek*, vol. 1, p. 152; Noordtzij, *Gods Woord*, p. 363.

[174]The Hebrew literally reads "better better," i.e., "much better."

[175]Literally, "in Israel's occupation of Heshbon . . . are three hundred years."

330-32), in Heshbon, Aroer, their surrounding settlements, and all the towns by or near the Arnon.

Heshbon, Sihon's capital city, is identical to modern Tell Hesban, 12½ miles east of the northernmost point of the Dead Sea. Aroer lay far south of this on the north bank of the Arnon; it is mentioned here because it was the most important city on the border with Moab.[176] Since Israel had occupied this region for centuries, even a legitimate Ammonite claim to it would have long since expired. For all these years, the nation had made not a single attempt to take back what it now claimed as its own.

11:27-29

I have not wronged you, but you are doing me wrong by waging war against me. Let the LORD, the Judge, decide the dispute this day between the Israelites and the Ammonites.

28 The king of Ammon, however, paid no attention to the message Jephthah sent him.

29 Then the Spirit of the LORD came upon Jephthah. He crossed Gilead and Manasseh, passed through Mizpah of Gilead, and from there he advanced against the Ammonites.

The answer to the dispute is thus obvious: Ammon was in the wrong. The Ammonite king had no grounds for his charge that the Israelites had violated his nation's rights (v. 13). On the contrary, Ammon was perpetrating an injustice against Israel. Jephthah closed his case by calling on Yahweh, the true Judge over all people, to pronounce a just decision and end the dispute.

In spite of Jephthah's persuasive words and convincing arguments, the Ammonite king ignored him and chose to fight, no matter what the cost. The Spirit of the Lord then came on Jephthah. Filled with great enthusiasm and inner strength, he marched through Gilead and Manasseh, i.e., the land north of the Jabbok, to rally behind him as many Israelites as he could from that region.[177] He then returned to the camp at Mizpah with his new reinforcements and advanced against the

---

[176] See Joshua 13:9, 16. This is a different Aroer than that of Judges 11:33 and Joshua 13:25, which lay east of Rabbah, Ammon's capital city, and therefore could not have belonged to Israel during Jephthah's day (if it indeed ever did).

[177] The name Gilead in verse 29 refers only to the territory of Gad. Jephthah therefore did not march through Reuben, which extended southward of Gad from Heshbon to Aroer. Perhaps this region already was in Ammonite hands (see under v. 24).

Ammonites in full strength. Judges 12:2 shows that Jephthah had also sent an unsuccessful plea for help to the tribe of Ephraim.

11:30–31 *And Jephthah made a vow to the* LORD: *"If you give the Ammonites into my hands,* ³¹ *whatever comes out of the door of my house to meet me when I return in triumph from the Ammonites will be the* LORD'*s, and I will sacrifice it as a burnt offering."*

Jephthah probably made his vow to the Lord before he marched out from Mizpah. He solemnly declared that if the Lord granted him a total victory over the Ammonites, he would in return make a full offering of thanksgiving to the Lord. The words that Jephthah used for the content of this offering are rather peculiar. He literally says, "the one coming out, who comes out the doors of my house to meet me." The Hebrew language knows only the masculine and feminine genders, but it is permissible to translate this phrase in the neuter: "whatever comes out." When the neuter is intended, however, a feminine form is generally used. Since a masculine form is used here and the whole context indicates that Jephthah had a human being and not an animal in mind, it seems better to translate "the one," or "whoever."[178] Sheep or cattle would never come out the door of a house, and still less would they be said to "come to meet" someone. Moreover, Jephthah clearly intended to present an unusual offering, and an animal could have been sacrificed in thanksgiving for the victory without making a special vow. Whether or not he had a member of his own family, or at least someone from his household, in mind is impossible to determine.

Perhaps Jephthah did not consider the implications of his vow carefully enough, but his aim was to leave the choice of the offering to the Lord. The first person who came from his house to meet him would "be the LORD's"; and to explain what he meant by this, Jephthah added that he would "sacrifice him [NIV, 'it'] as a burnt offering." The main question is whether or not he meant this literally. If he did not, we must ask why he used these words. If he did, it is puzzling, to say the least, that a judge inspired by God's Spirit could have promised the Lord a human offering, something that He had forbidden most emphatically (Lev. 18:21; Deut. 12:31).

At the end of this section, I will discuss this question at length. Here I will confine myself to the remark that Jephthah's vow strikes us as extremely ill-considered and reckless. He grossly overestimated his

---

[178]The RSV has "whoever"; KJV and NIV have "whatever"—TRANS.

own willingness to give to the Lord, if necessary, his dearest possession (see v. 35; Hannah's words in 1 Sam. 1:22–28 are entirely different). Moreover, the fulfillment of his vow would cause pain not only to himself but also to the sacrificial victim. This was not the proper way to make a vow to the Lord. Jephthah was guilty of making a thoughtless boast, and the Lord brought this home to him by causing his daughter to be the first person to come from his house to meet him.[179]

11:32–33 *Then Jephthah went over to fight the Ammonites, and the* Lord *gave them into his hands. ³³He devastated twenty towns from Aroer to the vicinity of Minnith, as far as Abel Keramim. Thus Israel subdued Ammon.*

Jephthah engaged the Ammonites in battle and, with the Lord's help, won an overwhelming victory. The battle must have been followed by a lengthy pursuit, for he is said to have devastated twenty towns. Apparently, Jephthah was not satisfied merely to defeat the Ammonite army; he also wanted to recover the land that they had unlawfully occupied and permanently discourage them from reattacking. In this he was completely successful. The Aroer that verse 33 speaks of was probably the town east of Rabbah, Ammon's capital city. The locations of Minnith and Abel Keramim are unknown, but they presumably lay between Rabbah and Heshbon. Whereas the Ammonites had once encamped on Israelite soil (10:17), they now were forced to retreat behind their own borders.

11:34–37 *When Jephthah returned to his home in Mizpah, who should come out to meet him but his daughter, dancing to the sound of tambourines! She was an only child. Except for her he had neither son nor daughter. ³⁵When he saw her, he tore his clothes and cried, "Oh! My daughter! You have made me miserable and wretched,[180] because I have made a vow to the* Lord *that I cannot break."*

³⁶"My father," she replied, "you have given your word to the Lord. *Do to me just as you promised, now that the* Lord *has avenged you of your enemies,*

---

[179]H. Rosier rightly points to Ecclesiastes 5:1 in this connection (*Opwekkingen*, p. 113). I believe Noordtzij's claim (*Gods Woord*, p. 366) that vows were products of a pagan mentality goes too far (see Lev. 27; 1 Sam. 1:11; Isa. 19:21; see also footnote 185 on p. 397).

[180]The KJV translation—"thou art one of them that trouble me"—is far too literal and gives only a weak impression of Jephthah's strong words. The Hebrew really means "you, more than anyone, have the marks of those who trouble me," i.e., "you especially make me wretched." Psalm 54:4 (v. 6 in the Masoretic text) contains a similar expression.

the Ammonites. *37 But grant me this one request,"* she said. *"Give me two months to roam*[181] *the hills and weep with my friends, because I will never marry."*

The author gives a vivid description of Jephthah's return home. When he arrived at his house in Mizpah, his daughter, who was his only child, came out to greet him, dancing to the sound of the tambourine. Jephthah at once remembered his vow (his daughter obviously was unaware of it); and in great sorrow he cried out, "Oh! My daughter! You have made me miserable [literally, 'brought me low'] and wretched." His unconditional obligation to fulfill his vow pierced him to the heart, for he had opened his mouth (the same word is used in Job 35:16) before the Lord and could not back out of his promise. Jephthah's sudden outcry indicates that the appearance of his daughter took him completely by surprise and that he had not thought of her when he made his vow. Had he been able to withdraw his rash words, he certainly would have done so; but the Lord would not allow this (Deut. 23:21–23). His daughter, in an exemplary spirit of self-denial and submissiveness, answered that he should do to her as he had promised.

Since the Lord had granted Jephthah such an overwhelming victory, no offering of thanksgiving was too great. His daughter was therefore willing to accept her fate as the victim of her father's vow. She asked only for a two-month delay so that she could roam with her friends in the solitude of the hills and bewail her virginity. Although she managed to maintain her composure, her father's words were a severe blow; and she needed time to prepare for her fate and to abandon her youthful feminine hopes, something that would cost her many tears. The joys of marriage and motherhood no longer awaited her, and her virgin state would never reach its natural fulfillment. Jephthah's daughter's words indicate that the fulfillment of her father's vow would prevent her from marrying, but they do not necessarily imply that she would be put to death. Although she could have used the same words if the latter was her fate, it would have been more appropriate for her to say "weep for my life" or "weep for my youth." This is worth noting, since her unmarried state receives so much emphasis in these verses (see v. 39).

---

[181]The Hebrew verb literally means "descend." Even if Mizpah stood in an elevated place, to "descend upon the hills" is a rather odd expression in this context; and it is used elsewhere only of God (see Exod. 19:11, 20). Possibly the text originally had *raḏtî* (from *rûḏ*, "to roam") and that the yod in *yāraḏtî* ("descend") is the result of a copyist's error. See Rudolf Kittel, *Biblia Hebraica*.

11:38–40 *"You may go," he said. And he let her go for two months. She and the girls went into the hills and wept because she would never marry. ³⁹After the two months, she returned to her father and he did to her as he had vowed. And she was a virgin.*[182]

From this comes the Israelite custom ⁴⁰that each year the young women of Israel go out for four days to commemorate the daughter of Jephthah the Gileadite.

Jephthah accepted his daughter's request. Her dignity, her childlike self-surrender, and her inner strength no doubt had a soothing effect on him. For two months he let her wander in the hills and weep over her virginity. Then she returned at the appointed time, just as she had promised, and "he did to her as he had vowed." The meaning of these words from verse 39 will be discussed below, and I will also come back to the following words—"and she was a virgin"—which can be translated in two different ways (see footnote 182). It became an annual custom in Israel for the young women (apparently these included more than just the women from Mizpah) to "commemorate" Jephthah's daughter for four days (the verb, which is the same as that in 5:11, could also be translated "celebrate in song, recite"). She thus came to be widely praised for the rare act of self-surrender by which she allowed her father to fulfill his vow to the Lord.

In comparison to the detailed account of the meeting between Jephthah and his daughter in verses 34–38, verses 39–40 are extremely sketchy and brief. It seems as though the author wanted to be done with the story as quickly as possible. He reported that Jephthah performed his vow, but we are not told how exactly he did this or what impression it made on the people. Nor do we learn where the young women of Israel went for their annual ceremony. This might be because the custom that verse 40 speaks of had lasted till the author's own day and did not need a fuller description.

We can only guess why the author wrote so briefly in verse 39. Some see this as evidence that Jephthah's daughter was literally slaughtered

---

[182]It is hard to translate these words without opting for a particular interpretation of the text. The most obvious translation would be "and she had never known a man" (cf. RSV), but the preceding clause would then have to mean that Jephthah sacrificed his daughter. A more neutral but equally permissible translation would be "she had no relations with a man," or "she was a virgin." The meaning then would be that she remained celibate her entire life and died a virgin. Such a translation is therefore preferable. It does not contradict the thought that she was killed, but it also leaves open the possibility that she lived on as a virgin. See the comments on pp. 396–97, 399–400.

like a sacrificial animal; the author supposedly did not wish to dwell on this appalling event, so he reported it in as few words as possible. There are two objections to this, however. First, the Book of Judges elsewhere recounts the most shocking and revolting events in great detail (e.g., 3:22; 4:21; 9:5; 15:6; 19:22–29; 21:10, 23). Second, it would be strange that neither the people nor the elders—nor even a priest or prophet—tried to prevent Jephthah's abominable act (compare how the Israelite men acted when Saul tried to fulfill his oath by killing Jonathan, 1 Sam. 14:45).

Some scholars have concluded with equal justice that the author's meaning in the first part of verse 39 comes out in the final sentence.[183] Since we have already been told that Jephthah's daughter was a virgin, it is argued that these final words must mean something different, namely, that Jephthah fulfilled his vow by keeping her unmarried and having her live a life of chastity before the Lord. This explanation leaves something to be desired, since it does not tell us what Jephthah did himself. He of course would have had to give her up and renounce his hope for descendants, but the text says nothing about how this happened or what took place at the end of the two months (on this view). One could at least expect a statement of how she dedicated herself to the Lord, for voluntary chastity in itself was no more pleasing to God than marriage.

Another objection to this view is that, according to some Hebrew scholars, the translation "and she knew no man [i.e., after that]" is entirely unacceptable. The meaning is, rather, that she had had no previous relations with a man; i.e., she was sacrificed as a virgin. Other Hebrew authorities reject this linguistic argument, however; so we cannot be certain how the translation should read.[184] Because of the lack of evidence, both interpretations—namely, that Jephthah's daughter was sacrificed, and that she was spared—can be regarded as consistent with the text; and neither can be declared the sole correct one.

The view that Jephthah's daughter was actually sacrificed has the

---

[183] See G. Ch. Aalders, "Jephthah," *Christelijke Encyclopedie*.

[184] According to Noordtzij, "This translation [viz., the former] is completely contrary to Hebrew idiom" (*Gods Woord*, p. 364). The same view is held by Mader (see footnote 186) and Oettli (*Buch der Richter*, p. 296), who bases his argument mainly on the use of the personal pronoun *hî*. But König counters this by pointing to Isaiah 1:2, where the personal pronoun *hēm* is used similarly in a context that cannot be understood as a circumstantial clause referring to the past (*Geschichte der alttestamentlichen Religion*, p. 233). See also footnote 182.

advantage of being the most natural choice. If verses 34–40 are taken alone, this interpretation seems to flow directly from the text itself. Luther therefore wrote, "One would like to think that he did not sacrifice her, but the text clearly says that he did." Nothing in the text contradicts this view, and the brevity of verse 39 does lead us to suspect that something horrible happened, not that Jephthah's daughter was specially dedicated to the Lord. For a true Israelite to belong to the Lord was a position of honor, and the tragic picture that the author draws in these verses would therefore be inappropriate if she had merely been committed to lifelong service in the tabernacle. Both Jephthah's grief and that of his daughter indicate that she met a pitiable fate. We have no other examples of Israelite women being bound to a life of special service to the Lord.[185] Some have pointed to Exodus 38:8 and 1 Samuel 2:22 in this connection, but these verses only show that there were women who performed routine chores at the entrance to (and thus outside) the tabernacle; they are not called virgins, and they probably were not. Indeed, if it was common for young women to dedicate themselves (or be dedicated) to the Lord in this way, there would have been nothing unusual about Jephthah's vow.

As I have already observed, one who wishes to maintain that Jephthah's daughter received a special vocation in the sanctuary must face the fact that we read not a word about it. The only possible support for this view would be Jephthah's vow that the first person who came from his house "will be the LORD's (v. 31), but the following words clearly indicate that he had a bloody sacrifice in mind. The words "sacrifice . . . as a burnt offering" cannot be understood metaphorically; so there is no way to escape the conclusion that Jephthah's rash vow obligated him to offer a bloody sacrifice. It is therefore not surprising that many commentators have concluded from verse 39 that his daughter indeed was sacrificed.

Nevertheless it also is completely understandable that others recoil from this interpretation and either seek another solution or leave the matter undecided. It is true that the verses in question offer little direct evidence for an alternate view. Besides the words "and she was a virgin" (or "and she had no relations with a man"), which I have spoken of above, the thing that is appealed to most often is Jephthah's daughter's weeping over her unmarried state in verses 37–38. I have

---

[185]Leviticus 27 is irrelevant in this regard. This chapter does speak of vows in which persons are dedicated to the Lord, but it directs that such persons must be redeemed (e.g., a female for thirty shekels of silver, v. 4).

already observed that this says more for a condemnation to a life of celibacy than a condemnation to death. Nevertheless, she still could have used the same words in the latter case; for her virgin nature and youthful feminine hopes would have remained unfulfilled whether she had to take leave of marriage and motherhood or of life itself. If she was sacrificed, she died as a virgin; and she thus had good reason to weep over her virginity. The words of Jephthah's daughter therefore do not allow us to decide between the two interpretations.

Jephthah's daughter's wish to retreat into the hills for two months also offers no solution. Many suppose that the girl would have stayed with her father if she was indeed condemned to die, but one can look at this in two different ways. In my view, Jephthah's vow deprived him of the right to keep his daughter at home for two months to enjoy her company. Moreover, it was prudent to begin their separation at once. To argue that the custom of the young Israelite women proves that Jephthah's daughter was not sacrificed is equally unconvincing. This annual ceremony only shows that something unusual had happened, and the verse does not say that the women actually went out to meet Jephthah's daughter. All these arguments are too weak to overcome the literal meaning of verses 30–31 and 34–40.[186]

Those who choose to reject the literal interpretation find their strongest argument in what Scripture says elsewhere about Jephthah, for the abominable act of sacrificing his own daughter seems incompatible with this. Judges 11 and 12 portray him, not only as a capable and courageous general, but also as a man of high principles. When the elders of Gilead called on him, he was bitter for a moment; but he quickly realized that he had to forget the past and join forces with them against Israel's enemy (vv. 6–9). He frequently gave spontaneous expression to his utter dependence on God (vv. 9, 11, 30), and he stood in deep reverence of the Lord's majesty and justice (vv. 27, 35). He patiently tried to convince the Ammonites of their injustice to avert a bloody war, and in these negotiations he displayed an outstanding knowledge of Israel's history (vv. 14–26). It is therefore unthinkable that he was unacquainted with the story of Abraham's sacrifice (Gen. 22) or with the Mosaic laws in general.

---

[186]Outside of Judges 11, there is no evidence that human sacrifice was practiced in Israel before the time of the kings (2 Kings 16:3; 21:6). See E. Mader, *Die Menschenopfer der alten Hebräer* (in *Biblische Studien,* XIV, 5 and 6, 1909); J. Ridderbos, *Israël en de Baäls,* p. 77; E. König, *Geschichte der alttestamentlichen Religion,* pp. 179, 230. On child sacrifices to Molech, see p. 122.

No doubt Israel's religious decline during the period of the judges affected Jephthah, too; but this could never explain how he could have approved of something as abominable as human sacrifice, especially since he was no ordinary man but a judge appointed by God. True, the Book of Judges does not conceal the sins of its heroes. Nevertheless. it still presents them as the Lord's instruments for leading the people in the paths of obedience (2:16–18), and this could hardly be said of Jephthah if he had stooped so low. It is worth noting here that Samuel granted Jephthah a place of honor (1 Sam. 12:11), and Hebrews 11:32 lists him among the heroes of faith.

In view of the unity of Holy Scripture, all this has a significant bearing on our interpretation of Judges 11:30–31, 34–40. It is hard to understand how a man like Jephthah could have taken a vow that obligated him to offer a human sacrifice, but verse 31 clearly shows that he did so. However repugnant and barbarous this may strike us, his strong words at the end of verse 31—even if these were uttered in a moment of carelessness—indicate that the thought of human sacrifice was not completely foreign to his mind. But it is even harder to imagine that Jephthah actually carried out his original intention. We should not forget that he had two months to reflect after his unfortunate meeting with his daughter. He could have realized during this time that to keep his vow would be a greater crime than to break it, or at least to fulfill it in a different manner than he had initially intended.

Jephthah obviously made his vow to please the Lord, but the least reflection should have convinced him that God would never take pleasure in a bloody human sacrifice. If he indeed came to be persuaded by the advice of others and by his own study of the law that he could never appear before the Lord's face with such an offering (see Lev. 18:21; 20:2–5; Deut. 12:29–31; 18:9–10), he may have sought an equivalent offering that closely resembled human sacrifice. Possibly he decided to banish his daughter from human life by condemning her to a lonely and barren existence, apart from marriage, motherhood, and all human intercourse. After her friends had comforted her during the two months' postponement, she could have been ostracized to an uninhabited part of the country, where she lived out her life in utter isolation. This would not literally have been a burnt offering, but it would have been the costliest offering possible for Jephthah: permanent separation from his only child and the end of his hope for progeny.

In my view the words of verse 39, which conceal more than they reveal, do not absolutely rule out the possibility of permanent separation. Jephthah's daughter could indeed have been put to death, but there could also have been a mournful ceremony in which she was sent off into the desert to wither and die. The words "and she was a virgin" would then make clear what Jephthah's decision did to her, and the custom reported in verse 40 could have been a means to lighten her unbearable fate a little by allowing her to have company for four days a year.

Recapitulating my argument, the view that Jephthah's daughter was indeed sacrificed finds its strongest support in the literal words of verses 30–40; but the picture of Jephthah given elsewhere in Scripture (11:1–29; 12:1–7; 1 Sam. 12:11; Heb. 11:32) makes it hard to believe that he actually stooped to offer a human sacrifice. It is difficult to make a definite decision, and the dearth of evidence compels us to exercise caution. Although the former view may seem the most likely on first consideration, the latter remains possible. Indeed, the mere fact that Jephthah retained his office of judge after verse 39 speaks in its favor. The Mosaic law had imposed the death penalty on anyone who sacrificed one of his children to Molech (Lev. 20:2). If Jephthah had sacrificed his daughter as a burnt offering—not to Molech, it is true, but to the Lord—it is hard to imagine that the Israelites would not have reacted against this in some way (compare footnote 186). Even the Ephraimites did not rebuke Jephthah for his vow, however, and there is no evidence that his prestige was diminished in the least. We should not conclude too much from this, but it has to be taken into consideration in our interpretation of 11:34–40. The issue is discussed more fully in the extensive literature on this passage.[187]

---

[187]The view that Jephthah's daughter, who according to an extrabiblical tradition had the name Seila, was not sacrificed dates from the Middle Ages and was first advocated by the rabbi David Kimchi (ca. 1232). The ancient versions and commentaries and the church fathers unanimously held to the literal interpretation. The same is done by many Roman Catholic exegetes (e.g., E. Mader, see footnote 186), but not by all.

Protestant scholars differ on this question as well, though the orthodox ones generally tend to reject the thought of a bloody burnt offering. Examples are Keil, *Kommentar*, who on p. 315 cites much older literature on the question; P. Cassel, "Jephthah," *Protestantische Realenzyklopädie*, 1st ed.; E. König, *Geschichte der alttestamentlichen Religion*, p. 233. The literal view is taken by A. Noordtzij, *Gods Woord*, pp. 364ff.; K. Dronkert, *Het mensenoffer*, pp. 46ff., 137ff.; and more reservedly by W. H. Gispen, "De gelofte," *Gereformeerde Theologische Tijdschrift* (1961). G. Ch. Aalders leaves the question unresolved (*Christelijke Encyclopedie*). Lists of additional literature can be found in the commentaries of Moore and Oettli, and in the article on Jephthah by F. Buhl in *Protestantische Realenzyklopädie*, 3rd

3. JEPHTHAH'S QUARREL WITH THE EPHRAIMITES; THE JUDGES IBZAN, ELON, AND ABDON (12:1-15)

12:1 *The men of Ephraim called out their forces, crossed over to Zaphon[188] and said to Jephthah, "Why did you go to fight the Ammonites without calling us to go with you? We're going to burn down your house over your head."*

Soon after the events of chapter 11, Israel's new peace was upset by a violent fraternal quarrel. Jephthah's success against the Ammonites and his fame as head of all Gilead (11:11) rekindled the Ephraimites' jealousy, and they begrudged the honor of victory even to their brother-tribe of Manasseh. They had behaved similarly under Gideon (8:1-3), but here their actions were much more drastic. They mustered a sizable army; crossed the Jordan by Zaphon, a city of Gad near Succoth (Josh. 13:27);[189] and entered the territory of Gilead. There they confronted Jephthah and reproached him for not calling them to join in the battle against the Ammonites, adding that they intended to burn down his house over his head. This message must have been brought by a deputation from Ephraim, for Jephthah had time to rally an army of Gileadites after he made his response (v. 4). The threat in verse 1 should therefore probably be regarded as conditional; in other words, the Ephraimites might not have carried it out if Jephthah had submitted to them or stepped down as leader of Gilead.

12:2-3 *Jephthah answered, "I and my people were engaged in a great struggle with the Ammonites,[190] and although I called, you didn't save me out of their hands. ³When I saw that you wouldn't help, I took my life in my hands and crossed over to fight the Ammonites, and the LORD gave me the victory over them. Now why have you come up today to fight me?"*

Jephthah did not even consider stooping to the Ephraimites' demands. He forcefully exposed the falsehood in their allegation; and

---

ed. (1900). These three scholars take a critical view of Scripture and assume that Jephthah's daughter was sacrificed. Also see the list of literature in Mader's book cited in footnote 186.

[188]I.e., crossed over the Jordan. "To Zaphon" could also be translated "northward" (cf. KJV), but this would be too vague and has to be rejected for geographical reasons.

[189]The Talmud identified Zaphon with Amanthus, a place mentioned by Josephus that is identical to modern Tell 'Ammata, slightly north of the Jabbok in the Jordan Valley (see Keil, *Kommentar*, p. 321; Moore, *Judges*, p. 306).

[190]The Hebrew literally reads "a man of struggle was I . . . very." Some Septuagint manuscripts have "they oppressed me" after the word "Ammonites";

as in his dispute with the Ammonites (11:14–27), his arguments were incisive. First, he set them straight on a few points. He and his people (i.e., the inhabitants of Gilead, 10:17) were engaged in a fierce struggle with the Ammonites; and because they were hard pressed, they had to act at once. They therefore could not have been blamed had they not sent messengers to Ephraim. But in fact they had done this anyway. The Ephraimites' complaint was thus completely unfounded and was tantamount to a lie. "I called," says Jephthah, but "you didn't save me out of their hands." Since chapter 11 neither affirms nor denies that an appeal was sent to Ephraim, no one can maintain that these two chapters are inconsistent. The Ammonites had harassed Ephraim along with the other tribes (10:9); so Jephthah had every reason to ask for their help. Their former indifference to Gilead's plight made their current behavior all the more reprehensible.

Jephthah then said, "When I saw that you wouldn't help [literally, 'were not helping,' i.e., were unwilling and unready to offer the help he was awaiting], I risked my life and fought the battle alone." He humbly gave the Lord credit for his victory and ended by asking why the Ephraimites had come to fight him. Jephthah's question certainly had much better grounds than theirs. They had profited from his victory but still came to reproach him, thus making it only too clear that their motives were dubious. We are not told where the verbal exchange in verses 1–3 took place, but it was probably at or near Mizpah (11:34). The words "come up" (12:3) may form indirect evidence of this, for Mizpah lay high up in the hills (see under 10:17).

12:4 *Jephthah then called together the men of Gilead and fought against Ephraim. The Gileadites struck them down because the Ephraimites had said, "You Gileadites are renegades[191] from Ephraim and Manasseh."*

The Ephraimites were dissatisfied with Jephthah's response; so they turned from talk to action. The issue would have to be decided by force of arms. Jephthah thus marshalled his army, which apparently had

but although this might make the sentence read more smoothly, we do not have sufficient grounds for emending the text this way.

[191] The word translated "renegades" (*pālîṭ*) usually means "fugitive," "escapee," "survivor"; but here its meaning is somewhat different. Possibly the Hebrew text is corrupt in verse 4 and the words "because they had said, you are renegades from Ephraim" were mistakenly copied from verse 5; for the very same Hebrew words appear there (only a single consonant is different), where they are translated "whenever a survivor of Ephraim said." A serious problem for this view, however, is that the final words in verse 4 would then be left hanging.

already disbanded, and won an overwhelming victory. Verse 4 is clear up to this point, but the words translated "because the Ephraimites . . . and Manasseh" are rather obscure. First of all, this clause seems out of place, since it gives the reason why the conflict started, not the reason for the Ephraimites' defeat. Second, an entirely different reason for the battle has already been given in verses 1–3.

Possibly, of course, verse 4 is stating a secondary cause of the battle, but the meaning of the clause is still obscure. A literal translation would be "because the Ephraimites had said, 'You are renegades from Ephraim'—Gilead lies between Ephraim and Manasseh" (cf. NEB margin). This could be paraphrased: "You are renegade Ephraimites and have no right to wage an independent war; for Gilead, which lies between Ephraim and Manasseh, belongs to one of these two tribes and is not their equal."[192] If the sentence is read literally, this is the only possible interpretation.

The fact that the Hebrew term *pālîṭ* would then have an uncommon meaning ("renegade" instead of "fugitive" or "survivor"; see footnote 191) presents no serious problem, but it is unclear why the Gileadites would be called renegades from Ephraim and not from Manasseh. The population of Gilead was partly from the half-tribe of Manasseh and partly from Gad (see Josh. 13:24–25, 31), and the Ephraimites had no right to deny these tribes the independence that they claimed for themselves. Possibly the Manassites and Gadites had intermingled in a section of Gilead, but this would not explain the words "renegades from Ephraim." Some suppose that Jephthah's army contained a large number of freebooters who were originally from Ephraim, but the Ephraimites' taunts are directed at Gilead as a whole, which is said to lie between (literally, "in the midst of") Ephraim and Manasseh. Ephraim did in fact lie to the west of Gilead and Manasseh to the north and northeast, but the region of Gilead as a whole did not lie between Ephraim and Manasseh.

There is no completely satisfactory solution for the problems in verse 4. Possibly the clause in question is spurious and has to be emended.[193]

---

[192] According to Keil, Oettli, and others, the word "Gilead" toward the end of verse 4 is a vocative and should be translated "you Gileadites" (as in the NIV). This seems unlikely, however, since the Hebrew noun then should be in the plural so that it would agree with the plural personal pronoun ("you"). In addition, "Gilead" has to be the subject of the final part of verse 4 (see the literal translation in the text above).

[193] The NEB omits the clause altogether. The NIV offers an alternate translation that avoids the problems discussed by Goslinga—TRANS.

It seems to me, however, that the Ephraimites' derisive comment about the Gileadites should be regarded as authentic. This remark could never have been added by a later hand, for the final words of the verse have to be original (see footnote 191). If my interpretation is correct, verse 4 not only contains a striking example of the Ephraimites' arrogance; it also sheds light on verse 5, where the words "survivors [or 'fugitives'] of Ephraim" are ironically (and correctly) applied to the defeated Ephraimites themselves.

12:5-6 *The Gileadites captured the fords of the Jordan leading to Ephraim, and whenever a survivor of Ephraim said, "Let me cross over," the men of Gilead asked him, "Are you an Ephraimite?" If he replied, "No," ⁶they said, "All right, say 'Shibboleth.'" If he said, "Sibboleth," because he could[194] not pronounce the word correctly, they seized him and killed him at the fords of the Jordan. Forty-two thousand Ephraimites were killed at that time.*

The Gileadites were not content merely to push the Ephraimites back into their own territory. They took violent revenge even on those who attempted to flee. By occupying the fords of the Jordan along the territory of Ephraim, they prevented them from crossing back over the river unmolested (we are not told whether the Ephraimites had left a garrison by the fords, but this seems likely). But since the men of Ephraim were not easily recognizable, it was necessary to employ a cunning trick to expose those who tried to conceal their identity. All who wanted to cross the Jordan were asked to say the word "Shibboleth" (i.e., "torrent"). If anyone said "Sibboleth," his Ephraimite accent gave him away and he was seized and killed. The number of Ephraimites who died in this civil war totalled forty-two thousand.

12:7 *Jephthah led Israel six years. Then Jephthah the Gileadite died, and was buried in a town in Gilead.*

Jephthah's authority was not challenged again after this victory. He held the office of judge in Israel for a total of six years. He probably had direct control only over the Transjordan tribes, for the Philistines continued to harass the western tribes in spite of Samson's resistance. Jephthah's reign was shorter than that of any of the other judges. His

---

[194]The Hebrew term *yāķîn* here does not make good sense. Following a number of Hebrew manuscripts, it perhaps should be changed to *yāḇîn*, which in Isaiah 32:4 similarly means "be able" before an infinitive.

office brought little joy to his personal life. The author's vague reference to his place of burial ("a town [literally, 'towns'] in Gilead") shows that the precise site had been forgotten.

12:8–15 *After him, Ibzan of Bethlehem led Israel.⁹ He had thirty sons and thirty daughters. He gave his daughters away in marriage to those outside his clan,¹⁹⁵ and for his sons he brought in thirty young women as wives from outside his clan. Ibzan led Israel seven years.¹⁰ Then Ibzan died, and was buried in Bethlehem.*

¹¹After him, Elon the Zebulunite led Israel ten years. ¹⁰Then Elon died, and was buried in Aijalon in the land of Zebulun.

¹³After him, Abdon son of Hillel, from Pirathon, led Israel. ¹⁴He had forty sons and thirty grandsons, who rode on seventy donkeys. He led Israel eight years. ¹⁵Then Abdon son of Hillel died, and was buried at Pirathon in Ephraim, in the hill country of the Amalekites.

Chapter 12 ends with a brief report on each of the three judges that followed Jephthah. The words "after him" in verses 8, 11, and 13 in no way imply that they also reigned over Gilead, for none of them lived or was buried in that part of Israel. Clearly their judgeships were later than that of Jephthah. Ibzan's birthplace, Bethlehem, was not the well-known town in Judah (17:7 and 19:1 call this "Bethlehem in Judah") but a place of the same name in Zebulun (Josh. 19:15), northwest of Nazareth, that is identical to modern Beit Lahm. He was buried in the same place after a seven-year judgeship that probably was limited to the tribe of Zebulun and the bordering regions of the other northern tribes.

Ibzan's successor, Elon, was likewise a Zebulunite and must have reigned in the same area. After leading Israel for ten years, he died and was buried in Aijalon, a place whose location is unknown. Some have identified it with modern Jalūn, east of Acco,¹⁹⁶ but in any case it has to be distinguished from the Aijalon of Joshua 10:12. Here again we see that the judgeship was not hereditary, but we are not told why Ibzan was not succeeded by one of his sons or how the office passed to Elon.

Our information on Abdon is scanty as well. He did not reign in Zebulun but in the tribe of Ephraim. His home, Pirathon, was in the hill country of the Amalekites (see 5:14), which probably was a region in the Ephraimite hill country where an Amalekite settlement had existed before Israel's conquests. Pirathon perhaps should be identified with

---

¹⁹⁵Literally, "sent his daughters outside."
¹⁹⁶See Keil, *Kommentar*, p. 323; Oettli, *Buch der Richter*, p. 272.

modern Far'ata, six miles southwest of Shechem.[197] Benaiah, one of David's mighty men, was also a Pirathonite (2 Sam. 23:30). In the person of Abdon, the tribe of Ephraim regained its prominence after its crushing defeat at the hands of Jephthah.[198] Like Ibzan (and also Gideon and Jair), Abdon had a great number of children and must have been a polygamist. His children's seventy donkeys are a sign of his affluence. As a final observation, since Elon and Abdon had such large families and brief reigns, they probably assumed their office at an advanced age. See also the Introduction, pages 209 and 231–36.

F. Samson
(13:1–16:31)

As I observed in the Introduction (p. 209), the story of Samson in chapters 13–16 forms a self-contained literary unit. In spite of this, there have been numerous attempts to demonstrate that this part of the book too is an assemblage of fragments from a variety of narratives. In other words, the theory of source criticism is thought to be applicable even to this part of Scripture. No text-critical evidence has ever been adduced to support this view. Instead, it takes its cue from the presumed contrast between the historical material itself and the "religious schema" that allegedly serves as its frame.[199] A man like Samson supposedly could never have been a judge, and the reckless adventurer described in chapter 14 could never have been a Nazirite. According to this view, then, he never really was either of these; later generations turned Samson, who was merely a popular hero, into a judge and a man set apart for God, placing him on the same level as Othniel, Ehud, and the other judges. Everything in these chapters that points to Samson's divine calling as judge was allegedly added later, and only if we remove these elements do we recover the original story of Samson and the true historical figure.

On the basis of these premises, chapter 13, and sometimes chapter 16 as well, were detached from the other chapters and assigned to a later hand. A variety of "sources" was distinguished even within chapter 13 itself and in chapters 14–16; whatever speaks of the Lord and His

---

[197] See Oettli, *Buch der Richter*, p. 272; Moore, *Judges,* p. 311.

[198] Some scholars (e.g., Ewald) conjecture that Abdon was the same person as Bedan (see 1 Sam. 12:11 in the KJV and the NIV marginal note). But see footnote 36 on p. 236.

[199] See the Introduction, p. 204.

special assistance was declared to be a later addition. The limited scope of this book will not permit me to deal with this often destructive "research" at length. Indeed, it seems unnecessary to refute these efforts, for their approach to the text is extremely arbitrary.[200] Leading scholars have continually pointed out that the inner coherence of chapters 13–16 is so obvious that their literary unity is beyond question, and that it would be impossible to divide them into different sources.[201]

In the commentary on these chapters that follows, I will discuss whatever seeming inconsistencies are present within the biblical text itself (see, e.g., in 14:8–10 and 16:27). It will not do, however, to read certain inconsistencies into the text and then to deny the text's unity on this basis. Such an approach sidesteps the real problems and eliminates the true exegetical questions. We shall see that to hold to the unity of the text presents no insurmountable problems. We do not even have to make a distinction here between material drawn from ancient sources and introductory and closing remarks added by a later author (e.g., 13:1; 15:20; 16:31b); for it seems plausible to me that the story of Samson was written by the very same person who composed the Book of Judges as a whole. My reasons for this are found in the Introduction, pages 209–10 and 219.[202]

I here will devote only brief attention to the peculiarities in Samson's person and behavior that have given rise to the divergent views of this individual, some of which are extremely dubious. Samson is a unique figure in the Old Testament. Chapter 13 foretells the birth of a great

---

[200] I here have in mind the arguments of A. van Doorninck, *Theologische Tijdschrift* (1894), pp. 15–19; Fr. Seyring, *Die altisraelitische Religion in den "Heldengeschichten" des Richterbuches* (Hamburg, 1902); and especially H. Stahn, *Die Simsonsage* (Göttingen, 1908), pp. 12ff.

[201] E.g., Wellhausen, Kuenen, Nowack, Moore, Zapletal, and, more hesitantly, Budde and Eissfeldt. In 1925 Eissfeldt wrote a monograph entitled *Die Quellen des Richterbuches* in which he distinguished different sources within the book of Judges as a whole but still maintained that chapters 13–16 are a literary unity. See also A. Schulz, *Das Buch der Richter*, pp. 6–7.

[202] I should add here that 15:20 points to the same conclusion. If one maintains that 15:9–19, or at least verses 18–19, is an old tradition that the author interpolated into his story, he could not explain why verse 20 was added here, since this verse would fit only at the end of the story of Samson (cf. 3:11, 30; 12:7; 16:31). If we assume, however, that chapters 13–16 are not a mere compilation of ancient traditions but the author's own telling of the story of Samson, it is easy to think that he had a particular reason for placing verse 20 after verses 18–19. See the comments on this verse.

religious and national leader, but chapters 14–16 disappoint our expectations on first reading. The man they portray was indeed extraordinary, but he apparently was not a zealous servant of the Lord who made war against Israel's enemy to lead the people back to a life of obedience.

There is very little evidence of a close bond between Samson and his fellow Israelites. On the contrary, he at first was on very friendly terms with the Philistines; and when he turned against them, he did this, not for religious reasons, but to seek revenge for their insulting treatment of him. God had given him great physical strength so that he could accomplish his divinely appointed task, but he seems to have squandered this on reckless adventures that were of no benefit to Israel. Rather than being guided by higher principles, he acted on momentary impulses and was controlled by his sensual desires and thirst for revenge, even in his prayers.

In reading the story of Samson, we therefore cannot help asking questions like the following. Why does the Book of Judges devote so much space to this individual? Can he really be considered a judge? Wasn't he a total failure as a Nazirite? How can we reconcile all the inconsistencies in his character?

None of these questions can be adequately answered if we begin by questioning the historical reliability of Scripture. The proper approach to the final question, for example, is not to ask whether the biblical data allow us to form a harmonious picture of Samson and, if not, to reject certain things as unhistorical. We simply are not free to refashion the story in accordance with our own views and standards. A mere respect for tradition should prevent us from doing this, not to mention the fact that whatever picture of Samson is arrived at by this route would be a product of pure fantasy. Things that seem incompatible to our own minds could certainly have coexisted in a single individual or life. Real people are seldom, if ever, perfectly harmonious; and outstanding personalities in particular often combine diverse traits that seem utterly inconsistent. It would therefore be wrong to cast doubt on any tradition for reasons like these. Beyond this, however, the authority of Holy Scripture demands that we accept its picture of Samson without reservation. To arrive at a true understanding of Samson, we must not mutilate this picture but begin from the assumption that it is fundamentally correct.

Our starting point demands that we reject every view that regards Samson as a mythical rather than a historical person. According to some scholars, what Judges is offering to us as history is actually a nature myth— specifically, a solar myth that bears much resemblance to the solar myths found in the literature of other ancient peoples. Samson, whose name is probably related to the Hebrew word for sun,[203] is supposedly a solar hero who wages war against the powers of darkness and loses his strength in winter. His long hair represents sunbeams, and the lion in 14:5-6 is the constellation Leo. His heroic deeds correspond to those of the Greek demigod Hercules, and Delilah is reminiscent of his beloved Omphale. This mythical interpretation finds not the least support in the Old Testament; and since it has already been refuted more than once, there is no need for me to treat it in detail.[204]

We also must reject the view that Samson indeed existed as a historical figure but was nothing more than a "noble savage" or popular hero of extraordinary physical strength who became the subject of a variety of myths or legends and was later transformed into a Nazirite and a judge.[205] This position, which regards the various biblical data on Samson as mutually incompatible, is itself incompatible with the respect that is due to the historical material in Scripture. The same can be said about the view that holds that Samson was clearly subject to a religious vow and was therefore indeed a Nazirite but that he could not have been a judge since we find no hint that he ever acted as one. Here again the truth of a particular statement in Scripture is arbitrarily denied, and an important feature is eliminated from the picture that it draws of Samson. Moreover, one who adopts this view would have to explain why a person who was not a judge and did not

---

[203]The meaning of the name is discussed in 13:24.

[204]Proponents of this interpretation include Steinthal, Goldziher, Völter, and Stahn (see footnote 200). For arguments against it, see V. Zapletal, *Der biblische Samson* (Freiburg, 1906), who gives a detailed account of the variant forms of the mythical interpretation; C. von Orelli, "Simson," *Protestantische Realenzyklopädie,* 3rd ed. (1906), who presents a clear summary of the different views of Samson that I mention in the text; J. F. Driscoll, "Samson," *Catholic Encyclopedia;* A. Noordtzij, "Simson," *Christelijke Encyclopedie.* The mythical interpretation is also opposed by Gunkel, *Reden und Aufsätze* (Göttingen, 1913), who still thinks the story of Samson contains fictitious elements; the article on Samson in *Religion in Geschichte und Gegenwart* (1931); and the commentaries of Budde, Moore, Nowack, and Oettli. Lists of relevant literature can be found in Zapletal, Stahn, von Orelli, Moore, and Oettli.

[205]This view too has different versions; it can be found in Hitzig, Ewald, Kittel, Jeremias, Baur, Gunkel, Nowack, Budde, and Schulz. Moore combines it with the mythical view.

even resemble one was later made out to be a judge by including his story in the Book of Judges and explicitly granting him this title (see the NIV marginal notes in 15:20 and 16:31).

Some hold that 15:20 and 16:31 were only added so that the story of Samson would conform to the narratives of the other judges.[206] Samson was very much different from the other judges, however; and it is altogether unthinkable that the author would have included a man like Samson among the judges if he had not been certain of God's having called him to be a judge. That Samson is called both a Nazirite and a judge in spite of his many flaws actually forms internal proof for the truth of the entire historical narrative.

In attempting to answer the questions that I asked on page 404, we must start by observing that the author did not write chapters 13–16 to draw a picture of Samson or to present his complete biography. His purpose was rather to preserve for later generations an account of what God did for Israel through Samson.[207] We should therefore not expect to find a final answer to every question about Samson's life or about the secrets of his personality. It would be more than enough merely to demonstrate that this unique figure was the appropriate instrument to realize God's purposes and plan at that time.

Chapter 13 makes it abundantly clear that God chose Samson and set him apart as His servant in a very special way. The angel of the Lord himself announced his birth to a childless couple, and he commanded the mother to abstain from anything that would have an unholy influence on her child during her pregnancy. He also prophesied that the boy would be "a Nazirite, set apart to God from birth." This therefore was no ordinary Nazirite vow, one that was voluntary and temporary, but a permanent Nazirite separation that was ordained by God.[208] The angel went on to disclose Samson's task and destiny as a judge by stating that "he will begin the deliverance of Israel from the hands of the Philistines." Samson's separation as a Nazirite was intimately related to his office as judge. Because he would be a judge with exceptional physical endowments, he, unlike all the other judges, had to be consecrated to God as a Nazirite from the time of his

---

[206]This is the opinion of von Orelli; see his article on Samson in *Protestantische Realenzyklopädie*, vol. 18, pp. 372, 374. Oettli expresses the same thought somewhat differently in *Das Buch der Richter*, p. 283.

[207]See, e.g., A. Noordtzij, *Het probleem van het Oude Testament* (1927), p. 58; G. Ch. Aalders, *De geschiedschrijving in het Oude Testament* (1928), pp. 15f.

[208]See, e.g., Noordtzij's article "Nazireër" in *Christelijke Encyclopedie*.

conception. We should not ignore this in our evaluation of his behavior in chapters 14–16.[209]

Samson was not unaware of the task he had been called to or of the source of his superior strength. He knew that it was the Spirit of the Lord that drove him and took hold of him at certain times, making him invincibly strong. The story in 15:9–20 shows that in spite of his seemingly rash and adventurous behavior, he still had a sober mind, a sense of solidarity with his own people, and an awareness of his dependence on the Lord. Therefore it would be wrong to discount his sense of his calling and to explain his enmity toward the Philistines purely in terms of baser motives such as a lust for revenge. His words to Delilah in 16:17, where he revealed his Nazirite separation, give quite the opposite impression. This confession was certainly a major failure on his part, but the entire context shows that he was not easily persuaded to give it. We can infer from this that he had kept his secret up till chapter 16 and had largely remained faithful to the Nazirite vow he had made.

We also should not overlook the statement in 14:4 that Samson acted as he did because he was seeking an occasion to confront the Philistines (see the comments on this verse). He wanted to let the Philistines know that he regarded them as enemies, not as friends, and that he was not afraid of them like the other Israelites. Here we can see that he was indeed conscious of his calling to take a stand against the Philistines and break the curse that their yoke had laid on Israel. He welcomed every opportunity to show the Philistines his strength and their own weakness. Samson's lot was to fight them alone, without human help or support and without an army. Because of this, his encounters with the Philistines always looked like personal quarrels and acts of revenge (e.g., 14:19; 15:3, 8, 11).[210] Even here, however, Samson was acting as a judge who inflicted harm on Israel's oppressor. What he did as an individual cannot be separated from what he did as a judge, and often the two cannot even be distinguished.[211]

Samson unquestionably was a judge dedicated to God, as was clearly revealed to friend and foe alike in the great battle at Lehi. There is no question that he fulfilled his mission as judge. He began the deliverance

---

[209] Noordtzij's assessment of Samson in *De Geschiedenis der Godsopenbaring op onze scholen* (1933), p. 12, manifests such a bias.

[210] R. E. van Arkel makes some insightful remarks on this in *De wolk der getuigen* (1931), pp. 153f.

[211] See J. Schelhaas, *Simson de Richter en Nazireër Gods* (1937), pp. 68, 73.

of Israel from the Philistines (13:5); and by pulling down the temple of Dagon at his death (16:30), he inflicted such heavy losses on them that their tyranny over Israel was temporarily ended.[212] The manner in which he carried out his task was extremely peculiar and highly original, to be sure, but this was a direct result of the rare physical strength that God had given him and the unusual conditions in Israel.

The Israelites were living under Philistine tyranny (13:1, 5; 14:4), and their spirits had sunk very low. The decline of the sanctuary at Shiloh and the appalling example set by the priests (see 1 Sam. 2:12–25) may have contributed to this. Their words to Samson in 15:11 show that they considered it foolhardy and futile to stand up against the Philistines.[213] It would therefore have been impossible for Samson to lead an Israelite army against them, as Barak and Gideon had done.[214] On the other hand his astonishing strength and the special divine protection he enjoyed enabled him to move about among the Philistines without fear, to attack them on his own, and even to defeat an entire army. Samson not only inflicted enormous losses on the Philistines (see 16:23–24); he also made an amazing display to this pagan nation of the indestructible, supernatural power that lay hidden in their Israelite subjects. The Philistines were so frightened of this power that they resolved to take Samson captive at any price, even though they knew that they were too weak to do this without using treachery and deceit. His obvious superiority and the way he constantly embarrassed them— sometimes by means of his wit—must have been a severe blow to their pride.

Samson no doubt eventually managed to revive the courage of his fellow Israelites, for he led them as judge for twenty years. It matters little that we find no specific information on how he did this; the mere fact that he laid the foundation for Israel's deliverance during the darkest years of the period of the judges says enough. And even though Samson might not have been the same type of judge as Gideon or Samuel, for example, we have to respect God's decision. It would be wrong to form a preconceived notion of what a true judge should be and then to use this as a standard for determining whether Samson should be included in that select group. We have to recognize God's sovereign

---

[212]See the remarks on this in section IV of the Introduction.

[213]Samson must have been an older contemporary of Samuel; see the Introduction, pp. 222, 235–36. Their births have to be dated around 1125 and 1100 B.C., respectively.

[214]See Oettli, *Buch der Richter*, p. 282.

right to choose His own instruments, and we can only stand amazed at His wisdom in granting Israel a man like Samson at that time.

It is true that Samson proved to be unworthy of God's favor and of his position of honor. In spite of his great strength, he was not strong enough to control his own impulses. He was unable to withstand Delilah's seduction; and even when it became obvious that she was laying a trap for him, he still succumbed to her temptations and walked into it with open eyes. This was nothing less than a betrayal or even a disavowal of both his Nazirite separation unto the Lord and his office as judge. Samson's extreme foolishness to fall for Delilah's trap after all that had happened (16:2–3, 9, 13–14) is not the only thing in his life deserving of blame. Nevertheless, none of this makes his story unacceptable or impossible.

Insofar as God uses sinful human beings to accomplish His plans, His instruments are always far from perfect. Samson's fall into sin was no less possible than David's, and 16:1–15 shows that it was a result of common human passions. He was able to fall so deep precisely because God had placed him so high. His subsequent repentance shows that his betrayal of the Lord had been preceded by a severe struggle and that he had not taken this step wholeheartedly. Languishing in prison, Samson was able to reflect on his errors. The Lord then restored his strength; and, in answer to Samson's prayer, He permitted him to crown his life's work by pulling down the temple of Dagon as a proof of the power of Israel's God. In his death, therefore, Samson was once again a true Nazirite and a true judge of Israel.

Anyone who overlooks the tragedy in Samson's downfall and the sincerity of his repentance, and who thinks his prayer in 16:28 was motivated merely by a personal desire for revenge, misses the whole point of the stirring story in chapter 16.[215] Only if we read this chapter as an account of the final victory of the Spirit of God over Samson's sinful nature and of Samson's willingness to meet death for the sake of his Lord and the deliverance of his people do we understand the end of his life rightly.

We also should keep in mind what was said in section V of the Introduction about the period of the judges in general and about Samson as the "typical Israelite" of this period (see p. 246). Samson's sins and personal flaws were inexcusable, of course, but they still were used to serve God's purposes. God wanted to demonstrate that man's

---

[215]This is done, e.g., by D. J. Baarslag in his book *Richters, Rovers, en Filistijnen*, pp. 119, 122, 126.

natural strength and abilities were incapable of bringing deliverance unless they were totally subjected to the Spirit of the Lord[216] and, because of this, that the judgeship in itself was inadequate. Both the strengths and the weaknesses of this office are brought out most clearly in the person of Samson.[217] His story illustrates how Israel's sinful weakness toward the temptations of its pagan neighbors was the cause of much misery and shame, but also how the Lord maintained His claim on His people, chastened them for their unfaithfulness and ingratitude, and brought them back to Himself.

All this should provide an adequate answer to the questions posed on page 404, in particular, the question of why the Book of Judges devotes so much attention to Samson. It also should be clear why Hebrews 11:32 includes Samson along with Gideon, Barak, and Jephthah among the heroes of faith.[218]

1. THE ANGEL OF THE LORD'S PROMISE OF A SON TO MANOAH AND HIS WIFE; SAMSON'S BIRTH AND YOUTH (13:1-25)

13:1 *Again the Israelites did evil in the eyes of the LORD, so the LORD delivered them into the hands of the Philistines for forty years.*

Samson's life fell completely within the years of the Philistine oppression. Because he was destined to stand up against the Philistines

---

[216] See von Orelli's article on Samson in the *Protestantische Realenzyklopädie*.

[217] See Keil, *Kommentar* (1874), p. 326, whose view of Samson (pp. 323–27) is absolutely faithful to the biblical data. The same can be said about D. Hoek, *Het boek der Richteren*, p. 335; S. G. de Graaf, *Promise and Deliverance*, tr. H. E. and E. W. Runner, 4 vols. (St. Catharines, Ontario: Paideia 1978), 2:38–48; R. E. van Arkel, *Het wolk der getuigen*, p. 158. According to van Arkel, "Samson's sin was Israel's sin. For it was Israel that had violated and desecrated . . . its call to live in holy isolation among the nations. This is what comes out in Samson, Israel's representative."

[218] In *Richters, Rovers, en Filistijnen*, p. 124, D. J. Baarslag says that the question "Samson, a hero of faith?" presents an extremely difficult problem. However, it would be much harder to maintain that Samson was a man without faith. Baarslag magnifies the problem needlessly by depicting Samson as a pure brute, a barbarous, vindictive, and foolish sensualist, and by ignoring the evidence that shows him in a different light. It is therefore no surprise that his answer to the above question leaves much to be desired. According to him, Samson was only called a hero of faith because he was an instrument for "reviving Israel's national-religious sentiment" (p. 125). Hebrews 11:32–40 speaks much differently about Samson and the other heroes of faith, however, and gives them credit for much more than this. The biblical characters should not be mutilated but accepted as the Bible presents them.

as the champion of Israel, his story begins with a brief statement of the reason why the Israelites had to endure this foreign tyranny. They had stubbornly persisted in acting contrary to the Lord's will, no doubt by committing the sins mentioned in 2:11–13; 3:6–7; and also 10:6. Chapter 13:1 actually picks up the story from this latter verse, for 10:7 has already stated that the Lord sold the Israelites into the hands of the Philistines because of their sins. The author has earlier recounted the Ammonite oppression and the history of Jephthah and his successors (10:7–12:15). Now he returns to the Philistine oppression, which coincided with that of the Ammonites at least in part. The latter began in 1126 B.C. and lasted eighteen years, while the Philistine oppression began at the same time and lasted forty years, or perhaps even a bit longer, since Samson grew to manhood and judged Israel for twenty years under their tyranny. Samson was born in 1125 B.C. and died in 1085.[219] In this connection see also section IV of the Introduction and the comments in 10:6–7.

The Philistines were a people of European origin who had emigrated to the coastal plain of Palestine, probably from the island of Crete. The Book of Joshua mentions them only briefly (13:2–3), and for a large part of the period of the judges it seems that they did not have much contact with the Israelites. Judah occupied the cities of Gaza, Ashkelon, and Ekron for a time (1:18), and Shamgar repulsed a band of Philistines (3:31). They probably grew in strength through the constant arrival of new immigrants, however, and the time had finally come for them to fulfill the task for which God had allowed them to remain in Canaan (3:1–4).[220]

13:2–4 *A certain man of Zorah, named Manoah, from the clan of the Danites, had a wife who was sterile and remained childless. ³The angel of the Lord appeared to her and said, "You are sterile and childless, but you are going to conceive and have a son. ⁴Now see to it that you drink no wine or other fermented drink and that you do not eat anything unclean,*

The author first introduces Samson's parents. His father, Manoah, was from the clan of the Danites. Dan was in fact a tribe (18:1, 30), but

---

[219]Van Gelderen arrives at nearly the same dates in *Bijbels Handboek,* vol. 1, pp. 128f. He places the beginning of the Philistine oppression in 1122 B.C. and Samson's birth in 1120.

[220]For information on the Philistines, see A. Noordtzij, *De Filistijnen* (Kampen, 1905), and the articles by Gispen in *Christelijke Encyclopedie* and Böhl in *Bijbels-Kerkelijk Woordenboek.*

it appears that the tribe comprised only a single clan (Num. 26:42). Manoah lived in Zorah, a town that had first belonged to Judah but was later assigned to Dan (Josh. 15:33; 19:41). After the kingdom was divided, it fell back into the hands of Judah (2 Chron. 11:10). Zorah has been identified with modern Sarʻah, north of Beth Shemesh.[221] Manoah and his wife had no children. This does not necessarily mean that they were already old, but their hopes for offspring certainly must have been disappointed for a long time. By choosing a barren couple, the Lord made clear that deliverance would only come through a special dispensation on His part and that His people, who were powerless in themselves, could only receive it as a gift from above (cf. 1 Sam. 1:2; Luke 1:7).

The angel of the Lord appeared to Manoah's wife and announced to her that she would give birth to a child. He did not tell her who He was or where He had come from, but He spoke decisively and with authority. He commanded the woman to look after herself and to abstain from all intoxicating drinks and all foods that would make her unclean. Unclean animals were forbidden to all Israelites (see, e.g., Lev. 11:4, 7, 24), but the angel repeated this to Manoah's wife to make her doubly cautious in this regard. The reason she was to stay away from wine and other fermented drinks comes out in verse 5.

13:5 *because you will conceive and give birth to a son. No razor may be used on his head, because the boy is to be a Nazirite, set apart to God from birth, and he will begin the deliverance of Israel from the hands of the Philistines."*

Manoah's wife had to abstain from those things because she would give birth to a son who would be dedicated to God in a very special way. The Hebrew literally reads "you *are* conceiving and will give birth," just as the angel said to Hagar in Genesis 16:11. Hagar's pregnancy had already begun at that time (Gen. 16:4), however, while in the present case we must regard "are conceiving" as a reference to the near future (see v. 3). In other words, the angel's promise would be fulfilled very soon. The emphasis here falls on the second verb: the woman would give birth to a son who would be a Nazirite of God. The angel added that no razor was to be used on the boy's head. Samson's long, flowing hair would be his special mark; it would be a symbol of his

---

[221] See Garstang, *Joshua, Judges*, pp. 334f. Zorah lay on the north bank of the brook Sorek (modern Wadi es-Sarar).

consecration to the Lord, and later on it would assume an extremely important role in his life (16:13–20).

This was not the only thing that set Samson apart, however. A Nazirite, i.e., a man or woman who took a voluntary vow to be consecrated to the Lord for a certain length of time, had to obey three specific requirements: he had to abstain from wine and other fermented drinks, to leave his hair uncut, and to avoid contact with any dead body, even if it was a member of his own family (Num. 6:1–7). Samson's Nazirite consecration was unique in two respects: it was not voluntary but was commanded by God Himself, and it lasted for his entire life. We should not infer from this, however, that his obligations were less strict than those that accompanied a voluntary and temporary Nazirite vow. Samson undoubtedly had to abstain from wine and all fermented drinks, for this prohibition had been imposed on his mother in its strictest form. Like the Nazirites, she could not even eat grapes (v. 14; see Num. 6:3–4). Since all intoxicants and stimulants that would hinder the working of God's Spirit had to be avoided even during his mother's pregnancy, the same rule certainly would have applied to him after he was born.[222] Samson's inspiration had to come from above, not from below.

The second sign of his Nazirite consecration was his long, flowing hair, uncut by any human hand, which also symbolized the full blossoming of his vitality and strength. Samson seems to have been exempted only from the prohibition against touching corpses, for this would have prevented him from carrying out his divine mandate to

---

[222]J. Schelhaas takes the opposite view in *Simson de Richter en Nazireër Gods,* pp. 16ff. He maintains that the prohibition of liquor did not apply to Samson himself, so that the only sign of his Nazirite consecration was his uncut hair. Although Schelhaas's arguments have merit (his main one is that the prohibition applied emphatically to his mother but was not prescribed for her child), they remain unconvincing because he overlooks the angel's statement to Manoah's wife that "the boy is to be a Nazirite, set apart to God from birth." Schelhaas rightly observes that "the angel takes it for granted that the woman is acquainted with the Nazirite vow," but this means it would have been obvious to her that her son would have to abstain from fermented drink just as much as she did. Since the prohibition of liquor is implied by the very word "Nazirite," the angel otherwise would have explicitly exempted him from this rule. It would be very strange indeed if an ordinary Nazirite had to abstain from wine, while a man who had been called by God to a life of Nazirite separation from his mother's womb was permitted to drink it. Chapter 14 contains no evidence that Samson took part in the drinking at his wedding feast (as Schelhaas supposes). But his divine calling to deliver Israel (v. 5) implies that he was in fact exempted from the prohibition against touching corpses.

begin Israel's deliverance from the yoke of the Philistines. This task was the ultimate purpose of his Nazirite consecration. Since Israel's deliverance could come from the Lord alone, the human instrument for this would have to be a man who belonged to the Lord in a special way right from his conception. The angel of the Lord's appearance formed a clear sign that God was deeply concerned with Israel's fortunes (see also 2:1–5; 6:11); and to a certain extent it also announced the advent of a new period. The painstaking steps that the Lord took to provide His people with a judge are more evident in Samson's case than with any of the previous judges (e.g., Othniel, Gideon).[223] Here He was intimately involved even at the moment of Samson's conception, and it was not too much for Him to send His angel to the mother twice.

13:6–7 *Then the woman went to her husband and told him, "A man of God came to me. He looked like an angel of God, very awesome. I didn't ask him where he came from, and he didn't tell me his name. ⁷But he said to me, 'You will conceive and give birth to a son. Now then, drink no wine or other fermented drink and do not eat anything unclean, because the boy will be a Nazirite of God from birth until the day of his death.' "*

After the angel had departed, the woman went in to her husband at once and excitedly told him what she had seen and heard. She was certain that she had received a message from God, for she called her visitor a "man of Elohim," i.e., a man who was in direct touch with God (Moses was called the same thing, see Deut. 33:1 and the superscription of Ps. 90; also Elisha, 2 Kings 4:9, 40). He even looked like the angel of God, very awesome, by which she did not mean frightening but exalted and imposing. But she did not know who he was, since she did not ask and he did not tell her. The important thing was his message, and the woman remembered this well and repeated it almost word for word. Surprisingly, however, she did not mention her promised son's mission to begin Israel's deliverance, something that she certainly would not have kept secret from her husband.

13:8–10 *Then Manoah prayed to the LORD: "O Lord, I beg you, let the man of God you sent to us come again to teach us how to bring up the boy who is to be born."*

⁹*God heard Manoah, and the angel of God came again to the woman while she was out in the field; but her husband Manoah was not with her. ¹⁰The*

---

[223] Keil discusses this at greater length (*Kommentar*, pp. 195f.)

woman hurried to tell her husband, "He's here! The man who appeared to me the other day!"

Manoah was as certain as his wife that the announcement came from God, but he prayed to the Lord and asked Him to repeat it. This was not a sign of unbelief, for his faith comes out clearly in this prayer. But since the angel had spoken only to his wife and the announcement had placed a great responsibility on himself as well, it is understandable that he wanted to learn exactly what their duties were in regard to the promised son. Manoah's prayer was heard (note how the divine names "Yahweh" and "Elohim" are used interchangeably here); but the angel again appeared first to his wife, who naturally would have known of his desire. She quickly ran back to her husband and told him that the visitor had returned.

13:11–14 *Manoah got up and followed his wife. When he came to the man, he said, "Are you the one who talked to my wife?"*

"I am," he said.

[12] *So Manoah asked him, "When your words[224] are fulfilled, what is to be the rule for the boy's life and work?"*

[13] *The angel of the LORD answered, "Your wife must do all that I have told her.* [14] *She must not eat anything that comes from the grapevine, nor drink any wine or other fermented drink nor eat anything unclean. She must do everything I have commanded her."*

The angel waited patiently and willingly answered the questions asked by Manoah, who had prepared himself well for this meeting. This does not mean that the angel told him exactly what he wanted to hear. Manoah still thought he was speaking to a human being (see v. 21). He first asked his visitor whether he was the same person that had come to his wife, and the angel answered affirmatively. This actually should have been enough for Manoah, since it showed that his prayer had been answered and that the messenger had been sent by God. But when he requested further details about the rule for the boy's life and the nature of his work, the angel (who from then on is always called "angel of the LORD") did nothing more than repeat the instructions that he had previously given to Manoah's wife (v. 4) in slightly different words and emphasize that these had to be obeyed.

The prohibition of wine and fermented drink was extended even to

---

[224] Following many of the manuscripts and ancient translations, this word should perhaps be read as the singular (in pause).

grapes, which had also been forbidden to Nazirites in Numbers 6:3;[225] but the angel said nothing about the boy himself. No doubt this was because Manoah's question evinced a certain premature curiosity that had to be discouraged. The angel's second appearance was only intended to confirm the first, not to add something new to it. Manoah knew enough and his wish had been granted, for the angel had come back to teach him "how to bring up the boy" (v. 8); i.e., he told Manoah that he must obey his previous instruction scrupulously. This was Manoah's responsibility as well as his wife's, and he did not need to know more about the future than had already been announced.

13:15-18 *Manoah said to the angel of the LORD, "We would like you to stay until we prepare a young goat for you."*[226]
16 The angel of the LORD replied, "Even though you detain me, I will not eat any of your food. But if you prepare a burnt offering, offer it to the LORD." (Manoah did not realize that it was the angel of the LORD.)
17 Then Manoah inquired of the angel of the LORD, "What is your name, so that we may honor you when your word comes true?"
18 He replied, "Why do you ask my name? It is beyond understanding."

Realizing that he should inquire no further, Manoah asked permission to prepare his visitor a meal (cf. 6:17-19; Gen. 18:3-5). But the angel said that even if he stayed, he would not taste any of the food. If, however, Manoah wanted to present a burnt offering to the Lord to show his gratitude, *He* was willing to wait for that. The angel's words could also be construed to mean that if Manoah were to prepare a burnt offering, he should offer it to the Lord (this is how the NIV understands v. 16).[227] This would introduce a rather strange contrast into the text, however. Manoah had spoken not of a burnt offering but of a meal. The angel rejected this offer; but he gave Manoah to understand that he had every reason to present a burnt offering to the Lord, the source of the glad tidings that he, as the messenger, had conveyed.

The translation "offer it to the LORD" (as in the NIV) puts the main emphasis on "the LORD," but there was no reason for the angel to say

---

[225] Scripture offers no support whatsoever for Noordtzij's view that the angel's prohibition was intended to put the woman on her guard against "demonic powers" (*De Geschiedenis der Godsopenbaring op onze scholen*, pp. 15f.). Such a thought could never have been in the angel's mind, and the prohibition finds a sufficient explanation in the rules for Nazirites (see in v. 5).

[226] Literally, "let us detain you and prepare a young goat in your presence."

[227] Goslinga's translation of verse 16 reads "but if you want to prepare a burnt offering for the Lord, you may offer that" (cf. NAB)—TRANS.

this to Manoah, since he would never have considered presenting his burnt offering to anyone else. The angel's meaning was therefore, "If you wish to make an offering to the Lord, go ahead and do so; and I will be present out of respect for Him who sent me." The end of verse 16 sheds light on Manoah's offer to his visitor and also on the angel's response, in which he concealed his identity and simultaneously paved the way for its disclosure. Since he was not a human being, he wanted an offering rather than a meal. Manoah did not comprehend this (his wife had displayed a keener intuition, v. 6), however; so he did not hasten to prepare an offering. Instead, he first asked the stranger for his name so that he would be able to reward him with gifts and other honors (see Num. 22:17, 37; 24:11) when his word came true and the child was born.

The angel's mysterious response contains a mild reprimand; but in refusing to disclose His name, He simultaneously gave a subtle hint of His true, exalted identity. Manoah was not to ask for His name because it was "beyond understanding" or "wonderful" (see NIV margin). The angel of course did not mean that "Wonderful" is His name[228] but simply that His name, as an expression of His nature, was as wonderful as that nature itself. It was divine and therefore transcended human understanding (cf. Gen. 32:29).

13:19–23 *Then Manoah took a young goat, together with the grain offering, and sacrificed it on a rock to the LORD. And the LORD did an amazing thing while Manoah and his wife watched:* ²⁰*As the flame blazed up from the altar toward heaven, the angel of the LORD ascended in the flame. Seeing this, Manoah and his wife fell with their faces to the ground.* ²¹*When the angel of the LORD did not show himself again to Manoah and his wife, Manoah realized that it was the angel of the LORD.*

²²*"We are doomed to die!" he said to his wife. "We have seen God!"*
²³*But his wife answered, "If the LORD had meant to kill us, he would not have accepted a burnt offering and grain offering from our hands, nor shown us all these things or now told us this."*

Manoah responded to his visitor's suggestion by taking a young goat that he had set aside for a burnt offering and the grain offering that had to accompany it (Num. 15:3–4) and sacrificing these to the Lord on a rock. "And the LORD did an amazing thing" translates two Hebrew

---

[228]Schelhaas understands verse 18 this way in *Simson de Richter en Nazireër Gods,* pp. 31f., although he rightly observes that "both views are in essence very much the same."

words that are almost grammatically independent (they literally mean "doing wonderfully" or "amazing in doing"), but they undoubtedly refer to something that happened while Manoah was offering his sacrifice. Their subject obviously is not Manoah but the Lord or the angel of the Lord (who were one and the same).[229]

What the Lord did on this occasion is not completely clear. Some commentators think He caused fire to flare from the rock as in Gideon's offering (6:21); but the text does not say this, and we should not overlook the differences between these two appearances of the angel. Since verse 19 says that Manoah offered the sacrifice, we have to assume that he ignited it himself. The "amazing thing" was therefore simply that the angel of the Lord ascended in the flame as it rose from the altar toward heaven, thereby revealing His amazing divine nature. All this happened before the eyes of Manoah and his wife, who fell to the ground dumbfounded.

The angel of the Lord did not return again after His sudden disappearance, and Manoah finally realized who his visitor had been. In great dismay, he cried out to his wife that they were doomed to die because they had seen God. The Hebrew term '^{e}lōhîm here should perhaps be translated "a divine being" (cf. NEB margin), but this does not have to be understood polytheistically. In fact the word means "God"; but without the definite article, it can also have a more general meaning that might have been more appropriate coming from Manoah on this occasion. Manoah expressed his alarm in stronger words than those of Gideon in 6:22. But his wife pointed out that his fear was unfounded in words that displayed her wisdom and calm faith. The Lord's acceptance of their offering, His miraculous sign, and especially His promise of a son who would begin to deliver Israel all showed that God did not want them to die. Never could He contradict Himself this way. The story brings out some subtle differences between Manoah and his wife. Although Manoah acted as her superior and even became a little headstrong, he more easily succumbed to fear and doubt. His wife, in contrast, gladly put her trust in God's promise without asking

---

[229]The text may be slightly corrupt here. We have to assume *hû'* ("he") as the tacit subject, and it is tempting to suppose that the waw ("and") was originally the definite article *ha* (this would then be an instance of haplography). The Greek and Latin translations support such an emendation, which yields the meaning "the Lord, who acts amazingly, did an amazing thing." This would leave the final clause of the verse in an awkward position, however. The manuscripts contain no evidence for the view of some that this clause was inadvertently copied from verse 20.

questions and clearly surpassed him in spiritual strength and knowledge of the Lord.

13:24-25 *The woman gave birth to a boy and named him Samson. He grew and the LORD blessed him, ²⁵ and the Spirit of the LORD began to stir him while he was in Mahaneh Dan, between Zorah and Eshtaol.*

These final verses of chapter 13 tell how God's promise began to be fulfilled. Manoah's wife gave birth to a son who with the Lord's blessing grew and prospered (compare what is said about Samuel and John the Baptist in 1 Sam. 2:21; Luke 1:80). The child's name, Samson, is almost unanimously thought to be derived from *šemeš*, the Hebrew word for "sun."[230] Its meaning would thus be "sunny" or "sun's child," which probably expressed his parents' (particularly his mother's) hope that through this child a new dawning of freedom would come to Israel. Possibly the final words of the song of Deborah (5:31) were also in their minds at this time. Already during his youth, Samson began to experience the special influence of the Spirit of the Lord that would take hold of him again and again in his later life (14:6, 19; 15:14).

The Hebrew term translated "stir" appears here only in the Old Testament and seems to denote a powerful impulse or push. It thus indicates that Samson would receive overpowering impulses from the Spirit of the Lord that would drive him on and enable him to do amazing feats of great strength (see under 14:4). The first time this happened was at Mahaneh Dan (literally, "camp of Dan"), a nearby place in Judah west of Kiriath Jearim, which lay northeast of Zorah. Eshtaol lay east of Zorah and has been identified with modern Eshwa' (see 18:12).[231]

2. SAMSON'S MARRIAGE AND CONSTANT STRIFE WITH THE PHILISTINES (14:1–15:20)

Judges 14 and 15 present a thrilling account of Samson's unusual relationship to the Philistines. To confront them he even went so far as to marry a Philistine woman. This became a source of constant quarreling and strife in which the Philistines displayed their savagery

---

[230] See Noordtzij's article on Samson in the *Christelijke Encyclopedie*, vol. 5. The derivation from *šemeš* suggests itself so strongly that it is clearly preferable to Keil's derivation from *šāmam* ("destroy").

[231] See Garstang, *Joshua, Judges*, pp 334f.

and depravity, while Samson had the opportunity to demonstrate his obvious superiority.

14:1–5 *Samson went down to Timnah and saw there a young Philistine woman.* *²When he returned, he said to his father and mother, "I have seen a Philistine woman in Timnah; now get her for me as my wife."*

³His father and mother replied, "Isn't there an acceptable woman among your relatives or among all our people? Must you go to the uncircumcised Philistines to get a wife?"

But Samson said to his father, "Get her for me. She's the right one for me."

In reading verses 1–2 we have to keep in mind what was said in 13:24–25 and also the parenthetical remark that follows in verse 4. Samson was full-grown, and the Spirit of the Lord had whetted his appetite for action. Verse 4 explains why he turned his eyes toward the Philistines at this point. As a young man of twenty years at most, he traveled from Zorah to Timnah (modern Tibneh), which lay about 3½ miles west in the western foothills. Timnah had been allotted to the tribe of Dan (Josh. 19:43), but they failed to take possession of it (1:34); and the town was then controlled by the Philistines. It seems that in Israel's border regions the Philistines' power was unchallenged (see v. 4). Samson saw a Philistine woman at Timnah whom he wanted to marry.[232] He returned to his father and mother and asked them to get her for him as his wife. Quite understandably, they had serious objections to this, which apparently were voiced by the father ("our people" is "my people" in the Hebrew, and see Samson's answer). The Philistines were a foreign people; and since they were also uncircumcised, they were even more unclean than the other neighboring peoples with whom the Israelites were forbidden to marry (Exod. 34:16). Samson refused to change his mind, however, and the events that follow show that his parents finally dropped their resistance.

14:4 *(His parents did not know that this was from the LORD, who was seeking an occasion to confront the Philistines; for at that time they were ruling over Israel.)*

The author here inserts a parenthetical remark (compare the similar statement in 1 Kings 12:15) that reveals God's special purpose in this

---

[232] It seems odd that she is not called a girl even though she still lived with her father. There is no obvious reason for this, but perhaps the word "woman" is mildly contemptuous in this context (cf. 16:4). See Schulz, *Das Buch der Richter*, p. 77.

and explains both Samson's behavior and that of his parents. His parents were certain that their son was acting wrongly and that "this" (i.e., Samson's desire) could not be from the Lord.[233] The Lord's will was, in fact, at work here, however. He wanted to do something with Samson that He had never done with any of the previous judges. He wanted him to confront Israel's enemy in an entirely new way. For the first time, the confrontation had to be eminently personal. The Lord's hidden purpose, of course, could not have been realized without Samson's cooperation. He was conscious of the fact that he was an instrument in the Lord's hands. His parents certainly would have told him about his calling to deliver Israel and his Nazirite consecration. The Spirit of the Lord therefore must have led him to and look for an opportunity to confront the Philistines. The way he did this, however, shows that he was a sinful person and an imperfect instrument.

The Hebrew word that the NIV translates as "occasion" does not appear elsewhere in the Old Testament. It is derived from a verb stem meaning "come on time," which has derived forms that mean "befall" (Ps. 91:10; Prov. 12:21) and "pick (a quarrel)" (2 Kings 5:7). The word could therefore be rendered as "meeting," "opportunity," or "occasion." Verse 4 literally says that Samson "was seeking an occasion from the Philistines,"[234] which must mean that he was on the lookout for something that would give him an opportunity or motive to attack them. "Confront" thus has a hostile meaning here, and Samson certainly was not wrong to seek such a confrontation. His parents did not understand this either, however. They could not comprehend that Samson's desire for the Philistine woman was from the Lord, nor could they understand that in his heart he really wanted to carry out his mission against the Philistines. Like most children with an unusual destiny, he remained an enigma to his parents.

Verse 4 ends with a reminder that the Israelites were living under Philistine tyranny, for this of course had a direct bearing on Samson's birth and calling (13:5). In showing how God's sovereign will serves as the background for men's actions, the verse is typical of Old Testament historiography (cf. 1 Sam. 2:25; 1 Kings 12:15).

---

[233]They were certainly correct in thinking that Samson's desire to marry a Philistine was in conflict with God's revealed will. See Schelhaas, *Simson de Richter en Nazireër Gods,* pp. 44f.; de Graaf, *Promise and Deliverance,* 2:42–44.

[234]In Goslinga's translation, the subject of "was seeking" is Samson, not the Lord (cf. KJV, RSV)—TRANS.

14:5–7 *Samson went down to Timnah together with his father and mother. As they*[235] *approached the vineyards of Timnah, suddenly a young lion came roaring toward him.* [6] *The Spirit of the LORD came upon him in power so that he tore the lion apart with his bare hands as he might have torn a young goat. But he told neither his father nor his mother what he had done.* [7] *Then he went down and talked with the woman, and he liked her.*

After Samson had won his parents over, the three of them traveled together to Timnah, apparently to make a marriage proposal to the Philistine woman. It seems that near Timnah Samson briefly turned off the main road alone (see v. 8). There he was attacked by a full-grown, roaring lion, but the Spirit of the Lord filled him with power and enabled him to tear the animal apart with his bare hands as if it were a young goat. The Hebrew verb translated "came upon . . . in power" literally means "penetrated mightily, rushed into" (see v. 19; 15:14; 1 Sam. 10:10; 16:13). With Samson, it always indicates a supernatural but temporary action of the Spirit that filled him with overwhelming strength. The extraordinary help he received on this occasion (compare David's and Benaiah's killing of lions, where the Spirit of the Lord is not spoken of, 1 Sam. 17:34; 2 Sam. 23:20) served as a sign that the Lord was with him and would also enable him to defeat the Philistines without human assistance.[236]

Samson rejoined his parents but told them nothing about his adventure with the lion. They arrived in Timnah together, where Samson talked with the Philistine woman and found that she continued to attract him. The events that follow indicate that they must have become engaged on this visit and agreed on a wedding day. We are not told what part Samson's parents played in this.[237]

---

[235] Following the Septuagint and other ancient versions, this perhaps should be emended to the singular pronoun "he." Samson confronted the lion alone. The plural suffix *û* could be a copyist's error.

[236] According to de Graaf, "this showed him what he would be able to do against Israel's enemies in faith, relying on the strength of the Lord. Thus he saw his calling" (*Promise and Deliverance,* 2:43).

[237] The traditional text of Judges 14 contains a number of problems that have never received an adequate explanation. Although these problems affect verses 5–10, it is best to discuss all of them here. As I observed above, verse 7 is strangely silent about Samson's parents, even though they were supposed to arrange the wedding and make the proposal (see vv. 2–3, 5). It also is odd that verse 8 gives the impression that Samson went back to Timnah alone, while verse 9 indicates that his parents accompanied him this time, too. Verse 10, in contrast, speaks only of Samson's father and gives the impression that he arrived in Timnah shortly after

14:8–9 *Some time later, when he went back to marry her, he turned aside to look at the lion's carcass. In it was a swarm of bees and some honey, ⁹which he scooped out with his hands and ate as he went along. When he rejoined his parents, he gave them some, and they too ate it. But he did not tell them that he had taken the honey from the lion's carcass.*

Some time after the visit in verses 5–7, Samson returned to Timnah to marry the Philistine woman. He again turned off the main road, this time to see what had become of the lion. He found a carcass, dried up by the heat of the sun, in which a swarm of bees had made a nest and had begun to produce honey. Scooping out some of the honey with his hands (the verb here, which appears elsewhere only in Jer. 5:31, probably can also mean to remove bread from an oven), he returned to his parents, eating it as he walked. Although he shared the honey with them, he did not tell them where he had gotten it.[238] He did not wish to

Samson. But Samson is suddenly the subject again in the second half of verse 10; after this we hear nothing more about his parents.

All these inconsistencies might lead us to suspect that the original text has been corrupted at various points. Some things may have been omitted and others added, with the result that the story has lost its coherence. Such a suspicion finds no support in the text-critical evidence, however (the minor discrepancies that exist [see footnote 236] have no significance). Even the ancient versions are in total agreement with the text as we have it, and in my view the major changes that some commentators would make in this text are therefore unwarranted. Budde and Moore, for example, delete the words pertaining to Samson's parents from verse 5 and have Samson going to Timnah alone (Schulz even deletes vv. 1b—4a and 6b, and he rearranges some clauses as he sees fit). In verse 8 they delete the words "to marry her" and regard this trip as Samson's return from Timnah to Zorah. And in verse 10 they delete "his father" and either replace it with "Samson" or just translate the pronoun "he" that is contained in the verb. Instead of this arbitrary and biased deletion, we should rather expect an additional word or two at this point.

The problem with verse 10 is not only its failure to mention Samson's mother but also its statement that his father went "to see the woman." One would rather expect to read that his father went to Timnah, as in verse 5. The words "to see the woman" would only make sense if Samson were the subject, for she was his bride. And since Samson is in fact the main actor in verses 5–9 and the subject of every verb (except in v. 6a), it is highly probable that he was originally also the subject of the verb in verse 10a. If we assume, therefore, that the original text contained the word "and" or "with" before *ʾābîhû* ("his father"), the biggest problem in the story has been removed. Verse 10 would then read "now he and his father went down to see the woman." This is only a hypothesis, of course, but it makes better sense than the text as it stands. The other inconsistencies mentioned above do not make the text unintelligible, and they can be explained fairly well by the author's desire to put Samson in the foreground.

[238] Samson's parents apparently again stayed on the main road. If he had been returning home to Zorah here, as Budde and Moore maintain, the verb that the NIV

divulge his adventure with the lion, for he was too modest; and the experience he had had was too intimate and personal to speak of. Since Samson's parents accompanied him to the wedding, they must have been reconciled to the marriage; but they perhaps did not stay for the full seven days of the feast.

14:10–13a *Now his father went down*[239] *to see the woman. And Samson made a feast there, as was customary for bridegrooms.* [11] *When he appeared, he was given thirty companions.*
[12] *"Let me tell you a riddle," Samson said to them. "If you can give me the answer within the seven days of the feast, I will give you thirty linen garments and thirty sets of clothes.* [13] *If you can't tell me the answer, you must give me thirty linen garments and thirty sets of clothes."*

When he arrived at Timnah with his parents, Samson arranged a feast; for this was the custom of bridegrooms at that time. This was naturally the bridegroom's responsibility, but he needed others to help him with the actual work. Samson was thus given thirty attendants, one of whom seems to have been in charge (see v. 20). The words "when he appeared" most likely refer to the moment of his arrival at the bride's house.[240] The family had been awaiting him; and when they welcomed him, they offered him the thirty companions who would serve him and contribute to the merrymaking. Whether or not thirty was the usual number is not known (Song of Sol. 3:7 says that there were sixty warriors at Solomon's wedding). It is a little surprising that these helpers were invited by the family of the bride rather than by the bridegroom himself (see v. 15). Perhaps this was a departure from the normal custom, since the Philistines would not have wanted too many Israelites at the wedding.

On the first day of the feast, Samson offered to tell a riddle and proposed a wager. He acted very friendly, but verse 4 no doubt sheds light on his true motive. Samson was slyly throwing down the gauntlet to the Philistines; for although he began with a game, this could easily

---

translates as "rejoined" would be *bā'* rather than *hālak*. For *hālak*, which means "go, walk," indicates that he was traveling.

[239]Goslinga offers "he and his father went down" as a possible emendation here. See footnote 237—TRANS.

[240]The Hebrew literally reads "when they saw him." Some manuscripts of the Septuagint read "since they feared him," which would indicate only a minor change in the Hebrew text. This reading therefore could be acceptable on text-critical grounds, but it does not fit with the context. At this time the Philistines did not yet have any reason to fear Samson.

take a serious turn. Conscious of his own superiority, he defied them by stacking the odds against himself: he alone would stand up to thirty of them. He gave them seven days to guess the answer to his riddle; and if they succeeded, he would give each of them a linen garment and a set of clothes. If they failed, however, each of them would have to give him only one linen garment and set of clothes.[241]

14:13b–16 *"Tell us your riddle," they said. "Let's hear it."*
[14] *He replied,*

"Out of the eater, something to eat;
    out of the strong, something sweet."

For three days they could not give the answer.
[15] *On the fourth[242] day, they said to Samson's wife, "Coax your husband into explaining the riddle for us, or we will burn you and your father's household to death. Did you invite us here to rob us?"[243]*
[16] *Then Samson's wife threw herself on him, sobbing, "You hate me! You don't really love me. You've given my people a riddle, but you haven't told me the answer."*

"I haven't even explained it to my father or mother," he replied, "so why should I explain it to you?"

Samson's Philistine companions accepted his challenge and the terms he had set; so he proceeded to tell them his riddle. He presented it in a poetic verse containing two parallel lines—short, pithy, and very puzzling. Anyone who did not know of Samson's experience with the lion and the honey (vv. 5–9) could never have guessed the meaning of these obscure words. It was somewhat reckless of Samson to use this incident as the basis for his riddle. To a certain extent he was "playing with something God had given him, something he should have kept secret."[244]

For three days the Philistine wedding attendants pondered the riddle

---

[241] It is not explicitly stated that these garments had to be costly. The word translated "linen garments" (literally, "undergarment" or "shirt") appears elsewhere only in Proverbs 31:24 and Isaiah 3:23. The word translated "sets" is also found in verse 19 and in Genesis 45:22; 2 Kings 5:5, 22–23. The derivation and precise meaning of the latter word is uncertain, but the contexts in which both words appear show that they generally referred to items of value (but see under v. 19).

[242] The Hebrew reads "seventh"; the NIV follows the Septuagint and the Syriac translation.

[243] The Hebrew word $h^a l\bar{o}$' at the end of verse 15 does not make good sense standing alone like this. The NIV therefore emends it to $h^a l\bar{o}m$ ("here") following several Hebrew manuscripts.

[244] S. G. de Graaf, *Promise and Deliverance,* 2:43.

in vain and failed to find the solution. Then they changed their tactics and sought the help of Samson's wife.[245] Since the woman is called his "wife" here (literally in the Hebrew, "the woman belonging to Samson"), the wedding clearly took place at the beginning of the seven-day feast (15:1 also shows that there had been a legitimate wedding). They told her that she must "coax" (the same verb is translated "lure" in 16:5) her husband into explaining the riddle to them. These last words are rather remarkable. They cannot mean that the Philistines wanted Samson to divulge the solution to them directly, for then they would clearly lose the wager. Rather, they wanted Samson to explain the riddle to his wife so that they could get the answer from her surreptitiously and convey it to Samson before the end of the seven days. In that way they could at least pretend they had won the contest. This base and childish ploy assumed that Samson's wife would take their side, but to force her hand they threatened to burn her and her family if she did not comply. They also added the vile insinuation that she had invited them to the wedding only to plunder them, apparently forgetting that they had freely accepted Samson's wager.

The attendants' words had the desired effect. The young wife sided with her countrymen against her husband and moaned to her husband. The Hebrew word translated "sobbing" literally means nothing more than "weep" (it is translated "cried" in v. 17); but when followed by the preposition "against" or "on" (*'al*), it means "burden with moaning, whine, wail" (see Num. 11:13). It seems that Samson's wife had done this from the first day of the feast (v. 17),[246] but now she increased the pressure by complaining that his unwillingness to trust her showed that he did not love her. Samson was well aware that his secret would not be safe with her, and he countered her accusation by pointing out that he had not even explained the riddle to his parents.

---

[245]The Hebrew text of verse 15 has "on the seventh day," but this does not fit with the number "three" in verse 14. Keil tries to explain this by assuming that after struggling with the riddle for three days, they let it rest until the seventh. But this would have been a strange way to act, and the Septuagint and Syriac translations offer another solution (see footnote 242). The Hebrew words for "seventh" (*šᵉbî'î*) and "fourth" (*rᵉbî'î*) differ by only a single consonant; so a copyist easily could have erred here. Moreover, Samson's confession to his wife (v. 17) would be easier to understand if she had been pressing him for several days.

[246]Verse 17 of course does not mean that she cried unceasingly for the whole seven days. Schelhaas's translation—"she cried on the seventh day"—is wrong (*Simson de Richter en Nazireër Gods*, p. 59). Had this been his meaning, the author would have used the standard ordinal number (see vv. 15, 17b).

14:17–18 *She cried the whole seven days of the feast. So on the seventh day he finally told her, because she continued to press him. She in turn explained the riddle to her people.*
¹⁸Before sunset²⁴⁷ on the seventh day the men of the town said to him,

> *"What is sweeter than honey?*
> *What is stronger than a lion?"*

Samson said to them,

> *"If you had not plowed with my heifer,*
> *you would not have solved my riddle."*

The woman continued to moan and complain to Samson whenever they were alone. The Hebrew verb that the NIV translates "continued to press" can also mean "oppress"; in Isaiah 29:2, 7 it means to "besiege" a city. Finally, in the course of the seventh day, Samson succumbed to her pressure, thus revealing his vulnerable spot for the first time. She immediately betrayed the secret to her countrymen. Before sundown they (the thirty attendants are here called "men of the town" because Timnah's honor was at stake in the wager) gave the solution to Samson in the form of a double rhetorical question that refered to the second line of his riddle: "out of the strong, something sweet." This of course simultaneously explained the first line ("out of the eater, something to eat").

Although the men of the town tried to give the impression that they had found the answer themselves without much difficulty, Samson at once realized what had really happened. He responded with an alert riposte, once again couched in poetic verse. Although the ends of the two lines rhyme, this is lost in the translation: "If you had not plowed with my heifer, / you would not have solved my riddle." Samson may have invented this imagery himself, but it is also possible that it was a proverb already in use. Although its exact meaning is uncertain, the drift is completely clear. The men of Timnah surely understood his words, but his reproach would not have troubled them since they had won at least an ostensible victory. Samson himself acknowledged this in his answer; so he was thus obliged to deliver the clothing that was wagered.

---

²⁴⁷Some commentators have suggested that *harsâ(h)*, an unusual, poetic word for "sun," should be emended to *hadrâ(h)*. The verse then would read "before he went into the room" (cf. NEB). Since the Hebrew text makes eminently good sense as it stands, however, we have no warrant for changing it.

14:19–20 *Then the Spirit of the LORD came upon him in power. He went down to Ashkelon, struck down thirty of their men, stripped them of their belongings and gave their clothes to those who had explained the riddle. Burning with anger, he went up to his father's house. ²⁰ And Samson's wife was given to the friend who had attended him at his wedding.*

Samson made no attempt to shirk his obligation. Although things had turned against him, he at least found "an occasion to confront the Philistines" (v. 4). The men of Timnah had won his contest by means of deceit and trickery, and they would indeed get their prize; but it would come at the expense of their own countrymen. Samson thus went down to Ashkelon,[248] where he overpowered thirty Philistines, stripped them of their clothes, and brought these back to the men of Timnah.[249] The author explicitly states that the Spirit of the Lord drove him to do all this. The Spirit seized him and filled him with power so that he could punish the Philistines and show them his superior strength. Samson therefore was not seeking personal revenge. Rather he was acting as a judge called by God who wanted to demonstrate to the Philistines that he was their most formidable foe. It was really the Lord, Israel's covenant God, who was fighting through Samson against the oppressors of His people.

When Samson returned with his spoils to Timnah, he became incensed at his wife and rushed off in a foul mood to the home of his parents, who probably had left earlier during the week of the feast. His angry departure was hardly praiseworthy, especially since his wife had only been able to deceive him because of his own weakness. Worse by far, however, was the response of the bride's father. Insulted by Samson's fury, which humiliated his daughter and brought the feast to an untimely end, he suddenly decided to get rid of Samson once and for all by giving his daughter to the groomsman (cf. John 3:29), who had been in charge of the thirty attendants (v. 11). It seems that this young man instantly took Samson's place so that the wedding feast could carry on. The Philistines obviously did not place a high value on

---

[248] Presumably, this was not the well-known city on the coast, which lay far to the southwest of Timnah, but a smaller place of the same name about an hour's journey south (see Moore, *Judges,* p. 338).

[249] The "linen garments" Samson had spoken of (vv. 12–13) are not mentioned here, but the word that is used is undoubtedly an inclusive term for all articles of clothing. The Hebrew *hᵃlîpâ(h)* might mean simply "garment," like the possibly related Assyrian term *nahlaptu.* Since Samson stripped the men of whatever they were wearing, verse 19 could not be speaking of costly or festal garments.

conjugal fidelity (see also 15:2), and it certainly was in Samson's best interest that his ties with this woman and her family were broken so soon. Through the failure of Samson's marriage, the Lord was showing him that true friendship could never exist between Israel and the Philistines.

To a certain extent chapter 14 is still introductory in character. The battle between Samson and the Philistines has begun, and Samson's strength and his weakness have been brought to our attention. Both of these things come more into the open as the story unfolds in chapters 15 and 16.

15:1 *Later on, at the time of wheat harvest, Samson took a young goat and went to visit his wife. He said, "I'm going to my wife's room." But her father would not let him go in.*

Some time later Samson returned to Timnah. We are told that this was at the time of the wheat harvest because of what follows in verse 5. His anger had cooled, and to appease his wife he took along a young goat as a gift. There is no basis for assuming that Samson intended to leave his wife in Timnah and only to pay her an occasional visit, as some commentators have inferred from this verse.[250] According to them, Samson became involved in a so-called "sadiga" marriage, in which the husband and wife did not form a new family unit, but the wife stayed in her parental home and only received periodic visits from her husband. Such marriages are found only in matriarchal societies, however; and neither the Israelites nor the Philistines had that kind of society.

The story of Samson provides no evidence that matriarchal marriage did in fact exist there. Some have argued this by pointing out that Samson brought his wife a young goat, the same payment that Judah sent to Tamar (Gen. 38:17), but this proves nothing more than that a young goat was regarded as a welcome gift in Israel. That Samson's wife did not go home with him proves even less, for this happened only because of his sudden, angry departure from the feast on the seventh

---

[250] E.g., Budde, *Das Buch der Richter,* pp. 97f., 100, 102; Moore, *Judges,* p. 340. According to Moore, who cites much other literature, the Arabs also engaged in such marriages. He grants that Samson's marriage is the sole example of this found in the Old Testament, but even this one is "found" only by reading it into the text. We should remember that the proponents of this view delete everything that pertains to Samson's parents from 14:5–6 and the words "to marry her" from verse 8 (see footnote 237).

day. The text actually does not even say that the woman was still living in her father's house, even though Samson came looking for her there. She indeed might not have been, since she had been given to another man. The marriage proposal that was made with Samson's parents' consent, the wedding and feast, and Samson's return to Timnah to claim his wife all show that his marriage was completely legitimate, though it is true that there was not much respect for the norms of marriage on the Philistine side (14:20).

15:2–5 *"I was so sure you thoroughly hated her," he said, "that I gave her to your friend. Isn't her younger sister more attractive? Take her instead."*

³Samson said to them, "This time I have a right to get even with the Philistines; I will really harm them." ⁴So he went out and caught three hundred foxes and tied them tail to tail in pairs. He then fastened a torch to every pair of tails, ⁵lit the torches and let the foxes loose in the standing grain of the Philistines. He burned up the shocks and standing grain, together with the vineyards and²⁵¹ olive groves.

Samson's father-in-law refused to allow him into his wife's room. He informed him that he had given her to Samson's best man because he thought Samson no longer wanted the woman and had intended to leave her for good. But since he seemed to have some awareness that this was unfair to Samson, he offered him a younger, more attractive daughter in his wife's place. Apparently he thought that Samson's morals were no better than his own. Samson naturally did not stoop to this insulting offer. Turning menacingly to his father-in-law and those with him, he said that this time he had "a right to get even with the Philistines," literally, "I am innocent in regard to the Philistines when I do them harm" (see 14:4). He sensed that the Philistines' treatment of him showed their contempt for his own people and that Israel as a whole was being insulted. In relation to him, an Israelite, his father-in-law and the men of Timnah (14:18) felt no obligation to be loyal or truthful. And he realized that he was being offended not merely as an individual but also as a judge.²⁵²

Samson therefore took vengeance, not merely on his wife's family, but on the Philistines in general by destroying their harvest. First he captured three hundred foxes. The Hebrew word can also mean "jackals" (see Ps. 63:10). Some commentators prefer this translation

---

²⁵¹The Hebrew *wᵉ* ("and") has been added between *kerem* and *zāyit* following the Septuagint and the Vulgate.

²⁵²See Schelhaas, *Simson de Richter en Nazireër Gods,* p. 68.

since jackals are social animals that run in packs, which would have made it easier for Samson to capture three hundred of them. Foxes are more likely, however, because of their long, bushy tails. Samson used these tails to tie the foxes together in pairs, and to each pair of tails he fastened a torch. He ignited the torches and let the animals loose in the fields so that they dragged the flame behind them and spread it to the wheat. Some of the grain was still standing in the fields, and some had been gathered into shocks. The foxes, straining at the cords that bound them together, probably first ran about in the vicinity of Timnah and later spread the fire far out into the countryside. By the time they were finished, the grain harvest had been destroyed and great damage had also been done to the vineyards (see 14:5) and olive groves.

15:6–8a *When the Philistines asked, "Who did this?" they were told, "Samson, the Timnite's son-in-law, because his wife was given to his friend."*
   So the Philistines went up and burned her and her father[253] *to death.* [7]*Samson said to them, "Since you've acted like this, I won't stop until I get my revenge on you."* [8]*He attacked them viciously*[254] *and slaughtered many of them.*

The Philistines could not allow the loss of their crops to go unpunished. They soon discovered that the person responsible was "Samson, the Timnite's son-in-law," who had used this novel but extremely effective method of destruction to get revenge for the injustice he had suffered. The words that are used for Samson show that persons outside of Timnah were speaking and, therefore, that a great part of the Philistine nation had been affected by his angry measure. But instead of banding together against their Israelite adversary, they marched to Timnah and savagely murdered Samson's wife and her father (or family, see footnote 253), their own countrymen, probably by shutting them up in their house and then burning it. Regarded from a higher perspective, this was no doubt a fitting punishment for their previous betrayal of Samson (14:17, 20). Samson, however, who welcomed any chance to fight the Philistines, saw the Philistines' action as proof that they were too cowardly to fight him

---

[253]The Masoretic text has "father," but many of the Hebrew manuscripts and ancient versions have "house [or 'family'] of her father." A copyist easily could have accidentally omitted the word *bêt* ("house") after *'et*, since both end with the same consonant.
   [254]Literally, "thigh on hip." The same construction appears in Genesis 32:11 and Exodus 12:9.

openly but still wanted to cause him pain. He therefore resolved also to take revenge for the murder of his wife.

Samson probably spoke the words of verse 7 to himself when he learned what the Philistines had done; "to them" would then merely mean that his words were meant for them. It also is possible, however, that he shouted these words directly to the band of Philistines who had set the fire, for they indeed would have been the main victims of his vicious attack and slaughter (v. 8). The Hebrew literally says that he struck them "thigh on hip," which probably was a popular expression that indicated ruthlessness or total annihilation. Samson seems to have won this victory without using a single weapon, which would mean that he had enormous physical strength even when the Spirit of the Lord did not take hold of him and infuse him with power. Remarkably, he made no attempt to organize his fellow Israelites and lead them against the enemy, as Gideon and the other judges had done. No doubt the explanation for this lies in his Nazirite consecration. He knew that he had been called to a special task in which he would need no human help and that he was a unique instrument of the Spirit of the Lord. It also is possible, however, that his aim was merely to provoke a Philistine attack against Israel so that his own people would rise to the challenge of battle. If so, the following verses show that he was not successful.

15:8b–9 *Then he went down and stayed in a cave in the rock of Etam.*
⁹ The Philistines went up and camped in Judah, spreading out near Lehi.

Samson retreated into a cave in the rock of Etam. Since verse 8 says that he "went down," this could not be the Etam in Judah (2 Chron. 11:6), a town that lay in the hill country. It could possibly be the Etam in Simeon (1 Chron. 4:32), which was located in the Negev near Ain Rimmon; but it is hard to believe that Samson would have traveled that far south. More likely is a place near modern 'Artuf, east of Zorah, where an almost inaccessible cleft is found in a steep wall of rock.[255] One indeed had to "go down" to reach this place (see also vv. 11, 13), and it was located in the general area where Samson was active. Samson certainly did not withdraw to the rock of Etam out of fear. We must assume that he was reluctant to endanger the inhabitants of Zorah or other Israelite towns by staying near them, and he may even have

---

[255] The site was discovered by Schick, who is cited by Budde and Moore. But since we have no evidence that this place has ever been called Etam, the identification remains uncertain.

felt that many Israelites would not take kindly to his presence (however much they may have admired him), because they themselves feared the Philistines' vengeance. Samson willingly accepted his calling to fight the Philistines alone, but he waited for them to make the first move. Once again he remained true to his policy of going to battle only when he had been challenged or treated unjustly (see his words in v. 11).

15:10–13 *The men of Judah asked, "Why have you come to fight us?"*

"We have come to take Samson prisoner," they answered, "to do to him as he did to us."

¹¹ *Then three thousand men from Judah went down to the cave in the rock of Etam and said to Samson, "Don't you realize that the Philistines are rulers over us? What have you done to us?"*

He answered, "I merely did to them what they did to me."

¹² *They said to him, "We've come to tie you up and hand you over to the Philistines."*

Samson said, "Swear to me that you won't kill me yourselves."

¹³ *"Agreed," they answered. "We will only tie you up and hand you over to them. We will not kill you." So they bound him with two new ropes and led him up from the rock.*

Realizing that things had taken a turn for the worse, the Philistines decided that Samson's harassment of them had to be ended once and for all. They therefore marched into Judah with a large army and set up camp near Lehi, a place whose name is explained in verse 17 (see NIV margin). There may have been permanent Philistine garrisons at various points in Israel, for they undoubtedly exacted an annual tribute from the people. In any case the invasion that they now undertook tightened their stranglehold, but the Israelites did not even raise a finger against them. The men of Judah's question—"Why have you come to fight us?"—is an expression of abject fear, almost as if they were saying, "We have done you no harm and would not think of revolting." The Philistines responded by saying that they were only after Samson and would be content when they had him. The two sides almost sound like friends here.

The Philistines indeed had no desire to fight, and obviously they did not expect the least resistance from the men of Judah. Samson alone was a threat; so he would be the only one punished. The men of Judah were even more reluctant to go to war. They refused to take the side of their fellow Israelite even though he had good reason to retaliate against the Philistines. Like the Philistines, they regarded Samson as a rebel against the legitimate authorities, not as a judge. They even took it on themselves to go and seize Samson, a favor that the Philistines gladly accepted.

Samson's hiding place apparently was no secret; so three thousand men from Judah marched down to the rock of Etam to capture and hand over the "troublemaker." Their first words were a harsh rebuke: "Don't you realize that the Philistines are rulers over us? What have you done to us?" Apparently, the men of Judah had fallen so low that they no longer felt humiliated at being subjects of the uncircumcised Philistines. They considered it a crime that Samson had provoked their masters (vv. 5, 8), and they called him to account for this. Samson's defense was brief: he did not begin the fighting but was treated unjustly by the Philistines and merely repaid them in kind. He did not even speak of the antagonism between Israel and Philistia, for such words would have been wasted on men who were so lacking in national awareness.

The men of Judah did not argue with Samson's response. Instead they told him that they had come to surrender him to the Philistines. Samson demanded that they take an oath not to attack him once he was tied up. He did this, not because he feared them, but because he did not want to be forced to shed the blood of a fellow Israelite. The men of Judah did not take an oath, but they did make a firm promise that they would not attempt to kill him (they literally said, "We will indeed tie you up . . . but we surely will not kill you"; the words "tie up" and "kill" are marked for strong emphasis). To their credit they at least kept this promise. This whole experience must have been extremely disappointing for Samson; his own people failed utterly to understand that he had been sent to deliver them (cf. the Israelites' attitude toward Moses in Exod. 5:20–21; Acts 7:25). His only consolation was that the Philistines had once again given him an occasion to confront them, the very thing he was looking for (14:4). The men of Judah bound him with two newly braided ropes and led him off to his enemies, subjecting him to the same fate that Jesus later received when He was handed over to the Gentiles (John 18:28–30).

15:14–15 *As he approached Lehi, the Philistines came toward him shouting. The Spirit of the LORD came upon him in power. The ropes on his arms became like charred flax, and the bindings dropped from his hands. 15 Finding a fresh jawbone of a donkey, he grabbed it and struck down a thousand men.*

Verse 14 presents a vivid description of Samson's plight. He was dragged toward the Philistines, bound and apparently defenseless, while they rushed forward to seize him, shouting triumphantly. But suddenly the tables were turned. The Spirit of the Lord took hold of Samson and filled him with superhuman power. He broke the strong, new cords that bound him almost without effort—they are said to have melted from his hands like wax held to the fire—and a moment later he was inflicting a crushing defeat on the fleeing Philistine army.

The divine humor in this stirring picture cannot be missed: "The One enthroned in heaven laughs" (Ps. 2:4). At Samson's feet lay a donkey's jawbone that was still fresh, and thus hard and strong. Before the Philistines had time to overcome their amazement, he picked the jawbone up and struck down those nearest to him with fierce blows. They were too shocked to fight back, and a huge number were killed. The number "one thousand" probably should not be taken literally, however; perhaps it was borrowed from the triumphant song that Samson uttered after he stopped his pursuit.

15:16–17 *Then Samson said,*

> *"With a donkey's jawbone*
> *I have made donkeys of them.*[256]
> *With a donkey's jawbone*
> *I have killed a thousand men."*

17 When he finished speaking, he threw away the jawbone; and the place was called Ramath Lehi.

This song, which consists of two poetic lines, contains a pun in the first line that is based on the fact that the Hebrew words for "donkey" and "heap" are homonyms, but it is impossible to preserve this in the translation.[257] An attempt has been made to compensate for this loss by using meter and rhyme in the English. The entire song expresses Samson's amazement at the fact that he had been able to defeat such a multitude. Perhaps he remembered the words from Moses' song of

---

[256] The Hebrew words for "donkey" and "heap" are homonyms; so the translation could also be "made a heap or two" (see NIV margin—TRANS.). Another possibility is to follow the Septuagint and repoint the final two Hebrew words in this line as an infinitive absolute followed by a finite verb form, both based on a stem *ḥmr*, which is the root of the noun *ḥᵃmôr* ("heap") . The meaning then would be "heap up." Moore thus repoints these words *ḥāmôr ḥimmartîm*. (Goslinga accepts this hypothesis and translates the line "with a donkey's jawbone I have made them into a heap"—TRANS.)

[257] Gressmann offers an approximate equivalent in his German translation, "mit dem Backen eines Esels schlug ich das Eselspack" (*Die Anfänge Israels* (1922), p. 235).

farewell: "How could one man chase a thousand?" (Deut. 32:30; cf. Josh. 23:10), for he indeed had brought this to fulfillment. The song would be even better if it gave God the glory for Samson's victory. The Israelites obviously did not help him; so it was only through the extraordinary strength that he received from the Lord that he was able to accomplish his astonishing feat (see under v. 18). After Samson had exulted over his victory, he threw away the jawbone and named the site after it: Ramath Lehi, or "Jawbone Hill."[258] The use of the name "Lehi" in verses 9 and 14 is thus proleptic. See also footnote 280 at the end of this section.

15:18–20 *Because he was very thirsty, he cried out to the LORD, "You have given your servant this great victory. Must I now die of thirst and fall into the hands of the uncircumcised?"* [19] *Then God opened up the hollow place in Lehi, and water came out of it. When Samson drank, his strength returned and he revived. So the spring was called En Hakkore, and it is still there in Lehi.* [20] *Samson led Israel for twenty years in the days of the Philistines.*

Samson apparently was alone again, for nothing more is said about the men of Judah. There was no water, and he was so overcome by thirst that he feared he would lose his strength. Conscious of his deep dependence on the Lord, he turned to Him for help. He acknowledged that "this great victory" had come from God and that he had merely been acting as His servant. Samson's prayer in verse 16 thus makes up for what was lacking in his song of triumph (v. 18). Here we see him at his best—a humble suppliant who knew that he was nothing but an instrument in the Lord's hands, but who for this very reason made bold to demand that the Lord be faithful.

Samson asked how the same God who had used him to defeat the Philistines could permit him to die of thirst and thus fall into their hands after all. Would this not defame the name of the Lord? Would it not seem that the Lord had abandoned him, or that he had not truly been a Nazirite consecrated to God? The Lord answered Samson's prayer by performing a miracle. For the God of Israel to whom he called was also the Creator who was able to use the forces of nature as He pleased. Before Samson's very eyes, He caused the ground to split open and

---

[258] Verse 17 can be translated either "the place was called" (NIV) or "he called the place" (Goslinga, KJV). But since Samson is the subject in verses 18–19, we have every reason to think that he was also the subject here. His song shows that he attached great importance to his victory; so it is likely that the name that memorialized it came from him.

water to come forth (cf. Exod. 17:6; Isa. 48:21). The "hollow place in Lehi" was not a cleft that was already there; the Lord's answer to Samson's prayer brought it into being. "Hollow place" translates a rare Hebrew word (it appears elsewhere only in Prov. 27:22; Zeph. 1:11) that literally means "mortar"; so the place undoubtedly was shaped somewhat like a mortar.[259]

After Samson had drunk, his strength (literally, "spirit") returned and he was quickly revived. In gratitude to God he named the spring En Hakkore ("Caller's Spring") to preserve the memory of his prayer and the Lord's answer for later generations. The spring still existed in the author's day. Like verse 17, verse 19 can read either "the spring was called" or "he called the spring."[260]

It is highly significant that verse 20 makes the statement that Samson led (or "judged") Israel for twenty years. This is not a stray remark that just happened to be added at this point in the story and that really belongs only at the end of chapter 16. Rather, it is intimately connected with the preceding events and forms a fitting conclusion to chapters 14 and 15. The episodes from Samson's life that are recorded in these two chapters happened within a relatively short span of time and were designed by God to prepare him for his work as judge. The last two events at Lehi (vv. 14–17 and vv. 18–19), in particular, completed his training and showed Samson where he stood both in relation to the Israelites and in relation to the Lord Himself. Thus it became clear to friend and foe alike that Samson was God's appointed man who had been sent to protect the Israelites and to defend their interests.[261] Verse 20 is therefore completely in place here. It would be different if

---

[259]The rabbis hold that the word means "tooth cavity" and translate Lehi literally as "jawbone," thus, "then God opened the cavity in the jawbone." On this basis many of the church fathers and even some modern exegetes think that Samson drank water from the donkey's jawbone. Such a notion is ruled out, however, by the words themselves, by the entire context, and especially by the final clause in verse 19 (see Keil, *Kommentar,* p. 338; Moore, *Judges,* p. 347). Cavities in Palestine's rocky ground were in fact often used as mortars for crushing grain (see Schulz, *Das Buch der Richter,* p. 83).

[260]See footnote 258. Keil prefers "the spring was called"; and if the words "to this day" (NIV, "it is still there") are read with this first part of the sentence rather than with "in Lehi," this would be the only possible translation (i.e., "it is called En Hakkore in Lehi to this day").

[261]Compare de Graaf's statement: "It was made clear to the Philistines that a deliverer had arisen in Israel, that there was someone in Israel who was stronger than all of them together, because the Lord was with him" (*Promise and Deliverance,* 2:44; cf. p. 45).

the author had intended to present an orderly account of Samson's judgeship. This was not his aim, however, and it has rightly been observed that verse 20 already forms a provisional conclusion to his work as judge. As Keil points out, the story in chapter 16 belongs to the time of Samson's downfall and must be placed at the end of his life.[262] He did remain a Nazirite till his death, but there were interruptions in his judgeship (see 16:31, however).

Although we are not told exactly what Samson did during his twenty years as judge, this has also been the case with most of the other judges. The words "in the days of the Philistines" show that the Israelites continued to live under foreign tyranny throughout his judgeship. There never was a widespread rebellion or any organized resistance. In all likelihood, however, there were frequent passing confrontations like those described in chapter 15, which would have kept the Philistines in perpetual fear of Samson (16:23–24) and caused them to stay on the lookout for an opportunity to capture him (16:2). See further the remarks on pages 408–9.

There is no ground whatsoever for the view of some commentators that the stories in verses 14–17 and 18–19 are mere instances of folk etymology, i.e., legends that became attached to certain places and gave a popular but incorrect explanation of their names. According to this view, the name Lehi really arose because the place had a shape reminiscent of a jawbone, not because Samson defeated the Philistines with a donkey's jawbone there. But if this fanciful explanation is true, where then did Samson's song in verse 16 come from? As a second example some scholars hold that the author understood the name Ramath Lehi as "throwing away of the jawbone," even though the obvious meaning is "hill of Lehi [i.e., 'Jawbone']." For if that is what the author had meant by the name, he surely would have used *rāmâ(h)* (rather than *hišlîḵ*) for "threw away" in the first part of verse 17.

Finally, it is thought that the name En Hakkore should be translated "spring of the partridge." Even apart from the question of whether this translation is correct, however, there is not the slightest indication that either the spring or its name ever had anything to do with a partridge. This derivation too is therefore obviously motivated by the desire to reduce the story in verses 18–19 to a mere legend. Such "explanations," which are indulged in by Moore, Budde, Gressman, and Schulz (see their commentaries on these verses), drain the soul out of Israel's

---

[262] *Kommentar*, p. 339.

history and declare the text to be fictitious without a shred of objective evidence for doing so.

3. SAMSON'S CAPTURE AND TRIUMPH OVER THE PHILISTINES (16:1–31)

16:1–3 *One day Samson went to Gaza, where he saw a prostitute. He went in to spend the night with her. ²The people of Gaza were told,*[263] *"Samson is here!" So they surrounded the place and lay in wait for him all night at the city gate. They made no move during the night, saying, "At dawn we'll kill him."*

³But Samson lay there only until the middle of the night. Then he got up and took hold of the doors of the city gate, together with the two posts, and tore them loose, bar and all. He lifted them to his shoulders and carried them to the top of the hill that faces Hebron.

Within the story of Samson as a whole, verses 1–3 form the transition to the account of his downfall and death, which is deliberately introduced by the words "some time later" in verse 4. These three verses therefore stand more or less alone. In no case are they to be attached directly to chapters 14–15, for 15:20 marks the end of that part of Samson's life. They rather serve to foreshadow Samson's fall and prepare the reader for the final act in his life, which also unfolded in Gaza (v. 21).

Toward the end of his reign as judge, Samson went to Gaza ("strong place"), the southernmost city on the coast of Palestine, which had been conquered by Judah (1:18) but later fell back into the hands of the Philistines. He seems to have been alone again, and he moved about in this Philistine stronghold freely and without fear. We are not told whether he had any particular reason for going there. Possibly, his reckless impulses again got the better of him, and he certainly took a false step when he went in to spend the night with a prostitute. By yielding to his sinful passions, he also placed his life in danger. Before long, the people of Gaza found out that Samson was in their city and where he was staying. Their first step was to surround the prostitute's house, and they also placed a watch at the city gate. Because of their fear of Samson, however, they did not dare to attack him; so they merely stayed in hiding and put off the moment of truth till dawn. But

---

[263]This word is lacking in the Hebrew text, but on the basis of the Septuagint it is almost unanimously assumed that *wayyuggad: ku* ("it was told"), or, according to Schulz, *wattaggêd: ku* ("she told"), has been omitted.

although they did not make a move during the night, Samson did not wait till morning.[264]

At midnight Samson arose and proceeded unmolested to the city gate. We hear nothing more about the Philistine ambushers and sentries, but this silence is eloquent. Samson merely walked on as if they were not there. The gate, which was secured by a crossbar, also presented no serious problem. He simply ripped the two doors, posts and all, right out of the ground, hoisted the entire mass to his shoulders (presumably with the Philistines looking on, breathless and silent), and carried it all to the top of a hill that is vaguely described as "facing Hebron" (NIV, "that faces Hebron").

It is a good question whether these words are to be taken literally. Hebron was located almost forty miles east of Gaza; so one cannot help wondering whether it made any sense for Samson to carry the gates so far. Some (e.g., Keil) think it did not and hold that the word "facing" merely means "toward, in the direction of," an interpretation that is at least possible in view of Genesis 18:16, where the same word does mean "toward (Sodom)." On this basis it is assumed that he carried the gates to the peak of El-Muntar, a hill about a half hour's walk southeast of Gaza that has also been accepted by the tradition as the place where he left them. But if this is true, why did the author even mention Hebron instead of simply saying "facing the city [viz., Gaza]" or something similar? We also should note that Samson's heroic act would lose much significance if he left the gates in Philistine territory.

I believe that Samson indeed brought the gates back to Israelite soil, and that the author included the name Hebron to show that he deposited them in the center of Judah so that Israel would have tangible proof of his victory. The citizens of Hebron would have had a clear view of the gates lying on the hilltop. The words "facing Hebron" therefore should be taken literally. The author apparently felt that the mention of the hill near Hebron was clear enough and sufficient for his purpose. It was indeed a great distance from Gaza to this hill, but we should not attach too much weight to mere numerical computations. For Samson to carry the gates away was a miracle, regardless of whether he carried them four miles or forty miles.

Although we do not read in these verses that the Spirit of the Lord came on Samson, the Lord obviously had not yet left him. Once again

---

[264]Schelhaas's assumption that the woman's house stood near the city gate is plausible, but the text offers no support for his thought that the watchmen fell asleep (*Simson de Richter en Nazireër Gods,* p. 85).

He enabled Samson to escape danger and to terrorize Israel's enemies with a display of the power of his God. Nevertheless, Samson's experience at Gaza also contained a warning for him. The occasion that he chose "to confront the Philistines" (14:4) was a dishonor to God and endangered his life so greatly that only a miracle could save him.[265] By turning down a sinful path and trusting that his strength would protect him, he was tempting the Lord. Samson failed to understand this lesson, however, and his visit to Gaza proved to be the beginning of the end for him (see also footnote 280).

16:4–5 *Some time later, he fell in love with a woman in the Valley of Sorek whose name was Delilah. ⁵The rulers of the Philistines went to her and said, "See if you can lure him into showing you the secret of his great strength and how we can overpower him so we may tie him up and subdue him. Each one of us will give you eleven hundred shekels of silver."*

Samson's love affair with Delilah began shortly after his victory at Gaza. This too was an improper way for him to "confront" the Philistines. We are not told that there was a legitimate wedding, as in chapter 14, and Samson seems to have been driven mainly by his carnal desires. Although Delilah is not explicitly called a prostitute, it is obvious that she was not a woman of high morals. We also are not told that she was a Philistine, but there is no doubt that she was. Had she been an Amorite, the author certainly would have reported this; and he does tell us that she lived in the Valley of Sorek. This was the valley of the brook Sorek, modern Wadi es-Sarar, which flowed through Philistine territory about an hour's journey west of Zorah. Samson probably still lived in this town, and he therefore easily could have paid regular visits to Delilah.

Once the relationship between Samson and Delilah became known, the Philistines made plans to trap him so that they could finally put an end to their dreaded Israelite foe. Delilah was approached by the five Philistine rulers (see 3:3; 1 Sam. 6:4, 16), who persuaded her to try to lure Samson into divulging the secret of his prodigious strength. If she could discover the mystery or magic that lay behind this and, more importantly, the means by which he could be overcome, they promised each to give her 1,100 shekels of silver, a considerable sum (about 5 x 40 = 200 pounds of silver if a shekel was equal to approximately ⅖ of

---

[265] According to de Graaf, "in that sinful unfolding of his life he was also an antitype of the Christ—and thus a type of the people, with their sinful desires and their unfaithfulness to the Lord" (*Promise and Deliverance,* 2:39).

an ounce; but see NIV margin in v. 5, which indicates 5 x 28 = 140 pounds). The rulers themselves would take care of Samson's capture. The Hebrew in verse 5 literally reads "a thousand and a hundred" shekels, which according to some commentators is a more or less indefinite number meaning "a thousand and more," or "a thousand and something" (see also 17:2).

16:6–9 *So Delilah said to Samson, "Tell me the secret of your great strength and how you can be tied up and subdued."*

⁷Samson answered her, "If anyone ties me with seven fresh thongs that have not been dried, I'll become as weak as any other man."

⁸Then the rulers of the Philistines brought her seven fresh thongs that had not been dried, and she tied him with them. ⁹With men hidden in the room, she called to him, "Samson, the Philistines are upon you!" But he snapped the thongs as easily as a piece of string snaps when it comes close to a flame. So the secret of his strength was not discovered.

When Delilah began to ask Samson about the secret of his strength, she took care not to arouse his suspicion. She no doubt pretended to be playing a game and gave the impression that she wanted to see him tied up and helpless only for fun. As Samson's beloved, she certainly could demand to know more about him than others. Samson nevertheless remained on his guard and did not divulge his secret. He was still conscious of his Nazirite consecration, and he even hinted at this in a way by naming the sacred number seven. Was he thinking of his seven braids of hair? One has to wonder why he did not flee Delilah's seduction right at this point.

Samson's weakness was clearly evident here; he was unable to master his sensual desires, which indeed are often stronger in a man in the prime of life than in a youth. Unwilling to break his relationship with Delilah, he struck a compromise by joining in her game and trying to mislead her. He thus told her that he would be rendered powerless if he was bound with seven fresh thongs (or bowstrings) that had not been dried. Such cords could be tied the tightest and were the hardest to break when they were new and moist. By turning his secret into a game, Samson became even more guilty than his pagan woman; for she, at least, knew nothing about his divine consecration and calling. He had acted more honorably and more manly in relation to his former wife (14:16, 19) than he did in relation to Delilah.

The Hebrew words translated "as any other man" (v. 7) literally mean "as one of the men" or "one of mankind" (the same words appear in v. 11, while v. 17 literally means "as all men"). A similar expression appears in Psalm 73:5. The Philistine rulers provided Delilah with the fresh thongs that she asked for, and they also sent her a group of men who would take Samson captive once he had been tied up. She hid them in a nearby place (perhaps in a side room), where they could keep watch and pounce on him when she gave the signal. The next time Samson arrived, Delilah gave her plan a try. She tied him with the seven thongs, probably while he was asleep (cf. v. 14), and then called out, "The Philistines are upon you!" Samson awoke, found he had been bound, but snapped all the thongs with a single movement as easily as a string of tow could be snapped when it had been singed by fire (cf. 15:14). Delilah's first attempt to discover the secret of Samson's strength thus failed, and the Philistines undoubtedly did not even venture from their hiding place.

16:10–12 *Then Delilah said to Samson, "You have made a fool of me; you lied to me. Come now, tell me how you can be tied."*

¹¹He said, "If anyone ties me securely with new ropes that have never been used, I'll become as weak as any other man."

¹²So Delilah took new ropes and tied him with them. Then, with men hidden in the room, she called to him, "Samson, the Philistines are upon you!" But he snapped the ropes off his arms as if they were threads.

Undaunted by her failure, Delilah renewed her efforts. She scolded Samson for deceiving her and insisted that he tell her his secret. Again he could not resist playing along with her and continued his deception. He was confident that he was strong enough to win the game but careful enough not to say too much. This time he told her to tie him with new ropes (the same Hebrew words as in 15:13) that had never been used. Delilah may have only half-trusted Samson (cf. v. 18), but she had to give it a try. She kept up the game if only to give him a false sense of security, the better to surprise him later. Once again the result was the same: the new ropes were no match for Samson's strength.

16:13–14 *Delilah then said to Samson, "Until now, you have been making a fool of me and lying to me. Tell me how you can be tied."*

He replied, "If you weave the seven braids of my head into the fabric on the loom and tighten it with the pin, I'll become as weak as any other man." So while he was sleeping, Delilah took the seven braids of his head, wove them into the fabric ¹⁴and tightened it with the pin.[266]

---

[266]In the Hebrew text, verse 13 ends with the words "into the fabric [on the loom]," and verse 14 begins "and she tightened it" (see KJV, NIV margin). Obviously,

Again she called to him, "Samson, the Philistines are upon you!" He awoke from his sleep and pulled up the pin and the loom, with the fabric.

Delilah still did not lose heart. She did not want to give up on the silver shekels, and she believed that persistence would win out in the end. Samson, on the other hand, was too blind to realize that the longer he played Delilah's game, the less he would be able to hold out against her. He even became overbold and relaxed his guard a little by drawing her attention to his hair. What he told her and what she then did are clear for the most part; but some of the details are obscure because we do not know exactly how the looms of that day worked, and a few of the Hebrew terms are uncommon. In addition, the traditional text presents some difficulties that can only be partially solved by following the Septuagint translation (see footnote 266). Samson told Delilah to weave his long, braided hair into the fabric that was stretched out on the loom; the fabric was the warp, and his hair would serve as the woof. She then was to tighten the weave, probably not with a pin (as in the NIV),[267] but with a flat, pointed wooden instrument for beating the woof down so that the entire fabric would be tight and closely knit. After Samson had fallen asleep, probably on the ground near to the loom, Delilah carried out his instructions to the letter. Anyone other than Samson would have been rendered completely helpless by this; but when Delilah cried out and he awoke, he once again managed to free himself without difficulty.

This much is clear, but the end of verse 14 presents a problem. The Hebrew text says that Samson pulled up three different things when he suddenly arose: (1) the wooden beater (or pin); (2) a word that appears

---

something is missing here. Verse 13 contains Samson's instructions and verse 14 tells how Delilah carried them out, but both of these things are described much less fully than in her other attempts to subdue him (vv. 7, 11, 17 and vv. 8, 12, 18). The Septuagint has a fuller text here that contains everything that is missing in the Hebrew, and it is easy to explain how the Hebrew words that it presumably is based on could have been omitted from the text. The final words of the omitted passage are identical to the end of verse 13 (in the Hebrew), and the opening words are like the beginning of verse 14; so the eye of a copyist very easily could have strayed from the one group of words to the other. In my view the Septuagint reading therefore has to be regarded as a translation of the original Hebrew text. The Hebrew text does not say that Samson fell asleep but only that he awoke. This problem too is cleared up by the Septuagint text where it begins verse 14.

[267]The Hebrew term generally does mean "pin" or "peg," but that would not fit here. The Septuagint tries to make the meaning more acceptable by adding the words "into the wall."

elsewhere only in Job 7:6, where it means "weaver's shuttle"; and (3) the fabric (i.e., the warp). The third item presents no difficulty, but it is not clear how Samson could have pulled loose the beater and the shuttle, since these were separate from the loom itself.[268] In addition, the vocalization of the Hebrew text suggests the translation "beater of the shuttle," which makes no sense and in fact does not fit with the definite article attached to "beater." The text thus contains a grammatical inconsistency that seems to indicate that it is not completely intact. In my judgment the word "beater" (or "pin") does not belong and is probably a later addition that was motivated by the misconception that the Hebrew term indicated a pin by which the fabric was fastened to the wall (see footnote 267). The second Hebrew term could well mean something different than "shuttle." Since it comes from a root meaning "weave," some think it denotes a loom;[269] but this is unlikely because it is followed by the word "fabric." It seems very plausible to me, however, that the word should be translated "woof," which in fact would be consistent with the meaning "shuttle." Verse 14 then would mean that Samson pulled loose both the woof (i.e., his hair) and the warp, in other words, the entire cloth that had been woven on the loom.

16:15–17 *Then she said to him, "How can you say, 'I love you,' when you won't confide in me? This is the third time you have made a fool of me and haven't told me the secret of your great strength."* [16] *With such nagging she prodded him day after day until he was tired to death.*

[17] *So he told her everything. "No razor has ever been used on my head," he said, "because I have been a Nazirite set apart to God since birth. If my head were shaved, my strength would leave me, and I would become as weak as any other man."*

Samson once again managed to elude Delilah's attempt to snare him. Nevertheless, by succumbing to her pressure little by little, he lost his power to resist; and Delilah's supreme cunning enabled her to capitalize on her advantage. So she pretended to be hurt and chided Samson for his insincerity; he had told her that he loved her but refused to confide in her and continually misled her. The words translated "you won't confide in me" literally mean "your heart is not with me," where "heart" does not denote his affection but the most intimate secrets of

---

[268]Notice that the NIV has "loom" instead of "shuttle," which would change the situation—TRANS.

[269]This is how Moore translates it (*Judges*, p. 354; also the RSV and NIV—TRANS.). I agree with his understanding of these verses in all other respects.

his mind.[270] The opening words of verse 17 similarly have the literal meaning "so he told her his whole heart." Delilah did not want Samson to keep a single secret from her, and she harped on this daily and prodded him till he could not stand it any longer (cf. 14:17). The Hebrew term translated "prod" appears here only in the Old Testament, but its cognates in related languages mean "beset, oppress."

Finally, when Delilah had tormented Samson to death and his life had been made bitter (cf. 10:16), he decided to tell her what she wanted to know. He told her that he had been a Nazirite since birth, a man set apart to God. The sign of this was that no razor had ever been used on his head; but if he were to lose his hair, his strength would also depart.

16:18–19 *When Delilah saw that he had told her everything, she sent word to the rulers of the Philistines, "Come back once more; he has told me*[271] *everything." So the rulers of the Philistines returned with the silver in their hands. 19Having put him to sleep on her lap, she called a man to shave off the seven braids of his hair, and so began to subdue him. And his strength left him.*

Delilah could tell from Samson's deep earnestness and especially from the nature of his words that this time he had told her the whole truth. She therefore immediately sent to the Philistine rulers and told them to come back once more, for she finally had discovered the secret of his strength. From this we can infer that she had had doubts the previous times she sent for them and had expected from the beginning that Samson would not at once tell her everything she wanted to know. The rulers and their henchmen must have come on a day when Delilah knew that Samson would visit her and arrived before he did. They brought the promised silver with them (probably on pack animals, since it was such a large amount). After Samson had divulged his secret, Delilah undoubtedly did everything possible to assure him that it was safe with her and that she would not misuse it. But he obviously was very foolish to continue visiting her. In a sense the Lord had already abandoned him at this point; since he refused to take warning, he would have to suffer the consequences of his sinful folly.

When Samson arrived, Delilah allowed him to fall asleep on her knees or lap and then called a man to come and shave off the seven

---

[270]See F. H. von Meyenfeldt, *Het hart in het Oude Testament* (Leiden, 1950), pp. 25f.

[271]The Masoretic text reads "her" here, but the *Qere*, along with numerous Hebrew manuscripts and ancient versions, has "me." The latter obviously is correct, since Delilah was speaking.

braids of his hair. A few Greek manuscripts actually call this man a barber; and although there is not much support for this reading, shaving undoubtedly was his trade. Delilah obviously would have arranged this beforehand and hidden the man in a side room. The Hebrew text literally states that "she shaved off the seven braids of his hair," but this of course merely means that she was responsible for the act, not that she handled the razor. Her only job was to sit quietly so that Samson would not awaken too early.

The end of verse 19 has to be read in connection with verse 5, where the Philistine rulers said that their aim was to "subdue" Samson. The same Hebrew word is used here to show that Delilah was the one who began to do this. This of course does not mean that she attacked him physically, for Samson remained fast asleep till she called him. Some commentators think that she tied him up and point to his words "shake myself free" in verse 20; but if she had done this, it would have been stated more explicitly. The only meaning can be that Delilah overpowered Samson in principle by depriving him of his long hair. The final words of the verse confirm this by stating that his strength left him at that moment.

16:20–22 *Then she called, "Samson, the Philistines are upon you!"*

He awoke from his sleep and thought, "I'll go out as before and shake myself free." But he did not know that the Lord had left him.

*²¹ Then the Philistines seized him, gouged out his eyes and took him down to Gaza. Binding him with bronze shackles,*²⁷² *they set him to grinding in the prison. ²² But the hair on his head began to grow again after it had been shaved.*

When Delilah awakened Samson in the usual manner, his strength was gone. At first he thought that he was as strong as ever and would be able to tear himself free, just as he had done the previous times he was tied up. He did not realize, however, that this time the Lord had left him. By saying that it was the Lord that left him and not merely his hair, the author makes clear that Samson's enormous strength did not come from his hair as such but from the fact that the Lord was with him and was using him as His instrument. Once Samson had forsaken his calling to harass Israel's enemy and had squandered his energies in the pursuit of sensual pleasure—even going so far as to join hands with the enemy by revealing the source of his strength to a Philistine woman and placing the sign of his Nazirite consecration in jeopardy—the Lord

---

²⁷²The Hebrew term is dual; Keil therefore translates it "double fetters" (Goslinga has "pair of bronze fetters"—Trans.).

punished him by causing his strength to leave him along with this external sign. Samson needed to realize that he could not trifle with Israel's God or treat His gift to him as a plaything. He had to find out that his strength had not been given to him unconditionally. He had abandoned the Lord; so the Lord in turn abandoned him and left him powerless, or at least no stronger than any other man.

The Philistines sprang out of their hiding place and quickly overpowered Samson. Then they gouged his eyes out and led him off to Gaza, where he was kept under close guard. Their aim was not to kill him but to render him harmless so they could have fun torturing him. So in the very city that had stood dumbfounded as he carried off its gates, he had to sit in prison, bound with two bronze shackles, and perform the work of a slave. The disarming of Samson, which had begun in Delilah's lap, was brought to a cruel completion in the city of Gaza. But although this was his nadir, it was not his end. The Lord did not forsake him entirely. He merely wanted to remove him from his ruinous friendship with Delilah and bring him to repentance through a harsh punishment.

In his humiliation Samson came back to himself and also rediscovered his God (see v. 28). As a sign that the Lord had not really left him, his hair began to grow back at once. This can only mean that from the moment of Samson's fall, God began to raise him up again and to prepare him for the hour when he would erase the stain of dishonor that he had brought on both himself and the name of the Lord. It is not implied that his hair grew back to its former length before the events of verses 23–30 took place. There was not enough time for that, and the Philistines would have shaved his hair again if it had grown too much.

16:23–25a *Now the rulers of the Philistines assembled to offer a great sacrifice to Dagon their god and to celebrate, saying, "Our god has delivered Samson, our enemy, into our hands."*

²⁴ When the people saw him, they praised their god, saying,

> *"Our god has delivered our enemy*
> *   into our hands,*
> *the one who laid waste our land*
> *   and multiplied our slain."*

²⁵ While they were in high spirits, they shouted, "Bring out Samson to entertain us." So they called Samson out of the prison, and he performed for them.

Samson's capture inspired the Philistine rulers to organize a great sacrificial feast in honor of their god Dagon. This seems to have been the national god of the Philistines (see 1 Sam. 5); but since his name shows that he was Semitic in origin, they must have taken him over from the Canaanites.[273] The rulers told their subjects that they had gathered to celebrate (literally, "for joy") because their god had delivered Samson, their enemy, into their hands. The people then took up those words and expanded them into a song of praise to Dagon in which four or five lines can be distinguished, each ending with the same rhyming suffix.[274] The two final lines obviously refer to events like those in 15:4–8, 14–15.

According to verse 24, the Philistines sang this song when they saw Samson; but since these words seem to run ahead of the story (Samson does not enter till v. 25), some think that verse 24 and verse 25 have been transposed. There is no text-critical evidence to support this, however, and it does not even offer a real improvement; for the poem in verse 24 naturally follows the rulers' words in verse 23, while verse 25 leads directly into verse 26. The words "high spirits" (v. 25) were often used in connection with the drinking of wine (e.g., 1 Sam. 25:36; 2 Sam. 13:28; also Judg. 19:6 in the Hebrew).

Samson was hauled out of the prison to "entertain" the Philistine spectators. The Hebrew verb here literally means to "joke" (Prov. 26:19), but it can also mean to dance with song and music (1 Sam. 18:7; 2 Sam. 6:5), to celebrate, or to play (Prov. 8:30–31; Zech. 8:5). Psalm 137:3 is reminiscent of Samson's plight here. Since the spectators probably could only see him without hearing him, he must have been led about and compelled to "perform" (the Hebrew verb here is closely related to the one translated "entertain") certain dances or tricks in which his blindness made him a laughingstock.

16:25b–28 *When they stood him among the pillars,* [26]*Samson said to the servant who held his hand, "Put me where I can feel the pillars that support the temple, so that I may lean against them."* [27]*Now the temple was crowded with men and women; all the rulers of the Philistines were there, and on the roof were about three thousand men and women watching Samson perform.* [28]*Then Samson prayed to the LORD, "O Sovereign LORD, remember me. O God, please strengthen me just once more, and let me with one blow get revenge on the Philistines for my two eyes."*

Samson was made to stand among the pillars, either to give him a moment's rest or because the spectators had a better view of him there.

---

[273]See Noordtzij's article on Dagon in the *Christelijke Encyclopedie.*

[274]The suffix *-ênû* occurs five times, but there probably are not more than four lines, of which the second is extremely brief. It seems that the name "Samson" has been omitted, but this remains uncertain.

His words to his guide show that these were the pillars that supported the entire temple, particularly its roof. He seems to have had some knowledge of the building's structure, for he asked the guide to put him near these pillars (see v. 29). The author adds that the temple was filled with men and women who looked on in delight at Samson's "performance." Many sat inside the building along with the Philistine rulers, and three thousand more sat on the roof.

The words "all the rulers . . . three thousand men and women" could perhaps be regarded as a parenthetical remark within verse 27 that explicates the first part of the verse; in that case "watching Samson perform" should be connected with the first "men and women." This in no way implies, however, that these intervening words are a later addition that should be deleted from the text, as some commentators assume.[275] The roof must have been open in the middle so that those sitting on it would have a view of Samson on the floor below.[276] Perhaps the roof rested on crossbeams that were propped up by wooden pillars standing in the center of the building.

When Samson had been led to these pillars, he at once turned to the Lord, the God of Israel, knowing that He ruled also within the land of the Philistines and could enable his servant to perform mighty deeds even in the temple of Dagon. His urgent prayer shows that his humiliation had brought him back to God and that he once again put his trust in Him alone.[277] He realized that if God saw fit to strengthen him, he would have his final chance to inflict a crushing blow on the Philistines. Calling on Him with His twofold name ("Lord, LORD," or "Sovereign LORD"), he implored Him to remember him, i.e., to be gracious to him, and to give him back his strength one more time so that he could with one blow get revenge on the Philistines for his two eyes. Verse 28 could also be translated "let me get revenge on the Philistines for one of my two eyes," as if vengeance for both of them would have demanded an even greater punishment.[278]

---

[275] E.g., Moore, *Judges*, pp. 363f.; Schulz, *Das Buch der Richter*, p. 88; Gressman, *Die Anfänge Israels*, p. 237.

[276] Gressman offers this hypothesis and points out that temples in this style have been unearthed in Crete, the Philistines' fatherland (*Die Anfänge Israels*, p. 249). Noordtzij argues, however, that Samson was standing in the courtyard in front of the temple ("Dagon," *Christelijke Encyclopedie*).

[277] B. Balscheit completely misunderstands the meaning of Samson's prayer in *Simson ein Retter Israels* (Zurich), p. 46.

[278] Goslinga used this latter translation (see also RSV). The NIV translation finds support in the Septuagint and the Vulgate; but according to him, it is based on a less natural grammatical construction—TRANS.

16:29–30 *Then Samson reached toward the two central pillars on which the temple stood. Bracing himself against them, his right hand on the one and his left hand on the other, ³⁰Samson said, "Let me die with the Philistines!" Then he pushed with all his might, and down came the temple on the rulers and all the people in it. Thus he killed many more when he died than while he lived.*

Samson's prayer was answered, and he once again felt within himself the presence of an invincible power that would enable him to do the impossible. He grasped the two central pillars (the word translated "reach," which does not appear elsewhere, has also been interpreted as "embrace" [cf. NEB], but the context seems to indicate that Samson grasped the pillars strongly) and braced himself against them with his right and his left hand so that he could thrust outward in both directions. Then he uttered his death cry, "let me (literally, 'my soul') die with the Philistines!"[279] and at the same moment he pushed against the pillars with all his might. The pillars slid off their stone pedestals, and the entire temple collapsed, killing the Philistines on the roof and those within the building almost to the last man.

The author does not describe the agony caused by Samson's final act of vengeance. He merely adds the telling comment that Samson killed more people in his death than he had during his life. This succinct and sober remark is enough to show how great a victory Samson had won and to provide a striking illustration of the supreme power of Israel's God. God brought down the Philistines and their god in a humiliating defeat at the very height of their power, using as His instrument a broken and seemingly impotent man. Just as in 15:14, one cannot fail to appreciate the divine humor that is here.

16:31 *Then his brothers and his father's whole family went down to get him. They brought him back and buried him between Zorah and Eshtaol in the tomb of Manoah his father. He had led Israel twenty years.*

It is remarkable that Samson's family had the opportunity to remove his corpse from the ruins. Perhaps the Philistines left them alone because of some superstitious fear that they had.[280] Nevertheless, this

---

[279] Samson probably cried this aloud. There are various details in the story that it seems could only have become known to the author through direct revelation. Samson sought an occasion to confront the Philistines (14:4) even in his death, and his death therefore formed a perfect conclusion to his life.

[280] D. Hoek offers this suggestion in *Het boek der richteren*, p. 389. This is but one of the many unanswered questions concerning the story of Samson. Because of the mystery that surrounds Samson, the extravagant and miraculous features of his

was still an act of courage that we should not have expected to find among the Israelites of this time. Samson thus received an honorable burial in the tomb of his father, Manoah, and at least received the respect he deserved after his death.

The final words of chapter 16 are not a needless repetition of 15:20. They rather make clear that Samson's final victory over the Philistines was as much a part of his judgeship as his previous confrontations with them. Although his work as a judge had been interrupted, he became a judge once again in his death. He died for the honor of his God and for the benefit of his people and was herein a type of Christ, whose death likewise meant the defeat of God's enemies and the salvation of His people (Col. 2:15; Heb. 2:14–15).

This ends the history of the judges insofar as it is recounted in the Book of Judges. See also the comments on Samson's judgeship on pages 406–10.

---

person and life, it is impossible for us to conceive exactly how events like those in 14:19; 15:5, 15; and 16:3 could have happened. He simply transcended human measure.

Part Three

The Origin of the Idol Worship in Dan and the Civil War Against Benjamin
(17:1–21:25)

In the Introduction to this commentary, I discussed the significance of chapters 17–21 within the Book of Judges as a whole and why they are placed at the end of the book (see especially pp. 210, footnote 14 on p. 211, the note on pp. 214–17, and pp. 219–21). Although these chapters do form an integral part of the book, they differ in character from everything that precedes them. Instead of carrying the history of the judges further, they shed a unique light on the whole period by presenting two stories that give an impression of Israel's condition at that time. And although they contain almost nothing that could inspire us, they have great value because they give us a fuller picture of how things actually were during the time of the judges. As I observed in the Introduction (p. 210), these final chapters reveal how soon after the death of Joshua and the older generation Israel succumbed to the process of religious and moral decay that caused the period of the judges to contrast so unfavorably with the early years of the monarchy.[1]

---

[1] According to Noordtzij, chapters 3–16 present a longitudinal cross section, and chapters 17–21 a vertical cross-section of the period of the judges (*Bijbelsch Handboek*, vol. 1, pp. 444–45).

This does not mean that chapters 17–21 form a literary unit. The stories in chapters 17–18 and 19–21 are completely independent of one another. The recurrent statement "in those days Israel had no king," which is found in both stories, undoubtedly comes from the author of the book and in no way proves that the two stories in their original form were written by the same hand. We have to assume that the author of Judges, who lived at the end of the period that he wrote about, was too far removed from the events recounted in these chapters to describe them on his own. He must have made use of ancient documents (which perhaps had been supplemented at various points by oral tradition), probably copying them verbatim and adding a few brief comments of his own (e.g., 17:6; 18:1, 31; 19:1; 21:25). It is well possible that the two stories were in fact originally written down by the same person; there is nothing in these chapters that definitely rules this out.[2] Since we have no real evidence as to the writer's identity, however, the issue remains in doubt.

The two stories undoubtedly did unfold during roughly the same period. Judges 20:28 indicates that the events of chapters 19–21 fell during the lifetime of Phinehas, the son of Eleazar; and the background for chapters 20–21 in fact has much in common with the beginning of the period of the judges. There was still a strong sense of Israel's religious and national unity, and the leadership of the tribe of Judah was willingly accepted (20:18–20; cf. 1:1–2). Chapter 20 is even strongly reminiscent of Joshua 22:10–34.[3] There are differences, of course. The nation as depicted in Judges 20–21 had declined from the high spiritual

---

[2] The following things could be adduced in support of this position:

1. The two stories unfold at approximately the same time (see above).

2. Chapters 17 and 19 both speak of a Levite who had connections with Bethlehem in Judah. The first was born in Bethlehem and the second took a concubine from there. Since there are only vague references to the hill country of Ephraim as the home of these Levites (17:1; 19:1, 18; cf. 19:16), whoever wrote these chapters must have had only a superficial knowledge of this region. It is therefore not improbable that chapters 17 and 19 were originally written by a single person who lived in or near Bethlehem and gathered the necessary details from the families involved. This also would explain why the stories were preserved together. See also the introduction to Ruth, p. 513, footnote 4.

[3] It is therefore only because of their dogmatic, critical standpoint that commentators like Wellhausen, Kuenen, and Moore emphatically deny the historicity of chapters 19–21, contending that there was no sense of national unity whatsoever during the time of the judges, and assign them to the postexilic period. See Moore, *Judges,* pp. 403ff., who at least admits that the story has a historical nucleus. Such a viewpoint is also incompatible with Hosea 10:9 (see the comments on 19:28).

level of the Twelve Tribes in Joshua 22, and the high priest thus stood more in the background. In addition, the people's behavior in 20:23, 26 and 21:2–4 has more in common with their attitude in 2:4–5 than with that of Joshua and the elders in Joshua 7:6–9 (see pp. 263–64 and the comments below in 20:26). Nevertheless Israel's national and religious decline had not yet become so serious as it was, for example, during the time of Deborah (5:8, 16–17). Chapters 19–21 therefore took place before the oppression of Cushan-Rishathaim (3:8).

We also have some fairly precise evidence for the date of chapters 17–18. The mere fact that this story precedes chapters 19–21 has some significance, but it does not tell us enough. More important is that 18:30 calls Jonathan a son of Gershom, and thus a grandson of Moses. Possibly a name has been omitted between Gershom and Jonathan, as often happened in genealogical lists; and since 17:7, 11 calls Jonathan a young man, it is in fact hard to imagine that he could have been a grandson of Moses. But he still would have lived near the beginning of the period of the judges even if he had been Moses' great grandson. Further evidence for such an early date is found in 18:1, where it is said that the Danites were looking for a place to settle. When this tribe tried to take possession of their allotted territory, the Amorites forced them back into the hill country (1:34), where they did not have enough room to live. This situation could not have lasted long, and the Danites must have very soon set out to find a home elsewhere. Their northern expedition therefore in all likelihood took place around the same time as the battle with the Benjamites, namely, between Joshua's death and the first foreign invasion. It probably even happened before the latter event, for 20:1 uses the phrase "from Dan to Beersheba" to indicate the entire extent of Israel's territory.[4] The name Dan must have replaced Laish some time before this verse was written, and chapters 18–19 must have been written shortly after the events they describe.[5]

A. The Origin of the Idol Worship in Dan (17:1–18:31)

1. MICAH'S IDOLS (17:1–13)

Chapter 17 gives the background for the story in chapter 18. There the tribe (or at least a clan) of the Danites set up a private sanctuary

---

[4]The name Dan could not have been used proleptically for Laish in this fixed phrase, for the phrase would only have arisen after Dan's northern settlement had become Israelite territory. A proleptic use of the name is found in Genesis 14:14.

[5]See also footnote 47 on p. 475.

that contained idols and was served by an illegitimate priest. Here the same was done by an individual person.

17:1–2 *Now a man named Micah from the hill country of Ephraim ²said to his mother, "The eleven hundred shekels of silver that were taken from you and about which I heard you utter a curse—I have that silver with me; I took it." Then his mother said, "The LORD bless you, my son!"*

The name of this person was Micahyehu ("who is like Yahweh?"), the Hebrew form of the name in verses 1 and 4, which elsewhere is abbreviated to Micah. We are told nothing about his ancestry; but since he lived in the hill country of Ephraim, he must have been a member of that tribe. The story picks up abruptly with a conversation between Micah and his mother, who apparently was an aged and prosperous widow, in which he confesses that he had stolen from her 1,100 shekels of silver (i.e., about forty pounds, see under 16:5; but see NIV margin). Three things can be inferred from his words: (1) his mother did not know who had taken them; (2) she had pronounced a curse against the thief, or, more likely, adjured each member of her household to tell what he knew by threatening him with a curse;⁶ (3) the curse had been spoken in Micah's presence. The literal reading of the Hebrew leads us to expect to find the actual words of the curse, and perhaps these have fallen out of the text. In any case, Micah did not dare to hide his crime. After he had confessed it, his mother wished him the Lord's blessing; but although she may have done this to express her forgiveness, she probably also dispelled his sense of guilt.

17:3–4 *When he returned the eleven hundred shekels of silver to his mother, she said, "I solemnly consecrate my silver to the LORD for my son to make a carved image and a cast idol. I will give it back to you."*

⁴So he returned the silver to his mother, and she took two hundred shekels of silver and gave them to a silversmith, who made them into the image and the idol. And they were⁷ put in Micah's house.

---

⁶The Hebrew verb, which is rather rare, can mean either "curse" or "swear an oath." In view of Leviticus 5:1, where the related noun is used, it seems likely that she solemnly announced the theft and invoked the name of Yahweh to compel each person to testify what he knew (cf. Prov. 29:24). Anyone who willfully kept silent would therefore have been subject to the Lord's curse. The imprecation naturally would have fallen first of all on the thief himself if he did not speak up.

⁷Or "and it was."

When Micah tried to return the silver to his mother, she surprised him by announcing that she had consecrated it to the Lord on his behalf. She did not mean that she had consecrated it already, but that she had decided to do so at that moment to atone for her son's guilt and to undo the effects of the curse she had pronounced. The silver was to be used to make an idol (see below), and since Micah already had a private shrine (v. 5), she declined to take it back. Micah, however, had no desire to keep the silver, perhaps because of some superstitious fear that he then would still be subject to the curse, or perhaps because he thought that the offering would only be effective if his mother brought it herself. He therefore returned it to his mother, and she gave two hundred shekels of it to a silversmith so that he could make what she had promised to the Lord: a "carved image and a cast idol" (v. 3).[8]

---

[8]This phrase (and the words "the image and the idol" in v. 4) translates two Hebrew words, *pesel* and *massēkâ(h)*, that are joined by the conjunction *û* ("and"). The first term usually denotes an image that is carved or hewn (from wood or stone), but it sometimes also can refer to an idol cast from metal (Isa. 40:19–20; 44:10). The second term always denotes a cast idol, and it is used particularly for Aaron's golden calf (Deut. 9:12) and the golden calves of Jeroboam (2 Kings 17:16). The most natural explanation of the two terms would thus be that Micah's mother had two idols made, one carved from wood and one cast from the silver. There are a number of objections to this, however.

1. The Hebrew text at the end of verse 4 speaks of but one idol that was (singular) in the house of Micah (see footnote 7 and the RSV).

2. The silver was given only to the silversmith, and no other craftsman is mentioned.

3. It is hard to understand why Micah's mother would have promised two idols and why the costly silver one would have been accompanied by a simple wooden one.

4. If there were in fact two idols, the cast silver *massēkâ(h)* would have been the primary one. The more prominent of the two terms, however, is *pesel;* it comes before *massēkâ(h)* in 17:3, 4 and 18:14; and in 18:20 and 30, *massēkâ(h)* does not appear at all. In these latter two verses, the *pesel* thus includes the *massēkâ(h)*, and the *massēkâ(h)* therefore could not have been a separate idol. All this points toward the conclusion that the combination *pesel-massēkâ(h)* actually denotes a single idol, but one that consisted of two distinct parts (Goslinga thus has "carved and cast idol" in vv. 3, 4 et al.—TRANS.). It had to have two parts, since in 18:17 and 18 *pesel* and *massēkâ(h)* are separated by the words *'ēpôd* ("ephod") and *terāpîm* ("household gods"); the *pesel* and the *massēkâ(h)* are thus two distinct objects here. These two verses present a problem that has no satisfactory solution. Moore thinks that the author of chapter 18 used only the word *pesel* and that a later redactor or copyist added the word *massēkâ(h)* from chapter 17. There is no evidence for this, however; and such an approach, which merely side-steps the problem, is in general completely unacceptable.

17:5-6 *Now this man Micah had a shrine, and he made an ephod and some idols and installed one of his sons as his priest.* ⁶*In those days Israel had no king; everyone did as he saw fit.*

The author sheds light on the preceding event by telling us that Micah already had a private shrine that was partially furnished. It contained an ephod, the costly upper garment worn by the priest when he pronounced oracles (see the comments on 8:27), and also teraphim (NIV "idols") or small household gods. The latter were sometimes shaped like human beings (cf. 1 Sam. 19:13-16), but some have proposed that they were mummylike masks.⁹ Micah completed this collection by adding his large, costly new idol cast from silver. It seems that he did this to give honor to the Lord; and in that case, except for the household gods, his sin was not idolatry. He was guilty, however, of establishing an arbitrary, new form of worship, a worship of images that showed contempt for the sanctuary at Shiloh where the ark stood.

The author connects Micah's disregard for the law of Moses (Deut. 12) with the absence of a kingship in Israel, tacitly assuming that the king's duties would not be limited to affairs of state, but that he also would take action against idolatry and image worship (see Deut. 17:18-20). During the time of the judges, everyone could violate the cultic laws with impunity and was free to do as he pleased. Micah thus arbitrarily installed one of his own sons as his personal priest, since an illegitimate shrine needed an illegitimate priesthood. The word "install" translates a Hebrew phrase that literally means "fill the hand" (probably with an offering) and is the standard expression for the ordination of priests (e.g., Exod. 28:41; 29:9; 1 Kings 13:33). Since Micah appointed his own son, it is clear that he must have been a middle-aged man.

The main question that has to be answered is this: If the *pesel* and the *massēḵâ(h)* constituted a single idol, what two parts of it are designated by these terms? Calvin, Hengstenberg, and Keil think that the *pesel* was the idol itself and the *massēḵâ(h)* was its pedestal, but Moore rightly points out that this does not fit with the meaning of *massēḵâ(h)*. The view of Schulz and others that the *massēḵâ(h)* was a silver case for the carved wooden idol is more likely. If so, it is possible that the calves of Aaron and Jeroboam were also wooden idols enclosed in a casing of precious metal. In any case, Micah's idol then would have been separable into two distinct parts, and the word *pesel* could indicate either the carved wooden inner section or the entire idol (as in 18:20, 30, 31).

⁹See the articles on "Terafim" in the *Christlelijke Encyclopedie,* 1st ed. (Noordtzij) and 2nd ed. (Oosterhoff).

17:7-10 *A young Levite from Bethlehem in Judah, who had been living within the clan of Judah,* ⁸*left that town in search of some other place to stay. On his way he came to Micah's house in the hill country of Ephraim.*

⁹*Micah asked him, "Where are you from?"*

"I'm a Levite from Bethlehem in Judah," he said, "and I'm looking for a place to stay."

¹⁰*Then Micah said to him, "Live with me and be my father and priest, and I'll give you ten shekels of silver a year, your clothes*¹⁰ *and your food."*¹¹

These next verses show that Micah himself was aware that the priesthood of his son was somewhat improper. He met a young Levite who had been living in the town of Bethlehem in Judah.¹² The Hebrew verb that the NIV translates as "living" literally means "live as a sojourner"; it is used because Bethlehem was not one of the Levitical cities where the Levites were supposed to live. Perhaps he settled in Bethlehem because the Canaanites still controlled his assigned city,¹³ but it is more likely that he was driven there by the need for food.

The author does not tell us the name and ancestry of this Levite till 18:30. The Levite left Bethlehem and roamed through the land, intending to settle somewhere where he could find a livelihood. On his way he passed through the hill country of Ephraim and reached a group of houses of which Micah's must have been the most prominent (see 18:14). Micah welcomed him; asked where he was from; and, when he was pleasantly surprised to find that the traveler was a Levite, at once offered to make him a priest in his personal shrine. His words "be my father" show that the Levite would have a position of great honor; he would be the spiritual leader and adviser in Micah's house. His task would not merely be to present offerings but also to inquire of the Lord (see 18:5). The word "father" is similarly used as a title of honor in

---

¹⁰Literally, "a set of clothes."

¹¹In the Hebrew text verse 10 ends with the words "and the Levite went." Since this makes no sense, it might be appropriate to add a word like "in" (cf. KJV), but perhaps the words are an erroneous repetition of the beginning of verse 11.

¹²The Hebrew in verse 7 literally reads "a young man from Bethlehem in Judah, from the clan of Judah" (cf. RSV). It is quite surprising to find the latter phrase here. The text-critical support for the words "from the clan of Judah" is not decisive, but they are probably authentic since it is hard to see why someone would have added them. Since a Levite could not have been a descendant of Judah, most commentators think the words must mean that the man was one of the Levites who lived in the territory of Judah and were thus counted as citizens of this tribe (hence the NIV translation—TRANS.).

¹³See Keil, *Kommentar*, pp. 350f. According to Joshua 21:9–19, only the Aaronite line of Levites was assigned to Judah, while this Levite was a Gershonite (18:30).

18:19 (cf. Gen. 45:8 [Joseph], 2 Kings 6:21 [Elisha], and Isa. 22:21 [Eliakim]). Micah promised to provide the Levite with an annual salary and the necessities of life.[14]

17:11–13 *So the Levite agreed to live with him, and the young man was to him like one of his sons.* [12] *Then Micah installed the Levite, and the young man became his priest and lived in his house.* [12] *And Micah said, "Now I know that the* LORD *will be good to me, since this Levite has become my priest."*

The Levite gladly accepted Micah's offer. He apparently had no qualms about participating in this illicit private cult, even though he must have known better. His only concern was his personal well-being (cf. 18:20). Micah was so pleased with him that he regarded him as a son (the title "father" thus does not imply that the man was old). He formally installed the Levite as a priest and allowed him to live in his own house.[15] The fact that Micah still believed that the Lord would be with him and bless him is probably the best illustration of how far Israel had fallen. He apparently regarded his new housemate as a legitimate priest, even though his whole private cult was completely out of line and only the descendants of Aaron were eligible for the priesthood (Exod. 28:1; Num. 17). For Micah, the Levite was a guarantee that the curse of his mother (v. 2) would not fall on him and that the Lord would cause his family to prosper. Chapter 18 will show how wrong he was.

2. THE CAPTURE OF MICAH'S IDOLS AND THE LAND OF LAISH BY THE DANITES (18:1–31)

18:1 *In those days Israel had no king.*
And in those days the tribe of the Danites was seeking a place of their own where they might settle, because they had not yet come into an inheritance among the tribes of Israel.

[14] The Hebrew literally reads "for the days," but the meaning is clearly "a year" or "annually" (cf. Exod. 13:10; 1 Sam. 1:21). The Levite sinned in accepting Micah's offer, of course; but the nation was also guilty, for it had neglected its duty to provide for the Levites (Num. 18:24; Deut. 12:19).

[15] In my opinion this implies that priestly functions of Micah's son (v. 5) came to an end; but since the text says nothing about this, we can only speculate. It is therefore extremely strange for Th. W. Juynboll to argue in his article "De Leviet in Richteren 17–18" (*Theologische Tijdschrift* [1900]) that since nothing is said here about Micah's son, he must not have been discharged, when he also holds that the installation of the Levite, which is indeed spoken of, is an unhistorical later interpolation. There is not a shred of text-critical evidence for Juynboll's deletion of 17:7–18:1.

Chapter 18 begins by observing that Israel had no king in those days. Although this refers to the time of the events in the previous chapter, it has to be read as an introduction to chapter 18, not as the end of chapter 17. The compiler of the Book of Judges added this statement to the story that he found in his ancient source to prepare the way for the following illicit deeds of the Danites. They were seeking an inheritance where they could settle down. The area where they were living was too small for them; and although they had originally been allotted a larger territory (Josh. 19:40–46), the Amorites soon drove them back into the hill country (Judg. 1:34). The end of verse 1 therefore really means that the inheritance that had been allotted to them (which lay between Judah and Ephraim and extended westward to the Mediterranean Sea) never actually came into their possession. The Hebrew literally reads "it [viz., an inheritance] had not fallen to them." The writer does not express himself too clearly here, but there is no doubt as to his meaning.

18:2–3 *So the Danites sent[16] five warriors from Zorah and Eshtaol to spy out the land and explore it. These men represented all their clans. They told them, "Go, explore the land."*

The men entered the hill country of Ephraim and came to the house of Micah, where they spent the night. [3] When they were near Micah's house, they recognized the voice of the young Levite; so they turned in there and asked him, "Who brought you here? What are you doing in this place? Why are you here?"

The Danites sent out five men to explore the land and find a suitable area for them to settle. The Hebrew literally says "five men from their clan" (cf. NEB); the tribe of Dan is also called a clan in other places (vv. 11, 19; 13:2; cf. Num. 26:42–43). "These men represented all their clans" translates a Hebrew phrase that simply means "from their borders." The phrase cannot refer to the area where the five men lived, for they were all from Zorah and Eshtaol. Rather, it has to denote the entire extent of the tribe's territory and thus means that the men were sent out on behalf of the whole tribe, as representatives of all its clans (cf. Gen. 19:4; 1 Kings 12:31; 13:33, where the same Hebrew phrase is used). The men chosen were able warriors who had battle experience. Zorah and Eshtaol are also mentioned as Danite cities in the story of Samson (13:2, 25; 16:31).[17]

The men were commanded to explore the land of Canaan, and they

---

[16]The Hebrew text adds the words "from their clan"—TRANS.
[17]Their location is discussed under 13:2.

set out toward the north. They arrived at the house of Micah and spent the night there. The story is a little disjointed here, and it is not clear whether the events in the next few verses happened on the evening before or on the morning after their one-night stay. Verses 6–7 seem to indicate that their encounter with the Levite took place just before they departed the next morning, but verse 3 gives the strong impression that the Levite was the reason why they stopped at Micah's house in the first place. As they passed a group of houses along the road, they heard the voice of the Levite, who perhaps was reciting ritual prayers and formulas. This drew their attention, and the fact that his dialect was not Ephraimite may have heightened their curiosity (cf. 12:6). If they knew that there was a private shrine somewhere in the area, their desire to consult the oracle could have induced them to turn off the road.[18] In any case they entered Micah's house and found the well-furnished shrine attended by the Levite. Full of surprise they asked him who had brought him there and what his business was.

18:4–6 *He told them what Micah had done for him, and said, "He has hired me and I am his priest."*

⁵Then they said to him, "Please inquire of God to learn whether our journey will be successful."[19]

⁶The priest answered them, "Go in peace. Your journey has the LORD's approval."

The Levite readily told the five men what a good position Micah had given him. They in turn asked him for an oracle so that they might know whether their exploration would be successful. His answer was encouraging. The Levite, who here is called a priest because of the task he performed, probably tried to consult the deity by means of Micah's ephod and household gods. He told the Danites that their journey was under the eye of the Lord and had His approval (cf. Ps. 1:6; Isa 40:27; Jer. 16:17). It might be significant that the Danites used the general name God (Elohim) in verse 5, not the special, covenantal name Lord (Yahweh). It seems they did not really believe that this was a legitimate

---

[18] We are not told what exactly it was in the Levite's voice that drew the Danites' attention. It is not impossible that he was an acquaintance of theirs, but the fact that he was from Bethlehem makes this unlikely. Since it also does not seem likely that they entered merely because of his Judean dialect, the explanation given in the text above seems best.

[19] The verb *ṣālaḥ* ("be successful"), which is in the *Hiphil*, should be vocalized as the imperfect *Qal* following the Septuagint.

sanctuary of Israel's covenant God. Nevertheless, they still participated in the sin of Micah and the Levite. The latter spoke boldly of "the
LORD's approval," implicitly claiming that he had the same right to
speak on God's behalf as the legitimate priests through whom the Lord
revealed Himself (see the comments on 1:1–2).[20]

18:7 *So the five men left and came to Laish, where they saw that the people
were living in safety, like the Sidonians, unsuspecting and secure. And since
their land lacked nothing, they were prosperous. Also, they lived a long way
from the Sidonians and had no relationship with anyone else.*

After their one-night stay at the house of Micah, the five Danites
again traveled northward till they reached the city of Laish (or Leshem,
Josh. 19:47), a place identical to modern Tell el-Qadi that lay north of
Lake Huleh near the headstreams of the Jordan.[21] The life of the native
population of Laish is described in a series of words and phrases that
are only loosely strung together. They "were living in safety, like the

---

[20] Although the author's style in this pericope is somewhat wordy and not
especially clear, the thought that these verses contain two distinct stories that have
been awkwardly melded together is completely unfounded. Commentators like
Moore, Budde, and Nowack adopt this view almost as their starting point and find
evidence for it in even the slightest possible irregularities in the text. According to
them, the author (or rather redactor) used two parallel sources and combined as
much of their material as he could, which caused him to repeat himself frequently.
Even though they constantly have to admit that it is often extremely difficult to
identify these two "sources" and to divide the story between them, they hold fast to
this view as if it were an axiom. Their method proceeds as follows: "from their clan"
in verse 2 (see footnote 16) is supposedly from source A, while "these men
represented all their clans" is from source B; "five men" is from A and "warriors"
is from B; and "to spy out the land and explore it" is from A, while "they told them,
'Go, explore the land' " again is from B (or vice versa). How arbitrary this
procedure can become is illustrated by their analysis of verse 3, where the three
questions allegedly could not have been written by the same hand, and the first two
have to be assigned to source B, the third to source A. Apparently these
commentators cannot comprehend the fact that it would have been the most natural
thing in the world for the five men to ask the Levite several similar questions.
Verses 7 and 9 are "analyzed" in similar fashion. Juynboll takes an equally
arbitrary approach in his deletion from chapter 18 of everything that pertains to the
Levite (see footnote 15). There is no need to refute these scholars in detail, since the
text (apart from a few obscure places where it perhaps has been corrupted) is
sufficiently clear as it stands; and there are no major problems in interpreting it.
Oettli thus remarks in connection with verses 8–10 that "there is great confusion
only in Budde's distribution of the words, not in the text itself" (*Buch der Richter*,
p. 300).
[21] The location of Laish is discussed further under verse 28.

Sidonians,"[22] who were only concerned with their material welfare, were not bent on conquest, and trusted that others would likewise leave them in peace. The phrase implies that the citizens of Laish were related to the inhabitants of the Phoenician city Sidon; so Laish may have been a Sidonian settlement.

The people of Laish are further described as "unsuspecting and secure."[23] The latter term, which literally means "trusting," is here almost equivalent to "careless," since the people at least should have been on guard against thieves. They lived a peaceable life, probably engaging in farming and cattle-raising; and since the land was rich, their prosperity increased.[24] The Sidonians lived too far away to come to their aid, and they had no ties with any other nation. In other words, although the citizens of Laish were without enemies, they also had no friends; their city was completely unprotected.

18:8-10 *When they returned to Zorah and Eshtaol, their brothers asked them, "How did you find things?"*[25]

[9] They answered, "Come on, let's attack them![26] We have seen that the land is very good. Aren't you going to do something? Don't hesitate to go there and take it over.

---

[22] Since the feminine form of the participle "living" is used in the Hebrew, this phrase is grammatically connected, not to "people," a masculine noun, but to "Laish." In itself this presents no problem, since a city is often named in place of its inhabitants (cf. Isa. 47:8; Zeph. 2:15); but it is odd that the following participles are all in the masculine (see footnote 23). The feminine participle *yôšebet* must either be a careless slip of the author, who may have been misled by the preceding word *beqirbāh* ("within her"; the NIV leaves this out); or it is a copyist's error and should be emended to the masculine form *yôšēb*.

[23] The masculine form of these two participles contrasts with the preceding feminine participle (see footnote 22). Along with the following participle *yôrēš* ("acquiring"; see footnote 24), they are attributive modifiers of the noun "people." Oettli's conjecture (*Buch der Richter*, p. 300) that the words from *yôšebet* to *ṣidônîm* ("living . . . like the Sidonians") originally followed "Laish" merits attention, but it has no text-critical support.

[24] The Hebrew words translated "they were prosperous" literally mean "acquiring wealth." "Prosperous" translates a rare noun derived from a verb that can also mean "rule." Some versions therefore understand the word in this sense (e.g., KJV, NASB); but since the Septuagint and Vulgate reading "riches" fits well in the context, it seems better to follow this. (The Hebrew that the NIV translates "since their land lacked nothing" is obscure [see marginal note]. Goslinga translates this "no one molested anyone in the land"—TRANS.).

[25] The Hebrew literally reads simply "How you?" or "What you?" Some translate this "What do you report?" (e.g., RSV) or "What have you done?"

[26] Literally, "against them." These words are a little odd, since the men do not say who they mean. The reading in some Septuagint manuscripts ("against her") is no

> [10] *When you get there, you will find an unsuspecting people and a spacious*
> *land that God has put into your hands, a land that lacks nothing whatever."*

When the scouts returned from their mission, their fellow tribesmen asked them what they had found. The question is very abrupt (see footnote 25), as if it were asked in great suspense; and the men answered it with a series of quick, broken exclamations. They were so excited that they almost stumbled over their words, beginning with what should have come last. The lack of order in verse 9 makes good psychological sense, but it is remarkable that the men did not even mention the name Laish (but see footnote 26). They began by urging their tribesmen to march out: "Come on, let's attack them!" (i.e., the people they had in mind). Then they gave the reason: "We have seen that the land is very good." They had achieved their goal of finding a suitable place to settle, and they expected that their brothers would at once become as enthusiastic as they were. Thus they cried out, "Aren't you going to do something?" (literally, "and you are still," i.e., "you do nothing"). The other Danites should join them and attack without delay, for they would find an "unsuspecting people and a spacious land" (literally, "spacious on both hands," i.e., in all directions). Moreover, the land was so rich and fruitful that they would have all they needed there. In a word, God Himself had given the land into their hands, and they would be foolish not to seize this opportunity. The five scouts undoubtedly also told their tribesmen about the auspicious oracle they had received at the house of Micah.

18:11–15 *Then six hundred men from the clan of the Danites, armed for battle, set out from Zorah and Eshtaol.* [12] *On their way they set up camp near Kiriath Jearim in Judah. This is why the place west of Kiriath Jearim is called Mahaneh Dan to this day.* [13] *From there they went on to the hill country of Ephraim and came to Micah's house.*

[14] *Then the five men who had spied out the land of Laish*[27] *said to their brothers, "Do you know that one of these houses has an ephod, other household gods, a carved image and a cast idol? Now you know what to do."* [15] *So they turned in there and went to the house of the young Levite at Micah's place and greeted him.*

---

better. Some scholars therefore would emend the text to "to Laish," but this is nothing but an arbitrary conjecture. The words "against them" are not inexplicable (see the comments at this verse).

[27] The name Laish, which is absent in some manuscripts of the Septuagint, is a little odd here, since the scouts' task was to spy out all of Canaan. Perhaps it was added as a gloss.

Six hundred Danites answered the scouts' call to arms and marched out from Zorah and Eshtaol along with their families (see v. 21). Their first stopping-place was west of (literally, "behind") Kiriath Jearim, a town a few hours west of Jerusalem that many identify with modern Qaryet el-'Inab on the road to Jaffa.[28] The site of their camp became known in the area as Mahaneh Dan (i.e., "camp of Dan," see 13:25; the author no doubt added this comment to explain why a place in Judah was named after the tribe of Dan). From here the Danites marched on into the hill country of Ephraim. As they approached Micah's house, the five scouts, who must have been leading their tribesmen, told them about the treasures in his shrine. They needed to say no more.

The word "houses" (literally "these houses"; NIV "one of these houses") indicates that Micah's dwelling was actually a complex of buildings, probably circled by a low wall that allowed them to be seen from the road. In this wall was the gate that verses 16–17 speak of. The house where the Levite was quartered belonged to this complex and formed only a part of the whole house of Micah, as is evident in verse 15; so the five men easily could have gone in to him without Micah's knowledge. Having entered, they greeted him.

18:16–17 *The six hundred Danites, armed for battle, stood at the entrance to the gate.* [17]*The five men who had spied out the land went inside and took the carved image,*[29] *the ephod, the other household gods and the cast idol while the priest and the six hundred armed men stood at the entrance to the gate.*

The five men pretended that they were only paying the Levite a passing visit. They probably told him the outcome of their first journey; and since in verse 17 he was standing outside with the other Danites, they must also have informed him that they were traveling back to Laish with some of their tribesmen. Meanwhile, the six hundred armed men stationed themselves by the entrance to the gate.[30] The plan was to plunder Micah's shrine without violence and without causing a stir; the men therefore waited outside for their comrades, but they were ready to make an instant attack if necessary.

The word "Danites" in verse 16 (literally, "who were of the Danites") may seem superfluous, but there is no reason to regard it as

---

[28] See Garstang, *Joshua, Judges,* pp. 166f., 171, and Van Deursen's article in the *Bijbelse Encyclopedie.*

[29] See footnote 8.

[30] The Hebrew here uses a word that never denotes the door of a house; it must therefore refer to the gate in a wall that encircled Micah's property.

spurious. Verse 17 also is rather wordy and a bit unclear, but it is not too difficult to infer what happened. Between these two verses the Levite must have gone outside to see the large company that was traveling with his visitors. Instead of following him, the five men went into Micah's shrine and seized the goods (the Hebrew literally says that they "went up"; the shrine must have been on a higher level of the house). The author changed the verb tense here to show that the theft took place during the short time that the Levite was outside; he also omitted the conjunction "and" between the clauses, which is very unusual in Hebrew. Both these things make his account more vivid. We can almost see the five men sneaking into the shrine and gathering up the idol, the ephod, and the household gods, while the priest unsuspectingly chats with the Danites outdoors.

18:18–21 *When these men went into Micah's house and took the carved image,[31] the ephod, the other household gods and the cast idol, the priest said to them, "What are you doing?"*

[19]They answered him, "Be quiet! Don't say a word. Come with us, and be our father and priest. Isn't it better that you serve a tribe and clan in Israel as priest rather than just one man's household?" [20]Then the priest was glad. He took the ephod, the other household gods and the carved image and went along with the people. [21]Putting their little children, their livestock and their possessions in front of them, they turned away and left.

The Levite noticed soon enough that his five guests had stayed behind; and when he saw them come out of the house with his master's treasures, he asked in alarm, "What are you doing?" They immediately commanded him to be silent and offered to take him with them and give him the position among them that he had held in Micah's house. This of course would be a good exchange for him: he would be promoted from a household priest to the priest of an entire tribe (or at least clan). The Levite, who here is consistently called a priest, showed his true character by gladly accepting their offer. Turning his back on his benefactor, he took the ephod, the household gods, and the idol in his own hands and joined the Danite community. They in turn took to the road again and continued their journey, putting their children, livestock, and possessions in front in case they were pursued.[32] Their

---

[31]See footnote 8. The definite article should be added before *pesel* and the object marker before *hā'ēpôd*, following the Septuagint and Vulgate.
[32]"Possessions" translates a rare Hebrew word that is rendered as "carriage" in the KJV, "goods" in the RSV. Since the word means "glorious" or "wealth" in Psalm 45:13, "valuables" would perhaps be the best translation (see NASB, NEB).

wives obviously would have been put there too, and it is odd that they are not mentioned (cf. Exod. 12:37 KJV).

Like chapter 17, this entire pericope shows that the Israelites of that day had a strong desire for local shrines. They had succumbed to the purely pagan notion that the mere possession of an ephod or idol, even if it was stolen, would guarantee them safety and prosperity. Apparently they believed they would be even better off if they secured the services of a priest who at least possessed a trace of legitimacy, even though he was a man without character. The religious and moral decline of Israel went hand in hand, and there is no one in this story that deserves our respect or sympathy.

18:22–26 *When they had gone some distance from Micah's house, the men who lived near Micah were called together and overtook the Danites.* ²³ *As they shouted after them, the Danites turned and said to Micah, "What's the matter with you that you called out your men to fight?"*

²⁴ *He replied, "You took the gods I made, and my priest, and went away. What else do I have? How can you ask, 'What's the matter with you?'"*

²⁵ *The Danites answered, "Don't argue with us, or some hot-tempered men will attack you, and you and your family will lose your lives." ²⁶ So the Danites went their way, and Micah, seeing that they were too strong for him, turned around and went back home.*

Some commentators relate these next verses to Jacob's flight from Laban and Laban's pursuit (Gen. 31); but although there are indeed some similarities (e.g., the theft of the household gods), the differences are far more numerous. Verse 22 begins with a circumstantial clause that modifies the main clause; the Danites had not traveled very far when Micah called out his neighbors to pursue them, either as his underlings or simply as good friends. Since he would not have been able to do anything on his own, he wisely kept still at the moment of the theft (assuming that he even saw it). He felt strong enough when his family and friends had joined him, however. They all shouted out to the Danites, and the latter turned back in seeming surprise and asked, "What's the matter with you that you called out your men to fight?" The Hebrew literally reads "What is with you [sing.], that you [sing.] have assembled?" The entire group was thus addressed in the person of its commander Micah.

Micah did not hesitate to express how outraged he was at their brazen act, and he spoke first of what was closest to his heart. They had taken the gods that he had made (here again we see how debased his spiritual life had become) and abducted his priest. What did he have left? His most treasured possessions had been stolen; so how could they be so insolent as to ask, "What is the matter?" The Danites indeed could say nothing against this; but for them, might made right, and therefore they responded with threats. Micah had better keep still, or he and his family would otherwise be attacked by "hot-tempered men" and would lose their lives as well as their possessions. The Hebrew phrase translated "hot-tempered," which appears also in 2 Samuel 17:8 (NIV, "fierce"; cf. 1 Sam. 22:2, "discontented"), here denotes unscrupulous men who have nothing to lose. Knowing that Micah did not stand a chance against them, the Danites turned their backs to him and walked on, while Micah wisely chose to return home and swallow his deep disappointment. Things had turned out quite differently than he had hoped (17:13).

18:27–29 *Then they took what Micah had made, and his priest, and went on to Laish, against a peaceful and unsuspecting people. They attacked them with the sword and burned down their city.* ²⁸ *There was no one to rescue them because they lived a long way from Sidon and had no relationship with anyone else. The city was in a valley near Beth Rehob.*

The Danites rebuilt the city and settled there. ²⁹ *They named it Dan after their forefather Dan, who was born to Israel—though the city used to be called Laish.*

The Danites, trusting in their idols as blindly as Micah had done, took the stolen goods and their new priest and resumed their journey. They attacked the peaceful, unsuspecting citizens of Laish and put them all to death with the sword.³³ Then they burned the city to the ground, superstitiously fearing that they would be harassed by its guardian deity if they simply moved into the existing dwellings. The Danites were able to carry out this massacre without interference, since Laish was far from Sidon and its inhabitants lived in total isolation.

The author sheds further light on this by noting that the city lay in the valley that led to Beth Rehob (see Num. 13:21; 2 Sam. 10:6). The location of this latter town is uncertain; but it is usually identified with modern Baniyas (Caesarea Philippi, Mark 8:27), since this was the most important town in the valley that stretches northward from Lake Huleh. A road ran through this valley to Damascus, and Laish lay northwest of this road on the Nahr Leddan, one of the headstreams of

---

³³ The Israelites had a right to conquer Laish, but this should have been done by Naphtali, the tribe that had been allotted the land around the upper reaches of the Jordan. The Danites attacked the city out of sinful motives.

the Jordan.[34] The author probably added this geographical note because Laish would thenceforth be the northernmost extremity of Israel. The new inhabitants rebuilt the city and renamed it after their forefather Dan.

18:30–31 *There the Danites set up for themselves the idols, and Jonathan son of Gershom, the son of Moses,[35] and his sons were priests for the tribe of Dan until the time of the captivity of the land. [31] They continued to use the idols Micah had made, all the time the house of God was in Shiloh.*

The final two verses of the story tell how the Danites used Micah's idols to institute an unlawful cult that had been forbidden in the second commandment. They set up the idols in their new home, and Jonathan and his sons supervised the rites that were performed there. This Jonathan could be none other than the priest who had served Micah. He is called the son of Gershom, but it is generally assumed that a generation has been skipped here (see p. 459) and that Jonathan was a grandson of Gershom (who had only one son that we know of, 1 Chron. 23:16) and a great-grandson of Moses. Gershom had been born in Midian, long before the Exodus (Exod. 2:22; 18:3); and since the Levite was still a young man in this story, he certainly could not have been born before the Israelites entered Canaan.

The end of verse 30 states that the descendants of Jonathan continued as priests for the tribe of Dan "until the time of the captivity

---

[34] See Garstang, *Joshua, Judges,* p. 392; also pp. 103 and 246f., where a photograph of Laish is found.

[35] The Hebrew text has the name Manasseh here, which in the ancient consonantal script differed from the name Moses only by the letter *n* (Hebrew *nûn*). This letter is written a little above the line of the other Hebrew consonants, and it has therefore been called a "suspended *nûn.* " According to a very ancient Jewish tradition, it was deliberately inserted to express the fact that this Jonathan was not worthy to be called a descendant of Moses and that his deeds were more characteristic of a son of the godless king Manasseh. A rabbi has stated that the name Moses originally did stand in the written text (*Kethib*), but that this should be pronounced as "Manasseh" (*Qere*). The Syriac version and most manuscripts of the Septuagint have Manasseh, while the Vulgate has Moses. The latter undoubtedly was the original reading. The name Manasseh would never have been changed to Moses, but it is conceivable that the reverse could have been done, with the *nûn* being added above the other consonants out of respect for the sacred text. Further evidence for this is found in the fact that Gershom the son of Moses was a well-known person (e.g., Exod. 2:22; 18:3; 1 Chron. 23:15–16), while we nowhere hear of a son of Manasseh named Gershom. In addition, a Levite could never have come from the tribe of Manasseh, the son of Joseph. The commentaries of Keil, Moore, and Bertheau discuss this question at greater length.

of the land," which of course means "captivity of the people of the land" (similar expressions are used in Gen. 9:19 [see NASB margin] and 10:25). Most commentators naturally take this as a reference to the deportation of the people of Gilead, Galilee, and the whole land of Naphtali (where Laish was located) by Tiglath-Pileser, king of Assyria (2 Kings 15:29),[36] which probably took place in 732 B.C.[37] Several serious objections have been raised against this view; but before we can examine these, it is necessary to turn to verse 31.

Verse 31 is completely separate from verse 30; it speaks of something different and in fact forms a second conclusion to the story. Its opening words form an approximate repetition of the opening words of the previous verse, for the Hebrew in both cases means "and they set up for themselves" (cf. NASB). Verse 31 uses a different verb, however, which seems to connote the setting up of something for a long time (cf. 1 Kings 12:29). It is necessary to bring this out in the translation, since this verse is not speaking of the moment when Micah's idol was set up but rather of the length of time that it remained standing in Dan.

The temporal clause at the end of verse 31 is rather remarkable. First of all, it speaks of the "house of God," which can only mean the Mosaic tabernacle;[38] and this has not been mentioned before in the Book of Judges. In the second place, it regards the period in which this tabernacle stood at Shiloh as already over. Now, although we do know when it was that the ark was taken from Shiloh and fell into the hands of the Philistines (1 Sam. 4:4-11, 18), we do not know for sure how long after this the tabernacle remained in Shiloh. It could not have stayed there for long, however, since Shiloh is not mentioned again during Samuel's judgeship; and the ark was never brought back there. The judgment of Shiloh (at the hands of the Philistines?) alluded to in Psalm 78:60 and Jeremiah 7:12, 14; 26:6 probably happened soon after Eli's death, and in Saul's time we find the tabernacle and its priestly attendants in the town of Nob (1 Sam. 21:1-9; 22:9-19). But this

---

[36] Some commentators think the verse might be speaking of the captivity of all Israel after the Fall of Samaria in 722 B.C. The difference is minor, since the two deportations were separated by only a few years, but the fact that 2 Kings 15:29 explicitly names the region where Laish was favors the first deportation.

[37] See Van Gelderen's comments on 2 Kings 15:29 in the *Bible Student's Commentary*.

[38] Joshua 18:1 states that this tabernacle was set up at Shiloh. First Samuel 1:9 and other verses seem to imply that it was later replaced by a more permanent structure. If so, "house of God" in verse 31 would mean this building.

means that verse 31 must have been written after the end of the period of the judges.

Nothing forbids us to assume that verse 31 was not part of the original version of chapters 17-18, which must have been written by someone who lived early in the period of the judges, but was a later addition by the author of the Book of Judges,[39] who took over this earlier story and expanded it with a few brief comments of his own (e.g., 17:6; 18:1a; perhaps the sentence about Beth Rehob in 18:28; and v. 31). This would explain why verse 31 follows so loosely after verse 30 and in effect forms a second conclusion to the story.

The end of verse 31 deserves our attention for still a third reason. The temporal qualification that it makes is not limitative, like the end of verse 30 ("until the time of"), for it leaves the possibility open that Micah's idols remained in Dan even after the house of God in Shiloh had been destroyed. It merely states that the idolatrous cult in Dan continued for as long as the tabernacle stood in Shiloh, but we are not told what happened later. Apparently the author heard nothing more about Dan after the fall of Shiloh, and from this we can infer that verse 31 was written not too long after this event.

Verse 31 therefore in no way forbids us to understand the end of verse 30 as a reference to the Assyrian deportation under Tiglath-Pileser. There is no reason why the descendants of Jonathan could not have remained as priests in Dan even after the fall of the tabernacle in Shiloh. They could have continued to perform their priestly functions either with or without the idols that had been stolen from Micah; for if the idols were removed for any reason, the Danite priests still could have retained their prestige and continued to lead an illegitimate cult (perhaps using only an ephod). Verse 31 says nothing against this, since it does not even mention the descendants of Jonathan; nor does it state that the cult connected with Micah's idol came to an end.

There are other, more serious objections to the view that verse 30 is speaking of the Assyrian deportation.[40] First, it is considered unthinkable that an unlawful cult could have continued to exist in Dan during and after the reforms initiated by Samuel (1 Sam. 7:2-4) and carried through by David. Second, how could the priesthood of Jonathan's descendants have continued this long when, according to 1 Kings

---

[39] Namely Samuel or one of his contemporaries; see section III of the Introduction, p. 221-23.

[40] See especially Keil, *Kommentar*, pp. 357f.; H. Mulder, *Gereformeerde Theologische Tijdschrift* (1948), pp. 109f.

12:28–33, King Jeroboam set up two golden calves at Dan and Bethel and installed priests who were not Levites? Third, the author of Judges lived no later than the beginning of the monarchical period; so he could not have written of Tiglath-Pileser's deportation as an historical fact.

This third objection would indeed be decisive if it were not possible that the final words of verse 30 were added after 732 B.C. (see below). The second objection comes to nothing in my view; 1 Kings 12:31 does not rule out the possibility that Jeroboam also appointed apostate Levites to the priesthood, and verse 30 does not imply that Micah's idols were still in Dan at that time.[41]

The first objection is harder to deal with. It is indeed difficult to imagine that Samuel, and especially David, would not have taken action against the unlawful cult at Dan. The main question that we have to face, however, is what the words "captivity of the land" at the end of verse 30 refer to. They clearly are not speaking of the destruction of the idolatrous cult by Samuel or David but of something that was done by one of Israel's enemies. But we know nothing about any foreign captivity during this period, and the author seems to be referring to a well-known event.[42] We therefore would have to assume that verse 30 is alluding to a deportation of the people of Dan shortly after the fall of Shiloh, of which no record has been preserved. But since Dan was an undisputed Israelite city during the time of Samuel and David (1 Sam. 3:20; 2 Sam. 3:10), it then would have had to have been recaptured and rebuilt very soon after this. All this seems much less likely than that Jonathan's descendants managed to maintain their unlawful cult in this remote corner of the land, even if it flourished much less under David, for example, than it did later during the time of Jeroboam. We should also note that the word "land" in verse 30 has to refer to a larger area than a mere city.

All in all, there does not seem to be a better solution to the problem presented by verse 30 than to understand the words "until the time of the captivity of the land" as a later addition that dates from after the

---

[41] See footnote 23 in section III of the Introduction, especially the quotations from Van Gelderen's commentary on 1 Kings.

[42] Some exegetes think verse 30 is alluding to the events in 1 Samuel 4 and suggest that "captivity of the land" actually means "captivity of the ark," the ceremonial center of the land. This is quite far-fetched, however. The view of Noordtzij (*Bijbels Handboek,* vol. 1, p. 445), Schulz (*Buch der Richter,* p. 95), and others that *hā'āreṣ* ("the land") should be emended to *hā'ārôn* ("the ark") is at least more plausible than this, even though there is not a trace of text-critical evidence to support it.

invasion of Tiglath-Pileser in 732 B.C. (or even the conquest of Samaria in 722). This is by far the most natural interpretation of the words. In addition, we should note that this temporal clause at the end of verse 30 is really unnecessary. If it had been included in the ancient document that the author used,[43] he certainly would not have followed it with the completely different, and much broader, temporal qualification in verse 31. The fact that he did add verse 31 (see p. 472) thus forms an indirect proof that verse 30 originally did not end with a temporal clause. It probably was inserted later by a scribe, possibly from the time of Hezekiah or Ezra (see Ezra 7:6; Prov. 25:1), who happened to know that Jonathan's descendants continued as priests in Dan until the captivity. Although this view finds no text-critical support, such evidence is not strictly necessary, no more than in other cases where we find a chronological or ethnographic comment that is an obvious interpolation from a later era.[44] This does not detract from the canonicity or historical reliability of chapter 18, for it is only through such later interpolations that the books of the Old Testament received the finished form that God had intended for them.[45]

B. The Civil War Against Benjamin (19:1–21:25)

1. THE ATROCITY OF THE MEN OF GIBEAH (19:1–30)

19:1–2a *In those days Israel had no king.*
Now a Levite who lived in a remote area in the hill country of Ephraim took a concubine from Bethlehem in Judah. [2] *But she was unfaithful to him.*[46] *She left him and went back to her father's house in Bethlehem, Judah.*

---

[43] I am assuming that the author of Judges did not write chapters 17–18 himself but took them over virtually unchanged from an ancient source that he had access to. See the Introduction, pp. 207, 212, and 454.

[44] E.g., 1 Samuel 9:9. See the *Bible Student's Commentary* on Genesis by G. Ch. Aalders, 1:39; also the comments in 1 Samuel 9:9 in the *Korte Verklaring* on 1 Samuel by C. J. Goslinga.

[45] In this context the reader should keep in mind what I have said in the Introduction about the unity, composition, and date of the Book of Judges. See especially pp. 217–23.

[46] The construction of the verb *zānâ(h)* with the preposition *'al* is unusual, but we have no reason to regard the Hebrew text as corrupt. The ancient versions cannot be followed here; their readings differ and are probably attempts to explain the Hebrew phrase.

The beginning of chapter 19 is quite similar to that of chapter 18, but there is a difference. A more literal translation of 19:1 would be "in those days, when there was no king in Israel" (cf. RSV). "In those days" refers back to the events of chapters 17–18, while the absence of a king is noted in a parenthetical clause. Apparently the author meant to say that the events he was about to recount happened at approximately the same time as those of the preceding two chapters. He then added that this was before the monarchial period, the time when he himself lived and wrote his book, incorporating these two ancient stories into his previous sketch of the period of the judges (chs. 1–16).

As I explained in my introductory comments to chapters 17–21 (pp. 453–55, these stories take us back to the time between the death of Joshua and Israel's first oppression at the hands of a foreign enemy.[47] The main actor in chapter 19 is a Levite who was living as a sojourner "in a remote part of" (literally, "inmost part of") the hill country of Ephraim. His situation was thus similar to that of the Levite in 17:7–8 (see the comments there). We are not told the precise place where he lived, and there is no need for us to hazard a guess. At the point where the story starts, he had taken a concubine from Bethlehem in Judah who became "unfaithful to him" (literally, "played the harlot against him"). She then returned to her father's house, probably partly out of fear and partly out of a need for love and acceptance.

19:2b–7 *After she had been there four months, [3] her husband went to her to persuade her to return. He had with him his servant and two donkeys. She took him into her father's house, and when her father saw him, he gladly welcomed him. [4] His father-in-law, the girl's father, prevailed upon him to stay; so he remained with him three days, eating and drinking, and sleeping there.*

[5] On the fourth day they got up early and he prepared to leave, but the girl's father said to his son-in-law, "Refresh yourself with something to eat; then you can go." [6] So the two of them sat down to eat and drink together. Afterward the girl's father said, "Please stay tonight and enjoy yourself." [7] And when the man got up to go, his father-in-law persuaded him, so he stayed there that night.

The deceived spouse accepted this separation at first, but after four months he traveled to Bethlehem to "persuade her to return." The

---

[47] A later date is also excluded for the following reason. According to 3:15, Ehud, the second judge, was from the tribe of Benjamin. In the civil war recounted in chapters 19–21, however, this tribe was largely annihilated, and it became an object of general contempt because it had sided with Gibeah. A considerable amount of time must therefore have passed before Ehud, a Benjamite, gained enough of a reputation and following to be recognized as a judge.

Hebrew phrase translated "persuade" literally means "speak to her heart"; more than mere persuasion, it thus denotes an intimate and tender talk in which the Levite tried to dispel her fear and rekindle their old love.[48] He brought with him his servant and a pair of donkeys, one of which must have been for his concubine and her belongings. It seems that they became reconciled as soon as he arrived. The young woman received him at once and brought him in to her father, who welcomed him gladly. It was easier for the Levite to regain her love, however, than it was to gain her father's permission to take her home with him. The father-in-law (the Hebrew uses this word and calls the Levite his "son-in-law," even though the man was only the father of a concubine)[49] implored him to stay and won him over with a generous display of hospitality.

After three days the Levite prepared to depart early in the morning. When he and his two companions were just about to leave, however, his father-in-law invited him to sit down and eat. He dared not refuse, and the result was that he again was prevailed on to remain another night. His father-in-law's words were persuasive, and the Levite was unable to resist the temptation of a good meal. The Hebrew phrase translated "refresh yourself" literally means "strengthen your heart [i.e., vital powers]." Neither the concubine nor the other members of the household were present at this meal. Verse 7 shows that it was not easy to persuade the Levite to stay; the word translated "stayed" could also mean "came back," which would imply that he had already left the house (this is Goslinga's translation—TRANS.).

19:8–10 *On the morning of the fifth day, when he rose to go, the girl's father said, "Refresh yourself. Wait till afternoon!"[50] So the two of them ate together.*

[9] Then when the man, with his concubine and his servant, got up to leave, his father-in-law, the girl's father, said, "Now look, it's almost evening. Spend the night here; the day is nearly over. Stay and enjoy yourself. Early tomorrow morning you can get up and be on your way home." [10] But, unwilling to stay

---

[48] See F. H. von Meyenfeldt, *Het hart in het Oude Testament,* pp. 26, 131f.

[49] The Hebrew term used in these verses usually just means "girl," but it can also denote a married young woman (e.g., Ruth 2:6 RSV).

[50] Goslinga's translation of verse 8 corresponds to the KJV and NEB: "so they tarried until afternoon." He adds the following note: "The Hebrew verb for 'tarry' or 'wait' could also be read as an imperative (as in the NIV), but the context seems to rule this out. The words 'until afternoon' could not be the father-in-law's, and there has to be a statement that they accepted his invitation"—TRANS.

another night, the man left and went toward Jebus (that is, Jerusalem), with his two saddled donkeys and his concubine.[51]

It is not hard to understand that the Levite finally resolved to turn a deaf ear to his father-in-law's pleas to stay. The fifth day began just like the previous days, and he shared a meal with the girl's father till it was almost too late to leave. But he finally stood up from the table to depart with his concubine and his servant. His father-in-law showered him with invitations to stay yet one more night, but this time his efforts were in vain. The Levite refused to listen, and he and his small caravan set out towards the north.[52] They apparently took the road from Bethlehem to Shechem, which went west of Jerusalem, the first place that they passed. The latter city was called Jebus here because it was then inhabited by the Jebusites, a non-Israelite tribe. The parenthetical remark that this was identical to Jerusalem seems to be a later insertion by the author. Jerusalem lay approximately thirty miles from Bethlehem, about a two hours' journey.[53]

19:11–14 *When they were near Jebus and the day was almost gone, the servant said to his master, "Come, let's stop at this city of the Jebusites and spend the night."*

[12] His master replied, "No. We won't go into an alien city, whose people are not Israelites. We will go on to Gibeah." [13] He added, "Come, let's try to reach

---

[51] A few manuscripts of the Septuagint add the words "and his servant" here.

[52] According to Oettli (*Buch der Richter*, p. 290), he may have left then because if he waited another day, he would have had to travel on the Sabbath.

[53] Because of the prolixity of the narrative, the frequent recurrence of the same or similar phrases, and the constant alternation between singular and plural in verses 5–9 (especially v. 9), some commentators think that this chapter is a combination of two distinct "sources." These sources are supposedly recovered by dividing the material somewhat as follows: "father-in-law" always belongs to source A, "the girl's father" to source B; source A contains the singular, and source B the plural forms; "look now, it's almost evening" (v. 9) belongs to source A, and "the day is nearly over" to source B. Such a method can be used to prove almost anything, and I report this only as an example of how arbitrarily the biblical text is dealt with by some scholars. The style may be rather wordy in this passage, but the author had to relate his story in great detail to show why the Levite was delayed for so long. The alternation between singular and plural makes perfect sense if one keeps in mind that three persons were traveling, while the decision when to go rested solely with the Levite. The father-in-law therefore spoke sometimes to all three and sometimes only to his son-in-law. His repetitive words in verse 9 present no problem at all; on the contrary, they make the story more vivid and even give the impression that it was written by an eyewitness.

Gibeah or Ramah and spend the night in one of those places." ¹⁴So they went on, and the sun set as they neared Gibeah in Benjamin.

Since the day was almost gone when they approached Jebus,⁵⁴ the servant suggested to his master that they spend the night there. The Levite, however, objected to staying in an alien city where there were no Israelites.⁵⁵ He must have motioned toward the city as he said this, for the Hebrew text contains the word *hēnnâ(h)* ("here"). They would instead go on to Gibeah. The travelers probably stood still for a moment during this discussion. The servant still hesitated, but his master insisted that they move on and pointed in the direction of Gibeah and Ramah. Both towns stood on hills north of Jerusalem. Gibeah has been identified with modern Tell el-Ful and Ramah with er-Ram, which lay approximately three miles and five miles from Jerusalem, respectively. The Levite thus wanted to travel as far as possible before nightfall; but the sun set as they neared Gibeah, and they had to halt their journey.

19:15–19 *There they stopped to spend the night. They went and sat in the city square, but no one took them into his home for the night.*

¹⁶*That evening an old man from the hill country of Ephraim, who was living in Gibeah (the men of the place were Benjamites), came in from his work in the fields. ¹⁷When he looked and saw the traveler in the city square, the old man asked, "Where are you going? Where did you come from?"*

¹⁸*He answered, "We are on our way from Bethlehem in Judah to a remote area in the hill country of Ephraim where I live. I have been to Bethlehem in Judah and now I am going to⁵⁶ the house of the LORD.⁵⁷ No one has taken me*

---

⁵⁴The Hebrew in verse 11 literally reads "the day had descended very low." The Hebrew *rad* has to be regarded as a rare variant of the perfect form *yārad* ("to descend").

⁵⁵It seems that *'îr*, the Hebrew word for "city," is here construed as a masculine noun in spite of its normal feminine gender; for the adjective "alien" is in the masculine. The only other possibility would be to read the words as "city of an alien," a rather forced translation in my view. The emendation to "city of aliens" is a mere conjecture with no text-critical ground.

⁵⁶The Hebrew text has the object marker *'et* here, which is very unusual and does not make good sense in this context. It therefore seems better to follow the Septuagint and emend this to the preposition *'el* ("to").

⁵⁷The Hebrew reading "house of the LORD" is questionable. The Septuagint simply has "my house." Although we cannot be sure how the original text read, the reading presupposed by the Septuagint translation seems preferable for several reasons. First, the Levite's home has only been referred to vaguely up to now (v. 1), even by the Levite himself (v. 18); so the author probably did not know its precise location. Second, the Levite was not traveling to the house of the Lord but to his

> *into his house.* ¹⁹ *We have both straw and fodder for our donkeys and bread and wine for ourselves your servants—me, your maidservant, and the young man with us. We don't need anything."*

The travelers entered Gibeah with a feeling of security. But although they were among brothers there, no one welcomed them at first. Finally, an old man returning from his work in the fields walked up and spoke to them. The author's statement that this man was not a Benjamite indirectly casts an unfavorable light on the citizens of Gibeah, who were given to lawless and deviant behavior (cf. Exod. 22:21; Judg. 3:15; Job 31:32). The man was nonetheless a fellow Israelite, and he even came from the same region as the Levite, viz., the hill country of Ephraim. He asked the Levite where he was going and learned that the latter had made a trip to Bethlehem and was returning home. In footnote 57 I gave my reasons for rejecting the translation "to the house of the LORD" in verse 18. Some have suggested that this verse be translated "my place is by the house of the LORD," but the verb in question can never have this meaning;[58] moreover, if he had wanted to tell the man his position he could simply have said "I am a Levite."

The Levite's answer expressed his disappointment; no one had welcomed him into his house, even though the people of Gibeah could not have missed him sitting in the city square. To invite the man's hospitality, he went on to say that he had all the necessary provisions: straw and fodder for the donkeys and bread and wine for himself, the girl, and the young man (he calls himself and his companions "your servants" in courtesy to the old man). All they needed was lodging for the night.

---

own house (vv. 3, 9, 29). Third, it seems odd that the author would not have named the place where the "house of the LORD" stood. The word "LORD" could have been erroneously inserted by a copyist who mistook the first person singular suffix for an abbreviation of the name "Yahweh." (Goslinga thus emends v. 18 to "my house"; cf. RSV—TRANS.).

[58] Keil and Schmidt adopt this translation and suggest that the Levite was giving the reason why no one from Gibeah welcomed him: they opposed the Lord, in whose house he served. This strikes me as quite far-fetched, however; no one could have known that he was a Levite, and the old man did not ask what he did but where he was going.

19:20–21 *"You are welcome at my house," the old man said. "Let me supply whatever you need. Only don't spend the night in the square."* ²¹ *So he took him into his house and fed his donkeys. After they had washed their feet, they had something to eat and drink.*

The old man's response was generous. He welcomed the Levite into his home and regarded him as his guest, promising to provide the travelers with whatever they needed. Well aware of the dangers outdoors, he warned him against sleeping in the city square. The travelers thus entered the man's home. The donkeys were given fodder (probably a tasty mash, Isa. 30:24), and the Levite and his companions washed their feet and sat down to eat. This passage is reminiscent of the Lot's reception of the two angels in Sodom (Gen. 19:1–3).

19:22–24 *While they were enjoying themselves, some of the wicked men of the city surrounded the house. Pounding on the door, they shouted to the old man who owned the house, "Bring out the man who came to your house so we can have sex with him."*
²³ *The owner of the house went outside and said to them, "No, my friends, don't be so vile. Since this man is my guest, don't do this disgraceful thing.* ²⁴ *Look, here is my virgin daughter, and his concubine. I will bring them out to you now, and you can use them and do to them whatever you wish. But to this man, don't*[59] *do such a disgraceful thing."*

The next part of the story also has much in common with Genesis 19. The differences are so great, however, that there is no way we can accept the claim of Wellhausen and others that Judges 19 is a mere imitation of the former chapter (a few scholars even think that the present chapter came first and Gen. 19 was the later imitation). The similarities between the two chapters nevertheless do indicate that the author of Judges 19 was well-acquainted with Genesis 19.[60] He probably followed the latter so closely to remind the reader of the earlier story and provide a subtle hint that the wickedness of the men of Gibeah was equal to that of the Sodomites.

While the travelers were eating and "enjoying themselves" (literally, "did their heart good"), some wicked men from the city gathered outdoors. The word "wicked" translates a Hebrew phrase that literally

---

[59] The reading of the Masoretic text and the Septuagint, *lō'* ("not"), is followed here.

[60] Compare, e.g., verse 22 with Genesis 19:4–5; verse 23 with Genesis 19:7; verse 24 with Genesis 19:8. See the *Bible Student's Commentary* on Genesis by G. Ch. Aalders, 1:37–38.

means "sons of Belial" (cf. KJV), i.e., base and worthless men. They surrounded the house and pounded on the door, demanding that the owner surrender his male guest to them so that they could "have sex with him" (literally, "know him"). Their unnatural lust (cf. Gen. 19:5; Rom. 1:27) shows how corrupt these men of Gibeah had become. The old man nevertheless went out to them and calmly tried to dissuade them from committing such a vile act. The Levite had a sacred right to his hospitality; so he never could allow them to do such a "disgraceful thing." These words translate *nᵉbālâ(h)* , a word that literally means "foolishness" and often denotes a scandalous sexual sin (e.g., v. 24; 20:6; Gen. 34:7; 2 Sam. 13:12).

Knowing that the men of Gibeah were stronger than him, the old man tried to appease them by instead offering to let them satisfy their lusts on his virgin daughter and the Levite's concubine. However repugnant this offer may strike us, we at least have to respect the old man's adamant resolve to protect his guest; he would rather hand over his own daughter than allow the Levite to be shamefully abused. But he still violated his guests' right to hospitality by also offering to surrender the concubine.[61] The only explanation for his behavior could be a desire to choose the "lesser of two evils"; it at least would be better for his degenerate townsmen to have sexual relations with the two women than with a man. The old man's decision was firm, and his final words to the men outside were even stronger than his first words: "but to this man, don't do such a disgraceful thing." He may have also suspected that the men would kill the Levite if he resisted them (see 20:5). It seems that the Israelites generally did not regard it as a mortal sin to sacrifice a woman's honor in order to save the life of a man; Abraham and Isaac too chose this route to save their own lives (Gen. 12:11–16; 20:2; 26:7). It always is wrong, however, to embrace one sin to avert another. Time and again such a course has led only to disaster.

---

[61] Some commentators argue that the words "and his concubine" in verse 24 are spurious. There is reason to think this, since we would not expect the host to offer one of his guests; and it seems unlikely that the men would have been content with one woman if two had been offered. Others would delete all of verse 24 for similar reasons, claiming that it is a duplication of Genesis 19:8. The text-critical support for the verse as it stands is overwhelming, however. Moreover it differs from Genesis 19:8 in numerous details, and the similarities are perhaps due to the fact that the man consciously followed the example of Lot. The men of Gibeah may have been content to forgo his offer of his daughter because they regarded him as their fellow townsman, for we find no reply like that in Genesis 19:9, where Lot was reproached because he was an alien. For all these reasons, verse 24 in its entirety has to be considered authentic.

19:25-28 *But the men would not listen to him. So the man took his concubine and sent her outside to them, and they raped her and abused her throughout the night, and at dawn they let her go.* [26]*At daybreak the woman went back to the house where her master was staying, fell down at the door and lay there until daylight.*

[27]*When her master got up in the morning and opened the door of the house and stepped out to continue on his way, there lay his concubine, fallen in the doorway of the house, with her hands on the threshold.* [28]*He said to her, "Get up; let's go." But there was no answer. Then the man put her on his donkey and set out for home.*

Disaster is in fact what happens in the present story, which is so frightfully eloquent in its sober account of the events that follow. The men of Gibeah refused to listen to the old man, and a conflict threatened to break out. The Levite, who had been listening to the discussion from behind the door, decided to come to his host's aid, but without endangering his own life. He grabbed his concubine callously and shoved her out the door. The men of Gibeah seem to have been content with the woman, for they showed no further interest in either the Levite or his host. They regarded her as their prize and turned her into the object of their foul passions, obviously against her will; for in the author's graphic words, "they raped her and abused her throughout the night." When they finally released the ravaged woman, it was no wonder that she could barely drag herself back to the house where her master was staying and collapsed at the door. The words "and lay there" in verse 26 are not found in the Hebrew but have been added for clarity.

Those within the house slept through the night without looking out for the woman. The next morning, when the Levite opened the door and stepped outside to continue his journey (this does not necessarily mean that he did not intend to look for his concubine first), he found her lying at the entrance with her hands on the threshold, "as if, even at the point of death, she still wanted to be let inside."[62] Although the author might not have intended it this way, the Levite's words to her—"Get up, let's go"— sound cold and crude. The woman did not answer; and when he realized that she was dead, he put her on his donkey and set off for home.

Although the narrative is very terse and sober here, it provides a shocking illustration of the depth of moral depravity into which some of

[62]Oettli, *Buch der Richter*, p. 292.

the Israelites had fallen so soon. As chapter 20 will show, the men of Gibeah's atrocity made a deep impression and opened the eyes of God's covenant people to the evil that was festering in their midst. Hosea mentioned the sin of Gibeah as one of Israel's low points (Hos. 9:9), a dreadful event that marked the beginning of their apostasy from the Lord (Hos. 10:9). This was the first major, outrageous sin of Israel since she had settled in Canaan. And the men of Gibeah were by no means the only persons who were blackened by the author's account. The Levite too was not spared, even though he was better than the others.

The story illustrates how sexual sins receive their just reward. As one commentator appropriately put it, "Nemesis stalks onward through the unembellished narrative. The woman became a harlot and sinned against the Levite (v. 2). This crime could not be annulled by a mere tipping of the wineglass (vv. 3–9), and the Levite, who was himself sensually inclined, had to surrender his unfaithful spouse to sexual abuse and death. She died by her own sin."[63] In other words, God's punishment matches the sinner's transgression, and each person is repaid according to his deeds (Ps. 62:12).

19:29–30 *When he reached home, he took a knife and cut up his concubine, limb by limb, into twelve parts and sent them[64] into all the areas of Israel.* *[30]Everyone who saw it said, "Such a thing has never been seen or done, not since the day the Israelites came up out of Egypt. Think about it! Consider it! Tell us what to do!"*[65]

These final two verses show how little regard the Levite had for his deceased concubine, but they also illustrate the harshness of the times in which he was living. The men of Gibeah's crime could not be kept

---

[63] Oettli, *Buch der Richter*, p. 292.

[64] Literally, "her."

[65] In the manuscript of the Septuagint contained in the Codex Alexandrinus, verse 30 reads as follows: "And he commanded the men he sent to say to every Israelite, 'has such a thing as this ever happened from the day the Israelites came up out of Egypt until this day? Think about it, consider it, and speak'" (cf. NEB). Moore thinks that this reading is clearly preferable, since the final words of the verse (which are almost identical in both readings) make better sense coming from the Levite than from those who received the message (*Judges*, p. 421). In my view this argument is not decisive, since these final words can also be easily understood as what the Israelites said to each other. Chapter 20:1 seems to indicate that verse 30 has already said something about the people's reaction to the Levite's message. But it is difficult to make a final decision between the two readings, and the reading of the Codex Alexandrinus is so attractive that it at least deserves mention.

hidden or allowed to go unpunished. The Levite chose the most drastic means to make it known. As soon as he reached home, he cut up the corpse, "limb by limb,"[66] into twelve parts in accordance with the Twelve Tribes, just as if it were an animal (compare what Saul did in 1 Sam. 11:7). He then had these carried throughout all Israel by messengers, who spread the news of what had happened to the woman in Gibeah. His gruesome method achieved its goal. The verb tenses at the beginning of verse 30 indicate repetitive action: literally, "and it happened that whenever someone saw it, he said. . . ." All Israel cried out in indignation. Knowing that the crime brought disgrace on the entire nation, the people urged one another to take counsel and consider together what they should do.

2. THE ISRAELITE CAMPAIGN AGAINST BENJAMIN (20:1-48)

20:1-3a *Then all the Israelites from Dan to Beersheba and from the land of Gilead came out as one man and assembled before the* LORD *in Mizpah.* ²*The leaders of all the people of the tribes of Israel*[67] *took their places in the assembly of the people of God, four hundred thousand soldiers armed with swords.* ³*(The Benjamites heard that the Israelites had gone up to Mizpah.)*

Chapter 20 gives us a clear picture of how things were in Israel shortly after the death of Joshua: the national and religious unity of the Twelve Tribes was still quite strong, and the people were keenly aware of their obligation to take strenuous, concerted action against the atrocity that had been committed in their midst. It is remarkable that we do not hear of a leader who called the people together on this occasion. The Levite's message, and especially the manner in which he conveyed it, must have been so effective that the Israelites came to this solemn national assembly of their own accord. It was probably because of Mizpah's location that the meeting was held there rather than at Shiloh or Shechem (Josh. 18:1; 24:1). Mizpah in all likelihood was located at the site of modern Tell en-Nasbeh, a high hill (Mizpah means

---

[66]Literally, "in relation to her bones." The Hebrew word for "bones" or "limbs" often indicates the entire body; Gesenius (*Handwörterbuch* [Leipzig, 1899], p. 633) thus translates it as "completely" here. (Goslinga disagrees with the translation "limb by limb" and instead has "with her bones and all"; cf. KJV—TRANS.)

[67]Goslinga's translation corresponds to the NEB: "and all the tribes of Israel." He adds the following note: "The word 'and,' although missing in the Hebrew text, is present in the Septuagint. It seems indispensable here, since the number 400,000 could not apply to the leaders alone"—TRANS.

"watchtower") about 4½ miles north of Gibeah; therefore it probably was on the border of Benjamin and near to the city where the crime was committed.

Verse 1 probably says that the people assembled "before the LORD" there because Mizpah had a place of worship (cf. 1 Sam. 7:5–7, 11, 16). The meeting was attended by virtually all Israel. They came out "as one man" all the way from Dan (18:29) to Beersheba, the northernmost and southernmost cities of the land west of the Jordan, and also from Gilead, a name that here denotes the entire Transjordan.

Verse 2 describes the nature of the assembly more closely. It was composed of the leaders of the people and men who represented the nation as a whole. The Hebrew term translated "leaders" usually means "corner" or "corner-tower," but here it has the metaphorical meaning "head" or, in a military sense, "chief" (also in 1 Sam. 14:38; Isa. 19:13). These commanders and the men who followed them from all the tribes constituted themselves as an official assembly of the people of God; they numbered 400,000 foot soldiers, each armed with a sword and ready to fight (see v. 17). We should not conclude from the size of this number that all the Israelite men were present at the assembly (there were 600,000 men twenty years and older at the time of the Exodus, Num. 26:51), but it certainly must have included all the heads of families. There could not have been room for all of them at Mizpah; so the encampment must have spread out far to the north and west. Mizpah was the site of the headquarters and the assembly itself, however, which must have been attended by the family heads and as many others as there was room for.

Only Benjamin was not represented, which reflects very unfavorably on that tribe. The brief comment about the Benjamites in verse 3a implies that they immediately took a hostile attitude toward the other tribes. They knew that all Israel (of which they also were members) had come together; and by not joining the assembly, they consciously chose the side of Gibeah. Verse 3a thus anticipates verses 12–13.

20:3b–7 *Then the Israelites said, "Tell us how this awful thing happened."* *⁴So the Levite, the husband of the murdered woman, said, "I and my concubine came to Gibeah in Benjamin to spend the night. ⁵During the night the men of Gibeah came after me and surrounded the house, intending to kill me. They raped my concubine, and she died. ⁶I took my concubine, cut her into pieces and sent one piece to each region of Israel's inheritance, because they committed this lewd and disgraceful act in Israel. ⁷Now, all you Israelites, speak up and give your verdict."*

Once the assembly had convened, the Israelites sought to determine exactly how the crime happened, for up until then they had only heard about it indirectly through the Levite's messengers. Before they could take action, they had to establish where the guilt lay. Their command—"Tell us how this awful thing happened"—was not addressed to a specific person but to anyone who could give them further information. The Levite stepped forward as the chief witness against the men of Gibeah, who had no advocate of their own at the assembly. Without going into details, he briefly described the crime of the citizens of Gibeah. The men of the city had not all had a direct hand in the atrocity, but they all shared in the guilt.

Although chapter 19 does not explicitly state that the men of Gibeah intended to kill him, the Levite was not wrong to say this. They immediately took a hostile attitude toward him by leaving him alone in the city square; then, with malicious intent, they surrounded the house where he and his companions were staying, and they certainly would have killed him if he had fallen into their hands and resisted their shameful designs on him. And indeed they abused his concubine so harshly that she died. This is the crime he was accusing them of and which he had made known by sending one part of her body "to each region of Israel's inheritance" (his words here are almost solemn). They had not committed a misdemeanor but a "lewd and disgraceful act in Israel" that was a sin against the whole people of God, an atrocity so perverse that it could bring a curse on the entire nation.

The words translated "in Israel" also have the connotation "against Israel" (cf. v. 10). The word translated "lewd" appears also in Leviticus 18:17 (NIV, "wickedness"), where it denotes a sin whose perpetrator must be "cut off from the people" (Lev. 18:29; cf. Job 31:11). The phrase "disgraceful thing in Israel" is found also in Genesis 34:7; Deuteronomy 22:21; Joshua 7:15 (cf. 2 Sam. 13:11–12). Because the men of Gibeah's crime affected the whole nation, the Levite ended by asking all the Israelites to "speak up" (literally, "give your word") and give their verdict.

20:8-11 *All the people rose as one man, saying, "None of us will go home. No, not one of us will return to his house. ⁹But now this is what we'll do to Gibeah: We'll go up against it as the lot directs. ¹⁰We'll take ten men out of every hundred from all the tribes of Israel, and a hundred from a thousand, and a thousand from ten thousand, to get provisions for the army. Then, when the army arrives*[68] *at Gibeah*[69] *in Benjamin, it can give them what they deserve for all this vileness done in Israel." ¹¹So all the men of Israel got together and united as one man against the city.*

The people's response was unanimous. They all took a solemn vow that not one of them would return to his house.[70] They would remain together till justice had been done for the atrocity. Gibeah's guilt was clear, and its citizens had to be punished. Their sentence is expressed in a short Hebrew phrase that is not completely clear (v. 9). Although the NIV translates this "we'll go up against it as the lot directs," the literal meaning is simply "against it by lot!"[71] This probably means "we will take action against it with the lot," i.e., treat it like the Canaanites, whom Israel had destroyed and then divided up their territory by lot. In support of this interpretation, we should note that this is how Gibeah was actually dealt with: the city and its inhabitants were utterly destroyed, just like the pagan cities that were put under the ban when the Israelites entered Canaan (vv. 37, 40, 48; cf. Deut. 13:15-17). Obviously it would take more than one or two days to carry

---

[68] Since the Hebrew text here is rather hard to translate as it stands, the sequence of the words should perhaps be changed. The Hebrew word translated "army" is followed by two infinitive constructs, the first meaning "to do" (NIV, "give") and the second, "that they arrive." These two words are then followed by "at Gibeah in Benjamin," which clearly goes with "to do." It is therefore strange that the second infinitive construct comes between these two (the problem here is more obvious in the KJV—TRANS.). The solution may be provided by a group of Septuagint manuscripts that read the two words in the reverse order (although these also have another slight difference: "that they arrive" is changed to "for those arriving," a participial modifier of "army"). Possibly this was also the original sequence in the Hebrew text.

[69] The Hebrew text has "Geba" here (cf. NIV margin), but this is probably a copyist's error. The Septuagint has the same name here as in verses 4, 5, and 9.

[70] Literally, "turn aside to his house"; the verb implies that to return home would be a faithless departure from the chosen course, a betrayal of one's calling.

[71] Goslinga disagrees with the NIV translation because the following verses say nothing about the casting of lots. In verse 18 the people rather ask the Lord for advice. He admits that the Septuagint reading, which contains the verb "we will go up," supports the translation found in the NIV; but since the other ancient versions read differently, he thinks the verb must have been absent in the original text— TRANS.

out this decision. The people therefore also decided to give one-tenth of their number the special task of finding provisions for the army. This would have to be done at once so that the rest of the people would be free to fight against Gibeah and give its citizens their just deserts for "all this vileness done in Israel."

The account of the national assembly at Mizpah ends at this point. The fact that more must have happened there is clear from 21:1. The people also must have decided to send men into Benjamin to search for the criminals (vv. 12–13) and have taken the oaths spoken of in 21:5 and 18. Verses 8–10 are concerned only with the main proceedings. Verse 11 then adds that all Israel's soldiers united as one man against the city. This is not an anticipation of verse 19, as some commentators maintain. It simply means that the Israelites who had gathered at Mizpah took a common stand against Gibeah and, with complete unity of purpose, prepared for war. The eleven tribes were on good terms with one another, but their relationship to the Lord and also to Benjamin left something to be desired (see in vv. 18, 21, 25, 26–28).

20:12–13 *The tribes of Israel sent men throughout the tribe of Benjamin, saying, "What about this awful crime that was committed among you?* 13 *Now surrender those wicked men of Gibeah so that we may put them to death and purge the evil from Israel."*

But the Benjamites[72] *would not listen to their fellow Israelites.*

With a commendable sense of justice and desire for peace, the Israelites first sent messengers through all the tribe of Benjamin (the Hebrew term literally means "tribes," but there is reason to think that it at times can refer to the divisions of a tribe; cf. Num. 4:18) to express their outrage at the crime and demand that those responsible for it be handed over. By "purging the evil from Israel" (this phrase is borrowed from the Mosaic laws; cf. Deut. 13:5; 17:12; 22:22), they would avert God's wrath from the entire nation (cf. Josh. 7). But the Benjamites refused to listen to the brotherly offer of their fellow Israelites. Instead of seeking justice, they simply took the side of their tribesman and thus came to share in the guilt of the murderers among them. The inevitable outcome was civil war.

---

[72] The Hebrew text merely has "Benjamin" here. The NIV follows the *Qere* and adds *bᵉnē* (i.e., "sons of Benjamin," or "Benjamites"), a reading that is supported by a number of Hebrew manuscripts and the ancient versions.

20:14–16 *From their towns they came together at Gibeah to fight against the Israelites. 15At once the Benjamites mobilized twenty-six thousand73 swordsmen from their towns, in addition to seven hundred chosen men from those living in Gibeah. 16Among all these soldiers there were seven hundred chosen men74 who were left-handed, each of whom could sling a stone at a hair and not miss.*

The Benjamites immediately mobilized their troops at Gibeah for the impending war. Although verses 14–15 speak only of the towns, this does not mean that the villages were left out; the men from the various regions naturally would have gathered first in the towns and then marched from there to Gibeah. Twenty-six thousand armed men arrived at the city, and this number was increased by 700 chosen men from Gibeah itself.75 The latter probably formed a separate company that would guard the city. There was an equally large group of slingshot artists: 700 left-handed men. The Hebrew phrase translated "left-handed" here (also in 3:15) probably literally means "closed on the right hand" (a verbal form of the word for "closed" is found only in Ps. 69:15), which must mean that they were not adept with their right hands and were thus left-handed. The translation "with lame right hands" goes too far in my view. On the other hand, the Septuagint translation "with two right hands," i.e., ambidextrous, is certainly wrong. The special dexterity and skill of the Benjamites, which is also spoken of in 1 Chronicles 12:2, was at least an indirect cause of their partial success in the civil war.

The beginning of verse 16 shows that the 700 slingers are included in the total of 26,000. Benjamin thus had 26,700 soldiers in all. There is a discrepancy between the numbers in these two verses and the numbers

---

73 The Septuagint has 25,000, the Hebrew text 26,000. Which number is correct cannot be determined on text-critical grounds alone, but it is best to stay with the Hebrew reading. See footnote 74.

74 Most ancient versions lack the words "among all these soldiers there were 700 chosen men." This can be readily explained by the fact that the words "700 chosen men" are identical to the final words of verse 15; a copyist's eyes could therefore easily have strayed from the first to the second occurrence of these words, causing the intervening words to be inadvertently omitted (homoeoteleuton). The Hebrew text therefore has to be regarded as authentic. The fact that the numbers in verses 15–16 do not tally with the 25,100 in verse 35 has no significance in this regard (see in v. 15).

75 The Hebrew text repeats the words "they were mobilized [or 'numbered']" in the second half of verse 15 (cf. KJV, NASB). This should be read as a relative clause in which the relative pronoun has been omitted, since the words would otherwise be a pointless repetition and the end of verse 15 would be left hanging.

that appear later in the story. According to verse 35, 25,100 Benjamites fell in the third battle; and verse 47 says that there were 600 survivors. This gives a total of 25,700 men, a difference of exactly 1,000. The most obvious explanation of this discrepancy, namely, that 1,000 Benjamites were killed in the first two battles, is probably correct. The Septuagint has 25,000 instead of 26,000 in verse 15, but this gives the impression of being a deliberate change to make the number agree with verses 35 and 47. A few other minor discrepancies are discussed in verse 35.

20:17–21 *Israel, apart from Benjamin, mustered four hundred thousand swordsmen, all of them fighting men.*
18 The Israelites went up to Bethel and inquired of God. They said, "Who of us shall go first to fight against the Benjamites?"
The LORD replied, "Judah shall go first."
19 The next morning the Israelites got up and pitched camp near Gibeah.
20 The men of Israel went out to fight the Benjamites and took up battle positions against them at Gibeah. 21 The Benjamites came out of Gibeah and cut down twenty-two thousand Israelites on the battlefield that day.

Benjamin was able to mobilize its men without interference because the eleven other tribes still had to muster their own troops as well. Their army numbered 400,000, all of them armed with swords and able warriors. We are not told whether this muster exposed the absence of any troops from Jabesh Gilead (21:9), nor how such a colossal army could have encamped. Since the 400,000 soldiers obviously could not be used at the same time, the Israelites had to decide which tribe should attack first. They thus went to Bethel in order to inquire of God and provoke Him into making the decision. They did not implore Him for His help, and we read nothing about the bringing of offerings. Since Shiloh was too far away, they first had the ark of the covenant brought to Bethel, a town about three miles north of Mizpah along the road from Jerusalem to Shechem. Phinehas supervised the ritual worship there at that time and inquired of God on behalf of the people (vv. 27–28; cf. Josh. 22:12–13). The Lord's answer was "Judah shall go first."

There is a striking resemblance between verse 18 and 1:1–2; but the former is by no means a mere copy of the latter, and the differences are not without significance. The Lord's answer, in particular, sounds very curt, and He did not give His approval to what the people were doing (although some commentators think He did). In 1:2, in contrast, He immediately promised victory. It also is not insignificant that the Israelites are here said to inquire of "God," whereas in 1:1 the name

"Lord" is used; this indicates that their relationship to the God of the covenant was less intimate and pure than on the former occasion (see also under vv. 23 and 26). The trip to Bethel naturally would not have been made by the entire army but only by a deputation of elders and military leaders.

The next morning, after they had received their answer, the Israelites (undoubtedly these were mainly men from Judah) marched out against Gibeah. Their aim was not merely to besiege the city but, if possible, to take it by storm and conquer it. But the outcome was a bitter disappointment to them. As they approached Gibeah, the Benjamites made a sudden attack and won a crushing victory in which 22,000 Israelites were cut down ("on the battlefield" in v. 21 could also be translated "to the ground"; cf. RSV). We are told nothing about how the battle unfolded or what led to the Israelites' defeat. The men of Israel did come to understand, however, that the Lord was not with them in this battle and that there had to be some reason for this.

20:22–25 *But the men of Israel encouraged one another and again took up their positions where they had stationed themselves the first day.* 23 *The Israelites went up and wept before the Lord until evening, and they inquired of the Lord. They said, "Shall we go up again to battle against the Benjamites, our brothers?"*

The Lord answered, "Go up against them."

24 *Then the Israelites drew near to Benjamin the second day.* 25 *This time, when the Benjamites came out from Gibeah to oppose them, they cut down another eighteen thousand Israelites, all of them armed with swords.*

The impression we get from these next two verses is a little ambiguous. First, we are told that the defeated soldiers encouraged one another and "took up their positions"[76] in the very same place where they had stationed themselves before the first battle. This indicates that they were overly bold and bent on concealing their fear at all costs and getting revenge for their wounded pride. The next verse, however, says that the Israelites returned to Bethel, where they wept till evening and then meekly asked the Lord whether they should venture to attack their brother Benjamites again.

It is hard to harmonize the two attitudes evident in these verses. The

---

[76] Although the Hebrew words here are the same as in verse 20, Goslinga translates them "prepared for battle" this time because he thinks this was done in the evening right after their defeat. According to him, R. Breuer's translation, "offered battle" (*Das Buch der Richter* [1922]), is also attractive—Trans.

usual solution for those who critically question the divine origin of Scripture is to assign verses 22 and 23 to different sources. Such an approach is too arbitrary to be acceptable, however; and it does not remove the problems contained in the text as it stands. Much more plausible is the hypothesis offered by a few commentators that a copyist inadvertently reversed the order of the two verses. If verse 22 is read after and in the light of verse 23, it gives a better impression of the Israelites, since their bold action in the former verse then would be the fruit of their humble submission to God in the latter. But this solution creates a new problem: why would a nation that had repented and humbled itself have to suffer another defeat? In addition, the Hebrew manuscripts and the ancient versions unanimously place verse 22 before verse 23. The traditional order of the two verses therefore has to be maintained.

The problem can still be solved, however, if we assume that what is said in verse 23 did not follow verse 22 temporally. Rather we here are confronted with two different things that happened at the same time, and the Hebrew text brings this out by beginning verse 23 with the word "also." One therefore can only gain a correct understanding of the Israelites' mood or attitude if the two verses are read together. Their behavior expressed uncertainty, for the shock of defeat had upset their self-confidence and their belief in their cause. On the one hand, they told themselves that their defeat was an unacceptable mistake and that they must make amends by reattacking at once, and with greater force. On the other hand, they suspected that it may have somehow been wrong for them to make war against a brother tribe; and they decided to consult the Lord again to make sure.

On this view the people did not really display any true humility. Their tears were not a sign of repentance but more a means to provoke the Lord (this time the covenant name for God is used) into giving a favorable answer. The ambiguity in the text is thus merely a reflection of the people's indecision. The Lord's brief and guarded answer to the Israelites' question supports this interpretation. By simply saying "go up against them," He implied that they would have to wait to see what happened; and we can only take this to mean that another humiliation was in store for Israel (see also in vv. 26–28).

The second battle thus ended in defeat for the Israelites as well. As they marched toward Gibeah on "the second day," i.e., the day of the second battle, the Benjamites overwhelmed them again and cut down another 18,000 men. The Israelites probably took flight early during both battles (see the words "as before" in v. 32), giving the Benjamites the opportunity to slaughter them so decisively without suffering any significant losses of their own.

20:26–28 *Then the Israelites, all the people, went up to Bethel, and there they sat weeping before the LORD. They fasted that day until evening and presented burnt offerings and fellowship offerings to the LORD.* [27]*And the Israelites inquired of the LORD. (In those days the ark of the covenant of God was there,* [28]*with Phinehas son of Eleazar, the son of Aaron, ministering before it.) They asked, "Shall we go up again to battle with Benjamin our brother, or not?"*
The LORD responded, "Go, for tomorrow I will give them into your hands."

The Israelites had lost all confidence in themselves. Finally they had come to understand that victory could be won, not by their own power, but only by the grace of Yahweh.[77] They realized that they should go no further till they were absolutely sure of the Lord's help, which obviously had left them. Even the civilians knew this, for verse 26 seems to indicate that not merely the soldiers but also other men and women made the pilgrimage to Bethel. There they wept and fasted till evening and offered burnt offerings and fellowship offerings (or peace offerings; see NIV margin, KJV, and RSV). The burnt offering was completedly consumed by the fire as a sign of complete self-surrender to God.

The other offering is sometimes regarded as a thank offering, but this translation is definitely wrong in the present context. Peace offering is a better name and fits perfectly with the most probable derivation of the Hebrew term in question. The purpose of these offerings was to honor God and give expression to one's close fellowship with Him.[78] But they could also serve to express one's desire for a restoration of peace with God. This indeed was the reason why the Israelites presented such offerings on this occasion. In keeping with this, the offerings at least partly had an atoning function, for they were bloody offerings in which (in contrast to the burnt offering) a portion of the meat was returned to the offerer for a sacrificial meal.[79] There is no basis for regarding them

---

[77]See Oettli, *Buch der Richter,* p. 294.

[78]The NIV name, "fellowship offering," thus accords with the purpose of the offering and its accompanying sacrificial meal. See the *Bible Student's Commentary, Leviticus,* by A. Noordtzij (tr. R. Togtman [Grand Rapids: Zondervan, 1982]), pp. 47–49—TRANS.

[79]Burnt offerings are described particularly in Leviticus 1. For the fellowship offerings, see Leviticus 3 and 7:11–34. The latter are divided into praise offerings, votive offerings, and freewill offerings. The offerings in verse 26 and 21:4 can be

as offerings of prayer and supplication,[80] for we are not told that the people turned to God with a humble, heartfelt prayer. On the contrary, we get the impression that their tears, fasting, and offerings were merely an attempt to appease the Lord (compare their similar behavior in the assembly at Bokim, 2:4–5, which must have taken place during this same period). Hence, even here (as in v. 23), we should not think that the people truly humbled themselves and repented for their sins.

The Israelites' attitude here is not nearly as commendable as that of Joshua after the defeat at Ai (Josh. 7:6–9). Joshua and the elders were deeply dismayed by the fact that the people's relationship to the Lord had been broken, and for them it was absolutely necessary that this be restored. At Bethel, in contrast, the Israelites were more overcome by the pain of their losses and regret for their defeat. Their religious display remained more or less external, for they were more interested in their own victory than in God Himself. They should have had a sense of their complicity in the sin of Gibeah, since Gibeah was one of their own cities. The crime of the men of Gibeah had cast a shadow over the whole nation, and the behavior and way of life of the Levite was also reprehensible. The people's behavior may have been in conformity with the law (cf. the end of Deut. 22:22), but they were at fault for the Pharisaic attitude that lay behind their attack on Benjamin, for their lack of a sense of guilt before God, and for their reliance on their own strength.[81] This mentality also led them to take an unreasonably harsh and cruel attitude toward the whole tribe of Benjamin. They were more interested in vengeance than in justice. They did in fact feel sorry for this later on, but even then they did not comprehend the true depth of their sin, which consisted mainly in a false, insincere relationship to God that came out especially in the underhanded way that they escaped their vows (ch. 21). Chapter 21 confirms my negative view of the Israelites' behavior in verse 26.

---

considered freewill offerings, but they were definitely not thank offerings. For a discussion of these offerings, see, e.g., Gispen's article in *Bijbels Handboek*, vol. 1, pp. 281f.

[80] This is the view of Keil, *Kommentar*, p. 368, and D. Hoek, *Boek der Richteren*, p. 458.

[81] See Keil, *Kommentar*, p. 367; De Graaf, *Promise and Deliverance*, 2:55. According to the rabbis, the Israelites had to suffer the first two defeats in order to pay for their sin of allowing Micah and the Danites to practice their idol worship with impunity. But although it is true that there were sometimes specific punishments like this for specific sins (see 2 Sam. 21:1), we cannot accept this explanation here because there is no support for it in the text.

The next two verses offer further support. The only result of the pilgrimage to Bethel was that the people again asked the Lord what they should do. The question of verse 23 is repeated almost verbatim, but the additional words "or not" show that they felt a little smaller. No longer were they driven by pride; and if it was God's will, they would stop fighting. This time, however, the Lord's answer contained a promise of victory. This does not necessarily mean that the Lord was completely satisfied with them; but Benjamin's wickedness also had to be punished, and the Israelites had suffered enough. In commenting on this, De Graaf writes: "Now, in humble faith, they were to be nothing other than agents carrying out the Lord's judgment upon Benjamin."[82]

20:29–35 *Then Israel set an ambush around Gibeah. [30] They went up against the Benjamites on the third day and took up positions against Gibeah as they had done before. [31] The Benjamites came out to meet them and were drawn away from the city. They began to inflict casualties on the Israelites as before, so that about thirty men fell in the open field and on the roads — the one leading to Bethel and the other to Gibeah.[83]*

[32] While the Benjamites were saying, "We are defeating them as before," the Israelites were saying, "Let's retreat and draw them away from the city to the roads."

[33] All the men of Israel moved from their places and took up positions at Baal Tamar, and the Israelite ambush charged out of its place on the west of Gibeah.[84] [34] Then ten thousand of Israel's finest men made a frontal attack on

---

[82] *Promise and Deliverance,* 2:55.

[83] Although the Hebrew text has Gibeah here, Goslinga thinks (along with some other commentators) that the original reading must have been Gibeon, a name that differs by only one consonant. He gives two reasons: (1) it makes no sense to say that men who had come from Gibeah went onto a road leading to Gibeah; (2) at a point northwest of Gibeah, which itself stood beside the main road, a road to Gibeon did in fact branch off from the road to Bethel—TRANS.

[84] Goslinga translates this "caves of Geba" and adds the following note:

The Hebrew text here has the word *ma'ᵃrēh,* a term that appears nowhere else and is often taken to mean "nakedness" or "plain, open place" (from the stem ' *rh*). The latter meaning is forbidden by the fact that the ambush certainly would not have been stationed in a plain. The former also cannot be right, since the whole phrase clearly modifies the words "out of its place," and the Hebrew text does not read "Gibeah," but "Geba" (cf. NIV margin). Some Septuagint manuscripts and the Vulgate translate "on the west" (cf. NIV), which would indicate that the Hebrew text read *ma'ᵃrab,* but this word is never joined to a place name in this manner. Following the Syriac translation, it seems best to regard the word *ma'ᵃrēh* as a derivative of the stem ' *rr* and a variant form of *mᵉ'ārā(h),* the word for "cave" used in 6:2. Here it should be regarded as a

Gibeah. The fighting was so heavy that the Benjamites did not realize how near disaster was. ³⁵ *The LORD defeated Benjamin before Israel, and on that day the Israelites struck down 25,100 Benjamites, all armed with swords.*

NOTE ON VERSES 29–48.

Up to this point the historical narrative has been fairly well-organized. No doubt one could wish that it were clearer at some points, and a few unresolved problems do remain. In addition, some commentators have spoken of needless repetitions or "doublets": e.g., verses 2 and 17, 11 and 19. Closer inspection reveals that these are not pointless redundancies, however, and nothing can be found that actually distorts the account of what happened. At most, one could say that the style is a little incoherent and somewhat dull. In verses 29–48, however, which recount the final battle, the problems are more serious. Even a superficial reading reveals that the same event is described twice. The outcome of the battle and the number of slain is reported already in verse 35, but the story is then resumed. Verses 44–46 give some numbers that are a little different, while several things in the battle (the Israelites' feigned flight, the ambush's attack, the thirty slain Israelites) are simply repeated. Various commentators (e.g., Budde, Moore, Gressmann) thus assume either that an original nucleus of the story has been repeatedly revised and amplified, or that two independent stories have been joined together by the author and, to a certain extent, interwoven. Attempts have been made to recover the stories in their original form by dividing the text as it stands between the two alleged sources, but this remains a hopeless and rather useless task.

The main question that confronts us is the meaning of the text as it stands, which the author undoubtedly wanted us to read as a unity. In other words, even though verses 29–35 and 36–46 undeniably give us two accounts of the third battle, we have to read and interpret these pericopes as parts of a single whole, in which the second, longer account merely serves to supplement the first. Interpretation is made more difficult because a few of the geographical references are rather obscure, and because there are some unclear passages that lead us to suspect that the text is corrupt, while we have no certain clues as to how these should be emended. In addition, the style is something less than transparent, and there is inconsistency in the verb tenses and the use of singular and plural forms (e.g., in vv. 31, 33). I do not mean to deny that the main outlines of the battle can easily be gathered from the text as it stands. The purpose of this note is only to point out some of the peculiar problems in these verses and to clarify the task that lies before us in interpreting them: namely, to seek to understand all the data in terms of their context, without discounting certain passages as later in date and less reliable. It is possible that the author of

---

collective noun referring to a group of caves near Geba, a place northeast of Gibeah. The ambush's hiding place is discussed further under verse 29—TRANS.

Judges could have written a more orderly account himself. Since he preferred, however, to allow his ancient documents to speak for themselves as far as possible (even though this had a harmful effect on his style), we have to accept the text as his own product and try to do full justice to it in our interpretation.

As a final observation, just as verses 19–25 are reminiscent of Israel's defeat at Ai (Josh. 7:4–5), verses 29–48 display great similarity with the account of Ai's conquest (Josh. 8:1–29). In spite of this, Wellhausen's claim that these verses are a mere copy of the earlier story has no grounds whatsoever. Other cities easily could have been captured in the same manner.

The Lord's promise did not cause the Israelites to act recklessly. On the contrary, they made careful preparations for the next battle with their formidable opponents, who had confirmed the truth of Jacob's prophecy that Benjamin would be a ravenous wolf (Gen. 49:27). First, they set an ambush around Gibeah.[85] The main army was probably encamped north and west of the city (see below in v. 33), and the troops most likely took a roundabout route to their posts during the night. The city was surrounded. On the third day after the previous battle, the Israelites marched against Gibeah for the third time, pretending that they were going to use the same tactics as before. The Benjamites, who had become overconfident because of their earlier successes, expected that this battle would go the same as the other two; and they seemed to be right, since they at first gained the upper hand and put Israel on the defensive. The Israelites' sudden retreat was intentional, however. It served to draw the Benjamites too far from their own city and into the open field, where Israel's superior forces could be put to better use. The Benjamites did not realize this and thought that they merely had to press on with the pursuit of their defeated enemy, of whom they had already killed some thirty men. But the Israelites, who had abandoned their former positions, suddenly stopped their retreat and took a stand at Baal Tamar, an otherwise unknown place that must have lain northwest of Gibeah (see footnote 83; Eusebius mentions a Baal Tamar near Gibeah; the name Tamar indicates there were palm trees there). The Hebrew verb tenses in verse 33 indicate that the ambush acted at the same time as the main army. They charged from their hiding place (the same verb is translated

---

[85] If the NIV's emendation of verse 33 ("on the west of Gibeah") following the Septuagint and Vulgate is correct, the main part of this ambush was stationed west of Gibeah. Goslinga, in contrast, has "from the caves of Geba" in verse 33 (he points to 1 Sam. 14:5, 11 in this connection), which would put the ambush northeast of the city—TRANS.

"burst forth" in Job 38:8) and rushed toward Gibeah, arriving at the city gates ten thousand men strong.

The author then returns to the battle at Baal Tamar, where the main Israelite army was making a gallant stand. At first the Benjamites were still oblivious of their impending doom. The Lord Himself then gave Israel a total victory. The outcome of the battle is stated already in verse 35, but it is described at greater length in verses 40–48. By evening 25,100 Benjamites lay dead on the field. According to verses 44–45, 18,000 men fell first, while 5,000 and then 2,000 more were cut down as they attempted to flee. Since the author was only giving round numbers here, the difference of 100 men is not important.

20:36–41 *Then the Benjamites saw that they were beaten.*

Now the men of Israel had given way before Benjamin, because they relied on the ambush they had set near Gibeah. [37] The men who had been in ambush made a sudden dash into Gibeah, spread out and put the whole city to the sword. [38] The men of Israel had arranged with the ambush that they should[86] send up a great cloud of smoke from the city, [39] and then the men of Israel would turn in the battle.

The Benjamites had begun to inflict casualties on the men of Israel (about thirty), and they said, "We are defeating them as in the first battle." [40] But when the column of smoke began to rise from the city, the Benjamites turned and saw the smoke of the whole city going up into the sky. [41] Then the men of Israel turned on them, and the men of Benjamin were terrified, because they realized that disaster had come upon them.

After having reported the outcome of the battle in verse 35, the author proceeds to enlarge on his previous account by describing the progress of the battle in detail. Verse 36 thus returns to the situation described in verses 33–34. Those commentators who suppose that the author has simply juxtaposed two independent narratives usually regard verse 36a as the end of the first story and connect it directly to

---

[86]The Hebrew text contains the imperative form *hereb* ("make great") here. But this does not fit in the context, since the verse is using indirect discourse. The witness of the ancient versions is divided; the word is missing in the Vulgate and Syriac translations, while some Septuagint manuscripts seem to have read it as (or emended it to) *hereb*, "sword," which makes no sense at all. The problem is that *hereb*, a second person singular form, clashes with the third person plural suffix on the infinitive construct ("send up") that follows it. Some commentators would omit the suffix, but there are no text-critical grounds for this. It seems better simply to omit *hereb*, since the word is very obscure in this context and completely redundant. It could easily have slipped into the text as a misspelled dittograph of *hā'ōrēb* ("ambush").

verse 35. This could not have been the author's intention, however. After a great army has been cut to pieces, it would be silly to say of the survivors that they noticed they were beaten. The problem contained in verse 36a can best be solved if we assume that the author is here going back to verse 34, where he had said that the fighting was heavy and the Benjamites were oblivious of the danger that threatened them from behind.

In verses 36b–41, the author describes how the Benjamites finally came to realize that their cause was lost. The main Israelite army had only given way before the Benjamites because they were counting on the ambush to make a surprise attack, not because they were afraid. The men in ambush proved worthy of their confidence. With great speed they rushed to attack the city, which apparently had been left unguarded and easily fell into their hands. Everyone found in the city was put to the sword (see under vv. 9, 13). Then, as had been arranged previously with the main army, they set the city aflame so that a great column of smoke rose skyward. This was the signal for the Israelites to stop their retreat (the same signal was used in the battle at Ai, with the important difference that Joshua himself gave the sign for the ambush to make their move; Josh. 8:18).

Although verses 38–39a do not explicitly state that Gibeah was set aflame and that the main Israelite army saw the smoke rising, this is indeed implied by the text.[87] It is therefore a little confusing for the author to return in verse 39b to an earlier point in the battle. The first part of verse 39 implies that the Israelites faced about and took a stand against the pursuing Benjamites (at Baal Tamar, v. 33).[88] The second part of the verse begins a digression, however, in which the author goes back to the beginning of the battle in verse 31. The change in the verb tenses indicates that this digression is a sort of parenthesis, which runs till verse 41a and ends at the same point in the battle as verse 39a. This repetition might seem rather superfluous, but we should note that the author was here describing exactly how the Benjamites came to realize that their cause was lost (v. 36a). Apparently he wanted to bring out

---

[87] Goslinga's translation of verse 39a corresponds to the NASB and NEB: "Then the men of Israel turned in the battle." The translation in the NIV and RSV, "would turn in the battle," clears up the problem he is dealing with—TRANS.

[88] The KJV translation of verse 39a is clearly wrong. The verse is not speaking of the moment when the Israelites were pushed back from Gibeah and began to retreat, for that does not fit here. The turning about in verse 39a has to be the same as that in verse 41a; it is a turning *toward* the Benjamites, not away from them. The use of the perfect tense in verses 39b–41a indicates that this is a parenthesis—TRANS.

how they saw disaster threatening them from both sides. They saw the smoke rising from their city in verse 40, and in verse 41 they saw the men of Israel turn about to attack them. The Benjamite army was thus seized by panic; they were trapped on both sides, and their end was at hand.

20:42–45 *So they fled before the Israelites in the direction of the desert, but they could not escape the battle. And the men of Israel who came out of the towns,[89] cut them down there.[90] 43 They surrounded the Benjamites, chased them and easily overran them in the vicinity of Gibeah on the east. 44 Eighteen thousand Benjamites fell, all of them valiant fighters. 45 As they turned and fled toward the desert to the rock of Rimmon, the Israelites cut down five thousand men along the roads. They kept pressing after the Benjamites as far as Gidom and struck down two thousand more.*

The Benjamites obviously had no choice but to flee at this point. Their enemy was overwhelming them, but they at least had a chance to escape if they could only reach the desert, which stretched eastward from Gibeah toward the Jordan Valley and contained numerous caves and ravines where they could hide. This last hope was thwarted at once, however; for the battle overtook them, and the men who had captured and burned Gibeah rushed on them (see footnote 89). They were surrounded; and whichever way they turned, they were hunted

---

[89] Goslinga emends this to "town" (cf. NEB) and adds the following note:
The Hebrew text has the plural form "towns" here, which makes good sense by itself but is hard to understand in its context. For the battle was fought entirely within the territory of Benjamin, and any towns that the Benjamites passed on their flight would have been their own. Verse 48 thus says that when the Israelites returned, they burned down all the towns that they passed. It is unthinkable that the citizens of these towns would have attacked the fleeing Benjamites. Even if we assume that the towns spoken of did lie in other tribes, their fighting men would have already been in the Israelite army. We also should keep in mind that verse 42 is speaking only of the beginning of the Benjamites' flight. They fled because they were threatened on both sides—by the main Israelite army, and also by the ambush troops that had captured Gibeah and now attacked them from behind (cf. Josh. 8:22). In my view, the end of verse 42 is therefore speaking of the attack of the ambush from the town of Gibeah. The emendation to the singular form, "town," is supported by the Vulgate and accepted by many commentators. The plural form could have arisen through dittography with the first letter (*mēm*) of the following word—TRANS.
[90] The Hebrew literally reads "in his midst." The word "his" has to refer to Benjamin; but this makes no sense, since the Benjamites were rather trapped in the midst of the Israelites. Most translations therefore follow the Septuagint and emend the phrase to "in their midst."

down without being permitted a moment's rest and easily overrun. By the time they had reached a point slightly east of Gibeah, the bulk of the Benjamite army, 18,000 men, lay slaughtered on the field.

Although the Israelites had already won the battle, they still pressed on with the pursuit. A group of Benjamites managed to break through toward the desert in the direction of the rock of Rimmon, a place mentioned by Eusebius, identical to modern Rammun, which lay three or four miles east of Bethel atop a high limestone outcropping. It was situated northeast of Geba, which itself lay northeast of Gibeah.[91] But the Israelites overtook and killed 5,000 of these fugitives along the roads leading there—a mere gleaning compared to the initial slaughter of the 18,000 (cf. v. 45 in the KJV)—and then 2,000 more on the way to Gidom. The location of Gidom is unknown.[92]

20:46–48 *On that day twenty-five thousand Benjamite swordsmen fell, all of them valiant fighters. [47]But six hundred men turned and fled into the desert to the rock of Rimmon, where they stayed four months. [48]The men of Israel went back to Benjamin and put all[93] the towns to the sword, including the animals and everything else they found. All the towns they came across they set on fire.*

Verse 46 repeats the number of fallen Benjamites, here rounded off to 25,000 (cf. v. 35). The total of course would not have been known by counting the corpses but by comparing the size of Benjamin's initially large army to the small number of survivors at the end. Only 600 men were able to escape by reaching the rock of Rimmon, which apparently was an almost inaccessible and impregnable natural stronghold. Instead of going after these survivors, the men of Israel turned back against the civilian population of Benjamin. The entire tribe had to be punished, for they all had taken the side of the men of Gibeah (see vv. 9–13). Old men, women, children, and animals—whatever was found alive—were killed without mercy; and all the towns of Benjamin were set on fire.

---

[91] This shows that the Benjamites, who at first fled eastward (v. 43), turned toward the north.

[92] The Hebrew word might not even be a place name; with a slight change in the vowels, it could be translated "until they had cut down" (cf. NEB).

[93] The Hebrew word here, $m^e t\bar{o}m$, literally means "sound, unhurt, whole." It thus could be translated "entire" or "all" (NASB, NIV), but it often is emended to $m^e t\hat{i}m$, "men, people," a word that appears in a similar context in Deuteronomy 2:34; 3:6. Goslinga accepts this emendation, as do the KJV, RSV, and NEB—TRANS.

3. WIVES FOR THE BENJAMITE SURVIVORS (21:1-25)

Chapter 21 tells how the Israelites came back to their senses after their extraordinarily harsh punishment of the Benjamites and tried to escape the consequences of what they had done. This story, more than the others, provides a clear picture of the hypocritical, almost childish mentality of the people at that time. Afraid to accept the responsibility for their cruel slaughter, they did not turn to God and sincerely confess their guilt. Instead, they tried to save themselves through a subterfuge that seemingly left their oath intact but in reality reduced it to a mere sham. The chapter begins by reporting this oath, which sets the stage for everything that follows.

21:1-4 *The men of Israel had taken an oath at Mizpah: "Not one of us will give his daughter in marriage to a Benjamite."*

² The people went to Bethel, where they sat before God until evening, raising their voices and weeping bitterly. ³ "O LORD, the God of Israel," they cried, "why has this happened to Israel? Why should one tribe be missing from Israel today?"

⁴ Early the next day the people built an altar and presented burnt offerings and fellowship offerings.

The men of Israel had taken an oath at Mizpah that not one of them would give his daughter in marriage to a Benjamite. By this act they had in effect excluded the tribe of Benjamin from the community of Israel and placed it on the same level as the Canaanites (see Deut. 7:3). But when they returned to Bethel after the civil war in chapter 20, it dawned on them that one of the Twelve Tribes was all but missing from Israel. The people at Bethel, who perhaps had gathered there to thank God for His help, were thus overcome by sorrow and grief and sat weeping before the Lord till evening. But their excessive tears seem a little mawkish, since the Israelites showed no awareness of their own guilt. Instead, they demanded an answer from God, as if He was the one who had brought this evil on them. Their grief was completely understandable, but they had no reason to call God to account. If they had been right to punish Benjamin so severely, it was pointless to bemoan the consequences; and if they had been wrong, then they should have humbled themselves instead of indirectly accusing God. Their lament therefore did not bring them an answer, and the next day they could do nothing more than present to the Lord the offerings He deserved for granting them victory.

The fact that the Israelites built a new altar even though Bethel already had one (20:26) shows how grateful they were. Their burnt offerings and fellowship offerings show that they thought their relationship to the Lord was normal and proper, but the offerings were also motivated by the Israelites' desire to propitiate Him and move Him to heal the wound in their nation. They had yet to learn that obedience is better than sacrifice (1 Sam. 15:22).

21:5–9 *Then the Israelites asked, "Who from all the tribes of Israel has failed to assemble before the Lord?" For they had taken a solemn oath that anyone who failed to assemble before the Lord at Mizpah should certainly be put to death.*

⁶ Now the Israelites grieved for their brothers, the Benjamites. "Today one tribe is cut off from Israel," they said. ⁷ "How can we provide wives for those who are left, since we have taken an oath by the Lord not to give them any of our daughters in marriage?" ⁸ Then they asked, "Which one of the tribes⁹⁴ of Israel failed to assemble before the Lord at Mizpah?" They discovered that no one from Jabesh Gilead had come to the camp for the assembly. ⁹ For when they counted the people, they found that none of the people of Jabesh Gilead were there.

A plan had meanwhile been brewing among the leaders, and they decided to see whether there was any way that they could carry it out. They asked the people if any of the tribes had failed to appear at the assembly at Mizpah (20:1–11). Apparently all the Israelites had been obliged to attend this assembly under penalty of death, and a solemn oath had been pronounced in the name of the Lord against any who were absent. The reason for this question appears in verses 6–7, although what the leaders actually intended to do does not come out till verses 10–11. They asked it because they had pity on their brothers, the Benjamites, who had been nearly annihilated in the civil war and would soon die out altogether, since all the survivors were men. The Israelites were thus tormented by the question of how wives could be found for the few men who remained alive. This was a serious problem, since they had sworn to the Lord that none of their daughters would be given in marriage to a Benjamite. They must have secretly regretted this oath, but none of them dared say this openly; and they were even less willing to break it. In hindsight they realized how thoughtless and unnecessary the oath had been. The best course for the Israelites would have been to ask forgiveness for their oath and to pray to the Lord that

---

⁹⁴Literally, "who is the one among the tribes . . . ?" The question makes clear that it could be only one.

He would ignore it.[95] For it was gross insincerity for them to look for a way to provide wives for the Benjamites hiding at Rimmon in spite of what they had sworn.

After this interruption the author returns in verse 8 to the question asked in verse 5. It comes out that no one from Jabesh Gilead had been present at the assembly, even though Gilead as a whole had been well represented (20:1). Their absence was a serious mistake. The Israelites must have discovered it through a careful investigation that was even more rigorous than the muster spoken of in 20:17; for this time they had to determine, not who was present, but who was absent. The name Jabesh is preserved in the Wadi Yabis, a tributary that flows into the Jordan River opposite the site of ancient Bezek (1 Sam. 11:8). Some have identified it with the ruins at ed-Deir, south of the Wadi Yabis.

21:10–14 *So the assembly sent twelve thousand fighting men with instructions to go to Jabesh Gilead and put to the sword those living there, including the women and children. ¹¹"This is what you are to do," they said. "Kill every male and every woman who is not a virgin."[96] ¹²They found among the people living in Jabesh Gilead four hundred young women who had never slept with a man, and they took them[97] to the camp at Shiloh in Canaan.*

¹³Then the whole assembly sent an offer of peace to the Benjamites at the rock of Rimmon. ¹⁴So the Benjamites returned at that time and were given the women of Jabesh Gilead who had been spared. But there were not enough for all of them.

Once the guilt of Jabesh Gilead had been established, the Israelite assembly sent twelve thousand soldiers there with orders to kill the entire population except for the young virgins. It is almost incomprehensible that they could have decided so soon after the slaughter of the Benjamites to massacre their own countrymen without an express command from the Lord. To be sure, they did this because of the oath mentioned in verse 5, but this oath would have applied either to the men alone or to the entire population including the virgins. The exemption of the latter was completely arbitrary,[98] and the Israelites honored one oath only to escape the other.

---

[95] See D. Hoek, *Het boek der Richteren*, p. 476; also Keil and De Graaf.

[96] The Septuagint and Vulgate add at the end of verse 11: "but the virgins you shall let live. And they did this." Although these words are not found in the Masoretic text, they probably represent the original reading. Otherwise the more important, positive part of their task would be left out.

[97] The Hebrew text oddly uses the masculine form of the pronoun here.

[98] See the authors mentioned in footnote 95.

The twelve thousand soldiers carried out their mission, and at Jabesh Gilead they found four hundred virgins, or, as the Hebrew puts it with overstated clarity, "young virgins who had not known a man by lying with a male" (v. 12). The virgins probably were recognizable by their clothing. Since they were brought to Shiloh rather than Bethel, the assembly must have decided beforehand to await the outcome of the soldiers' mission there. Perhaps the ark of the covenant had been moved back to Shiloh because of the approaching festival (v. 19), and the national assembly went with it. In any case the fact that we are not told this directly forms a gap in the story.

Shiloh was the site of the tabernacle, and it was actually the usual place for national assemblies (Josh. 18:1; 21:2; 22:9; it is not clear why it is called "Shiloh in Canaan" here and in the latter two verses, since we know of no other Shiloh). After the virgins had been brought back, a delegation was sent to the six hundred Benjamites, who were still hiding at the rock of Rimmon (20:47 says they stayed there four months), to invite them to return and live in peace among the Israelites. Peace was thus restored, and the Benjamites took as their wives the four hundred virgins from Jabesh Gilead who had been so cruelly deprived of their families.[99] Since there were six hundred Benjamites, however, the women were not enough for all of them.

21:15-19 *The people grieved for Benjamin, because the LORD had made a gap in the tribes of Israel. [16]And the elders of the assembly said, "With the women of Benjamin destroyed, how shall we provide wives for the men who are left? [17]The Benjamite survivors must have heirs," they said, "so that a tribe of Israel will not be wiped out. [18]We can't give them our daughters as wives, since we Israelites have taken this oath: 'Cursed be anyone who gives a wife to a Benjamite.' [19]But look, there is the annual festival of the LORD in Shiloh, to the north of Bethel, and east of the road that goes from Bethel to Shechem, and to the south of Lebonah."*

Different tactics were used to get the two hundred women who were still needed. Some commentators think that verses 15-23 are a separate story that gives a completely different account of how wives were found for the Benjamites than the story in verses 1-14. This supposedly is the reason why verses 15-18 repeat some of the things found in verses 6-7. The repetitions here do in fact indicate that the author had access to two distinct sources, which he used quite liberally. As far as

---

[99]This undoubtedly was one of the reasons why the later Benjamites had such great sympathy for Jabesh Gilead (1 Sam. 11).

we are able to determine, however, neither of these sources was complete; the first told only of the abduction of the four hundred women from Jabesh, and the second did not mention that the Benjamites were brought back from Rimmon. The story in the second source thus presupposed the first (see v. 22), while the first source demanded a sequel.[100] Here again, only the biblical text as we have it contains the full, authentic story; and it is only of secondary interest to hypothesize about how the author got his information on these events, which were already ancient history by his day. Verses 15–18 are not a mere repetition of verses 6–7; they contain much new information.

If we regard chapter 21 as an integral whole, verse 15 means that after the Benjamites had returned and the Israelites saw the abject remnant who still had no hope for descendants, they again were filled with grief and pity "because the LORD had made a gap in the tribes of Israel." The author expressed himself this way only to show how the people saw things (cf. v. 3). The Lord had done it, they thought, but they could not reconcile themselves to the fact and now tried to escape the consequences. Once again they thus confronted the question of verse 7, which the elders now expressed in somewhat different words. The raid on Jabesh Gilead had served its purpose, but it did not provide a full answer. The elders did agree that the few survivors would be recognized as the tribe of Benjamin and allowed to have an inheritance and heirs,[101] but this did not solve the problem created by Israel's destruction of the Benjamite women (chapter 21 thus confirms 20:48 here). The Israelites could not give them their own daughters, for this was forbidden by their oath, which verse 18 repeats in even stronger words than are found in verses 1 and 7.

After their deliberations in verses 16–18, the elders finally found their answer in verse 19. In itself this verse is incomplete, but their full plans come out in their instructions to the Benjamites in verses 20–21. Engaging in the sophistical hairsplitting characteristic of the later rabbis, the elders reasoned that their oath did not forbid them from helping the Benjamite survivors to abduct some Israelite women. The

---

[100] It is therefore groundless for Moore and Gressmann to claim that verses 15–23 are more ancient and the only believable story, whereas verses 1–14 are a pure fiction based loosely on Numbers 31.

[101] They therefore did not intend to divide Benjamin's territory by lot. To this extent the harsh decision of 20:9 (see the comments there) was not carried out against either the tribe as a whole or the town of Gibeah.

annual festival of the Lord at Shiloh presented a perfect opportunity for this. We can only guess as to what festival this was.[102]

There is no obvious reason why the elders should have described the location of Shiloh so precisely, since that is exactly where they were at the time. The Benjamites too would not have needed such a precise description, since they must have been at Shiloh as well. Verse 19b therefore has to be regarded as a later insertion that was put there for the sake of the reader, perhaps to make clear that the proximity of Shiloh to Benjamin's territory made the elders' plan easily feasible.[103] It may have been inserted by the same person who added the temporal clause in 18:30 (see the comments there). Shiloh was identical to modern Seilun and lay slightly east of the road running from Jerusalem, through Benjamin and Bethel (modern Beitin), to Shechem. Northwest of Seilun lies El Lubban, which is identical to ancient Lebonah.

21:20–21 *So they[104] instructed the Benjamites, saying, "Go and hide in the vineyards 21 and watch. When the girls of Shiloh come out to join in the dancing, then rush from the vineyards and each of you seize a wife from the girls of Shiloh and go to the land of Benjamin.*

When the elders had agreed on their plan, they summoned the Benjamites, or at least their representatives, to give them the necessary instructions. Neither of the parties seems to have had any qualms of conscience about using a festival of the Lord for this piece of knavery. The Benjamites who still needed wives were to lie in wait in the vineyards near Shiloh, and when the girls of the city came out to dance, they would each be able to seize one and make a dash for their own territory. The other four hundred Benjamites, who were still in the Israelite camp, undoubtedly intended to help cover their retreat. Since

---

[102] It could have been either the Passover or the Feast of Tabernacles. Keil suspects it was the first, since the girls' dancing seems to have been like the dance of Miriam's companions in Exodus 15:20. The text gives the impression that the festival was at hand when the elders made their decision. Baarslag's claim that it was merely a local harvest festival is groundless (*Verdeeld land*, p. 135).

[103] This implies that the description of Shiloh's location must have been written long after the place was destroyed. Even after its destruction, many Israelites naturally would still have known where Shiloh had been (as can be seen from Jeremiah's words in Jer. 7:12, 14; 26:6, 9). But when the people no longer went to worship there, there also would have been many, especially from the south, who would have needed such a precise description.

[104] The Hebrew consonantal text has the singular here, but the NIV translates "they instructed" following the *Qere* and all the ancient versions.

the Israelites rested from their daily tasks on feast days, the girls were free to amuse themselves outside the city, probably at about the same time each day. One would expect that others would have been watching, but the text is brief here. It also is strange that the elders did not seem to have figured on meeting resistance, not even from the girls themselves, who would be treated almost like cattle. Apparently no one but the daughters of Shiloh took part in the dancing, even though other Israelites undoubtedly came to the festival as well. The citizens of Shiloh alone would suffer the loss—a gross injustice.

21:22–23 *When their fathers or brothers complain to us, we will say to them, 'Do us a kindness by helping them, because we did not get wives for them*[105] *during the war, and you are innocent,*[106] *since you did not give your daughters to them.' "*

[23] *So that is what the Benjamites did. While the girls were dancing, each man caught one and carried her off to be his wife. Then they returned to their inheritance and rebuilt the towns and settled in them.*

The elders naturally expected that the people of Shiloh would complain to them as soon as they found out that their daughters had been abducted. If this happened, they would try to calm the girls' fathers and brothers by pointing out that the latter at least had not broken their oath (as if this would be enough to overcome their complaint!). They would tell them "do us a kindness by helping them [i.e., the Benjamites], because we did not get wives for them during the war."[107] In other words, the elders wanted the citizens of Shiloh to

---

[105] The Hebrew merely has "them" (literally, "each man"), but the verse makes no sense unless this is read "for them." For in the war with Jabesh Gilead, the Israelites were not getting wives for themselves but for the Benjamite survivors.

[106] The Hebrew text is problematic here, and any translation should be regarded as tentative. The Hebrew words, which literally mean "at this time you are guilty," come at the end of verse 22 and are grammatically unconnected to the previous part of the verse. Since a literal translation makes no sense, two main interpretations have been offered: (1) "At this time" is interpreted as "now," and the verse is translated "neither did you give your daughters to them, that you now would be guilty" (Breuer; cf. RSV, NASB); (2) "At this time" is interpreted as "in that case," and the translation reads "in which case you would be guilty" (Bertheau, Keil, Oettli, Schulz, and others [this also is Goslinga's translation—TRANS.]). Although the ancient versions support the Hebrew text, it also is possible to make two minor emendations and translate as follows: "for if [*lû* instead of *lō'*] you had given your daughters to them, then [*kî 'attâ(h)* instead of *kā'ēt*] you would have been guilty." Fortunately there is no real difference of opinion as to the author's meaning.

[107] Verse 22 uses the masculine pronoun where one should expect the feminine: "their fathers," "their brothers." The verb *ḥānan* ("do kindness") is used with a

508

renounce their claim to the girls. They had no intention of pursuing the thieves, since their abduction of the girls was in effect legitimated by the Israelites' slaughter of their own wives and failure to find enough replacements in the war against Jabesh Gilead. The people of Shiloh therefore had no reason to complain. They needed not to fear that they had violated their oath (v. 1), since the girls were stolen by the Benjamites and not freely given to them.

The elders' intended defense was poor indeed. They merely were heaping injustice on injustice, and they did not seem to realize that they were playing a hideous game with the oath they had sworn. However they might look at it, they were responsible for causing Israelite daughters to be given to the Benjamites. Nevertheless they did not show the least concern for this. The Benjamites carried out the plan, which doubtless had been given to them in secret. They captured as many girls as they needed (viz., two hundred)[108] and returned together to their inheritance, where they rebuilt the towns that had been burnt down and resettled them. Since the author does not speak of any resistance on the part of the citizens of Shiloh, we can infer that they did nothing or at least did not cause any serious problems.

21:24-25 *At that time the Israelites left that place and went home to their tribes and clans, each to his own inheritance.*

²⁵ In those days Israel had no king; everyone did as he saw fit.

Verse 24 also shows that everything went smoothly. The national assembly had served its purpose, and everyone could return home. The words "that place" are a little vague; they have to refer primarily to Shiloh, but it is hard to think that the entire Israelite army had been moved there. A great number must have stayed behind at Mizpah to await the end of the Benjamite affair. Finally, they received word that each could return to his tribe, clan, and home. The author ends his book by observing one final time that it was because of the absence of a king that such lawless things could happen in Israel.

The picture of Israel in chapters 17–21 is certainly not inspiring. To

---

double accusative, "us" and "them" (cf. Gen. 33:5; Ps. 119:29). (Because of the irregular use of the pronoun genders, Goslinga also regards the masculine form ʾ ôṯām ["them"] as feminine and translates this "give them to us"; cf. RSV, NASB. He disagrees with the interpretation found in the KJV and NIV, "do us a kindness by helping them [or 'on their behalf']"—TRANS.).

[108]Certainly not six hundred, the number that would have been necessary if Moore's claim that vv. 15–23 is the only plausible story in chapter 21 were true.

be sure, there is no evidence of Baal worship, and the people's sense of national unity remained strong. Nevertheless none of the main characters deserves our undivided sympathy, and no one became the representative of a nation that sincerely feared the Lord. Fortunately there were more pleasant episodes in the period of the judges. In this regard we can point to some parts of Judges 1–16 and, above all, to the beautiful Book of Ruth, examined in the commentary that follows.

Ruth
Introduction

This introduction to the Book of Ruth can be brief. Brevity is a goal of this entire series of commentaries; and the tiny Book of Ruth happily allows this, since it contains no serious problems in either its structure or its content. In reading the introductory remarks in the various commentaries, one continually encounters the same data and points of view. Opinions differ, to be sure, when these data are evaluated, and solutions are offered for the various questions that arise. But it is remarkable that arguments that are decisive for one commentator— e.g., linguistic arguments for determining the book's date—mean nothing to another. Whether a commentator is guided by respect for the biblical tradition or takes a radical (or at least critical) point of view makes a great difference. I will not pretend to shed any new light; and it seems pointless to me to discuss all the views that have been taken, some of which are quite far-fetched. Instead I will confine myself to a simple exposition of what is necessary for a proper understanding of the Book of Ruth. Here again my starting point is the firm conviction that the book is inspired by the Spirit of God and is therefore absolutely trustworthy. Furthermore, it is an account of actual history, forms an organic unity with the other books of the Old Testament canon, and still has a unique position within them.[1]

---

[1] On the main questions, I am in full agreement with the introduction to Ruth in the *Tekst en Uitleg* commentary by G. Smit (*Ruth, Ester en Klaagliederen* [Groningen, 1930]), although he is a little too brief. Smit also gives an extensive list of fine literature, to which I only need add the following: Ph. S. van Ronkel, *Het boek Ruth in Bijbellezingen* (Amsterdam); J. C. Sikkel, *Onder de vleugelen des Heeren* (1921); J. C. de Moor, *Ruth* (Kampen, 1915); M. David, *Het huwelijk van Ruth* (see footnote

I. *Place in the Canon*

To begin with the most external question, there is no consensus on where the Book of Ruth should be placed. In the Septuagint, the Greek translation of the Old Testament, the book is placed after Judges; and this sequence has been preserved in the Vulgate (the Latin translation) and later translations. There are definite indications, however, that this was not the original sequence. As far as we know, Ruth always belonged to the third division of the Hebrew canon, the Writings or *keṯûḇîm*. Judges, in contrast, was put in the second division, the Prophets or *neḇî'îm*. [2]

The position of Ruth within the Writings, however, was not always the same. One of the Talmud tractates puts it at the beginning of the whole division, but in some ancient manuscripts it is merely the first of the five *megillôṯ* or Festival Scrolls. Most commonly, however, Ruth stood second among the Scrolls (i.e., Song of Songs, Ruth, Lamentations, Ecclesiastes, Esther), each of which was read every year in the synagogue at an annual festival or day of commemoration (e.g., Song of Songs at Passover, Ruth at the Feast of Weeks). These differences have only secondary importance. The main thing to notice is that the pure Jewish tradition unanimously puts Ruth in the third part of the Canon,[3] and therefore it did not originally stand between Judges and 1 Samuel. It only came to be inserted there when the Greek translators of the Septuagint rearranged the books of the Old Testament according to a definite historical scheme.

There are a few scholars who think that Ruth originally did stand

---

49 at the end of this commentary). A thorough discussion of all the introductory questions is found in S. Oettli, *Das Buch Ruth* (in Strack and Zöckler's *Kurzgefasster Kommentar*, 1893). Some of my arguments in the pages that follow are borrowed from this book.

[2] The first division was called the Torah (*tôrâ[h]*) or Law and contained only the Five Books of Moses. The second division contained both the Latter and the Former Prophets, i.e., Joshua, Judges, 1 and 2 Samuel, 1 and 2 Kings. The name "Writings" for the third division dates from the third century A.D. The New Testament calls it the Psalms (Luke 24:44), while the Greek name is *Hagiographa* ("sacred writings"). See G. Ch. Aalders, *Bijbels Handboek* (Kampen, 1935), 1:337f.

[3] I do not count Josephus as a witness to this tradition. His totals for the canonical books imply that he put Ruth by Judges, but he was merely following the Septuagint in this. Josephus in turn was followed by Origen and other church fathers. Jerome, however, in his preface to the Book of Daniel, followed the Jewish tradition and included Ruth in the *Hagiographa;* elsewhere he tried to take an intermediate standpoint. See C. F. Keil, *Josua, Richter, und Ruth, Biblischer Kommentar über das Alte Testament*, vol. 3 (Leipzig, 1874), note on p. 383.

where the Septuagint puts it, but the vast majority disagree. In the first place, the correct order of the books was most likely preserved in the Hebrew canon, not in a translation. Furthermore, if Ruth originally stood among the historical books, it would be hard to explain how it could have been moved from there and placed among the more poetic Writings. On the other hand, it is easy to see why the Septuagint would have transferred it from the Writings to its present position between Judges and 1 Samuel; for the content of the book is historical, and the story that it tells took place during the period of the judges (see 1:1). If a historical arrangement is used, there could be no better place to put the book. Therefore there is no need to move the book to another position in our modern translations. Indeed, this could not be done without adopting the Jewish arrangement as a whole. Nevertheless, it is good to keep the original position of the book in mind, since this is our best evidence that Ruth is not a mere appendix to the Book of Judges.[4] In spite of its small size, it has to be regarded as an independent work.

It is worth asking why the Jews included Ruth among the Writings. The answer need not be that the division of the Prophets was already closed when Ruth was written; indeed, we cannot be sure about this

---

[4]This is the view of Bertheau, *Das Buch der Richter und Rut* (Leipzig, 1845), p. 233, and especially of Auberlen, whose article well in *Theologische Studien und Kritiken,* 33 (1860), pp. 536–68, is otherwise well worth reading. According to Bertheau, Ruth is a fragment from a lost writing that was more of a historical novel than an accurate account of history. Auberlen, in contrast, argues on the basis of a close analysis that Ruth and the two appendices to the Book of Judges (chs. 17–21) were designed and written as a single whole, and that all three stories almost certainly came from the same hand. Judges 17–18 was allegedly written in order to expose the roots of the later idol worship in Ephraim, while the purpose of Judges 19–21 was to reveal how Saul was descended from the survivors of a band of criminals and covenant breakers who were only spared out of pity. These two narratives thus contain the prehistory of the aberrant, untheocratic forms of the monarchy that appeared after David (the kingdom of the Ten Tribes) and before him (Saul). Over against this, Ruth gives the prehistory of the true, theocratic monarchy. These observations unquestionably contain a strong element of truth, but it cannot be demonstrated that the author of Judges 17–18 and 19–21 consciously wrote these stories for the reasons given by Auberlen. His purpose was rather to point out the disastrous things that happened because of the absence of a king. Auberlen fails to see this, and his arguments are sometimes quite far-fetched (e.g., he thinks it is significant that when the Danites [18:12–13] and the Levite [19:10–12] left Judah for Ephraim, things went wrong for both). We should remember that the divine Author of Scripture can have purposes beyond those of the human authors, which only become apparent to later readers (see, e.g., footnote 99 on p. 505 of the Judges commentary). This, however, can form no argument against the independence of the Book of Ruth.

(see the next section). But the readers of the book must have perceived at once that it had a unique character that separated it from books like Joshua and Judges. Whereas the narrative there is quite objective, in Ruth it is more subjective and focuses, not on the entire nation, but on what seems to be a single family. The Jews undoubtedly had definite reasons for including Ruth in the Writings, and I offer one suggestion in this regard in footnote 7 on page 515. Very little is known, however, about why exactly they arranged the Canon as they did.[5]

II. *Author and Date*

The question of who wrote the Book of Ruth cannot be given a definite answer. The author does not tell us his name, and the rest of the Bible speaks of him neither directly nor indirectly. However much we might like to know who was responsible for this unusually beautiful writing, we can only grope in the dark. The basis for the Talmud's claim that Samuel authored Judges and Ruth is not known;[6] and since this tradition is hard to reconcile with the end of chapter 4, it is unanimously rejected.

This final part of chapter 4, verses 17–22, sheds some light on the book's date. To begin, we should note that 1:1 sets the events that follow "in the days when the judges ruled." These words show that the author regarded the period of the judges as a time long past. His purpose was to illumine the earlier history of the family of David. He thus tells how at that time in Israel's history a young Moabite woman named Ruth was adopted into a family from Bethlehem and, having herself become a daughter of Abraham through her faith in the God of Israel, later became the great grandmother of David by her marriage to Boaz. His words about David in 4:17 and the genealogy that he adds in 4:18–22 clearly indicate that this was no longer the shepherd boy from the fields of Ephrathah who had been anointed by Samuel. By the time the book was written, David must rather have already become famous as the great theocratic king who enjoyed the Lord's special favor.

It is not impossible that the Book of Ruth was written while David was still alive. More likely, however, it dates from his son Solomon's reign, the "golden age of Israel," when the general peace and prosperity provided ample opportunity for the cultivation of scholarship and the fine arts, and particularly historical research. Solomon

---

[5] See G. Ch. Aalders, *Bijbels Handboek,* 1:340f.
[6] See p. 217 in the preceding commentary on Judges.

may even have played a direct or indirect role in the writing of the book, for it was concerned with the history of his own ancestors. Up till that time, this history had probably only been preserved orally within close family circles, and it could not be allowed to sink into oblivion. The hypothesis that Solomon was somehow involved in the production of the book might seem somewhat bold, but we have every reason to believe that there was a strong impulse during his day to research and preserve in writing the past history of the house of David, which had been so richly blessed by God. And Ruth can best be placed in the time when the splendor of David's reign had not yet fallen under a shadow, thus, "before the decline that set in at the end of Solomon's reign and in the division of the kingdom."[7]

Although the issue must remain in doubt, the objections that have been raised against such an early date for the Book of Ruth are far from convincing. Again and again, one encounters the argument that certain linguistic forms in the book indicate a postexilic date. This argument only has validity, however, if one assumes a priori that a disproportionately large part of the Old Testament was not written till during or after the Exile. It cannot be demonstrated that the linguistic forms in question were not already in use much earlier, and those related to the Aramaic language in particular could have been present centuries before the Exile in dialects. Keil has rightly pointed out that the disputed phrases are always put into the mouths of the book's actors and are not used when the author himself is speaking. This could be a sign that the story is reported very faithfully, almost verbatim.[8]

In my view the claim that 1:1 and 4:7 could only have been written after Deuteronomy (the first because it allegedly presupposes knowledge of the so-called Deuteronomic edition of Judges; the second in view of Deut. 25:9) also has little significance. It certainly has not been established that Deuteronomy was not written before the seventh

---

[7] G. Ch. Aalders, "Ruth," *Christelijke Encyclopedie*, 1st ed., (Kampen: Kok, 1925). The fact that Ruth stands near the Psalms and the Song of Songs in the Hebrew text leads one to suspect that the author was part of the royal household or at least had close connections to it (e.g., as a court prophet). This could be one reason the book was put in this part of the Hebrew canon.

[8] Keil, *Kommentar*, p. 385. The Book of Ruth contains much dialogue, and it is natural to assume that such conversations preserved from the past would contain archaic and dialectical expressions rather than late-Hebrew forms. Outside these conversations virtually the only questionable phrase is *nāśā' nāšîm* in 1:4, but one would have to prove that this was not used before Chronicles. See also the commentaries of Nowack, Bertholet, Oettli, and Keil.

century B.C., a notion that is in utter conflict with the testimony of this genuinely Mosaic (in terms of its content) book. The author does mention in 4:7 a custom that no longer existed in his own day, but this is something quite different from what is found in Deuteronomy 25:9.[9] This verse indeed must have been written long after the events of the book took place; but if we date the book in Solomon's day, the interval of 180 years (which included, among other things, the Philistine oppression) certainly would have been enough time for the custom to have fallen into disuse.

We also need not concern ourselves with the notion that Ruth has to be assigned a much later date because it idealizes the turbulent period of the judges and presents a decidedly unhistorical picture of it. For this "Sturm und Drang" period in Israel's history certainly could have had its peaceful years in which life went on (especially in Judah) in relative tranquility. There is nothing in the book that indicates that its story took place later than the time of the judges. Its style resembles that of the best stories in the books of Samuel and Kings; and in its beauty, simplicity, purity, and power, it fits much better in Israel's early halcyon days than in the arid years after the Exile. Significantly 1 Samuel 22:3 seems to presuppose a knowledge of Ruth, for it makes no attempt to explain why David turned to Moab in his time of need. If the readers of this passage knew about David's family relations with the Moabites from the Book of Ruth, no explanation was necessary. The fact that 1 Samuel contains no genealogy of David (at ch. 16 or elsewhere), while it does contain one of Saul (9:1), points in this same direction. The absence of such a genealogy would be a definite defect in the book unless we assume that its readers were acquainted with Ruth 4:8–22. And since the books of Samuel have to be dated during (or perhaps after) the reign of Rehoboam,[10] Ruth also must have been written early in the monarchical period.

III. *Purpose and Meaning*

The Book of Ruth cannot be considered a polemical or problem piece that distorts the facts in accordance with a preconceived plan or fits them into some controlling scheme. In that case it would be either an

---

[9] According to Gressmann (*Die Schriften des Alten Testaments,* part 1, vol. 2, 2nd ed. [Göttingen, 1922], p. 275), 4:7 proves the opposite, viz., that Ruth is older than Deuteronomy!

[10] See my *Korte Verklaring* on 1 Samuel, 2nd ed. (Kampen: Kok, 1959), pp. 16ff.

edifying sermon or a tract that served some national or party interest, but it would not allow the voice of history to speak for itself. The latter, however, is the clear purpose of the book. Its overall design and especially its conclusion show that its aim was to make known the history of David's ancestors. It discloses the genealogical line by which God's favorite king was descended from the patriarch Judah and, no less, the true piety and nobility that were the marks of his forebears. Since the book's main character is a Moabite who is presented in a very favorable light, we can also discern another purpose. It reveals how even heathendom played a role in the formation of the royal house chosen by God and how this did not put a blemish on David's family, since Ruth, his great grandmother, wholeheartedly accepted the God of Israel and gladly became a member of His chosen people.

This purpose is so evident, even though it is not expressly stated, that one cannot mistake it without simultaneously doing violence to the book. Any attempt to ascribe it another purpose is condemned from the start, since one can only do this either by butchering the text or by denying the book's independence and regarding it as a part of a larger whole. As an example of the first, numerous commentators hold that the genealogy in 4:18–22 was added at a later date. This, however, is like breaking the point off an arrow. It is true that David is mentioned already in 4:17, but the fact that the book's purpose is to tell the history of his ancestors only becomes fully clear in verses 18–22.[11] These verses are not at all a loose appendix that could just as well be missing. Their connection to the preceding material appears, for example, in the fact that the genealogy begins with Perez, whom the elders have spoken of in 4:12. The notion that the Book of Ruth originally formed part of a larger whole remains an unproven hypothesis (see footnote 4, p. 513).

Those who question the book's integrity and separate it from the canon of the Old Testament come to all kinds of dubious conclusions, some of which are mutually contradictory. Some thus suppose that it was written in order to illustrate the importance and desirability of

---

[11] Some think that these verses are an excerpt from 1 Chronicles 2:5–17. If so, however, why did the person who added this excerpt stop with David? One could answer that he was only concerned with David's ancestry, but this purpose could just as well be attributed to the author of the book. To say that this purpose is not prominent enough is foolishness (F. E. Gigot, "Book of Ruth," *The Catholic Encyclopedia*). To return to my above analogy, the point of an arrow is always small, but that does not stop it from being the most important part. One also should not overlook the fact that there is system in the genealogy (see the comments in 4:17–22).

levirate marriage,[12] while others regard precisely those passages that speak of such a marriage as later interpolations.[13] Some read the book simply as an edifying tale of tested and rewarded loyalty without granting it any historical reality.[14] Others think the book's claim that David was descended from a Moabite is indisputable but regard the story merely as a protest against Ezra's and Nehemiah's "rigoristic" stand against marriage with non-Israelites (see Ezra 9 and Neh. 13).[15] I mention this latter view partly because it is the most common one in critical circles and partly because it provides a striking illustration of the amazing conclusions that the critical standpoint leads to and of how it prejudices one's perception of his material and bars the way to good exegesis. The Book of Ruth contains none of the marks of a polemical writing, and there is no conflict at all between the marriage of Boaz and Ruth (who left her nation and her gods and accepted Naomi's people and God) and the divine prohibition that Ezra and Nehemiah held before the people. Such interpretations fail utterly to do justice to the obvious intention of the author.

I have already observed that the purpose of the Book of Ruth is to disclose David's noble ancestry and to show how God did not despise David's pagan great grandmother but graciously admitted her into the line of Judah. This, however, does not exhaust the significance of the book. Like the entire Old Testament, the book has a messianic character, and this comes out particularly in the way it points to David,

---

[12] E.g., Benary, *De Hebreeuwse leviratu* (1835); Bertholet, *Einleitung*, pp. 231f.

[13] Bewer in *The American Journal of Semitic Language and Literature* (1903 and 1904) and *Theologische Studien und Kritik* (1903).

[14] Bertheau already leans this way in *Das Buch der Richter und Rut*, pp. 238f. Köhler goes much further in *Teyler's Theologische Tijdschrift* (1904). The most extreme position is taken by Gressmann (*Die Schriften des Alten Testaments*, pp. 276f.) and Gunkel (*Reden und Aufsätze* [Göttingen, 1913]; "Ruth" in *Religion in Geschichte und Gegenwart* [Tubingen, 1927]), who regard the book as a poetically embellished folk legend. This is quite out of line, since there is no doubt that David was a historical personage.

[15] E.g., Kuenen, Wildeboer, Bertholet, Nowack, Böhl. But this view is opposed by Oettli, Wright (*Encyclopaedia Brittanica*), von Orelli (*Protestantische Realenzyklopädie*), Gigot, Gunkel, Gressmann, and Smit. The fact that this view is almost too arbitrary for its own proponents can be seen in Bertholet's amusing statement that "the meaning that we claim to find in the book can only be discerned with great subtlety" (p. 54). In other words, it almost cannot be found at all. These scholars show so little concern for the problem of how such a book came to be admitted to the Canon that Schulz was led to exclaim: "The inclusion of such a 'protest book' would almost be as strange as the inclusion of Luther's 95 theses in the lawbook of the Catholic church" (*Das Buch der Richter und Ruth* [Bonn, 1926], p. 113).

the preeminent type of Christ.[16] It is necessary to exercise caution here and not to embark on a reckless search for typological discoveries,[17] but we also should not close our eyes to the splendid perspective that is afforded by this tiny but priceless book. Here we see Boaz, the kind redeemer, who raises Ruth from her poor estate and marries her—an obvious image of our Savior, who accepts the unworthy church as His bride and enriches each of her members with the treasures of His grace. As in a shadow, we see how Christ preserves our names from oblivion and ensures that we receive an inheritance in the new earth.[18] We see how heathendom comes into contact with Judaism and finds the way to the Savior of the world, who was not ashamed to count not only Tamar and Rahab but also Ruth among His forebears, because He wanted to be like us in all things (Matt. 1:3, 5).

At the same time the book provides a powerful confirmation of how God watched over His holy line and shows how everything in the Old Testament, even institutions like redemption and levirate marriage, basically pointed to Christ and found their full meaning in His coming. Everything that we read here was "put in writing by the Holy Spirit in order to teach us how God prepared the way for the Messiah's coming, not merely to acquaint us with an interesting story, but to bring us to repentance and strengthen our faith."[19] In the Book of Ruth, we receive an extraordinary revelation of God's wisdom, faithfulness, and grace. It contains a rich proclamation of Christ.

IV. *Literary Form*

The Book of Ruth is neither a product of fantasy nor a mixture of truth and fiction. Nevertheless it clearly is the work of an artist. In its vivid narrative style, its firm control of its material, its masterly drawing of its characters, and its overall organization, it has to be considered one of the most beautiful parts of the Old Testament.

---

[16] See, e.g., Jeremiah 30:9; 33:15; Matthew 12:41–42; Revelation 22:16.

[17] Van Ronkel goes much too far in this; he finds a religious meaning in every feature of the book and thus ends up spiritualizing the story. For example, the field of Boaz is an image of the church, the meal signifies the Lord's Supper, the six measures of barley point to total assurance of faith, the kinsman-redeemer symbolizes the inability of the law to redeem, the handing over of the sandal is like a sacrament, etc.

[18] S. G. de Graaf, *Promise and Deliverance,* tr. H. E. and E. W. Runner, 4 vols. (St. Catharines, Ontario: Paideia, 1978), 2:57–58.

[19] J. C. de Moor, *Ruth,* p. 12.

Herder and Goethe try to outdo one another in extolling the charms of this "village idyll."[20] Commentators unanimously pay tribute to the simplicity and naturalness of its style and to the love and skill with which it depicts its main characters.[21] The entire story glows with a special radiance. It begins so darkly; but through Boaz's intervention the light breaks through more and more brightly on Naomi and her daughter-in-law, who was "better to [her] than seven sons" (4:15). A particularly exquisite stroke is the contrast between the tragic deaths at the beginning of the book and the table of births that ends it, one of the many genealogies in Scripture that form an indispensable link between the primeval promise to the seed of the woman in Genesis 3:15 and its fulfillment in Luke 2.

Here we touch the real beauty of the book, which is more spiritual than literary and lies more in its content than its form, although its noble image is still reflected in the form. The book contains a resounding sermon about God's providence over all things, even the seemingly insignificant products of chance (e.g., 2:3), and tells how things small and great work together in His will. It proclaims how richly He rewards acts of godliness and faith. Yet none of this is stated explicitly; at most, it is hinted at with a few brief strokes. But if the reader perceives this subtle voice of history by reading between the lines, he cannot help but exclaim, "The LORD has done this, and it is marvelous in our eyes" (Ps. 118:23).

The artistic manner in which the book organizes the diverse parts of its story has been pointed out especially by H. Gunkel, who observes that each of the four chapters contains both a main and a secondary scene. He offers the following outline (my captions are not literal translations):

Introduction, 1:1–6

First main scene, 1:7–18—Naomi and her daughters-in-law

First secondary scene, 1:19–22—Naomi's return to Bethlehem

---

[20] Goethe has called it the "loveliest miniature whole that has been preserved for us in epic and idyllic literature" (quoted from Schulz, *Das Buch Richter und Ruth*, p. 114).

[21] Especially Oetti (*Das Buch Ruth*), who also calls attention to the clear portrayals of the secondary figures: the women of Bethlehem (1:19–20; 4:14–15), Boaz's foreman (2:5–6), the kinsman-redeemer (4:3–8). Schulz too praises the book highly. He points out that a relatively large part of it consists of dialogue but says that "there is good reason for this: first, it is about women; second, it concerns a man whose heart is set aflame; third, it tells of a purchase and marriage contract that had to reckon with all kinds of details" (*Das Buch Richter und Ruth*, p. 115).

Second main scene, 2:1–17—Ruth gleans in Boaz's field
Second secondary scene, 2:18–23—light first shines for Ruth and Naomi
Third main scene, 3:1–15—Ruth goes to Boaz on Naomi's advice
Third secondary scene, 3:16–18—Ruth's talk with Naomi
Fourth main scene, 4:1–12—legal transaction
Fourth secondary scene, 4:13–17—conclusion: a son for Naomi[22]
This outline fits so well with the text that we can adopt it completely, with the one difference that 4:18–22 be retained as the conclusion. In both its form and its content, Ruth can thus indeed be called a "rare jewel" among the books of the Bible.

V. *Outline*

A. Ruth the Moabitess Led to Israel (1:1–22)
   1. Introduction: The Death of Elimelech and His Sons in Moab (1:1–6)
   2. Ruth's Return With Naomi and Her Pledge of Fidelity (1:7–18)
   3. Naomi and Ruth's Arrival in Bethlehem (1:19–22)
B. Ruth's Meeting With Boaz (2:1–23)
   1. Gleaning in Boaz's Field (2:1–17)
   2. New Hope for Naomi (2:18–23)
C. Ruth's Request to Boaz for Redemption (3:1–18)
   1. Ruth and Boaz at the Threshing Floor (3:1–15)
   2. Boaz's Answer (3:16–18)
D. Boaz's Marriage to Ruth and the Birth of Obed (4:1–22)
   1. Ruth's Kinsman-Redeemer and Husband (4:1–12)
   2. Boaz the Father of Obed and Forefather of David (4:13–22)

---

[22] Gunkel deletes 4:17b–22; see his article "Ruth" in *Religion in Geschichte und Gegenwart*.

Ruth
Commentary

A. Ruth the Moabitess Led to Israel (1:1–22)

1. INTRODUCTION: THE DEATH OF ELIMELECH AND HIS SONS IN MOAB (1:1–6)

1:1–2 *In the days when the judges ruled, there was a famine in the land, and a man from Bethlehem in Judah, together with his wife and two sons, went to live for a while in the country of Moab. ² The man's name was Elimelech, his wife's name Naomi, and the names of his two sons were Mahlon and Kilion. They were Ephrathites from Bethlehem, Judah. And they went to Moab and lived there.*

The history that is recorded in the Book of Ruth took place "in the days when the judges ruled." The word translated "ruled," *šāpaṭ*, literally means "to judge" (see NIV margin). Here it denotes the unique work of those men who were called by God after the death of Joshua to perform a twofold task: to serve as Israel's commanders in its wars for freedom, and to administer justice and lead the government at home. The judges thus sought to uphold the justice of the Lord both in Israel's domestic life and over against its enemies.[1]

The story of Ruth in all likelihood took place toward the end of the period of the judges, since 4:17 says that Obed was the grandfather of David. David's birth can be dated to 1040 B.C. at the earliest;[2] so Obed must have been born near the end of the twelfth century. The date remains in doubt, however, since it is possible that a generation has been left out between Obed and Jesse in 4:17.[3] The mention of a famine at 1:1 offers little help in this regard. There is no indication that this was

---

[1] See section 5 of the Introduction to the preceding commentary on Judges.
[2] See Van Gelderen, *Bijbels Handboek*, 1:133.
[3] See the comments on this verse.

a result of the Midianite raids in Gideon's day (Judg. 6); more likely is the time described in Judges 10:6–7. In any case, famine generally came on the Promised Land as a special judgment of God against the people's sin (see Deut. 28:15–18). The present famine apparently was not a mere local disaster but affected a large part of Canaan. Otherwise a family from Bethlehem in Judah (there was another Bethlehem in Zebulun, Josh. 19:15) would not have gone so far as to take refuge in the land of Moab, beyond the Jordan and the Dead Sea.

The Israelites apparently were on friendly terms with Moab at that time. They could live there as aliens, a position in which they were not equal to Moabite citizens but still enjoyed certain rights, could practice their religion, and were able to support themselves. The head of this family was Elimelech ("my God is king") and his wife's name was Naomi (*no'°mî* "pleasant"; the name is related to Naamah in 1 Kings 14:21). The meaning of their sons' names, Mahlon and Kilion, is uncertain; nor is it clear which of the two was older, since they appear in the reverse order in 4:9. By calling the family Ephrathites (Ephrathah was the district around Bethlehem, Mic. 5:2), the author emphasizes their pure Israelite descent. The end of verse 2 perhaps contains an element of contrast: in spite of the fact that they were from Ephrathah, they went to Moab and settled there.

1:3–6 *Now Elimelech, Naomi's husband, died, and she was left with her two sons. ⁴They married Moabite women, one named Orpah and the other Ruth. After they had lived there about ten years, ⁵both Mahlon and Kilion also died, and Naomi was left without her two sons and her husband.*

⁶When she heard in Moab that the LORD had come to the aid of his people by providing food for them, Naomi and her daughters-in-law prepared to return home from there.

Elimelech soon died in his adopted home, and Naomi was left behind with her two sons. They did not yet think of returning to Israel; and the sons married Moabite women, one named Orpah and the other Ruth (these non-Hebrew names have been interpreted differently, but they have no real significance for the story). Although marriages to Moabites were not explicitly prohibited, the Israelites had indeed been forbidden to marry Canaanite women to keep them from succumbing to foreign gods (Deut. 7:3–4). Mahlon and Kilion therefore did not disobey the letter of the law, but they did ignore its spirit; for the Moabites too were idol worshipers and had been excluded from the assembly of the Lord (Deut. 23:3). It seems, however, that their wives agreed to worship the

God of Israel (this at least is true of Ruth, but probably of Orpah as well, since she also at first wanted to leave Moab).

Although the domestic life of Naomi's sons did not openly conflict with God's commandments, they also received no blessing. No children were born to them, and approximately ten years after Elimelech had left Bethlehem, Mahlon and Kilion both died at about the same time. Naomi thus was virtually alone in a foreign land. One should expect that her daughters-in-law would have wanted to stay there and that their ties to her would have grown weaker, especially if they remarried. In addition, Naomi's heart yearned for her own people and the home of her youth. She received news that the Lord had come back to His people and made Canaan's soil fruitful again. Everything was telling her to leave Moab, and her two daughters-in-law at first went with her. The Hebrew verb translated "return" in verse 6 is singular, and strictly speaking it here applies only to Naomi (cf. KJV). Nevertheless, in later verses it is applied more broadly to all three women (v. 7, "take them back"; vv. 10, 22 [cf. KJV]).

2. RUTH'S RETURN WITH NAOMI AND HER PLEDGE OF FIDELITY (1:7–18)

1:7–10 *With her two daughters-in-law she left the place where she had been living and set out on the road that would take them back to the land of Judah.*

8 Then Naomi said to her two daughters-in-law, "Go back, each of you, to your mother's home. May the LORD show kindness to you, as you have shown to your dead and to me. 9 May the LORD grant that each of you will find rest in the home of another husband."

Then she kissed them and they wept aloud 10 and said to her, "We will go back with you to your people."

Naomi's two daughters-in-law not only escorted her from Moab; they wished to accompany her all the way to Judah and stay with her there. But Naomi sought to dissuade them from this in their own interest. Realizing how difficult it would be for the Moabite women to make their home in Israel, she stopped on the road and told them kindly but firmly to return, each to the house of her mother. That she spoke of their mothers rather than their fathers, even though Ruth's father was still alive (2:11), is not unusual; the young widows belonged with other women, and they naturally would have first sought comfort with their mothers. She then wished them the kindness of the Lord her God, who reigned also in Moab. In particular, she expressed the hope that they each would find security in the home of a new husband. But when Naomi kissed Orpah and Ruth good-by, they began to weep loudly and protested that they would not let her go on alone but wanted to return with her to her people.

1:11–13 *But Naomi said, "Return home, my daughters. Why would you come with me? Am I going to have any more sons, who could become your husbands? ¹²Return home, my daughters; I am too old to have another husband. Even if I thought there was still hope for me—even if I had a husband tonight and then gave birth to sons— ¹³would you wait until they grew up? Would you remain unmarried for them? No, my daughters. It is more bitter for me than for you, because the LORD's hand has gone out against me!"*

Naomi refused to change her mind. However comforting the deep love and fidelity of the young women may have been to her, she could not allow herself to be swayed by her feelings. As a woman of greater maturity, she considered it her duty almost to compel her daughters-in-law to go back to their own people. She might also have reflected that it would be easier for her to live alone in Bethlehem than to provide for three persons; but if so, she said nothing about this. Her arguments were concerned solely with the possibility of new marriages for Orpah and Ruth. She herself was done with life, but they still could find fulfillment with a husband and family. But if they wanted this, they should not go with her, since she had no other sons to replace Mahlon and Kilion.

The basis for Naomi's argument here was the Israelite practice of levirate marriage, which had existed as a custom long before it became a legal requirement (Deut. 25:5–6; cf. Gen. 38:6–11). If a man died childless, his brother had to marry the widow in order to produce offspring for him. The first-born son of such a marriage was then considered the child of the deceased brother (see the comments in 3:1). For Naomi nothing would have been better than to preserve the line of her husband this way; but, alas, such a route was closed to her, and the ancient Israelite custom offered no hope. She examined all the possibilities. She had no more sons in her womb who could become husbands for Ruth and Orpah. She was too old to have another husband of her own (literally, "to be for a husband"). Even if she clung to an impossible hope for a husband—indeed, even if she had intercourse or gave birth to sons that very night—she could not expect her daughters-in-law to wait for them to grow up and "remain unmarried" for them. The Hebrew verb here literally means "stay withdrawn," i.e., lead a life of strict isolation (like Tamar, Gen. 38:11); although it appears nowhere else in the Old Testament, its meaning is clear from the cognate Aramaic term.

The only hope for Orpah and Ruth was in their homeland of Moab (Naomi apparently had no hope at all that the Moabite widows could marry other Israelite men). She therefore insisted that they go back, saying that it was extremely bitter to her for their sake that the hand of the Lord had gone out against her.[4] The latter words refer to Naomi's harsh lot in life, which to her formed proof that the Lord did not look favorably on her. The death of her husband and two sons showed that their emigration to Moab had not been in accordance with His will. Of this she was well aware, and it was her deepest sorrow. But it grieved her also that her daughters-in-law had been afflicted by her fate. If they were to leave her then, her sorrow would be lightened in at least one respect; she would be free of the painful thought that they had to share in her bitter judgment.

1:14–18 *At this they wept again. Then Orpah kissed her mother-in-law goodbye, but Ruth clung to her.*

[15]"Look," said Naomi, "your sister-in-law is going back to her people and her gods. Go back with her."

[16]But Ruth replied, "Don't urge me to leave you or to turn back from you. Where you go I will go, and where you stay I will stay. Your people will be my people and your God my God. [17]Where you die I will die, and there I will be buried. May the LORD deal with me, be it ever so severely, if anything but death separates you and me." [18]When Naomi realized that Ruth was determined to go with her, she stopped urging her.

Orpah finally was persuaded by Naomi's words, and she kissed her mother-in-law good-by amid a flood of tears. Ruth still "clung" to Naomi, however. The author here uses a graphic verb meaning "hold fast, stick, cling to"; in Genesis 2:24 it is translated "united," but here it should be taken literally. The widow of Mahlon thus showed that she was willing to stay with her mother-in-law at any cost. Naomi's love for Ruth still led her to deny her own interests. She tried a third time to persuade her daughter-in-law to return, this time by pointing to the

---

[4]Goslinga follows Oettli and others in rejecting the translation of verse 13 found in the NIV, "it is more bitter for me than for you" (cf. also the NASB and NEB). According to him, this does not fit the context, since Naomi was not concerned to arouse pity for herself by calling her lot the most grievous. His translation thus corresponds to the KJV and RSV: "it is exceedingly bitter to me for your sake"— TRANS.

example of Orpah, who in the end was unwilling to exchange her people and her gods (the two went together; cf. v. 16) for a life in Bethlehem.

Ruth, however, remained immovable. Naomi's arguments were no match for the firm resolve and the unswerving loyalty of the Moabite widow, who revealed the nobility of her soul in a moving response of sublime poetic beauty. She absolutely refused to bend before her mother-in-law's pressure and bound her fate to Naomi's for all time, assuring her that she would remain with her in life and in death. The heart of her answer (which was far more sublime than the common protest of Orpah and Ruth in v. 10) came when she made her life decision at the end of verse 16: "Your people will be my people and your God my God." Here she revealed that she did not have a merely human desire to return with Naomi to a foreign people but regarded her mother-in-law's nation as her own and felt bound to her God in the depths of her heart. The knowledge of this God that she had gained during her marriage had not been something superficial and external; it had deepened into a personal bond of love of which she only now became fully conscious.

To show how serious she was, Ruth swore by the name of the Lord with a type of oath that was found only in Israel (see 1 Sam. 3:17; 25:22; 1 Kings 2:23). Such an oath, which may have originally been accompanied by certain signs or ceremonies, was actually a self-malediction in which the speaker invoked the wrath of the Lord on himself if he should prove unfaithful to the solemn condition that followed it. Ruth thus swore that nothing short of death would separate her from Naomi. Naomi was reduced to silence. She finally realized how deadly earnest Ruth was in her determination to go with her; so she stopped urging her to return to Moab.

3. NAOMI AND RUTH'S ARRIVAL IN BETHLEHEM (1:19–22)

1:19–21 *So the two women went on until they came to Bethlehem. When they arrived in Bethlehem, the whole town was stirred because of them, and the women exclaimed, "Can this be Naomi?"*

20 "Don't call me Naomi," she told them. "Call me Mara, because the Almighty has made my life very bitter. 21 I went away full, but the LORD has brought me back empty. Why call me Naomi? The LORD has afflicted me; the Almighty has brought misfortune upon me."

Naomi and Ruth continued the journey to Bethlehem together. When they arrived, Naomi was recognized at once; but the misfortunes she had suffered had changed her appearance so much that the entire town asked in astonishment and pity, "Can this be Naomi?" The gender of the pronoun indicates that it was particularly the women of Bethlehem who asked this. Alluding to the auspicious meaning of her name ("pleasant"), she answered that they should not call her Naomi but Mara ("bitter"), because the Almighty had bitterly afflicted her. The world "Almighty" in verses 20–21 is a translation of the ancient divine name Shaddai (see Gen. 17:1 NIV margin).

Reading between the lines, one can gather that Naomi had not yet fully reconciled herself to God's will. She realized that she must submit to it, but it was not easy for her to accept. She had left Bethlehem "full" (i.e., rich), not in material wealth, but in the company of her husband and sons; but the Lord brought her back destitute. He Himself had afflicted her or testified against her (see NIV margin; the same phrase is used in Exod. 20:16) and declared her guilty. Someone who has forfeited the Lord's grace this way could no longer be called "pleasant."

1:22 *So Naomi returned from Moab accompanied by Ruth the Moabitess, her daughter-in-law, arriving in Bethlehem as the barley harvest was beginning.*

Naomi's bitter words underestimated the treasure that God had given to her in the love of her daughter-in-law Ruth.[5] The author corrects her oversight by mentioning Ruth at this point, and he adds another remark that contains a subtle hint that the Lord would soon lighten her burden in another way. The barley harvest was just beginning, which marked the start of the harvest season in general; so Naomi would have no lack of food. Day was beginning to dawn for her.

---

[5] The Hebrew text of verse 22 remarkably says that Ruth returned (literally, "the returning") from the country of Moab (see RSV). Was the author here divulging one of the central themes of his book by implying that Ruth, the pagan, returned to the one true God? I see no better explanation; and if the author had not meant this, he could have omitted the words entirely.

B. Ruth's Meeting With Boaz
(2:1-23)

1. GLEANING IN BOAZ'S FIELD (2:1–17)

2:1 *Now Naomi had a relative on her husband's side, from the clan of Elimelech, a man of standing, whose name was Boaz.*

The author interrupts his story to make a brief statement about Naomi's relationship to Boaz, one of the main characters in the book. The name Boaz probably means "in him is strength," though this actually presupposes the spelling Booz, the form of the name found in the Septuagint and Vulgate (see KJV of Matt. 1:5). There is another derivation of the name that would give it the meaning "fiery." Boaz is portrayed as a "man of standing," literally, "mighty in wealth," which no doubt refers mainly to his property holdings. He was a relative of Naomi's husband Elimelech and thus came from his clan.

The Hebrew term translated "relative" actually means "kinship," but here it has the concrete sense of "kinsman" (compare the use of the English word "relation"). We can infer from it that Boaz did not belong to Elimelech's immediate family. All this information has great importance for our understanding of Naomi's position and the remarkable train of events that follows.

2:2–3 *And Ruth the Moabitess said to Naomi, "Let me go to the fields and pick up the leftover grain behind anyone in whose eyes I find favor."*
Naomi said to her, "Go ahead, my daughter." ³ So she went out and began to glean ⁶ in the fields behind the harvesters. As it turned out, she found herself working in a field belonging to Boaz, who was from the clan of Elimelech.

These remarkable events appear at once when Ruth first went out to the fields. She was not ashamed to perform the most menial labor to earn her keep, and she therefore asked Naomi's permission to follow the reapers and glean among the ears of grain that they left behind. It would be an overstatement to call such gleaning a *right* of the poor in Israel. The Mosaic law merely instructed the owners of land not to harvest their fields too carefully but to leave something behind for the poor and the alien (Lev. 19:9–10; 23:22; Deut. 24:19). But the custom could easily have arisen for the harvesters to allow needy persons to follow them and, as it were, gather the "crumbs that fell from the

---

⁶Literally, "and came and gleaned"; "in the fields" goes with both verbs.

table" (Luke 16:21).[7] One could thus perhaps call this a customary right.

Ruth wished to take advantage of this right but said that she would only do so if she were allowed to by someone "in whose eyes I find favor." Verse 7 shows that she politely asked the foreman for permission. After receiving Naomi's consent, she went out and "by chance" found herself in a field belonging to Boaz. The words "as it turned out" (the same Hebrew phrase appears in 1 Sam. 6:9) are not a denial of God's providence but merely mean that Ruth was not acting deliberately.

2:4–7 *Just then Boaz arrived from Bethlehem and greeted the harvesters, "The Lord be with you!"*

"The Lord bless you!" they called back.

[5] *Boaz asked the foreman of his harvesters, "Whose young woman is that?"*

[6] *The foreman replied, "She is the Moabitess who came back from Moab with Naomi. [7] She said, 'Please let me glean and gather among the sheaves behind the harvesters.' She went into the field and has worked steadily from morning till now, except for a short rest in the shelter."* [8]

Boaz himself traveled from Bethlehem to his field somewhat later in the morning (see v. 7). The greetings that he and his harvesters exchanged show that they were on very friendly terms with one another (similar greetings are found in Judg. 6:12 and Ps. 129:8). Boaz was a model of the God-fearing Israelite who took his social responsibilities seriously. When he saw the foreigner working in his field, he asked the servant in charge of his hired men about her and received a lengthy and very favorable report. The foreman was especially struck by Ruth's modesty and great diligence. Following behind the harvesters, she had

---

[7] A survey of the Mosaic laws pertaining to the poor can be found in W. A. van Es, *De eigendom in den Pentateuch* (Kampen: Kok, 1909), pp. 359ff.

[8] The final words of verse 7 are unclear in the Hebrew. One could translate them literally, "her rest at home was short" (cf. KJV), but this makes no sense since Ruth had not gone home at all. The word *bayit* ("home, house") is extremely difficult to deal with (the NIV translates it "shelter"—TRANS.), and it easily could have been accidentally added to the text as a dittograph of the preceding word. The Septuagint and Vulgate may offer a solution. Their translation assumes the negation *lo'* at the beginning of the phrase and repoints the verb (they also have "in the field" instead of "at home" or "in the shelter," but this seems to be a mere conjecture), which changes the meaning to "without a moment's rest in the field" (cf. RSV, NEB). This reading perhaps should be adopted (omitting "in the field"), since it fits so well in the context.

gleaned the entire morning without permitting herself a moment's rest (see footnote 8).

2:8–9 *So Boaz said to Ruth, "My daughter, listen to me. Don't go and glean in another field and don't go away from here. Stay here with my servant girls. ⁹Watch the field where the men are harvesting, and follow along after the girls. I have told the men not to touch you. And whenever you are thirsty, go and get a drink from the water jars the men have filled."*

Boaz, who had already heard many good things about Ruth (v. 11) but did not yet know her by sight, spoke to her kindly. His words "my daughter" show that he must have been a middle-aged man (see also 3:10). He told her never to go and work in another field (probably for the same reason that Naomi gave in v. 22, and also because he wanted to help her) and also not to depart and stop her gleaning. Instead, she should attach herself to his servant girls who bound the grain into sheaves, not to help them, but so that she would be in a better position to watch the field and gather what she needed; for the servant girls followed directly behind the harvesters. She needed not fear his hired men, for he had ordered them (probably through his foreman) not to touch her. Boaz also gave Ruth permission to drink water from the jars that had been provided for his workers. He thus did everything he could to make her feel welcome and showed his respect for her diligent efforts to provide for her own support.

2:10–13 *At this, she bowed down with her face to the ground. She exclaimed, "Why have I found such favor in your eyes that you notice me—a foreigner?" ¹¹Boaz replied, "I've been told all about what you have done for your mother-in-law since the death of your husband—how you left your father and mother and your homeland and came to live with a people you did not know before. ¹²May the Lord repay you for what you have done. May you be richly rewarded by the Lord, the God of Israel, under whose wings you have come to take refuge."*

¹³"May I continue to find favor in your eyes, my lord," she said. "You have given me comfort and have spoken kindly to your servant—though I do not have the standing of one of your servant girls."

Astonished at Boaz's kindness, Ruth bowed to the ground and humbly asked why she had found such favor in his eyes. She was a mere foreigner and was no different from anyone else. There is a minor play on words here in that the Hebrew terms translated "notice me" and "foreigner" resemble each other; a rough English equivalent would be "respect a reject." Boaz's answer reveals that she had earned his deepest respect by all that she had done for her mother-in-law Naomi. In leaving her family and her native land for an unknown nation, she had done the same thing that God had commanded Abraham. Boaz did not mention Abraham here, but his words have rightly been regarded as an allusion to Genesis 12:1 (v. 12 similarly is reminiscent of Gen. 15:1).

Ruth already had shown that she was a daughter of Abraham; so Boaz generously wished her the blessing of Abraham's God. He beautifully described her arrival in Bethlehem as a "coming to take refuge under the wings of the LORD, the God of Israel," words that are reminiscent of the image of the eagle in Exodus 19:4 and Deuteronomy 32:11. We can see Boaz's profound joy at the fact that a Moabite had turned to the true God and his confidence that Ruth's hopes would not be deceived. Ruth then commended herself to Boaz's good will (v. 13), using exactly the same words that Jacob had said to Esau in Genesis 33:15, and humbly thanked him for his kind and comforting words. In her own eyes she was not even equal to his servant girls.

2:14–17 *At mealtime Boaz said to her, "Come over here. Have some bread and dip it in the wine vinegar."*

When she sat down with the harvesters, he offered her some roasted grain. She ate all she wanted and had some left over. [15] *As she got up to glean, Boaz gave orders to his men, "Even if she gathers among the sheaves, don't embarrass her.* [16] *Rather, pull out some stalks for her from the bundles and leave them for her to pick up, and don't rebuke her."*

[17] *So Ruth gleaned in the field until evening. Then she threshed the barley she had gathered, and it amounted to about an ephah.*

Boaz's words were no mere pious wish. At mealtime he called Ruth back from her work and invited her to eat with him and his harvesters and servant girls, a favor that doubtless was not often granted to women gleaners. The meal consisted of bread and vinegar diluted with wine, a drink that is still today used as a thirst-quencher in the Near East. Pieces of bread were broken off and dipped into the wine vinegar. Boaz even treated Ruth as his equal by personally giving her some roasted kernels of grain, a tasty side-dish. So generous was he that she ate her fill and had some left over. His kind treatment of her thus not only made her feel like an honored guest but increased her intake that day. Ruth nevertheless maintained her modesty. She did not take a prominent seat but ate alongside the harvesters; and as soon as she was done, she went back to look for more grain.

Boaz granted Ruth yet another privilege. He told the harvesters to let her glean among the sheaves. Thus she not only could work where the harvest was finished but was also allowed to gather where the stalks were still on the ground and were just being bound together. No one was permitted to take offense at this. Instead, the harvesters were told to encourage her by pretending to leave some of the stalks behind inadvertently so that she could pick them up, and they were not to rebuke her for this. Boaz thus resorted to a sly but friendly trick to give Ruth an occasional bonus, without letting her know that it was his doing. As a result she gathered an exceptionally large amount for one day. After she had beaten out the grain with a stick at evening (cf. Judg. 6:11), the total came to about an ephah of barley, i.e., twenty to twenty-two liters by the latest reckoning.

2. NEW HOPE FOR NAOMI (2:18–23)

2:18–20 *She carried it back to town, and her mother-in-law saw how much she had gathered. Ruth also brought out and gave her what she had left over after she had eaten enough.*

¹⁹ *Her mother-in-law asked her, "Where did you glean today? Where did you work? Blessed be the man who took notice of you!"*

Then Ruth told her mother-in-law about the one at whose place she had been working. "The name of the man I worked with today is Boaz," she said.

²⁰ *"The LORD bless him!" Naomi said to her daughter-in-law." He has not stopped showing his kindness to the living and the dead." She added, "That man is our close relative; he is one of our kinsman-redeemers."*

Ruth lifted her load to her shoulders and returned home. Naomi was astonished when she saw how much Ruth had gathered, and Ruth also handed her the leftovers from her meal (literally, "from her satiety"). Naomi asked her daughter-in-law where she had gleaned; and before learning the answer, she pronounced a blessing on the man who had so richly favored her. Ruth then revealed the name of her benefactor. The man was not unknown to Naomi, and she could not suppress her joy when she realized that the merciful hand of God was behind this. Once again she blessed Boaz, but her words became even more exultant when she praised the Lord for His kindness to the living and the dead. Once she thought that His mercy had left her (1:13, 20–21), but now she saw that He had remembered both her and Ruth (the living), and Elimelech and his sons (the dead) by caring for their widows.

It was because of the Lord's goodness and faithfulness that Ruth met Boaz and made such a favorable impression on him. Boaz was a close relative, one of their kinsman-redeemers. Naomi mentioned this so that Ruth would understand her joy, and we can only guess what thoughts and plans began to enter Naomi's mind at this point. Apparently she had already considered the possibility of getting help through the law of redemption, but she had not yet investigated who the nearest kinsman-redeemer would be (see 3:12; 4:3). "Kinsman-redeemer" is the best translation for the Hebrew term *gō'ēl* when the uniquely Israelite practice of redemption is spoken of. The word "kinsman" alone (cf. KJV, RSV, NEB) is too general.

2:21–23 *Then Ruth the Moabitess said, "He even said to me, 'Stay with my workers until they finish harvesting all my grain.' "*

²²Naomi said to Ruth her daughter-in-law, "It will be good for you, my daughter, to go with his girls, because in someone else's field you might be harmed."

²³So Ruth stayed close to the servant girls of Boaz to glean until the barley and wheat harvests were finished. And she lived with her mother-in-law.

Instead of asking what Naomi meant by this, Ruth went on to tell how Boaz's kindness guaranteed that they would have food for the time being. With excitement in her voice, she told her mother-in-law about his promise to her in verses 8–9. The word "workers" refers to all his personnel, both men and women. The Hebrew words that are used emphasize Boaz's ownership of "my workers" and "my grain" (v. 21); in other words, among all that Boaz owned, Ruth also had a place. Naomi rejoiced in this news and advised Ruth to take advantage of Boaz's kindness. In another field she could receive harsh treatment, which must have happened often in view of Boaz's words in verses 9 and 15–16.

The final verse of chapter 2 summarizes Ruth's life for the next three months. Every day she gleaned in Boaz's fields, first in the barley harvest and then in the wheat harvest. She lived faithfully with her mother-in-law, and there were no changes in her daily routine.

C. Ruth's Request to Boaz for Redemption
(3:1-18)

1. RUTH AND BOAZ AT THE THRESHING FLOOR (3:1-15)

3:1-4 *One day Naomi her mother-in-law said to her, "My daughter, should I not try to find a home for you, where you will be well provided for? ²Is not Boaz, with whose servant girls you have been, a kinsman of ours? Tonight he will be winnowing barley on the threshing floor. ³Wash and perfume yourself, and put on your best clothes. Then go down to the threshing floor, but don't let him know you are there until he has finished eating and drinking. ⁴When he lies down, note the place where he is lying. Then go and uncover his feet and lie down. He will tell you what to do."*

Naomi next took the initiative. A plan had been ripening in her mind, and she had contemplated it from all angles and carefully considered how best to carry it out. Once the harvest season had ended, she presented it to Ruth. The questioning form of her words implies that she could not have been expected to act otherwise. Her plan, in short, was to find a husband for her daughter-in-law. The Hebrew phrase translated "find a home" (v. 1) literally means "find rest" (cf. 1:9), i.e., a place where Ruth would have a secure future. But Naomi did not intend for her to act rashly or dishonorably but in accordance with the Israelite custom that was sanctioned by the Mosaic law.

Ruth had an obligation to preserve the line of Elimelech from extinction, if possible, by entering into a levirate marriage. This gave her a certain right to demand that the appropriate member of the family marry her, for male relatives had obligations in regard to a childless widow. The law stated that this obligation rested exclusively on one of the brothers of the deceased man (Deut. 25:5-6; cf. Matt. 22:23-24), although the brother was in fact allowed to decline (Deut. 25:7-10). In Naomi's time, however, it seems that the custom had greater latitude than the law. Apparently it extended the obligation—although this was not absolutely binding—to the nearest relatives if there were no brothers (see 4:5-6). In the present case the obligation rested on Ruth and one of the members of Elimelech's clan.

Naomi also was guided by another thought. Because of her poverty she could demand help under the law of redemption. This right to redemption, which will be dealt with further in chapter 4, imposed a duty on more than a person's immediate brothers (see Lev. 25:23-28). Naomi thus asserted two rights simultaneously: the right to redemption and the right to a levirate marriage. We need not ask whether there had been any precedent for this combination.[9] It certainly could not have been a binding rule, but chapter 4 shows that Naomi's action aroused no public disapproval. Naomi could assert these two rights only through Ruth, of course, since she herself was too old to marry (1:12). Since Boaz was a kinsman-redeemer and had already shown great kindness to Ruth, he was the obvious answer to her hope for someone who would perpetuate Elimelech's line and keep the family estate intact.

Naomi thus wanted Ruth to go to Boaz to remind him both of his obligation as a kinsman-redeemer and of his calling to keep alive the line of Elimelech.[10] Her instructions to her daughter-in-law place more emphasis on the latter aim, but Ruth's words in verse 9 show that Naomi also had the former in mind.[11] Ruth may have regarded Boaz mainly as a wealthy landowner, but Naomi explicitly pointed out that he was a kinsman to whom they could make a legitimate appeal for help. She then told her daughter-in-law that Boaz was planning to winnow barley on the threshing floor that very night (i.e., from evening into the night).

Grain was winnowed after it was threshed. After it had been beaten from the stalks and lay mixed with the chaff on the threshing floor, the two were thrown upward with the winnow; and the chaff was blown away by the evening wind, leaving only the grain behind. This work seems to have been done by the landowner himself, who then would sleep the night on the threshing floor (a large, open area where the ground had been stamped hard) to guard his harvest. One would expect that Boaz would have been winnowing wheat; but it appears that the entire harvest, both barley and wheat (2:23), was gathered before the winnowing was begun.

Ruth needed to present herself to Boaz as a relative seeking her rights, not as a destitute gleaner; so Naomi told her to wash and perfume herself and to put on her best clothing. Then she was to go down from the town to the threshing floor and hide herself there. When Boaz had finished his meal and had lain down to sleep, she was to approach him silently and lie down at his feet under the tip of his

---

[9] Keil claims this was an established custom (*Kommentar*, pp. 395f.), but 4:5 does not say this.

[10] See footnote 18 on p. 540 and the note at the end of the book.

[11] The same thing comes out in 4:3–4. Chapter 3 does not explicitly mention the property transaction, but Naomi and Ruth certainly must have spoken about this; and Ruth must have told Boaz.

blanket. This act had a symbolic meaning. By sharing the same blanket with Boaz, Ruth made known that she was claiming the place of his wife; but her position at his feet signified that she did not yet have that status. Before that could happen, Boaz himself had to acknowledge her right.[12] Naomi probably also told Ruth what to say, but the most important thing was that she listen to Boaz's advice. As an upright Israelite with a sincere respect for justice and law, he certainly would know the right thing to do.

Naomi no doubt had considered the possibility that Boaz would decline Ruth's request. So she made sure the meeting occurred at a time and place where no one would see them. That way his potential refusal would remain a secret, and the good names of Ruth and Boaz would not fall into disrepute.

3:5–6 *"I will do whatever you say," Ruth answered. 6 So she went down to the threshing floor and did everything her mother-in-law told her to do.*

With a few brief words, Ruth promised to follow her mother-in-law's instructions exactly. She willingly accepted the obligations that were placed on her by Israelite law and custom. Her prompt decision speaks well of her. So noble was she that she could approach Boaz in this manner without compromising her virtue. And she was well aware that Naomi would not ask her to do anything that would offend her womanly honor, just as she trusted that Boaz would not treat her disrespectfully. A widow left without her natural guardian had no choice but to use an unusual method if she wanted to lay claim to her rights.

Naomi's advice and Ruth's behavior might strike us as somewhat scandalous and risky, but our feelings cannot be the criterion here. Commentators have rightly pointed out that we have to look first to the reactions of the persons involved; Boaz did not despise Ruth for what she did but respected her all the more (v. 10).[13] The moral standards of the Bethlehemites must have been lofty indeed if Naomi and Ruth could have acted this way without tarnishing anyone's conscience. What an exalted commentary on the hearts and lives of Boaz and Ruth, ancestors of our Savior! Ruth thus went down to the threshing floor and did precisely as her mother-in-law had told her.

---

[12] This is roughly De Moor's view (*Ruth*, p. 82).

[13] See, e.g., De Moor, *Ruth*, p. 78, and also the commentaries of Keil and Schulz.

3:7-9 *When Boaz had finished eating and drinking and was in good spirits, he went over to lie down at the far end of the grain pile. Ruth approached quietly, uncovered his feet and lay down.* [8] *In the middle of the night something startled the man, and he turned and discovered a woman lying at his feet.*

[9] *"Who are you?" he asked.*

"I am your servant Ruth," she said. "Spread the corner of your garment over me, since you are a kinsman-redeemer."

The Lord's blessing was with Naomi and Ruth, for the plan started off well. Ruth managed to approach Boaz undetected. Boaz fell asleep at once; but in the middle of the night he was startled (the verb literally means "he trembled, shuddered"), perhaps by an inadvertent movement of Ruth, and woke up. He turned over,[14] sat upright, looked and felt about him, and discovered a woman lying at his feet. Apparently it was not completely dark under the clear sky. He asked who she was; and Ruth immediately told him, again with becoming modesty. She then made a request that clearly revealed her intentions, even though her words were utterly respectful. She called herself Boaz's servant; but since she belonged to him, she had the right to appeal to him for help. Actually she did more than this, for her humble command was a veiled request that he marry her.

No unseemly word passed Ruth's lips. On the contrary, Boaz must have heard in her response an echo of his former blessing in which he spoke of the wings of the Lord. The Hebrew noun translated "corner of garment" in verse 9 is the same word that is translated "wings" in 2:12. If the correct translation is "garment" or "skirt" (NIV, KJV, RSV), Ruth's request was even more direct—"marry me, let me share your covering"[15]—but her further words, "you are a kinsman-redeemer," argue for the translation "spread your wing over me" (this is how Goslinga translates v. 9—TRANS.). Ruth thus informed Boaz of his obligation to redeem her, which was placed on him both by popular custom and, more importantly, by divine law. This obligation, however, did not demand that he marry her. None of the laws pertaining to redemption spoke of such a duty, and the law concerning levirate marriage did not use the word "redeem."[16] A redeemer was someone

---

[14] This verb (v. 8) is often translated "bent forward" (see NASB); but in Job 6:18, its only other occurrence in the Old Testament, it means "turn aside." The same meaning could apply to someone who rolls over on awaking.

[15] See G. Smit, *Ruth (Tekst en Uitleg)*, p. 28.

[16] H. Visscher's notion that there was a law of redemption that instructed the redeemer to marry is therefore groundless (*In Israel vermaard* [Kampen: Kok, 1911] pp. 250f.). De Moor takes a similar view (*Ruth*, p. 107).

who came to a person's aid by ransoming him or his property (Lev. 25:25, 48–49), but this did not make the redeemer a marriage candidate.

If Boaz understood his obligation as redeemer as broadly as possible and wanted to help Ruth, not merely financially, but in all her needs, he then could not stop at redeeming the family property but also had to marry her. This is in fact how he saw things (see the comments in 4:5), but the latter duty was not strictly incumbent on him as a redeemer. In my view, Ruth's request to Boaz in verse 9 should therefore be understood as follows: "Take me completely under your protection; I make bold to ask this because you are a kinsman-redeemer." He could infer from her behavior that she really wanted him to marry her (see footnote 49 at the end of the book).

3:10–13 *"The LORD bless you, my daughter," he replied. "This kindness is greater than that which you showed earlier: You have not run after the younger men, whether rich or poor. [11] And now, my daughter, don't be afraid. I will do for you all you ask. All my fellow townsmen know that you are a woman of noble character. [12] Although it is true that I am near of kin, there is a kinsman-redeemer nearer than I. [13] Stay here for the night, and in the morning if he wants to redeem, good; let him redeem. But if he is not willing, as surely as the LORD lives, I will do it. Lie here until morning."*

Boaz grasped Ruth's meaning at once. First he praised her behavior by wishing her the Lord's blessing. The "earlier kindness" that he spoke of was the way she had followed Naomi to Bethlehem (2:11). But she had surpassed even this by being willing, again out of love for Naomi, to marry whatever man was designated for her by Israelite law. This indeed was an act of great love, self-sacrifice, and respect for custom and law. For Ruth showed no concern for her own interests. She did not follow her personal desires or sensual passions and seek a man her own age, whether rich or poor. Instead she was "dedicated to the memory of her husband and bowed to the demand of Israelite law, submitting without protest to the desire of Naomi,"[17] even though this meant she had to marry a much older man.

Boaz was as modest as Ruth and realized at once that he would not be the most desirable mate for a young woman. His words reveal that he already felt a warm affection for her. Undoubtedly he could tell from her trembling voice that she feared he would misunderstand her behavior and refuse her request. He thus kindly reassured her and told

---

[17] De Moor, *Ruth*, p. 92. Cf. Oettli's fine remark: "She followed the voice of piety rather than the voice of nature" (*Das Buch Ruth*, p. 223).

her not to be afraid. He basically promised to do all that he could for her as a redeemer. He too was willing to accept his legal obligations; and her virtue was so well-known among his "fellow townsmen" (literally, "the whole gate of my people," i.e., everyone who sat and talked in the gate; cf. Prov. 31:31) that there could be no doubt that her intentions were noble. He had no reason to refuse her request, but one thing stood in the way: Ruth had a kinsman-redeemer who was a closer relative than Boaz.[18] This person could not be passed by, for he had the strongest obligation and also the first claim to her.

Since Boaz had no desire to ignore established custom and law, he had to first give this other person the opportunity to fulfill his obligation as a redeemer. The Hebrew text of verse 13 literally reads "if he wants to redeem *you*," i.e., if he did not conceive his duty too narrowly and decided to redeem not only the family property but also Ruth herself by marrying her (see in v. 9), thus giving her the chance to fulfill her obligations to the line of Elimelech. Boaz promised to go to this person the very next morning and asked Ruth to stay at the threshing floor till then. He could not send her away at night, and she would be able to rest in the meantime. Calling on the name of the Lord, he vowed that he surely would redeem her if the other man refused.

There is remarkable drama in the story here. Even though the author uses no stylistic devices, he keeps the reader in constant suspense about what will happen next (see, e.g., also 4:4).

3:14–15 *So she lay at his feet until morning, but got up before anyone could be recognized; and he said, "Don't let it be known that a woman came to the threshing floor."*

[15] He also said, "Bring me the shawl you are wearing and hold it out." When she did so, he poured into it six measures of barley and put it on her. Then he went back to town.

Ruth lay down again at Boaz's feet;[19] but before daybreak, he warned her that she had better depart so that their meeting at the

---

[18] This sheds further light on Naomi's behavior. One could ask whether she should not have waited till the kinsman-redeemer extended his help and offered to marry Ruth. Was it not unwomanly for Naomi to take the initiative? Apparently, however, the kinsman-redeemer was not obliged to step forward. Boaz was willing to do so, but he was not the nearest kin; and since the nearest kinsman-redeemer was not greatly inclined to help (4:6), he merely let matters ride. Naomi therefore had no choice but to take the first step (cf. Deut. 25:7).

[19] They undoubtedly also spoke about Elimelech's land (4:3), but the author does not mention this.

threshing floor would remain a secret. If it became known, Ruth's name would be tarnished, and the other kinsman-redeemer would then be unable to accept her request. It still was dark enough for her to return home unrecognized. Before she left, Boaz gave her a sign—a pledge, as it were, of his good intentions—that would also make clear to Naomi that he would not neglect his duty toward her. He naturally was well aware that Ruth was acting on her mother-in-law's instructions (see v. 17). Ruth held out the large shawl she was wearing; and Boaz poured into it six measures of barley (although we are not told how large a "measure" was, the amount perhaps came to six omers, i.e., ⅗ of an ephah or ca. thirteen liters; cf. 2:17). She carried this off on her shoulders, and even someone who recognized her could not have known where she had been during the night. Boaz then went back to the town.[20]

2. BOAZ'S ANSWER (3:16–18)

3:16–17 *When Ruth came to her mother-in-law, Naomi asked, "How did it go, my daughter?"*

Then she told her everything Boaz had done for her [17] *and added, "He gave me these six measures of barley, saying, 'Don't go back to your mother-in-law empty-handed.'"*

Like chapter 2, chapter 3 ends with a brief scene in Naomi's house, where Ruth brought a report of her meeting with Boaz, and Naomi responded with some comments and advice. In the Hebrew text Naomi's question in verse 16 is literally "Who are you, my daughter?" (cf. KJV); but this clearly means "How did it go, what is the outcome of your meeting?" There is no reason to follow Schulz in changing the text here (the question in Judg. 18:8 also sounds strange to our ears; see p. 464, footnote 25, in the commentary on Judges).

Ruth told her mother-in-law everything that Boaz did for her, how he calmed her fear and vowed to redeem her. She naturally also must have mentioned what he said about the other kinsman-redeemer. The six measures of barley served as a sign to Naomi that her time of emptiness

---

[20] Many Hebrew manuscripts and a few ancient versions have "then she went back to town" (v. 15). Since Boaz is the subject of the two previous verbs, there is no reason to prefer this reading to the Masoretic text. In addition, the verb *wattābō'* ("she went") then would occur twice in succession. The Septuagint has the male pronoun.

(1:21) was past. Her daughter-in-law's glad report took a heavy load from her heart.

3:18 *Then Naomi said, "Wait, my daughter, until you find out what happens. For the man will not rest until the matter is settled today."*

Naomi ended by advising Ruth patiently to await the outcome of Boaz's action. She was certain that he would reach a favorable settlement that very day.

D. Boaz's Marriage to Ruth and the Birth of Obed (4:1–22)

1. RUTH'S KINSMAN-REDEEMER AND HUSBAND (4:1–12)

4:1–2 *Meanwhile Boaz went up to the town gate and sat there. When the kinsman-redeemer he had mentioned came along, Boaz said, "Come over here, my friend, and sit down." So he went over and sat down.*
²Boaz took ten of the elders of the town and said, "Sit here," and they did so.

Naomi was right in her expectation that Boaz would act promptly. Although verse 1 could simply be translated "and Boaz went up" (cf. RSV), both the verb tense and the entire context indicate that a translation like "had gone up" (NEB) or "meanwhile Boaz went up" (NIV) is more appropriate; for he did this after he went back to the town (3:15). The verb "went up" does not indicate that Bethlehem stood higher than the threshing floor (3:3). "Going up to the town gate" was probably, rather, the standard expression that was used when someone went to seek justice (cf. Deut. 17:8; 25:7 [RSV]). The town gate not only was the place where persons were praised or blamed (Prov. 31:23, 31); it also was the site where contracts were made (Gen. 23:10–11, 17–18) and legal cases were conducted (Prov. 22:22; Amos 5:12, 15 [RSV]). Since anyone entering or leaving the city had to pass through it, it was the best place to find someone one was looking for. This is why Boaz sat at the town gate (i.e., the open place in front of it).

Boaz did not have to wait long before the kinsman-redeemer he had mentioned (3:12–13) came by. He called the man aside and invited him to sit down. Undoubtedly he addressed him by name, but the author does not tell us what this was. Instead he uses an indefinite expression that means something like "a certain one" or "so-and-so" (the same expression appears in 1 Sam. 21:2). Perhaps he wanted to conceal the man's identity or thought his name was not worth mentioning. In any case, once Boaz had found him, he called ten of the elders of the town, who perhaps were already in the area, and asked them to come and sit down. He needed them not only as witnesses but also as expert observers who could make sure that everything was done according to law. Apparently morning was the time for handling legal affairs.

4:3–4 *Then he said to the kinsman-redeemer, "Naomi, who has come back from Moab, is selling the piece of land that belonged to our brother Elimelech. ⁴I thought I should bring the matter to your attention and suggest that you buy it in the presence of these seated here and in the presence of the elders of my people. If you will redeem it, do so. But if you* ²¹ *will not, tell me, so I will know. For no one has the right to do it except you, and I am next in line."*
"I will redeem it," he said.

Boaz was ready to speak his mind. First, he turned to the other kinsman-redeemer and told him something about Elimelech's property that we have not heard till now. The word "brother" is used loosely here, since both men were merely members of Elimelech's clan.²² Like every Israelite, Elimelech had had a hereditary right to part of Canaan's soil (cf. 1 Kings 21:3).

There is a question about how Boaz's words in verse 3 should be translated. The Hebrew text with the Masoretic vocalization literally says that Naomi "sold the piece of land." In itself this presents no problem, although it is odd that the author would not have spoken earlier about such an important event in Naomi's life.²³ There was no need for him to mention it directly, however, since Naomi had already brought up the topic of kinsman-redeemers in 2:20; and the law stated that such a redeemer was to come forward after the impoverished property owner had already been forced to sell (Lev. 25:25). The thought that Naomi had already sold her land, therefore, is not inconsistent with 2:20 or 3:9, 12–13.

---

²¹ The Masoretic text has "he," but this has been emended to "you" following many Hebrew manuscripts and the ancient versions.

²² The rabbinic tradition states that Boaz was a nephew and the other man an actual brother of Elimelech, but it is obvious that we cannot attach much value to this.

²³ If she had indeed sold it, this could not have happened before her departure for Moab; for the famine in Israel would have made the field virtually worthless. Rather, the sale would have had to take place after her return in poverty, and the question of who managed the land in the interim then must remain unanswered. But see the further comments on verse 3.

There are other problems, however. In the first place, if Naomi had sold the land, it is incomprehensible that chapter 4 does not mention the buyer and that he was not heard from at the legal proceeding. How could his property have been disposed of and purchased by Boaz (v. 9) without his consent to the transaction and the price? In the second place, it then would make no sense for the author to say that the land was bought "from Naomi" (vv. 5, 9). She would have had nothing to sell, and the author certainly would not have left out the name of its new owner. In the third place, if the land had already been sold, it is hard to imagine why Boaz would have wanted to see it redeemed in Naomi's behalf (v. 4). For she then would have already received a sum of money, and the redemption price would have been paid, not to her, but to the new temporary owner. This would not have done Naomi any good. At most, she would have gotten the field back; but to derive any benefit from it, she would have had to pay someone to farm it, and that would have eaten up her profits almost entirely. She had no funds to start this anyway. Getting back the field would not have alleviated Naomi's and Ruth's poverty,[24] and it therefore would have made little sense for Naomi to request the redemption of property she had sold.

For these three reasons, I agree with the numerous commentators who reject the notion that Naomi had already sold the field. The Hebrew text actually does not demand this interpretation, since the vowels added by the Masoretes have no absolute authority. Without changing a single consonant, the perfect form *māḵᵉrâ(h)* ("she sold") can be read as the active participle *mōḵᵉrâ(h)*, which means "she intends to sell, is about to sell" (the NIV thus has "is selling"—TRANS.). If this reading is adopted, the situation must have been as follows. Naomi had kept possession of the family property up to this time (whether or not she derived much benefit from it is unknown). Once the harvest was over (2:23) and Ruth could no longer glean, however, Naomi saw no other way to provide for their support during the coming season than to sell the land. She told this to Boaz, her "business adviser," and he decided he should keep the property from going to a new owner outside the family.

Boaz's proposal in verse 4 therefore had precisely the same motivation as that of Jeremiah's cousin Hanamel in Jeremiah 32. In both stories we are confronted with a custom that was an indirect product of the Mosaic law concerning redemption. According to G. Ch. Aalders, it seems "to have been a custom that the impoverished

---

[24] See G. Smith, *Ruth,* p. 31.

landowner, before selling to a stranger, first offered his property for sale to the legally designated 'redeemer,' who thereby was given the opportunity to fulfill his obligations immediately without allowing an outsider to become involved in the affair."[25] The advantage of this was that the land then would remain in the family, and the seller probably could obtain a better price from a relative than from a stranger.[26] In any event Jeremiah 32 unquestionably shows that such a custom existed, and there therefore can be no objection to the thought that Naomi and Boaz also intended to follow it. If this is indeed what they had in mind, there is no problem in understanding the transaction in verses 3–11. We also should note that Jeremiah 32:8 calls the transaction that it speaks of an act of redemption.

In verse 3 Boaz was thus declaring that Naomi planned to sell the property of her deceased husband. No one present questioned her right to do this.[27] In fact her intentions were wholly in keeping with the Old Testament's numerous statements about the rights of widows, the respect that was their due, and the Lord's special care for them (e.g., Exod. 22:22–24; Deut. 10:18; Ps. 146:9; Isa. 1:17, 23).[28]

In verse 4 Boaz made his actual proposal. His opening words literally mean "I thought I should uncover your ear," an expression used in 1 Samuel 9:15; 20:2 et al., to denote the communication of an important, confidential message to a specific person. Here the element of confidentiality is missing, but the phrase still means to reveal something that had been hidden. Boaz suggested to his fellow kinsman-

---

[25] *Korte Verklaring* (Kampen: Kok, 1925) on Jeremiah 32:6–7.

[26] See G. Smit, *Ruth,* p. 32.

[27] This undoubtedly was related to the fact that the sale of land in Israel was never permanent (Lev. 25:23). The Lord Himself was the owner of the land, and the people were merely its users (somewhat comparable to medieval vassals). If someone was driven by need to sell his inherited property and no one redeemed it for him, he received it back in the Year of Jubilee. This had an automatic influence on the price. Strictly speaking, one did not sell the land itself but only the number of crops it would produce until the next Year of Jubilee (Lev. 25:15–16).

Elimelech's sons had inherited his property after his death; but since they both died childless, it had to be given back to the family of the father (Num. 27:8–11). By general consent, however, the family could not take possession till the owner's widow had died. The law did not command this, but it undoubtedly was a consequence of the unwritten law of mercy. Naomi and Ruth (Orpah did not enter the picture) therefore had the right to use the land till Naomi's death; and this implied that they also could sell this right if they were in need. Like all land sales in Israel, this sale had "more or less the character of a *lending of use* that could be revoked at any time" (W. A. van Es, *De eigendom in den Pentateuch,* p. 242).

[28] See van Es, *De eigendom in den Pentateuch,* p. 358.

redeemer that he fulfill his obligation by buying Naomi's land.[29] If he agreed, he was to do this at once in the presence of the citizens seated there and especially the elders, whose word had authority in Bethlehem. If he did not agree, he was to say so and let Boaz decide what to do; for Boaz was the next nearest relative, and there were no other potential redeemers besides these two. The kinsman-redeemer, confronted with his obligation, had no desire to evade it; and he declared that he was willing to redeem, i.e., he would pay Naomi for the number of crops till the next Year of Jubilee, when the land would become his own (see under v. 6). This unexpected answer gives a new twist to the story.

4:5–8 *Then Boaz said, "On the day you buy the land from Naomi and from Ruth the Moabitess, you acquire the dead man's widow,* [30] *in order to maintain the name of the dead with his property."*

[6] *At this, the kinsman-redeemer said, "Then I cannot redeem it because I might endanger my own estate. You redeem it yourself. I cannot do it."*

---

[29] This is something different than we would have expected from chapter 3, and it was not the uppermost thing on Boaz's mind. For tactical reasons, however, he did not start with his main concern. De Moor explains Boaz's procedure as follows: "First, it would have been indelicate to begin by speaking of Ruth; second, Boaz here puts the case on a better legal basis than if he had immediately spoken of marriage. For . . . the legal obligation applied only to the children of a single father, and as we know, this redeemer was not Elimelech's son" (*Ruth*, p. 107).

[30] Goslinga's translation of verse 5 corresponds to the NIV marginal note (cf. also RSV, NASB, and NEB): "On the day you buy the land from Naomi, you also acquire Ruth the Moabitess, the dead man's widow." He adds the following footnote:

This translation is based on a slight emendation of the text. The Hebrew consonantal text has the verb "acquire" in the first person, but this unquestionably should be changed to the second person following the *Qere*, numerous Hebrew manuscripts, and the ancient versions. A bigger problem is that the Hebrew text literally reads "and you acquire from Ruth the Moabitess, the dead man's widow." This usually is translated "you also acquire [or 'buy'] it from Ruth" (cf. KJV). If this is what the author meant, however, he undoubtedly would have used the adverb "also" (*gam*) instead of the conjunction "and." In addition, he probably would have added *miyyad* ("from the hand of") before "Ruth" (cf. RSV, "from the hand of Naomi"), while the verb "acquire" would have been given an object suffix. Agreements made at a purchase had to be stated unambiguously. Although these arguments are not decisive in themselves, their strength is increased by the fact that the above (KJV) translation does not have Boaz say what he undoubtedly meant to say, namely, that the redeemer had to take Ruth along with the land. The Vulgate and Syriac translations apparently read *gam-'ēt* instead of *ûmē'ēt* before "Ruth," which changes the meaning to "you also acquire Ruth the Moabitess" (see NIV margin). It is obvious that such a translation makes much better sense and fits the context perfectly; the condition of the

> [7](*Now in earlier times in Israel, for the redemption and transfer of property to become final, one party took off his sandal and gave it to the other. This was the method of legalizing transactions in Israel.*)
> [8]*So the kinsman-redeemer said to Boaz, "Buy it yourself." And he removed his sandal.*

Boaz was not yet finished, however. To use Schulz's words, "he still has a trump in his hand."[31] He next brought up the name of Ruth and pointed out to his relative that the case of Naomi had something special about it. Whoever bought Naomi's field also had to take the young widow of Mahlon, who was tied to the land, as it were. The verb that the NIV translates as "acquire" literally means "to buy." To apply such a concept to Ruth may seem a little strange, but it is understandable in the context; and we should note that Boaz used the same verb with himself as the subject in verse 10.[32]

There was a certain encumbrance, so to speak, on Elimelech's estate; whoever bought it had to accept the obligation to preserve the line of Elimelech from extinction by marrying the widow of his son. Things would have been different if Mahlon and Kilion had not both died childless. Since they had, however, the only way to maintain the name of the dead with his property was for the kinsman-redeemer to enter into a levirate marriage with Ruth, so that their first son could be counted as a son of Mahlon (see Deut. 25:5–6 and the comments on 3:1). In verse 5 Boaz was thus setting a condition that had to be satisfied by the buyer of Elimelech's estate.[33] Since the land to be redeemed belonged to a family that was on the verge of extinction and one of its owners was still young enough to produce offspring, the redeemer had a moral obligation to marry her.

We need not ask whether Boaz put the case this way on his own or was following a scheme devised by Naomi, but the former seems more likely. Nevertheless he undoubtedly proceeded with great tact and completely in Naomi's spirit (see 3:1). The other kinsman-redeemer probably had considered that such a proposal would be made to him,

---

purchase is clearly stated, the verb is given a suitable object, and the sentence closely resembles Boaz's words in verses 9–10. This reading is therefore definitely preferable to that of the Masoretic text. Only one consonant has to be changed, the *wāw* to a *gîmel*, and these easily could have been confused by a copyist because of their similarity—TRANS.

[31]*Das Buch Richter und Ruth,* p. 126.

[32]The verb is translated "acquire" to avoid giving the impression that Ruth was treated as a slave.

[33]See G. Smit, *Ruth,* p. 32.

and this could be the reason why he did not come forward on his own. In any case he had his answer ready at once. He declined to redeem, figuring that it would harm his interests to marry Ruth. Buying Naomi's land would cost him some money, but it would enlarge his property holdings; and since the field eventually (after the deaths of Naomi and Ruth) would revert to Elimelech's clan, i.e., to himself and perhaps partly to Boaz (see Num. 27:8-11), his wealth probably would be increased permanently. If he were to marry Ruth and father a son by her, however, Mahlon's inheritance would pass to the son; and he would lose both his money and the land. This he could not accept.[34]

The fact that the kinsman-redeemer would preserve the line of Elimelech from extinction by marrying Ruth and fathering a son by her meant nothing to him. He thus withdrew his offer and told Boaz to redeem the land himself (his words in v. 6 literally mean "you redeem for yourself my redemption"). The man's attitude did not do him credit, but we should remember that he apparently had every right to refuse. The elders neither rebuked him nor held him liable. From this we can infer that the condition set by Boaz and Naomi's broad conception of the obligation to enter into a levirate marriage were prescribed neither by law nor by national custom. The condition of marriage was considered eminently reasonable in this case, and the other kinsman-redeemer indeed did not question it; but no one was absolutely required to go to this length to help Ruth and Naomi (see footnote 49 at the end of the book). It is important to keep this in mind if one wants to read the next two verses in an unbiased way.

To clarify what happens in verse 8, the author makes a parenthetical comment about a custom that no longer existed in his own day. His description is clear enough. When an agreement was reached concerning the redemption or transfer of property, one party would take off his sandal and give it to the other to confirm and legalize the transaction. The custom undoubtedly was pregnant with meaning. When one took over some land, he would signify this by walking across it on foot; and the sandal or shoe thus became a symbol of power or authority (see Ps. 60:8). Handing over a sandal thus signified the transfer of title from one

---

[34] According to Jewish tradition, the man was already married and was afraid that another wife would upset his home life. Calvin thinks he had a superstitious fear of marrying Ruth, since her first husband had died so young. It also is possible that he simply found a Moabite wife unacceptable. All such suggestions are largely conjectural, however, and they have no bearing on the interpretation of the text. The man's excuse (v. 6) explains his refusal well enough.

party to another. In the present case it undoubtedly was the nearest kinsman-redeemer who took off his sandal, saying, "Buy it yourself" (v. 8). The text does not expressly state that he gave the sandal to Boaz, but this obviously is implied (the Septuagint has "and gave it to him" at the end of v. 8, but this probably was added later).

Some commentators have misconstrued what happened here by relating it to the symbolic act of the spurned widow in Deuteronomy 25:9, which also involved the removal of a sandal. According to them, Boaz took off the other man's sandal as a sign of his contempt for him. There is no evidence for this view, however, and it in fact conflicts with the context (see p. 515–16).

4:9–10 *Then Boaz announced to the elders and all the people, "Today you are witnesses that I have bought from Naomi all the property of Elimelech, Kilion and Mahlon. ¹⁰I have also acquired Ruth the Moabitess, Mahlon's widow, as my wife, in order to maintain the name of the dead with his property, so that his name will not disappear from among his family or from the town records. Today you are witnesses!"*

Boaz got right to the point. These two verses form the climax of the book, for we here find the answer to the question of what would happen to the property and lineage of Elimelech. Our mounting suspense is finally released. The crucial pronouncement flowed from Boaz's mouth in words that are solemn and legally precise but also earnest, kind, and devout. He wholeheartedly accepted his duty as a kinsman-redeemer, and he also declared that he was willing to fulfill the added obligations that were involved in the special case of Naomi and Ruth. With utter selflessness he submitted unconditionally to the demands of the divine law and the custom that it had inspired. He declared that the elders and all the people present were witnesses to his purchase of all the property of Elimelech, which had passed to his two sons after his death. They also could attest that he had acquired Ruth the Moabitess as his wife, so that the name of Mahlon might be carried on and not disappear from the town records (the Hebrew literally has "from the gate of his place" [cf. KJV], i.e., their first son would be spoken of in the town gate as a son of Mahlon).

Boaz here stood revealed as a great and selfless man, a splendid contrast to the petty, self-seeking figure of the nearest kinsman-redeemer. A touch of irony can be detected in that while the latter was afraid he would harm his interests if he bought the land, Boaz spoke as if he had acquired considerable wealth ("all the property . . . also . . .

Ruth''). The field itself could not have meant much to a man like him, especially since it cost him some money up front. In Ruth, however, who would be a noble and faithful wife, he had received a great treasure; and she was precisely the reason why the other man had declined to redeem the property. Boaz saw Ruth with completely different eyes, however.

This turn of events forms a splendid illustration of the fact that the heart of the law is the commandment of love, and this cannot be obeyed by someone who looks solely to his own material interests, like the nearest kinsman-redeemer, but only by a man like Boaz, who was inspired by love for God and his neighbor. The far-reaching obligations involved in the case of Naomi and Ruth, which flowed more from the spirit than the letter of the law, demanded a person of noble character who did not ask "How little is enough?" but "What can I do to live up to the Lord's law as fully as possible?" Boaz was such a man, and he thus formed an outstanding example of the upright Israelite in whom the Lord took pleasure (Ps. 11:7). In this he was clearly a type of our Lord Jesus Christ. For when the human race had rejected God and fallen into a hopeless state, Christ alone was good enough to fulfill the high demands of divine justice and, in sacred love, to raise humankind from its fallen condition and bring it salvation. No more than Boaz did He hold Himself back. Willingly He gave Himself for His bride, the church, freely offering His treasures to end His people's desperate poverty. In the words of de Graaf, "just as the redeemer Boaz preserved the name and the place of Elimelech in Israel, the Christ restores the names of His own for all time and gives them an eternal inheritance."[35] In these two verses, the climax of the book, we thus see that while Ruth's life was fulfilled in Boaz, Boaz himself found his fulfillment in Christ. This comes out even more clearly in the final verses of chapter 4.[36]

---

[35] *Promise and Deliverance*, 2:63.

[36] Some have pointed out that we are not told what price Boaz had to pay for the field. Perhaps this is because the price was not negotiable but fixed by some accepted guideline (see Aalders' comments in Jer. 32:9 in the *Korte Verklaring*). Boaz certainly would not have paid too little, for he accepted full responsibility for Naomi's and Ruth's support.

4:11–12 *Then the elders and all those at the gate said, "We are witnesses. May the* LORD *make the woman who is coming into your home like Rachel and Leah, who together built up the house of Israel. May you have standing in Ephrathah and be famous* [37] *in Bethlehem.* [12] *Through the offspring the* LORD *gives you by this young woman, may your family be like that of Perez, whom Tamar bore to Judah."*

When Boaz finished, the entire assembly answered him. Undoubtedly, one of the elders spoke first and the others chimed in to express their agreement, probably adding a few words of their own. Everyone was happy about how the case turned out, and there was obvious affection for Boaz and Ruth. Their words "we are witnesses" completed and ratified the act of redemption. This was followed by a blessing, reminiscent of Genesis 24:60, in which they wished Boaz a large and famous progeny. Rachel and Leah had built up the house of Israel as the mothers of Jacob's sons. Now, by starting a family of his own, Boaz would be able to increase his standing and fame in Bethlehem (both of these expressions in v. 11 refered mainly to the fathering of a numerous and illustrious progeny; cf. Ps. 127:4–5) and build the house of Israel further.

The elders finally expressed the wish that Boaz's family would be like that of Perez, son of Judah and Tamar. This was a natural comparison, since Boaz was a descendant of Perez,[38] and perhaps also because there was a certain similarity between Ruth and Tamar, who had also been childless in her first marriage. The differences between the two women were rather large, however.

---

[37] Literally, "call [or 'name'] a name," viz., by having children who would carry on his name.

[38] In the *Encyclopaedia Brittanica* article "Ruth," W. R. Smith and S. A. Cook state that 4:12 definitely implies that Boaz and Perez did not share the same lineage. They offer not one argument to support this bold claim. Is it so strange for someone to wish Boaz that his family would be like that of one of his forefathers? The blessing probably meant "may your family be as renowned as that of Perez" (Perez's descendant Nahshon was especially famous; see Num. 1:7; 2:3; 7:12, 17; 10:14; 1 Chron. 2:10), though this is not explicitly stated. If Boaz had no connection with the family of Perez, there would have been no reason to mention the latter after verse 11.

2. BOAZ THE FATHER OF OBED AND FOREFATHER OF DAVID
(4:13–22)

4:13–15 *So Boaz took Ruth and she became his wife. Then he went to her, and the* LORD *enabled her to conceive, and she gave birth to a son.* [14] *The women said to Naomi: "Praise be to the* LORD, *who this day has not left you without a kinsman-redeemer. May he become famous throughout Israel!* [15] *He will renew your life and sustain you in your old age. For your daughter-in-law, who loves you and who is better to you than seven sons, has given him birth."*

The Book of Ruth here comes to a happy ending in the marriage of Boaz and Ruth. Their relationship was blessed by the Lord; and the marriage was consummated when Ruth, the childless one, conceived and gave birth to a son. Without this, the solution to the plight of Elimelech's family (see in vv. 9–10) would have remained incomplete. It is remarkable, but completely consistent with the story as a whole, that the significance of this birth for Naomi is spoken of first of all. It was to her that the women of Bethlehem (cf. 1:19) addressed their congratulations.[39] They praised the name of the Lord because, against all expectations, He had not left Naomi without a kinsman-redeemer.

It is quite surprising that the newly born child is already called a redeemer here. The reason is not hard to imagine, however. Boaz indeed had redeemed Elimelech's estate; but if his marriage to Ruth had remained childless, Elimelech would have had no posterity and his property would have reverted to his clan. In view of this, the child was the real kinsman-redeemer, a word that here has the broad sense of "deliverer" and "helper" (a hint of this meaning is already present in 3:9). Only through this child was the yoke of affliction that the Lord had laid on Naomi completely removed.

The women of Bethlehem also expressed the wish that the child would become famous in Israel, i.e., that he would grow up, assume his own place among the families of Israel, and perpetuate his name as the son of Mahlon and grandson of Elimelech. His significance for Naomi was eloquently expressed in the assurance that he would renew her life (literally, "cause your life to return," i.e., rejuvenate and revivify her) and care for her in her old age. The women were confident this would happen because the son was born to Ruth, who loved Naomi and was

---

[39]The *Encyclopaedia Brittanica* article on Ruth calls it an inconsistency that whereas Ruth married, Naomi was congratulated. This is wrong, since Naomi remained a member of Elimelech's clan, while Ruth now was taken entirely into the clan of Boaz.

dearer to her than seven sons. Ruth's love guaranteed that she would also teach her child to love Naomi; and since Naomi in turn was so fond of Ruth, her daughter-in-law's son would also be a source of great joy to her.

To have seven sons was a special and full blessing for a mother (cf. 1 Sam. 2:5), and "better to you than seven sons" was therefore the highest praise that the women of Bethlehem could award Ruth. It probably was a popular expression that was particularly appropriate on this occasion, since Ruth had been an extraordinary blessing to Naomi. She had remained faithful to her mother-in-law and surrounded her with love; and now, by giving birth to a son, she had turned her sorrow into joy, her darkness into light, and her old age into youth. Through Ruth, Naomi again had a future.

4:16–17 *Then Naomi took the child, laid him in her lap and cared for him.* [17] *The women living there said, "Naomi has a son." And they named him Obed. He was the father of Jesse, the father of David.*

Naomi listened in silence to the words of the women of Bethlehem. She had no reply; but by taking the child in her lap, she showed that she regarded and loved it as her own. She naturally accepted the responsibility of caring for him (cf. RSV, "became his nurse"), and from this we can infer that she was living with Ruth. But it would be wrong to conclude that Naomi adopted the child as her own.[40]

The women of the neighborhood gave the son a name. This may seem a little meddlesome, but custom probably granted them a certain say in the matter. The women were representatives, so to speak, of the citizens who had approved the marriage of Boaz and Ruth and pronounced the Lord's blessing on it (vv. 11–12; cf. Luke 1:59–65). Seeing Naomi with the child on her lap, they thus said, "Naomi has a son"; and at once they knew what his name should be. The name Obed appropriately means "servant," for he was born for Naomi's sake: to amend her loss, brighten her darkness, and sustain her in her old age (v. 15). His task and his destiny were to serve, namely, to keep alive his lineage, which otherwise would have died out. The author immediately adds that he was successful in this, for he became the father of Jesse, the father of David. The hopes expressed in verses 11–12 and 14 were thus realized in a most striking way. Obed was not

---

[40]G. Smit rightly takes issue with this notion of Köhler and others (*Ruth*, p. 36).

one among many in Israel; he was the forefather of the great and famous king who became the object of the Lord's special favor.

Since the end of verse 17 is not an actual genealogy, it is natural to assume that the word "father" is used literally in both cases. No generations, then, would be skipped between Obed and Jesse or between Jesse and David (Jesse clearly was the immediate father of David; see 1 Sam. 16:1). We cannot be absolutely sure about this, but Obed probably was David's grandfather; and he certainly was his forefather, which is really all that counts.

4:18–22 *This, then, is the family line of Perez:*

> *Perez was the father of Hezron,*
> *19 Hezron the father of Ram,*
> *Ram the father of Amminadab,*
> *20 Amminadab the father of Nahshon,*
> *Nahshon the father of Salmon,*
> *21 Salmon the father of Boaz,*
> *Boaz the father of Obed,*
> *22 Obed the father of Jesse,*
> *and Jesse the father of David.*

That Obed was David's forefather is placed beyond doubt by the fact that the author ends his story with a genealogy of David's ancestors. Since the genealogy begins with Perez (see v. 12), it draws a connection between Judah, the patriarch of the tribe of royalty (see Gen. 49:8, 10), and the man in whom the ideal of a truly theocratic monarchy was most fully realized. The author's purpose was to show the line that ran from Perez to Boaz to David, and he therefore only listed as many descendants of Perez as seemed necessary for this. There is no reason whatsoever, text-critical or otherwise, to regard this genealogy as a later addition to the book (see section 3 of the Introduction).[41] A table of names like this fits perfectly in a book that

---

[41] The previously cited article on Ruth in the *Encyclopaedia Brittanica* forms a good example of the thoughtless arguments that have been made for this view. There it is said that the genealogy of Perez has little value, since 1 Chronicles 2:51, 54 show that Salma (or Salmon, v. 20; see NIV margin) was a Calebite clan head in Bethlehem, not Hebron, and this was not possible till during or after the Exile. This argument is rendered worthless if we merely note that the Salma in 1 Chronicles 2:51 was a different person than the Salmon (or Salma) in 1 Chronicles 2:11. Equally groundless is Oettli's claim (*Das Buch Ruth*, p. 216) that the genealogy in Ruth has to be an excerpt from 1 Chronicles 2:5–17 and that its heading and form show that it conformed to the "Priestly Codex." The exact relationship between the two

evinces such an obvious respect for family lines. Its purpose was to show, more clearly than verse 17 would do alone, that God saw to it that His promise to Judah was fulfilled.

The line of Perez was the bearer of this promise, and the story of Ruth has shown how carefully the Lord watched over that chosen lineage in Boaz's day. The sacred line could not be allowed to die out with Boaz. Boaz had to "become famous in Bethlehem" by becoming the father of Obed and forefather of David, for from his offspring Christ was destined to be born according to the flesh. Everything that happened in the Book of Ruth, even the seeming products of chance, was therefore controlled by God in order to lead Boaz to Ruth. He took her as his wife out of respect for God's holy law to maintain a family line in Israel. And the genealogy that ends the book shows how richly God rewarded him for this; by his selfless act he became a forefather of David and earned a name that is still held in honor today.

The heading of the genealogy (v. 18a) corresponds to Genesis 5:1; 10:1; 11:10 et al. It begins with Perez because it is not concerned with the whole tribe of Judah but only with the particular clan that gave birth to David. To start earlier than Perez would have been a superfluous repetition of what was already known. The birth of Perez is recorded in Genesis 38:29 and that of his son Hezron in Genesis 46:12 and Numbers 26:21 (1 Chron. 4:1 lists Hezron alongside Perez as a descendant of Judah). Ram, the next descendant, appears elsewhere only in 1 Chronicles 2:9–10; then follows Amminadab, the father-in-law of Aaron (Exod. 6:23) and father of Nahshon. Nahshon was a contemporary of Moses and the leader of the tribe of Judah during the journey through the desert (Num. 1:7; 7:12; 10:14). Next in the list is Salmon. Since the Hebrew text has Salma in verse 20 and Salmon in verse 21 (see NIV margin; he also is called Salma in 1 Chron. 2:11), these must have been alternate forms of the same name (Salma is presumed to be a shortened form of Salman).[42] Matthew 1:5 says that this Salmon was married to Rahab, information which the author must have gotten from a reliable extrabiblical tradition. Here he is called the father of Boaz.

There is no need to comment further on the names in this genealogy.

---

genealogies is unclear, but I see no reason why the author of 1 Chronicles 2 could not have used ancient records that were also available to the author of Ruth; perhaps he even got some of his information from the Book of Ruth itself (see Aalders' article on Chronicles in the *Christelijke Encyclopedie,* 1st ed.). Oettli's argument is probably now found unconvincing even by members of the critical school.

[42] See, e.g., E. Bertheau, *Richter und Rut,* p. 255.

All the persons mentioned appear in the same order in Matthew 1:3–6, where some of the names have slightly different forms that are closer to the Septuagint spellings (some of these spellings are quite inexact, e.g., Perez becomes Phares, Hezron becomes Esrom, Ram becomes Aram; see the kjv, which transcribes the Greek spellings).

A closer inspection of the list reveals that it contains ten names in all. It is easy to see that these could not cover all the generations between Perez and David. For when Jacob and his family traveled to Egypt, Perez was still very young;[43] and after the Israelites had lived there for 430 years,[44] Nahshon was among those who marched out. But Nahshon is only the fourth name after Perez, and four generations certainly are not enough to fill these four centuries. Further evidence that names have been omitted can be found in the fact that Salmon is called the father of Boaz. Salmon indeed must have been the son (or at most grandson) of Nahshon; for the latter led the tribe of Judah on the desert journey, and Salmon must have married Rahab soon after the fall of Jericho (Josh. 6:25). But he then could not have been Boaz's immediate father, for it is unthinkable that Boaz lived near the beginning of the period of the judges. The narrative that is related in the Book of Ruth presupposes a background of centuries of Israelite life in Bethlehem. And even if Boaz were in fact Salmon's son, a whole series of names would have to be added between Obed and Jesse; for more than 350 years passed between the fall of Jericho and the birth of David, probably more time than could be covered by four generations.

There is no doubt, therefore, that the genealogy is incomplete.[45] How many names were omitted, why this was done and according to what system, why precisely these ten names were chosen above others—these are questions that cannot be answered. It is clear, however, that similar omissions were made in other genealogies and that this was not done arbitrarily but for a specific reason. This is

---

[43] See, e.g., G. Ch. Aalders' comments on Genesis 46:12 in the *Bible Student's Commentary* on Genesis (tr. William Heynen, 2 vols. [Grand Rapids: Zondervan, 1981], 2:247).

[44] See Exodus 12:40. Van Gelderen thinks that another reading of this verse that would shorten the stay in Egypt considerably is more plausible (*Bijbels Handboek,* 1:110), but there is no need for us to go into this view and the serious objections that can be raised against it (see, e.g., Gen. 15:13).

[45] Some commentators have also argued on the basis of 1 Chronicles 2:25 that Ram was not a son but a grandson of Hezron, but this is a different Ram than the one in 1 Chronicles 2:9–10.

obvious above all in the genealogy *par excellence*, —that of Jesus Christ in Matthew 1, which clearly is based in part on Ruth 4:18–22.[46]

Even in the present genealogy, however, we can at least find hints of a system. In the first place, it certainly is no accident that the author summarized David's ancestry in ten names. This signifies that God's work of forming this lineage was finished and complete and reached its goal in David's birth. And in the second place, the ten names can be divided into two groups of five. The first five names embrace the period of Israel's sojourn in Egypt and the desert journey, while the latter five (from Salmon to David) all lived in Canaan. This symmetry gives expression to the orderly manner in which God prepared the way for the theocratic monarchy and also to His faithfulness in fulfilling His promise that He would grant Abraham's descendants a home in Canaan.[47]

In conclusion we should briefly notice that some commentators have questioned the fact that the genealogy calls Obed a son of Boaz, while the earlier part of the book implies that he was counted as a son of Mahlon. For consistency's sake, should not the author here have included the genealogy of Elimelech? Such a view (which some commentators use to dispute the authenticity of vv. 18–22)[48] is merely the result of a doctrinaire conception of levirate marriage and its consequences. Although it is true that Obed became the heir of Ruth's first husband, that does not alter the fact that Boaz fathered him (as v. 21 says). The same could not be said of Mahlon. The book's primary concern is not the line of Elimelech but the line of David, and God so arranged things that Boaz received an honorable position in the latter. He, even more than Ruth herself, is the book's main character; but it is only as David's forefather that he occupies this position. Regarded in the whole context of sacred history, the Book of Ruth thus shows us that whereas Ruth's life was fulfilled in Boaz, Boaz's was fulfilled in David, and David's in Christ.[49]

---

[46] See, e.g., F. W. Grosheide, *Het heilig Evangelie volgens Mattheüs* (Amsterdam, 1922); H. N. Ridderbos, *Matthew* (in the *Bible Student's Commentary*).

[47] See Keil, *Kommentar*, p. 405.

[48] See, e.g., Gunkel's article "Ruth" in *Religion in Geschichte und Gegenwart*, cited above.

[49] Because of the importance of the matter, I here will discuss at some length M. David's monograph on the marriage of Ruth (*Het huwelijk van Ruth* [Leiden: Brill, 1974]), which devotes special attention to the legal problems involved in the book. David argues that there are serious objections to the notion that the marriage of Boaz and Ruth was a kind of levirate marriage based on a family obligation

prescribed by law. First of all, he points out that according to Deuteronomy 25:5–10 only the actual brothers of a deceased husband were eligible for a levirate marriage. For Naomi to imagine that a half brother who might be born to her later would have to marry her daughter-in-law (Ruth 1:11–13) is therefore inconsistent with this law. According to David, this shows that the author of the book (who he claims lived during or after the Exile) no longer had a clear understanding of the institution of levirate marriage. But surely the author could have read the rules pertaining to such marriages in Deuteronomy 25 just as well as we can! David attaches too much importance to what Naomi said in these verses. In her great sorrow she merely was imagining an unreal possibility, and we therefore should not press her words too far. And even if we assume that Naomi really thought a half brother born to her later would be eligible for a levirate marriage, this still could be explained by the fact that Israelite custom understood the family's obligation more broadly than was strictly required by the law (see pp. 535, 538–39, 548).

This brings me to David's second argument, namely, that a kinsman-redeemer only had financial obligations and did not have to enter into a marriage. No doubt this is true, and on p. 538, footnote 16, I thus rejected the notion of a "redeemer's marriage." David is wrong, however, to conclude that Ruth had no desire for Boaz to marry her. If this was not in her mind, what was the purpose of her nocturnal visit? If Naomi had only wanted financial help, she could simply have discussed this with Boaz herself. In 3:1 (also 1:9) she clearly was speaking of marriage, as David himself admits. But he places great emphasis on the fact that neither Boaz nor the other kinsman-redeemer had a legal obligation to marry. Again, he is correct; but the Book of Ruth shows that true piety in Israel was not satisfied with a legalistic adherence to the letter of the law but instead sought to act according to a broad conception of the law's spirit. Therefore it would be inconsistent with the whole story to think that Boaz attached an arbitrary condition to the institution of redemption that took the other kinsman-redeemer completely by surprise. On pages 547–48 I argued that quite the opposite was the case. The mere fact that David's position implies that Boaz acted improperly shows that he has not done justice to the story. His argument, although sharply reasoned, is overly legalistic and underestimates the importance of custom as a norm for conduct. Moreover, it betrays the desire to date the Book of Ruth as late as possible.